Michael Shichor

Dearest Clare,

A chance to learn of a great land. Enjoy it!

with love,

George

Sept 89

MICHAEL'S GUIDE

SOUTH AMERICA

By
Michael Shichor

*I**NBAL*
Travel Information Ltd.

Inbal Travel Information Ltd.
P.O. Box 39090 Tel Aviv Israel 61390

© 1988 edition
All rights reserved

No part of this publication may be reproduced, stored in a retrieval system, or transmitted in any form or by any means, electronic, mechanical, photocopying, recording or otherwise, without the prior written permission of the publishers.

ISBN 965-288-009-4

Graphic design: Rivka Brisk & Yaron Gilad
Maps: Benjamin Blustein
Cover photo: Obremski/TIB
Typesetting: Inbal Travel Info. Ltd.
Plates, printing & binding: Havatzelet Press

Distributors:
U.S. & Canada: Hunter Publishing Inc., 300 Raritan Center Parkway, Edison, New Jersey 08818; **U.K.:** Kuperard (London) Ltd., 30 Cliff Rd., London NW1 9AG; **Australia:** Rex Publications, 413 Pacific Highway, Arparmon, N.S. Wales 2064; **Belgium:** Geocart, Breedstraat 108, 2700 Sint-Niklaas; **Bolivia:** Los Amigos del Libro, Casilla 450, Cochabamba; **Denmark and Finland:** Scanvik Books aps, Store Kongensgade 59 A, DK-1264 Copenhagen, K. Denmark; **Netherlands:** Nilsson & Lamm bv., Pampuslaan 212-214, 1382 JS Weesp Nederland; **New Zealand:** Roulston Greene, Private Bag, Takapuna, Auckland 9.

CONTENTS

Preface	11
Using this Guide	16

INTRODUCTION 19

A special place for tourists 19

PART ONE – Our First Steps 21
Making the decision to go
Who's going (21), How to go (22), Where to go (24), When to visit and how long to stay (27), How much does it cost? (29)

First Steps
Documents and papers (31), Health (33), Finances (34), What to take (36), Photography (39), Language (40)

PART TWO – Setting Out 40
How to get there (40)

PART THREE – Easing the Shock: Where have we Landed? 43
Accommodations (43), Food and drink (44), Domestic transportation (46), Personal security (48), Local currencies 48), Altitude – How to cope with thin air (50), Discounts for Students and young travelers (51), Behaviour and manners (52), Keeping in touch (52), Shopping and souvenirs (53), Overland border crossings (54), Taxes and custom duties (55), Working hours (56), Holidays and festivals (56), Weights and measures, temperatures, electricity, time (56)

ARGENTINA 59

Getting to Know Argentina
History (60), Geography and Climate (69), Population, Education and Culture (72), Economy (73), General Information (74)

Buenos Aires	81
The Iguacu Falls	98
Northern Argentina	103
Central Region	110
The Lake District	115
Patagonia	121
Tierra del Fuego	127

BOLIVIA 131

Getting to know Bolivia

History (131), Geography and Climate (134), Population (136), Economy (137), General Information (139)

La Paz	145
Short Trips around La Paz	157
Longer Excursions from La Paz	162
Other Bolivian Cities	169
Sucre	173
Potosi	178

BRAZIL 183

Getting to know Brazil
History (183), Geography and Climate (191), Population (194), Government (196) Economy (197), Language (201), Brazilian music (201), General Information (202)

Rio de Janeiro	213
Around Rio	240
Sao Paulo	252
The Iguacu Falls	267
Minas Gerais	273
Along the Coast from Rio to Salvador	283
Nordeste: Northeast Brazil	287
The Amazon Basin	313
The Midwest	325
Brasilia	331

CHILE 339

Getting to know Chile
History (339), Geography and Climate (342), Population, Education and Culture (344), Economy (344), General Information (346)

Santiago de Chile	349
The Northern Deserts	362
The South-Central Region	369
The Far South	387

COLOMBIA 397

Getting to know Colombia
History (397), Geography and Climate (401), Population (402), Economy (403), General Information (404)

Bogota	**410**
From Bogota to Cucuta	**420**
The Caribbean Coast	**424**
San Andres Island	**436**
Darien Gap	**439**
The Cordillera Central	**440**
Southwest Colombia	**445**
The San Agustin Civilization	**453**
The Amazon Jungle	**462**
The Savanna – Los Llanos	**466**

E *CUADOR* 469

Getting to know Ecuador
History (469, Geography and Climate (472), Population (475), Economy (475), General Information (476)

Quito	**480**
Guayaquil	**499**
The Galapagos Island	**505**
From Guayaquil to Quito – up the Andes	**511**
El Oriente	**517**
From Quito to the northern coast	**522**
North of Quito	**533**

P *ARAGUAY* 537

Getting to know Paraguay
History (537), Geography and Climate (539), Population, Education and Culture (541), Economy (541), Folklore (542)

Asuncion   **542**

P *ERU* 553

Getting to know Peru
History (553), Geography and Climate (556), Population, Education and Culture (558), Economy (559), General Information (560), Personal security (566)

Lima	**568**
North of Lima	**584**
The Amazon Basin	**597**
South of Lima	**603**
The Coastal Axis	**604**
From Lima to Cuzco by the Mountain Route	**613**
The Incas	**618**
Cuzco – Capital of the Inca Empire	**627**
Short Excursions in the Cuzco Area	**640**

Extended Tours in the Cuzco Area   652
Lake Titicaca   658

*U*RUGUAY   663

Getting to know Uruguay
History (663), Geography and Climate (666), Population (667), Economy (667), General Information (668)

Montevideo   670
Punta del Este   678

*V*ENEZUELA   681

Getting to know Venezuela
History (681), Geography and Climate (683), Population and Government (685), Economy (685), General Information (686)

Caracas   689
Western Venezuela   705
Southeast Venezuela   709

*I*NDEX   716

*N*OTES   724

TABLE OF MAPS

SOUTH AMERICA	14
ARGENTINA	70
BUENOS AIRES	88
IGUACU FALLS	99
NORTHERN ARGENTINA	105
BOLIVIA	135
LA PAZ	150
BRAZIL	188
RIO DE JANEIRO – CENTROA	224
RIO DE JANEIRO – ZONA SUL	230
SOUTH EASTERN BRAZIL	241
SAO PAULO	256
THE IGUACU FALLS	270
OURO-PRETO	279
NORDESTE	288
SALVADOR	290
THE AMAZON BASIN	314
THE PANTANAL	326
BRASILIA	332
CHILE	343
SANTIAGO	353
THE LAKES	371
COLOMBIA	400
BOGOTA	414
SOUTHWEST COLOMBIA	446
ECUADOR	473
QUITO	486
GUAYAQUIL	502
THE GALAPAGOS ISLANDS	509
PARAGUAY	540
ASUNCION	548
PERU	557
LIMA	575
NORTHERN PERU	585
CUZCO	634
INCA SITES	642
URUGUAY	666
MONTEVIDEO	674
VENEZUELA	684
CARACAS	695

Preface

Writing this guide, I have aimed at coming out with a comprehensive, in-depth companion to the tourist who wants to get to know the South American continent in a direct and personal way. People who travel to South America come from a variety of places and go for a variety of reasons, each with his or her own traveling style and on different schedules and budgets. An attempt has been made to create an information pool, which would combine material relevant to understanding the **what**, while contributing to the practicalities of the **how**.

Tourism towards the 90's has changed. We are no longer dealing with the superficial style of maximum-area-minimum-time. Today's tourists are sophisticated, serious and experienced. Their aims and goals are wider, more far-reaching. The modern traveler is interested in a significant, relevant, first-hand experience when touring foreign lands. He wants to get to know new and different worlds and is well aware of the effort involved. This book is written for this traveler — curious, intense, experienced and open-minded — the tourist who really and truly wishes to meet South America, face-to-face.

While writing the guide with special emphasis on enlarging upon and clarifying general areas, I have not done so at the expense of the plethora of practical details which are of vital import, if you are to fully succeed in your venture and truly enjoy the experiences awaiting you.

Aware of the responsibility involved in being guide and companion to all who choose to see South America "through my looking glass", I have tried to compile as many facts and details as possible. From this pool of information, let each person take what fits best, what is most appropriate. This guide includes a vast selection of data, suitable for all tastes. Therefore, feel free to "browse" through the material offered and choose those topics which interest you and which contribute most to your traveling style.

In the course of this work, I have labored to separate the wheat from the chaff and have tried to be as precise as possible. Naturally, many of the impressions and recommendations included in the guide are subjective, and reflect my personal tastes and preferences. However, I feel certain that they do contain those elements which will fulfill the expectations of the kind of tourist mentioned, and will guide and assist you in making the most of your trip, in as enjoyable, comprehensive and pleasant a way as possible.

I have written this guide in great affection for the South American continent, her scenic splendors and her people. I have therefore allowed myself the liberty of detouring from the formal, informative framework, and endowing this book with a more personal hue. I have attempted to balance between the practical aspects of traveling and those which enrich us, giving us a "feel' for the place, which is what essentially makes our tour a truly memorable experience.

Much effort has gone into the compilation of the practical information, as well as the rest of the text, in order to enhance your awareness and ease your way along the highways and byways of an unfamiliar land — one whose splendor and enchantment will sweep you along in dynamic intensity.

The task of putting this Guide together has spread over months of labor, months during which I was fortunate to benefit from the assistance and encouragement of a great many people — both family and friends.

I am grateful to the members of my family, who stood by me and supported me all along the way.

Thanks are due also to all my wonderful friends whose encouraging support never faltered, and whose constructive advice and caring efforts were so valuable.

Special appreciation goes to my good friend Aaron Young, from New York, without whose special help and support it is highly unlikely this project would ever have come to be, in the manner in which it has evolved today.

I wish to express my thanks to the loyal and dedicated staff at Inbal Travel Information Ltd., who worked so enthusiastically, making my long nights their days, as well.

To these, and all the other people who assisted and gave of themselves — my heartfelt thanks.

Michael Shichor

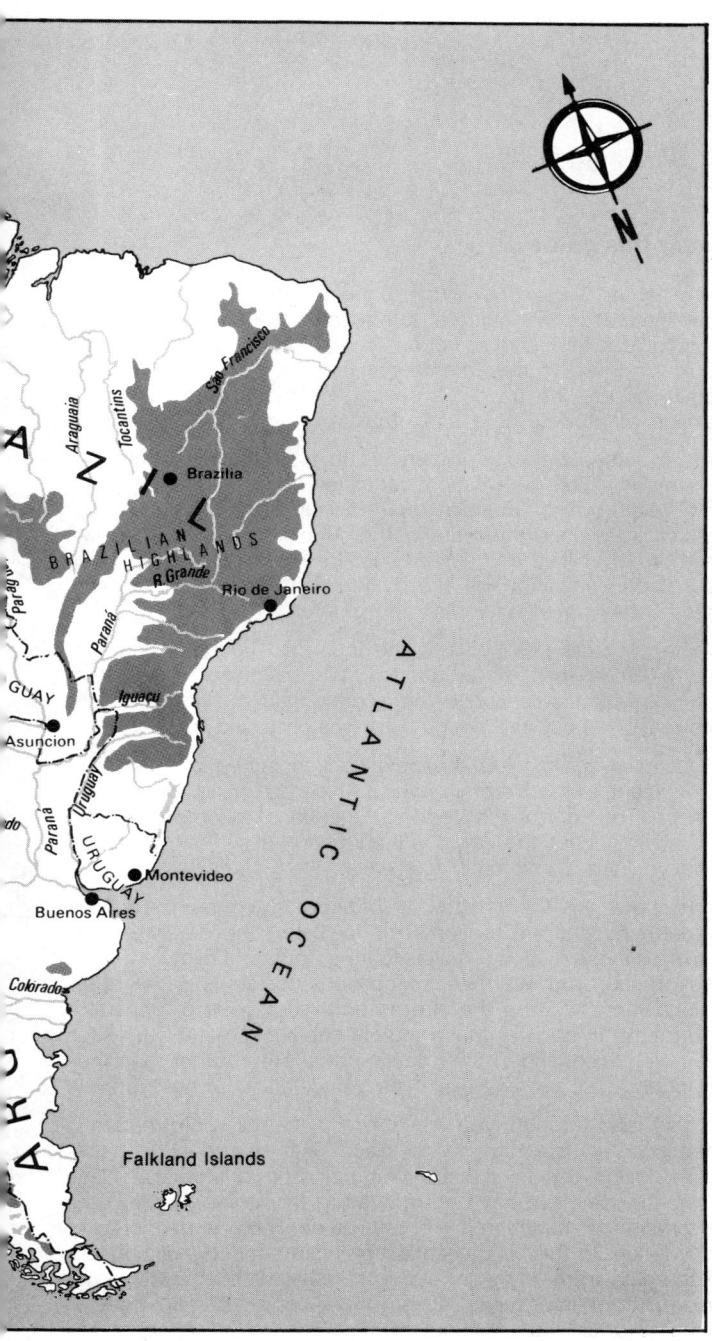

Using this guide

In order to reap maximum benefit from the information concentrated in this guide, it is advisable to read the following material carefully and act upon it. The facts contained in the book are there to help the tourist find his or her way around and to assure the traveler's seeing the most, with maximum savings of money, time and effort.

Before setting out, it is imperative to read the Introduction in its entirety. The information contained there will supply you with details which will help you in making early decisions about your trip. Covering the material thoroughly means that you will be more organized and set for your travels. Once you arrive at your destination you will already feel familiar and comfortable there, more so than would otherwise be the case.

In the chapters dealing with the individual countries you will find a broadly-based Introduction, whose first section deals with general topics, while the second part includes practical information about the country, its customs and ways.

The country's capital is the next section in the chapter, with the exception of Brazil in which this section is on Rio de Janeiro. The information here — suggestions, recommendations and advice about the city — will guide and assist you from the time you arrive and until you leave.

From here on, the chapter is organized geographically: the different regions are presented in logical sequence, with each region surveyed along major touring routes. Following main sites noted, you will find suggestions for touring the areas around them — using the site as both your point of departure and return. In each of these touring sub-sections too, the sites are noted according to their geographical order rather than their importance, so as to make it easier to follow along the way.

As you read through, you will notice that similar information is mentioned in more than one place. This is meant to assist tourists who decide to start their tour from a particular place along the way, but have not arrived at this point via the route described or suggested in the guide, and with no prior knowledge. In this way each traveler can begin his or her tour of the area from any point along the way, without missing out on important information. This allows for greater flexibility in planning your tour, without being tied to the geographical divisions or considerations of this guide, i.e., whether you go from north to south, or the other way around, it makes no difference. This is especially helpful for *mochileros*, who make their way along the roads, coming overland rather than via major airports; or for those who decide to fly from place to place, arriving at different locations without having toured the vicinity or places along the way.

For travelers crossing by land, you will find in each border city discussed a section on the procedures required for continuing into the neighboring country. Treat this as you would treat a plan to go from one site to another: **read the material dealing with both places** – the city from which you are coming and the one to which you are heading. Only in this way can you be sure to have covered all the information necessary.

The geographical index at the end of this guide includes those sites reviewed in special chapters or sections. Smaller tourist attractions are not mentioned there, but can be easily located within their relevant chapters. In the various countries, towns and areas we have included first-quality maps to assist you in finding your way around. These, I believe, will make your way much easier and will prove essential both in planning your journey and executing it.

I have included several blank pages in the guide. These are for you, to jot down special experiences of people and places, feelings you may have had, or any other significant happenings along the way. You will always be able to look back on these words, and remember.

When mentioning information about transportation, accomodations, food, etc., I have tended to simplify and have preferred to give general guidelines, placing more emphasis on existing possibilities than on variable specifics. It is always disappointing to find that what you have counted on seeing or doing, according to advice given in a guide, is not available once you finally get to the location. I have therefore tried to avoid, as much as possible, giving specific details about subjects given to frequent change, preferring rather to advise you of those places where relevant, here-and-now information can be obtained once you are actually on the spot. Thus, for example, I mention that a bus line operates between two cities or towns several times a week. I note the name of the bus company, the address (in both cities) and the telephone numbers. Yet I avoid mentioning that these buses run on Monday, Wednesday and Friday, as this is a flexible schedule, tending to change every so often. So too, in the case of a hotel noted in a guide as "cheap and friendly"; yet an upsurge in tourism by the time the book is published, may mean that you will find the same hotel no longer as inexpensive, and as for friendly, well...

Therefore, an important rule of thumb should be to consult the local Tourist Office in each place you visit. Their addresses are mentioned in the text. They can advise you of the latest updated information for the specific time of your visit.

The shaky economic infrastructure characterizing Latin America in recent years, has caused me to avoid quoting prices. These tend to vary from one day to the next – in both directions. It is for this reason that I have decided to categorize whatever fees are involved by using general terms, describing them in price categories relevant to the specific country in which you are traveling. You will therefore find, for example, that a hotel charging the same price for accommodations, will be classified as "inexpensive" in one country, yet described as a "big splurge" in another.

As for updating – this kind of guide to these specific countries cannot afford to march in place. A technical update from year to year is not enough, either. A finger on the continent's pulse is ever necessary, and not just on the technical, practical pulse, but even more on the emotional pulse, feelings, outlooks, attitudes, etc. Up to the day this guide went to press, I attempted to confirm its relevance and up-to-dateness. However, it is only natural that due to frequent changes which occur, travelers will find certain time-related facts somewhat less than precise when they arrive at their destinations, and for this I apologize in advance.

To this end, cooperation and assistance from you who have enjoyed the information contained in this guide, is necessary and vital. It ensures, first and foremost, that those who travel in your wake will also enjoy and succeed in their ventures, as much as you have. For this purpose, we have included a short questionnaire at the end of the Guide and we will be most grateful and appreciative to those of you who will take the time to complete it and send it to us.

Have a pleasant and exciting trip – Bon voyage!

INTRODUCTION

A Special Place for Tourists

The third world countries, avoided by Western visitors, have been among the less "touristy" places for many years. Americans have traditionally preferred European vacations, while Europeans have favored destinations in North America. In recent years, however, significant changes have begun to take place in the patterns of thinking and touring of western travelers. They've begun to place emphasis on getting to know remote worlds, encountering foreign cultures, absorbing the life styles of other societies, and forming impressions of uncommon ways of thought and existence. The worldwide growth in tourism – more tourists on the one hand and a broader range of destinations on the other – has contributed to putting South America on the world tourist map. It attracts more and more visitors each year.

South America's exciting, exotic charm combines forces with the veteran tourist's natural curiosity. When these are reinforced by a significant drop in the costs of touring and by a constantly developing tourist infrastructure, it's no wonder that South America has become a new and captivating destination for travelers. Here is a continent that offers innumerable experiences, sights and impressions. On the one hand, it has incredible untamed scenery – canyons, deserts, mountains, jungles, rivers, and glaciers; on the other hand there's an astonishing and varied "human landscape" – a blend of cultures and races woven into a fragile and enchanting social fabric. Anyone seeking an encounter with rare worlds – a fascinating harmony of nature and scenery, man and animal, progress and antiquity – will find it here. It is a continent abounding in contradictions, where no day resembles its predecessor and no man his neighbor.

A trip to South America, whether for business or for pleasure, is wholly different from a trip anywhere else. Before we set out we must prepare, investigate, interpret, comprehend. As we travel, too, we engage in a process of learning, becoming acquainted and adjusting. Our ordinary ways of life and thought, attitudes to time, people, and things are simply not the same as those found in South America. Its languages, foods, clothing and customs are all quite remote from those we know. As we head

INTRODUCTION

for South America, we must disabuse ourselves of many biases; we must open ourselves up, both emotionally and intellectually, to wholly different messages and impressions. Though it's certainly true that the transitions are not so sharp between New York and Caracas or between Paris and Buenos Aires, the contradictions remain in full force. They accompany the tourist every step of the way, and place him in daily confrontation with his own values, opinions, and habits. The greatest return one can expect from a trip through South America is the knowledge of the existence of another world, one which lives, thinks and behaves differently, a world no better and no worse – merely different.

South America invites the tourist to share numerous experiences and ordeals – cosmopolitan cities, ancient villages that have not changed in centuries, untamed scenery of mighty grandeur, massive power projects, and all the rest. Here you'll find a fantastically wealthy elite beside shameful poverty, incomparably primitive scenes alongside technological wonders. Wonderful outings on foresaken trails will take you to Indian tribes who still go about naked, fish with harpoons, and hunt with bows and arrows. Other journeys will lead you to some of the world's best-known and most important archeological sites.

South America has it all – for the family on their an annual vacation, for the youth out to wander with a backpack, or for the retired couple on their second honeymoon. Each will find what he is seeking here. There's enough here for everyone, on every topic and in every field. On every itinerary, every form of travel, visitors are sure to find what they want – and more.

It is important to mention again that the substantial difference between "North" and "South", which accounts for Latin America's exotic splendor, requires fundamental and thorough preparation. The sharp transition obliges you to be open and tolerant, and to reinforce those qualities with advance study and suitable intellectual and emotional preparation. These guarantee a successful tour, out of which you'll get the most enjoyment; in their absence you're liable to encounter many difficulties which may well spoil your pleasure. Under all conditons and in any event it's worthwhile to behave with great patience and to accept South America for what it is – beautiful, wild, fascinating. This, after all, is the purpose of our visit, one unequalled anywhere on Earth.

INTRODUCTION

Part One – Our First Steps

Before we set out we must consider a number of important points: deciding upon our route, destinations, and the like. The paragraphs that follow will guide you in these matters.

Making the decision to go

Who's going

Anyone can visit South America. Due to the great variety of sites, plentitude of things to see, and abundance of areas of interest on the way, there's almost no one who won't find what he's seeking. A great many **young tourists** spend several months exploring South America from one end to the other, wandering along the roads with backpacks and a few coins in their pockets. It's a nice "timeout" from the rat race, in addition to being an enjoyable and fascinating experience. These backpackers, known in local parlance as *mochileros*, come to know the continent perhaps better than most natives, and enjoy unrestricted mobility on all of South America's highways and byways.

More and more **middle aged** tourists have been frequenting South America in recent years, generally after having come to know both the United States and Europe. Now, in search of new and interesting places to visit, they've packed their bags and wandered to the faraway southern continent. Faraway? Not really. For the tourist, South America is closer today than it's ever been. It's no longer a backward continent hidden behind dark mountains, but rather a bustling and popular place, connected to the rest of the world by excellent air service.

There is no longer anything to fear about going to South America. Sanitary conditions and the public services offered tourists are constantly improving, and today are not significantly inferior, in the large cities, to those we're used to in the West. Transportation services, hotels and restaurants have also conformed to a great degree to the new tourist's demands and, though difficulties still occur, the experienced tourist has no reason to refrain from visiting. Vacation and resort sites, too, are flourishing, and many people combine rest and recreation with their visit.

As trade between Latin America and the rest of the world expands, a great many **business people** have been combining business and pleasure, enjoying the experience of getting to know different economic systems. The Latin American business world is lively and effervescent, and has adopted Western work

INTRODUCTION

patterns and behavior in the large cosmopolitan cities. Grand hotels, superb restaurants, and office, guide and rent-a-car services are available for the businessman and tourist of means. The South American ambience, the "flexibility" of the clock, and the tendency to do things lightheartedly and at leisure leave their impact here, too, though when you get down to it, business is conducted strictly and thoroughly.

Bringing the children along requires special preparation. In many places – mainly in Andean countries such as Bolivia, Peru, Ecuador, and Colombia – it is difficult, for example, to obtain milk products. Sanitary conditions are not the best, and are liable to cause problems for adults as well. At the same time, do not hesitate to take children from the age of 7-8 years old to the large cities or the famous tourist sites. These are served by convenient access roads beside which you'll find visitors' facilities. There is no problem in touring with children in Argentina and Chile – quite the contrary.

How to go

The most comfortable way to go is, of course, with **organized group tours**. Many companies specialize in providing this kind of service – generally rather expensive – in a number of Latin American countries. Here you'll be assured that your trip will involve a minimum of difficulties and breakdowns, though you'll be deprived of personal contact with the natives, the ability to set your own timetable and itinerary, and more. It's nevertheless important to remember that there are few English speakers in South America, and visitors who don't speak Spanish or Portuguese are liable to find themselves in tight spots, especially when meandering in remote locations outside the cities.

South American group tours are varied and diverse, so that it is hard to relate to them as a single unit. Every visitor should draw up a list with a number of destinations and objectives, carefully examining the means by which he'll reach them with the greatest success and least expense.

Another way of going, of course, is the private, individual trip, where you're free to choose your own dates, destination, pace, budget, etc. Indeed, there's no greater freedom than that of a long, extended tour, where one has no obligation to preset an itinerary and timetable, but can suit these to the needs and desires of the moment.

Backpack tourism is especially popular among the young, and the young in spirit. Many spend several months in South America, making their way through the continent from country to country and site to site. It's a fascinating and pleasant way

*I*NTRODUCTION

to travel. Most such visitors pick up some Spanish or Portuguese en route, get to know the natives, and get to interesting places that few visitors reach.

Backpack tourism is cheap, pleasant, and easy. The visitor should not expect many difficulties, and excluding a few countries where the police pick on tourists – such as Peru, Colombia and, to a certain extent, Argentina – it's highly improbable that you'll encounter any problems that will mar the pleasure of your trip.

Mochileros, with their packs on their backs, are usually received cordially. Tourists of all nationalities tend to meet anywhere on the continent and continue together. Those who set out alone are bound to meet up with many other travelers, so it's hard to imagine that they'd suffer from loneliness. I think it is good idea to set out in pairs. This is the most convenient format for traveling – in terms of planning flexibility, social considerations, and practical concerns involving accommodation and transportation, where it's easier and cheaper to go about in twosomes.

Women, too, have nothing to fear in South America. Apart from several places which I wouldn't advise young women to enter alone, and apart from the fact that they shouldn't go about in dangerous urban areas late at night, I find no reason to be deterred. Two women traveling together, at any rate, will resolve these problems.

By traveling in this manner, you won't have to carry a lot of money; a few ten dollar bills per week will enable you to get along fine and in relative comfort. At the same time, bear in mind that such a journey does involve difficulties: the means of transportation you'll use aren't very good, the hotels will offer no more than the bare essentials, and so on. Hence, you'll need extra time, more strength, and lots of patience, openness, and good humor.

Well-off tourists, and those whose time is limited and who want to get in a lot of sites comfortably without wasting precious time on the road, can get the most out of their visit by careful advance planning and by making reservations. I would recommend that you carefully select the sites you consider most important to visit, and draw up a timetable for your trip.

Reservations are not always essential, a fact which allows for greater flexibility en route. In this book we've noted the places, routes, and dates that attract crowds. If you've placed these on your itinerary, I recommend that you have a reliable travel agent make reservations before you set out. Make sure he obtains

INTRODUCTION

written confirmation since overbooking is a common phenomenon in South America and is liable to cause you great unpleasantness.

Business people would do well to arrange all matters beforehand. The big cities frequently experience unexpected pressure on hotels, flights, and car-rental firms; though ordinary vacationers would hardly notice these problems, they are apt to cause delays and annoyance to a businessman on a tight schedule.

Where to go

In our opening paragraphs we noted that South America is rich in all kinds of places to visit. I therefore think it important to determine and locate the types of places that attract you in particular.

Mochileros setting out on an extended visit can expect to discover many of the beautiful continent's hidden secrets on the way, and will meet and enjoy its abundant treasures. Others, especially those whose time is limited, will prefer – correctly, in my opinion – to designate one or several countries, and do them throughly. Both sorts of tourists might give preference to subjects in which they are particularly interested, and plan their trips so as to achieve the maximum in these spheres. We will survey below a number of **categories** in which we'll try to sketch out various directions of interest. Individual tourists will choose the categories that attract them, and draw up a plan that includes one or several.

The first possibility involves those **natural and scenic attractions**. which are found throughout South America. They are divided into several types:

Glaciers and lakes are located chiefly in the continent's southern section, in southern Argentina and Chile. Here you'll find some of the world's most beautiful tour routes, enchanting scenery, friendly people. Many Andean peaks in the region feature well-developed ski areas, which, because the seasons are reversed, are in top condition, when in Europe, holiday-makers are tanning themeselves on the beaches. North of Lima, Peru, in the vicinity of Huaraz, you'll find lovely hiking trails that demand good physical condition, the ability to adapt to unusual climatic conditions and a willingness to live primitively. All these routes require first-class camping gear.

For a pleasant stay on the **seashore** there's nothing like Brazil. Resort towns with pristine beaches abound along the Atlantic coast, especially between Vitoria and Puerto Alegre and between Recife and Salvador. These are especially popular

INTRODUCTION

among Brazil's wealthy, and tourists frequent them primarily at Carnival time in February and March. Their great advantage – like that of the ski areas – is in the reversed season. Here you can swim and sunbathe from January to March, while most of Europe is buried in snow. The few coastal sites in Argentina and Chile serve mainly the local population. Peru and Ecuador have lovely beaches, though these lack a developed service infrastructure. There are developed beaches in Colombia and Venezuela, with the popular ones located along the Caribbean. Hotel occupancy and prices are high during the summer months (June-August), and it's important to make advance reservations.

A long strip of exclusive resort clubs has sprouted along the Caribbean coast, where you can spend a seaside vacation under ideal conditions, renting gear for fishing, sailing, diving, and more. Some of the beaches, especially those in the Caracas area, are rather neglected; their level of upkeep has deteriorated perceptibly.

About one-third of South America is covered with thick **jungle**, most of it unexplored. On the exceedingly popular jungle excursions tourists can encounter out-of-the-way cultures and get a first-hand impression of ancient ways of life that are rapidly disappearing. It's important to remember that jungle trips require special effort, organization, and experience. You can take such trips in Brazil, Bolivia, Peru, Ecuador, Colombia and Venezuela. Each of these countries has extensive jungle regions, most of which, despite the massive resources invested in their development in recent years, remain basically as they were when the first Spanish *conquistadores* arrived.

The jungle's harsh and unpleasant climate – an oppressive combination of high temperatures, high humidity, and frequent rainfall – explains to a large extent why the area has not been settled, though it also deserves credit for the lush wild vegetation. This flora, watered by giant rivers such as the Amazon, the Orinoco, and their tributaries, is of decisive importance in reducing air pollution and maintaining the natural environmental equilibrium in all of South America. An outing to the jungles must be planned carefully and with great caution. Though most of the jungle is free of malaria, I would recommend taking medication against that disease, along with water purification tablets and mosquito repellent.

Travelers visit the jungle cities of Peru and Brazil in great numbers, either on organized tours or on their own. Though the former are very expensive, it's worth remembering that the "unattached" visitor, too, will find a visit to these areas far from

INTRODUCTION

cheap. Prices in and around the jungle towns are far higher than elsewhere as goods must be imported from far away. Be prepared for this, and bring along a sufficient amount of the local currency.

The jungles in Ecuador's eastern region are home to a number of Indian tribes, and are accessible as a relatively "short hop" from the capital. Personally, I think the jungles in Ecuador offer a maximum return of enjoyment and interesting experiences while demanding minimum investment of time, effort, and expense.

Wildlife: Though the jungle might appear to be **the** place for observing wildlife in its natural habitat, this is in fact not the case. It is true that jungle tours can give you a glimpse of thousands of strange and varied species of birds, insects, butterflies, and even reptiles, monkeys, and wild boars, but you can't assume so. You must penetrate deep into the jungle, and there's no guarantee that you'll find what you've come for there, either.

By contrast, the Galapagos Islands off Ecuador are famous for their abundant wildlife, most of it unique. It is rather expensive to visit, and it's best to make reservations for a flight to the islands, and on the ships and boats that sail among them. This is undoubtedly a unique place and a visit here may be the highlight of your trip to the entire continent. The lovely nature reserve on the Paracas Islands off central Peru has thousands of birds and sea lions, and is far less expensive and more convenient to visit. Bolivia and Chile, too, have nature reserves with a multitude of wild animals, primarily of the llama family.

In Brazil, in the area of the Bolivian border, there are vast stretches of marshes inhabited by an abundance of birds, alligators and other animals. The best time to visit here is during the dry season, between May and September, when one can really appreciate the variety and profusion of wildlife.

The Valdez Peninsula in southern Argentina is another fascinating reserve, with penguins, whales, sea lions, and more. The best time for visiting it is October or November, when the animal population reaches its annual peak.

Another planning strategy places the emphasis on South America's **complex social structure**, concentrating on sites from **the continent's past**, as well as those which accent its special present.

Archeology: The glory of pre-Columbian settlement in the southern half of the Americas is, of course, the Inca Empire and its center, the city of Cuzco, Peru. From these, the Inca

INTRODUCTION

(emperor) and his men dominated the tribes from Ecuador in the north as far as central Chile in the south. Few pre-Incan remains have survived in South America. Remains of what is thought to be the oldest settlement in all the Americas have been discovered at Puerto Varas (Southern Chile), and are being studied thoroughly. Pre-Incan civilizations existed primarily in Tiwanaku, Bolivia, around the village of San Agustin in southern Colombia, and in various locations in Peru. While the tourist will certainly want to visit San Agustin and Tiwanaku, the pinnacle of his archeological experience will undoubtedly be a visit to the Inca sites, with the lost Inca city of Machu Picchu as the highpoint.

Folklore and folk culture: Age-old Indian traditions have blended with the Spanish influence to produce a unique and extraordinary compendium of folklore and culture. All of South America, and the Andean countries in particular, excel in uncommonly beautiful handicrafts of unique character and style. Visiting these countries is like an extended shopping trip. This activity centers on the marketplaces – in large cities, country towns, and remote villages. In some, the barter system is still practiced. The markets of South America are colorful, effervescent, lively, and enchantingly beautiful. Most commerce is carried on by women, and they are most skillful at it. As you meander through the markets choose carefully, check quality, compare prices, and bargain, **always** bargain.

Most South American countries have a rich and varied folklore. Folk music varies from country to country: while quiet cowboy songs typify Argentina and Venezuela, Brazillian music is usually stormy and rhythmic. Music and dance in the Andean countries draw on Indian sources; typical musical instruments are the *charango*, the drum, and the reed flute. Music and dance dominate Latin American life. Numerous holidays and festivals are celebrated on the continent every year, and there's hardly a month when some part of the continent isn't gearing up for a festival. National festivities reach their peak with folk festivals, most in February or March. The largest and most famous is the Brazillian Carnival in Rio de Janeiro, unequalled anywhere in the world for beauty and joy. The most important festivals in Peru and Bolivia are held in February-March and June-July.

When to visit and how long to stay

Determining how long to stay is one of the most important decisions a tourist must make. For an extended tour you'll need to organize in a totally different manner than for a short visit, vacation, or business trip, and it's worth your while to do so before setting out.

INTRODUCTION

Getting to know South America inside and out is a matter of month after month of intensive touring. The first condition for success is command – albeit of the most rudimentary nature – of Spanish (or, for Brazil, Portuguese). *Mochilero* touring of this sort usually lasts from three months up to a full year, and allows you to visit most countries on the continent, exploring them exhaustively and comprehensively. Eight to ten months seems to me the optimal length for such a trip, broken down more or less as follows: two to three months in Argentina and Chile, three to five months in the Andean countries (Bolivia, Peru, Ecuador, and Colombia); two to three months in Brazil; and one more month for the remaining countries.

The tourist with this much time available can fix his original port of entry at whatever point is cheapest to reach, and move around in accordance with weather conditions and the various special events that take place throughout the year.

Argentina and Chile
The period from September to March is best; plan to visit the southernmost regions close to the middle of that period, when the weather there is best. Before September and after March the continent's southern reaches suffer harsh and unpleasant wintry weather, when touring is almost impossible. These countries' central and northern areas can be visited the year around.

Brazil and Venezuela
The period from October to June, the hot season, is recommended. Then you can go most places with ease, tan on the beach, roam the jungles, visit the cities, and so on. The desire to participate in the Carnival, celebrated annually in February or March determines for most tourists when they go to Brazil, and this is how it should be. Participating in the Carnival is undoubtedly an experience not to be missed; what's more, it's held at the best time of the year for a visit.

The Andean countries
These may be visited the year round, though the summer months (November-February) are the wettest, with showers liable to mar your enjoyment. During those months excursions to the mountains and jungle are difficult, so it's a good idea to make the effort to come during the winter (May-September), when although it's a bit cooler, the skies are clear and the weather excellent.

On the Galapagos Islands (Ecuador), as in the countries along the equator (Ecuador, Venezuela, and parts of Brazil, Colombia,

*I*NTRODUCTION

and Peru), the weather is stable the year round, with no extreme differences among the seasons.

These climatic details describe somewhat generally the course of the season according to a rough division of the continent, and are meant for those traveling for extended periods. Those making shorter visits (the majority of tourists, after all) will find a more precise description of the climate in the chapters on each country; furthermore, a section dealing with local weather is included for each of the large cities.

Tourists who want to know as much as possible of South America within a limited time period, may opt for a number of different possibilities, according to their special interests. In all events, it seems to me that any visit to South America, even if you wish to focus on a certain region and a simple field, requires at least three to four weeks. It's most desirable that it be planned with enough flexibility to allow for possible changes in your intinerary.

None of this applies, for example, to those coming for a week-long organized tour of Brazil to attend the Carnival, or for ten days of sailing among the Galapagos Islands. But apart from such limited frameworks you should allow a longer period. The great distances, extreme variation from place to place, range of sites, and tour and holiday possibilities make this much time necessary. One must always bear in mind the chance of delays on the way, so that a packed and precise timetable – reminiscent of one's last visit to Switzerland – would be wholly inappropriate here.

How much does it cost?
Until the early 1980s, the air routes from Europe and the United States to South America were among the world's most expensive. Governmental intransigence concerning charter flights, and objections to price competition among the various airlines gave rise to a situation in which, while airfare between Europe and North America was significantly reduced, the lines to Latin America remained very expensive. This naturally deterred tourists from coming.

All this has changed recently; since the mid-1980s fierce competition among the various airlines has led to tremendous cuts in airfares. Today they are not much higher than for flights of similar length to other destinations and we are the fortunate beneficiaties.

On top of this drop in fares there's another factor – the depreciation of the local currencies. The difficult economic situation of the Latin American countries finds expression in

INTRODUCTION

inflation and frequent devaltuations of their currency against the dollar, which has gained greatly in strength in recent years even in comparison to stable European currencies – and all the more so in comparison to the South American currencies, which generally serve as legal tender in rickety economic systems that have been in a distressed state for some time.

From the tourist's viewpoint, of course, there's a distinct plus to this situation. Domestic price rises do not keep up with the rate of devaluation, so that with each passing year South America becomes cheaper for the tourist who has dollars or a stable European currency to spend. A meal that had cost $10 two or three years ago will today cost the equivalent of $5 – and sometimes even less.

South America is, therefore, a better tourist bargain then ever before. On the one hand, airfare is cheaper than in the past; on the other, expenditures for transportation, accommodation, food, shopping and so forth are far lower than they used to be. The cost of living is not uniform everywhere, and prices, of course, vary from country to country. The cheapest countries to visit are the Andean ones, especially Bolivia, while the most expensive are Venezuela, Uruguay, and Paraguay. Even the last three, however, which in the not-too-distant past were expensive even by European and American standards, have become significantly cheaper, and a visit there today is no more expensive than an intermediate-priced tour in Europe or North America. Countries once considered prohibitive, such as Argentina, Chile, and Brazil, have become much less expensive, and the devalutation of their currencies gives you the chance to enjoy a tour of reasonable standards at truly rock-bottom prices.

The young and thrifty tourist who has brought a tent, sleeping bag and cooking stove can get by, counting his pennies, on about $50 a week. His less parsimonious fellows can do very well indeed for less than double that amount. More mature tourists will find that a night in a reasonable hotel can be had for no more than $10, and that living expenses need not exceed about $10 per person per day. Obviously, the tourist who wishes to spend $50 or even a $100 a day will succeed with no trouble, but he will have to be almost outrageously extravagant to do so. That's how it is – it just isn't expensive here.

True luxury tourism does not come cheap here, either. The best hotels in Bogota, Caracas, Lima, Rio, Sao Paulo, Buenos Aires and the like are rather expensive, especially at peak tourist season or at holiday or Carnival time. Car rental rates resemble those the world over, but first-class restaurants tend to be less expensive than their counterparts in the Western world.

*I*NTRODUCTION

In conclusion, it can be said that the range is broad; each of us must choose a path in accordance with our means. On every budget, though, tourists will find South America open, ready to meet them, and easy on the wallet.

First Steps
Once you've decided how, when and where to go, all that's left is to make practical preparations for the journey. The next section deals with these matters, spelling out everything that must be done before leaving home, in order to make the trip as successful, easy, comfortable and inexpensive as possible.

Documents and papers
Anyone going to South America requires a valid passport, except for citizens of certain South American countries who may cross into neighboring states with nothing more than an identity card. Some of the Latin American states require that your passport be valid for at least six months beyond your date of entry. It's best to get your passport some time prior to your trip, for some of these countries require you to obtain an entry visa in advance, and issuing this visa generally takes several days.

In our chapters on each country, we've spelled out the relevant regulations and documents you'll need; study them before you go. We should again mention that immigration regulations in the South American countries are in a constant state of flux; you **must** consult the embassy, consulate or tourist bureau of the country you intend to visit, shortly before your trip, in order to obtain up-to-date and reliable information.

Countries that require an entry visa have fixed procedures for issuing them. You'll need to present a passport, an entry and departure ticket, a photograph, and relevant travel documents (reservations, a letter from your place of work, etc.) The visa takes from one to three days to be issued, and usually involves no difficulties. All visa matters should be seen to in your own country, but if necessary, they can be obtained en route, in each of the countries you visit on the way.

A tourist card issued by airlines or distributed at frontier posts to those arriving by land has replaced visas in many cases. This card, which is free, must be filled out before you land or at the border station, and handed to the immigration officials along with your passport. A stamped copy will be attached to your passport, and returned when leaving the country.

We must stress that, as a rule, government clerks, police and military personnel check documents punctiliously, so keep them on you at all times, properly stamped and arranged. Many

INTRODUCTION

tourists have found that letters of reference (for example, a letter confirming that you were sent on business by your employer), various certificates (preferably with your photograph), and documents that have an official look to them are frequently of help in getting pesky clerks or policemen to leave you alone.

Proof of immunization against malaria, smallpox, and other diseases is no longer required in South America, apart from special and rather infrequent cases.

A tourist's national driver's license is accepted in most South American countries, on condition that a Spanish translation has been attached. Even so, we recommend that you obtain an International Driver's License and make sure that one of its languages is Spanish.

A Student Card is good for certain discounts and benefits. In Argentina and Chile students are granted discounts on public transportation, though foreign students may have to engage in lengthy bargaining to receive them. In Peru, significant discounts are given to students on tickets for museums, archeological sites, and more. Venezuela discounts certain domestic flights. The essential condition for using your Student Card is that it be valid and bear your photograph.

One should not go to South America without an **insurance policy** covering health and baggage. Theft has become a common occurrence throughout the continent, and the uninsured tourist is liable to suffer great financial damage. The matter of health insurance, however, is even more serious. Because disease is rife, and medical care and drugs are expensive, under no circumstances should one leave a matter as important as health insurance to chance or luck; no knowledgeable tourist would ever set out without being properly insured.

Though it can hardly be described as a document, you'll find in your travels that an MCO card is as important as if it were one. An MCO is a flight voucher issued by airlines that are members of IATA, and is honored by all other IATA members. At many border points where you'll be asked to show a departure card, and when you apply for a visa, an MCO will satisfy the requirement in most cases. It's important to check that its value is specified in dollars and in no other currency, for the voucher is calculated according to the value in the currency in which it was paid. At the end of your trip you can apply your MCO to pay for the flight ticket you want, or you can redeem it where it was issued or at the airline office.

INTRODUCTION

Health

Most serious diseases have been totally eradicated in South America, and linger on only in the most remote jungles. Malaria no longer strikes in the cities and towns, though those wishing to penetrate deep into the jungles should bring malaria pills as a preventive measure.

Intestinal diseases are very widespread in South America, due to the poor sanitary conditions and inappropriate food storage methods. Be prepared for the near certainty that at some stage you'll come down with intestinal trouble. It's worth your while to bring along any medication you're used to taking. Don't hesitate to consult a doctor in serious cases, for common diseases such as hepatitis are liable to cause you great distress if not discovered in time.

Drink bottled water only. Despite the fact that in most large cities the water undergoes filtration and purification, its still contains pollutants and bacteria, which not infrequently cause stomach aches and more serious ailments. Carbonated drinks and bottled water will help you overcome the problem (we're not referring to mineral water but to ordinary water that has been boiled and purified). When you're in the country or in places where bottled drinks are unavailable, boil your drinking water and purify it with chlorine tablets.

Mosquitoes and other flying pests are especially common in tropical areas, and are a real menace. **Don't go there** without large quantities of mosquito repellent and – no less important – ointment to spread on the bite when the repellent fails to work. A visit to Asuncion, Paraguay, or the jungles of eastern Ecuador cannot but end with dozens or hundreds of painful bites.

Every tourist must bring along a small kit with first-aid supplies and medicines. Many kinds of medication are hard to find in South America, and those which are available are expensive and not always usable due to their age or storage conditions. Before you set out, see your doctor in order to obtain an adequate stock of essential medications. A short list of essential drugs and medical items follows:

Medication for intestinal diseases.
Painkillers.
Fever pills.
Anti-malaria pills.
Chlorine tablets for water purification.
Antibiotic ointment.
Antiseptics.
Gauze pads, bandages and adhesive tape.
Medication for chronic illnesses.

INTRODUCTION

The chronically ill, and heart and asthma patients, should consult their doctors concerning the treatment they may require in the climatic conditions and altitude of the lands they're going to visit. Asthmatics should be doubly cautious when going to high elevations, where even healthy people find it hard to adjust to the thin atmosphere.

Women should bring tampons and birth-control pills in sufficient quantity since these items are difficult to obtain in Latin America, except in some of the large cities.

Before setting out, it's best to have a thorough checkup to ascertain that your health permits you to take the trip. Medical care in South America is generally not of the highest quality, and it's best to try not to need it. See your dentist for preventive treatment to forestall problems that might arise during your tour. I would definitely not recommend South American dental care, except in truly urgent cases.

For the trip itself, I'd recommend bringing an extra pair of eye glasses and the lense prescription. Contact lenses, though generally convenient to use, are liable to cause problems and discomfort in dry areas and at high elevation.

Thus far we've been speaking of the continent in general. It's obvious that in certain places – mainly cosmopolitan capital cities – the sanitary conditions are good and medical services advanced. Nevertheless, do yourself a favor and set out well-equipped and prepared for most eventualities.

Finances

The most popular and convenient currency to use and exchange in South America is the U.S. dollar, recognized and sought after everywhere; converting it presents no problem in the large cities. The Pound Sterling, Deutsch Mark, and Swiss Franc are also recognized, but exchanging them can involve problems, especially on the black market.

Currency laws vary from country to country. How much money to take and in what form depends to a great extent on the regulations in effect in the countries you decide to visit.

Brazil, Argentina, Bolivia and, to a large extent, Paraguay, Peru and Colombia, have black markets in foreign currency. For cash dollars, moneychangers will give you local currency at higher rates than the banks offer. When visiting these countries, it's worthwhile to carry more cash and fewer travelers' checks. Credit card transactions and bank transfers involve the official exchange rate, since charge slips are calculated according to that rate and the transfers are paid in it – in local currency. Given

INTRODUCTION

that the difference between the official and "black" rates may reach 50% it's only wise to take advantage of this discrepancy.

The theft epidemic that has spread through some of the South American countries – especially Colombia, Peru, Brazil, and Venezuela – has led many banks to refuse to cash travelers' checks out of fear that they may be stolen, and, at times, tourists are put through an exhausting bureaucratic procedure. A letter of credit is not efficient either; getting it honored is a slow and complicated affair and here, too, payment is made at the official rate.

Those traveling for short periods can make it easier on themselves by carrying cash, whereas long-term travelers would do well to divide their resources into a number of baskets, to minimize risk.

In certain countries – Uruguay, Venezuela, and at times Bolivia and Ecuador – travelers' checks can sometimes be converted into cash dollars for a fee, but the regulations in these matters are always changing and cannot be relied upon. This point is particularly important for tourists who want to stock up on cash en route to countries with black markets.

It's worth your while to bring a credit card. Their use is widespread throughout South America, and can be used to purchase goods, services, and for cash withdrawals. It's important to note that cash withdrawals involve a 4%-5% commission – $40 or $50 per thousand; you should consider whether this service is worth the price. In any case, using your credit card is worthwhile only in countries where there is no black market, so that your account will be debited at the same rate as that at which you would change money on the spot.

The alternative to carrying cash or using a credit card is travelers' checks. We recommend using small denominations – nothing over $50; hundred-dollar travelers' checks are harder to cash. In small towns, it is difficult to exchange travelers' checks in any case; not only is the exchange rate low, but there is a high commission as well. It's best to stick to travelers' checks issued by Bank of America, Thomas Cook, and American Express.

Always keep your money, credit cards, and documents **well-hidden** in your clothing. Guarding against theft here requires precautionary measures that we're not accustomed to in Europe and North America; nevertheless they are essential, and mustn't be scorned.

35

INTRODUCTION

What to take
As on any trip, the question arises here, too: what to take and what to leave behind? As a rule, I suggest taking as little as possible. In my opinion, the advantages of traveling light immeasurably outweigh the satisfaction of wrapping yourself in extra garments, for, after all, we've set out on a trip, not a fashion show. My personal view, acquired after many and extended tours, is that we don't use a considerable portion of what we've brought along, and that during a short tour most of it proves wholly unnecessary. True, it's hard to leave a house bursting with everything and reduce your world to a suitcase or a single small backpack, but there's no getting around it. When we travel we leave behind an entire world – family, friends, places – and our belongings as well.

Almost everything you need can be procured during the trip. Perhaps not the same kind, style, or quality, but I've yet to meet even one tourist who's walked the world's highways naked. During the trip you will accumulate many souvenirs and gifts, so it's truly worthwhile to start out with the lightest load possible – replacing necessary items with resourcefulness.

Clothing
Pack clothes in accordance with the season and destination of your trip. Businessmen must pay strict attention to their dress, though jacket and tie are usually not necessary. In large cities formal evening dress is customary for men and women, as is sportswear for the young. *Mochileros* will feel at ease in jeans and casual wear, though they should pack more festive clothing for occasions that require it.

Simple, light clothing is always appreciated, and is easy to carry and wash. It's best to refrain from carrying around elegant evening attire that must be carefully packed and protected. The effort simply isn't worth it.

I wouldn't recommend setting out with more than one pack or suitcase, and this, too, should be no larger than medium-size. Luggage weighing more than 30 pounds or so becomes a heavy burden, and past 44 pounds (20 kilograms) it becomes expensive as well. Many South American airlines are strict about baggage limitations and charge for excess weight.

Comfortable walking shoes are perhaps the most important item of all. You'll need them for any kind of hike or excursion, and it is no exaggeration to say that a poor pair of shoes can ruin an entire tour. Don't skimp here!

I recommend that you pack the following:
Change of clothes for daily use.
Two light shirts.

Introduction

Underwear, socks, handkerchiefs.
Walking shoes.
Evening shoes.
Sweater.
Evening clothes.
Jacket.
Raincoat, umbrella.
Swimsuit.
Shower kit, sewing kit, first aid supplies.

Camping Gear

Those embarking on an extended tour and intending to explore the entire continent should put everything in a backpack, including camping gear. When buying camping gear, be sure that its quality is appropriate for your needs. Remember that it must serve you for long months, and that cheap equipment, saving you money at the time of purchase, is liable to prove a painful impediment when you're on the road.

A list of essential items follows:

A lightweight **backpack** with **internal** metal frame, lots of pockets, and laces to which a sleeping bag, mattress, and other gear can be tied.

A **sleeping bag:** Chose one appropriate for the season and the area to which you are headed. For a lengthy trip through a number of climatic zones (-5 or -20 degrees Centigrade) you should get a warm sleeping bag made of down. It must be of excellent quality, well sewn, and with a reliable zipper. Sleeping bags come in various sizes and shapes; be sure that yours matches your dimensions. The "mummy" style, wide at the shoulders and narrow around the legs, is the best of all. It holds body heat well and is easy to carry. Synthetic-filled sleeping bags are much cheaper, but are much larger, bulkier, and heavier. Remember that you'll have to carry it on your back – week after week and month after month – and the inconvenience will outweigh your savings. On the other hand, bear in mind that the down bag has one great disadvantage: when it gets wet, it loses its efficiency and special qualities; sleeping in it then is downright unpleasant.

A **mattress:** To soften the bed of rocks on which you'll spend many a night, we recommend – highly, if you've got a down sleeping bag – an easy-to-carry mattress. There are two common types: foam-rubber and inflatable (especially made for capming). The latter costs more, but provides comfort and ensures a good night's sleep, essential after a full day of walking.

INTRODUCTION

A **tent:** We recommend a two-man, two-layer model with a floor. A one-man tent isn't enough, for you're unlikely to find yourself alone on outings into the country. A two-layer tent provides better protection against rain, retains heat, and repels moisture.

A **cooking stove:** This is essential on hikes through the countryside, and economical in town. Since gas for camping stoves is almost unavailable in South America and comes at great cost when it is at hand, we think it best to use a kerosene stove. The most popular models are made by Colman and the Optimus company of Sweden. They are reliable, safe, and easy to carry. Remember to exercise great caution when using them. Flammable materials may cause disaster if you don't treat them with the caution they deserve.

Utensils: Bring the minimum, but choose good ones. Metal or aluminium is best. Food should be kept in plastic or cloth bags, since cans take up more space in your pack.

A **canteen:** Preferably of aluminium. It's worthwhile to bring a collapsible water container, essential on extended trips in remote areas.

Miscellaneous: Pocketknife, flashlight, rope, etc.

Buying equipment represents one of the largest expenditures of your trip. It's therefore worthwhile to do some comparison shopping and not buy hastily. At the same time, I must again stress that economy must not be at the expense of quality, for the "saving" is liable to cost you dearly on the road. It's also worth noting that camping equipment is in great demand in South America, so that at the end of your trip your gear can be sold for a reasonable price; not much lower than what you paid for it.

The traditional centers for buying camping gear are London and New York, where you'll find the widest selection and the most attractive prices. Though London has many stores that handle camping gear, the best, in my view, is the Youth Hostel Association store at 14 Southampton Street (Tel. 836-8541). This is a gigantic store where you'll find it all – from shoelaces to emergency dehydrated rations. A tourist could enter this store stark naked and come out a few hours later with everything needed for a trip around the world. YHA members receive a 10% discount on all purchases.

In New York you can pick up your gear at any of hundreds of camping and sporting goods stores. The largest, Paragon, offers a seemingly inexhaustible selection of merchandise, at prices suitable for all budgets.

INTRODUCTION

Photography

One of the most enjoyable aspects of a trip is reliving it. The thrill of viewing photographs of familiar scenes and showing them to friends and relatives can be just as great as that of the tour itself. So make your photographic preparations in advance, acquiring appropriate equipment and learning at least the basics of how to use your camera.

Lots of people travel around South America with complex and complicated photo systems. South America is a paradise for photographers who will find it fertile ground for expression and creativity. Such experienced "shutterbugs" tend to bring along a number of cameras, lenses, and types of film.

To the tourists who wish to record their trips without dragging around a portable studio I recommend taking a single camera and two lenses – wide-angle and telephoto. It's worth your while to buy good and reliable equipment, to pack it carefully and to **insure** it. It's best to avoid bringing expensive, fancy equipment since during your trip it is apt to get bounced around in a way that may damage it, and may well tempt the sticky fingers of thieves. Film is expensive in most South American countries, excluding a few isolated areas where it can be bought duty-free (chiefly in Chile and Argentina). So bring an adequate supply with you; you can always sell anything left over on the spot. As a rule, ASA 64 film is the most convenient since this speed is sure to be appropriate for almost any light and weather conditions on the continent. ASA 400 is also worth having along; it's hard to get in South America and comes at an especially high price when it can be found. Purchases of photo supplies in South America itself should be limited to the large cities. Elsewhere you'll find that in addition to the problems of actually finding film and of coping with its price, some of what is on the shelf may have expired.

Film developing in South America is done at laboratories of various kinds, and the risk isn't always worth running. As a rule, it's best to send undeveloped film by **registered mail** to Kodak or Agfa labs in the United States or Europe. In certain places – Buenos Aires, Sao Paulo, or La Paz, for example – you can be relatively confident about having film developed in the local Kodak labs. Slide film whose purchase price includes processing should be sent directly to the company's lab, from which it will be returned to your home address.

The best type of film is a matter of personal preference. For myself, I've found that slides, though slightly complicated to view, convey sensations, shapes and sizes far better than prints. By this method, which is also less expensive, you can take lots

INTRODUCTION

of pictures, and decide afterwards which to include in your "viewing" collection, and which to file away or discard.

Language

You won't have any language problems in South America's large cities. Most people dealing principally with tourists have sufficient command of English to help you get what you want, and it can be assumed that shortly after your arrival you'll pick up enough of the local conversational "code" to express basic needs. The problems begin when you venture outside the professional tourism framework, and even on its fringes – taxis and restaurants. Few taxi drivers or waiters speak English. Communication is in Spanish only, as are most restaurant menus.

It's even worse in outlying areas. English-speakers are few and far between in the towns, and in villages – nonexistent. On the roads, too, and even in tourist bureaus, airline offices, and banks, it's hard to find someone fluent in the language of Shakespeare, Keats and Milton, or even with enough English to understand a request for a glass of water.

Nor will a command of Spanish or Portuguese solve the problem altogether. In many places – Paraguay, northern Bolivia and the mountain towns of Peru, for example – ancient Indian languages are used. Although most locals speak Spanish at one level or another, it's hard to maintain verbal communication with them in the accepted sense of the term.

Those who've set their hearts on a long, thorough exploration of the secrets of the South American continent absolutely must acquire the basic linguistic skills before setting out. It's true that one picks up a language during a trip, and that within a month or two one is able to carry on a basic conversation with the locals, but advance preparation will make things much easier and increase your enjoyment. No less important is the fact that advance study will establish a correct grammatical foundation, to which a large vocabulary will be added as you go. On-the-road study, though easier, is built atop a shaky foundation, whcih will demand great efforts to repair afterwards.

Part Two – Setting Out

How to get there

By air: This is the fastest and most convenient way of reaching South America from Europe or the United States. Most

INTRODUCTION

European airlines maintain service between their respective capitals and various destinations in South America, as do the national airlines of the South American countries. The latter also fly to various destinations in the United States, as do Eastern and Pan American.

A number of ticket options are available to and from South America; their terms and fares vary from airline to airline and from country to country. Excursion tickets, limited in time, are generally the cheapest, followed by youth and student tickets. The most expensive are ordinary tickets sold at IATA prices. A combined ticket, by which different sections of the route are flown on different airlines, is usually more expensive than flying all sections with the same airline.

Planning your flights requires thorough preparation and comprehensive market research. Careful investigation and resourcefulness can save lots of money and cut the price of your trip by 20% or more. The open market and fierce competition have led to a situation in which passengers aboard the same plane on the very same flight may well have paid completely different fares.

As a rule a round-trip ticket is worthwhile, unless you're making an extended trip and don't want to commit yourself about where and when it's going to end. Airline tickets bought in South America are subject to excise taxes at rates that vary from country to country; this makes them significantly more expensive. A round-trip ticket purchased outside the country from which you're returning is exempt from tax.

Those who want a one-way ticket should check which routes and combinations may make the trip cheaper. Such routes, for example, go via the Carribean islands, Central America, and so on. Certain destinations are traditionally more expensive than others. Flights to Sao Paulo, Buenos Aires, Santiago, La Paz, and elsewhere are far more expensive than those to Lima, Rio de Janeiro, and Bogota. Relatively low-cost flights reach the latter group of cities from London, Paris, and Miami. It's a good idea to inquire at travel agencies which specialize in these destinations about the cheapest and best way to get there.

Ordinary tickets are more expensive one-way than round-trip. Their great advantage lies in the fact that they are calculated on a mileage basis. Holders can change dates and arrange for stopovers on the way, so long as these remain within the permitted mileage. Thus, for example, a New York – Buenos Aires ticket gives one the right to stop over in Miami, Caracas, Belem, Rio, and Sao Paulo at no extra cost.

*I*NTRODUCTION

London and Miami are known as preferred ports of departure for Latin America; here you can usually find the cheapest tickets. A significant portion of these tickets are sold over-the-counter only, and travel agents in other countries are not permitted to sell them. A stopover in one of those cities and a visit to some of these agencies may be worth your while, even though you must remember that two days in London cost money too, as does a separate ticket to London. At times it may be cheaper to buy a slightly higher-priced ticket where you live, with the margin offset by the savings in time, stopover expense, and the effort involved in getting around a foreign city.

The national airlines of Venezuela (Viasa), Colombia (Avianca) and Peru (Aero Peru) are known for being less expensive than the other South American flag carriers. They fly to numerous destinations, but you must change planes in their respective capitals. European airlines such as Air France, Iberia, and the Portuguese TAP also offer seasonal packages worth taking advantage of. Never buy until you've checked and compared prices!

When buying discounted tickets, be very, very careful about their validity and reliability. Remember that any change involves additional payment, and it's best to know how much is in question in advance. Avail yourself of the services of reliable travel agents – there are charlatans in this field too. Best of all are travel agencies that specialize in tourism to South America, and have package deals with various airlines.

London abounds in travel agencies offering discounted air tickets. I recommend checking airfares at Worldwide Student Travel, Ltd., at 37 Store Street (Tel. 580-7733), where you'll frequently find attractive and reliable offers.

By land: An overland trip from North America via Central America is a unique experience. It can be done by car, bus, or train, and you'll need to do the Panama-Colombia stretch by sea or air. The highway there still isn't suitable for traffic, and is impassable several months out of the year. Due to political tensions in Central America, you should check exactly when and how to cross various countries, and, even more so, when and how not to. If you're driving, bring along plenty of spare parts, and have someone along with mechanical knowledge. Your car papers must be in good order, since they'll be inspected every time you turn a corner.

INTRODUCTION

Part Three – Easing the Shock: Where Have We Landed?

Previous sections of this introduction have dealt with the preparations and arrangements necessary before the trip begins. Now we shall survey some relevant details concerning the trip itself, to make the experience of landing in this alien world a bit easier. The material we're about to present is meant first of all to facilitate your adjustment to South America, but reading it before you go may be of great importance in determining the form and nature of your tour. Here you'll find much **useful information** about all spheres of your trip which will help you overcome quickly, comfortably, and efficiently the range of problems liable to arise at the very beginning of your trip.

The paragraphs that follow offer some general advice, and in the chapters on each respective country, you'll find more specific information on those countries and their sites.

Accommodations

South America offers a wide variety of accommodation possibilities. All the large cities have luxury hotels, some of which belong to the world's great hotel chains; standards here equal those in the Western countries, with prices set accordingly. In the large cities you'll also find locally owned luxury hotels, whose prices are lower although the level of service is in no way inferior.

Intermediate-class and inexpensive hotels abound. Almost all hotels outside the cities charge intermediate or low rates, and many are very inexpensive. Lodging is significantly cheaper in the Andean countries than in the lowland countries. (Brazil and Venezuela), but conditions there, too, are far worse.

Be careful when choosing a hotel that is not first-class. In many places these are not regulated in any way. At the same time we must note that the Ministries of Tourism in most South American countries are making an effort to enforce hotel regulations. In the large cities and major tourist centers you'll find that most hotels are clean, reliable, and altogether satisfactory.

Away from the big tourist centers and along the roads, there are always places to stay. Almost every village has a house that serves as a hotel, but don't expect much here – at best a creaky bed and rickety chair. Sanitation and cleanliness, too, are not the best. In most hotels outside the luxury class, rooms with

INTRODUCTION

private bath are a rarity. Even a basin and mirror, are luxuries that cannot be taken for granted here.

Youth hostels aren't popular in South America, though you will find them in some places, generally small towns. On the other hand, it's customary to put up young travelers in churches, schools, youth clubs, and even fire stations – for no charge.

Camping grounds are rather rare. In some countries – mainly Argentina, Chile, and Brazil – they do exist and can serve the tourist public. They aren't organized along North American lines, and the tourist must provide his own tent and sleeping equipment. On many routes tourists spend their nights under the stars in improvised campgrounds and an informal atmosphere.

Food and drink

In the culinary field, too, we've landed in a very strange place. We've all heard the legends about Argentinian steaks and Brazilian coconuts, but we should also be ready for what comes along with them – guinea-pig (*cuy*) in Peru, eel in Chile, and similar terrors elsewhere.

The South American kitchen, like everything else on the continent, combines Indian tradition with Spanish influence, and its national character is determined by what's grown where. A lot of meat is eaten in Argentina, Uruguay, Paraguay and Venezuela; lots of fish and seafood in Chile and Peru; and tropical fruit in Brazil. Potatoes and rice are standard side-dishes in every restaurant; so is soup a very popular item throughout the continent and many varieties are served.

Milk products are hard to get in the Andean countries, in contrast to Argentina, Chile, and Brazil where they are plentiful – and excellent. *Empanadas* (stuffed pastry), *mate* (South American tea), and many other delicacies are only some of the contents in the bursting menu of excellent food and drink enjoyed by the local populace. We'll cover them in detail and at length in our Introduction to each country.

South American restaurants are innumerable. Every second house serves as one, and every street corner has two more. In the cities, a variety of food is served at all levels of quality, while in towns and villages native and peasant cooking is the most common fare. Hygienic conditions aren't the best, but that's something you get used to as time and upset stomachs pass... Western manners and dress are customary in the better restaurants, while the more popular ones favor a free and informal atmosphere. Eating at streetside stands, kiosks, and

INTRODUCTION

market stalls is a common practice. It's a quick and cheap way to get a meal, and how most of the locals get their nourishment. Try it, but remember to check how clean, or perhaps how "undirty" the place is. Mealtimes vary from country to country, according to the climate.

Fruit and vegetable lovers will have problems in the Andean countries, where most produce may be tainted with various diseases Even if they appear healthy to the eye, their insides are liable to be infested. You must therefore adopt an ironclad rule about fruit and vegetables: peel them, cook them, or throw them out. If you can't peel or cook it, don't try it!

Vegetarians will manage quite well. Although vegetarian restaurants aren't very common, the major foods on which a vegetarian diet is based are available in abundance, and can be prepared yourself. Tourists who abide by Jewish dietary laws are in for a harder time: kosher restaurants exist only in Buenos Aires, and the rest of the continent is slim pickings.

To help you avoid embarrassing mistakes in restaurants – getting a side-dish when you thought you'd ordered a hefty steak – we've appended a basic list of foods in Spanish:

English	Spanish
Breakfast	Desayuno
Lunch	Almuerzo
Dinner	Cena
Wine	Vino
Beer	Cerveza
Juice	Jugo
Milk	Leche
Butter	Manteca
Jam	Dulce
Cheese	Queso
Eggs	Huevos
Bread	Pan
Salt	Sal
Pepper	Pimienta
Sugar	Azucar
Gravy	Salsa
Soup	Sopa
Salad	Ensalada
Fish	Pescado
Meat	Carne
Chicken	Pollo
Steak	Bife

INTRODUCTION

Grilled Meat	Asado
Mixed Grill	Parrillada
Chips/Fries	Papas Fritas
Dessert	Postre
Cake	Torta
Fruit	Frutas

Domestic transportation

Airlines link the South American countries with one another. International flights are frequent and convenient, and prices resemble those of short international flights in the West. Domestic flights are another story. Here the range is broad, complications are rife, and confusion reigns.

In Brazil, Argentina, Peru, and Colombia the airlines offer an open ticket for unlimited flights during a predetermined time period. In these countries, where covering distances overland requires many days, this is an offer certainly worthy of consideration. To go from Rio de Janeiro to Manaus or from Buenos Aires to Bariloche takes days or weeks by land, and the cost of an individual flight is high. In addition, Aerolineas Argentinas has reduced-price night flights, which cost no more than equivalent trips by bus. You must therefore weigh the alternatives well and decide accordingly. An unlimited-flight ticket may be bought only **outside** the country in which you intend to fly.

The armed forces of the South American countries also operate flights that carry civilian passengers. These are cheaper than their civilian counterparts, but take off at irregular intervals and generally involve antiquated aircraft.

Another typical problem of domestic flights is overbooking. Airlines are not reliable when issuing tickets, and frequently sell more tickets than the number of seats at their disposal. You must therefore get to the airport early; otherwise the flight is liable to fill up and leave you waiting for another. Cancellations, delays, and changes of routes are also common occurrences, for which the tourist must be prepared.

Be very sure to mark your gear, although even this doesn't guarantee that it will reach its destination. The care of passengers' luggage, especially in Peru, is negligent and contemptuous. Try to carry as much as possible, and relegate to the baggage compartment only the necessary minimum, **after** you've packed and marked it properly.

Driving a private or rented car is widespread in all South American countries. More and more tourists choose this way to

INTRODUCTION

get around, and avail themselves of the large international car-rental companies or local firms.

If you want to bring your own car, you should stock up on spare parts and make sure your documents are in order. Bureaucratic difficulties are especially frequent at border crossings, and garage services are rare in the hinterlands. Consult Auto Club experts in the United States or Europe before you set out for up-to-date material, including maps and the addresses of local auto clubs (which we've provided in the chapters pertaining to each country). Auto Clubs in South America are very active, and their personnel provide assistance and guidance to members of similar clubs abroad.

Your car must be in top mechanical condition before you set out. In the Andean countries many roads reach thousands of meters above sea level, where engines must be specially tuned. Note that the road networks of Colombia, Venezuela, Brazil, and Bolivia are undeveloped (apart from main highways) and difficult to drive on. My experience is that it's better to avoid driving there, and find another way of getting around. When traveling off the main roads, be sure to have enough fuel for the return trip, plus spare parts – service stations are almost nowhere to be found. A breakdown here is both unpleasant and expensive.

Car-rental rates vary from country to country, but usually don't exceed $100 per week for mid-sized cars. The minimum age for renting a car is 22 (25 in some countries), and the customer must leave a sizeable deposit or a credit card. It's important to insure the car when you rent it.

River boats are a common means of transportation in a number of areas, especially the eastern portions of the Andean countries and northwest Brazil (the jungles). Here you'll find that the only way to get from one settlement to another is by boat or ship along the river, and not infrequently you'll have to rent your own to reach your destination. Rental fees are high, but energetic bargaining will drive them down to something almost reasonable.

The major means of **public transportation** include trains, buses, trucks, and taxis. **Trains** operate only in some of the countries, and most are old, slow, and uncomfortable. They are not as common a way of getting around as they are in Europe, and I wouldn't recommend planning a tour based on the railways. **Buses**, by contrast, are the most popular form of transportation, and connect all places of settlement. In several countries – Brazil, Chile, Colombia and Argentina, for example – the buses are modern and comfortable; in others they're

INTRODUCTION

motorized crates. Differences in quality and service are extreme, precluding a uniform and precise description. On some routes, you'll find smiling stewardesses; elsewhere you'll find terrible overcrowding and rampant theft. In any case, the bus remains the cheapest and most efficient way of getting around on land. **Shared taxis and minibuses** run on many intercity routes. Their fares are higher than the buses, but their advantage lies in far greater speed, comfort and safety. **Trucks** (*camions*) carry passengers mainly in the poorer countries, where they ply remote dirt roads with their loads of shoulder-to-shoulder animals and people, the latter seated on piles of freight and clinging to their baggage lest it tumble off. It's a unique experience by all accounts – a cheap way (sometimes the only way) of reaching many remote places.

Hitchhiking is common in Chile and Argentina, chiefly in their southern regions. Hitchhikers there – especially women – get lifts easily, and vast distances can be covered quickly and cheaply. In the Andean countries, an accepted practice is to demand payment from a passenger, even if he thought he was getting a free ride. In Brazil and Colombia tourists have been attacked and their gear stolen: be careful.

Urban transportation is efficient in most large cities. Bus lines, subways, taxis, and *colectivos* (shared taxi service) contribute to mobility in densely-populated urban areas and are usually rapid and reliable. In many countries, particularly the Andean ones, taxis have no meters and the fare must be agreed upon with the driver – **before starting out.**

Personal security

One of the most severe problems that visitors to South America are liable to encounter is protecting themselves and their belongings. A combination of social and political ferment, plus the desperate poverty, makes violent outbursts all too common. Sometimes these are directed at the authorities, in the form of hostile underground activity, and sometimes aimed at the tourist, whose valuable baggage attracts thieves. The problems are especially serious in Colombia, Peru, Brazil, and Venezuela – in that order. In the Introduction to each of those countries, we have included guidelines on appropriate behavior and preventive measures. Argentina, Uruguay, Paraguay, Chile, Bolivia, and Ecuador are considered to be tranquil and relaxed; have no fears about touring there.

Local currencies

The various South American currencies are noted for their worrisome instability. In recent years they've been considerably

INTRODUCTION

devalued against the dollar; for the tourists, this has lowered the cost of a stay there significantly. If on an extended visit, you'll find that for every dollar you change on your last day you'll receive more local currency than you got when you arrived. Accordingly, it's worthwhile to change money only to cover your immediate needs since within a few days you are likely to get more for your dollars.

Banks and moneychangers (*Casa de Cambio*) change currency; the latter usually offer a slightly higher rate and far less bureaucratic red-tape than the former. Though several countries do not allow private dealing in foreign currency, and restrict activity to the major banks, black-market moneychangers will always find a way to offer you a more attractive rate. Be extremely careful about dealing with them – verify their reliability and be sure to count what they give you.

Most airports also have some arrangements for converting foreign currency. If you've arrived on a weekend or holiday, change enough to cover your needs until the next business day. In the city itself you probably won't find a bank open, and may be forced to change money at a poor rate. Cash dollars are always preferred, but it's best to hold onto these for countries where a black market operates, and use travelers' checks elsewhere.

When entering a new country by land, don't change more money at the border checkpost than you'll need to reach the nearest large city, where you can expect to get a better rate. In any event, check and compare rates carefully with a number of moneychangers before you decide; differences among them are by no means small. Count the money you're given very carefully, making sure you get what you paid for. Many moneychangers will try to exploit your innocence by holding back a few bills from the stack they hand you.

When leaving a country, get rid of any remaining local currency; it's worth considerably less in other countries, even those right across the border.

Tourist services

A well-arranged and efficient system of services awaits the tourist in most South American countries. As tourism increases, governments become more aware of its tremendous economic impact. They have begun investing in expanding and improving the infrastructure and services which will help tourists get oriented and acclimated. This infrastructure includes not only hotels and restaurants, but also information centers, transportation services, guides, various publications, and more.

INTRODUCTION

Major airports will greet you the moment you touch down with counters to provide information, hotel reservations, car rental, and baggage checking. The bus and taxi fares from the airport into town are usually fixed by the government.

Almost every city has a tourist information bureau which offers guidance, maps, and other material. One of the noticeable drawbacks of these bureaus is the lamentable fact that their personnel often speak only Spanish, so that a tourist who cannot get along in that language will find it hard to avail himself of their services.

In addition to the tourist bureaus, several other organizations offer tourists information and assistance. The most important are the various Auto clubs (*Aotomovil Club*), which will keep you updated in matters of transportation and tour routes. There are also the military geographical institutes (*Instituto Geographico Militar*), where you can obtain maps for hiking tours, the nature reserve authorities, etc.

Medical and health services

The most common health problems that a tourist to South America is liable to suffer are intestinal problems and difficulties in adjusting to the thin air at high altitudes. In both cases you'll probably need nothing more than short and routine treatment, which can be obtained at any regional clinic.

For more serious problems you'll have to go to a hospital. In national capitals and other large cities there are British or American hospitals, to which tourists should turn in case of need. In other cases, it's best to turn to English-speaking private physicians to whom you can describe your ailments, though you must be cautious about accepting treatment which seems inappropriate to you.

First-aid services in South America aren't the best, and still can't treat many health problems. You must therefore be doubly careful, and seek out qualified medical help in any case of suspected illness.

Dental treatment that can be put off should be put off. When that is impossible, visit a qualified dentist who has modern equipment.

Altitude – how to cope with thin air

The high elevation of South America's mountains requires one to take appropriate measures. Remember that the atmosphere is thin at these altitudes. The amount of oxygen is less than at sea level, upsetting the body's equilibrium. If you breathe at your

INTRODUCTION

normal rate you'll simply take in less oxygen, and consequently suffer from asthma-like sensations of choking and weakness. A certain amount of attention or caution may alleviate the problem and lessen its impact. Common side-effects are dizziness, nausea, headaches, and at times fainting. To avoid these reactions – which involve a certain discomfort even if they are not dangerous – you must take a number of precautionary measures. First, it's best to reach the mountains by an overland route, in order to moderate the rate of ascent and give your body a longer period of time to acclimatize. If you arrive by air, there will be a sharp transition which results in a quicker and stronger impact. In any event, be sure to set aside the first twenty-four hours for rest, relaxation, and reduced food intake. This will grant your body a suitable interval to adapt to the lower percentage of oxygen in the atmosphere.

At high elevations you should refrain from physical effort, including that considered insignificant under normal conditions. Walk slowly, do not run or carry heavy loads, slow down even more when walking uphill or climbing stairs, and take frequent rest stops. Keep physical activity to a minimum: don't smoke, and avoid large, heavy meals. If necessary, you can buy special medication in drugstores which expand the blood vessels, thus increasing the amount of oxygen supplied to the body. Asthmatics, heart patients, and pregnant women tend to suffer more at high altitudes and it's recommended that they stay away from these areas as much as possible.

In most cases, as we have said, rest will help but sometimes this may have to be augmented by medical care and short periods of oxygen treatment. Hospitals, clinics, and even ordinary institutions recognize the problem, are experienced at treating it, and will be glad to help. As time passes, the body grows accustomed to the new situation and can resume normal activity – if more slowly and cautiously, and less strenuously.

Discounts for students and young travelers

In South America students are eligible for discounts on public transportation and admission to various sites. The discounts are not offered on all occasions, and certainly not automatically. For details, consult the section on documents, and the text, where you will find these discounts mentioned wherever they are offered.

In regard to accommodation, few places offer reduced youth rates and those which do, are mentioned in the relevant chapters.

INTRODUCTION

Behavior and manners

The rules of manners accepted in the West apply here as well. The "dress code" is similar, though less formal. Both men and women wear sporty evening wear for official events, concerts or dinner in an elegant restaurant. In the daytime, light and airy clothing is wholly acceptable. For men, shorts are out of place except on the beach. In certain places, such as Caracas, the police can fine anyone who's improperly dressed in public. In Brazil, seashore dress is acceptable, but only in town and not on an intercity bus, for example. Women should dress modestly and avoid revealing garments. At holy places, those improperly attired are not allowed to enter.

Behavior toward women is somewhat archaic here, a matter which carries with it a certain grace and charm. Among descendants of the Indians as well, whose women bear the brunt of the physical burden, women are accorded respect and are treated with great consideration.

Latin Americans are friendly and hospitable. Many tourists are warmly welcomed into local homes, where they are made to feel at ease.

Among the European communities in Argentina and other countries it is customary to greet guests with a friendly kiss on the cheek. It's a gesture of friendship, and expresses no intimacy of any kind. The South American way of life is conservative and restrained; conspicuous permissiveness is nonexistent here.

In Spanish it is accepted practice to address people with the formal *usted* rather than the familiar *tu*. This serves to express respect and esteem rather than distance and estrangement.

It's customary to tip restaurant waiters (10%-15% of the bill) and service personnel (a small amount). Taxi drivers with whom you've negotiated a fare at the beginning of your trip do not expect a tip.

Keeping in touch

Postal and telephone services in Latin America are far from efficient. They are slow and clumsy, unreliable, and some are expensive. An airmail letter sent to South America is liable to spend an extended period (up to several weeks) en route, perhaps not arriving at all. *Poste Restante* (General Delivery) service is available in national capitals, but I wouldn't rely on it too much. Mail which arrives for you at the post office will only be kept for one month. American Express offices accept mail for their customers, and I recommend this method: have your

INTRODUCTION

correspondents send letters to an American Express office, where they will be kept for you until you get there.

Sending postal items from South America also requires attention. Mail letters only at post offices; use airmail, preferably registered. Film and important items should be sent registered, and only from main post offices. Avoid stamps in favor of a post-office cachet, since stamps not infrequently catch the eye of the sorter, who appropriates them for himself; more seriously, he destroys the contents. Letters encounter prolonged delays on the way, and if your tour lasts for two or three weeks your letters are likely to reach friends and family when you're already back at home, planning your next vacation.

Sending parcels involves much effort, time, and trouble. Parcels must be of fixed weight, and need to be boxed and wrapped. Those weighing more than one kilogram require inspection by a customs clerk, who sits – of course – somewhere other than the post office. The parcel has to be left open for inspection; only then can you seal it. Parcels may be sent by air or surface mail. The former is fast and sure, but is immeasurably more expensive than surface mail. Though surface is cheaper, it is far slower, and your parcel may spend six months in transit. It also happens that surface-mail parcels "get lost" and do not arrive at all. Surface mail is considered reliable from Argentina, Chile, Ecuador, and the Brazilian coastal cities, but not from Peru, Colombia, or Bolivia.

South America has telephone links to the rest of the world. International phone service is slow and expensive, but the connections are usually of satisfactory quality. Placing an international call from your hotel is liable to involve a wait of several hours. It's therefore wise to make most such calls from the telephone exchange found downtown in the large cities. These have several booths to which callers are summoned, each in his turn. The minimum length for such a call is three minutes. Collect calls are not always possible; it depends on where you are and to where you're calling. This is not the case in Brazil, where the International phone service is quick and efficient, and one can make collect calls from any public phone.

Shopping and souvenirs

Any tour of South America will add many kilograms of souvenirs and purchases to your luggage, whether it's a Dior suit from Buenos Aires, a poncho from La Paz or jewelry from Brazil. Every traveler, even the most frugal, will end up buying at least a few of the innumerable souvenirs encountered on the way. And this acquisitiveness is perfectly justified. In South America you'll find

INTRODUCTION

an amazing concentration of crafts and other artifacts, called *artesania*, most hand-made – the glory of local craftsmen and artists. Their beauty and the special character of these items will have you digging into your wallets time and again, to buy for yourself, relatives, friends, and anyone else on your list.

Those touring only one or two countries will find information on the characteristic wares of each country in the relevant chapters, and will soon discover the wealth of possibilities. Keep in mind a number of important rules so as to avoid later problems with budget and weight (or rather excess weight). Firstly, remember that all of South America resembles one gigantic market. It's hard to find a product exclusive to a single place, though there are, of course, differences in quality, types, and the like. Accordingly you'll be able to compare styles, prices, and quality, to ponder the various options... and to bargain! Bargaining is essential here; if you accept the stated price, not only will you pay more than you should but you'll also hurt the vendors' feelings, for they look forward to this give-and-take with their customers.

Each of the South American countries has its own characteristic forms of *artesania*. These give artistic expression to the economic condition of the country in question and the sources of its treasures. Thus Chile abounds in metalcrafts, Argentina in clothing, Brazil in precious stones, and the Andean countries in woolen fabrics and woodcrafts.

Andean *artesania* is noted for its strong Indian influence. In this region you'll find lovely woollen products, musical instruments, pottery, and astonishingly beautiful woodcarvings. Wall hangings, various garments, and antique fabrics are only some of the local treasures, and it's only natural that we'll cram them into our suitcases in considerable quantities. It's best, in my opinion, to send these home by mail (see above), for otherwise they're liable to interfere with the rest of your trip, getting in your way and causing problems.

In the cities you'll find tourist shops that offer top-quality merchandise at prices to match. As you travel you're bound to find these where they're made, closer to their natural environment and at their natural prices.

Overland border crossings

To explore South America properly, we must cross borders rather frequently. Whether during a combined tour of Argentina

INTRODUCTION

and Chile, a journey from Colombia to Ecuador, or on any other route, we'll encounter a number of traits common to all these inspection points.

All frontier stations are staffed by immigration officers in charge of the gates to their respective countries. They allow traffic to pass only during certain hours, which vary from station to station. In most cases border crossings are open from morning to nightfall, sometimes closing for an afternoon *siesta*. Some stations are open for only half a day on weekends. Check out the situation thoroughly before you reach the border, so as not to lose a full day's touring.

The main crossing points have separate lines for tourists and local citizens; crossing procedures here are simpler and quicker. In most countries you'll have to fill out a tourist card, stamped by the immigration clerk, which indicates how long you are permitted to stay. Always be sure to request the maximum time allowed – generally 90 days. Though getting an extension once you're in the country is possible, it can be very time-consuming.

Moneychangers congregate near crossing points. When changing money with them beware of being misled as to the exchange rates or in counting the bills.

Border posts can be reached by taxi or local bus. Direct bus routes from one border town to its counterpart on the other side are more expensive. It's therefore best to get to the border, cross on foot, and continue by vehicle on the other side after having taken care of the formalities.

Taxes and custom duties

Tourists must pay duty only on valuable items brought in as gifts, cigarettes and alcohol in excessive quantities, or commercial samples. These excluded, tourists can bring in personal belongings, including all required gear.

Among the many taxes imposed in South America, tourists are obliged to pay two: a port tax when leaving the country, and in some countries an excise tax on air tickets purchased there. Port taxes vary from country to country, as do the rates of the air ticket tax. When planning your return trip, it's therefore best to try to end your tour in Argentina, Chile, Brazil, Uruguay, Paraguay, or Venezuela, where no such tax is imposed. In the

INTRODUCTION

Andean countries taxes can add more than 10% to the price of the ticket.

Working hours

The afternoon *siesta* is almost the Latin American trademark. In every country, businesses, shops, and offices close for two or three hours in the afternoon; during that time it's hard to find a seat in a restaurant, and even the streets seem more crowded.

Most businesses open early in the morning and stay open until evening. Office reception hours are usually only before noon. On weekends most businesses and offices are closed. Shops are open half-day on Saturdays, and are closed Sundays. Many museums are closed on Mondays.

Holidays and festivals

South America's holiday season, on a continent-wide basis, lasts the entire year, though most special occasions tend to be concentrated in February-March, June-July, and December, when you can celebrate the carnivals in Rio and elsewhere, Inti Raimi (the Sun Festival) in Peru, and Christmas everywhere. During those seasons, much of the local population are themselves on vacation, and the general ambience isn't conducive to business. On national holidays, most services and many institutions are closed. When planning your tour, be sure to keep the dates of holidays in mind, and arrange matters so that your visit won't suffer on their account.

Weights and measures, temperatures, electricity, time

The metric system is used throughout South America, with the meter (slightly more than a yard) as the unit of distance, and the kilogram (2.2 pounds) for weight. Temperature is measured and reported in degrees Celsius. The voltage varies from country to country, and sometimes even between different parts of one country. The most common is 220 V, but 110 V is used in many places.

South American clocks lag behind Greenwich: GMT is three to five hours ahead of South American time, depending on location. The following table gives the time difference between South America and New York and London:

*I*NTRODUCTION

12 Noon	New York time	(GMT) London time
Asuncion	11:00	16:00
Buenos Aires	11:00	16:00
Bogota	12:00	17:00
Caracas	11:00	16:00
La Paz	11:00	16:00
Lima	12:00	17:00
Montevideo	10:00	15:00
Quito	12:00	17:00
Rio de Janiero	10:00	15:00
Santiago de Chile	10:00	15:00

ARGENTINA

The Republic of Argentina, the eighth largest country in the world and the second largest in both area and population in Latin America, is an important tourist center. Tourists to these parts will find a wide range of places to visit and plenty to capture their imagination: they can explore the exquisite countryside with its spectacular scenery, and experience a wide variety of cultural and social life and local folklore – not to mention enjoying this gourmet's paradise, with its cuisine based on meat, meat, and more meat.

Argentina is undoubtedly one of the most interesting countries in South America. It is a land of contrasts, with a strife-torn history of intermittent foreign and civil conflicts. A country that only a few decades ago was among the richest in the world is today, due to incompetent administration, in critical economic straits, with massive unemployment, a three-digit inflation, and foreign debts totaling tens of billions of dollars. But the roots of the problem strike much deeper.

During your stay in this country, a vast range of sights will greet you: from the tropical forests in the north to glaciers in the south, from the Atlantic beaches in the east to the peaks of the Andes in the west. You will encounter giant rivers, lakes, glaciers, and other natural phenomena, as well as huge cities, small villages, and isolated farms. Along with intellectuals and cultural and artistic giants, you will find gauchos (cowboys) and colorful Indians.

Argentina combines European traditions and mores with a Latin American way of life – with all its advantages and disadvantages. You will notice the mixture of colonial architecture, restaurants specializing in Italian or French cuisine, western apparel and mannerisms, and native music and dress, – all representing a glamourous social and national mixture.

Argentina will swiftly capture the heart of the newly arrived tourist. You will find a warm welcome, and will be quickly embraced into the fold. You cannot fail to notice the essential difference between this country and those around it, especially when you reach Buenos Aires – one of the largest and most beautiful cities in South America. The Argentinians themselves are convinced of their superiority over their neighbors, and act

ARGENTINA

accordingly. In South America, the joke goes that if you buy an Argentinian at the price he is **worth** and then sell him at the price **he thinks he's worth** you will have made the deal of a lifetime... There is something to that.

In any case, whether you come for a short visit to Buenos Aires – and there is no doubt that such a trip is worthwhile – or whether you intend to explore in depth the mysteries of this vast country, which only a few even of its own inhabitants are fortunate enough to know intimately, you can count on having a rich and varied experience. Argentina, more than any other South American country, is equipped to handle tourists. The sophisticated network of public services makes it easy for visitors to find their way around, thus transforming your trip into a pleasant and exciting experience for the entire family.

History

The dominant motif in the history of this country, from the day the Spaniard Juan de Solis first landed on its shores in 1516, is the continual domestic strife. Argentina was discovered by the Old World nearly five centuries ago, (with an indigenous population estimated to have been approximately 300,000 people at the time). Since then, the country has suffered many years of military, political, and economic instability.

Juan de Solis was killed by the Indians as soon as he landed on the shores of La Plata. It was only in 1536 that the first Spanish force of any significance arrived. Numbering several ships and hundreds of men, led by Pedro de Mendoza, it laid the foundations of Buenos Aires. However, the settlers, weakened by continuous attacks of the local Indians, soon left the area. Under the leadership of Domingo Irela they moved to Asuncion, conquering large areas of Paraguay on the way. Pedro de Mendoza's expedition brought horses with them, and cattle which thrived on the fertile pastureland, and became the basis for Argentina's prosperous meat industry.

At the same time as Buenos Aires was abandoned, and the Rio de La Plata left to the Portuguese (who had already conquered Brazil), groups of Spanish began infiltrating Argentina from the north (arriving from Peru, which was already in the hands of Pizarro) and Chile in the west. These pioneers founded several towns, the most important of which are Tucuman, Salta, Jujuy and Cordoba in the north, and Mendoza and San Rafael in the west. It was only in 1580 that Buenos Aires was again resettled, this time by Juan de Garay. The inhabitants gained their livelihood, until 1594 (when the Spanish government enforced trade restrictions), from the harbor through which gold and silver

ARGENTINA

from the Peruvian mines were exported. In 1617 a local semi-autonomous administration was set up, headed by Arias de Saavedra as Governor, with its capital in Buenos Aires.

The trade restrictions, which remained in force for nearly two hundred years, naturally gave rise to a small-scale smuggling industry. However, this did not contribute to the economic or population development of the town. At the same time, serious battles were being waged against the Portuguese from Brazil, who held a strong military outpost in Colonia, on the Uruguayan side of the gulf, and attempted to stem the development of this important port. In 1776, when it finally became clear that the area could not be dominated from Peru, which is some 4000 km away, Buenos Aires was declared an autonomous viceroyalty including within its borders Uruguay, Paraguay, and Bolivia. Two years later, all trade restrictions were rescinded and Buenos Aires once again became a free port – a change that paved the way for its development and prosperity. The population of the town soon doubled and its inhabitants, the large majority of whom were Creoles (Spaniards born in South America), grew in power. From posts of limited influence in the Cabildo (town council), they soon achieved positions of real importance.

The year 1806 marked the begining of the conflict between Argentina and Great Britain when the British, in pursuit of Napoleon's allies, captured Buenos Aires. However, the British were soon ousted, thanks to the stalwart resistance of the Creoles. A further attack in 1807 was also repulsed. The memory of these attacks, as well as the subsequent British domination over the Falkland Islands, has remained a thorn in the side of the Argentinians.

Their success in repulsing the invaders strengthened the self-confidence of the inhabitants. Therefore, when the French conquered Spain in 1810, exiling King Ferdinand VII and attempting to impose their authority on Spain's South American colonies, the Cabildo of Buenos Aires convened and on the 25th of May, 1810, decreed the establishment of a "Council for Self-Rule". They deposed the viceroy, entrusting the administration to Manuel Belgrano, the designer of the Argentinian flag and one of the country's great national heroes. To this day, Argentinians celebrate the 25th of May – the day on which Spanish rule was abolished – as their Independence Day. They also celebrate the 9th of July, since it was on this day in 1816 that the National Congress met in Tucuman and declared Argentinian independence.

During the Napoleonic wars, instability reigned in the European colonies in South America. The Spanish viceroy, exiled to Peru,

ARGENTINA

attempted to conquer the rebellious Argentina, but the small armies led by Generals Belgrano and San Martin overcame him, and the danger of renewed Spanish domination receded. However, this victory was accompanied by radical changes in the structure of Argentina: Paraguay broke away and declared herself an independent republic (1811) and Bolivia was re-annexed by the viceroy in Peru. The most severe problem was the internal polarization within Argentina itself. The split between the inhabitants of Buenos Aires – mainly cultured Europeans, merchants and professionals – and the provincial landowners and rich cattle breeders, who could call out armies composed of the gauchos employed on their ranches, continued to widen. The city-dwellers aspired to set up a united state with a central government in the capital, whereas the landowners sought a confederation that would formally unite the various provinces while preserving their rights to administer their own ecomomic and internal affairs.

The harsh struggle between city and province, between centralized state and confederation, continued throughout most of the 19th century, and was accompanied by political disputes and military uprisings, years of oppressive despotism, and r peated rebellions.

At the same time the capital continued to develop and grow. Bernardino Rivadavia, who in addition to being Argentina's first president was also mayor of Buenos Aires in the 1820's, enacted far-reaching reforms that contributed to the social and cultural development and prosperity of the town. The most important of these reforms were those encouraging immigration from Europe, and the institution of freedom of religion and freedom of the press. Rivadavia, whose term in office contributed greatly to growth and stability in this stormy century, was forced to resign and leave Argentina in 1827, when his army was unsuccessful in a war against Brazil. Although the Brazilian army was repulsed by the Argentinians in the Uruguayan lowlands, the Brazilian naval blockade of the Rio de la Plata had a catastrophic effect on Argentinian trade, and Rivadavia had to pay the price. After a short period of anarchy, Manuel Rosas was elected governor; by harsh and oppressive measures he managed to restore order in Argentina. Rosas, a federalist, was brutal towards his opponents, while entrusting wide powers to his supporters in the provinces.

At the same time, Rosas waged war against Bolivia's territorial annexations and involved himself in Uruguayan domestic struggles. His policies led to a confrontation with France and Great Britain, and in 1838 these countries sent warships to blockade the Plata, causing serious damage to Argentina's

ARGENTINA

economy and fostering unrest and rebellion among the Argentinian population. Urquiza, governor of Entre Rios Province, who had signed a pact with Brazil and Uruguay, raised an army of over 20,000 men and overthrew Rosas.

Urquiza, like his predecessors, was unable to bring peace or stability to Argentina. Under his influence, the establishment of a federation on the lines of the United States was approved and treaties were signed with France, England and the United States. Some of the agreements granted these powers free movement along Argentina's rivers. This proved detrimental to Buenos Aires' economy, which was based on customs revenues and port services. As a result, the city rebelled and seceded from the federation; only in 1859 was Buenos Aires re-annexed into the federation, by Urquiza – but not for long! Bartolome Mitre, who was mayor of Buenos Aires, led another rebellion and defeated President Derqui Urquiza's successor. Mitre was subsequently elected president of Argentina in 1862.

The next twenty years laid the foundations for Argentina as we know it today. The five-year "War of the Triple Alliance", between Paraguay on the one hand and Argentina, Uruguay and Brazil, on the other, broke out in 1865. The war ended without a decisive victory for either side, despite the unprecedented losses in life and property on both sides.

Following the war, the internal situation improved, in spite of the continuing strife between the various provinces. At the end of the 1870s, when the skirmishes with the Indians of the south intensified, General Julio Roca expelled them with great brutality, killing thousands. This opened the way for new settlements in the south, in faraway Patagonia and Tierra del Fuego. The people of Buenos Aires, who opposed Roca's policy on the division of the new territories, rebelled, but the revolt was swiftly quashed by the General's army. The status of the city was changed; formerly both the national capital and capital of the province, it now became an autonomous district (like Washington D.C.) and the capital of the federal republic. The town of La Plata was designated capital of the province. This change finally stabilized the relationship between Buenos Aires and the rest of Argentina. Roca, who was considered a national hero, was elected president of the country. His moderate policy, which favored peace and economic growth, was welcomed by most of the power groups in the country. The ensuing boom served to widen his support and increase his power and influence in subsequent years.

Roca devoted the ten years of his rule to strengthening Argentina's economy and furthering its technological and

ARGENTINA

industrial development. The mass immigration from Europe, especially from Italy and Spain, brought with it a cultured and progressive element. This immigration was further supported by foreign investors, especially the British. It was during these years that the basic export economy was established. Meat refrigeration methods were introduced and a rail network was built to facilitate the transport of goods from the north and center of the country to Buenos Aires. From there they were sent to Europe, particularly to England. The fruits of these huge investments and the concomitant boom in agricultural development, together with a hundredfold expansion in the area of cultivated land and increased sophistication of meat processing and storage methods, all contributed to Argentina becoming one of the most important and richest grain and meat exporters in the world by the beginning of the twentieth century.

These processes were accompanied by territorial stabilization. Ranches and pasturelands were fenced off which curbed the greed of the landowners; their legions of workers gave up their nomadic existence on the boundless pampas for the organized discipline of the restricted *estancia* (ranch), large though these were. At the same time, there was a new trend towards greater political participation by the general public, in particular that of the middle class, which essentially consisted of the recent immigrants from Europe. They organized as a bloc, clamoring against the ruling landowners for free universal suffrage. They did not hesitate to use violence in order to achieve their aim; the results shook the regime, which was forced to gradually yield to their demands. But the pace of reform was too slow for the public's liking.

Only in 1916, did the birthpangs of democracy end when the first general elections were held in Argentina. Irigoyen, a leading activist for democratic reform, was elected as president. His term of office, during the First World War, was characterized by far-reaching social changes. In the process, the landowners and industrialists lost some of their traditional power. Irigoyen was careful to adopt a neutral stance in Argentina's foreign policy, and refused to support the United States against Germany.

During the war, the country enjoyed an economic boom, since the countries of Western Europe and the United States bought huge quantities of meat and grain. In fact, until the Wall Street crash of 1929, when the West stopped buying, the Argentinians continued to enjoy prosperity. By the outbreak of the Second World War the economy had recovered, and except for occasional radical agitation that was quickly suppressed, Argentina continued the process of internal consolidation while

ARGENTINA

restricting her involvement in the affairs of the continent or the West.

When war broke out in 1939 a new polarization was evident, between the opponents of fascism and Nazism, led by the Socialist and Radical parties, and the more conservative government, which aligned itself with Germany and Italy, and adopted a policy of isolationism. With the entry of the United States into the war, this polarization intensified, leading, in 1943, to Argentina's first military coup. This coup paved the way to power for Argentina's best-known modern leader, Juan Domingo Peron.

On the 4th of June 1943, a group of officers forced President Castillo to resign, appointing in his stead General Arturo Rawson, who was himself replaced, by General Ramirez after only two days in office. Less than a year later he was also forced to resign, accused of being a puppet in the hands of the allies. Throughout this period, Peron, then a young colonel, was head of the War Office in the Junta. At the same time, he was gathering popular support, especially among the trade unions, with which he was involved in his additional capacity as Minister of Social Welfare. Peron saw to the well-being of the workers, and won for them huge salary increases, social and retirement benefits, and the like. When Ramirez was deposed and replaced by General Parel, Peron was appointed defense minister (May 1944) and, a few months later, vice-president. Peron equipped the army and expanded its ranks, at the same time continuing to improve the lot of the workers. The economic situation of the country, which supplied the United States and Britain with vast quantities of food throughout the war years, steadily improved, and her economic independence enabled Argentina to adopt a nonaligned position in the war. Nevertheless, when it became obvious that Germany was about to be defeated on the battlefield, Argentina swiftly declared war on her, at the end of March 1945, thus appeasing her critics and ensuring her entry into the United Nations.

Within the country itself agitation against Peron, particularly on the part of the industrialists, landowners and radicals, intensified. On the other hand, Peron enjoyed the unqualified support of the president, the loyalty of the army and the police, and the affection of the people. Peron, aware of the significance of this agitation and its latent threats, moderated to some extent his harshness towards his opponents, granted the universities a certain amount of autonomy, sanctioned political organizations and freed hundreds of political prisoners. This liberalization encouraged his opponents to take action. In September 1945, they staged a huge demonstration in the streets of Buenos

ARGENTINA

Aires, in which 300,000 people participated, demanding a curtailment of Peron's powers. The government reacted harshly by arresting hundreds of people, among them some of Argentina's leading personalities. When the wave of arrests reached the top echelons of the army, opposition to Peron intensified. On the 9th of October, Peron was arrested by presidential decree and imprisoned, but as a result of strikes organized by his supporters in the trade unions he was released after a week. Peron's arrest gained him a permanent place in the national pantheon as the hero of the workers, championing their cause and preventing their exploitation by the rich, and also as the man who gave their country an independent foreign policy.

In February 1946, Peron was elected president by democratic vote and immediately began implementing his national aims. His main ambition was to strengthen the economy in order to enhance Argentina's international standing. He used the vast sums that had accumulated from export profits during the war years to purchase industrial equipment, to improve the railway system, to set up power plants, and to further industrialization. Aided by his wife, Eva Duarte Peron, a film actress whom he married in 1945 (known by the affectionate diminutive Evita), Peron continued his openhanded social policy, distributing company profits to the workers and lavishly honoring his public commitments. Eva Peron, who as head of the "Eva Peron Fund for Social Aid" distributed vast sums of money to the needy, enjoyed considerable political influence. Her death, in July 1952, traumatized the country, and considerably influenced her husband's political outlook.

Peron continued his policy of giving industrial and urban development priority over agriculture. He nationalized the banks and public utilities and increased government involvement in the economy. In 1949, he had the Constitution amended, abolishing the clause prohibiting re-election of a president; in 1952 he was elected for a second six-year term. Argentina began to experience economic difficulties, mainly in the form of a galloping inflation and financial difficulties. Peron turned to foreign financiers for help, while stubbornly pursuing his spendthrift policies. The economic collapse, the opposition of students on the one hand and industrialists on the other, and his attempts to stifle the Church's criticism of him, all contributed to his downfall in 1955.

Peron's opponents, who understood the problems inherent in his economic policy, concentrated on obtaining foreign credit and capital and on encouraging export, at the same time limiting and even reducing wages. In spite of the efforts of the interim

ARGENTINA

president, Lunardi, to forge an understanding with Peron's supporters and the Church in order to reinstate liberal constitutional government, the military managed to seize power again and establish a military dictatorship. The new rulers adopted a violently anti-Peronist stand, disbanded the remnants of the Peronist party and swiftly suppressed a military uprising by the supporters of the ousted president. Over succeeding years, Peron's supporters limited themselves to restricted participation in the new regime. Successive presidents pursued a moderate economic policy, devaluing the local currency to attract foreign capital and encourage export. The war against inflation, which involved limited credit and imposing various restrictions and prohibitions, created a political and economic situation that was new to a nation that had been accustomed to wild extravagance. Strong pressures were exerted on the government, which was increasingly forced to rely on the army to preserve its authority. The anarchy led to a quick succession of governments and presidents, each of whom had to contend with the problems left by his predecessor. Lack of public support meant that they were unable to implement any significant changes. The question of how to deal with the Peronists also contributed to the national chaos. The military's intermittent seizures of power helped control tempers for short periods, until 1966 when a strong military government was once again established.

This government held power until 1973. During its existence, the economic, social and political fabric of the country was destroyed, leading to major riots in May 1969. The swift decline of the economy, civil unrest and fear of the future led the military government to allow the return of Peron from his exile in Spain. Peron arrived in Argentina in November 1972, staying only a month. Under his influence his candidate Hector Campora was elected president in the elections that were held a few months later. Two months after taking office he resigned, thus opening the way for Peron's return from exile and his subsequent election as President in October 1973.

President Peron died on July 1, 1974; it is rumored that he did not die a natural death. His widow, Maria Estela Peron known to the crowds as Isabelita, who was her husband's vice-president, assumed the reins of power, assisted by some of his advisers. Her rule was characterized by internal anarchy, harsh violence, mass arrests, and the liquidation of political opponents.

This state of affairs led to another military coup. At the begining of 1976, Maria Estella Peron was overthrown, and replaced by a military Junta. The Junta dissolved the Congress, and abolished all democratic institutions. Throughout 1976-1977 civil war raged

ARGENTINA

between the Peronist underground and the military, during which thousands of people were killed. Tens of thousands of people were arrested, many of whom have not been seen since and whose fate still remains a mystery to this day. Entire families of Peronists or of suspected anti-government activists were arrested, and many young people were jailed for long periods. International organizations and political pressure were unable to penetrate the conspiracy of silence regarding the fate of those who had vanished, the *desaparecidos*. Even though occasional reports filtered through, regarding the existence of anonymous graveyards containing hundreds of corpses, the Argentinian government continued to turn a blind eye. It was only in April 1983 that a government spokesman in Buenos Aires declared that the missing people should be considered "as if no longer alive". His announcement led to a furor in the West.

The rule of the military Junta brought with it a relative calm, although this was accompanied by internal tension and a harsh regime. Until 1982 the government maintained its moderate policies in an attempt to stabilize the tottering economy and to strengthen the currency, which had been devalued a thousand fold. When it failed in this task – a failure that was accompanied by severe internal unrest – the government headed by General Galtieri, attempted to divert public attention from internal and economic problems to foreign affairs. In April 1982, Argentinian forces invaded the Falkland Islands, or, as they are known to the Argentinians, the Malvinas, in an attempt to capture them from the British, who had controlled them for over one hundred and fifty years. A desperate war was waged for these small islands, inhabited by some 2000 English-speaking citizens of British extraction. The British Army, obliged to defend the islands against the Argentinian invasion, fought under harsh conditions, far from their home base and in stormy and treacherous weather conditions. The war lasted for several months, during which time both sides suffered heavy losses. In the end, Her Majesty's Army routed the Argentinian forces, who were suffering from shortages of food, arms and vital equipment.

As a result of this heavy defeat on the battle field, General Galtieri was forced to resign. His successor scheduled free elections. The unity and fervor that had characterized the months of war vanished, as Argentina lapsed into yet another economic crisis.

The election compaign was dominated by the Junta's political and military failures and the issue of the *desaparecidos*. On October 30, 1983, the Radical candidate Raul Alfonsin defeated the Peronist Italo Luder. This was the first defeat ever suffered

ARGENTINA

by the Peronist party, a fact which has far-reaching political and social implications.

Since taking office, Alfonsin has been diligently fulfilling his campaign promises: the restoration of civil liberties, stabilization of the economy and investigation of criminal activity by the Junta. A number of former generals and presidents have been arrested and charged with murder and other serious offences. The new president is making great efforts to obtain international financial backing so that Argentina can meet its foreign debt, and has so far been supported in this effort by the Western nations.

Although Alfonsin's first year in office was plagued by political and economic difficulties, by 1985 a positive trend in both fields could be felt. His government initiated numerous administrative and constitutional changes, resolved the long-standing border dispute with Chile, and introduced financial and monetary reforms, all with widening public support. Despite the oppressing financial difficulties and national anger and frustration regarding the crimes of the military regime, a positive mood now prevails in Argentina. The general opinion, in the country and abroad, is that the country is finally on the right path; a path that can lead Argentina back to prosperity, growth and peace.

Alfonsin's liberal policies were demonstrated during the crisis which arose with Chile in 1984 over the sovereignty of the three islands in the Beagle Straits, south of the country. The crisis intensified and almost led to war between the two countries. Alfonsin held a referendum whereby it was decided to cede the islands to Chile, and he thus prevented any further deterioration of the situation.

Geography and Climate

Argentina is the eighth largest country in the world. It stretches over an area of 2.77 million sq/km in the southern half of South America. It is 3500 km long and 1400 km at its widest. The Republic is divided into 22 provinces whose borders have been historically, rather than geographically, determined.

On the east, Argentina borders on the Atlantic Ocean for some 2500 km; its western border runs more or less parallel to the continental divide in the Andes. In the north, Argentina borders on Bolivia and Paraguay, and in the northeast, on Brazil and Uruguay. These boundaries generally follow large rivers.

Argentina's topography is extremely varied. It is characterized by climatic extremes and marked differences in flora and fauna.

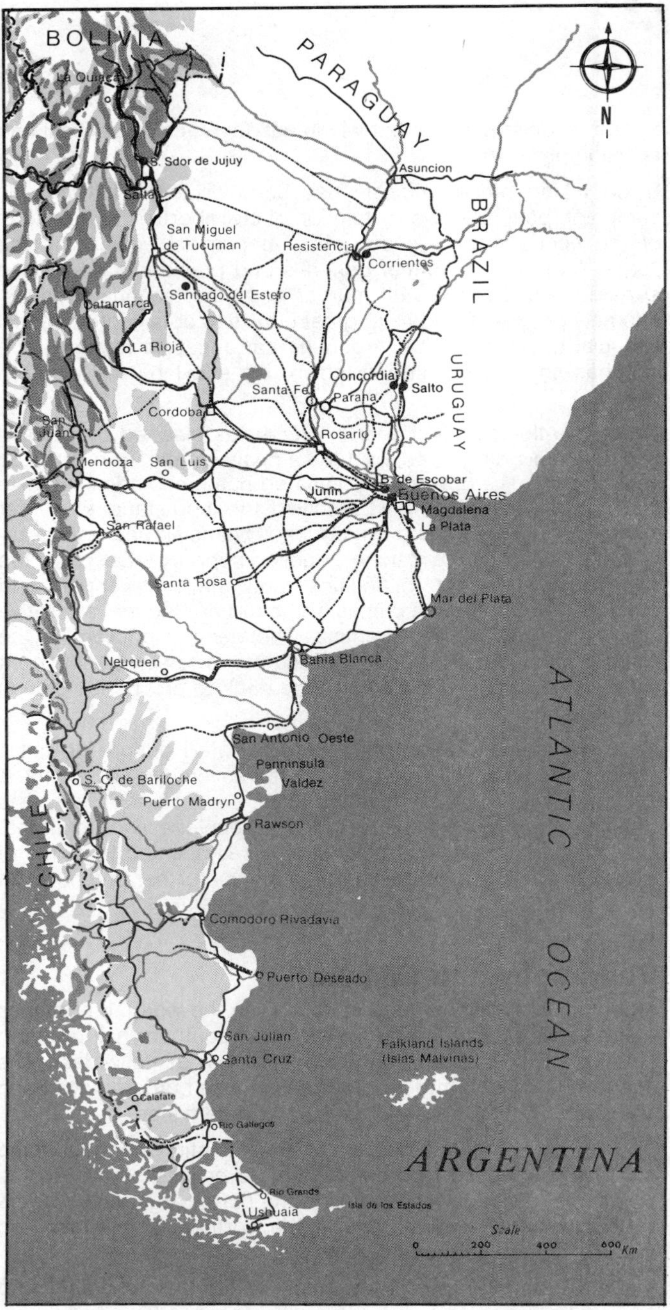
BOLIVIA
La Quiaca
PARAGUAY
S. Sdor de Jujuy
Asuncion
Salta
BRAZIL
San Miguel de Tucuman
Resistencia
Corrientes
Santiago del Estero
Catamarca
La Rioja
URUGUAY
Concordia
Salto
Santa Fe
Parana
Cordoba
San Juan
Rosario
Mendoza
San Luis
B. de Escobar
Junin
Buenos Aires
Magdalena
La Plata
San Rafael
Santa Rosa
Mar del Plata
Bahia Blanca
Neuquen
ATLANTIC OCEAN
San Antonio Oeste
Penninsula Valdez
S. C. de Bariloche
Puerto Madryn
Rawson
CHILE
Comodoro Rivadavia
Puerto Deseado
San Julian
Santa Cruz
Falkland Islands (Islas Malvinas)
Calafate
Rio Gallegos
ARGENTINA
Rio Grande
Isla de los Estados
Ushuaia
Scale
0 200 400 600 Km
N

ARGENTINA

Its western border is flanked by the Andes range, which reaches a height of 3000-4000 meters above sea level. The highest peak is Aconcagua, 6960 m above sea level, which is the highest in the Americas. The eastern slopes are not as steep as the western ones, and form a broad mountainous region which at its widest point extends for some 500 km, including the inner range of mountains. To the east of these mountains are the lowland regions: the Chaco (which continues into Paraguay) in the north, extending from the Paraguayan border to Cordoba; the pampas in the center extending from Cordoba to the region of Bahia Blanca; and Patagonia in the south, extending from Bahia Blanca to the Straits of Magellan. The lowland plains are fertile, consisting of alluvial soil deposited by rivers, and loess soil in the more rainy areas.

In contrast to the aridity of the Andes slopes, with their canyons and nature sites, the pampas are known for their fertility. Most of Argentina's grain is grown in this area. It is the agricultural development of this region that has made Argentina into one of the world's most important food suppliers. The Andean foothills stretch across the pampas through the center of the country (the provinces of Mendoza and San Juan). This area is rich in vineyards, and its grape harvests supply most of Argentina's wine. The "Gran Chaco" in the north (capital: Resistencia) with its temperate climate, is covered with forests, and serves the lumber industry and as pastureland. Argentina's "Mesopotamia", which includes the provinces of Misiones, Corrientes and Entre Rios, sandwiched between the Parana and Uruguay rivers, is also extremly fertile. In fact, the only non-arable area is the rocky dunelands of Patagonia, – this is mainly due to its cold, harsh climate and the strong winds that hinder the growth of any kind of plants.

Argentina is carved up by a network of giant rivers, which also serve as important transportation arteries. The enormous amount of water that flows through these rivers, together with a relatively high precipitation rate (the rainy season is the summer, from November to March) make Argentina especially blessed with ground water, particularly in the plains.

Argentina's climate varies enormously from one part of the country to another. The northern region has a sub-tropical climate, the pampas (including the province of Buenos Aires) have a temperate climate, while sub-arctic conditions prevail in Tierra del Fuego. More details concerning the climate are given below.

ARGENTINA

Population, Education and Culture

Argentina has about 27 million inhabitants, mostly of European descent. Unlike her neighbors in Latin America, only a few of the indigenous inhabitants remain, while the Creoles (Argentinian-born Spaniards) have generally assimilated into the waves of mass immigration from Europe. Some married Indians, and these are the forebears of the legendary gauchos (cowboys), who live mainly in the northern provinces. Successive Argentinian governments opened their doors to "anyone in the world who wishes to settle on Argentinian soil" (as stated in the Constitution). In particular, they encouraged immigration from Italy and Spain. Over the last 100 years, the country's population has increased twenty-five-fold(!), and the immigrants, who settled mainly in the towns, have contributed in no small measure to urban growth and development.

Approximately 40% of the immigrants came from Italy, and another 30% from Spain. Together, these groups fashioned the image and character of the country. There was also an influx of immigrants from England, France, Poland, Russia, and Germany, but these have, on the whole, assimilated into other demographic groups.

Most of the Europeans settled in the large towns, where they created a cultural, social, and commercial life along European lines. School and university education, social welfare, artistic and cultural life, fashion, as well as forms of polite behavior are also borrowed from European norms. This is especially apparent in the capital, Buenos Aires. More than a third of Argentina's population is concentrated in what is known as "greater Buenos Aires", the huge metropolis that is home to 10 million people. An additional 35% of the population lives in towns with more than 25,000 inhabitants. A mere 19% of the population lives in agricultural settlements spread over the huge expanses of the Argentinian countryside.

The European immigration had a decisive influence on the social structure of the country. The illiteracy rate is low (around 7%) in comparison to other countries in South America, and the education network has been developed in an attempt to reduce illiteracy still further. Both primary and secondary education are free and many students go on to university.

Social security is yet another proof of the preponderance of Western values in Argentina. The national insurance system has created an economic security which in turn has led to a socio-economic stability unparalleled in Latin America.

Freedom of worship allows members of all religions to practice

ARGENTINA

their beliefs as they see fit. In fact, 95% of the population are professing Catholics, and Christianity is the official religion.

The official language is Spanish, which is spoken in various dialects. In certain areas, especially in the north, Indian dialects are spoken, but these tend to be mixed with Spanish. European languages, in particular English and German, can be heard in the large towns.

Economy

In her economy, Argentina also stands apart from her neighbors. In spite of an extremely shaky economy, the Argentinians have one of the highest standards of living on the continent. Although Argentina is traditionally thought of as a meat and grain producer, and is still one of the world's main storehouses of grain, a trend towards increased industrialization has made itself evident during the past few decades. Although the strength of this trend has fluctuated according to the policies of successive governments, there is nevertheless a clear tendency to expand the country's industrial infrastructure, to increase the production of export goods, and to manufacture products locally rather than import them.

The main economic bastion remains, as always, agriculture. Around 12% of the land is cultivated, and of this, 60% is devoted to cereal crops, especially corn (nine million tons per year) and wheat (eight million tons). About 80% of the corn and wheat crops are exported. As far as livestock is concerned, the poultry industry has developed considerably over the last few years, alongside a corresponding increase in the number of cattle and sheep. At present Argentina boasts some 60 million head of cattle and some 35 million head of sheep, which are used for meat and for the flourishing dairy products industry. The quality of the meat is world renowned, and a huge industry has evolved for processing, freezing and exporting meat.

Industry is advancing by great strides, and this has been accompanied by the construction of an increasing number of power plants to lay the groundwork for the establishment of a large-scale industrial network in many varied fields. Argentina's main industrial production is still based on processing agricultural products, although recently efforts have been devoted to developing high-technology fields such as electronics, machinery and petrochemicals. Quarries, mines and oil wells have become a pivot of the economy, and much effort and capital have been invested in their development in the last few years. Today 36% of the gross national product is derived from industry, which employs 25% of the national workforce.

ARGENTINA

Approximately 80% of Argentina's exports are agriculture-based, and her imports are, on the whole, restricted to raw materials, spare parts, arms, machinary, etc. Argentina's trade balance has been in the red for many years now, and enormous debts have been accumulated, amounting to over 50 billion dollars.

The severe economic crisis that followed in the wake of the Falklands War in 1982 had grave consequences, and total economic collapse was averted only by massive international assistance and the intervention of the U.S. banking system. (The U.S.is one of Argentina's main creditors.) The exchange rate of the dollar changed daily and reached astronomical levels, with inflation soaring to 418% in 1983. In 1984 it reached an all time high of 647%, but that year marked the beginning of the national struggle to stabilize the Argentinian peso and economy. Economic guidelines were established, and their positive effect was already felt by mid-1985. The Argentinian government conducted fierce and stubborn negotiations with the International Monetary Fund. Several of the Fund's recommendations, if put into effect, would have had disastrous social repercussions, and were therefore rejected by the government. However, austerity measures were introduced, despite internal dissent, and in June 1985, economic guidelines were enforced, and the currency was changed – the austral replacing the peso. Inflation, running wild at 30% in the first half of 1985 (1000% per annum), was checked, largely due to the introduction of the austral. This success, combined with Argentina's conscientious payment of foreign debts, enabled her to receive further financial aid from both the International Monetary Fund and private banks.

General Information

How to get there

By air: The easiest way to get to Argentina from Europe or the United States is by plane. Aerolineas Argentinas runs scheduled flights daily from New York and Miami (The flight from New York takes less than 11 hours). Some of the flights have intermediate stops at Rio de Janeiro and Sao Paulo. Eastern Airlines and most South American carriers also have scheduled flights between the United States and Buenos Aires, but they take a longer route with stopovers and changes of plane. If you are not taking a direct flight, you should book with the Brazilian airline, Varig, whose flights stop at Rio or Sao Paulo, since they offer extremely pleasant flights, excellent service and marvelous food.

ARGENTINA

Most European airlines fly to Buenos Aires, usually with intermediate stops. Aerolineas Argentinas and British Caledonian offer two direct flights a week from London to Buenos Aires, and Varig offers three. It is well to bear in mind that such flights are quite expensive, but they are based on mileage, which means you can have stopovers at no extra charge (see "Setting Out").

There are daily flights from most South American countries, either on the respective national airlines or Aerolineas. Anyone starting from a nearby country with the intention of touring Argentina, should consider buying a "Visit Argentina" air ticket (for more details, see "Domestic Transportation").

Airports: Buenos Aires is served by two airports. Flights from other South American countries land in several of the other large cities as well (see the section on the cities for further details).

By land: Argentina has many crossing points along her borders There are frequent bus services from frontier towns to their Argentinian counterparts, but they are fairly expensive. Further details are given in the sections on the individual cities themselves.

There are rail connections between Argentina, Bolivia and Paraguay. The rail service to Chile no longer operates due to lack of passengers and political tension between the two countries. Train trips are long and tedious, and the trains old and slow. If you intend to travel by rail through South America, consider buying an unlimited travel pass for a period of 20, 30, 60, or 90 days in the Pullman carriage (reclining seats), which is the most comfortable and, indeed, essential if you are traveling long distances. The pass is valid in Argentina, Uruguay, Chile, Bolivia, Paraguay, and Brazil, and will make traveling considerably cheaper. You can buy the pass at the Rail Office, Calle Florida 729, Buenos Aires (open all day till 8pm, half-day Saturdays, closed Sundays). You should, however, bear in mind that bus travel is much quicker and no less comfortable than by train (except in Bolivia).

You can also enter Argentina by car, provided you have international documents and a customs form from the Automobile Club. It is a simple procedure if your car has a license plate from a neighboring country. The driver must be in possession of a valid international driving license.

By ship: It is also possible to cross the Rio de la Plata from Uruguay by passenger boat. Daily service is available, with the boat leaving Montevideo each evening and arriving at Buenos Aires in the morning. The journey is convenient, pleasant and

ARGENTINA

cheap. There is another ferry from Colonia. For further details, see the chapter on Uruguay.

Documents
Argentinian immigration procedures tend to change frequently and it is advisable to check with Argentinian authorities shortly before departing. North Americans need visas. So do business visitors from all countries. Western European tourists do not require a visa, although British citizens are advised to check specific requirements in force after the Falklands War.

Tourist visas are provided by Argentinian Consulates worldwide, after applicants fill out forms and submit a passport photo, a letter of recommendation and a round trip ticket. The visa is valid for one year and grants you three months stay in the country with unlimited exit and entry. If you intend to travel overland through South America and have difficulties obtaining a visa for Argentina, you would be well advised to obtain a visa in one of the other Latin American countries, since the Argentinian Consulates there are less particular about formalities (in particular, the possession of a round trip ticket).

You **must** carry your papers with you wherever you go, as you will often be asked to show them. If you are unable to produce them upon request you may find yourself in a very unpleasant situation.

Traveling overland, entering the country from Chile, some tourists have been asked to give a detailed account of their planned itinerary in Argentina. This is then listed on a special form attached to one's passport. Should this occur, you will have to have the form stamped at the police station within 12 hours of your arrival at each town. You should be careful to follow this procedure, to avoid unpleasant repercussions.

When to Come; National Holidays
Given the size of the country and the variety of climate, this question loses some of its relevance. The best time to travel is between September and March. Touring is more difficult between April and August (winter), especially as one goes further south. The weather is very stormy in Patagonia and Tierra del Fuego and you should avoid visiting these areas during the winter. The weather in Buenos Aires is pleasant throughout most of the year. You would be well-advised to visit Peninsula Valdez during October-November.

The national holidays are as follows: January 1, May 1, May 25 (Independence Day), July 9 (Independence Day) (yes, there are two of them!), June 20 (Flag Day), August 17 (Death of San Martin), and December 25.

ARGENTINA

Where to Stay
Argentina offers a large selection of **hotels** of varying quality, classed by stars, as in most Western countries. In addition, there are many small, inexpensive pensions, which are usually clean and situated near a railway or bus station and near the town center. Breakfast is not usually included in the price. Star-graded hotels have a fixed maximum rate determined by the Ministry of Tourism, but a service tax (about 15%) and value added tax are added, and you should bear this in mind. You can avoid the service tax by paying for services within the hotel (meals, laundry, etc.) separately each time you use them.

Argentina has a well-developed network of **camp sites** which provide all amenities. The camp sites are spread all over the country, in parks and on the outskirts of cities. Although they are far from the city centers, they are cheap, clean, and safe, and it is well-worth putting up with this slight inconvenience. Recommended.

There are only a few **youth hostels** scattered round the country. In the smaller towns, though, young people can usually find free sleeping accommodations in schools, fire stations, youth clubs, etc. Another money-saving possibility is sleeping in gas stations. For further details, see below "Hitchhiking".

Wining and Dining
Argentina is without doubt a gourmet's paradise. We have already sung the praises of its meat dishes. Suffice it to add that a steak at an average restaurant weighs several times more than a "large" steak in other countries.

The most common offerings are *asado* (grilled meat), *churrasco* (a thick juicy steak), and *parrillada* (mixed grill including roast beef and sausages – recommended). The *empanadas*, pastries filled with meat and vegetables, are very popular in South America, as are *chorizos*, which are spicy sausages. The *milanesa* schnitzels are excellent, and so is the popular dish *arroz con pollo*, which consists of rice with pieces of chicken and vegetables in sauce.

Pizzas, and Italian dishes in general (especially the cheese dishes), are definitely recommended. In fact they are often tastier than the same dishes in Italy. There is a wide variety of pizzas: especially recommended are those with a thin crust and lots of extras. There is also an excellent selection of cakes, ice cream, chocolate, and candy. The *confiteria* (a cross between a cafe and a snack bar) offers light meals plus a wide choice of cakes that taste out of this world! Chocolate lovers would be extremely foolish to forego the pleasure of tasting the

ARGENTINA

chocolates of Bariloche, especially if you are still under the delusion that Switzerland has a monopoly in this area. As for *dulce de leche* (milk simmered with sugar until very thick), this is the national delicacy.

Breakfast and lunch are eaten at the usual times, but it is rare for dinner to be served before 9pm. Most restaurants are still packed with diners much later than that. Most of them tack on a whopping service charge (up to 25%), so keep this in mind!

Evening meals are often accompanied by domestic wines. Connoisseurs will order Chilean wines, which are superior to the local vintage. With dessert one drinks *mate* (pronounced ma-teh), a kind of tea which is very popular in South America.

Currency

In June 1985 the Argentinian peso was replaced by the *austral*, introduced as a stable currency in order to break, once and for all, the vicious inflationary circle which reduced, practically daily, the peso's buying power. Its exchange rate against the U.S. dollar is determined by market fluctuations. Even though the austral is now the official currency, many people still "think" in older currencies. Since the abolition of free currency transactions, a black market, mainly in dollars, has flourished, located chiefly in Buenos Aires and the other large cities. The black market deals mainly in cash (so you will not get a good price for travelers' checks), and the difference between the official and black market rates can reach 20% or more.

The use of credit cards is widespread in Argentina, but now that there is a black market, it is not worth your while to use them, since your account will be debited according to the official exchange rate. Bank transfers of foreign currency to Argentinian banks are paid out only in local currency, and at the official rate, so avoid them!

Business Hours

Most shops are open from 9am till 7pm, or even later in downtown areas. Restaurants and cafes generally stay open till the small hours of the morning, or even around the clock. Banks are usually open from 11am-2pm but each bank keeps its own hours. Government offices are open in the morning during the summer, and in the afternoon in the winter. Post offices are open from 8am-8pm, and on Saturdays until 2pm.

Domestic Transportation

There are many and varied ways to get around the country.

Hitchhiking: Hitchhiking has become increasingly popular, especially during the past few years when public transport has

ARGENTINA

become more expensive. Many young tourists prefer to hitchhike, since it is a quick, comfortable and cheap way of traveling almost anywhere. Other advantages of this method are that you get to know the local population and improve your Spanish. The further you are from a city, the easier it is to get a lift. If you get picked up by a truck traveling on a main highway, you can cover vast distances in no time at all. If you are going to hitchhike, take a tent with you and ask to be put down at gas stations. If you should get stuck there for the night they will let you pitch your tent behind the station, which is equipped with showers and lavatories. Remember though, that there have been numerous cases of hitchhikers being assaulted or robbed.

Buses: There are several private companies providing bus services to all parts of the country. Most roads are paved, so you can reach almost any destination conveniently and quickly. Students are usually offered a discount, but foreign students may find that this does not apply to them.

Train: Argentina has an extensive rail network that links the northern, western, and southern parts of the country with the capital. The trains have Pullman cars (reclining seats), and first and second classes. The Pullman cars are served by a steward who attends to the passenger's comforts. The dining cars offer good food at reasonable prices. Train journeys are long and slow, and the pampas (around Bahia Blanca) and the north, the Salta-La Quiaca route, are extremely dusty. The southern terminus of the railroad is Bariloche. Trains are cheaper than buses, and those who plan extensive journeys can obtain a train pass for unlimited travel around the country (see "How to get there").

Car rental: There are many car rental companies throughout the country, especially in the large cities and tourist centers. This is a comfortable, albeit expensive, way of traveling, and is especially suited to groups of four. The large international companies accept reservations from abroad, so that a car will be waiting for you at the airport. Bear in mind that driving in Buenos Aires makes midtown Manhattan seem like a country lane: if you can avoid it, do!

Private car: This is a convenient means of travel, since most roads in Argentina are paved, and there is no shortage of gas stations and garages. The Argentinian Automobile Club (*Automovil Club Argentino*) is located at Avenida Libertad 1850, Buenos Aires (Tel. 836-061/0). The club has many branches all over the country, which provide maps, information,

ARGENTINA

and guidance. It also owns hotels, motels, and hostels. If you are traveling by car, you should get in touch with the club; you will find them efficient and helpful, especially if you are a member of an automobile association.

Plane: Aerolineas Argentinas, Austral, and the military airline Lade fly all over the country. Although the flights are quite expensive, bear in mind that an overland journey from Buenos Aires to Bariloche, for example, takes 36 hours each way! Flights from Buenos Aires to Bariloche, Rio Gallegos, and the Iguacu Falls are the most heavily booked, and you should try to make reservations ten to fourteen days ahead. Aerolineas has night flights several times a week on the main routes, such as to Rio Gallegos, and these are 50% cheaper than the day flights. There is a large demand for these flights, but they are worth the effort. Aerolineas also offers a "Visit Argentina" ticket, which is good for free air travel on its flights for 30 days. The ticket costs $290, but cannot be purchased in Argentina or in any neighboring country (Chile, Brazil, Uruguay, Paraguay or Bolivia). It allows you to visit any place once only. Lade also provides service south from Buenos Aires in old military planes. The flights are slow and make many stops, but they are far cheaper than Aerolineas' flights. Lade flights operate in Tierra del Fuego and on some routes in Patagonia. These are not included in the pass, but are not all that expensive either.

Measurements, electricity and time

Argentina uses the metric system. Clothes sizes follow the European system, and shoe sizes the American, although the shopkeeper will understand if you tell him your European shoe size.

The voltage in Argentina is 220V. Argentinian time is GMT-3.

A Suggested Itinerary for Touring Argentina (including Chile)

So as not to miss places of interest, you should begin your trip from Brazil in the northeast, travel to the far south, and then back along the western side to the northwest and Bolivia. This is a basic outline for a logical, comprehensive travel route that will save you both time and money. You can, of course, adapt it to your requirements and means. The suggested itinerary is as follows:

From the Iguacu Falls to Buenos Aires.

From Buenos Aires south to Tierra del Fuego, via Mar del Plata, Peninsula Valdez, and Patagonia.

From Tierra del Fuego to Chilean Patagonia.

ARGENTINA

From southern Chile to the lake district and Bariloche.

From the lake district to Mendoza.

From Mendoza to Cordoba, and then north to Bolivia via Tucuman, Salta, and Jujuy.

Buenos Aires

Buenos Aires is known as "the Paris of South America", and with good reason. Its avenues are broad with a constant flow of noisy traffic day and night. Its buildings are imposing, from skyscrapers to single-story houses, the architecture a mixture of European styles with a strong Spanish influence. The people wear the latest fashions, dance to the latest music, and dine out on the best of international cuisine.

Buenos Aires is a bustling, multi-faceted city, full of opportunities for pleasure and entertainment, a city whose streets are never silent. Argentina's capital honors the principle of "living around the clock" more than any other European or American city. The cafes and discotheques in the Recoleta district are as full at five in the morning as they are before midnight. Here you can drink to your heart's content in the popular cafes, gorge yourself on food unsurpassed in quality and quantity the world over, attend cultural and folklore events on an international level, and more.

Buenos Aires was founded in 1580. Today its population, including the suburbs, is around 10 million. The city serves as the economic, cultural, and national hub of Argentina, and its central position in the life of the Argentinian people is evident in every sphere. The city is endowed with a large variety of cultural, artistic, scientific, and commercial institutions. While touring the city you can see the exclusive residential districts in the north, the bustling commercial zone in the center, and in the south, the picturesque quarters around the port area. Here in the south, in the neighborhoods of La Boca and San Telmo, you cannot fail to marvel at the gardens and public squares, the old harbor, and the nightclubs from which the strains of the tango issue forth, creating that unique atmosphere which makes Buenos Aires so special and so captivating.

How to get there
By air: Buenos Aires has two airports, with dozens of daily arrivals and departures. If you are coming from abroad (with the exception of Uruguay) you will land at the modern Ezeiza Airport. Once you have finished with passport control and customs, which should not take long, turn left to where most of

ARGENTINA

the airport facilities are situated, including public transport into town. By far the best way of getting to the city is the airport bus, which takes 40 minutes to reach downtown. You can buy tickets in the terminal itself. Ask the driver to let you off downtown, since the last stop is some distance beyond. The taxi fare downtown is fixed (not metered), and is approximately four times the price of a bus ticket. Agree on the price before you enter the taxi, and on no account pay before you reach your destination. If you wish to save, you can take bus 86 from the International Hotel near the airport. When leaving Argentina, you will have to pay a $10 airport tax.

The other airport, Aeroparque, is in Palermo, near the river bank, only five minutes from downtown. It handles mainly domestic flights, and occasional flights from neighboring countries. You can catch a taxi to take you downtown. The journey is quick and cheap, paid according to the meter.

By land: Buses link the city to other parts of Argentina and to neigboring countries. Most buses depart from and arrive at the downtown Retiro terminal, while others use the Once terminal, which is on the subway (line A). Trains from the center, north, and west of the country terminate at Retiro station (which has three terminal buildings). Those from the south go to Constitucion station, while those from the northeast go to Lacroze station. A few trains from the west go to Once station. There are buses to all parts of the city from every station.

By ship: Ships call at the port of Buenos Aires from Montevideo and Colonia. This is a cheap, pleasant and recommended way to travel. Passport control takes place on board the ship, and the customs check is simple and quick. When you leave the terminal on Paseo Colon, turn north to go downtown, which is within walking distance, or else take a taxi.

Accommodations

Buenos Aires has many hotels and pensions. Most hotels are located downtown, between Avenida de Mayo and Avenida Sante Fe, or between Avenida 9 de Julio and Avenida Alem. Among the first-class hotels we will mention only the *Sheraton*, with its fantastic view from the upper stories, the *Libertador* (corner of Cordoba and Maipu), and the *Plaza* which is, in my opinion, the best of all, because of its pleasant ambience and excellent location (Florida and Plaza San Martin). More modest, if still expensive, is the *Grand Buenos Aires* (Alvear 767), which is pleasant and has large rooms; its prices and location make it especially suitable for businessmen.

ARGENTINA

Cheaper hotels can be found in the streets parallel to Florida. In general, the standard of cleanliness and safety in hotels and pensions is higher than the average in Latin America, and there is no need to be unduly concerned. *Hotel Orei* is a very cheap hotel which is situated at Calle Lavalle near Florida street.

What to eat, where and when

And so we come to the most pleasant part of this guide. Gourmets (and who isn't?) can look forward to a varied, rich, and boundless gastronomical experience during their stay in Buenos Aires. In addition to the 6000 (!) restaurants scattered throughout the city, there are tens of thousands of kiosks, cafes, and outdoor stands that sell food and candy; you can hardly walk 100 meters without passing one. As a multi-faceted metropolis, Buenos Aires caters to almost every taste. One thing, however, it will not tolerate: a diet! Anyone who has not eaten or at least tasted its cakes, pizzas, ice creams, chocolates, custards, cheeses, and choice meats cannot claim to have visited Buenos Aires. To be in Buenos Aires without enjoying its wonderful food is like being in Paris without visiting the Louvre, or being in New York without seeing the Statue of Liberty. Therefore, be brave, forget your figure and, bearing in mind Oscar Wilde's remark ("I can resist anything but temptation"), allow yourself to be tempted, and enjoy it. Given this unlimited profusion of restaurants, it would be pretentious as well as superfluous to attempt to provide names and addresses of the most highly recommended. I will therefore restrict myself to giving general guidelines to help you choose which of the ten restaurants on the block you wish to try, and what food is worth ordering, although one choice is as good as another, so you can't go wrong no matter what you order.

Let's start with the simpler options. A galaxy of candy and ice cream will lure you at every step. Ice cream is sold in a special shop known as an *heladeria* which offers a wide variety of flavors. Select the size you want, but remember that the ice cream will tower twice the height of the cup. The various chocolate flavors are highly recommended (Bariloche chocolate, white chocolate, chocolate with nuts, etc.), as are the custard flavors. You should concentrate on these rather than on the fruit flavors. The ice cream is usually made from high-fat milk, and the fruit flavors, which have a sour-milk base, just aren't as good. The others, as we have said, are quite out of this world.

Most of the chocolate you will find in the kiosks is imported from Switzerland, and you are no doubt familiar with its taste. So make a point of buying from the shops specializing in the home-made product *(caseros)*, which offer a vast assortment of

ARGENTINA

chocolates sold by the kilo. You can find many such shops along Florida or in the galleria where Florida and Plaza San Martin meet. The Bariloche chocolate is the best of all, but almost impossible to obtain in the capital. Shops that claim to sell Bariloche chocolate usually sell chocolate based on a similar recipe, but manufactured in Buenos Aires.

There is an almost unlimited choice of superb cakes in cafes and pastry shops (*confiterias*). Cream cakes are generously filled with a brown cream, which is not always chocolate but often the local delicacy known as *dulce de leche*. In the confiterias you can order light meals, sandwiches, meat (*carne*) and cheese (*queso*) *empanadas*, as well as simple main dishes, all of them cheap and tasty!

Highly recommended are the pizzerias and Italian restaurants. The influx of Italian immigrants has left its mark on Argentinian cuisine, and pizza is considered an indigenous national dish.

Apart from the many extras that you can order on a pizza (mushrooms, onions, salami, various vegetables, etc.), there are two main types: those with a thin crust and those with a thick one. Although the thick crust is more filling, you should order the thin crust variety if you want to savor the other components.

The meat restaurants present of course the crowning glory of Argentinian cuisine. In these restaurants, spread all over the city, an individual portion is large enough to satisfy an entire regiment! There is a never ending assortment of meat dishes, accompanied by salads, rice, and fried potatoes. (For a more detailed description of the meat dishes, see "Wining and Dining"). You will find dozens of such restaurants along Corrientes and Lavalle streets in the downtown area. If you want to enjoy an excellent meal, in a pleasant spot and at an exceptionally reasonable price, visit the **Los Carritos district**, which is situated along the river near the Aeroparque Airport. Here dozens of superior restaurants can be found, open day and night, serving the choicest Argentinian dishes in a relaxed and informal atmosphere. The wide road (Costanera Norte) leading to Los Carritos is lit up with neon signs all along the way, so you can't miss the place. You can also hire a taxi or travel by bus from Retiro station in a few minutes. The restaurants offer superb food, and although large (some seat hundreds of people), they are always full, day and night. We ate there at 2:30 in the morning at a restaurant called "Happening" (the only place where we found room to park the car), and it certainly lived up to its name. Another excellent meat restaurant in Costanera is *Los Anos Locos*. Refer to the list of recommended dishes in the

ARGENTINA

Wining and Dining section – and start practicing what we preach...

American style fast-food restaurants, whose "specialty" is usually hamburgers, can be found all along Calle Florida. On Carlos Pelegrini street, in the Colon theatre areas are a number of cafes and restaurants, some of which have tables outdoors. The *Sheraton* has an excellent restaurant on its roof, with a fantastic view. The Recoleta district also has an abundance of cafes and restaurants, and so do the San Telmo and La Boca quarters. You owe yourself a supper in La Boca, in one of the huge restaurants seating hundreds of diners, and accompanied by boisterous orchestras for your pleasure.

Transportation

The streets of Buenos Aires are laid out in a grid pattern, and with the help of a map (given out free in hotels and tourist offices), you should have no problem in getting around.

Buses are frequent and fast, serving all parts of the city. The route number and destination are clearly marked on the front of the bus, and every bus stop has a list of the streets followed by that route. Many essential bus routes – essential especially for the tourist – begin or end at **Retiro station**, alongside Plaza San Martin.

The subway has five lines, which cover the busiest arteries. The C line goes between the Retiro and Constitucion stations, intersecting the other four lines en route. Subway stations are indicated by a sign post with *SUBTE* written on it, and the number of the line.

Black and yellow **taxis** are plentiful and easy to flag down, even during rush hour. Taxis are metered, and a ride in the center of town is fairly inexpensive.

The most convenient means of inter-city transport is train or bus. For longer distances, it is better to fly (see details in "Domestic Transportation").

Detailed timetables can be obtained at the Railway Information Center, Florida 29 (Tel. 311-6411/4), and at the Tourist Information Center. Most inter-city buses leave from the Retiro bus station.

Car rental is another possibility and cars can be rented from Hertz, Avis (at the Sheraton Hotel), and local companies. You can reserve a car via the international agencies or the doorman at your hotel. The minimum age for renting a car is 22; if you don't have an international credit card you will have to leave a large deposit.

ARGENTINA

Tourist services

As already stated, Argentina in general and Buenos Aires in particular have excellent tourist information services, which supply both verbal and written assistance and guidance. Avenida Florida has two **information booths** staffed by charming English-speaking young ladies, who will be happy to help you in matters of transportation, tourist sites, entertainment, and so on. They can provide you with pamphlets, maps, and computerized information on a variety of topics. The blue booths are centrally located. The first is at the Florida-Paraguay intersection, and the second is at the other end of Florida, near the Plaza de Mayo. The main office is on Avenida Santa Fe 883, (Tel. 325-550), but the Florida branches are perfectly satisfactory.

The **tourist offices** of the provinces are also within walking distance of Calle Florida. These will provide you with lots of maps and detailed information about the provinces, tourist sites, parks, nature reserves and the like. Their material is usually available only in Spanish. The addresses of these tourist offices can be obtained from the tourist information booths on Florida.

The National Parks Authority also runs an information office that can supply interesting and useful material about nature sites throughout the country. Their office is at Avenida Santa Fe 680 (Plaza San Martin).

The **airline** offices are concentrated near Calle Florida and on Avenida Santa Fe (near Plaza San Martin). The main office of Aerolineas Argentinas is at Calle Peru 2 (continuation of Calle Florida, Tel. 308-551/9). Aerolineas also has a large branch office on Avenida Santa Fe, near Plaza San Martin. The offices of the following companies are also situated along Santa Fe: Eastern, Aero-Peru (840), Alitalia (887), Avianca (865), Ecuatoriana, Sabena (816), and Swissair (846). On Florida are the offices of Air France (890), KLM (989) and SAS (902). The numbers in parenthesis indicate the street number.

The Pan American office is at Avenida Pena 838, Austral (internal flights) has an office on Florida, and Lade (army airlines) has one at Calle Peru 710 (Tel. 347-071/3).

Tourist sites
Downtown

Like Chicago's Loop, sharply demarcated by railroad lines, downtown Buenos Aires can be defined fairly precisely as the area bounded by Ave. de Mayo in the south and Ave. Santa Fe in the north, and by Ave. Alem in the east and Ave. 9 de Julio in the west. This is the nerve center of the capital, and contains

ARGENTINA

most of the government offices, commercial and financial institutions and exclusive stores. The popular pedestrian mall of Calle Florida, which bisects this area from east to west, is one of the most familiar arteries to tourists, and serves as a focal point for the whole city.

We will start strolling from the **Casa Rosada**, the seat of the government, at the intersection of Ave. Alem and Ave. Mayo. This majestic building serves as the office of the president of the Republic. Although it contains a large library and impressive halls, it is closed to the public, so one can only admire its impressive facade. The square in front of it **Plaza de Mayo**, is considered by many to be the heart of the whole country. This square has witnessed huge demonstrations proclaiming both joyful events and times of sorrow. A white pyramid in the center of the square symbolizes peace and liberty. Till 1983 the square was the meeting point for hundreds of mothers who would gather there each Thursday, petitioning the government for information regarding dear ones who had disappeared during the civil war of 1976-1977.

Around the square are some of the city's most important buildings, such as the **Cathedral**, where General Jose de San Martin is buried. San Martin died in exile in France, but his body was brought back for reburial in Argentina. Soldiers wearing the uniform of San Martin's army stand guard over his tomb. Nearby is the **Cabildo** or town council, which houses a museum dedicated to the revolt against Spain in 1810. Six blocks west along Ave. de Mayo, you will arrive at Ave. 9 de Julio, which the people of Buenos Aires swear is the widest in the world. Another 800 yards down Ave. de Mayo, is **Plaza Congreso**, which is the largest public square in the city. In the center are fascinating statues, and, at the western end, the **Congress Building**. This majestic building, whose facade includes a monument to the Independence Congress of 1816, serves as the seat of the National Legislature. In 1976, when the Congress ceased functioning, the building was sealed off, until it was reopened at the end of 1983 with the restoration of democracy. One can take a guided tour of the splendid halls of the Congress Building, and sometimes the tour includes a visit to the office of a member of Congress.

Turning north into Ave. 9 de Julio will bring us to cafes, restaurants, stores, and offices. The mighty **Obelisk** will be the first to catch our attention. Situated in **Plaza de la Republica**, the Obelisk, which is some 70 m tall, was erected in 1936 to mark the quarter centenary of the city and serves as a central landmark. Two blocks further on, on the west side of the street, looms the magnificent **Teatro Colon**, built in 1908 from materials

BUENOS AIRES

- BELGRANO
- POZOS
- ENTRE RIOS
- SOLIS
- VIRREY CEVALLOS
- LUIS SAENZ PEÑA
- SAN JOSE
- SGO. DEL ESTERO
- SALTA
- LIMA
- BDO. DE IRIGOYEN
- AV. 9 DE JULIO
- TACUARI
- PIEDRAS
- CHACABUCO
- MORENO
- PERU
- BOLIVAR
- DEFENSA
- ALSINA
- BALCARCE
- PASEO COLON
- ESPORA
- AV. ING HUERGO
- MITRE
- AV. RIVADAVIA
- RODRIGUEZ PEÑA
- SARMIENTO
- TALCAHUANO
- AV. CORRIENTES
- MONTEVIDEO
- LAVALLE
- PLAZA DEL CONGRESO
- AV. DE MAYO
- H. YRIGOYEN
- SUIPACHA
- CANGALLO
- FLORIDA
- SAN MARTIN
- RECONQUISTA
- 25 DE MAYO
- AV. ROSALES
- BOUCHARD
- TUCUMAN

Index
1. Government Palace
2. Plaza de Mayo
3. Cathdral
4. Plaza del Congresso
5. Congress Building
6. The Obelisk
7. Theatro Colon
8. Plaza San Martin
9. Ministry of Foreign Affaires
10. Air Force Plaza (Plaza Britania)
11. Retiro Station
12. Central Post Office

ARGENTINA

Teatro Colon

specially imported from all over the world. The most outstanding of its palatial halls is the *Salon de Oro* (golden hall) which is reserved for gala occasions. Its roof is covered with gold, and the hall itself is furnished with splendid crystal chandeliers and wall decorations. The auditorium is unusually impressive, with seats for 2500 people, and standing room for another 1000. The accoustics are superb, making amplifiers unnecessary. The audience occupies an elegant seating area and seven tiers of boxes upholstered in red velvet. The stage is huge – twice the size of the seating area. It is partitioned by a special metal screen, which is both fireproof and soundproof, so that while an orchestra is rehearsing on the front part of the stage, a dance troupe can practice behind the screen, without disturbing each other. Operating the stage is a difficult and complex procedure. The scenery can be suspended from the rafters, or stood on the revolving stage. The cellars of the theater are no less impressive. The three floors below ground level are used by 1000 employees for preparing costumes, wigs, shoes (the shoe department has tens of thousands of pairs of shoes!), jewelry, laundry, and more. The Teatro Colon is without doubt the largest and most impressive artistic institution in the whole of Latin America. You should definitely take a guided tour of the building, which must be booked in advance. And if you are a lover of culture,

ARGENTINA

attendance at one of the performances of the theatre is *de rigueur* (for details, see "Entertainment and cultural events").

You can take Calle Tucuman from the Teatro Colon, bringing you back to **Florida**. This pedestrian mall, full of stores, is the tourist's favorite shopping area, and yet, in spite of this, is not much more expensive than other parts of the city. There is an abundance and variety of goods, all according to the latest fashion (see Shopping, below). Calle Lavalle and Calle Corrientes, which run parallel to Calle Tucuman, are the nightlife and entertainment centers, with many movie theaters, restaurants, and nightclubs (see "Entertaiment and cultural events"). A few steps to the left (north) on Florida, is the main shopping area. Many of the entrances actually lead to the *galerias*, or huge enclosed shopping malls, containing dozens of stores and colorful stands. It will cost you some effort not to spend money here.

At the end of Calle Florida is Buenos Aires' most important and well-kept square, the **Plaza San Martin**, with its equestrian statue of the *Libertador*. To the right is **Plaza Britania** with its copy of London's famous Big Ben, and the **Retiro** train and bus terminal. (Incidentally, after the Falklands War, Plaza Britania was renamed Airforce Square.) The **Defence Ministry** and alongside it a **Military Museum** (separate entrances) are also situated in Plaza San Martin. Continuing westward, you can stroll along the impressive **Ave. Santa Fe** with its exclusive shops.

The northwest

Now that you are familiar with the downtown, you will want to visit other areas, which are no less interesting than the center itself. We will start with the northwestern sector of the city, the **Recoleta** district. Although the Recoleta is famous mainly for its nightlife (see "Entertainment and cultural events"), it is well worth a visit by day. Among its sights is the National Cemetery, with the tombs of many of the city's outstanding personalities amid well tended lawns and shrubbery. A stone's throw away is the **Museum of Fine Arts** (Ave. Libertador San Martin 1473, Tel. 838-817). This museum, which houses the works of Argentinian artists as well as a European collection, is the most important in the city. It is closed on Wednesdays, but open on all other days except for an afternoon break. A little further on is the imposing building of the **Law Faculty**, which is situated near the **Ital Parque** – a huge amusement park, also recommended for adults.

Continuing in the same direction, you will come across another park – **Parque Palermo** (on maps it is designated by its official

ARGENTINA

name: *Parque 3 de Febrero*). This huge park, which extends from the Aeroparque to Ave. Santa Fe, contains enchanting botanical gardens, a large zoo, sports fields, a luxurious racetrack, a bicycle track, a large observatory, and much more. If you are a sports fan, the park offers a wide variety of equipment for rent, especially on weekends.

Olivos and Tigre

To the northwest is the prestigious suburb of Olivos, home to diplomats, government officials, and the president himself. The neighboring suburb of Tigre is where the Nazi criminal Adolf Eichmann was captured. Both suburbs nestle on the edge of the river. Olivos boasts a large marina as well as a picturesque arts-and-crafts fair every Sunday (see "Shopping"). Tigre, which borders the river delta, has many sports and recreation clubs as well as a landing stage for small boats.

La Boca

South of the center is the port district of **La Boca**, where Pedro de Mendoza laid the foundations for modern Buenos Aires. The area is full of industrial buildings. La Boca's population is mainly of Italian extraction. Bus 33 from Paseo Colon (behind the Casa Rosada) will take you to this picturesque quarter in a matter of 15 minutes. Most of its houses are painted in bright colors and richly ornamented, often with curios brought back by sailors. Many of the houses are built of sheet metal, because it's cheap. In this quarter you can absorb some of the enchanting atmosphere of the Italian colony, see half-sunk ships that will never again venture on the open seas, stroll among the work of local artists and sculptors on **Calle Caminito**, and, if you are lucky, you will be able to catch performances of a street theater (the Tourist Information Center can provide you with details). Then towards evening, to round off your day, go into one of the many clubs dotting the area, for a meal and entertainment (see "Entertainment and cultural events").

San Telmo

Between La Boca and Plaza de Mayo nestles the small but no less interesting San Telmo quarter. With its colonial architecture, it has become an artists' and fun-seekers' paradise with an abundance of restaurants, clubs, antique stores, art galleries, etc. The heart of the quarter is Ave. Independencia, which is within walking distance of Ave. de Mayo (eight blocks south along Calle Peru – the continuation of Florida). You can also take bus 29 from La Boca. Stroll through the pleasant streets of San

ARGENTINA

Telmo with their red-brick houses, and enjoy the special atmosphere of the neighborhood. On Sundays mornings, there is an impressive flea market in **Plaza Dorrego**, intersection of Bolivar and Humberto (see "Shopping"). During the evening you can hear the rhythmic strains of the tango emanating from the open windows of the nightclubs – an experience you should definitely not miss (see "Entertainment and cultural events").

Entertainment and cultural events

Buenos Aires has a rich and varied nightlife. Whatever you fancy, you will find it here – and plenty of it. Details on current films, folklore presentations, plays, concerts, ballets, opera and other events can be found conveniently in the "Stage and Screen" section of the English language *Buenos Aires Herald*. We will begin here with an exposition of the various options.

Amusement park: Ital Park has its entrance on Ave. Libertador. It provides dozens of the latest rides. The young, and the young at heart, are assured of a good time.

Bars: These are found all over the city (some are called *whiscerias*). The bars in Calle Reconquista (parallel to Florida) are frequented mainly by students and young people. They are inexpensive and the atmosphere is casual. These bars represent an excellent opportunity for getting to know young Argentinians, many of whom speak English. Recoleta too has its liberal quota of bars and cafes, but these are more exclusive, more expensive, and have a less intimate atmosphere.

Cinema: Over 300 movie theaters are located in all parts of the city, open day and night. The most convenient (as far as location is concerned) are those situated on Corrientes and Lavalle streets, and their selection is more than adequate. The films are usually in the original language, with Spanish subtitles. Tickets for evening showings should be purchased several hours in advance.

Nightclubs and discotheques: These can be classed according to the neighborhood. Recoleta has a large number of discotheques with the latest music. The admission charge is high, but usually includes the first drink. The discotheques are crammed with young well dressed Argentinians, especially on Friday and Saturday nights. Then the whole area radiates a warm and pleasant weekend spirit. You will find an altogether different style of dancing in the La Boca and San Telmo districts. This is the cradle of the legendary tango; here the tango still rules, and from here its fame has spread throughout the world.

ARGENTINA

The nightclubs offer shows that include popular singers, musicians, comedians, and the like. Some of them serve drinks, and even meals. Among the best is the Michelangelo Club.

Plays, concerts and opera. The more traditional forms of evening entertainment are also available. Thirty theaters offer a wide variety of plays; of course in this case a knowledge of Spanish is essential. On the other hand, no knowledge of Spanish is required to enjoy the many excellent concerts, operas, and ballets performed in the capital.

Certainly, the most rewarding experience is to attend such a performance in the **Teatro Colon**. The high quality of its chorus and orchestra attracts world famous conductors, musicians and singers, who have set uncompromising artistic standards for the institution as a whole. It is difficult to obtain a seat. The box office is open each day from 10am, but usually only standing room is available, and even these tickets have to be bought a day in advance (at the box office, you can book only for that day's performance or the next day's). The vitality of the performance and the unforgettable experience it represents justify both your efforts to obtain a ticket and the discomfort of standing. Conventional evening dress is the rule for such performances. Concerts and ballets are given on days when there is no opera. The season at the Teatro Colon begins in April and continues into November-December. Performances begin at 9pm.

Banks and currency exchange

Since the ban on purchasing foreign currency, the black market has naturally grown and flourished. If you exchange dollars in a bank or foreign exchange office (*casa de cambio*) you will receive the official rate. On the other hand, you will have no problem in changing travelers' checks or in collecting bank transfers from abroad. U.S. cash dollars can be exchanged, illegally, at the black market at a much higher rate. The center of the black market is in Calle San Martin (parallel to Florida), in the stretch between Sarmiento and Cordoba. The moneychangers will identify you with ease and offer their services... but be cautious. If you have friends who are willing to exchange money for you – so much the better. When you buy in stores on Florida you can usually pay in dollars, and at the black market rate. Ask for the price of goods in pesos and then offer to pay in dollars – most shopkeepers will agree.

Before leaving the capital for other parts of the country, change enough money to cover all your expenses. In small towns you will encounter considerable difficulty in exchanging foreign currency, especially travelers' checks. Before changing money,

ARGENTINA

compare the rates of the various moneychangers: the rates can vary significantly.

Postal and telephone services
The central post office is in Ave. Alem, between Corrientes and Sarmiento; it is open from 8am-8pm, (Tel. 315-031). It offers telex, telegram, and international telephone services. Generally speaking, service is prompt and efficient. Sending a parcel, however, is a complex procedure, since the rates are based on weight classes, which change every so often, and an extra ounce can cause the price to shoot up. While sending parcels by air is very expensive, sea-mail, although slower, is as safe and cheaper. Customs and post office clerks' inspect parcels, and are likely to raise many objections, for example refusing to accept clothes unless you have a laundry ticket to prove they are clean, etc. etc. You must prepare a detailed list of all items in the parcel and leave it open for inspection at the post office. Only after this inspection will you be allowed to seal the parcel and hand it over for delivery. International phone calls can be made from the Telephone Company's offices at the point where Calle Florida becomes Calle Peru. Open till 10pm. There is no three-minute minimum on International calls, and on the weekend, calls are almost 50% cheaper.

Photographic supplies
You would be best advised to come equipped with photographic supplies; but if you haven't managed to do so, you will find Argentina far cheaper than her neighbors in this respect. Kodak has its central office near Teatro Colon, where you can receive advice and assistance, as well as buy supplies and have film developed.

Books and periodicals in English
The capital has 800 bookstores, which sell an impressive variety of books from all over the world. All the stores on Florida sell books in English. International magazines, such as *Time* and *Newsweek*, are sold in most kiosks, particularly along Calle Florida. The *Buenos Aires Herald* is the local English-language daily, with a broad coverage of international news.

Shopping
In this field too, as in all others, Buenos Aires is noted for the rich variety of its shopping malls and available goods. The Argentinians invested a lot of money and effort into making shopping a pleasant and agreeable experience, and simply walking around the stores and galerias is enjoyable in its own right. You will find an endless array of clothes and shoes, souvenirs, arts and crafts, to mention but a few. Your problem

ARGENTINA

will be not what to buy, but rather what not to buy. See for yourselves – you've been warned.

Let's begin with leather goods, which are the pride of the nation. Here you can find absolutely everything, from traditional leather goods such as shoes, belts, coats, and purses, to the latest fashion in leather shirts, slacks, suitcases, and even book-bindings. Argentina's leather goods are beautiful and contemporary, and cheaper than in Europe. On the other hand, their quality is moderate, more or less comparable to that of leather goods from the Far East. Calle Florida has many stores that sell leather coats and other leather goods – the largest and most impressive being the *Ciudad del Cuero* (city of leather) at Florida 940 (Tel. 311-4721), corner of Paraguay. The various boutiques of this magnificent galeria offer an impressive variety of exclusive high quality and limited edition designs. Alongside women's suits, jackets, and coats, you will find all sorts of leather accessories, including shoes, gloves, belts, purses and suitcases. On the second floor to the right is an art gallery with a fair selection of paintings, and a pleasant cafe. Further down the street (Florida 738) is *Bigs* which specializes in good quality coats and jackets at more reasonable prices.

Further on, you will pass by the famous shoe store, *Botticelli*, which has branches all over the world. Here you can purchase an excellent pair of shoes of superb design, workmanship, and material, at a price lower than at the New York, Paris, or Rome outlets (though still very expensive).

And finally the prestigious store, *Pullman*, which carries leather goods of superb quality at very high prices.

You can buy clothes in almost any store. Pierre Cardin and Yves Saint Laurent are prominent, and so are their prices, but they are still far less expensive than in other countries and they specialize in the very latest fashions. If you are a clothes-conscious male, you will find a good selection of top quality shirts, jackets, and trousers at *MacTailor's* – but again prices are high. At the giant branch of the British chain store, *Harrod's*, you will find absolutely everything somewhere among the four floors of tastefully displayed merchandise, and at reasonable prices.

Contemporary design quality leather goods can be had more cheaply than on Florida at *Campanera Dalla Fontana* on Reconquista 735 (Tel. 311-1229) The store offers a wide selection of styles in different kinds of leather. Recommended!

The larger woman will find superb quality wear, of the best and latest design at *Medigrand*, in the store on Paraguay 665 just

ARGENTINA

off Florida, or in one of the branch stores located throughout the city.

"Professional shoppers" whose appetite has merely been whetted in Calle Florida, can indulge themselves on Ave. Santa Fe, with its thousands of stores displaying an endless variety of goods. It is a good idea to make a tour of the stores first in order to compare prices (which are in any case expensive!). Bargaining is not proper here, but you need not feel ashamed of asking for a discount (*descuento*). If you are looking for arts and crafts or gifts, this is the place for you. But bear in mind that the nearer you get to the center and Calle Florida, the higher the prices. Nevertheless, this is the most convenient place to find such goods.

In addition to the prestigious stores downtown, the tourist will have an excellent opportunity to savor the special atmosphere of the various markets held here every Sunday. One of the most enjoyable and interesting is the antique market in Plaza Dorrego in San Telmo (see "Tourist sites"). The market opens in the morning and closes in the early afternoon. Here you can find a wide selection of antiques, ranging from furniture, telephones, coins, jewelry, and household items, to a variety of original souvenirs. You should, while in the area, also take a look at the various shops and pawnbrokers in the neighborhood. A marvelous arts and crafts fair is open every Sunday afternoon in the suburb of Olivos – excellent for handicrafts and souvenirs at reasonable prices. There are a number of markets in Buenos Aires itself which sell goods ranging from pets, books, coins and antique bank notes to second-hand clothes and just plain junk.

Important addresses

U.S. Embassy: Colombia 430, Palermo (Tel. 774-7611)

British interests, handled by the Swiss Embassy: Ave. Santa Fe 846 (Tel. 316-491)

Tourist Office (*Subsecretaria de Turismo*) Ave. Santa Fe 883 (Tel. 325-550/2232).

Emergency services:

Ambulance – Tel. 344-001/9.

Police – Tel. 101.

And so we come to the end of our stay in this enchanting capital, which we will miss even before we have left it. Nevertheless the time has come for us – somewhat fatter it is true (thanks to the excellent food), and our suitcases somewhat

ARGENTINA

heavier (thanks to our various purchases), not to mention somewhat poorer (thanks to both) – to explore new territory.

The Iguacu Falls

The Iguacu Falls are breathtaking in their grandeur, surpassing both Niagara and the Victoria Falls. When you stand near the plummeting water you cannot but be overawed at the majestic scene of Nature at her noble and impressive best. As Eleanor Roosevelt remarked, "Iguacu Falls make Niagara look like a kitchen faucet", and visiting the falls is an enthralling experience. The falls, an amazing sight of overwhelming height, gives the elusive phrase "natural wonder" a real and unforgettable meaning.

Of all the natural wonders and landscapes that South America has to offer the tourist, these gigantic falls, located on the border of Brazil and Argentina, near the common border with Paraguay, are surely the most impressive. As the falls can, and preferably should, be visited from the Argentinian as well as the Brazilian side, there is a chapter on Iguacu in the two relevant countries. Some of the information, applicable to Argentina and Brazil, has been repeated, while material specific to only one side is mentioned only once. It is advisable to read both chapters.

The falls are situated about 20 km above the confluence of Rio Iguacu with Alto Parana, over 300 km upstream from Posadas. It is not surprising that the falls draw more than two million visitors annually. Every second, nearly 450,000 gallons of water come crashing down over a distance of 4 km, in hundreds of subsidiary waterfalls that are 60 to 80 meters high. This magnificent sight, together with the clouds of spray that envelop the area and the incessant roar of the cascading waters, recreates primeval nature in all her glory. And as if to complete the legendary quality of the place, the whole area is covered by a luxuriant tangle of tropical growth, a study in bright green, a feast for the eye.

Travel to and from the Falls

From within Argentina: The falls are 303 km from Posadas, and many buses run from the Posadas train station to Puerto Iguacu (the town on the Argentinian side of the falls). A train leaves Buenos Aires daily for Posadas. The journey takes about

ARGENTINA

IGUACU FALLS

ARGENTINA

The incredible Iguacu Falls

20 hours, and from there you must continue by bus to the falls. Expreso Singer (Reconquista 866, Buenos Aires, Tel. 316-850), has a direct bus several times a day from Retiro Station to Posadas (20 hours) and on to Iguacu (4 more hours).

If you are coming from Bolivia, you must first enter Argentina via Jujuy, since you cannot reach the falls directly by crossing Paraguay's Chaco. From Jujuy you can easily find public transportation to Posadas, via Resistencia and Corrientes, and from Posadas to the falls.

Aerolineas runs regular and frequent flights from Buenos Aires to Posadas, from which buses leave frequently for Iguacu Falls. Direct flights to the falls, and especially return flights, are heavily booked. This is, of course, the fastest and most convenient way of traveling and if you have bought a "Visit Argentina" ticket in Brazil, you can begin your tour of Argentina from here. If you intend to cross into Brazil after seeing the falls, you should fly Aerolineas to Puerto Iguacu and then cross the border overland and by ferry. A direct flight to the Brazilian

ARGENTINA

side of the falls (Foz do Iguacu) is far more expensive than a domestic flight to Puerto Iguazu.

From Paraguay: Buses from Asuncion cover the distance to Foz in about seven hours, along Paraguay's only paved highway. The Nuestra Senora, Rapido Iguazu, and Pluma companies run several buses a day to the Brazilian side (Foz) and back. The buses are comfortable and the journey pleasant, usually with one intermediate stop.

Food and lodging

You have three options: to stay in Puerto Iguazu (Argentina), to stay in Foz do Iguacu (Brazil), or to stay in Puerto Stroessner (Paraguay). Your best bet is Brazil, since it offers the best tourist facilities. So, if you're coming from Brazil, stay there until you continue your journey. If you're coming from Argentina on the way to Brazil, cross the border and stay in Foz. And if you're coming from Asuncion, the same advice holds: cross the bridge to the Brazilian side (see Brazil chapter).

ARGENTINA

Puerto Iguazu

The town has many hostels and hotels of reasonable quality which are not too expensive. The most luxurious and expensive is the *Internacional Iguazu*, which boasts a swimming pool, casino and an excellent restaurant. The hotel is situated alongside the falls — some distance outside the town. The town itself has luxury hotels such as the *Libertador* (near the bus station), popular ones such as the *Parana* and *Residenciales Segoria* (100 m from the bus station), and cheap ones such as the *Hoteria Hoppe* (near the Internacional) and *Hospedaja Familiar Misiones* (behind the bus station). This last has our recommendation. There are also several camping sites nearby; the best is *Pindo*, about 1/2 km outside town in the direction of the falls (Buses from town to the falls pass by the entrance).

As far as food is concerned, you will not go hungry. All the large hotels have good restaurants — offering both Argentinian and Brazilian cuisine — and there is no shortage of restaurants in town. Behind the bus station you will find the popular restaurants where you can sit outside and enjoy a good and inexpensive meal.

Evening is a good time to visit *Puerto Stroessner* (named for Paraguay's President, General Alfredo Stroessner), with its streets crammed with stores, restaurants, and casinos. Prices here vary according to the changing value of the dollar in the neighboring countries, so that sometimes you will find "bargains" and sometimes everything is outrageously expensive.

How to tour and what to see

The falls are on the border, but more than 80% of them are in Argentinian territory. The best vantage point, where you can see the entire falls in all their vast splendor, the rich foliage, and the surrounding area, is undoubtedly from the Brazilian side (see "Foz do Iguacu" — Brazil).

The best time to visit the falls is between August and November. This is also the most popular time, especially on weekends, so try to come during the week and make hotel reservations in advance. From May to July, the river is usually in flood, so this is not a recommended time to come as one does not have close access to the falls, and because of the tremendous volume of water thundering down, a dense spray is thrown up, which obscures the view of the falls somewhat. At any time of the year, however, the magical beauty of the place is awesome. Besides the cascading falls one can see

ARGENTINA

over 25 species of brightly colored butterfly; orange, pink and red begonias; orchids and ferns.

You will need more time to do the Argentinian side of the falls. From this side you can see more clearly the detail of the individual falls. From here you also have a better vantage point for viewing the wildlife, flowers, forest and butterflies at fairly close range. Buses leave for the falls from Puerto Iguazu (near the Tourist Office in the main street); the trip lasts about half-an-hour. Here too you have to pay the admission fee to the park before getting off the bus. Then you can start walking the miles of concrete paths alongside the torrential falls. Walking along these narrow paths is an extraordinary experience, with water thundering by on all sides soaking you with its spray, and the wondrous sight of the falling arc that splits apart at the bottom of the falls. You can walk for hours and not tire of the sublime views, the breathtaking beauty, the unbridled power, the vastness of it all. On this side, the paths lead in various directions, all clearly marked. The last bus back to town leaves at 6pm.

The Argentinian and Brazilian waterfalls are situated on either side of the Iguacu River (raging waters in Guarani – the language of the Paraguayan Indians). In order to travel from one side to the other you must cross the border and the river. Crossing from Argentina to Brazil is a simple matter – all you have to do is walk to the river bank and take the ferry over. (Cars are also allowed on the ferry although not at all seasons). Once in Brazil your passport will be stamped, and then you can board any bus for Foz itself, and go on to the falls.

If you want to cross from Brazil to Argentina, take the bus marked Porto Meira from the central bus station to the river, and then the ferry over to Argentina. If you plan to return to your initial side of the border the same day, you don't have to have your passport stamped. Just tell the immigrations official what you're planning – if you're coming from Brazil, you can obtain a visa from the Argentinian consulate in Foz.

When you visit the falls wear comfortable walking shoes with skid-proof soles, and take along a plastic bag in which to put your camera and papers so they won't get wet.

Northern Argentina

The parched, mountainous region in the northwest of the country has its own enchanting character. The view, the canyons, the yellow sand and irritating dust, and the many

ARGENTINA

varieties of cactus give the impression of a desert, although in fact the climate here is mild and pleasant.

The local population is mainly Indian and Creole, and the influence of Bolivia and Peru to the north is evident in every aspect of the cultural and social life of the area. The white colonial houses with their large windows stand out in contrast to the ancient Indian traditions and folklore, which are apparent in the atmosphere, handicrafts and local songs.

How to get there

Regular rail and bus service connects the large cities in Argentina to Tucuman, Salta, and Jujuy – the main northern cities – as well as these three to one another. On weekdays, three trains a day leave Buenos Aires for Tucuman; over the weekend, there is only one train a day. The fast train (called *Independencia*) takes 17 1/2 hours, otherwise the trip can last 20 hours or more. From the Tucuman train station there are direct bus connections to Salta and Jujuy. You can reserve a seat on one of these buses when buying your train ticket in Buenos Aires, although there is usually no shortage of seats. The Buenos Aires-La Paz train also passes through all three towns. Trains (which are slow) and buses (which are fast) run between the three towns at all hours of the day. If you want to fly, Aerolineas and Austral both have several flights daily between Buenos Aires and Tucuman. Some international flights, mainly from Bolivia and northern Chile, have intermediate stops in Salta or Tucuman. Night flights to Buenos Aires are half-price, but they are very heavily booked and you must reserve a place well in advance.

From Bolivia (the border town is Villazon) you can catch many buses to Jujuy. There is only one passenger train a day, and it is slow, dusty and crowded. If you are traveling at night, bear in mind that it is very cold then, and dress accordingly.

Tucuman

San Miguel de Tucuman, which is 1312 km north of Buenos Aires, is the capital of Argentina's smallest province, yet it is the largest and most modern city in the north. This area once marked the southern border of the Inca Empire in what is now Argentina. The people of this town, which was founded in 1565 by Spaniards coming from Bolivia and Peru, lived mainly by trading with northern communities. Tucuman today boasts a population of some 400,000 people and serves as the urban center of the entire northern part of the country. The architectural remnants of the colonial period are swallowed up by the modern buildings and bustling commercial district. The

ARGENTINA

NORTHERN ARGENTINA

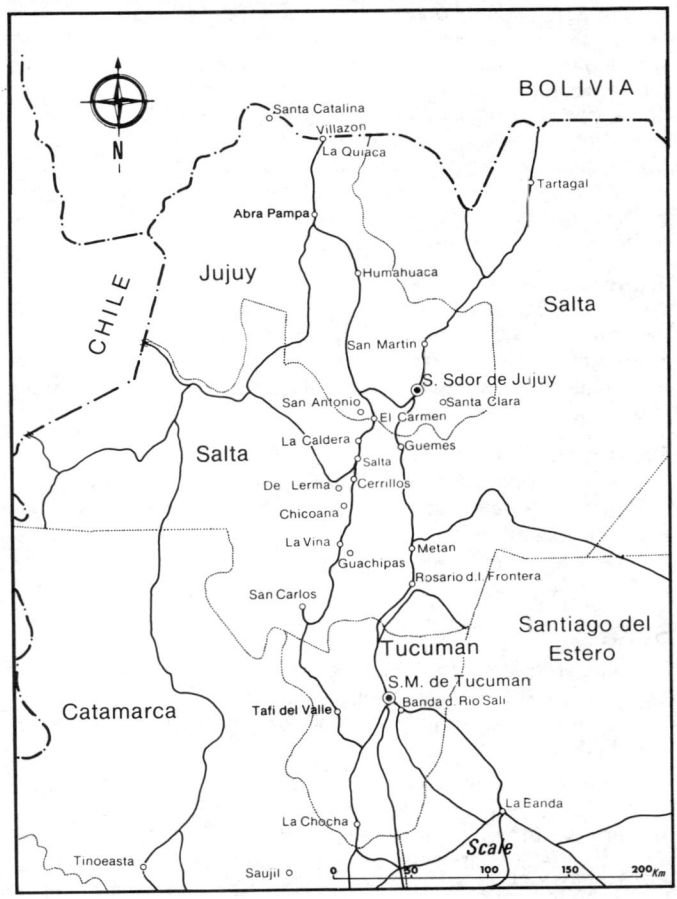

streets are laid out in a grid pattern, with **Plaza Independencia** (Independence Square) and its statue of liberty at the center. Around the square are the government buildings, the **Church of San Francisco** (which you can visit during services), the **Tourist Office**, and the **Argentinian Automobile Club (ACA)**. Behind the square (on Calle 24 de Setiembre) is the **Museum of Folklore**, named after General Belgrano, who won undying fame in the town where his army overcame those loyal to the Spanish crown. The museum houses handicrafts and local

ARGENTINA

works of art. The most important site in the city is the **Casa Historica** on Calle Congreso, corner of San Lorenzo. It was here that Argentina declared her independence from Spanish rule in 1816. The original building was destroyed, but the actual room where independence was declared survived intact. Today the reconstructed building serves as a museum exhibiting various items from the declaration ceremony, portraits and the like. In the street of the same name is the **Miguel Lillo Institute** (*Instituto Miguel Lillo*), which has an impressive collection of stuffed animals – well worth a visit. Tucuman's **University**, one of the first in Latin America, is at the corner of Ayacucho and General La Madrid streets.

Transportation
The town's **airport** is not far from downtown. The **central bus station** is in Ave. Pena, and the main railway station (General Mitre station) is at Catamarca 500. A centrally located, modern and comfortable **camping site** is situated at the edge of Parque 9 de Julio, near Ave. del Campo.

Tourist services
The address of the **Tourist Office** is: Calle 24 de Setiembre 484, in Plaza Independencia (Tel. 18591). It is open until late evening.

Salta

The road to Salta – the most beautiful and interesting town in the north – winds through a wilderness of cacti, huge cliffs, wild green countryside, and along small rivers and canyons, under a fiercely blue sky.

Although more than 400 years have gone by since Don Hernando de Lerma founded the town on April 16, 1582, Salta has remained true to the spirit of its founder; the dazzling white houses are still built in the colonial style. The town now has a population of 183,000. The top of **San Bernardo hill** (1454 m above sea level, and 250 m above the city) affords an unforgettable view of the straight avenues, the white houses and the red roofs, which typify Salta.

At the end of Ave. Guemes is the **statue of General Martin Miguel de Guemes**, the town's venerated hero who, together with the gauchos, routed the Spaniards in a frontal attack while General San Martin was attempting to outflank the Spaniards across the mountain range. This local battle, known as the Gaucho War (*Guerra Gaucha*), is celebrated each year by the local population during **Salta Week** (14-20 June), with a series

ARGENTINA

Salta - General Belgrano Square

of colorful events including firework displays, floats, popular songs and dances, and more.

Past the statue of the General and blending into the mountain is the **Archaeological Museum**, with exhibits from various parts of the province.

The heart of the city, the attractive **Plaza 9 de Julio** with its arched buildings, is busy day and night. It houses the government buildings and the beautiful **Cathedral**, which was rebuilt in 1882. Its impressive interior and the **statues of Jesus and Mary**, around which many legends have grown, make it into an interesting and important historical site. You can visit it during matins and vespers. On the other side of the square is the **Cabildo**, or Town Council, the oldest building in the city, and as old as Salta itself. Over the course of time the building has undergone many modifications, but the most notable and extensive renovation and expansion work, including the 14 arches and the high balconies, were carried out under Salta's first governor in 1780. The building houses two museums: the first, the **Historical Museum** of the whole northern region, is particularly impressive. It is on the ground floor and open several afternoons a week. Upstairs is the **Regional Art Museum**. Beginning at this building is the modern pedestrian mall of **Calle Alberdi**, full of people day and night, shopping, idling, or in search of entertainment.

A block from the square, at the corner of Calle Caseros and Cordoba, is the magnificent **Church of San Francisco**, which

ARGENTINA

also dates back to the origins of the town, but has been through many metamorphoses before attaining its present form with its conspicuous red and gold steeple. About 100 meters away, on the other side of Plaza 9 de Julio is a beautiful and well tended **square** named after **Manuel Belgrano**, dominated by his statue. The **San Martin park**, opposite the bus terminal, is popular with both children and adults in the afternoons, which is the best time to visit it. On the outskirts of the city is an interesting but relatively expensive **crafts market** (*mercado artesanal*), meant mainly for tourists (buses 2 and 3 from the center will take you there). The shops opposite the main building are marginally cheaper.

Salta has a variegated folklore, influenced by the popular music and costumes of her northern neighbors (Bolivia). A folklore event is a must while you are here. Details can be obtained at hotels or the Tourist Office.

The Salta region is full of nature sites and if you have enough time you should definitely pay them a visit. The national park, **El Rey** (The King), on the border of Salta and Jujuy provinces, is considered to be one of the most beautiful nature reserves in the country. Getting there is difficult and complicated, but you will be well rewarded for your efforts.

Food and lodging
Salta has about 40 hotels of varying quality, most of them in the downtown area. Plaza 9 de Julio has a number of the better hotels and restaurants. Around the bus station are several moderately priced hotels, including the *Motel Petit*. A friendly, comfortable, and very reasonably priced hotel is the *Residencial Astur*, which is located behind Plaza Guemes, one block from the automobile club ACA (Calle Rivadavia 752, Tel. 12107). Recommended! If you are looking for cheap accommodation, you will find plenty of really inexpensive hostels around the train station.

Tourist services
The **Tourist Office** is at Buenos Aires 93, very close to Plaza 9 de Julio. Its staff will be happy to provide you with maps, brochures, information about folklore performances, and assistance in finding inexpensive accommodations in private homes and hotels. From Salta a bus runs to Antofagasta in Chile several times a week.

Jujuy
San Salvador de Jujuy was founded on April 19, 1593, and serves as the capital of Argentina's northernmost province of

ARGENTINA

the same name. The town is divided by rivers, and the most interesting section for the tourist is the area bordered by the Rio Grande on the north and the Rio Xibi on the south. Jujuy is also built in a grid pattern, and the beautiful and well-tended **Plaza Belgrano,** with its fountain and citrus trees, serves as the focal point of the whole town.

On one side of the square is the imposing **Government Building**. Its second floor contains the **Hall of the Flag** (*El Salon de la Bandera*). On display in the purple and gold hall, in French Baroque style, is **Argentina's first flag**. It was designed by General Belgrano who gave the cloth flag to the inhabitants of Jujuy immediately after his victory in the battle of Salta in 1812, as a mark of appreciation of their contribution to his victory and to the struggle for independence.

On the other side of the square are **police headquarters** and the impressive **Cathedral** with its blue spire, dating from 1606 (the building itself has undergone many renovations and changes since then). Inside the cathedral is a breathtakingly beautiful carved wooden wall, the handiwork of local Indians. Downtown roads are narrow with many shops and old, two-story houses.

Jujuy does not offer the tourist much in the way of entertainment and in spite of a population of 100,000 people, is fairly quiet. There is the **Museum of History**, at Calle Lavalle 256, with exhibits of ancient pottery, weapons and portraits of governors of the town. It was here that General Lavalle was killed on October 8, 1941.

The area around Jujuy is blessed with interesting nature sites and landscapes, and dotted with small Indian villages where the ancient way of life is preserved down to the present day. The most famous of these is the village of **Humahuaca**, about two hours from Jujuy. It boasts an **Independence Monument**, a **crafts market** and **various museums**. If you're going on from here to Bolivia, don't spend time visiting these villages, since Bolivia has plenty of them.

Transportation
The **bus station** is in Ave. Dorrego, on the south bank of the Xibi River. There are several buses a day between Jujuy and La Quiaca (on the Bolivian border), Salta, Tucuman, and the surrounding villages. The trip to La Quiaca takes about 10 hours. The road is paved but narrow, and the scenery offers much of interest.

Tourist services
Jujuy has a few hotels and pensions of intermediate quality. The

ARGENTINA

Tourist Office on Calle Belgrano, corner of Lavalle, can give you details about them and provide brochures and maps, as well as explanations and suggestions for touring the area.

On to Bolivia

La Quiaca can be reached by train as well as by bus, from the station which is situated two blocks from the square. The ancient train leaves late in the evening, and the journey is slow and tiring. You should arrive early at the station and find yourself a seat on the train well before it leaves, since it is usually full. The route is extremely dusty, and you should wear warm clothes since it gets very cold at night. The transition from an elevation of 1200 m to 3600 m causes shortness of breath, and you should be careful not to exert yourself, and to walk slowly so as not to suffer from the thinness of the air (For information on how to cope with high altitudes, see "Introduction"). The train reaches the border early in the morning, but you will have to wait till 8am for the border point to open. Only then will you be able to cross the old bridge that spans the dried up river and leads to the Bolivian town of Villazon. The frontier point closes for an afternoon siesta, and on weekends is open only half a day. The Bolivian immigration official will grant you a visa for only 30 days, but this can be extended for an additional 60 days without payment at the Immigration Office in La Paz.

Money can be exchanged in local shops, but these will take only cash dollars. Beware of moneychangers at the train station and check the exchange rate. Change only as much as you will need till you reach the next big town, where you will almost certainly get a better deal. There is daily train service from Villazon to La Paz – a journey of some 24 hours. For this route, the train is the most comfortable, fastest and cheapest means of transport.

Central Region

Cordoba

The second largest city in Argentina, with its one million inhabitants, is an important commercial and economic center, although it offers little of interest to the tourist. Cordoba was founded in 1573, and its university, dating from 1614, is the oldest in the country. The modern office towers that have sprung up over the last decades have almost entirely replaced the colonial buildings and the city's numerous churches, but a few still stand in the shadow of these giant new edifices. The **Plaza San Martin**, with the **police headquarters** which once served as the **Cabildo** (Town Council) and the old **Cathedral**, which

ARGENTINA

took over a century to build, are perhaps the principal remnants of bygone days.

Cordoba has many hotels of various standards, which accommodate mainly businessmen and visiting Argentinians. The Tourist Office is situated in the modern bus station, and can provide you with ample information and advice. Buses link Cordoba to Buenos Aires (12 hours), Tucuman (12 hours), Salta (16 hours) and Mendoza (10 hours). Buses also run several times a week to Posadas and the Iguacu Falls; the journey takes more than 24 hours. There is train service from Cordoba to Buenos Aires in the south, and to Tucuman in the north.

Dotting the surrounding mountains are holiday villages and resort sites that are popular with many Argentinian vacationers.

Mendoza

This pleasant city, the Argentinian wine capital, is named after Pedro de Mendoza, who founded Buenos Aires in 1560. Mendoza was almost entirely destroyed by an earthquake in 1860 and was rebuilt – with low houses. Today, the city itself has a population of 140,000 and preserves an aura of quiet provinciality and friendliness. The province of Mendoza is richly endowed with natural reserves of petroleum, uranium, marble and lead, to mention but a few, all of which accelerated industrial development. The harvest of her many vineyards goes into her world famous wines. Mendoza has 1400 wineries, which have made Argentina into the fourth largest wine producer in the world.

How to get there

Mendoza lies on the highway linking Buenos Aires with Santiago de Chile. Route 7 from the capital will take you right to the Chilean border, 200 km west of the city. There are many buses from Buenos Aires to Mendoza's spacious central bus station (a 20-hour trip). There are also buses from Cordoba (10 hours), and from Santiago de Chile across the Andes. There are several buses a week to Bariloche (a day's journey) and Tucuman. There are two trains each evening to and from Buenos Aires. The route is extremely pleasant, passing as it does through green fertile plains. Aerolineas and Austral have flights to Mendoza from Buenos Aires, Santiago, Bariloche and Cordoba. Night flights are half the price of day flights.

Food and lodging

Mendoza being a popular tourist town, and its people most hospitable, there is no shortage of hotels and restaurants

ARGENTINA

catering to all tastes. The *Plaza Hotel* on Ave. Chile, with its majestic white facade, is quite luxurious and expensive, and very impressive. More modest hotels can be found downtown. An inexpensive and recommended hotel is the *Maxim* on Calle Lavalle, one block from San Martin, on the second floor. Budget-class hotels are concentrated around the train station. There is a camping site in the San Martin Park.

There are many restaurants downtown, especially along Ave. San Martin and the streets branching off it. Most restaurants serve typical Argentinian dishes and Italian food.

What to see

The beautiful streets of Mendoza are shaded by numerous trees that spread a pleasant atmosphere through the city. To these must be added the large, handsome **Park** named after **General San Martin**, which serves as a rest and recreation center for resident and visitor alike. In this spacious park, which lies at the foot of the mountains on the western side of the city, are a large lake, a zoo, and other attractions. The huge amphitheatre is the scene of the traditional **Wine Festival** celebrated each February – one of the most impressive festivals in the whole of Latin America. The large entrance gates to the park were imported from London in 1908. The camping site is located not far from them.

The city takes great pride in the fact that Mendoza was the launching point for General Jose de San Martin's campaign against the Spaniards across the Andes. During this campaign he helped Chile and then Peru (to which he traveled by sea) to achieve their independence. San Martin delivered an impassioned speech to the inhabitants of Mendoza, requesting their help in the war effort, and they gave generously of their jewelry and money. This historical event has been commemorated in the **huge monument** that stands in the middle of the park, which is within walking distance of **Plaza Independencia** in the town center. Plaza Independencia also has a small **Natural History Museum**.

Avenue San Martin, the main street, accommodates most of the city's public buildings, important offices, large stores, cafes and restaurants. In the afternoons and evenings the street is full of people, and its multicolored lighting blends in well with the atmosphere.

Mendoza's **Civic Center** is very impressive. It contains the district government buildings, the law courts and the municipal offices, with intervening stretches of well tended lawns, squares and fountains.

ARGENTINA

A visit to one of the many **wineries** is, of course, a must. Guided tours are available, in the course of which you will be able to follow the wine manufacturing process – starting with the initial fermentation, and going on to aging in vats, bottling, keeping the wine at a stable temperature and finally corking. The blend of up-to-date technology and traditional manufacturing methods is especially impressive. Wine tasting is usually offered at the end of the tour.

Tourist services
The **Tourist Office** is housed in a large building half way along Ave. San Martin (Block 11). Its staff will gladly supply you with comprehensive information and referrals to the wineries. You should definitely take advantage of their services.

During the winter, the surrounding villages and small towns turn into **ski resorts**. Ski buffs can hire equipment and indulge their passion.

On to Chile
You can fly or drive from Mendoza to Chile. Trains no longer ply this route due to lack of passengers. Aerolineas and Lan Chile run several daily flights between Santiago and Buenos Aires, stopping en route at Mendoza.

Traveling overland is a worthwhile experience, since the route passes through a number of interesting sites. Several companies have daily bus service to Santiago; you should buy your ticket at least one day in advance at the central bus station. The Ohiggins and Pluma companies have modern, fast buses (8 hours) and offer excellent service, with stewardesses to see to your comfort. The journey across the Andes is breathtaking in its beauty, especially in clear weather. The steep summits piercing the deep blue sky, the many tunnels carved into the mountainside, the winding road, take us through one of the largest and most famous mountain ranges in the world. As we travel west along Route 7 we are, in fact, taking the same route as that followed by San Martin's men. We pass Uspallata, a winter holiday resort, before reaching Punta de Vacas, where we will be subjected to Argentinian border formalities which may involve several hours wait. It is prohibited to bring fruit, vegetables, or fresh food into Chile.

Resuming our journey, we pass by the **Inca Bridge** (*Puente del Inca*), which, in spite of its shape, is a natural formation. It measures 20 m high, 20 m long, and 26 m wide, and is extremely impressive. From here you can see the distant peak of **Aconagua** which, at 7000 m, is the highest in South America.

ARGENTINA

After a stop in Las Cuevas, 4200 m above sea level, to complete Chilean immigration formalities, we can continue our trip. The road now twists and turns against a backdrop of a breathtakingly enchanting rocky landscape. The vegetation on this side of the mountains becomes increasingly thicker and greener because the western slopes enjoy abundant rain released by clouds that form over the Pacific Ocean. The rest of the journey takes you through holiday and ski resorts and farming villages along the approach to Santiago de Chile.

Mar del Plata

Mar del Plata (the Silver Sea) lies 410 km south of Buenos Aires. It is the Argentinians' favorite holiday resort. Spread along the shores of the Atlantic, with broad beaches and sunny weather, the city has become an important entertainment and tourist center, with hotels, casinos, restaurants and other attractions to delight the vacationer. Hundreds of thousands of people make the five-hour journey from Buenos Aires to Mar del Plata for a yearly holiday or short, weekend break.

The peak season is in the summer, from October to April/May, when the city's population of 400,000 swells to include an additional 2.5 million vacationers! If you can possibly avoid visiting Mar del Plata during this season, do so. If not, book your hotel well in advance.

The main attraction is of course the sea (bathing in Buenos Aires' Rio de la Plata is forbidden because of pollution). The beaches are equipped with deck chairs, cafes and other services. The **Playa Grande** (Large Beach) is the most prestigious, and has private beach clubs open to members only. Nearby are the most luxurious hotels and restaurants. **Bristol Beach** contains the city's largest and most famous casino. Near **Playa Perla** and around the bus station are the cheapest hotels and pensions. All the beaches rent a large variety of sporting equipment, such as scuba gear, boats, fishing tackle, water skis, etc.

Trains leave Constitucion station in the capital for Mar del Plata almost hourly, and the trip takes less than five hours. The trains continue south to Bahia Blanca and Bariloche. There are many buses on the same route. Aerolineas and Austral run daily flights to the capital (40 minutes). By car the trip takes about 5 hours on Route 2. The area around Mar del Plata has **lagoons** and **nature reserves** where you can camp and enjoy the quiet, tranquil and pleasant beaches.

ARGENTINA

The Lake District

Just as Mar del Plata is Argentina's most popular summer resort, the Lake District, which lies in the Andes some 1600 km southwest of Buenos Aires, is the country's favorite winter resort. Its distance from the capital means that it is less crowded than the seaside, but there is no self-respecting Argentinian who has failed to visit Bariloche, or at least does not dream of visiting there.

The fantastic scenery of blue lakes, forests and mountains offers vacationers a variety of nature hikes, ski resorts and up-to-date tourist services. All these together make the area very much like the Swiss Alps, and it is no wonder that the Argentinians refer to the place with pride and enthusiasm.

The Lake District extends almost the whole length of Patagonia, but the parks and main sites of interest are centered in the strip between San Martin de los Andes in the north and Esquel in the south, an area of some 500 km. The Lake District extends across the Chilean border, and a visit to the lakes on the Chilean side is recommended. Crossing the border presents no problems (for details, see below and the chapter on Chile).

This region is undoubtedly one of the most beautiful in Argentina, and has something for everybody: romantic hiking trails, mountain climbing, camping and complete retreat from the world. You can go off to the islands, sail on the lakes, enjoy the beautiful scenery from the comfort of buses, or for those who just want to rest, enjoy the pensions that offer good food in a pastoral setting. It is impossible not to fall in love with the Lake District. You can find everything here in exactly the right proportion: beauty, comfort, things to do, a carefree, relaxed atmosphere, good food, – and the prices are not too extravagant. This is the ideal place for couples, since the place positively demands a partner.

San Martin de Los Andes

This delightful town, some 200 km north of Bariloche, is composed entirely of small houses and straight streets and is surrounded by a number of interesting places to visit. The most important of these is the **Lanin Park**, which extends over a large area north of the town. In the center of the park is a giant volcano of the same name, which, reaching a height of 3740 meters, is one of the largest and most beautiful of its kind in the world. The road north to Junin de los Andes and on to Chile passes through the park. If you wish to explore its hidden

ARGENTINA

treasures, you can hike through its vast expanse dotted with lakes, or you can join a guided tour organized by one of the local tour companies.

Two roads link San Martin to Bariloche. The first is the paved highway used by the daily bus, and the second is the **Camino de los Siete Lagos** (The Way of the Seven Lakes). This tortuous road passes through beautiful scenery, including a desert where the wind and rains have carved the rocks into bizarre shapes resembling man and beast.

Traveling over this dusty track takes four hours. There are no buses and, as far as hitchhiking is concerned, I have heard of people who have traveled this way at the rate of one lake per day. The tour companies run organized minibus trips, which are by far the best way of visiting this area.

San Carlos de Bariloche

This popular holiday town, and the **Nahuel Huapi** Park which surrounds it, are the heart of the Lake District and contain the key to its magic. *Nahuel Huapi* means "Eye of the Tiger" in the local Indian language. Bariloche is the capital of the whole area, and the name is often used to refer to the entire Lake District.

The town lies on the shores of Lake Nahuel Huapi, which is the largest lake in the area (with an area of 536 sq/km). Its picturesque streets climb steeply from the shores of the lake up the slopes of the mountain. In the center of the town is the Municipality Square, surrounded by chocolate factories built in the form of Swiss chalets, which look as if they have been snatched straight out of a children's fairy tale.

How to get there

Bariloche is the transportation and tourist hub of the Lake District, and there are frequent air and overland services between it and Buenos Aires. Aerolineas, Austral, and Lade run frequent daily flights between Bariloche and Buenos Aires, and between Bariloche and Comodoro Rivadavia, and other cities in the south. Aerolineas also has a route to the north, via Mendoza. There is a train service from Bariloche (whose station is some distance from the town) to Buenos Aires several times a week, but the journey is long (over 30 hours) and exhausting, through the dusty and monotonous pampas. The train is not too crowded (no wonder!), and you should be sure to take enough food and drink with you. As I said, the trip is quite boring, and you should avoid it if at all possible. Although I have traveled farther by train, I cannot remember any journey as tedious as this one.

ARGENTINA

The buses present an entirely different picture. They are luxurious, most have charming hostesses who serve beverages and snacks, and the journey is far more interesting and quicker (a difference of about 10 hours) than by train. Some bus companies provide service to the capital, and others to Mendoza and Cordoba in the north, and to Comodoro in the southeast. There are frequent buses to the surrounding towns and to Chile (see below).

The fastest and most convenient overland route to Patagonia and Tierra del Fuego is via Comodoro Rivadavia and then on south to Rio Gallegos.

Food and lodging
One thing Bariloche definitely does not lack are hotels and restaurants. These can be found all over and cater to all tastes and budgets. Nevertheless, it is extremely difficult to find a hotel room during the peak seasons – summer and winter. In spring and fall it is quieter. The most pleasant hotels are actually situated out of town, on the lakeshores but these are more expensive, and inconvenient if you do not have a car.

When it comes to food, Bariloche's numerous restaurants specialize in all types of Argentinian as well as Italian cuisine. As for the famous Bariloche chocolate, see below: "what to buy".

What to see
The town itself offers the tourist mainly a chance to relax and take it easy. In the center, as we said, is the **Municipality Square**, home of the **City Hall** with its **clock tower**, the **Tourist Office** (on the ground floor of City Hall), and the **police station**, (to the right of City Hall). Most interesting of all, is the **Patagonia Museum**, which has a collection of stuffed animals including all species common to Patagonia, as well as geological specimens, ancient artifacts from the region and more. On the ground floor is a large exhibition of old military uniforms and weapons.

But the main attractions are to be found outside the town, in the natural beauty of the Lake District. The classic routes to follow are to **Cerro Tornador** and **Cerro Catedral**; the latter mountain is known for its ski slopes. A visit to **Victoria Island** is a must. This island is famous for its large red trees, and was chosen by Walt Disney as the inspiration for one of the best-loved children's films of our times – **Bambi**. You should book via one of the travel agents, since the boat fare alone is not much cheaper than the price of a complete guided tour, which includes visits to some of the other beautiful sites in the area.

ARGENTINA

City Hall

There is also plenty of scope for walking tours over different and varied routes. You can go hiking from two or three days up to a month, provided you are properly equipped with camping gear and food. The Club Andino Bariloche will supply you with information and maps, and inform you of altered routes, weather conditions, etc. If you are taking a trip through the mountains, you can spend the night in one of the hikers' *refugios* there, paying a small fee to the club to cover expenses.

One of the most beautiful routes is the one through *Cerro Catedral* (Cathedral Mountain). The hike takes three days, and passes impressive green forests, bubbling streams, blue lakes and towering Andean peaks. The route starts at the foot of the mountain at Vila Catedral, which is served by buses which set out a few times a day from Bariloche. The climb to *Refugio Frey* on the shores of Lake Frey begins here, and takes several hours. The second day of the hike is the most difficult, and includes the crossing of two high mountain saddles before you reach *Refugio San Martin* on the shores of Laguna Jacob. A short way up from the refugio is another enchanting lake, which is certainly worth the effort of the climb. The third day is devoted to the descent to Bariloche.

The best season for mountain hikes is in summer,

ARGENTINA

A street in Bariloche

December-March. Then the weather is pleasant, the skies are blue, and there is no snow to make walking difficult. In winter you can enjoy the ski slopes of Cathedral Mountain.

What to buy

The main street, leading off the Municipality Square, is lined with numerous shops offering a large selection of souvenirs typical of the locality, especially wood carvings, leather handicraft and wool products. Particularly noteworthy are the local sweaters, which are famous for their beauty and quality. You can find them in almost any store in town.

Bariloche is famous for its chocolate industry. The city and its outskirts are home to dozens of small chocolate factories, which produce an infinite variety of chocolates of unsurpassed quality. These chocolates are sold by weight in many shops. Just looking at their seductive displays will add to your waistline. Many shops sell home-made chocolate (*chocolate casero*), and generally speaking allow customers to sample the various kinds. The largest store, Turista, on Calle Mitre, is slightly more expensive than the others and does not allow you to sample their wares before buying. But you really can't go wrong! In a store like this, whatever you buy and however much you buy, you'll be sorry you didn't buy more!

ARGENTINA

El Bolson

This picturesque little town, 124 km south of Bariloche, is attractive in its own right, both for the special charm and character of its streets, and for the pastoral countryside in which it rests. El Bolson is chiefly known as the starting point for walking tours of the area, of varying lengths and difficulty. Its special feature is the fact that there are a large number of beautiful spots just outside the town. Even a short outing will give you a fair sample of them.

Esquel

This modern holiday resort located at an elevation of 540 meters above sea level, has a population of around 20,000 people. Esquel, too, serves as a starting point for various tours through the southern part of the Lake District, especially in the nearby **Los Alerces Park**, which is considered less "touristy" than the others. There are comfortable hotels, a wide selection of restaurants, a local food industry of high quality (specializing in jams and chocolate), fishing spots, etc. The Club Andino Esquel and the **Tourist Office** in the bus station will be glad to give you advice and directions, and provide you with maps of recommended hiking routes.

There is direct bus service from Esquel to Comodoro Rivadavia, and from there to the south. Lade also has flights to Patagonia in the south and to Buenos Aires in the north.

On to Chile

There are several frontier points between Argentina and Chile and your choice will depend on your destination there. You can travel over a fast, paved, and quite ordinary highway, or choose a more interesting route and make an experience of the trip itself.

There is one bus a day from Bariloche to Temuco in the north. The trip follows a difficult route and takes 10 hours. The bus passes through the outstandingly beautiful **Lanin Park**. The road climbs through the Andes to the frontier point at **Truman**. The border check points on either side are several kilometers apart. Once in Chile, you will be traveling through beautiful forests, passing by small farms which are still plowed by oxen, and crossing rivers and streams over shaky wooden bridges. During the winter, the border is sometimes closed due to snow drifts that block the road.

The Bariloche-Puerto Montt route is far less impressive, but much easier to travel. Several bus companies serve this route, and the ride is fast and comfortable. The travel agencies offer

ARGENTINA

one or two-day outings, which include a round trip to Puerto Montt, and provide a chance both to visit the city and to enjoy the lakes and landscapes en route. Another no less interesting possibility is to take a bus and then ride the ferry across *Todos Los Santos* lake, considered by many to be the most beautiful lake in the south.

Bear in mind that crossing the border depends to a large extent on the clemency of the weather, as well as on the political climate. As tourists, we have little say in either matter, so it is advisable to check which way the winds are blowing before setting out – and decide accordingly.

Patagonia

Almost devoid of vegetation, the ground bare and rocky, we set foot on the arid plains of southern Argentina – Patagonia. The climate here is extremely harsh throughout most of the year, and although the temperature never sinks below freezing, the biting cold and gale-force winds are enough to chase settlers much further north. No wonder then that Patagonia, which covers a third of Argentina, is sparsely populated (a population density of 2 people per square kilometer). The further south you go, the more virgin and undisturbed the landscape, until it becomes truly primeval. Unlike the jungle and other untamed spots, the horizon here is free of detail; you cannot fail to be overcome by a sense of infinite space. The outstanding beauty, the limpid sea in the east, and the lofty peaks of the Andes in the west, the awe-inspiring sunsets, the extreme contrasts of height and depth, and many other marvels of nature, as well as an abundance of birds and wildlife, combine to give this place a unique charm. Few settlements break up the vast open expanses, with large sheep ranches scattered among them.

Half of Argentina's sheep are raised in Patagonia and their thick, silky wool, as well as their meat and skins, provide the main source of income for the local population.

Traffic on the roads of Patagonia, most of which are unpaved, is sparse; on rainy days driving can be hazardous and difficult. The lack of industry means that most consumer goods must be imported from the north, and this is naturally evident in prices. The growing number of tourists over the past years has led to the development of tourist services, but these still fall short of what is needed. It can be very hard to find accommodation, especially during the summer influx of thousands of visitors.

ARGENTINA

How to get there
By air: Aerolineas, Austral, and Lade all run scheduled flights between the towns of Patagonia and Buenos Aires. There are daily flights leaving Buenos Aires, some are direct and others with intermediate stops. The southernmost terminus of Aerolineas and Austral is Rio Grande.

Night flights are half-price, but these are heavily booked and you have to make reservations at least a week in advance. Although Lade's flights are among the cheapest they are long and slow, with many stopovers en route. The planes are very old, most with piston engines, and there is usually no problem reserving a seat. Lade is the only company with local flights between the southern towns and to Tierra del Fuego, and these are no more expensive than bus journeys over the same routes. Reservations on Lade flights are not reliable, especially to remote destinations, and you will have to take this into account. Flights to and from Ushuaia are liable to be cancelled due to strong winds, which prevent planes from landing there.

Bus: The buses from Buenos Aires to Rio Gallegos ply the coastal route, and take at least two days to get there. The fare is only slightly cheaper than a night flight. Take a bus only if you want to visit places along the way.

Hitchhiking: If you have plenty of time on your hands and want to save, you can always hitchhike. You should allow 4-6 days, bearing in mind that this is one of the main hitching routes in the whole of South America. The gas stations along the route have showers and patches of lawn where you can set up a tent.

Come equipped with a good tent and sleeping bag, food, cooking utensils and most important of all – vast quantities of patience! The best lifts are from the huge trucks carrying goods south. Route 3 stretches for 3178 km from Buenos Aires to Ushuaia (Tierra del Fuego). Most of this length is paved.

The Valdes Peninsula
Half way between Buenos Aires and the south is Peninsula Valdes with its nature reserve, the center of an area rich in sea creatures and birds. The peninsula is a favorite haunt of sea lions, seals, penguins and whales, and these flock to its shores by the thousand. This rare concentration is what makes the nature reserve so interesting. It attracts tens of thousands of nature-lovers from Argentina and abroad each year. The best season to visit is September-December, in the spring, when you can see dozens of whales and thousands of other creatures.

ARGENTINA

Sometimes you can get really close to these huge animals, even within a few meters. The largest weigh hundreds of kilograms. The whales, some of which are truly gigantic, swim near the shore and can be seen quite clearly. Especially impressive are the jets of water they expel from their spouts and the sight of their tails sticking straight up out of the water when they dive. It is one you will never forget.

Several tourist agencies in the nearby town of Puerto Madryn, some 100 km from the reserve, organize guided bus tours to the peninsula, incorporating visits to other sites in the area. Getting around the reserve itself is difficult if you do not have a car, and there is not much hope of getting a lift. You can hire a car in Puerto Madryn, but the prices are far steeper than usual. Those who stay over can find accommodations in Puerto Piramides, at the entrance to the reserve, and a camp ground. Take food with you, since the restaurants are expensive and there are no stores. You can rent small boats, diving gear, water-sports equipment and the like in the vicinity.

The nearest airport is in the town of Trelew, and there are buses from there to Puerto Madryn.

Punta Tumbo

Punta Tumbo, situated about 100 km south of Trelew, has an enormous concentration of penguins which nest here during the summer. In the peak of the season, their numbers reach about three million! On the way to the penguin reserve you are likely to encounter other indigenous wild life, such as the *guanaco* (of the llama family) and the *nanu* (of the ostrich family). In the huge reserve one can wander around among the penguins, and almost get close enough to touch them.

From Trelew one can hire a car or take a taxi, which is not expensive if one organizes a group of five people.

Comodoro Rivadavia

This town of 115,000 is the transportation, industrial, military, and commercial center of the whole of Patagonia. Some 1800 km south of Buenos Aires, Commodoro underwent an economic boom due to oil and gas finds in the region, and is now enjoying a prosperity that is truly enviable. The area provides about a third of the national oil supply; derricks and pipelines are everywhere. Large military forces are based around the city, and it was from here that the invasion of the Falklands Islands was launched.

ARGENTINA

The town's airport is the largest and busiest in the south. There are daily flights to Buenos Aires, Bariloche, and other towns in Patagonia. The highway to Tierra del Fuego passes through the city and makes it an important road for all the regional bus lines.

Rio Gallegos

This southernmost town of Patagonia is the district capital for the tip of the continent. There's nothing particularly special about the place, and from our point of view its main importance is as a crossroads. Rio Gallegos has a small airport serving the few planes from Buenos Aires and elsewhere, including those half-price night flights we keep mentioning. Lade flies to Calafate, Rio Turbio, and Tierra del Fuego, and north to the large cities, including irregular flights to Bariloche. Lade also flies to La Plata, close to Buenos Aires. This is also the end of the line for buses on southern routes. There are two roads from Rio Gallegos to Chile, one to Punta Arenas, and the other to the border town of Rio Turbio. Route 3 from Buenos Aires continues south to the straits of Magellan and Tierra del Fuego, via Chile. Although buses travel these routes they are fairly expensive, in fact not much cheaper than Lade flights.

Calafate

This small country town has thousands of visitors each year, arriving en masse in the summer to feast their eyes on **Prito Moreno** – the huge glacier which is the only one in the world that is still growing. The glacier, more than 50 meters high, is one of the many relics of the Ice Age that can be found in the vicinity, and is the main attraction of the **Glacier National Park** (*Parque Nacional de los Glaciares*). On hot, clear days (hot for the glacier, we are still freezing...) sections of the ice wall melt and fall into the water with a tremendous crash, creating huge waves. You may have to stand around for hours till this happens, but it's worth the wait.

Because of the harsh climate, the tourist season here is rather short, running from the end of October to mid-March. During this period the local tourist agencies organize guided tours to the glacier, and offer additional trips to more distant glaciers in the park, including trips in motor boats. Although the fare from Calafate to the park is expensive, there is really no other way to reach the glacier. You could try hitchhiking, but you will need lots of patience. Public transport does not run out of season, but there are taxis (expensive). Park-service cars leave Calafate every day for the park and with a little luck and a smile, you can

ARGENTINA

usually persuade the driver to take you along. They do not leave at fixed times and there is not always room.

In the park itself there is an ACA bungalow site, but they are expensive and tend to be full during the tourist season. You can pitch a tent, if you have a permit, several kilometers away from the glacier, alongside the road that leads to town. Calafate itself has several hotels and a camping site, as well as restaurants and grocery stores. If you plan to spend more than a day in the park, stock up on food in the town, since the restaurant next to the glacier is expensive.

Calafate is linked to all towns in the south via Lade flights. The tiny airport is within walking distance of the town center. Buses cover the monotonous route to Rio Gallegos in 6 hours. Most other roads in the area are deserted, and hitchhikers run a risk of getting stuck. To get to Rio Turbio, you should backtrack to Rio Gallegos and then carry on from there, since there is hardly any traffic over the direct route west from Calafate.

Fitz Roy Mountain

Wild mountain scenery, majestic cliffs, glaciers and lakes – this is the Fitz Roy mountain region. Its peak is "only" 3375 m above sea level, but the cliff itself is a steep wall hundreds of meters high. Near Fitz Roy looms another imposing cliff, Cerro Torre, not quite as high as Fitz Roy, but no less impressive. The weather here is harsh, and it is only on a few days of the year, during the summer, that the skies are cloudless and the peaks of Fitz Roy and Cerro Torre exposed. Because of this combination of amazing cliffs and treacherous weather, these two peaks are considered by professional mountain climbers to be among the most difficult in the world to climb.

Access to Fitz Roy is complicated. It is a remote area, and the nearest settlement is Cala Fate, six hours travel away. There is no regular transport here, and very few cars travel the difficult road. The chances of hitching a ride are negligible. Farmers in the area depart from Cala Fate by truck from time to time, and will give you a lift for a fee. This is not a cheap option, but it may be the only way if one does not want to waste several days waiting for a lift which may never materialize.

At the site itself, there is an expensive *hosteria* (hostel) and a camping ground nearby. From here there are a number of walking routes, mostly for one day. Among the most beautiful are the walk to the observation point over Cerro Torre (one day) and the walk to the climbers' hut on Fitz Roy, where one should spend the night.

ARGENTINA

It is very important to bring enough food because there is no possibility of obtaining any at Fitz Roy, except in the hosteria, where it is very expensive. Take into account that you might be delayed several days, until there is a vehicle returning to Cala Fate.

As has been said, getting to Fitz Roy is not easy, and it is possible that you will spend days there without even catching a glimpse of the peaks of Fitz Roy and Cerro Torre. However, those who make the effort and to whom the weather is kind, will be privileged to see one of the most incredible views imaginable.

Rio Turbio

This border town is the last stop in Argentina before you cross into Chilean Patagonia. You can get here by plane or bus, or by hitchhiking from Rio Gallegos along a desolate road that passes through a few rather wretched settlements. The old-fashioned train that travels between the two towns carries coal from the Rio Turbio mines to Rio Gallegos and does not carry passengers. It is possible to find overnight accommodations in the town, but your best bet would be to carry on immediately to Puerto Natales in Chile and stay there. There are direct buses from the center of Rio Turbio (near the supermarket) to Puerto Natales. Another and cheaper alternative is to take a local bus to the Argentinian frontier point, cross the border on foot, and then board a Chilean bus. Generally speaking, crossing the border is a quick and simple matter, although there have been unpleasant cases of travelers being stopped and having luggage thoroughly examined.

The Argentinian and Chilean border points are several kilometers apart. Tourists crossing over from Chile to Argentina will sometimes be required to give a detailed list of their intended itinerary (see "Introduction" and "Documents").

Currency exchange

You will find it difficult to exchange dollars in the south; travelers' checks are virtually unacceptable, and cash is exchanged at a low rate and the commission charged is very high. You should try to exchange enough money before you leave the big city. If you nevertheless overspend and get "stuck", try changing in shops and private businesses rather than in official places. You'll find less beaucracy this way, and, more important, you'll get a better deal. Bear in mind that prices in the south run about 30% more than for the same items in the north.

Climate

The entire south has a harsh and treacherous climate. During

ARGENTINA

the winter (April-September) it's very hard to get around on the muddy roads, flights are delayed and sometimes cancelled and access to most places is blocked. In other words, either come in the summer, or don't come at all. Since touring this area requires so much effort, it would be a pity not to derive the maximum benefit. Always take with you a sleeping bag and the warmest clothes you can imagine – even those are not always enough! The notorious winds of Patagonia are frequent, and can reach a speed of 100 km an hour! During the summer the weather is slightly less hostile, and although the nights are cold, clear pleasant days are not uncommon. This is the peak tourist season, when accommodations are extremely hard to find.

Postal and telephone services

The large towns of Patagonia have post offices with letter and parcel service, as well as international telex and telephone services. However, the postal service is slow, so if you plan to return to Buenos Aires (in two or three weeks) hold on to your letters till you get there.

Tierra del Fuego

The magical name of this exotic island at the southern tip of the continent cannot but awaken associations. The island was named by the famous Portuguese navigator, Fernando Magellan (1480-1521) who, in November 1520, sailed through the straits that today bear his name, on his way from the Atlantic to the Pacific Ocean, during the first circumnavigation of the globe in history. There are several theories as to the origin of the name. One theory claims that Magellan called the island "Land of Fire" because the local Indians lit bonfires in his honor. I, however, prefer the explanation that the name was given on account of the red vegetation – especially the red tree-tops – which are due to the high concentration of iron oxide in the soil. It is impossible not to be impressed by the beauty of the foliage, which spreads like a lush, reddish carpet over slopes and valleys.

The island is divided between Argentina and Chile, and is sparsely populated. On the other hand, the area is famous for its abundance of fish and wildlife, including over 150 species of birds.

How to get there

Aerolineas and Austral fly as far south as Rio Grande, and Lade goes all the way to Ushuaia. Strong winds often cause serious alterations to timetables and even cancellation of flights. There are several buses per day from Rio Grande to Ushuaia (3 hours).

ARGENTINA

Hitchhiking is easy along this route: cross the large bridge south of Rio Grande and wait at the next junction. On your way back, wait at the northern exit of Ushuaia, but bear in mind that many vehicles travel only as far as the industrial zone several kilometers away. Buses run several times a week between Rio Grande and Puerto Porvenir in Chile (200 km – 5 hours). There are no problems crossing the border at San Sebastian. If you are traveling by car (Route 3), a ferry will take you over the straits between Patagonia and Tierra del Fuego. The road continues into Chilean territory, entailing the normal frontier road formalities. The ferry runs several times a day: the crossing takes about half-an-hour. There is also daily ferry service between Puerto Porvenir and Punta Arenas (3 hours).

Rio Grande

This small town lies on the shores of the Atlantic, on the northern bank of the river after which it is named. Its streets are empty and neglected, its houses low and its places of interest – non-existent. There are only a few hotels, and these are relatively expensive and full to capacity during the summer. If you are the sporty type, you can camp near the ACA service station on the beach (not to be confused with the expensive ACA luxury hotel in town). The station has showers and toilets, which are open all night. Outfit yourselves with warm, top-quality camping equipment. I spent one of the coldest nights of my life here.

Tierra del Fuego's proximity to the south pole results in drastic tidal flows; in the evenings, the sea recedes hundreds of meters. Make the effort to get up really early in order to see the waters "coming home" at sunrise, consuming the dry land once again.

Ushuaia

Welcome to the southernmost city in the world! On the strength of its latitude, the remote, insignificant town of Ushuaia has acquired international fame. The town, with its wooden houses and tiled roofs, its hotels, restaurants, charming harbor and factories, bears the mysterious stamp of "the end": you simply cannot go further south. Throughout its history Ushuaia has been mentioned in this context, and has been visited by throngs of people wishing to include it as a landmark in their lives.

Food and lodging

All the hotels in Ushuaia are expensive and usually fully booked, especially in the summer. The *Mafalda Hotel* at San Martin 5, near the navy base, is recommended. The *Ona Hotel*, on Calle

ARGENTINA

Ushuaia - a look at the southernmost city in the world

9 de Julio, is definitely **not** recommended. There is a cheap and good hostel on the road running parallel to the sea, in the red-turreted building visible from all points. There are plenty of restaurants, but these are also not cheap. If you are partial to seafood, don't miss Ushuaia's king crabs, known here as *centolla*. Several shops serve hot chocolate, home-made chocolate, and excellent pastries.

What to see
Avenue San Martin, which is the backbone of the town, contains the **municipality buildings**, the **tourist information office** (No. 524), **airline offices**, the best restaurants, duty-free stores, etc. Tierra del Fuego is a **duty-free zone** and as a result, many Argentinians do their shopping here.

Tourist agencies offer a wide selection of outings in the area, to look at the wildlife, glaciers and lakes. If you have a car you can stay in one of the motels along the Rio Grande-Ushuaia road, or south of the town on the road leading to the national park.

The **National Park** (*Parque Nacional Tierra del Fuego*) is extremely interesting, with an abundance of wildlife. The most famous of these is the beaver, who is the pride of the park. The park rangers will enthusiastically direct you to a point where you can see it, or at least the amazing constructions of which the beaver is the architect and builder. This spacious park is situated south of the town, and can be reached by car, hitchhiking, or organized tour.

BOLIVIA

Bolivia is certainly one of the most interesting countries in South America. Its geography, from the dense jungles in the east to the arid Andean plains in the west, and its Indian population, make it a fascinating country to visit. It is difficult to believe that Bolivia has experienced more political instability and unrest than any other country in the world.

Bolivia offers the rare opportunity of entering a strange, wonderful world, whose value system, customs, and outward appearance are unlike anything we are used to. Here primitivism, simplicity, a slow pace of life and an almost stoical apathy still reign. Everything seems to be a century behind. If we were to take away the cars and electricity, we would be thrown back five hundred years in time. Even in the suburbs of the large cities, single-story adobe houses, unpaved roads, wells, earthenware vessels, wood-burning stoves and other such relics from the past, are still very much in existence and, will probably be present in the future too.

History

Existing settlement atop the mountains, in the region currently known as the Altiplano, apparently dates back to the seventh century. Before then, the Tiwanaku culture flourished in the area, with a high level of social and material development.

Controversy surrounds the origins of this culture, and researchers have come up with dates hundreds of years apart. However, it is clear that the Tiwanaku civilization disappeared several centuries before the arrival of the Spanish conquerors. (See "Short trips around La Paz – Tiwanaku").

When the Spanish arrived in the 16th century, they found a large agricultural population in this region, who spoke mainly Aymara and Quechua. The Indian tribes warred among themselves, especially the Aymara against the Quechua. The Incas, upon conquering the area, settled in large numbers, intermarrying with the local Aymara people and thus laying the foundations of the Bolivian nation as it exists today.

When silver and rich deposits were discovered near the towns of Potosi and Oruro in the Altiplano (or Upper Peru as it was known then), the importance of the area soared. The Spanish, rejoicing in these promising discoveries, set thousands of workers to mine the metals and ores for export to Europe. Prosperity reached its peak in the mid-17th century, at which

BOLIVIA

time Potosi, then the largest city on the American continents, had some 150,000 inhabitants, living mainly off the mines.

The Spanish founded other cities, including La Paz and Chuquisaca, later renamed Sucre. These towns were intended to strengthen Spanish unity, while at the same time supplying the needs of the mining towns. In 1776, when Upper Peru was transferred from the jurisdiction of the Spanish Viceroy in Peru to the Spanish Viceroy in Argentina, the precious metals were exported through Buenos Aires. At the same time, the University of Chuquisaca developed into an important intellectual center, promoting ideas that had considerable influence in the more distant South American countries. In 1809, the call for independence rang out from Chuquisaca, calling for revolt against Spain, which was under the heel of Napoleon's conquering army at the time. Even though the revolt was suppressed by the legions of the Viceroy in Peru, the call was sufficient to kindle the spark of rebellion in neighboring countries, with the result that Argentina, Paraguay, Chile and Uruguay all declared their independence within a few years. Bolivia continued to bear the yoke of the Spanish, who refused to give up the rich mines. Only in 1825, one year after the young General Antonio de Sucre routed the Spanish in battle in Peru, did Simon Bolivar, one of the continent's foremost leaders and thinkers, declare the independence of the country that today bears his name. General Antonio de Sucre was elected as the country's first president.

Upon achieving independence, the newly-founded country was immediately confronted with serious economic problems, which, apart from short periods of prosperity, have dogged Bolivia to this day. These problems are largely responsible for her continuing reputation as a poor and backward country. The root of the problem lies in the fact that the national economy is almost exclusively based on mining, so that the country is at the mercy of the international market, with its sharp fluctuations and instability. As if to prove the point, at the end of the war of independence which had drained the national coffers, there was a significant decline in the world demand for silver, and Bolivia, as a result, entered a troubled economic and political era. In an attempt to solve these difficulties, President Andres de Santa Cruz sought union with Peru, but the protests of his Chilean neighbors thwarted his efforts. Chile continued "showing an interest" in its undeveloped neighbor, and when rich deposits of sodium nitrate were discovered in the Atacama desert – then Bolivian territory – Chile began exerting considerable pressure in order to gain a share in the profits. When these pressures proved ineffective, the five-year War of the Pacific broke out (1879-84). The Chilean army defeated Bolivia and Peru, captured

BOLIVIA

the Atacama Desert with its mines, and reached the outskirts of Lima.

Ironically, this defeat was a decisive factor in a temporary improvement in Bolivia's economic affairs. As a result of the war, Bolivia lost her outlet to the sea, and was henceforth dependent on her neighbors for exporting her goods. Consequently, more attention was given to internal affairs, and this internal political consolidation gave rise to social stability and tranquility, which in turn encouraged foreign investment and the development of the mines. New mining techniques were introduced and a railroad was laid. Towards the end of the 19th century, when there were signs of another decline in the world silver market, the demand for tin increased significantly among industrialized nations. Bolivia, which till then had neglected this metal, began investing considerable efforts in the development of her tin mines. To this day, tin constitutes a major export.

The change of emphasis from silver to tin mining had social as well as economic repercussions, since it lowered the status of the silver-mine owners. Development continued into the present century, and Bolivia began to deal with her social problems. However, this respite did not last long. Bolivia's neighbors continued exerting pressure in the border areas, coveting districts that seemed economically promising: Argentina annexed part of the Chaco, Brazil appropriated a large, rich stretch of land in the east, later forcing Bolivia to "sell" it to her, and Paraguay claimed a foothold in what was left of the desolate Chaco. The Bolivian government adopted a tolerant stance and conceded these territories. As compensation for damages incurred, Bolivia signed dependency and compensation agreements with her neighbors, which included the laying of railway lines from Bolivia to ports on the Pacific Ocean, to Argentina, and to Brazil.

During the First World War the mining industry reached its apex, but the ensuing prosperity brought with it political power struggles. In the early 1930s, when the economic situation deteriorated due to the 1929 Wall Street crash, fresh border skirmishes broke out with Paraguay. The Bolivian government, seeing war as a way of diverting public attention from economic problems, provoked a war that lasted for three years (1932-35). The war, having claimed thousands of lives, ended with the total defeat of the Bolivian army, and led to the loss of most of the Chaco. The ensuing domestic turmoil, brought about by this traumatic defeat, encouraged extreme political trends. The army seized power and subjected Bolivia to ten years of chaos and bloodshed (1936-46). The fascistic National Revolutionary Movement, which was the main political force of the times, led to the appointment of Colonel Villaroel as president in 1943. He

BOLIVIA

remained chief-of-state till 1946, when another violent revolt broke out, in the course of which Villaroel was hanged in the square facing the presidential palace.

Since 1946, Bolivia has suffered from continuing social and political strife, and except for short periods of peace, the country has been subjected to violent changes. Bolivia has had more than 180 (!) governments, with military men and civilians alternating as presidents. The most significant of these vicissitudes took place in the early fifties, when the National Revolutionary Movement again seized power in a bloody revolt. They nationalized the mines, instituted comprehensive reforms which altered the balance of power and the distribution of land, and established universal suffrage. However, their inability to stabilize the economy, together with rampant inflation and the ferment caused by groups who had suffered from these reforms, once again brought about a state of anarchy. In the 1960s and 1970s the power of the army as a moderating and stabilizing influence grew. In the early 1980s the country was again in a state of agitation, and in 1982, after protracted student riots, the army transferred the reins of power to an elected civilian president. During 1983-1984 the government attempted to deal with the critical economic situation, but without particular success, and the outlook for the future is none too bright.

Geography and Climate

Bolivia extends over an area of 1.1 million km in a distinctly tropical region. Since the loss of the Atacama desert in the war with Chile in 1884, Bolivia has been landlocked between Peru and Chile to the east, Brazil to the north and east, and Paraguay and Argentina to the south. Even though 70% of its territory lies to the east of the Andes, most of the population is concentrated in the *Altiplano* (high plain), which is wedged between two parallel mountain ranges: the Eastern Range (*Cordillera Oriental*) and the Western Range (*Cordillera Occidental*). The Altiplano is a deep and narrow valley, 3500-4000 m above sea level, bordered on east and west by high mountains. Some 65% of the population live in this area, which is 800 km long, 130 km wide, and constitutes only 10% of Bolivia's total area. Most Bolivians work in mining or mining-related industries. The weather is always chilly, both in winter and in summer, with an average temperature of 10 degrees Centigrade (50 degrees Fahrenheit). The annual rainfall of 600 mm is concentrated in the summer months; the rains drain into Lake Titicaca in northwest Bolivia. The Altiplano is arid, and the shrubs and groundcover which grow here are seasonal. Agricultural yields are sparse, and such crops as do grow require irrigation from the rivers flowing into Titicaca, or from the lake itself.

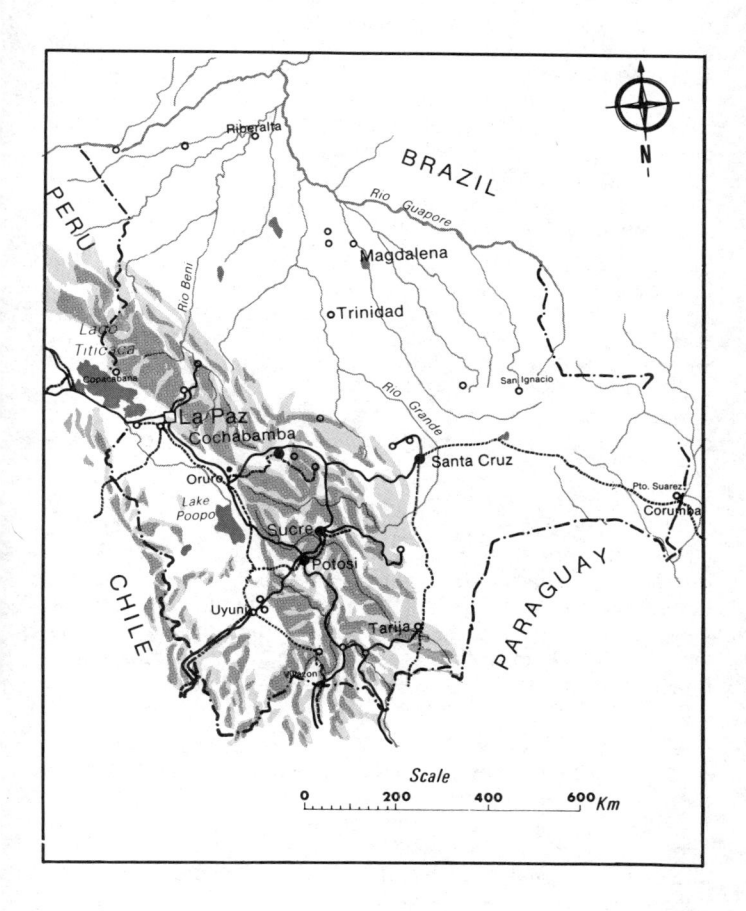

BOLIVIA

BOLIVIA

BOLIVIA

The towns of Oruro and Potosi are the center of the mining industry. These cities, like the rest of the Altiplano, are dependent on other parts of the country, in particular El Oriente (east) for food. El Oriente extends east of the Cordillera Oriental over 60% of the country, yet only 15% of the population live here. Although fertile, its geographical isolation makes it difficult to transport its agricultural produce to the markets of the large cities. A large part of El Oriente is covered in thick tropical jungle and mosquito-infested marshes. El Oriente is divided by a network of streams and rivers which together form part of the southern watershed of the Amazon.

The northern part of El Oriente, the El Beni region, is one of the remotest parts of the country, and most of it is unexplored territory. The El Beni River, flows between the many lakes, lagoons, and marshes – an untamed jungle region with many wild animals. Farms were set up in its endless expanses, but it was only in the late 1970s, when the Trinidad-La Paz road was opened, that significant development occurred, as it then became possible for local produce to be marketed in the capital.

To the south of El Beni, in the area north and east of the city of Cochabamba, is the rich and fertile Yungas region. The climate here is hot and humid, with an average temperature of 25 degrees Centigrade (80 degrees Fahrenheit). Heavy rain falls throughout the year (1300 mm annual average). The natural vegetation of the Yungas is luxuriant, and its forests are inhabited by a large variety of animals. The Cochabamba region is known for its fertility and its agricultural produce feeds the entire country.

The Chaco region – or that part of it which Bolivia managed to hold on to after her defeat by Paraguay in the 1930s – lies in the southern part of the country near the borders of Paraguay and Argentina. The climate here is hot and heavy and the land is arid. During the summer, when the rain falls, the Chaco turns into one huge, green marshland, but reverts to its former desert appearance as soon as the rains cease.

Bolivia is divided into 9 administrative districts, each with its own capital.

Population

Some 75% of Bolivia's total population of five million are Indians, and only 5% are of European extraction. Perhaps this disparity, which is the largest in South America, explains the unique character of the land. Although Spanish is the official language, it constitutes the mother tongue of only half the population. The other half still speak the languages of the pre-Columbian period

BOLIVIA

– Aymara and Quechua. Although 90% of Bolivians identify themselves as Catholics, Indian traditions from pre-Spanish times are still observed alongside Christianity. The ancient rituals are commonly practiced throughout the country, especially in rural areas. The Indian population, which is concentrated in the Altiplano, lives mainly off agriculture and mining. Most of them have distinctive facial features, and their clothes, houses, language and customs all reflect their strict adherence to ancestral traditions. The native costumes of the Indians, especially the women, are exceptionally colorful and unusual.

Only one third of the population are town-dwellers. The rest are scattered among thousands of small, extremely undeveloped villages, most of which have no electricity or plumbing. The educational and medical infrastructures are slowly but surely making headway, and cholera and malaria have been almost totally eradicated. In spite of this, the infant mortality rate is still almost 20%, average life expectancy is less than 50 years, and more than half the population are illiterate.

Since the agrarian reform that accompanied the 1952 revolution, settlement patterns have altered somewhat, and many former tenant-farmers are now landowners. Technological advances have led to a significant increase in output, but their distribution is restricted to the vicinity of the cities and to settlements that can be reached by road or rail. In many villages, especially the more remote ones, you will still find the barter system being used. Economic pressures and low income have led to massive emigration: it is estimated that hundreds of thousands of Bolivians are now living in neighboring countries.

Economy

National economic development along Western lines began in Bolivia only several decades ago. Previously, most of the population followed a regime of self-sufficiency. More than three-quarters of the population lived on subsistence agriculture, without participating in the national market, providing for their own needs through a system of barter. Only in the wake of the reforms of the early 1950s did an economic awakening make itself felt among this sector of the population, so that they too, like the urban sector, began consuming imported goods. The growing interest in industrial products among the exclusively Indian village population has led to the establishment of small factories, mostly textile plants, which supply cheap alternatives to imported clothes. However, in spite of the demand, industrial development has more or less remained static, and is unable to satisfy local consumption. The power plants that were erected have also failed to give industry

BOLIVIA

the needed impetus. Although Bolivia has the potential to enlarge its power supply, there have been no significant developments in this sector.

On the national level, the Bolivian economy is based on the export of natural resources, metals in particular. Bolivia is currently the Americas' most important ore producer and this alone explains the continued assistance of the United States. Bolivia is the world's second largest producer of tin-ore and a significant supplier of other minerals. Ores constitute 80% of total exports. Since the world market is subject to severe fluctuations, the economy suffers from chronic instability. Oil and natural gases have been extracted in the area around Santa Cruz for several decades, but production has declined in recent years. In the agricultural sector, domestic productions satisfy consumption. The settlements in the Yungas and El Beni valleys supply the Altiplano with most of its agricultural needs, but transport problems and the isolation of these areas make it difficult to transport food, so that food prices are high. In view of this situation, the government is attempting to expand the road network in order to reach places that are inaccesible by rail.

During the 1970s, Bolivia enjoyed a short-lived economic respite. Later, the political unrest frightened off foreign investors and discouraged new ones, and only the generous assistance of the International Monetary Fund and the United States prevented a total monetary collapse.

November 1979 marked the onset of a rapid devaluation in the national currency, and the dollar exchange rate rose thousands of percent in the space of a few years. The rise in the cost of living, inflation and unemployment that accompanied the accelerated devaluation, led to social unrest, strikes and riots which in the end brought about a change in government. In 1985, inflation reached 14,000%! In August of the same year there was a 95% devaluation of the Bolivian currency in an attempt to hold down the galloping hyper-inflation. Today, Bolivia is still struggling to stem inflation, reduce unemployment and obtain the foreign currency needed in order to survive. A two-pronged attack is being launched – on the one hand to restrict imports, and on the other hand, to develop, stimulate and broaden the export of natural resources and industrial and agricultural products. In June 1984, the Bolivian government announced a partial default on the country's debts, causing serious concern among the world financial community, to whom Bolivia owes 3.5 billion dollars. Urgent international meetings proposed new terms of repayment, which went some way towards easing the burden of the foreign debts. For its part, Bolivia was requested to adopt a policy of austerity and economic streamlining.

B OLIVIA

General information
How to get there
By air: The national airline LAB flies to most Latin American countries, and all South American companies have at least one flight a week to La Paz. There are daily flights from Brazil, Argentina, Chile and Peru. From Europe, Varig flies via Sao Paulo or Rio, and Aerolineas Argentinas flies via Buenos Aires. Lufthansa has flights from Europe to La Paz with at least one intermediate stop. Most flights to La Paz also stop at Santa Cruz. When leaving Bolivia, you will have to pay the $10 airport tax. Air tickets purchased in Bolivia carry a 13% tax.

By land: There are five rail routes between Bolivia and the shores of the Pacific and Atlantic Oceans and all are used by passenger trains. Buses travel along parallel routes, but given the bad condition of Bolivia's roads you should, if possible, avoid traveling by bus.

From **Chile** you can take a train from Antofagasta or Arica to La Paz – a long but pleasant journey. The first part of the journey is through dusty desert, but as the train climbs upwards to over 4000 m in its ascent through the Andes, the weather becomes extremely cold. Frequent buses also cover the same route.

From **Peru** most traffic goes via Lake Titicaca or the road that runs along its perimeter. There are daily buses between La Paz and Puno in Peru, which continue on to Arequipa, Cuzco and Lima. From Puno you can cross Lake Titicaca by boat to Copacabana on the Bolivian side, and then continue by bus to La Paz.

The train between Santa Cruz and Sao Paulo in **Brazil**, passes through the small town of Corumba. The stretch of track between Corumba and Santa Cruz is extremely old, and problems with the rails – especially in the marshy areas where derailing is not an uncommon occurrence – have earned it the nickname of "death train", though this is rather an exaggeration. Buses link the large towns of both countries, but from the point of view of technology and comfort they leave much to be desired.

The way to **Paraguay** passes through northern Argentina, since there is no public transport over the Chaco road. Thus, to travel directly to Asuncion you must drive or hitchhike, but in any case **not** during the rainy summer season. If you are hitchhiking, lifts are scarce and you will need plenty of food and patience. Take more than enough food with you, since once in the Chaco you will be unable to buy any, and you may have to wait several days by the roadside.

The train from Buenos Aires to La Paz takes three days. Buses

BOLIVIA

also cover the same route. From Villazon on the **Argentinian** border there is convenient transportation to most Bolivian towns. We suggest that you take the train from Villazon to La Paz. There is a train every day, and the journey lasts 24 hours.

Documents
Although regulations change periodically, holders of European and U.S. passports do not usually require a visa, and may stay in Bolivia for 90 days without a special permit. The immigration officials at the border will give you a visa valid for 30 days, which can be renewed at the Immigration Office (on Gonzales Street near Avenida Acre in La Paz), for a further 60 days. At the border check point you will be required to fill out a tourist card, which you should always carry with your passport, and which you will be asked to hand back when you leave the country. No immunization certificates are required to enter Bolivia.

When to come; National Holidays
The tourist season is generally the winter, when the skies are clear and temperatures low. The summer months, especially December and January, are quite rainy. During these months you will be more or less city-bound, since the mainly unpaved roads turn to mud with the first rains, making travel difficult if not impossible. The most important national holiday, Independence Day, is the 6th of August. Folk festivals are celebrated in the various towns and villages, especially in the Altiplano. The *Fiesta del Gran Poder* (Festival of the Great Power) is celebrated in La Paz in early June. This is one of the most beautiful folk festivals of South America. Many people dress up in costumes and the day is spent in dancing and relaxation. Thousands of stands selling food and sweets spring up around the city and people stroll about in obvious enjoyment. The fiesta reaches its climax in a gigantic dance parade along the main streets which are lined with thousands of spectators. The events of Mother's Day in Tiwanaku, at the end of May, are characterized by exceptionally colorful Indian celebrations, accompanied by music, dancing and traditional costume. This is perhaps one of the last authentic carnivals in South America, and one attended by few tourists. Highly recommended!

Where to stay
Accommodation is easy to find, but really good places to stay are far more difficult to come by. Hotels worthy of the name are found only in the four large towns, and even there not without difficulty. In all other small towns and villages the most you can expect to find is a modest – and with any luck, clean – hotel, hardly ever with a private bath. Hotels, with the exception of the *Sheraton* and *Plaza* in La Paz, are fairly inexpensive, and of a reasonable standard. The smaller hotels, used mainly by

BOLIVIA

backpackers (the *mochileros*), will provide you with a small, dilapidated room, a bed, a closet and occasionally – a sink. They are incredibly cheap, but the bedding and mattress are liable to be bug-infested. Extra caution should also be exercised in public showers and conveniences, which are far from clean. In most of the small hotels, shower water is heated via an electric element attached to the water pipe, which you must turn on yourself. Beware! The appliance is dangerous and caution should be exercised to avoid electrocution. In most of these places, the level of maintenance leaves much to be desired and the appliances are neglected, so that even a small amount of water can cause a short-circuit and disaster. Camping is not common except when hiking in the countryside. If you do camp out, be sure to take a good tent and an extremely warm sleeping bag! Spending a night in the Altiplano without suitable equipment will remain etched in your memory as a veritable torture.

Wining and Dining

In this sphere Bolivia is well provided for; indeed, sometimes every second building seems to house a small restaurant. The large cities have many quality restaurants that serve a wide variety of continental and popular food. Prices are cheap compared to other countries, and should definitely be taken advantage of. In the small towns and villages, and by the roadside, you will come across numerous eating places, whose culinary arts are mainly restricted to soup, rice and beef, and the level of hygiene is deplorable. Soup is usually the most tasty and safest dish to eat here. Due to the low sanitation standards in Bolivia, you should avoid tapwater as much as possible, and stick to mineral water (or fresh stream water when hiking through the countryside). In particular avoid eating fresh fruit and vegetables without first peeling them. Worms and other pests are a common occurrence, and even vegetables that seem to be clean are likely to be infested with germs. Stomach-aches and intestinal upsets are practically unavoidable in Bolivia; remember this and be suitably prepared. You should definitely take medicines with you, since these are expensive and hard to obtain in Bolivia. When leaving towns, you should stock up on canned goods, beans and durable foods, and do your own cooking.

Most restaurants throughout the country serve two meals – lunch and supper. Usually there is a fixed-price menu for each meal. If you order a la carte, you will pay more. Lunch (*almuerzo*) is served from 11:30am-2pm, and supper (*cena*) between 6-9pm. In the Altiplano, and especially around Lake Titicaca, trout fried in oil is a popular dish. This is a local delicacy and is highly recommended. Bolivian food, especially in the Altiplano, is spicy

BOLIVIA

and tasty. Most dishes are seasoned with *aji* (red pepper), which is the most popular spice and served along with each meal. Once you get used to its sharpness, you will become addicted to it. Meat is served in much smaller portions than in Argentina or the other lowland countries, and is of much lower quality. Steaks are usually thin, dry and tough. On the other hand, the soups are extremely rich, well-cooked and both filling and nutritious. Typical South American foods and beverages such as *empanadas* (pastry filled with meat or cheese) and *mate* (South American tea – pronounced ma-teh) are standard here too, and usually accompany local dishes. A uniquely Bolivian beverage is *api*, fermented from corn, which is commonly sold on city streets and markets.

Hygiene and health
Malaria has been almost completely eradicated. Nevertheless, we would advise you to take prescription anti-malaria pills if you are planning to visit areas like the El Beni region or the Yungas. Usually these pills should be taken for a week before you enter a malaria zone, and continued for six weeks after you leave the area. When staying in these places, be very careful regarding what you eat and drink. Water must be sterilized by both boiling and chemical means (chlorine tablets). Make sure that the water source is not contaminated. El Oriente is infested with mosquitos and bugs, so take along mosquito-repellents and soothing ointments. Even if you apply these liberally, you will no doubt be bitten as never before in your life. But if you do not use them and do not wear protective clothing (long sleeves, socks, scarf, etc.) you will be exposed to bites that will cause prolonged suffering and illness. At night, you should sleep under a mosquito net.

From a hygienic point of view, Bolivia is certainly far from satisfactory. Sewage networks exist only in large towns and villages; all other places, including city suburbs still use open sewer pipes and water is brought to the houses from central wells.

Living on high
Given the elevation of the Bolivian Altiplano, suitable precautionary and preventive measures must be taken. (see "Introduction – Altitude – how to cope with thin air".)

Currency
The national currency has in recent years been subject to constant devaluation, and its dollar exchange rate continues to soar. In December 1986 six zeroes were taken off the *peso*, and the new currency is the *Boliviano*. The restrictions on purchasing foreign currency have caused the black market to flourish, and the differences between the black market rate and

BOLIVIA

the official rate may run into hundreds of percent. As a rule, cash dollar notes are the most in demand in the black market. Moneychangers (*casas de cambio*) can sometimes be prevailed upon to cash travelers' checks into cash dollars for a commission. Credit cards are virtually unacceptable and you should not rely on them when planning your traveling budget. Bank transfers are possible only in local currency and at the official rate! Given the economic instability, such transactions are to be avoided.

Business Hours
Banks and commercial offices are open to the public both morning and afternoon. Nearly all places are shut between noon and 4pm. Shops are open until 7pm, with an afternoon siesta. Most places are open half-day on Saturdays. On Sundays the entire city is at a standstill and even traffic almost ceases.

Domestic Transportation
Buses and Trucks: Buses run between all the large towns and to most villages that are accessible by road. The roads are of poor quality, narrow, uncomfortable and incredibly crowded. Generally speaking, you should be at the bus station an hour before the bus leaves, since, although the driver will in all likelihood set out much later than scheduled, all the seats will be taken long before the official departure time. On interurban routes, tickets are sold a day or two in advance, so make sure to buy one in time. Bolivia's cheapest and most popular form of transport is the truck, into which dozens of passengers are squeezed, not to mention freight and animals. Although this is doubtless an interesting way to travel, it is by no means always pleasant. Travel by bus or truck is extremely cheap, but drawn-out, uncomfortable, and unreliable. Nevertheless, it is also the most authentic way of traveling, and if you don't mind "roughing it" you should certainly give it a try.

Train: Bolivia's rail system has improved considerably over the past few years and modern carriages now run on the antiquated tracks. Trains run only between the large cities, and are cheap, fast and comfortable. Night journeys on the Altiplano are very cold and you should be suitably prepared. There is also "ferrobus" service. This consists of two first-class carriages only, and is fast and comfortable. It is available only on inter-city lines.

Private and rented car: Travel by private car is not recommended. Most of Bolivia's roads are unpaved and in bad condition. Service stations and garages are scarce and one must stock up with fuel cans before leaving the large cities. For certain trips, a rented four-wheel drive car is recommended, but remember to take large quantities of fuel, at least two spare tires

BOLIVIA

and repair tools! The rental companies usually require your passport as a deposit, or $500 in cash, for which you will get a receipt. There are many road-blocks along the way, but most are not interested in tourists. Travel permits can be obtained without difficulty at any police station.

Plane: LAB has daily flights throughout Bolivia. The flights are ridiculously cheap – and heavily booked. You should reserve a place as early as possible, but bear in mind there may be delays, or even cancellations, due to weather problems, floods, etc. – especially in El Oriente, the Beni and the Yungas. Flying is the quickest and most comfortable method of interurban travel.

Measurements; electricity and time

The metric system is used. The standard voltage throughout Bolivia is 220V, except for La Paz, where the power grid still supplies 110V. Bolivian time is GMT-4.

Shopping

Bolivian products most in demand are local handicrafts and artifacts. These include attractive sweaters made of llama wool (coarser and cheaper) or of alpaca wool (finer and softer but more expensive), wall hangings, small sculptures and *mantas* (a special kind of intricately woven fabric). The Bolivian *mantas* are the most beautiful in South America, and the older they are, the more expensive they are too. The "antique" *mantas* are particularly beautiful, and if they are also in good condition and the embroidered patterns complete, they will in all likelihood be extremely expensive. Although the sweaters and woolen goods are beautiful, they are of medium quality. They must be washed in cold water and hung out to dry, without wringing, in a shady place.

Bolivia has many unusual markets. The giant market of La Paz is the largest, containing everything you could possibly wish for. Woven goods are cheaper elsewhere, such as the villages where they are made or in the market held on Wednesdays and Saturdays in Cochabamba. A market is also held on Sundays in Tarabuco, near Sucre, which is in my opinion, the most beautiful in South America. Prices are high, but can be bargained down to 20% of the initial quote. As a general rule **bargaining** is essential in the markets, and you should make a point of doing so everywhere.

A Suggested Itinerary for Touring Bolivia

La Paz is the starting point for most tourists. There are many places you can visit from La Paz, whether in the immediate surroundings, in El Oriente (jungle tracks and mountain villages), or in other towns. You can make the rounds of the cities and

BOLIVIA

their surroundings beginning and ending in La Paz, or on your way to or from neighboring countries. Suggested excursions accompany the section on each city.

La Paz

Although La Paz is not the official capital of Bolivia, it is the de facto one. The presidential palace, government offices and other national institutions are located here. Bolivia's largest city (nearly one million inhabitants) is the political, economic and commercial center of the country, and is the main tourist attraction.

This enchanting city nestles in a valley carved out of the mountain by a gigantic prehistoric glacier. The city center lies at the bottom of the valley, about 400 m below the Altiplano, and on either side clusters of small adobe houses ascend the steep slopes. The downtown area is modern: its main road, the Prado, has multi-story buildings and traffic is heavy. The first thing you notice is the walking pace of its inhabitants – a pace which is slower and more relaxed than in any other city. This phenomenon has its roots in the city's altitude. The paucity of oxygen in the atmosphere rules out strenuous exertion and a slower pace has become second nature. More than half of the city's population are Indians who have come from the surrounding villages, and they still wear their traditional garb and black hats (including the women). Many women carry their children in an embroidered cloth sack which they wear on their backs, and breastfeed their infants in public thoroughfares. Others sit on the sidewalks of the main streets selling sweets and cigarettes displayed on *mantas*.

Seen from above, as you look out of the train on its approach to the city or from the taxi bringing you from El Alto airport (the highest civilian airport in the world), your first impression of La Paz will be of a walled city. Although from afar the red-brown of adobe appears to be the dominant color, when you reach the city you will marvel at the wonderful variety of colors, the like of which few cities can boast. The small streets even those near the main avenues of the city, are exceedingly beautiful and picturesque, radiating simplicity and uniqueness. The inhabitants are friendly, and you can stroll safely through the streets at all hours of the day and night. Behind the city, which was founded on October 20, 1548, looms Mt. Illimani. Its snow covered peaks rise proudly to a height of 6700 m.

How to get there
El Alto, La Paz's somewhat old-fashioned airport, serves all internal and international flights. Although it has no banks, you will immediately be approached by moneychangers who will be

BOLIVIA

Mt. Illimani watching over the city of La Paz

happy to change your dollars for you. Change only a small amount, 10 or 20 dollars at the most, since you will receive a much higher rate in town. The 20-minute taxi trip to town, traveling on a wide freeway, will afford you an enchanting view of the town below. Trains, buses, and trucks travel right down to the city center. The central train and bus stations are within walking distance of the main street, but because of the altitude it would be wiser to take a cab and avoid carrying your luggage. Trucks and buses usually go as far as the central Plaza San Francisco, or to the area near the cemetery.

Accommodation
There are many hotels and pensions scattered throughout the city. Among the luxury hotels, the *Plaza* is especially recommended, due to its excellent situation. This five-star hotel has 200 rooms, excellent restaurants, a health club and other facilities. The hotel is located on Ave. 16 de Julio 1789 (Tel. 364-667). A little further, on Ave. Arce, you will find the *Sheraton* (Tel. 356-950), another luxury hotel, but not as central or pleasant as the Plaza. Other more central and cheaper hotels are: *The Sucre Palace* at Ave. 16 de Julio 1636 (Tel. 355-081); the *Gloria*, on Calle Potosi corner of Sanjines (Tel. 370-010/4); and the *El Dorado*, on Ave. Villazon (Tel. 363-403). These three hotels are far cheaper than either the Plaza or Sheraton, and almost as good. Another, even cheaper and extremely central hotel is the recommended *Copacabana*, directly opposite the Plaza, at Ave. 16 Julio 1802 (Tel. 351-240). All the above hotels

B OLIVIA

have private baths, telephones, room service and restaurants and are especially suited for families, businessmen and tourists.

As for cheaper hotels, I readily recommend the *Residencial Independencia* on Calle Comercio corner of Bueno. The hotel is extremely clean, neat and quiet. The owner of the hotel speaks English and is always ready to help. Another cheap hotel is the *Torino* at Calle Socabaya 457 (Tel. 341-487 and 329-688). This is a very large but simple hotel and costs only a dollar a night. Being so cheap it is very popular with the *mochileros* (backpackers) but one of its drawbacks is that it locks up at midnight and latecomers are not allowed in. The *Austria* at Yanacocha 531 (Tel. 328-915) is another cheap hotel. Another inexpensive hotel is the *Neuman* on Calle Loayza near the corner of Calle Comercio. It is well situated, the hotel is new with pleasant rooms, and the owners are friendly. Recommended.

What to eat, where and when

La Paz is one of the cheapest cities in the world and one should take advantage of this. There are several superb restaurants in the city, where you can get a meal at 10% of the price of a similar meal in the Western world. Therefore a wise tourist – and even thrifty one – would do well to indulge. It should be stressed that in spite of the low prices, dress and etiquette requirements are the same as in New York, Paris, or Rome.

The *Plaza's* roof restaurant serves a limited selection of main courses, mainly beef, chicken and fish, all of superb quality. The restaurant also has an open salad bar. Prices are moderate and the service excellent. The fantastic panorama from the windows is enough to justify a meal here, and when you add the excellent food and attractive prices, it is a special experience. The *Sheraton* also has an excellent roof restaurant. Its atmosphere is far more formal, with dimmed lights and background music (sometimes a trifle loud). This is the ideal place for an intimate meal, with the romantic background of the city's twinkling lights. The restaurant's chef specializes in famous dishes of international cuisine, including several exceptional delicacies to satisfy the palate of the most fastidious gourmet. Recommended! The Plaza and Sheraton restaurants also serve lunch, but evening is the best time to enjoy these restaurants.

There is a Swiss restaurant, *La Suissa*, opposite the Sheraton. Even though its entrance sports a plain Coca Cola sign, you will soon discover that this is one of the town's best restaurants. Although it offers a variety of meat dishes, I would suggest you stick to their speciality – fondue. The restaurant's manager owns one of the best butcher shops in town, so this is definitely the place to order a meat fondue or "Mongolian hot pot" (a more

BOLIVIA

delicate dish). Reservations are essential. The restaurant is closed on Sundays.

For lighter meals, go to *Elis* at Ave. 16 Julio 1497. This is a busy, noisy place, but the food is good and cheap. Not far from Elis, at the corner of Santa-Cruz and Colon, is the *Confiteria Verona*, where you can have breakfast, sandwiches and the like, or simply relax with a cup of coffee and cake. In the *Pena Naira* folklore club at Calle Sagarnaga 161 (the street leading to the market from the Plaza San Francisco) you will find a very good restaurant that serves an excellent and reasonably priced four-course lunch (*almuerzo*). Both lunch and dinner here are highly recommended.

In the markets you can get fairly satisfying meals at ridiculously low prices, but for health's sake you should be extremely selective or, even better, refrain from eating there altogether. Inexpensive restaurants can be found in every alley and street corner, but make doubly sure they are clean before eating in them.

Transportation

Urban: There is frequent minibus and regular bus service in the city. However, the buses are usually packed and the routes seem interminable. The most comfortable way of traveling in the city is by taxi. Taxis, which are abundant, are cheaper than buses in other countries. They are unmarked and unmetered. Within the downtown area the fare is fixed, regardless of the distance traveled. The price, though, is per passenger and the driver is entitled to pick up other passengers on the way. The first passenger determines the destination, and the driver will take only passengers who are going in the same direction. The fare jumps by 50% at night. For short day excursions from the city, it is a good idea to organize a group to share a taxi. Conventional public transport (buses and trucks) is slow and unreliable, and will waste much precious time.

Interurban: Most buses depart from the central bus station or nearby. Tickets should be bought several days in advance. The journey to Cochabamba takes 12 hours, to Potosi 14 hours and to Sucre 24 hours. Trains, which cover these routes several times a week, are far more comfortable. But by far the best way of traveling is the ferrobus, or express train service. If you are traveling to Villazon or Argentina, the train is your best bet. LAB flies between La Paz and all the other cities in the country, and even to some far-flung villages in the Beni and Yungas regions. Bear in mind that there are frequent delays, and that some flights to the less popular places may be cancelled for lack of passengers or due to bad weather conditions. Reserve your seat well in advance, for your return flight too, since the planes are

BOLIVIA

small and heavily-booked. The LAB offices are at the corner of Camacho and Loayza (Tel. 351-163 and 351-155).

To Peru: To reach Puno, the Peruvian town on the shore of Lake Titicaca, there are two options. The first is with a direct bus, which leaves La Paz several times a week and covers the distance in 10 hours. The second, which is cheaper, is to take one of the many local buses to Copacabana (4 hours) and then to cross the lake by ferry to Puno (see Copacabana).

Car rental: There are several rental agencies in La Paz, which can supply passenger cars, jeeps and vans. Prices vary, but in all cases make sure that insurance, two spare tires, a repair kit, water and fuel containers are included. The Hertz office is in the Sheraton Hotel (Tel. 355-592). Kolla Motors at Calle Rosendo Gutierrez 502 (Tel. 341-660/351-701) is recommended. They have a large fleet of reliable and well-maintained cars, are courteous and their rates are reasonable.

Tourist services

Most tourist services are concentrated around the Prado, Ave. Mariscal Santa Cruz. The blue booth of the Tourist Ministry is situated half-way down the street where it becomes Ave. 16 de Julio. Maps, guides, tourist material, brochures and any other information you may require are all available. The National Parks Authority is also represented here and will answer questions within its jurisdiction. *Instituto Geografico Militar* (The Military Geographical Institute) on Ave. Saavedra sells topographical maps of various areas which are especially useful for hiking.

Most travel agencies and airline companies are located on the Prado or on Calle Camacho (parallel to the Prado). The Exprinter travel agency, the largest in the city, has a large office on the Prado at the corner of Loayza. This company has branches throughout Latin America and also provides a package delivery and shipping service.

Tourist sites

La Paz's main street changes its name several times, but is known as the **Prado** along its entire length. We will begin our tour at the western end of the Prado, Mariscal Santa Cruz, with one of the city's most important squares, **Plaza San Francisco.** The **church** in this square is one of the largest buildings remaining from the colonial period, and is still, in spite of neglect, exceptionally beautiful. On Saturday mornings, Indian weddings are conducted here and the blending of ancient traditions with Christian rites is especially interesting. Plaza San Francisco is at one edge of the large **Indian market**, which continues uphill and south on Calle Sagarnaga (see "Markets"). We will now turn east along the Prado, walking along the flagstone street whose narrow sidewalks overflow with

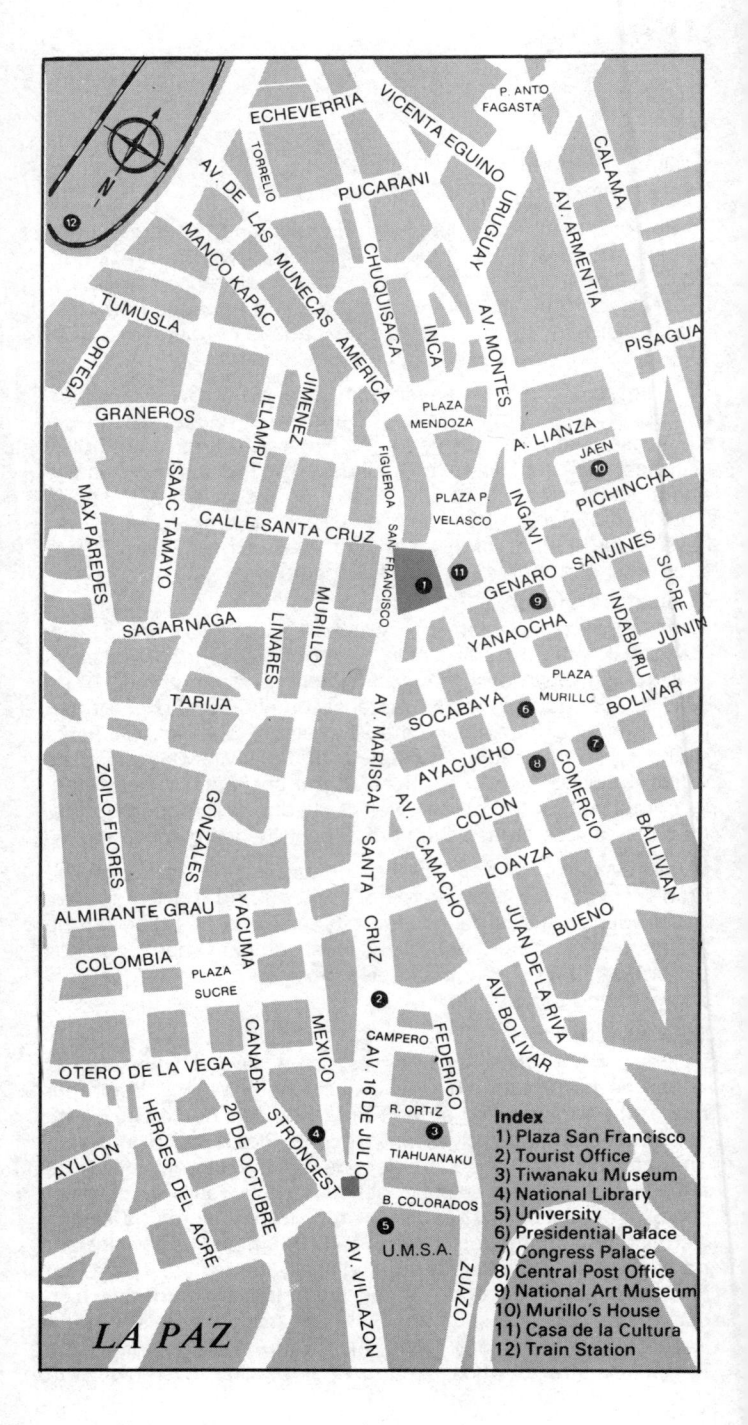

Index
1) Plaza San Francisco
2) Tourist Office
3) Tiwanaku Museum
4) National Library
5) University
6) Presidential Palace
7) Congress Palace
8) Central Post Office
9) National Art Museum
10) Murillo's House
11) Casa de la Cultura
12) Train Station

LA PAZ

BOLIVIA

pedestrians. To our left we will immediately catch sight of the lofty **Obelisk**, towering over the **Monument to the Unknown Soldier**. The Obelisk marks the beginning of **Calle Camacho**, which is a busy commercial street, more or less parallel to the Prado. Three blocks further down the Prado, in the middle of the road, is the Bolivian **Tourist Office** (*Instituto Boliviano de Turismo*) and alongside it the statue of **Simon Bolivar**. At this point the Prado widens, and becomes Ave. 16 Julio. A pleasant **promenade** separates the traffic lanes. Adorned with decorative trees and statues, the promenade is usually crowded during the afternoons, evenings and on weekends. The fourth street to the left is Calle Tiwanaku, with the **Tiwanaku Archeological Museum** which houses most of the finds from this important archeological site (see "Short trips around La Paz"). The museum, founded in 1922, is at the corner of Calle Suazo (Tel. 392-624), and is perhaps the most important of its kind in Bolivia.

A short way down the Prado is a large square dominated by a monument to the famous General Sucre. To the right of the square, at the corner of Calle Strongest, is the **National Library** building, and, to its left, the **University.** Its proximity to the university has earned the square the name of **Plaza de Estudiante** (Students Square), and it has been the starting point for many demonstrations and riots. Plaza de Estudiante marks the limits of the downtown area and beyond it extend attractive residential areas. We, however, return to the city center, turning north this time, to Calle Comercio, Plaza Murillo, and their surroundings.

Climb from the Prado along **Calle Colon.** Its intersection with Calle Camacho is the main haunt of the **black market** moneychangers. The steep road leads us to the corner of Calle Comercio, where the **Banco Minero** houses an interesting collection of minerals and ores. It is open Mon.-Fri. from 10am-noon and from 2-4pm.

A left turn onto Comercio will bring us to **Plaza Murillo**, named after one of the leaders of the 1809 uprising against Spain. The uprising failed and Murillo himself was executed. This pleasant square – one of the city's landmarks – is the seat of several of Bolivia's most important public institutions. The **Presidential Palace**, built 140 years ago, lies on the south side. Uniformed sentries guard its gates, and visiting is not allowed. Alongside the palace is the **Municipal Cathedral**, immense and neglected. A small plaque opposite the palace bears testimony to the fact that President Villaroel was hanged here in 1946. On the east side of the square stands the large **Congress Palace**, which, due to political instability, is used only on occasion. On the other side of the square, Calle Comercio becomes a

BOLIVIA

pedestrian mall lined with shops and small restaurants. At the beginning of this mall, at the corner of Calle Socabaya, is the stately home of the *Condes de Arana*, which currently houses Bolivia's **Museo Nacional de Arte** (National Art Museum). The museum has a collection dating from colonial times, as well as the works of contemporary Bolivian artists. It is open Tues.-Sat. from 9am-noon and from 2-5:45pm, and on Sun. from 10:30am-noon. It is closed all day Mon. (Tel. 367-283/4).

The Comercio pedestrian mall leads into Calle Sanjianes. Turn right at the top of the street to reach the **Museo Nacional de Etnografia y Folklore** (National Ethnographical and Folklore Museum). This interesting museum – which is housed in the Marquis de Villa Verde's residence – has a display of handicrafts, spun and woven fabrics, as well as exhibits of typical musical instruments. It is open Mon.-Sat. from 9:30am-12 noon and from 2:30-6:30pm (Tel. 358-559).

Not far off is **Calle Jaen**, a small alley closed to vehicles and sandwiched between Ave. Sucre and Calle Indaburu. Redone in colonial style, this picturesque street has a number of boutiques, three museums and a folklore club (see "Entertainment and folklore"). The most important museum on Calle Jaen is the **Casa de Murillo**, which has early 19th century exhibits, works of art, handicrafts, furniture, and more. (Tel. 375-273).

Moving away from the center, we come to **Plaza Arqueologia** (Archeology Square) in front of the **Municipal Stadium**. This square has an exact replica of the temple that was discovered at Tiwanaku, and some of the largest and most impressive statues that were uncovered there. Some distance from the center is the **Mirador Monticulo** (Monticulo Observatory), which is located in a small, pleasant park in the heart of Sopacachi suburb. En route, you will pass through one of the city's most beautiful neighborhoods, contrasting harshly with other parts of La Paz. From the observation point you have a wonderful view of the city on your left, and a breathtaking view of Mount Illimani on your right.

In addition to the above, we have yet to visit the **Indian Market**, which is an attraction in its own right. Even if you have no intention of buying anything you should definitely not miss this. No doubt your resolution will weaken once you set foot in the market. (see "Markets".)

Entertainment and folklore

If you are looking for nightlife, La Paz has little to offer. There are, it is true, a few discotheques, but these are exceptional landmarks in the town's cultural landscape. The best of these is at the Sheraton Hotel. There are a few movie theaters showing

BOLIVIA

mainly films with the original soundtrack and Spanish subtitles. The theaters along the Prado are modern and comfortable, but those farther out are old-fashioned and uncomfortable with poor quality projection equipment.

La Paz's main form of entertainment centers around local folklore and music – and not without reason. Although folklore clubs are a common feature in all large towns, those in La Paz are by far the best. Most of these clubs (known as *penas*) have shows Wed.-Sun., beginning at 10pm. The program lasts about 3 hours, during which seven or eight groups perform Bolivian folk music. All the instrumentalists, singers and dancers wear traditional Indian costumes, down to woolen hats with earmuffs. The instruments are authentic and always include drums, various types of flutes and the *charango* – a South American mandolin whose sounding box is made of an armadillo shell.

The best pena is *Pena Naira*, which has already been mentioned regarding its restaurant (see "What to eat, where and when"). This pena is not far from Plaza San Francisco, in the direction of the market, at Calle Sagarnaga 161 (Tel. 325-736). One of its owners, Ernesto Cavor, a virtuoso charangoist, sometimes performs for his patrons. The program is rich and varied, including songs, instrumental music and folk dancing. The audience is diverse, with local patrons as well as tourists. The cover charge is reasonable and includes the first drink. Although the show invariably begins late, you should be there early to be sure of getting a good seat.

Another excellent pena is *Marca Tambo* at Calle Jaen 710 (Tel. 340-146). Here you can combine a meal with the show – ordering drinks or dinner before or during the performances. Although the place is attractive, the serving of meals during the performances does little to enhance the atmosphere.

The *City* restaurant on the Prado also has performances, but is unappealing, the program bill unreliable and prices inflated. Definitely not recommended.

Concerts of Indian folk music are also held in the **Casa de la Cultura** just off Plaza San Francisco. The performers are usually amateur or youth groups but of extremely high quality and well worth hearing. Tickets are subsidized and therefore very inexpensive.

Banks and currency exchange

Banks exchange dollars at the official rate – and with tiresome bureaucratic red tape. Official exchanges (*casas de cambio*) will occasionally cash travelers' checks into dollars for a commission. When changing money into pesos at these places, you may be offered the official rate or the black market rate,

BOLIVIA

depending on the state of the economy and current government policy. A reliable *cambio* is Sudamer's on Calle Colon near Ave. Camacho. The black market moneychangers are mostly to be found on Colon and Camacho. They are easily identified: dozens of men and women carrying attache cases will approach you with an offer to purchase dollars. Do not use their services even if the rates they offer are tempting, because the danger always exists that you have been approached by an undercover policeman. The black market is illegal in Bolivia, and if you are caught changing money in this manner, you will have to bribe the police in order to avoid being arrested. Therefore, try to change your money in shops and businesses where you are bound to find someone who wants your cash dollars, and you can change money without running any risks. Before leaving La Paz for other areas, change as much money as you will be needing, since outside the three or four largest cities it is extremely difficult to change dollars.

Postal and telephone services

The Central Post Office is on Calle Ayacucho at the corner of Potosi, one block past Plaza Murillo. The usual stamps, postcards, envelopes and the like can be purchased here. At this branch, you can send letters by ordinary or registered mail and parcels weighing up to 1 kg. Everything should be sent by registered mail! Parcels weighing over 1 kg have to pass customs control, and must be taken to the Customs Office, on Calle Potosi. Be prepared to wait. The parcel should be open when you bring it, with a detailed list of its contents. Only once it has been searched and officially approved may it be sealed. Parcels weighing more than 15 kg are not accepted. The parcel must be wrapped in a bag, sewn shut and tied round with string. Delivery by sea mail can take months (sometimes over 6 months!) – so if you are sending clothes by sea, put in a few moth balls for good measure. The airlines also accept parcels and delivery takes only a few days. However, they are naturally far more expensive than the regular mail service.

International calls may be made from hotels, or at the Telephone Exchange in the Entel building on Calle Ayacucho. To some destinations there is no difference in price between a station-to-station and person-to-person call. Passports must be handed in when making international calls. There are 20 international call boxes along the hall and the wait is not usually very long. However, since this is also a domestic long-distance exchange, it is usually packed, especially at mid-day or in the afternoon, usually less so in the evening. It is open from 7am-9pm. On Sundays international calls are 25% cheaper. Entel also has a branch at the Sheraton Hotel which is open till

BOLIVIA

evening. Note that regular calls from hotels sometimes involve waiting several hours.

Books and periodicals in English
The large bookstore *Los Amigos del Libro* (Friends of the Book) has two branches in La Paz and one in Cochabamba. The store, whose owners are also publishers, offers a wide selection of books in English on subjects relating to Bolivia and Peru, as well as guides, maps and the like. The larger of the two branches in La Paz is on Calle Mercado near Ayacucho, and the other is on the Prado.

Photographical supplies
Film can be developed quickly and cheaply in La Paz, and the quality is good. The Kodak agency on Calle Potosi develops black-and-white and color film, as well as slides. Photo Lineares on Calle Loayza develops film of high quality, quickly and cheaply. Film can also be bought in the Thieves Market (see "Markets").

Weather
Due to high altitude, temperatures are low throughout the year, even though the sun may be shining in a clear and cloudless sky. The average daytime temperature throughout the year is 10 degrees Centigrade (50 degrees Fahrenheit), but at sunset, or even in the shade, you will immediately perceive a drastic drop in temperature. Take warm clothes: you will almost cetainly need them frequently. The summer months, especially November-January, are very rainy, but sudden changes in the weather are likely to occur. Always bear this in mind as far as clothes are concerned, since even a clear spring day is likely to end in a heavy downpour. The atmosphere is very dry, and you should use skin lotions and lip salve. The dryness may cause discomfort to contact-lens wearers.

Markets
La Paz has a superabundance of markets – so much so that it is virtually one immense market. No fashion shops or modern supermarkets here – La Paz is first and foremost an Indian market. A colorful, teeming market, offering everything from a cup of corn beer and charmed amulets to ward off the evil eye, to sweaters, ponchos, wood and metal ornaments, and jewelry.

The entire area southwest of Plaza San Francisco is in fact one giant market, which would take many days just to walk through. This is Bolivia's largest market – one of the largest in the world – and it lacks nothing. We will start our tour of the market at Plaza San Francisco and work our way up Calle Sagarnaga. You will immediately notice the dozens of small shops on either side,

BOLIVIA

packed with touristy trinkets. The goods in these stores are of extremely high quality, but their prices are commensurately high. Make a point of thoroughly checking the quality and type of product – and **bargaining**. Remember the iron rule here – always bargain!

You will not have to struggle uphill much longer. Only two blocks further, at the corner of Calle Linares, the market splits up into dozens of small alleys. However, before we come to this crossroad, turn right into a courtyard surrounded by shops. These offer a wide selection of knicknacks, jewelry, sweaters, and the like. Prices are relatively high, so, if you have the time, hunt around elsewhere. At the intersection, you can either carry straight on or turn right into Calle Linares, where the so-called **Mercado de Hechiceria** (Witches' Market) begins. Take a good look at the strange objects on display: bottles with unidentified contents, statuettes, dry bones and even desiccated llama fetuses. Further along Calle Linares are some quality stores whose prices are marginally cheaper than those already mentioned. A bit further on is Calle Santa Cruz (not to be confused with Ave. Santa Cruz) which is one of the most beautiful streets in the market. *Punchay* is located at Santa Cruz 156. It sells local arts and crafts and has an expensive music section which offers a wide selection of records and tapes. You can listen to them in the shop and ask the owner to record music for you.

A stone's throw from Linares down Santa Cruz and we are back in Plaza San Francisco. On our way to the square, on our left, is an enormous partially covered food market selling fresh bread, fruit, vegetables, sugar, canned goods, and more. Turning left from Linares, up Calle Santa Cruz, a few meters further on, our path crosses a small alley. To the left, in a small cul-de-sac more magic wares are sold, while to the right a small lane leads into the very heart of the market. The center of the market is crammed full of stalls overflowing with goods – down the hill on the right and up on the left. However alluring the descent may seem, and however unappealing the ascent, you will just have to grit your teeth and make your way through the stalls. At the top of the climb, you will notice that different types of goods are on display here – transistors, electrical goods and film. This section is known as the **Mercado Negro** (Thieves' Market) and prices here are relatively cheap. Compare prices before buying anything, and make absolutely sure that the goods you are buying are sound. When buying film, check the expiration date and make sure the manufacturer's seal has not been broken.

This is a good point from which to meander through the market. On all sides you will be immersed in a crowd of shoppers, vendors, porters, or simply idlers, and it will be some time before

BOLIVIA

you find your way out of the labyrinth of stalls, no doubt loaded with parcels...

Our tour has taken us through only a small section of this enormous market and there are many other places where you can shop. We have focused on this section because it represents far more than a mere shopping district or market. The customs and way of life of the local population are reflected in this unique quarter, and you will find no place like it in the whole world.

An important market is held on Sunday mornings in the Alto Lima neighborhood near the airport. From the early hours of the morning hundreds of Indians flock to this market with their wares: vegetables, fruit, sweaters and various artifacts. This large market spills out along the entire main street, and is so crowded that it is almost impossible to move. A unique experience, which should not be missed.

In conclusion, the inexhaustible richness and variety of the markets, and their attractive prices, make shopping here a truly delightful and worthwhile experience. La Paz is the ideal place for buying gifts and souvenirs.

Important addresses

U.S. Embassy: Banco Popular del Peru Building, cnr. Calles Mercado and Colon. P.O.B. 425 (Tel. 350-251, 350-120).

British Embassy: Avenida Arce 2732-2754. P.O.B. 694 (Tel. 329-401/4, 351-400).

Ministry of Tourism: Herrmann Building, 4th floor, (Tel. 367-464), opposite the main tourist office.

Emergencies: Tel. 118.

Short trips around La Paz

The area around La Paz has a wealth of interesting sites that can be visited on day trips. Some can be reached only on foot, but they can be incorporated into visits to more distant places. The following is a description of some of the more important and famous places.

Tiwanaku

A small portion of the ancient city of **Tiwanaku** was discovered here and is unquestionably Bolivia's most important archeological site. It is a 2 1/2 hour journey from La Paz (72 km).

Most researchers refer to Tiwanaku as South Americas's most ancient advanced civilization, but there is still considerable controversy regarding its age. No one can say for certain when

BOLIVIA

the Tiwanaku culture began to evolve, or when it reached its zenith. Different conclusions have been reached by researchers who base their analysis on architectural style, objects, artifacts, and potsherds, and those who prefer carbon-14 dating (which determines the age of an archeological find through the isotope breakdown rate). Nevertheless, the general assumption is that the roots go back to the Aymara civilization around 1600 BC, and reached a peak around 700 AD. The purpose of the city remains obscure, although the consensus is that Tiwanaku was originally intended as a port on Lake Titicaca. It began as a rural settlement and developed into a city and later into an empire. The reasons for the disappearance of so developed a civilization, which erected some of the largest stone structures in the Americas, are not very clear. Some theories point to a natural catastrophe, such as a flood or a plague. The generally accepted theory, however, is that social and economic decline in the kingdom led to famine and civil strife, after which the remaining inhabitants abandoned the site. Only a small portion of the town, less than 1% of its estimated area, has been uncovered. Nevertheless, this is unquestionaby one of the world's most important archeological sites. Visitors cannot fail to be impressed by the sophistication and technical expertise of this ancient civilization.

Every year at the end of May, the villagers celebrate Mother's Day (see "When to come; National Holidays"). It is a beautiful carnival and should not be missed.

Transport: Many daily buses make the round trip to Tiwanaku. Buses of the Ingavi Company, at Ave. Manco Kapac 445, leave every two hours. Buses from Tiwanaku to La Paz leave from the central square in Tiwanaku, near the church. Groups may prefer to share the cost and hire a taxi to Tiwanaku, which will wait for you and then bring you back to La Paz.

Literature: The bookstore, Los Amigos del Libro, has a selection of books on Tiwanaku. *Discovering Tiwanaku* by Hugo Rojo has detailed information interspersed with photographs of the site and various other places in the area.

Visiting the site: As we enter this arid zone, the first thing we see is the hill looming up in front of us. Buried beneath this hill is the **Akapana Pyramid**, which was one of the largest structures in the city, and is further proof of the outstanding achievements of this ancient civilization.

To the right of the pyramid is the central part of the archeological finds – the **Kalasasaya Temple**. Before entering this huge temple, take a look at the square "pool" slightly to its east. This is in fact the **Subterranean Temple**, some two meters deep. Many gargoyles peer out from its walls, but time has obscured

BOLIVIA

Mother's Day at Tiwanaku

their features. This subterranean temple was ingeniously designed to allow the rainwater to drain off. The monoliths that were found in the center of the temple now adorn the Archeology Square next to La Paz's soccer stadium.

Six huge steps lead from the subterranean temple to a gate in the wide stone wall, through which we enter the area of the Kalasasaya Temple. Before us stands the large monolith, 3.04 m high. Careful scrutiny reveals that the figure is holding ritual vessels. The pictures on its feet are thought to represent a calendar.

At the farther end of the temple is the **Sun Gate** – the most famous find of the entire site. Its eastern side, which faces the sun, is richly adorned and scholars have various theories concerning their significance. Most are of the opinion that the three rows of figures on the upper section of the gate on either side of the **Sun Man** represent some sort of calendar. The Sun Man himself holds two eagle-tipped scepters, and rays ending in figures of birds or serpents radiate from his head.

At the other end of the temple is a smaller monolith, also adorned with interesting shops. The figure's belt has pictures of crabs which do not live in the nearby Lake Titicaca, and are therefore assumed to symbolize the distant ocean. The restrained features and appearance of the figure have earned it the name of **The Priest**.

BOLIVIA

Silent remnant of ancient times - temple gate at Tiwanaku

Behind the temple is an unexposed area, divided into dig lots. This is **Putuni**, the western part of the temple. This area was excavated with extreme caution, and its finds transferred to the Museum of La Paz. Following the excavation, the area was once again covered over and further excavations left to future generations. From here we can return along the Temple's restored southern wall to marvel at its rainwater drainage system. Take a look at the drainpipes and tunnels that were carefully designed to prevent flooding. There are many South American cities that even today would envy such a drainage system...

Copacabana

This little town on the shore of Lake Titicaca is usually visited by tourists on their way to or from Peru. As well as being a transit point, the town also serves as a departure point for trips across the lake, in particular to the famous Sun Island. Its main square is dominated by a large, interesting church, and surrounded by shops, hotels, and inexpensive restaurants. Colorful celebrations are occasionally held here on weekends. Lake Titicaca, at an altitude of 3810 m above sea level, is the highest navigated body of water in the world. It is 192 km long and 80 km wide, with a maximum depth of some 300 m. You can travel across the lake in one of the large ships, or simply hire a boat. There are organized trips from La Paz, but these are rather expensive.

BOLIVIA

Sun Island itself, which is held by tradition to be the birthplace of the Inca dynasty, has a somewhat limited selection of archeological finds, including the remains of a temple and a port. It too has an impressive sun gate, although less ornate than the one at Tiwanaku. The other islands on this side of the lake are inhabited by Indians living in tribal villages. Seeing their unique way of life is an interesting experience. However, in my opinion, the islands on the Peruvian side of the Lake are more interesting (see "Peru – Puno").

Transport: Buses to Copacabana leave the La Paz central bus station each morning (the Flota Copacabana Bus Company, Tel. 322-888). Tickets should be purchased in advance. Early in the morning (5:30-6:30am) a minibus departs from a point near the La Paz cemetery, and it covers the 160 km to Copacabana in roughly 4 hours. The Expreso Manco Kapac Company at Calle Tumusla 506, and the 2 de Febrero Company, at Calle Manco Kapac 464 each run two daily buses to Copacabana.

On to Peru: From Copacabana you can cross over to Peru at Yunguyo. You can take a taxi from the town center to the border point, have it wait while you arrange your permit, and then continue with it to the main square of the village, from where you can catch a bus to Puno. You may be required by the Peruvian Immigration officials to show an exit ticket from Peru before you can obtain an entry permit. An MCO ticket is not always considered satisfactory. A safe bet is to buy a cheap bus ticket in La Paz from any Peruvian border town to a town in a neighboring country.

Diente del Diablo (Devil's Tooth)

This mountain, not far from La Paz, is known as the Devil's Tooth due to a huge rock similar in shape to an awesome tooth. The view from the top is simply dazzling. To get there you should first travel by bus to Cotacota, cross over the ravine, and then make the several hours' climb to the summit on foot. The path is steep. Take it slowly and carefully to avoid a feeling of suffocation and lack of air. On the way to Cotacota, you will pass through some of La Paz's luxury neighborhoods.

Valle de la Luna (Moon Valley)

Millions of years of geological and karstic evolution have fashioned this wondrous valley in the heart of the Andes. The rocks, rifts and mounds have wierd shapes. Moon Valley is a good few hours' walk from the end of the bus line in Florida or Calacoto. While there, it is well-worth visiting the Rio Abajo area, inhabited by a large Indian population who have been living in the same manner for centuries.

*B*OLIVIA

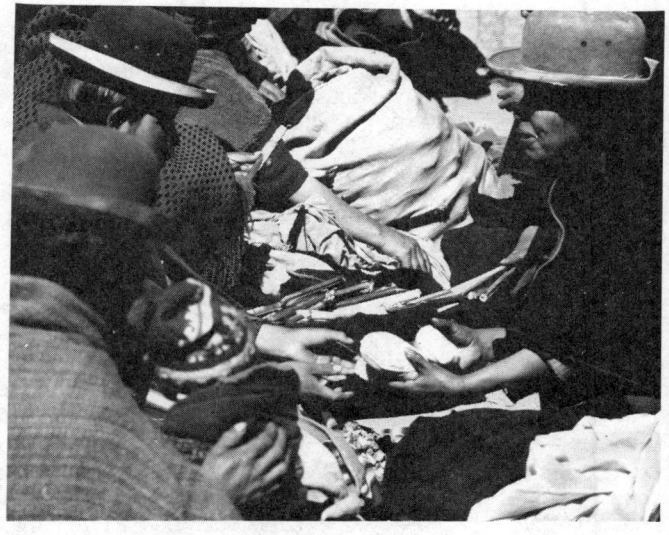

Special two-for-one offer in the barter market

Chacaltaya and the Ice Cave

About an hour's drive north of La Paz is the Chacaltaya ski resort, which is the highest in the world. The start of the slope is about 5500 m above sea level! The ski season is between the months of October and March. Even off season it is worthwhile going up to the observation point to enjoy a wonderful view of La Paz. During off season one can only reach the site by taxi.

Continue along the road which leads to *Cueva de Hielo* (Ice Cave) and to the foot of Huaina Potosi Mountain – recommended for mountain climbers. The cave is about an hour's walk from the main road. The path is steep, and the cave penetrates into a small glacier. It is only possible to get here by taxi. If a number of travelers share the cost, and one bargains vigorously with the driver, the trip is cheap. The road north to these mountains passes through the primitive Alto Lima Indian quarter. On Sunday mornings a large and colorful market is held here.

Longer excursions from La Paz

Here too we select only a few of the dozens of possible trips, each of which lasts several days. The places chosen are, in my opinion, the most beautiful, popular and accessible, and are

BOLIVIA

sufficient to give the tourist an authentic, impressive picture of the country. All the trips require physical fitness, since most incorporate hiking. Don't forget to take plenty of warm clothing, suitable camping equipment and sufficient food.

Lake Titicaca and the Northern Altiplano

One of Bolivia's most beautiful and lesser known areas is a large stretch of several hundred kilometers, north of La Paz. This area, characterized by enchanting lagoons and truly majestic scenery, is inhabited by Indians who are totally cut off from modern civilization. To tour this area you should preferably rent a car or jeep, have a good map, work tools, an extra spare tire and a reserve stock of gasoline, since there is no way of getting help if your car breaks down. The Transportes Arles Bus Company at Calle Tumusla 502 (Tel. 350-506) runs buses to Sorata only and there is no public transport from here to the more remote and more interesting places.

The route north from La Paz passes through Alto Lima, and from there follows the paved road to Lake Titicaca. To circle the lake you take the dirt track as far as Escoma, which is the last refueling point on the way. En route to Escoma you will pass many tiny villages along the shores of the lake, and see the inhabitants busy fishing or freezing potatoes. Incidentally, the method they use is the most ancient food freezing method in the world: the potatoes are spread on the ground, trodden on to express their juice, and then left to freeze at night. After several days, the potatoes harden and can be kept for many months.

From Escoma on, the road is very bad, and you must drive with extreme caution. Sorata, the largest settlement in the area, is a good base for walking tours to surrounding villages. Alternatively, you can continue to the village of Villa General Perez, more commonly known as Charazani, some 85 km from Escoma. The road is very steep and narrow, winding through an intoxicatingly beautiful scenery of mountains, valleys and streams, home to huge herds of llamas and alpacas (wild animals of the llama family).

The villages you will pass on the way consist of several rows of houses around the main square, inhabited by several dozen people only. Some of these villages are *pueblos*, i.e., villages in which each villager is responsible for himself. Others are known as *comunidades* – a sort of collective settlement, and the pride of the agrarian reform of 1952 which revolutionized agricultural settlements. The *comunidades* market their goods collectively. In the larger villages, market day is usually held once a month. These villages are one of the few places in the world where the

BOLIVIA

barter system is still in use. Commerce is entirely in the hands of women, and the rituals of displaying wares, haggling and exchanging goods is truly exciting. To all this must be added the colorful costumes, unusual customs and strange language – which together make this an unforgettable experience.

Charazani is also within a few hours' walking distance of many villages in the area. Pleasant paths through the mountains will take you across the considerable distances separating the villages. You will pass through areas cultivated by methods familiar only from history museums. One of the most beautiful villages in the area is Nino Corin, a rural idyll of adobe houses with thatched roofs. This peaceful village has neither electricity nor running water and cooking is still done in earthenware pots over small wood fires. The village is famous for the hand woven fabric made by its women and is one of the most interesting villages in the area. Cota is another charming village one hour's walk from Nino Corin.

At the end of July a number of *fiestas* are held in the villages in the Charazani area. These are authentic festivities in an area few tourists visit. The Indians don their wonderful festive clothes, and drink and dance to the sounds of the local music. On the 25th July this type of fiesta is held every year in the Calaya village. The village is about 3-4 hours' walk from Charazani, but the effort is certainly worthwhile.

After wandering through the mountains, return to Charazani, where the vehicular road ends. There are trucks taking passengers, supplies and food from La Paz to Charazani once or twice a week, but the journey is protracted and uncomfortable. The village itself has about 500 families and constitutes the center of the entire area. It has a health clinic that provides medical services for the local inhabitants, a small school and one policeman. Not far from the village is a pool fed by hot springs, where you can enjoy a bath in almost boiling water. The main square has a few stores, but these offer a poor selection of goods. In the central plaza there are two cheap hostels (*Alojamiento*); the better one is to the right of the church. Its owners are friendly and are happy to help with advice and information. Illiteracy is the norm – about 70% of the population can neither read nor write. Most of the population speaks Quechua, while others speak Aymara – both ancient Indian languages, and only a small percentage understand or speak Spanish. Charazani is the only village which has a power supply, and then only in the early evening. Although the past few years have seen the advent of transistor radios and tin roofs, the primitive isolation of this captivating area has remained unchanged.

BOLIVIA

From Charazani you can return to the main road and continue north towards the Vicuna Reserve of Ulla Ulla, near the Peruvian border. The herds of roaming vicuna, the fantastic scenery, the beautiful lakes and the ancient glaciers peering down from the surrounding ridges create a unique atmosphere. Make use of the information provided by the rangers at the entrance of the reserve. They can guide you through the meandering paths and tell you where to find concentrations of vicunas and llamas.

Camino del Inca (Inca Trail)

The mighty Inca kingdom left behind impressive ruins, palaces, cities and temples. However, no less impressive are the sophisticated Inca roads. The Incas' technology for cutting roads through even seemingly impassable places was one of the factors that contributed to the power of this great empire. To witness this expertise first-hand, we thoroughly recommend a 2-3 day hike along the Inca road near La Paz. This fascinating route still bears signs of the original Inca paving. The road begins with an exhausting climb through an arid countryside of black granite rocks criss-crossed with valleys and streams, and ends with a steep descent through a luxuriant jungle.

The hike begins in the village of Ventilla, which can be reached by bus or truck from La Paz, or by hitchhiking from Cotacota. Take a map, food, camping equipment and extremely warm clothing (!) At night the temperature drops far below freezing. Take the path from the village to the San Francisco mines, near where you begin the ascent.

The first day is spent climbing to the saddle, some 4682 m above sea level, along this splendid road, part of which is still covered with paving stones. Traces of hewn rock are still visible. Because of the high altitude you should climb very slowly, and if necessary take tablets to ease your breathing. On all sides, stark and rocky landscape soars towards the blue skies.

A few hours of climbing will bring you to the saddle, beyond which the scenery is radically different. The slopes on this side are covered in greenery, at first scant and sparse, but gradually becoming thicker until without warning, it becomes a wild, luxuriant jungle. Two kilometers past the saddle is a small village, whose humble abodes will offer you shelter for the night. Even a warm sleeping bag will not ward off the cold – you should sleep in socks and warm clothes.

The second day will be spent on the 2000 m descent, alternately above or beside the river, along a path meandering through wild forests and thick vegetation. If you walk fast you can reach the village of Chojilla on the same day. From this village, which lies on the slopes of a high hill, you can continue to La Paz, but you

BOLIVIA

Camino del Inca - The Inca Trail

will not regret an extra day in the heart of nature. Although the road descends, it is by no means easy. The descent is steep and painful, and you have to be careful all the time not to slip. My suggestion is that you make camp amid the tiny villages spread along the road – each of which consists of no more than 3-4 houses – and spend another, much warmer (due to the lower

BOLIVIA

altitude) night in the area. Then on the next day you can make the final steep ascent from the river to the village of Chojilla. There are several trucks a day from this village to La Paz.

This route is just one of several tracks which the Incas broke through in the La Paz area, and is known among travelers as the "short Inca trail". The "**long Inca trail**" is also very beautiful. It begins in **La Combre**, which can be reached by truck. The trucks leave La Paz at 9am every morning. La Combre is noted for its statue of Jesus, at 4650 m. One must alight from the truck at this point and climb to the saddle which is 4900 m above sea level. From the heights of the saddle one has a magnificent view of the immense snow capped peaks of the Andes, when suddenly the wide green valley between the mountains comes into view. From here the road continues downhill through small and remote Indian villages to a height of 1000 m above sea level. On the third day the scenery changes to mountainous jungle – dense and exquisite. The route, which takes 4 days, ends in the town of **Coroico** in the Yungas, and it is worthwhile resting here in this pleasant green mountainous area. Buses leave 3-4 times a week for La Paz along a road which is astonishingly beautiful.

The Yungas

A few hours' journey from La Paz brings us into the heart of a real tropical jungle. The road winds through the mountains northeast of La Paz. After crossing the mountain ridge at an altitude of almost 5000 m, it descends to a warm, humid area, rich in vegetation but scantily populated. Since the construction of the road to Trinidad in the late 1970s, the region has developed considerably, mainly because the inhabitants are now able to market their agricultural goods in La Paz. In spite of this, many villages have remained unchanged. When you visit them, you will have a glimpse of how they live in the heart of the jungle.

The Yungas stretches over the eastern section of the Cordillera Real mountain range, between La Paz and Cochabamba. It is an extremely fertile agricultural area, but due to its isolation has no great economic significance. Nevertheless, the government policy of supporting the expansion of the transport infrastructure has contributed considerably to its development. There are signs of increased progress, and the cultivation of agricultural lands is evident. The regional capital is Chulumani, a small village some 130 km east of La Paz, and 1000 m above sea level. The village has a few hotels and is surrounded by many coffee plantations and orchards. It is also the center of cocoa cultivation in the Yungas. This crop, after suitable chemical processing, is marketed the world over. The Flota Yunguena Bus Company on Ave. de los Americas in La Paz (Tel.

BOLIVIA

312-344) runs buses to Chulumani. You can also travel by car. The *San Bartolome Motel* is centrally located, modern and not too expensive.

With Chulumani as your base, you can tour nearby villages or penetrate the jungle.

El Beni

If your heart is set on true jungle, and you are not deterred by the thought of heat, humidity, millions of irritating mosquitos, wild animals, boat trips and long hikes through dense tropical shrubs and vegetation, you will no doubt enjoy a trip to the Beni region of northeast Bolivia. It should be pointed out that this is not an African jungle, with all its associations. But your encounter here with nature, and with the local population and their way of life, is no less exciting. The standard means of transport in the area are boat or ship. Dozens of these link the villages and Indian farms spread along the rivers and most take passengers. Take plenty of food, a mosquito net, mosquito repellent (!!!) and soothing ointment for when the mosquitoes are too hungry to mind the repellent. Most important, take water purification tablets and anti-malaria pills. The pills must be started at least a week before you enter the zone, and continued for six weeks after you leave it.

It is a good idea to come equipped with hunting bullets in order to give them to the local inhabitants who will gladly receive them as gifts, and sometimes even in lieu of cash payment. In La Paz they cost about one tenth of what they do in the jungle, where hunting bullets are a rare commodity in high demand. It is also a good idea to take modest gifts, such as candies, which you can distribute to the locals. This will assist in creating warm relations with them.

The regional capital is the friendly town of Trinidad, with 35,000 inhabitants. Trinidad can be reached from both La Paz and Cochabamba, so if you are planning to visit either of these two places, you should pass through this unusual area. LAB and TAM have daily flights from La Paz to Trinidad. Buses and trucks also cover the route, but are unreliable during the rainy season. Buses leave every morning from Cochabamba, (at the corner of Calle Lanza and Calle Brazil), for Puerto Villaroel. They cover the distance of 275 km in 6-7 hours. From Puerto Villaroel there are cargo ships to Trinidad, usually taking about a week (depending on the route, the depth of the river, the type of ship and the amount of cargo). A less adventurous but more comfortable mode of traveling is by plane – on the daily flight between the cities. Trinidad has a few hotels and restaurants, but these are generally more expensive than their counterparts in the rest of

BOLIVIA

the country. This is only to be expected, since transporting provisions to towns in the heart of the jungle entails considerable effort and expense.

Trinidad offers countless possibilities for penetrating the depths of the jungle. Whether by boat, on foot (only a little way), or by plane, you can visit remote enclaves reached by a mere handful of people. Trinidad itself, and even more so the area north of it, is a primeval landscape where time, as it were, has stood still.

Other Bolivian cities

La Paz is the northernmost large city in Bolivia. All the other cities – Oruro, Sucre, Potosi, Cochabamba and Santa Cruz – are south or east of La Paz. Each has its own unique features and a visit to them and their surroundings will reveal a wealth of interesting sites and tour possibilities.

Oruro

Oruro, about 200 km south of La Paz, has a population of over 150,000. The town, an important mining center, also serves as a main rail junction. In its center is a large market stretching on either side of the railway track, where Indian women sell their wares – mainly food brought from the many neighboring villages.

There is frequent bus service between Oruro and La Paz; the trip takes about 3 hours. Trains from Chile, Argentina, or the valleys of eastern Bolivia stop briefly at Oruro on their way to La Paz. The town has a large selection of hotels and cheap pensions.

Oruro is known particularly for its annual carnival, held in February. The three main figures of this carnival – devil, bear, and condor – symbolize the entire Bolivian tradition and are a constant motif throughout carnival week. The town's folklore groups are famous not only within Bolivia but also abroad.

Cochabamba

Cochabamba was founded in 1574. Since 1786, when it was officially declared a district capital, it has served as the capital of a fertile and densely populated area. Although situated on the eastern slopes of the mountain range, its altitude of 2570 m endows it with an excellent climate, with moderate temperatures and lower humidity than in surrounding settlements. The city has over 250,000 inhabitants and is the commercial center for tens of thousands more who live in the nearby villages and small towns.

BOLIVIA

How to get there
Cochabamba's airport is one of Bolivia's most active and is used by LAB for flights to most domestic destinations, including La Paz, Santa Cruz, Sucre, Potosi and Trinidad. Buses and trucks travel on the highways to the large cities, as well as to the numerous neighboring villages and settlements. The trip to Sucre takes 12 hours. There are several daily buses to Santa Cruz, a 14-hour journey over a paved road. There is a daily *ferrobus* train service to La Paz – the journey is far more comfortable and faster (8-10 hours) than bus or truck. The train station is at the western end of Calle 25 de Mayo, near the market.

Food and lodging
The *Ambassador Hotel* on Calle Espana is central and recommended (Tel. 48777). The rooms have private showers and conveniences and usually also telephones. Prices are moderate. A cheaper hotel is the *Gran Hotel Bolivar* on Calle San Martin (Tel. 22212), right off the main square. An budget-price hotel is the *Imperial* on Calle Arce (Tel. 28842), one block from the main square and near the market. Cheap pensions (*residenciales*) can be found near the main square and around the train station. For good food, try the restaurant at the *Bolivar Hotel*, or the *Continental* and *Napoli* restaurants, around the main square. The *Confiteria Zurich* on Calle San Martin, between Ave. Heroinas and Calle Colombia, serves excellent cakes, and the *Espana*, on Ave. Heroinas at the corner of Calle Espana (one block from the main square) serves good ice cream.

What to see
Downtown: The tranquil commercial center of the town is characterized by narrow streets lined with two-story buildings. The **Plaza Principal** (main square) is fairly modest, as is the **municipal church** on its western side. Near the church, one block south on Calle Sucre, is the **City Hall**, and to its east, on Calle 25 de Mayo, the **San Martin Church.** One block further along, at the corner of Calle Heroinas, is the **Culutral Institute.** Continuing along Calle 25 de Mayo, we come to the beginning of a promenade known as **El Prado**, which ends at the **Municipal Stadium.** As we walk along this promenade we will pass the **Tennis Club** on our right and, just behind it, the municipal **Archeological Park.**

The Portales Palace: This palace, perhaps the most beautiful in the town, is situated south of the stadium, at the intersection of Calle Potosi and Calle Buenos Aires. The palace, built at the beginning of the century, is surrounded by well-tended gardens.

BOLIVIA

It is open daily to the public for one hour only, on weekdays in the afternoon, and on weekends in the morning.

The University and the Archeological Museum: The University of San Simon is situated at the bottom of Calle Sucre. The pleasant campus is crowded with students who roam its attractive gardens, and many of the students speak English. The Anthropological Research Institute has an entire wing devoted to the Archeological Museum. The museum has exhibits from the locality as well as from all over Bolivia, including skeletons, pottery, work tools and a variety of ritual objects. The exhibits are well displayed and methodically documented. A visit to this museum is heartily recommended. You can obtain background material and explanatory pamphlets on ancient civilizations and the research conducted on them. The museum is open Mon.-Fri., from 8:30am-noon and from 2-6pm.

San Sebastian Hill: From the top of this hill – *Colina de San Sebastian* – south of the city center, there is a fantastic panorama. The hill has a monument commemorating the struggle for independence from Spain in 1812.

The market: Bustling commerce can be witnessed daily in Cochabamba's market area, within walking distance south of the main square, right next to the train station. Here various goods such as food, footwear, and housewares, to mention but a few, are sold. Market day is held twice a week, on Wednesdays and Saturdays. Indian men and women arrive from neighboring villages with their splendid handicrafts, renowned throughout the country. They are famous mainly for their marvelous wall hangings, which are woven and plaited from sheep, llama and alpaca wool. The sweaters, musical instruments and other typically Indian wares are also of outstanding design and artistry. Although I personally consider the La Paz market to be the best place for shopping, Cochabamba is definitely recommended for buying wall hangings – not only are they cheaper here, but also more beautiful and unusual.

Tourist services
The Tourist Office is situated at the corner of Heroinas and Aguirre, and supplies maps and brochures on places of interest and transportation.

Currency exchange
Unlike La Paz, the black market moneychangers here do not congregate in one place. Many stores will be only too glad to be paid in dollars, or even to change dollars into Bolivian pesos. Banks and official moneychangers pay the official rate. The black market rate in Cochabamba will probably be higher than that in La Paz, but not necessarily so.

BOLIVIA

Postal and Telephone service
The central post office is at the intersection of Ayacucho and Heroinas (Tel. 24479), and accepts regular letters, registered mail and parcels. Long-distance and international calls may be placed from the Entel Offices on Calle Gral. Acha. Both places are located two blocks from the main square.

Excursions
Cochabamba is a good base for short trips in the area. Of most interest are those villages and small towns that excel in hand-made items of the type that are sold in the town's market. Below is a brief survey of some of the better known places:

Punata: This small picturesque town, 48 km from Cochabamba, is home to expert craftsmen specializing in a variety of handicrafts. When walking through the town, ask the inhabitants to direct you to their houses. There are buses to Punata from Cochabamba every half-hour, from the corner of Calle 25 de Mayo and Honduras (not far from the train station).

Villa Rivero: Some 24 km beyond Punata is a small village whose inhabitants excel in woven wall hangings. Near the main square is a Weaving School, which is open to the public. The artists' work is quite impressive. In the small market held on Fridays you can purchase the local products at very low prices. There are buses from Cochabamba to Villa Rivero every ninety minutes, leaving from the same corner as those for Punata.

Arani: The town of Arani, whose population consists almost exclusively of potters, is 55 km from Cochabamba. Here you will find pottery and ceramics of outstanding quality and beauty, at fairly low prices. The town is located at the further end of the Cochabamba valley, against a backdrop of mountains, lending the final touch to the special atmosphere and rare beauty of the place.

Jungle: Cochabamba is a good starting point for jungle trips, especially to El Beni. For details, see "Longer excursions from La Paz – El Beni".

Santa Cruz
Santa Cruz de la Sierra, with a population of 375,000, is the second largest city in Bolivia. It is some 700 km from the Brazilian border on the east and about the same distance from La Paz in the west. Santa Cruz was founded by the Spanish in 1561, but has only enjoyed a spurt of development and prosperity during the last few decades. This was largely due to the discovery of natural resources – particularly oil and natural gas – in the vicinity. A by-product has been the development of a transport network linking the town to other places. The

BOLIVIA

weather is hot and disagreeable, but this is compensated for by the small houses and peaceful streets, which create a pleasant atmosphere. In the center is Plaza 24 de Setiembre, surrounded by some of the most important buildings, including the church and university. Over recent years, the population of the town and its suburbs has grown due to an influx of new settlers employed in the mining industries. The city is surrounded by several large oil fields, interspersed among farms and orchards.

Santa Cruz is a central crossroads for the eastern sector of Bolivia, with trains to Brazil and Argentina. There is a paved road to Cochabamba, used by both buses and trucks. The small and antiquated airport is used by LAB for domestic and international flights, and by several foreign airlines as an intermediate stop on the way to and from La Paz.

Warning: Because it is a central junction, the city has become the center for the Bolivian cocaine trade. It is difficult to imagine that a young traveler who sits down to relax in the central plaza will not be given a "tempting" offer from one of the local cocaine traders. As a result of this situation, the attitude of police to young foreigners is much harsher here than elsewhere in Bolivia.

On to Brazil

The Santa Cruz-Puerto Suarez rail link is extremely antiquated. It is not without reason that the train on this line is known as the "death train": the monotonous journey has been interrupted more than once by sudden derailing. The train runs several times a week and the trip takes about 24 hours. After passing through border checks, take a bus or taxi to Corumba in Brazil, where your passport will be stamped. You can then continue by bus or train to Sao Paulo, Rio de Janeiro, or any other destination in southern Brazil. Citizens of countries required to have visas to Brazil, should obtain them before reaching the border town.

Sucre

Although La Paz is Bolivia's de facto capital, Sucre remains it official one. It is home to some of the country's most important public institutions, notably the Supreme Court. Sucre was founded in September 1538 and for centuries has played an important and influential role in the development of the entire region. During the pre-Independence era, when it was called Chuquisaca, its progressive outlook had a crucial influence on the character of the struggle against the Spanish. It was not by chance that independence was declared – on August 6, 1825 – in Sucre itself. In spite of a population of 80,000, the city has preserved its provincial character. The narrow streets and white

BOLIVIA

A pristine street in Sucre

houses are a living memorial to the colonial era and make Sucre one of the most beautiful tourist centers in Bolivia.

How to get there
The quickest way to travel to Sucre is by plane. LAB has daily flights between La Paz and Sucre, as well as several flights a week to Cochabamba, Santa Cruz, Tarija and Camiri. The LAB offices are at Calle Bustillos 121-127 (Tel. 21140 or 23479). Trains from the Arce Train Station, behind Bolivar Park (Tel. 21114/5) leave for La Paz several times a week (18 hours), traveling via Potosi (6 hours) and Oruro. The ferrobus, a two-car express train, covers the distance in approximately two-thirds of that time – and in style! This is a recommended means of transport, but remember to purchase your ticket in advance. Buses travel along dirt roads to Potosi and Tarija in the south, and to Cochabamba and Santa Cruz in the north. The northern route consists of 240 km of dirt track, which, although difficult, to negotiate, takes you through breathtaking scenery as far as Empizana, which is located on the paved Cochabamba (128 km) – Santa Cruz (360 km) highway.

Food and lodging
The best hotels are the *Municipal* at Ave. Venezuela 1052 (Tel. 21074), near the train station, and the *Grand* at Aniceto Arce 61 (Tel. 22461). Cheap and centrally located hotels are the *San Francisco* at Arce 191 (Tel. 22117) and *La Plata* on Ravelo, one block from the Plaza 25 de Mayo. There are many restaurants off the main square and in the neighboring streets. The *Plaza*,

BOLIVIA

at Plaza 25 de Mayo 43, is recommended. For good cakes and ice cream, visit the *Sagitario* at Calle Arenales 17.

What to see

The town's main square, **Plaza 25 de Mayo**, is truly lovely. The trees and plants are interspersed with benches, where old and young rest from their afternoon stroll. Around the square are some of the city's most important buildings. Foremost among these is **Casa de la Libertad**, (Freedom House) on the northeastern side of the square. This building, where Bolivian independence was declared, is both a national shrine and a historical museum. In addition to its **Independence Hall**, in which the declaration was signed, it has a collection of portraits, flags, shields and the like. It is open Mon.-Fri. 10am-noon and 3-5pm, and on Sat. mornings.

On the other side of the square is the **Municipal Church**, built in 1559, and alongside it the **Church Museum**, which, in addition to a mediocre art collection, has a selection of holy vessels and treasures dating from the 16th and 17th centuries. The church is open daily from 7:30-9:30am. The museum visiting hours are the same as for Freedom House. **The National Library and Archives** are on Calle Espana, northeast of the square, while the **Old University**, founded in 1624, is northwest of it. Next to the university, at the junction of Calles Junin and Arenales, is **Iglesia San Miguel** (the Church of San Miguel), which was built in 1621. The Church has been renovated tastefully and is today one of Bolivia's most beautiful churches.

A further collection of interesting sites can be found around **Plaza del Obelisco** (Obelisk Square). To the south are the large **Santa Barbara Church** and **Hospital**, and to the north, the imposing building of the municipal **Theater**. Behind the theater is **Museo Anatomia Humana** (the Anatomical Museum), maintained and operated by the University's Medical School, with human anatomical and pathological exhibits. It is open Mon-Fri. 8:30am-noon and 2-6pm. North of the theater, towards **Bolivar Park**, is the contemporary building of the **Corte Suprema** (the Supreme Court). This is Sucre's sole remaining government body of any significance and is regarded with due respect by the entire population.

University Museums: The university runs an excellent network of museums, including some of the country's best. The three main museums are housed in a renovated colonial building on Calle Bolivar, one block from the main square and are open to the public Mon.-Fri. 8.30am-noon and 2-6pm, and from 9-11am on Sat. and Sun. The **Colonial Museum**, founded in 1939, has nearly 1000 exhibits, including pictures, sculptures, general

BOLIVIA

works of art and the like. The **Museum of Modern Art** has a collection of paintings and sculpture by Bolivian artists. The most interesting and important of the three is the **Anthropological Museum**, founded in 1943. This museum is divided into three main sections: Archeology, Ethnography, and Folklore. The Archeology section has an impressive collection of skulls, mummies, pottery and ancient artifacts, which depict the evolution of the local civilizations. The Ethnography section, on the other hand, has contemporary exhibits, mostly from the jungle cultures in the country's eastern sector. The Folklore section has an admirable display of traditional Indian costumes, pottery, jewelry and ritual ornaments, with emphasis on the evolution of the local culture and its influence on dress and customs.

Other museums: The **Santa Clara Museum** at Calle Calvo 212, has a display of religious vessels and pictures, including silver objects, pottery and a church organ. The **La Ricoleta Museum**, which is some distance from the city center, is housed in a 19th century colonial building, alongside the church of the same name. Next to the museum is an **observation point** from which you can see the entire city.

Tourist services

The **Tourist Office** is on Calle Audiencia, one block from the main square (Tel. 25983). Maps and pamphlets can be obtained here.

Currency exchange: Unlike the large cities, Sucre has no black market to speak of and you will have to resort to the shopkeepers, some of whom will doubtless agree to cash small amounts of dollars. Banks exchange currency at the official rate.

Postal and telephone service: The main post office is half a block from the main square, on Calle Argentina. Long-distance and international calls can be made from the Entel Building at the top of Calle Espana, corner of Urcullo.

Weather

Due to its altitude of 2790 m above sea level, the weather here is pleasant and temperate, with an average annual temperature of 16 degrees Centigrade (60 degrees Fahrenheit).

Tarabuco's Market

Perhaps the most beautiful Indian market in South America is held on Sunday mornings in the Indian village of Tarabuco, two hours' journey east of Sucre. This small village, which on ordinary days is indistinguishable from the many other villages in the area, is transformed on Sundays into something quite

BOLIVIA

'Who will buy...' - The market in Tarabuco

unique. Market day is a cause for celebration. People dress up in their festive clothes, put on jewelry and hats and fill the streets of the town with their colorful stalls. The large market teems with Indians walking around and selling ponchos, hats, and knitted and woven goods, among other things. These are all hand-made, in the original style characteristic of the region. Prices are usually high, but stubborn bargaining, especially towards closing time (early afternoon) is often rewarded with a considerable reduction. Bear in mind that there is no shortage of goods and that you, as a tourist, will be besieged on all sides, so you need be in no hurry to buy. You are sure to find what you want – and if you persist, at a good price. There are stalls that sell coca leaves, spices, fruit and vegetables, knives, mousetraps and more. The colorful clothes, the popular music occasionally played in the streets and the splash of colors make a visit here a truly exhilarating experience.

Transportation from Sucre: Buses, taxis and trucks leave Sucre for Tarabuco starting at 6am, from the square at the end

BOLIVIA

of Calle Calvo, behind the San Lazaro Church. The dirt track leading to the village is extremely dusty, and if you are traveling by truck, by the time you reach the village your face will have assumed a chalky pallor and your hair will have turned white! It is worth trying to organize a group to share a taxi. The driver will wait for you in Tarabuco and take you back to Sucre.

Potosi

Potosi's Spanish founders had great hopes for the town when they laid the cornerstone in April 1545. They had just discovered the *Cerro Rico de Potosi* – the mountain rising to the west of the town, with its great silver and tin deposits waiting to be mined. For 200 years Potosi was the largest mining center in the Americas. With 200,000 inhabitants at the start of the 17th century, it was the largest town on the continent. However, the drop in world demand for silver and the discovery of other silver deposits led to the town's near total collapse. Only improved mining techniques, and a growing demand for tin revived the town. Potosi is now reliving its glorious past, serving once more as an important center with considerable influence on the national economy. Potosi, which is situated 3976 m above sea level, currently has a population of 100,000. The town, which was built alongside the largest, most important silver mine discovered by the Spanish, is notable for its unique architecture, which has resisted the march of time. The public buildings and numerous churches have been preserved with their magnificent facades, which bear witness to the town's golden era.

Transportation

There is *ferrobus* rail service several times a week to La Paz (10 hours) and Sucre (5 hours). This is the fastest and most comfortable overland means of traveling to these places. The train station is in the northern part of the town, not far from the central bus station *(terminal de bus*, Tel. 26075). Several bus companies have daily service to La Paz – a journey of some 13 hours. There is also daily bus service to Sucre (6 hours), Oruro, Cochabamba, and Villazon (14 hours). Buses to Tarija leave several times a week. LAB flies several times a week to Cochabamba and La Paz.

Food and lodging

Potosi's hotels and restaurants are nothing special. The best hotels are the *Centenario*, on Plaza del Estudiante (Tel. 22751), and the *Colonial*, at Calle Hoyos 8 (Tel. 24265), near the main square. Cheap hotels are the *El Turista*, at Calle Lanza 19 (Tel. 22492), and the *Alojamiento Ferrocarril*, at Ave. Villazon 159 (Tel. 24292), opposite the train station. Very few restaurants

BOLIVIA

The city of Potosi from the top of Cerro Rico

deserve special mention. The *Sky Room* on Calle Bolivar (Tel. 26345) is centrally located and serves good lunches and dinners.

What to see

Downtown: The town has an abundance of churches, which have seemingly remained unaltered since they were first built centuries ago. Here too the streets are fairly narrow and the houses seem to sprout out of the curb, leaving a tiny sidewalk for pedestrians. The main square, **Plaza 10 de Noviembre**, a source of pride for the town's inhabitants and beautifully tended, has a refinement that is quite enchanting. On the north side of the square is the **Basilica Catedral** (Municipal Cathedral). One block further along to the left is one of Bolivia's most important buildings, the first **Casa de la Moneda** (mint) where, over the centuries, the silver mined from the mountain was transformed into legal tender. The mint is now a museum, with art collections, mostly of a religious nature, as well as an exhibit of tools and instruments used in the original mint. Behind the exhibition rooms are storehouses with archeological items and a collection of ancient weapons. The mint can be visited only on a guided tour. There are organized tours twice a day – in the morning and afternoon, lasting two hours.

The mines: The crowning experience is of course a visit to the Cerro Rico mines. The mountain has over 2000 mines, of which about 400 are active. Thousands of workers are employed in extracting tin ore: some work with machines, others with picks, and others with their bare hands. Although for over 4 centuries

BOLIVIA

A man's hammer in a child's hands - the Cerro Rico mines

the mountain's treasures have been plundered, the deposits have not yet been exhausted. Formerly, most of the mines were privately owned and the miners' working conditions and pay were nothing short of criminal exploitation. Basic safety devices, and medical and emergency services were lacking, and young children worked beside adults (who were old at 30). Constant

BOLIVIA

exposure to dust and soot considerably shortened their life expectancy. The scarity of oxygen at the high altitudes (over 4000 m above sea level) was merely an added aggravation to their other hardships, such as the extreme cold most of the year round, occupational hazards and so on. Many met their death through illness, uncontrolled dynamite explosions, or the frequent collisions between the ore laden carts. The unprotected miners were forced to fight for their survival under intolerable conditions. In recent years conditions have considerably improved. Although in some mines one is still reminded of Dickens' description of England's coal mines in the 19th century, many mines have been nationalized and reformed by the government in a truly remarkable manner.

There are guided tours to the Pailaviri mine Mon.-Sat. mornings. You will see modern mining and processing techniques and, to a lesser extent, the miners' working conditions. To reach the mine, hire a taxi downtown or take a bus that will take you to the entrance of the mine or, alternatively, hitch a lift on one of the trucks taking the miners to work. Getting into one of the private mines for a direct glimpse of how they work is forbidden and complicated, but if you succeed you will have a shocking, never-to-be-forgotten experience.

Tourist services
The **Tourist Office** is situated in a small building at the corner of the main square. Maps of the town and basic information are available here (Tel. 25288 or 26392).

Postal and telephone services
The central post office is at Calle Lanza 3. The Entel Building, for international calls, is at Calle Linares 15.

Weather
Potosi suffers from a harsh, cold climate throughout the year. Strong winds add to the feeling of oppression occasioned by the high altitudes and the open plains of the surrounding Altiplano. The average annual temperature is 8 degrees Centigrade (46 degrees Fahrenheit) – so take warm clothes with you. The lack of oxygen creates a feeling of asphyxiation, especially during climbs or exertions in the Cerro Rico mining area.

Tarija
Tarija, 376 km south of Potosi, is the largest town in southern Bolivia, with a population of over 30,000. Situated at an altitude of 1866 m, it is the heart of an extremely fertile agricultural area. Its geographical isolation from most of the rest of the country is responsible for a commercial and professional structure based largely on self-sufficiency.

BOLIVIA

Tarija is the transportation hub of the south and has a number of hotels and restaurants. There are two main bus routes from the town: the first is to Villazon (7 hours) and La Paz (30 hours), and the second is to Sucre (15 hours), Potosi (13 hours) and on to Cochabamba and Santa Cruz. LAB and TAM have numerous flights to La Paz, Cochabamba and other central towns. The Information Office on Calle Bolivar will give you up-to-date travel information, and recommend excursions around the town, in particular to the surrounding villages.

Villazon

This town on the Argentinian border, is 3443 m above sea level and almost 1000 km south of La Paz. The town is small (pop. 10,000), and fairly primitive – with unpaved streets, single-story adobe houses and a neglected and unattractive main square. From Villazon there is a train almost every day to La Paz – a 24 hour journey over the dusty Altiplano. The train is unheated and extremely cold by night. It is generally packed and you should preferably travel first class. This is the fastest and most comfortable way of traveling to La Paz, since bus journeys are not only arduous, dusty and uncomfortable, but longer than those by train. There are buses to Tarija and Potosi almost every day, but the road winds continuously and the journey is unpleasant.

The border crossing point to Argentina is on the outskirts of the town. You must already be in possession of an entry visa, since Villazon has no Argentinian consulate. The border point is closed daily for a two-hour siesta. Get rid of any Bolivian currency before crossing over and buy Argentinian pesos. However little the Bolivian peso is worth in Bolivia itself, it is worth even less outside the country. The Bolivian border officials are wont to levy unexplained fees – especially on weekends.

BRAZIL

A mere snatch of music instantly conveys the underlying magic and rhythm of Brazil, the largest country in South America. Brazilian music, the catchy Samba rhythm, and the national exhilaration of the annual carnival week are famous world over. The beauty of the Brazilian girls in their colorful costumes as they stroll down the streets of Rio de Janeiro, the wonders of the Copacabana beach, the famous Sugarloaf Mountain and the Corcovado are not easily forgotten.

Once a remote Portuguese colony in the New World, Brazil is today an important member of the international community, and a pillar of the Third World. A tangle of economic, political, social, and geographic problems prevent Brazil from real development and advancement. The tremendous potential is there, and if it is used wisely Brazil could have a brilliant future, where her beauty, her charm, and her social and economic potential will at last find full expression.

This vast and beautiful country offers the tourist a number of options: living it up in Rio de Janeiro, a turbulent cruise along the Amazon tributaries, a visit to the colonial town of Ouro-Preto or to the city of tommorrow – Brasilia. Brazil is a captivating country, one that is open and friendly, and unique.

History

Towards the end of the 15th century, when new sea routes and continents – which were to change the face of the world – were being discovered, Portuguese navigators were attempting to find a route to India and the Far East. While the Spanish navigators were sailing west to what was later called America – the Portuguese sailed south along the African coast. In 1487 they reached the Cape of Good Hope, and ten years later the Far East.

In 1494, two years after Columbus' momentous discovery, Spain and Portugal signed the Treaty of Tordesillas dividing up the newly discovered territories between them. An imaginary line was drawn from north to south pole, cutting through the eastern portion of South America. All that lay to the east of that line belonged to Portugal, while all that to the west was Spanish. This agreement provided the basis for Portuguese sovereignty over Brazil, which, incidentally, was not discovered for another six years. In 1500 the Spanish landed in Brazil, but did not stay. That same year, the Portuguese navigator Pedro

BRAZIL

Alvares Cabral's expedition landed on the coast of Bahia in northeast Brazil, and claimed the territory for the Portuguese crown. Unlike the Spanish, who encountered the rich and sophisticated cultures of the Aztecs and Incas, the Portuguese found only semi-nomadic Indian tribes subsisting off a primitive agriculture. These Indians lived in small and isolated communities and were extremely hostile towards the newcomers.

From an economic point of view, the newly discovered country was also somewhat disappointing. The only natural resource that could be exploited was the "coal tree" – *pau brasil* in Portuguese – which gave Brazil its name. The Portuguese were therefore in no hurry to expand settlement here, preferring to further their trade links with the rich markets of the Far East.

Only in 1530 did the first colonizing expedition reach Brazil, bringing the animals, seeds, and agricultural equipment needed to set up a permanent settlement. One after another, small coastal towns sprang up – initially in the Sao Vicente region (now the state of Sao Paulo), and later in the north, in the area of Salvador. Fear of Indian tribes prevented the colonials from penetrating inland. They settled mainly along the coastal strip between Bahia in the north and Porto-Alegre in the south. As the settlements grew, mainly during the 16th and 17th centuries, a new administrative policy was adopted to ensure control of the territory. The coastal strip was divided into administrative districts – *capitanias* – headed by powerful governors who were responsible for defending and developing their region.

Since the middle of the 16th century, the combination of the growing European demand for sugar, Portuguese navigational initiative, and the fertile lands of northeast Brazil (what is today the Pernambuco region) gave much impetus to settlement. Brazil became the world's largest sugar producer. The extensive sugar plantations were worked mainly by Black slaves imported from Africa, who laid the foundations for Brazil's unique ethnic structure.

In 1580, Philip II of Spain assumed the Portuguese crown and claimed the country for Spain. For 60 years, the two Iberian kingdoms were a single state. This situation had far-reaching repercussions on Brazil. The merger in practice nullified the Tordesillas agreement, making it possible for the Portuguese to settle further inland. At the same time, Spain, and consequently Brazil too, became involved in a 30-year war with Holland. The Dutch conquered large portions of northeast

BRAZIL

Brazil, where sugar – the prime economic resource – was grown. The westward extension of settlement laid the foundations for Brazil's immense size, since the Portuguese refused to yield the territories they had settled during the years of union, and expelled the Dutch in 1654.

Perhaps the most important outcome of inland settlement was the discovery of gold, and later diamonds. In the 18th century, colonial expeditions, called *bandeirantes*, sent north and west from Sao Paulo, discovered significant amounts of gold in what is today the state of Minas Gerais. This led to a gold rush similar to the one in the United States. Thousands left the coastal towns, and masses of immigrants arrived from Portugal and other parts of Europe, flocking to the mining towns that sprouted in the new regions. Agricultural settlements grew alongside them to provide for their needs. In a matter of decades Brazil was transformed from a remote and isolated corner of the world to a magnet for immigration, and a popular center that was developing at a galloping pace, and whose future was full of hope.

As the gold fever subsided and diamond export waned, tranquility returned to the country, and practicality replaced dreams. Coffee production soon overshadowed gold production as Brazil began cultivating top-grade coffee, first near Rio de Janeiro, and subsequently in the south near Sao Paulo and Porto Alegre. Because of a suitable climate, soil, and elevation, Brazil produces coffee beans of choice quality. Since the second half of the 19th century, coffee has been one of the most important components of Brazilian economy, and the country's most important export.

The frequent changes and accelerated development also brought about administrative and constitutional changes. At the end of the 18th century, equal rights were granted to the Indians, liberal immigration laws were promulgated, and Rio de Janeiro replaced Salvador as the country's capital. This was due to its command of the main routes to Minas Gerais, with its rich mines, and because of its proximity to the growing settlements in the south.

The desire for independence was already apparent at the start of the 18th century. Growing dissatisfaction was felt since Portugal effectively controlled Brazilian commerce, dictating its scope, terms, and profits. Toward the end of the century, during the 1770s and 1780s, ideas of independence began to take shape, and insurrections occurred in several areas. Freedom was in the air, just as in Europe and other Latin American countries. It was largely promoted by a new

BRAZIL

intellectual elite, which exploited the economic crisis, in particular the decline of gold and sugar exports, to further their ends. One of the rebel leaders of the period was Tiradentes, who is famous for his uncompromising stance in favor of ridding Brazil of the Portuguese crown. To this day he is a symbol of freedom and independence for Brazilians.

Unlike its neighbors which gained independence only after long and bloody battles, Brazil followed a gradual and moderate course, and managed to avoid armed confrontation. In 1808 Napoleon conquered Portugal. The Portuguese royal family fled Lisbon for Brazil, making it the seat of the monarchy, and they were welcomed with open arms. In 1815, Brazil was declared an independent state, federated with the mother country and subject to the Portuguese crown. Its ports were opened to free, large-scale trade. In 1821, the king returned to Portugal, where he vainly attempted to rescind some of the progressive economic and political concessions he had granted Brazil. His son, Dom Pedro I, joined forces with the secessionists. In 1822, when Brazil's independence was declared, he was chosen as its first Emperor.

Dom Pedro wanted to establish absolute monarchy, and tried to dissolve parliament. The parliament, on the other hand, tried to establish a liberal new constitution, but this resistance was met with force. On his father's death in 1826, Dom Pedro inherited the Portuguese crown. A short while later, he abdicated in favor of his young daughter, Maria de Gloria, who became Queen Gloria II of Portugal. In 1831, unable to come to an agreement with the Brazilian parliament, Dom Pedro abdicated the Brazilian throne as well, in favor of his young son, Dom Pedro II.

The period under the leadership of Dom Pedro II was far more tranquil. Internal affairs stabilized, substantial resources were channeled into development, many immigrants were absorbed from Europe, and Brazil embarked on an era of prosperity. Dom Pedro II ruled for 49 years, during which time he laid much of the foundations of modern Brazil. Dom Pedro improved the bureaucracy, expanded education, health, and welfare services, and advanced international trade and commerce. His liberal policies, the most significant being the abolition of slavery and the emancipation of 700,000 Black slaves in 1888, were strongly opposed by the landowners and the wealthy. In 1889 they banded together under the leadership of Marshal Fonesca, deposed Dom Pedro, and declared a republic.

At that time, northern Brazil was enjoying unprecedented prosperity. The discovery of the rubber tree in the Amazon

BRAZIL

region, and the eagerness with which this product was greeted in Europe, led to an extraordinary economic boom, which helped create a moderate political climate. Brazil's central government adopted liberal and conciliatory social and international policies, and with the help of one of Brazil's greatest leaders ever, the Baron Rio Branco, the country signed border agreements with its neighbors.

Brazil supported the Allies against Germany in both World Wars, winning it great sympathy in the West. The liberal government continued, but the economic crisis of the late 1920s brought about unpleasant political changes. The most important of these was the end of the "first republic" and the inauguration of the second, when, for the first time in its history, Brazil suffered a violent revolution. In 1930, a group of rebels led by Getulio Vargas, seized power and continued to rule Brazil for fifteen successive years. Vargas' first step was to alter the system by which the president was elected.

Formerly, electors had chosen the president under the direction of the powerful state governors. The strong opposition that initially greeted his rule slowly diminished. In 1934 Vargas drew up a new constitution by which, among other things, women were granted the franchise. In 1937, a short while before the presidential elections, the internal climate grew so heated that Vargas declared a state of emergency. He dissolved Congress, and concentrated most power into his own hands.

During his rule, Vargas instituted a number of far-reaching reforms in education and welfare. He narrowed the social gap, and developed the western sector of Brazil, which was virtually uninhabited till then. In the early 1940s, Vargas restored some civil liberties, and allowed the formation of political parties. In 1945, in the face of mounting opposition to his rule, he resigned.

General Dutra, Minister of Defense under Vargas, won the presidency in the ensuing democratic elections. Dutra drew up a new constitution safeguarding individual liberties. In 1951, Vargas was re-elected president, but his rule was beset with serious economic problems and heavy pressure from the opposition.

In 1954, Vargas committed suicide under scandalous circumstances, following the attempted murder of one of the leaders of the opposition. The new president, Juscelino Kubitschek, led the country into a period of slow but steady economic growth, continued the policy of settling the west,

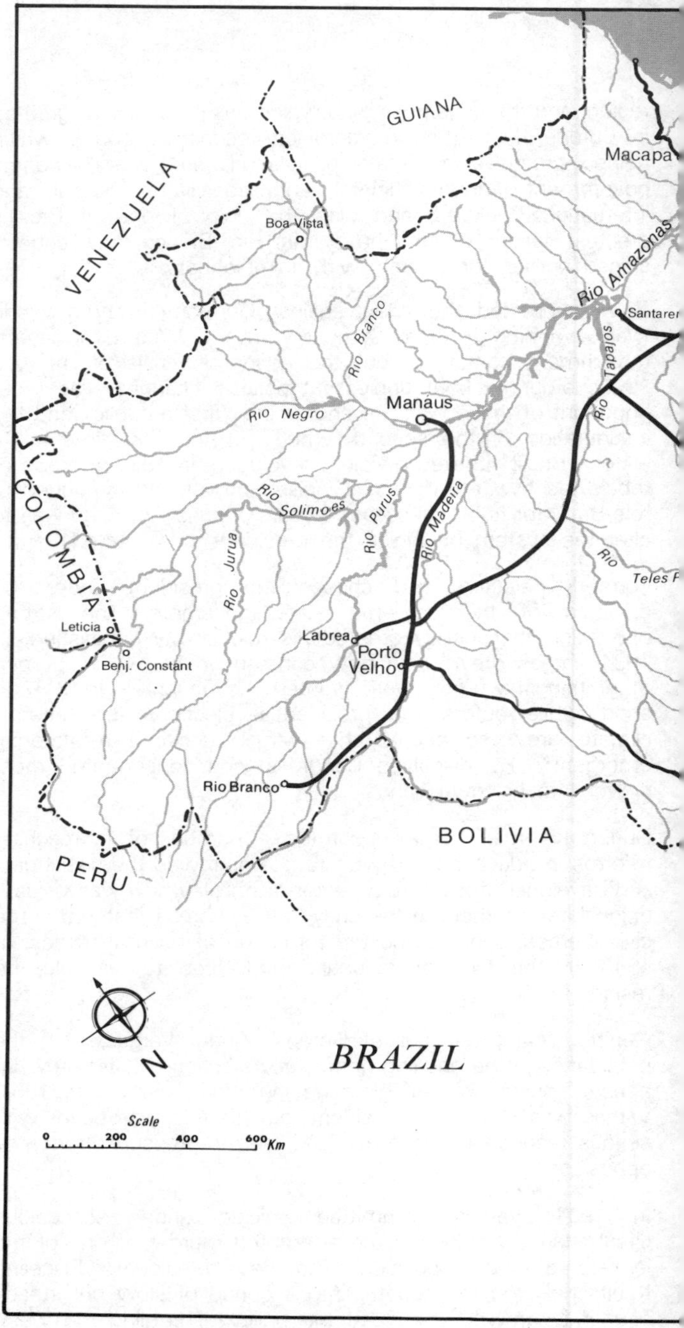
GUIANA
VENEZUELA
Macapa
Boa Vista
Rio Amazonas
Santaren
Rio Branco
Rio Tapajos
Manaus
Rio Negro
Rio
COLOMBIA
Rio Solimoes
Rio Purus
Rio Madeira
Rio
Teles P
Rio Jurua
Leticia
Benj. Constant
Labrea
Porto
Velho
Rio Branco
BOLIVIA
PERU
N
BRAZIL
Scale
0
200
400
600
Km

189

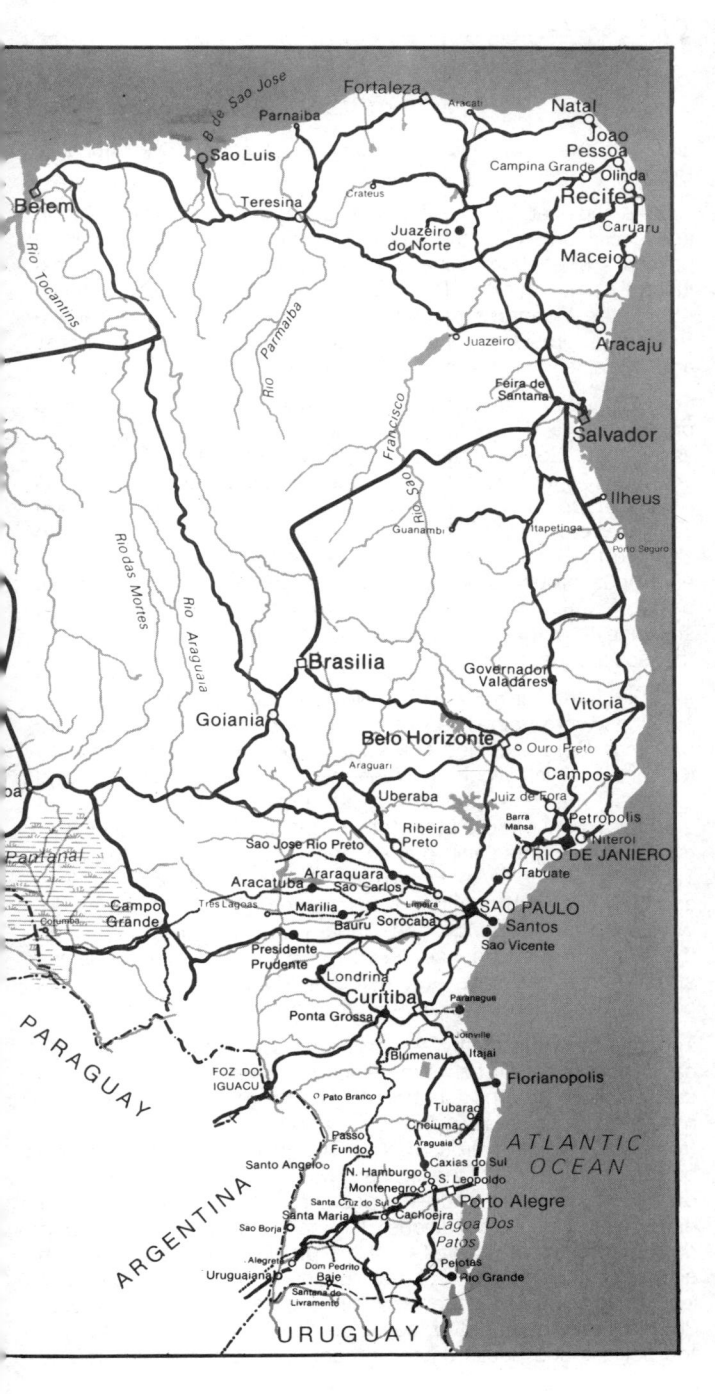

BRAZIL

and laid the foundations of Brazil's glorious new capital — Brasilia.

Brazil's rapid economic development led to galloping inflation and social unrest in the industrial cities. The 1960s began in political and economic chaos. An economic austerity policy was instituted, but this too failed. In April 1964, in an extraordinary move, the Congress elected a military man, General Castelo Branco, as president, with a mandate to stabilize the economy and social conditions.

For 20 years, a military junta ruled Brazil, suppressing opposition and restricting freedom of expression and association. Concurrently, attempts were made to develop the economy, agrarian reforms were instituted, power stations were set up, and unprecedentedly large amounts of foreign capital were raised. These measures, however, failed to alleviate the economic situation. The foreign debt grew to such enormous proportions that it was doubtful if it could ever be paid off, inflation surpassed government control, and a food shortage threatened to lead to a violent uprising on the part of the socially deprived.

In 1984, the army gave in to popular opinion, and new elections were held. The victor, Tancredo Nevas from the state of Minas Gerais, coined the slogan *Nova Republica* ("the new republic"), which would avoid showy but economically unsound projects, make a concerted effort to solve problems of unemployment, housing, nutrition, and agricultural settlement, restore civil rights, and put an end to oppression. Nevas (or Tancredo, as he was known by the masses) gained mass approval and public support for his program. But Tancredo, who had won the elections by a large majority, never reached the presidential residence, Planalto, in Brasilia. A fatal illness struck him a few days before the scheduled inauguration. His deputy, Jose Sarney, was sworn into office in his stead.

The day Tancredo died was one of the saddest and most bitter days modern Brazil has experienced — a day when hope was dashed and dreams shattered. Hundreds of thousands of mourners participated in the funeral cortege as it made its way from Sao Paulo towards Brasilia. The procession ended at his birthplace in Minas Gerais. Sarney, Tancredo's deputy, took over the presidency, and assumed the task of leadership under extremely difficult conditions. He had strong public support both at home and abroad, and his presidency has marked an economic, social, and political turning point. Under Sarney's leadership, Brazil's economy attained notable stability in 1985-86. Inflation was arrested, social unrest diminished, and faith in the political and public establishment was restored. A true and

BRAZIL

lasting solution to the serious economic problems has, however, yet to be found.

Geography and climate

Brazil has an area of 8,514,000 sq/km, which is half the area of the entire South American continent and as large as the whole of Europe. Brazil's border stretches for some 15,720 km, 7408 km of them along the Atlantic coast. Brazil borders on every South American country, except Chile and Ecuador.

Brazil is a federal republic, consisting of 24 states and two territories. The equator transverses the north of the country. Although about 90% of Brazil is located in the tropics, its climate is modified by the high altitude. Most of Brazil lies, 500-1000 m above sea level. North Brazil, or Amazonia, is covered in thick forest, while the center is mainly savanna land, with sparse, low vegetation.

Most of the plateau consists of extremely ancient granite rock, which has been eroded and leveled over the last 700 million years. The plateau is bordered by the Andes in the west, by the Amazon basin in the north, and by the coastal mountain range in the east. The huge Amazon basin, one of the largest basins in the world, is a vast plain of silt washed down from the Andes, and covered in thick forest. The mountains, on the other hand, are extremely steep, with peaks right on the coast. These steep mountains make inland Brazil virtually inaccessible, and explain why settlement is concentrated along the coast.

The Brazilian plateau is drained by three main rivers: the Amazon in the north, the Sao Francisco in the center, and the Parana. The tributaries of these rivers usually flow from north to south, emptying into the main rivers via a series of waterfalls, the most famous of which are the Iguacu Falls. These sudden changes in height make the rivers turbulent, and prevent them from serving as major transportation routes. The Amazon is an exceptionally deep river and large ships can negotiate it for 1500 km upstream, as far as Manaus. In terms of settlement, Brazil can be divided into five main areas, each with its own topography and climate.

Amazonia: The largest and most unique area of Brazil is its northern sector. Amazonia stretches over 60% of Brazil's area, but is home to only 4% of the country's population. The climate is tropical – hot and humid – with a high precipitation rate (more than 2000 mm of rainfall annually) and due to its proximity to the equator, there is little seasonal variation and the temperature is constant the year round.

BRAZIL

Amazonia is covered in dense forest, which comprises a third of the world's natural forests. A thousand species of trees and plants grow in it, and about 2000 species of fish and aquatic animals inhabit its rivers. Over the last decades, considerable effort has been put into developing the area, and particularly into exploiting its many mineral resources. Brazilian governments have done much to encourage settlement, build roads, and set up agricultural and industrial enterprises. Manaus, for example, was declared a free port, which led to a significant boom. Another huge government project was the Trans-Amazon highway. This project, which was intended to encourage settlement in the jungle, ended in bitter failure. Even though some parts of the road are still passable, most of this difficult route – which its planners saw as a true miracle of engineering – is neglected and overgrown by jungle vegetation. On the other hand, dozens of mining towns have mushroomed, full of fortune-hunters intent on discovering diamonds or other treasures in the area.

The Northeast: This area preserves remnants of its Spanish and Dutch colonial past. Many of the current population are descended from the Black slaves who worked the sugar plantations. Northeast Brazil is one of Brazil's least developed areas. Even though about one-third of the total population lives here, it has no real industrial or agricultural infrastructure. Over the last few years there has been a greater impetus toward development. The educational network has been expanded and a basis has been laid for improving the quality of life. In spite of this, the local inhabitants, in particular those who live far from the main towns of Bahia and Recife, still live in the primitive conditions of shameful poverty, gnawing hunger, and ignorance handed down by their ancestors. The weather is extremely fickle, sometimes dry almost to the point of drought, while in other seasons, awesome floods sweep away entire towns and villages.

The Southeast: This is Brazil's most developed, industrialized and populated area. Most of the country's economic activity takes place in the three cities of Rio, Sao Paulo, and Belo Horizonte. The reason for this is the pleasant climate in these areas – tropical to temperate – which enables the cultivation of top-grade agricultural products, and encourages settlement and broad industrial development. The area has many mineral resources, whose exploitation and sale has a major effect on the country's economy.

The South: The climate of southern Brazil is temperate in the main. The fertile plains are used as pastureland and for cultivation of a variety of crops. There is also some light

BRAZIL

Bird's-eye view of Rio

BRAZIL

industry here, and ports through which the local produce is exported. The south has always attracted European immigrants, who make their presence felt. Most Europeans here work in agriculture and live on farms or small rural settlements, living a lifestyle similar to the one they had in Europe.

The West: This is definitely Brazil's least-known or most "neglected" section. The huge states of Mato Grosso and Goias are almost entirely uninhabited. Only in recent years has public attention been directed to these places. Most of the land is savanna and marshland, known as *pantanal*. In the heart of this area lies Brazil's new capital – Brasilia – which, since it was built, has done much to assist this difficult and problematic region and give new hope to its inhabitants. The area has a hot climate and the precipitation increases as one goes further south.

Population

Since Brazil covers half the South American continent, its population, currently estimated at about 130 million, correspondingly accounts for nearly half the total population of South America. The people are a mixture of various races, which accounts for Brazil's rich and diversified cultural life.

Brazil's population has grown at an astonishing rate since the start of the century, when the population was a mere 17 million. Only five million were Europeans (a third Portuguese, a third Italian, and the remaining third Spanish, German, etc.). The other 12 million were Blacks and Indians. During the 17th and 18th centuries, the Portuguese colonists "imported" millions of Black slaves, mainly from West Africa, to work the sugar plantations. These Blacks became an important demographic factor. They intermarried with the Portuguese, producing a distinctive ethnic group, whose social imprint is felt to this day.

Most immigration to Brazil took place in the 19th and 20th centuries, when millions of immigrants from all over the world landed on its shores. Most of the immigrants settled in the large cities and along the coastal strip. They began to intermarry, and the population grew rapidly. The Portuguese language and Catholicism are dominant. Some people see these as the main factors in overcoming ethnic and communal differences and creating the country's strong sense of unity (90% of Brazilians are Catholics, making Brazil the largest Catholic country in the world).

Nowadays, the population consists of about 60% Whites, over

BRAZIL

Colorful street celebrations during the Carnival

20% *Mestizos* (mixed Portuguese and Indian) and Mulattos (mixed Portuguse and Blacks), 15% Blacks, and the remaining minority are Indians, Japanese, and other minorities. The Whites live mainly in south Brazil and along the coast. Most are "new" immigrants, having arrived since the second half of the 19th century. Only a few can trace their ancestry back to colonial roots. The Blacks are all descendants of the slaves who numbered an estimated 4-6 million at the end of the previous century, when slavery was abolished. Large concentrations of Blacks can be found in Bahia, Rio, and Minas Gerais, the regions of sugar plantations, industrial development, and mines, where the slaves were employed. Only about 200,000 Indians survive. They are mainly to be found in remote areas of the Amazonia and Mato Grosso States. Many Indians perished from disease and the impact of modernization, while others were absorbed into the immigrant population, abandoning their traditional roots. FUNAI, the national authority that deals with all matters relating to the Indians, watches over the assimilation process and attempts to control their exposure to the modern world, thus making the transition less painful.

Immigration from the Far East has also played an important part in Brazilian society. About half a million Japanese live in

BRAZIL

Brazil, mostly in Sao Paulo. Their presence is felt in industry and commerce.

In spite of the complex racial mixture, there are no racial or sectarian conflicts. Everyone speaks Portuguese, and religion is a personal matter. Even though the vast majority are Catholics, a variety of pagan traditions and rites have been preserved, in particular African voodoo. These traditions flourish alongside the Church, and often Christian and pagan rites intermingle.

The population distribution is by no means uniform. Almost the entire population – 90% – lives along the Atlantic coast, and in the states of Sao Paulo and Minas Gerais. About 80% of the population live in urban environments, and the other 20% in Amazonia and in the huge western states. Government attempts to encourage settlement in the west and inland, which culminated in the building of Brasilia in the center of the country, have had very limited success. The vast majority still prefer the cities, which are consequently expanding continually, without adequate urban planning. The consequences of uncontrolled urbanization are extremely painful. The most obvious are the slums, or *favelas* as they are known in Brazil, which surround almost every large city. Thousands of citizens live there in unhygienic, sub-human economic and social conditions. Poverty, distress, and the lack of job opportunities lead to crime, drug abuse, prostitution, and other blights and diseases. These have spread to sizable portions of Brazilian society, threatening to undermine its foundations.

To this is added the lack of Government policy concerning family planning. This leads to an extremely rapid population growth, at a rate of 2.5% per annum, i.e., an annual increase of three million. About half the total population are children, mostly of school age. In spite of untiring efforts, the government is unable to help all of them, and many children roam the streets. About a quarter of Brazil's population is thought to be illiterate.

Government

The country is led by a president and vice president, who are elected for a six year term. The legislative bodies are the Senate, which has three representatives from each state, and the House of Representatives, with 280 members elected every four years on a proportional geographical basis. The president has broad powers and a virtually unrestricted say in all matters relating to legislation and decrees, although his use of these prerogatives is being restricted by the process of democratization. In 1985 the military regime came to an end, and the country was once again headed by a civilian president.

BRAZIL

Each state of the federal republic has its own governor and legislature. They are responsible for internal affairs, administration, education, etc. The governor and members of the legislature are democratically elected on a party basis.

Economy

Brazil's economy is based on agriculture and industry, including sophisticated hydroelectric plants and oil-drilling rigs. However, the country also has gigantic foreign debts, and is dependent on imported energy sources, and other products.

Agriculture: Basically, Brazil is agriculturally self sufficient. About one third of the population makes its living from agriculture, which not only satisfies local needs (except for wheat), but also provides about one third of the world's coffee.

Brazil is one of the world's largest agricultural states. In addition to its famous coffee production, it produces soya, cocoa, tobacco, cotton, sugar, and meat. The agricultural sector is growing year by year, particularly as a result of the expansion of agricultural training. This growth is impeded every so often by fluctuations on the world coffee market, which have a direct effect on the entire Brazilian economy.

Since agriculture accounts for about 50% of total export revenues, it is not surprising that successive governments have invested large resources in developing and diversifying it. Government bodies are continually attempting to modernize techniques, which in most parts of the country (particularly the northeast) are still fairly primitive, due to the low educational level of the inhabitants. Over the past twenty years, however, there have been considerable achievements in this area. Unlike the north, the south, especially the coffee growing areas, uses the most up-to-date agricultural technology.

Cattle ranching is a major industry in Brazil, with an estimated 200 million head of cattle. Meat is a central component of the national diet, and dairy products are also important. Most livestock is raised in the south, from which a considerable amount of meat is exported to Europe, the United States, and other countries.

Half of Brazil is covered with virgin forest, much of it carved up by rivers and streams. This restricts the amount of land that can be used for farming. However, the Brazilians have managed to put this ready-made forest to commercial use. The export of various kinds of wood is a growing industry.

Minerals: Brazil has been blessed with an abundance of mineral wealth. Iron, oil, magnesium, uranium, gold, and silver

BRAZIL

are just a few of the metals and minerals that lie buried in its soil. Their extraction is very important from both the economic and social points of view.

The discovery of gold, diamonds and other minerals had not only economic repercussions, but also social and demographic ones. Formerly, the state of Minas Gerais was the major mining area, but today it has been overshadowed by Amazonia. However, wherever the location, the phenomenon is the same. When a natural resource is discovered in commercial quantities, and the infrastructure for its extraction and marketing has been laid down, there is a marked increase in immigration to the area, and accelerated economic development.

The most serious problem in exploiting the mineral resources is their distance from ports and industrial centers. This makes the mining process more difficult and the product more expensive, so that the commercial potential is restricted. However, iron, which is found in plentiful supply in Minas Gerais and Amazonia, has in the last few decades become the mining industry's most important metal and the most significant raw material used in national industry. Iron mining laid the basis for Brazil's heavy industry, in particular the automobile and weapons industries. It is growing in importance every year.

Industry: The history of Brazilian industry is marked by ups and downs that are not always the result of commercial success or failure. In an attempt to develop local industry and avoid almost total dependence on agriculture, Brazil's various governments, virtually since the start of the century, have given special consideration to the establishment of industrial enterprises. The basic idea was and is to supply local consumption, i.e., to manufacture rather than import, and eventually to export. In the 1960s and the 1970s, Brazilian industry made a huge leap forward, new factories were established, workers were trained, and production increased on an annual basis at a rate unparalleled in the entire world. However, the masterminds of this boom neglected to lay a suitable infrastructure – in particular with regard to energy sources, the utilization of raw materials and the development of transport routes. As a result, a sharp recession ensued in the 1980s, economic growth slackened off considerably, and many industrial plants ran into financial difficulties, which had repercussions on the entire national economy.

Strict import restrictions limit competition from foreign products and assist domestic industry in the battle for the local

BRAZIL

market. Today, Brazil manufactures almost all its own cars, many electronic goods, petrochemical products, and weapons. Brazil is the fifth-largest arms manufacturer in the world.

Industrial exports are slowly catching up with agriculture's hitherto unquestioned supremacy, and nowadays the two are more or less on an equal footing.

Energy: Oil, mainly from the Middle East, accounts for roughly half of Brazil's total imports. About three-quarters of Brazil's total oil consumption is imported, which explains the sudden shift in national priorities toward the development of alternative energy sources, and the expansion of the local oil industry.

The government oil company Petrobras is investigating with admirable thoroughness, all potential oil sources in Amazonia and along the coast. They are expanding drilling and pumping operations in existing oil fields, in particular around Bahia and Campos, and investing huge sums in setting up oil refineries.

At the same time special attention is being given to alternative energy sources. Many engines now run on alcohol instead of gasoline. This alcohol is obtained from sugar cane through a relatively inexpensive chemical process. Nuclear energy is also being considered, but its use is still rather limited.

The most important energy source after petroleum is hydroenergy, since water is so plentiful in Brazil. The huge hydroelectric plant at Itaipu, on the Paraguayan border, is merely the crowning glory of a series of similar plants, which already supply about 40% of all Brazil's energy, and about 90% of its electricity. Brazil is investing huge sums in developing hydroelectric energy in order to develop it into the country's main energy source, to free itself from its stifling dependence on oil.

Itaipu, a joint Brazilian-Paraguayan venture, is intended to be the largest hydroelectric plant in the world. At the end of the current decade, when it will be completed, its output is anticipated at some 12,000 megawatts. Twenty billion dollars have been invested in the project. The governments involved view it not only as a very significant economic development, but also as a justifiable source of national pride.

Transport and communication: One of the most serious economic and social problems which has to be faced by a country as vast as Brazil is how to overcome natural obstacles and vast distances. As settlement penetrated deeper inland, the need arose to build roads and establish a convenient and

BRAZIL

efficient communications network. In the last decade Brazil has invested billions of dollars in this field, and thousands of kilometers of paved roads and dirt tracks are built every year. About 90% of passenger transportation is overland. Many travelers use the comfortable and convenient public transport services. All the large cities have modern bus stations, and streamlined buses run to all parts of the country.

One of Brazil's controversial projects is the Trans-Amazonia Highway, which cost billions of dollars. The road was intended to promote settlement in Amazonia, but the plan — initially a source of national pride — failed abysmally. The plan met with fierce opposition from the local Indians, thousands of whom fell victim to diseases spread by the road builders. Over the past years, all attempts to encourage use of the route have failed, and the ongoing maintenance costs far exceed its economic benefits. Nowadays, vast stretches of the road are neglected, and the encroaching forest is swiftly reclaiming its rights.

In the field of civil aviation, Brazil is advancing at a rapid pace. Nearly every city and town has its own airport, with flight links throughout the country. Scheduled airlines operate alongside private companies which fly to remote destinations that lack regular commercial service. In addition, light aircraft may be rented. This method of transport is essential in a country of such vast distances, and it is becoming increasingly popular.

Brazil's seaports have also been developing continuously. The country's 20 ports, along the Atlantic coast and the Amazon River, handle most of the import and export trade.

The telephone network, datalines, databases, and other technological innovations are developing fast — but not fast enough — in Brazil. More rapid progress is held back because of the huge investment required. In spite of this, Brazil has launched its own communications satellite, and is able to boast sophisticated computerized systems in both the private and public sectors.

Conclusion: In the current decade, Brazil is showing signs of a severe economic crisis. Faulty planning has created a foreign debt of roughly one hundred billion dollars. Add to this the cumulative trade deficit, difficulties in obtaining credit, and social problems that in any case make it impossible to apply a policy of restraint to the tottering economy. During 1985-86 the new civilian government attempted to institute a policy of fiscal restraint, at the recommendation of the International Monetary Fund. Rather than improve matters, these measures further undermined a social fabric already so rent by the recession that

BRAZIL

it is hard to imagine how it can be pieced together again in the near future.

Rapid, unplanned urbanization without an economic base has increased the public pressure on the government. Unemployment is spreading and taking on a dangerous aspect in the absence of suitable mechanisms of unemployment compensation, supervision, and welfare. The disproportional distribution of incomes perpetuates a situation of social inequality, especially in the poorer regions of the country such as the northeast, where the average annual per capita income is a mere tenth of that in Sao Paulo.

Language

Unlike the other Latin American countries, where Spanish is spoken, Brazil's national tongue is Portuguese; the heritage of the Portuguese colonizers. However, the Brazilian accent is totally different from that heard in Portugal. Moreover, within Brazil itself, there are regional dialects. For example, the pronunciation and idioms of the south are quite different from those of the north, to such an extent that one Brazilian can easily identify where another comes from merely by his speech. English speakers will encounter the same problem as in the rest of South America: although English is spoken in all large cities, it is almost impossible to find anyone who speaks English in provincial towns and remote villages. So it is a good idea to try and master the basics of Portuguese before arriving in Brazil, or you will find it hard to make yourself understood.

Although the languages are different, Spanish speakers will probably learn Portuguese fast, at least enough to manage.

Brazilian music

Music plays a major part in the life of Brazilians, and Brazilian music is extremely rich and varied. Who doesn't recognize the famous samba, which is one of the national symbols of Brazil? However, contrary to what is commonly believed, the streets do not resound with the strains of the samba from morning to night, except during the Rio Carnival and other celebrations. On ordinary days, you can hear the samba only in clubs or at special events. The samba is popular mainly in southeast Brazil. In the north, other beats are more popular, such as the *forro or frevo*. These have a faster tempo, and the songs are accompanied on the accordion. The bossa nova, a variation of the samba, is slower and more lyrical, and most popular among the bohemian section of society. Among the most famous composers and musicians of the bossa nova are Vinicius de Morais, Toquinho, Antonio Jobim, Dorival Caimi, and Chico

BRAZIL

Buarque. Brazilian pop music has also won international acclaim. Some of Brazil's most famous pop singers are Gal Costa, Jorge Ben, and Gilberto Gil. The latter is particularly influenced by Jamaican reggae and African music. Caetano Veloso and Djavan are extremely popular in Brazil itself, as is Elba Ramalho, who specializes in northern music. Egberto Gismonti – the famous jazz musician – has also captured a wide audience.

The influence of western pop and rock is evident in Brazil. An ever increasing number of pop singers and rock groups are making their appearance in Brazil. Popular hits are played over the radio, on television, and in discotheques.

We have mentioned only a few outstanding names in Brazilian music. If you hear of a show featuring one of the above musicians, make sure not to miss it. The music – and watching the audience reaction – will give you an idea of the part music plays in the life of the Brazilians.

General Information
How to get there
By air: Brazil has excellent air links with most parts of the world. The national airline Varig runs daily flights to Brazil from various places in the United States, Europe, and the Far East. Eastern and Pan-Am also fly daily from the United States to Brazil. Most international flights land in Rio de Janeiro or Sao Paulo, but some fly to Belem, Recife, and Manaus. Varig and the South African airline SAA have weekly flights between South Africa and Rio and Sao Paulo. Varig has flights from various places in West Africa to Brazil's two major cities.

There are many flights each day from the major cities of Western Europe, both on Varig and the various European airlines. Varig and British Caledonian have several weekly flights from London to Recife, via Lisbon. Air France has one direct flight a week from Paris. There are flights to Manaus from Miami and Mexico City; and to Belem from Miami, New York, Montevideo, and Buenos Aires.

There is frequent daily service from other South American countries to a number of Brazilian cities.

By land: Good highways lead to Brazil from Argentina and Uruguay. There is regular bus service from Buenos Aires, Montevideo, Santiago (Chile) and Asuncion (Paraguay). From Santa Cruz in Bolivia you can reach the Brazilian border on the so-called "Train of Death". There is irregular transportation from Venezuela to Buena Vista, and from there you can continue southward. Only a long and tiring cruise on tributaries

BRAZIL

of the Amazon will get you, from Colombia and Peru, to Manaus and Belem.

Documents
Most foreigners require a visa, which can be obtained at any Brazilian consulate. The visa allows entry up to three months after date of issue; the actual entrance stamp on your passport is valid for a stay of three months from date of entry. A three-month extension can be obtained from the Immigration Bureau in any of the large cities. A tourist card must be filled out when you enter the country, and must always be kept with your passport thereafter. On entry to Brazil the authorities usually require a certificate of immunisation against yellow fever.

An international driver's license is valid in Brazil, but remember to attach your original license. A student card carries no great weight in Brazil, and will not usually confer any discount. Always carry identification papers (passport). Surprise checks by policemen are common occurrences, and the absence of ID can lead to harrassment and unpleasantness.

How Long to Stay
Brazil is so large you'll need several months to get to know it. Many tourists choose to come for short periods: a week during the Carnival season, a weekend in Rio, or similar flying visits. Tourists who travel within the country by air and tour intensively can see considerable portions of the country within 3 or 4 weeks. In this length of time you can get to know many of Brazil's cities and some of its countryside. If you have only a limited period at your disposal and wish to travel overland, concentrate on one part of the country only. In a short period it is impossible, and not worth trying, to get to know both the coastal region – in southern and northern Brazil – as well as the inland regions and the Amazon basin. The *mochileros* who spends months traveling through the country will tell you that even three or four months is not long enough to get to know the country really well.

When to Come; National Holidays
The weather in Brazil is very pleasant in the winter months, between May and September. During the summer, from October to April, it is very hot and rainy. It is easier to tour in the winter, but there are fewer events at that time. The Carnival takes place at the end of February, at the height of summer. This is also the vacation season, when the beaches are packed with young people taking their annual break from study or work. If you wish to tour Brazil extensively, try to

BRAZIL

come in winter, but if you are on a short vacation, a summer visit is recommended.

Businesses close for the following national holidays: January 1, the Carnival days (around Shrove Tuesday), Good Friday, April 21, May 1, Corpus Christi, September 7 (Independence Day), November 1, November 15 (the day the republic was declared), and Christmas.

Where to Stay

The development of the tourist industry has led to a considerable expansion in available accommodation. All the major cities have a very large selection of hotels, ranging from first-class luxury hotels to modest *pensions*, which are called *Pousadas*. The smaller places, such as the northern coastal villages, the Amazon region, and remote interior regions of the country, are equipped only with primitive guest houses, often without hot water, and in some there are either beds or hammocks. Hotels are classified by stars, under the auspices of the Brazilian Tourist Office, *Embratur*. However, classification seems to be somewhat inconsistent, and you are apt to come across two hotels with the same number of stars that bear only the most superficial resemblance. A five star hotel in Salvador may be the equivalent of a mere three star hotel in Rio, and so on.

The hotels are, however, clean and well kept, and hotel staff usually polite and helpful. Generally, the growing awareness of the importance of tourism has brought about a real change in tourist services, and improvements are noticeable from one year to the next.

There is no shortage of inexpensive accommodation. Such places are not always clean, and often not in the most attractive surroundings. Carefully check such places before taking a room, and never leave valuables in your room. No one speaks English in these places, so come prepared with a smattering of Portuguese and plenty of resourcefulness.

The tourist with modest requirements can always find intermediate class hotels in the cities. Although these are much less expensive than luxury hotels, the actual differences between them are not so striking. In these establishments, the staff does not speak English, but patience and persistence will go a long way.

In the coastal villages of Bahia and north Brazil, rooms can be rented for next to nothing. In some of these places, you can sleep in a hammock for a nominal charge. The owners of these

BRAZIL

pensions (known as *pousadas*) are usually very friendly and pleasant.

Wining and Dining

Brazilian cuisine is extremely varied, and the local dishes differ from one place to the next. In the south, for example, the influence of nearby Argentina and Uruguay is felt: prime beef is the staple diet, and the *Rodizho* restaurants, which serve "all you can eat", are part of the local scenery and folklore. In the Amazon area, by contrast, meat is a rarity, and locals live on fruit, fish, and rice. Bahia in the northeast has exotic and unique cuisine. Here you can find exquisite concoctions of seafood, prepared according to the African traditions brought over by the Black slaves.

The most popular dish in the southeast is *feijoada* – a stew based on black beans, cooked slowly with an assortment of meats, mainly beef and pork, and served over rice. Traditional Brazilian side dishes are rice and brown or black beans cooked in sauce, *feijao*, and a condiment known as *farofa*, made from dried and coarsely ground potatoes or yucca, is often sprinkled over foods.

Brazil has a rich assortment of fruits, especially tropical ones. Bananas, pineapples, mangos, and papayas are merely some of the choice fresh fruit you can find in abundance in the markets at ridiculously low prices, especially in northeast Brazil. On every street corner you will come across stands selling fruit juice: *suco* is a water based juice, and *vitamina* a milk based one. Brazilians prepare suco or vitamina from all fruits, even avocados. Sounds strange? Try it anyway – you may change your mind. Another drink is sugar cane juice, *caldo de cana*, prepared in large, complicated machines.

Brazil is also noted for its variety of alcoholic beverages. The south, especially the state of Rio Granada do Sul, is famous for its choice wines. Brazil also manufactures good, strong beer known as *cerveja*, which comes bottled, and a milder draft beer known as *chope*. The national beverage is *cachaca*. This is an extremely potent type of rum, made from sugar cane, and is usually an acquired taste. Easier to take is *caipirinha*, which is *cachaca* diluted with lemon juice, sugar, and ice.

Brazil's most famous drink, of course, is coffee. However, don't expect anything outstanding, since most of Brazil's choice coffee is exported. Only a few companies manufacture top quality coffee for local consumption. In most cases you will find acceptable coffee, but not much more than that. Coffee is a very popular beverage, and almost every restaurant, even the

BRAZIL

most modest, will bring you a *cafezinho*, a small cup of coffee, at the end of your meal — on the house.

Brazil's dairy industry is highly developed, and all supermarkets sell a variety of cheeses, yoghurts, and other dairy products. Restaurants, too, serve delicious ice cream, cakes, and confectionery.

As a general rule, the food in Brazil is excellent, and served in generous portions. The price of a meal at a modest restaurant is extremely reasonable. Even first class restaurants do not charge exorbitant prices. A meal at a fancy restaurant in Brazil costs no more than an average meal in Europe or the States. The cost of a meal in more popular establishments is correspondingly less.

Most restaurants serve local fare, as well as a selection of continental dishes, and portions are usually huge. Fixed-price meals are especially reasonable and one portion can easily satisfy two people.

The large cities have many restaurants, with a wide range of prices and cuisine, but the smaller towns have a more restricted, although perfectly adequate, selection. Really inexpensive restaurants are known as *lanchonetes*, and serve fixed-price meals, *comercial*, which usually consist of meat with rice and *feijao*.

Health

The Brazilian health services are far from satisfactory, with the exception of the major cities — Rio and Sao Paulo — which have modern hospitals and many clinics. In the villages and countryside there are only rudimentary health services, and you should refrain from availing yourself of them as much as possible. Most of the serious diseases that were endemic to Brazil a few decades ago have been eliminated in all but the most remote jungle regions. However, malaria is still common in the Amazon basin and the Pantanal; if you are planning to travel to remote areas, you must take anti-malaria pills with you. The immigration authorities at the border will usually ask to see a certificate of immunization against yellow fever, which you should obtain before leaving home.

The beaches in the northeast are infested with worms that penetrate under the skin *(bichos)*. In order to keep from getting infected, never walk barefoot on the beaches or in the adjoining villages. If you get infected despite these precautions, go to the local doctor, who will easily cure you of this problem.

A final word: never neglect even a slight wound. A scratch you

BRAZIL

could have safely ignored at home is likely to get infected here if neglected.

Currency
The Brazilian unit of currency is the cruzado, which is divided into 100 centavos. The cruzado is an unstable currency and its value against the dollar is always changing. Brazil has a flourishing black market, where the dollar rates are sometimes twenty percent higher (or more) than the official bank rate.

Currency exchanges *(casas-de-cambio)* are shops that trade in foreign currency. They are plentiful in all of Brazil's major cities, and most change foreign currency at the black market rate. This is the quickest and best legal method of purchasing cruzados. Private moneychangers may offer a slightly higher rate, but the extra time and hassle are not worthwhile.

Moneychangers will swoop down on you at the airport, especially in the offices of the taxi companies. They will invent 1001 fanciful reasons why you should change your dollars with them... In town the banks are closed, the situation is difficult, the dollar's falling, and so on and so forth. Don't panic: you will always be able to change your dollars at a better rate than the one they offer. I have yet to hear of a tourist who was unable to change dollars into local currency.

When leaving major cities for the hinterlands, be sure to take along sufficient local currency, since in the provinces changing money may prove somewhat complicated, and the rate will be lower than in the major cities.

Business Hours
Brazilian banks are open Mon.-Fri., 10am-4:30pm, and closed on weekends. Stores are open Mon.-Fri., 9am-6:30pm, and on Saturdays till 1pm. During the holiday season, in December, most stores stay open until 10pm or even later. In the large modern shopping centers, the stores are open till late at night.

Outside the major cities, the situation is somewhat different. Hardly anyone skips the famous siesta (the traditional afternoon break customary throughout the Latin world), and most offices are closed in the afternoon for two or three hours.

Domestic Transportation
Brazil has an excellent internal transportation network, both by air and overland. Air transport is highly developed due to the vast distances that have to be covered. The three major airlines, Varig-Cruzeiro, VASP and Trans-Brasil run frequent and

BRAZIL

reliable flights to all parts of the country. Service on internal flights is excellent, and even surpasses that in Europe and North America.

Varig offers tourists an Air Pass, permitting travel on 40 internal flights over three weeks for a mere $330, or on 4 internal flights over two weeks for $250. This arrangement is highly recommended, especially if one has little time and wants to visit several parts of the country. The Air Pass must be purchased outside Brazil, but routes can be decided upon once you are in the country. You can also alter the route as often as you please – as long as you don't visit the same place twice. During the summer, make advance reservations. This is not essential during the rest of the year.

Interurban bus service is also excellent. Brazil has dozens of competing bus companies, with modern, comfortable, air conditioned buses. The largest of these are Itapemirim and Penha. Remember, though, that the vast distances can make journeys somewhat tedious. (For example, the bus ride from Rio to Salvador takes more than 30 hours!)

The bus terminals *(rodoviarias)* are located on the outskirts of the towns. In the large cities, these terminals are modern and spacious, but in the villages they are often nothing more than small, miserable holes in the wall.

For interurban travel, buy tickets at least a day in advance. Always ask the exact price and count your change. Ticket clerks are not among the most honest of Brazilians.

Trains operate on a few main routes, but trips by rail are less comfortable and longer than bus trips. The Curitiba-Paranagua route is recommended, more for the scenery than for the journey itself. The train service between Rio and Sao Paulo is relatively efficient.

Driving in Brazil is no easy matter. Except for south and east Brazil, there are almost no roads, and those that do exist suffer from natural inclemencies and erosion. There are plenty of rent-a-car companies – in almost in every town – but the rates are extremely high. As for hitchhiking, the answer is an emphatic no. Before trying to save a nickel or two, remember the numerous cases of hitchhiking tourists who were robbed, assaulted, and even killed. In Brazil one has to be doubly careful. Since public transportation is efficient, comfortable and reasonable, there is absolutely no justification for putting one's life in danger.

Shopping and Souvenirs
Even confirmed tightwads will find it hard to resist the

BRAZIL

temptations of Brazil: the modern and luxurious shopping centers in the major cities offer the tourist a selection of high-quality goods at low prices, and the many markets to be found in every town are overflowing with attractive and interesting souvenirs and handicrafts (artesania) – each region with its own distinctive style.

Brazilian fashions excel in light, extremely colorful sportswear, which suit the tropical climate and the character of the people. Clothes are quite inexpensive, and you should certainly take the opportunity to renew your wardrobe with beautiful and comfortable summerwear. Leather goods, such as shoes and bags, are also inexpensive and of high quality.

Jewelry is a well-developed industry, thanks to the abundance of precious stones mined in Brazil. In the large cities there is a jewelry store on almost every street corner. These sell statuettes carved from various types of stone, all sorts of precious gems in various settings, and of course jewelry. All of these are extremely cheap in comparison to Western prices. Some of the largest jewelry chains in the world are Brazilian; the largest is H. Stern, which has a huge selection of jewelry of all kinds. Large stores too have a very wide selection – you will have no problem finding what you want – and they are less expensive than the jewelry stores.

As to souvenirs and handicrafts – each region in Brazil has its typical products: in the south, leather goods; in the southeast, particularly in Minas Gerais state, stone statuettes; in the northeast, beautiful, intricate lacework, wooden statuettes and wood carvings, and colorful hammocks. Pottery, typical Brazilian musical instruments, and shirts imprinted with local pictures or names can be found throughout Brazil. Indian souvenirs are found mainly in the regions where the Indians live, especially in the Amazon region, but they are ostentatious and reflect nothing of their lives. All types of handicrafts are sold throughout Brazil; for example, even in Rio you can find beautiful lacework. However, if you are intending to visit the north, wait until you get there – prices in the north are extremely low and you will be able to buy directly from the lacemaker herself.

In relevant sections you will find a detailed description of the various markets and villages and the typical handicrafts of each of them, as well as information about the large major shopping centers in the main towns. It would be hard to imagine that after visiting several of the places mentioned below you could leave Brazil empty-handed.

BRAZIL

Personal Security
As in the rest of South America, in Brazil you must take certain precautions to protect yourself and your equipment. In the large cities, robbery and theft are routine events. Police efforts to fight crime have not been very successful. The scope and seriousness of the problem are brought home by the permanent presence of at least two armed guards at every bank branch, and by the fact that late at night cars do not stop at red lights for fear of robbers who might attack stationary cars.

Anyone visiting Brazil should adopt the basic precautionary measures that the locals are already used to: don't wear jewelry; carry your camera in your bag and guard the latter jealously; don't carry large sums of money with you; any extra money or documents should be deposited in the hotel safe. Do not rely on hotels and their employees. In many cases valuables that were innocently left in a hotel room have been stolen. If you are staying in the less expensive hotels that do not have safes, always take your money, documents, and important papers with you safely hidden under your clothes. It is a good idea to sew an inner pocket in your pants to hide valuables. Don't carry all your money in cash — at least some should be in travelers' checks. Never put your wallet in the back pocket of your trousers — a sore temptation to pickpockets — but always in a front pocket. In the large cities, stick to visiting the central and more pleasant areas, and avoid visiting the slums, or *favelas*. A visit to such places with any valuables whatsoever is tantamount to tempting fate. Likewise refrain from hitchhiking — especially if you are a woman by yourself.

In spite of all the above cautions, there is no reason to panic. Simply adhere to the guidelines above, and keep alert. In this way you will be able to complete an enjoyable and successful tour of Brazil without mishap or unpleasantness. If you are nevertheless the victim of violence or crime, go to the nearest policeman or police station, and make sure to fill out the appropriate complaint form, in order to receive compensation from your insurance company.

Measurements, Electricity, and Time
Brazil uses the metric system. Clothes are sized according to European measurements. Electricity is usually 110V, but always check before using an electrical appliance, since many areas have gone over to 220V. Brazil's official time is set by the time in Brasilia, GMT-3, but due to the vast size of the country, in the west the clock is set an hour later.

BRAZIL

Suggested Itinerary for Brazil

Each chapter of the guide is based on a geographical route, and each new chapter continues from where the previous chapter ended. Thus there is a geographic continuity between the two main routes — the southern route and the northern route. Of course, you can compile your own itinerary according to personal preferences within different regions, or you can combine a selection of sites from different chapters.

Southern route — Rio de Janeiro, Sao Paulo, Southern Brazil, Foz do Iguacu.

Northern route — Minas Gerais, north to Salvador, north-eastern Brazil, Amazon Basin and south to the Midwest. This tour ends in the new capital of Brasilia.

For those who do not wish to explore the depths of the Amazon Jungle (which is particularly difficult to do overland), we suggest an alternative route from Rio de Janeiro westwards: Minas Gerais, Brasilia, Pantanal.

We will become acquainted with north-eastern Brazil through a tour of the coast from southern Salvador northwards to Sao Luis.

The tour of the Amazon Basin goes from Belem to Manaus, and there you can choose one of three possible directions to take: north to Boa Vista and on to Venezuela; west to Benjamin Constant, Leticia and on to Colombia or Peru; south to Porto Velho. It's a short way from Porto Velho to Bolivia or you can go towards the Midwest, to Cuiaba. We have detailed all these possibilities, but the main route along which we will continue our tour is that which goes to Porto Velho and to the Midwest.

BRAZIL

Rio de Janeiro

Many people consider Rio to be one of the most beautiful cities on earth. Its southern neighborhoods cluster between steep, verdant cliffs hundreds of meters high and broad sandy beaches. As if nature had not provided enough delights, the city's residents have added all kinds of attractions of their own. During the day shopping centers are bustling, and the wonderful beaches are packed, and at night the restaurants, clubs and discotheques overflow. The locals are nicknamed "*Carioca*", and they enjoy a reputation for being both amiable and good-looking, with their tanned complexions and bright and colorful dress.

The French were the first to settle here in 1555. During the subsequent 150 years or so, the city experienced many upheavals and reversals as it passed from French to Portuguese rule. Rio came under Portuguese control in the early 18th century, and by the middle of that century it had become the seat of the Portuguese Governor. It was declared capital of the Republic of Brazil in 1834, and retained this title until the establishment of Brasilia in 1960. Today the city has a population of over five million, and is constantly developing and growing. The presence of rich, elegant and exclusive neighborhoods alongside impoverished *favelas* (shantytowns) has given rise to great social tensions and Rio has a high rate of crime and violence.

Rio's summers are uncomfortably hot and humid, with temperatures up to 40°C (104°F) and frequent showers. Winter, from May to October, is more temperate, with warm weather and usually clear skies. Average maximum temperature in these months is 25°C (75°F).

How to get there
By air: Rio has two busy airports. The first is the **Aeroporto Internacional do Galeao** at Ilha do Governador, about half an hour out of town. The terminal has three sections: A for domestic flights, and B and C for international flights. It is an excellent, modern airport with heavy traffic every day from all over the world. Pan Am and Varig fly daily to New York, Los Angeles and Miami. Many European airlines also connect Rio to all major European cities, and there are weekly Varig and SAA flights to South Africa. There are also daily flights to all South American capitals. At the airport there are many radio-taxis that can convey you quickly and comfortably to any destination in town

BRAZIL

View from Corcovado – Botafogo and Sugarloaf Mountain

for fixed fares. Comfortable buses, with much lower fares, leave every few minutes for different parts of Rio.

The other airport is **Santos Dumont**, located downtown. This small airfield, serving only the shuttle service between Rio and

*B*RAZIL

Sao Paulo, is connected to the rest of Rio by many taxis, and regular and special buses.

By land: The new bus terminal, *Rodoviaria Novo Rio* in the Sao Cristovao neighborhood, is served by buses from all over Brazil

BRAZIL

and from Buenos Aires (Argentina), Montevideo (Uruguay), Asuncion (Paraguay), and Santiago (Chile). It's always busy and, despite its size, very crowded. There are many taxis in the vicinity, and many city bus lines start here too.

Tourist services

Two municipal tourist bureaus provide information for visitors to Rio. One is Embratur, the Brazilian Tourist Bureau at Rua Mariz Barros 13, close to Praca de Bandeira in northern Rio (Tel. 273-2212, open Mon.-Fri. 9am-6pm). The other bureau is Riotur, the Rio de Janeiro Tourist Bureau at Rua Assemblia 10 (Tel. 297-7117). Riotur has another office downtown, at Rua Sao Jose 90 (Tel. 232-4320), and provides 24-hour telephone service in English, French, and Spanish (Tel. 580-8000). There are also information booths at various locations around town such as the Sugarloaf cablecar, the Novo Rio bus terminal, and the International Airport.

Touring Club do Brasil is on Avenida General Serviano in Botafogo. Here you can find up-to-date information about Brazil in general and Rio in particular.

Most airline offices in Rio are concentrated around Avenida Rio Branco downtown. Varig, Brazil's national airline, has 9 offices throughout the city.

There are many car rental companies in Rio so you should have no problem finding a suitable car. The largest and most reliable international companies are Avis and Hertz, and the best Brazilian companies are Localiza and Nobre. All have branch offices at the International Airport. In town, their offices are on Avenida Princesa Isabel in Copacabana. The rates are much higher than in the United States or Europe, and bear in mind that gas stations are closed on weekends.

Where to stay

Rio has an abundance of hotels of all kinds, from the most superb and expensive to the very low-priced for young travelers. Downtown is not recommended, either for businessmen in a hurry or for youngsters wishing to economize. Although the area is crowded and bustling by day, it is deserted and lonely by night. Hotels here are cheap for good reason: the district is unpleasant at night and is far from the night-spots in the south of town. There are some very inexpensive hotels with basic facilities in the Catete Quarter, which is a cut above downtown.

Flamengo and Botafogo: For those who need to be primarily in the downtown area, *Hotel Gloria* will prove very convenient. Located at Praia do Russel 632 in the Gloria Quarter, it is close to the city center and maintains a high standard (Tel. 205-7272).

BRAZIL

Its neighbor, *Hotel Novo Mundo*, provides basic but good facilities. It is much cheaper, with an appropriate drop in standard, and is patronized by the young. Inexpensive hotels are found in the Catete Quarter in Flamengo. Most of these are not very good, and be sure not to leave your belongings in the room during the day. However, we can recommend two inexpensive places which are both clean and safe: *Vitoria*, on Rua do Catete, and *Monterrey* at Bernades 39.

Copacabana: Most tourists prefer to stay in this area rather than in any other part of Rio because of its excellent beach and its proximity to downtown and the Ipanema and Leblon neighborhoods, where most of the nightlife takes place. Some of the best and most expensive hotels in Rio are along the glorious Copacabana promenade. There are also some less expensive hotels here. The *Rio Palace* at Avenida Atlantica 4240 (Tel. 521-3232), at the southern end of the promenade, opened in 1979 and has since come to be considered the best hotel in town. It overlooks Copacabana and Ipanema, and has two very good restaurants, two swimming pools, an excellent night-club, a shopping center, and other first-class facilities. At the northern end of the beach, known as the *Leme*, is another excellent hotel: the *Meridien*, at Avenida Atlantica 1020 (Tel. 275-9922). It offers superb facilities, a swimming pool, sauna, cinema, and one of Rio's best French restaurants on the 37th floor. Two other luxury hotels on the same boulevard are *Copacabana Palace* at No. 1072 (Tel. 257-1818) and the *Othon Palace* at No. 3264 (Tel. 255-8812). The moderately priced *Debret* at Rua Goncalves 5 (Tel. 521-3332) overlooks the beach and has very good facilities. The *Astoria* is moderately priced but the facilities offered do not justify the price.

Ipanema and Leblon: The best hotel in the area is the excellent *Caesar Park* at Avenida Vieiria Souto 460 (Tel. 287-3122), on the boulevard parallel to the Ipanema beach. Another excellent hotel is the *Everest Rio* at Rua Prudente de Morais 1117 (Tel. 287-8282). It is relatively low-priced compared with the other luxury hotels in its class. The *Carlton* at Rua Joao Lire 68 in Leblon (Tel. 259-1932) is noteworthy for its pleasant, tranquil atmosphere. It is an intermediate-class hotel, close to the beach. The *San Marco*, at Rua Visconde Piraja 524 in Ipanema, is a cheap hotel near the beach, patronized mainly by the younger crowd looking for a nice, comfortable place to stay.

The *Rio Sheraton* rests on the mountainous slopes between Leblon and Sao Conrado at Avenida Niemeyer 121 (Tel.274-1122). Although it is far away from the "in" places, the hotel offers a variety of entertainment possibilities: sports center, private beach, swimming pool, tennis courts, discotheque, and even a small zoo.

BRAZIL

Sao Conrado: Despite its distance from the center of things, two large, luxurious hotels have been built here. The *Inter-Continental*, at Avenida Prefeito Mendes de Morais 222 (Tel. 322-2200) is first class, with three swimming pools, two bars, a good restaurant, discotheque, sports club, and tennis courts. The *Nacional Rio* at Avenida Niemeyer 769 (Tel. 287-5976) is outstanding in its class and has the largest convention center in Rio.

What to eat, where and when

Rio has many good restaurants and, as an international metropolis, provides excellent examples of cuisine from all over the world. In dollar prices, even the most luxurious restaurants here are not expensive. Most of the fancy restaurants are in Ipanema and Leblon, but those wishing to eat cheaply will find a lot of good, inexpensive *lanchonetes* mainly in Catete, Botafogo, and downtown. Fast-food fans will find dozens of McDonalds all over town.

Downtown: Many restaurants downtown serve low-cost business meals, and there are many fast-food places where office workers and business people eat during the day. *Cafe de Teatro* is one of the nicest restaurants in the area. It serves weekday lunches only, and the prices are high, but the food is good and the location – the municipal theater – is interesting. *La Tour*, at Rua Santa Luzia 651 on the 34th floor of a high-rise building, is a revolving restaurant commanding spectacular views. The food, however, is nothing special.

Mosteiro, close to Maua Square, serves very good continental food at lunchtime on weekdays. *Cosmopolita*, on Rua Mosquiera 4, close to Paseio Publico, looks very modest but has an excellent Portuguese menu.

Flamengo and Botafogo: As opposed to downtown, these quarters have a wide range of quality restaurants, some outstanding. Those on limited budgets can choose from one of the many low-cost eateries up and down Rua Catete, where one can eat well at little cost.

There are two excellent and expensive restaurants in Botafogo. One is the French *Clube Gourmet* at Rua General Polidoro 186, considered to be one of the best in Rio. The second is *Maxim's de Paris*, on the 44th floor of the Rio Sul building. The view is breathtaking. Also worth mentioning is *Casa de Suica* at Rua Candido Mendes 157 in the Gloria Quarter, with good Swiss food at moderate prices.

Copacabana: There is a range of restaurants here in every price range and a wide culinary range. Dozens of snack-bars are found alongside some of the best restaurants in town. The *Saint*

BRAZIL

Honore, on the 37th floor of the *Meridien*, is without doubt one of these – luxurious surroundings, an excellent French menu, and faultless service. The *Enotria* at Rua Constante Ramos 115, serves Rio's best Italian food at reasonable prices. At the *Trocadero Hotel*, Avenida Atlantica 2064, is the *Moenda* restaurant which serves a selection of Brazilian dishes, especially those of Bahia and the north. If you do not plan to continue to the north, try these exotic foods here.

This is not the city for superb Chinese food, but Copacabana has some good Oriental restaurants. *China Town* at Avenida Copacabana 435 is the best, and its prices are reasonable.

The *Shirley*, Rua Gustavo Sampanio 610, deserves special mention. Although it doesn't look very promising from outside, the food is excellent and the prices are very reasonable. The menu consists of seafood and very good Spanish cuisine, and the service is friendly. *Top-Set* is a good eatery with large, satisfying and tasty portions at low prices.

Ipanema and Leblon: Deluxe prestige restaurants abound in these neighborhoods, but those on tight budgets would do well to eat elsewhere. *Antiquarius*, Rua Aristedes Espinola 19 in Leblon, is one of the most popular restaurants in Rio. Enjoy its excellent continental cuisine and impressive decor. *Claude Troisgros* is a fine French restaurant in Lagoa, Rua Custodio Serrao 62. This restaurant, which opened a few years ago, has already claimed its place as one of the top restaurants in Rio because of its superb French cuisine. *Grottamare* is an excellent, moderately priced Italian restaurant at Rua Carneiro Gomez 132, in Ipanema. For good, reasonably priced continental food, try the *Gardenia* in the Jardim Botanico Quarter, at Rua Visconde de Carandai 9. The best Oriental restaurant in town is *Le Viet-nam*, Avenida Afranio de Melo Franco 131 in Leblon. *Entrecote* serves good meat dishes at low prices. For a refreshing change, try the Scandinavian *Helsingor* which serves delicious light meals and salads. On Sunday it has a smorgasbord with a rich variety of offerings.

Getting around town

Taxis are always available in Rio, and fares are very low. Regular taxis have two tariffs: one for regular trips, and another for service after midnight, on Sundays, or to the airport. Make sure the meter does not display Tariff 2 when making a regular trip. The sum shown on the meter is not the price you pay; it has to be multiplied according to the table of fares which the driver has. Be sure to check the price!

Another type of taxi is the radio-taxi – a large, air-conditioned vehicle ordered by telephone. The largest radio-taxi companies

BRAZIL

are Coopertramo (Tel. 260-2022), Cootramo (Tel. 270-1442), and Transcoopass (Tel. 270-4888).

Buses are fast, regular, and frequent, and they reach every corner of the city. Each bus is numbered and carries route details. Drivers are polite and always willing to give information. They usually stop for pedestrians who wave them down in between stops. Many routes start from the inter-city bus terminal.

Rio also has a new **subway** (metro) which, unlike those of many other cities, is clean and pleasant. There are only two lines, linking Botafogo with downtown and northern Rio. The metro runs 6am-11pm every day except Sunday, and is quick, comfortable and safe.

What to see

Before setting off to explore Rio's beaches and neighborhoods, visit two outstandingly beautiful observation points – perhaps the most famous tourist spots in Rio and indeed in all Brazil: the Corcovado and Sugarloaf Mountain. Each provides a spectacular view of the city. From these points it is clear why Rio is considered the world's most beautiful city.

Corcovado

This is certainly the place that springs to mind when Rio de Janeiro is mentioned. Corcovado is the famous mount whose summit, 709 m above sea level, bears a giant statue of Jesus that is clearly visible from almost any point in the city. (Many people mistakenly apply the name Corcovado to the statue, instead of the hill.) The statue is 30 m tall and is made of 1450 tons of concrete and granite, with an observation deck at its base. At night the statue is spotlit and stands out dramatically against the black sky. No visit to Rio would be complete without a visit to Corcovado.

The left hand of the statue points in the direction of the northern city, the commercial and business area. Notice in the distance the International Airport, the immense Rio-Niteroi bridge, the Maracana Stadium, the Santos Dumont Airport, and the wide avenues and skyscrapers of downtown. Opposite stands proud Sugarloaf Mountain. Between Sugarloaf and downtown is the Flamengo neighborhood, and between Sugarloaf and Corcovado is Botafogo. Copacabana is on the right.

The statue's right hand points in the direction of Ipanema and Leblon, and, at the foot of Corcovado, one can see the Botanical Gardens, the Jockey Club, and the lake – Lagoa Rodrigo de Freitas.

There are two ways of getting to Corcovado: by road and train.

BRAZIL

Statue of Jesus on the summit of Corcovado

The train station is at Rua Cosme Velho 513, and there are trains every half-hour between 8am and 10pm. They cover the 3.5 km distance in about 20 minutes, traveling through a beautiful landscape of thick, luxuriant foliage. The lower station is reached by Bus 583 from Copacabana. The road also winds up the mountain through wonderful scenery. There is a parking lot close to the summit and nearby there are cafes and souvenir shops.

The best time to visit Corcovado is toward evening, when the sun is setting behind you and the fantastic view is seen against the backdrop of spreading darkness and city lights.

Pao de Acuar – Sugarloaf Mountain
After the spectacular view from the Corcovado, no one will want to miss a visit to Sugarloaf Mountain, which gives a different perspective of the city. Sugarloaf is an immense granite slab at the entrance of the Guanabara Bay. Its walls rise steeply to a height of 396 m above sea level, from which the whole city can be observed. At twilight, crowds of amateur and professional photographers come here to catch the fabulous sunsets.

A cablecar starts out from Praca General Tubirco at the Vermelho beach, with departures every thirty minutes. Halfway up is Morro da Urca, where there is an entertainment center with a discotheque and samba performances (see "Nightlife").

BRAZIL

View from Sugarloaf Mountain – Copacabana neighborhood and beach

Do not choose a cloudy day for either of these observation points, since both are hidden in clouds.

Having seen Rio and its beauty from the heights, let us study it from close up.

The Northern City
This is a dreary, unpleasant concentration of industrial and poor neighborhoods, but there are two sites here that should not be missed: Quinta Boa Vista and Estadio Maracana.

Quinta Boa Vista (Boa Vista Palace) houses the **Museu Nacional**, Rio's most important and interesting museum. The impressive palace was built in 1803 by a wealthy Portuguese gentleman who presented it as a gift to his King in 1808. It was a residence of the Brazilian monarchs until the country became a republic in 1889. A few years later in 1892, it was turned into a National Museum. On display is a wealth of exhibits: archeology, botany, zoology, ethnology, and more. Most interesting of all are the South American archeology halls, especially that devoted to Brazil, and the exhibits of Indian ethnology and Brazilian folklore. In the entrance hall stands the largest meteorite ever found in the southern hemisphere, discovered in Bahia in 1888. (Open Tues.-Sun., 10am-5pm.) The Boa Vista Palace is in the Sao Cristovao neighborhood. Take Bus 472 or 474 from Copacabana, or 262 from downtown.

Close to the National Museum is the **Zoo**, and across from its

BRAZIL

entrance is an interesting **Zoological Museum** with a selection of wildlife from the different regions of Brazil, particularly from the Amazon and the Pantanal. (Open Tues.-Sat., noon-5pm.)

Not far from the National Museum, in Campo de Sao Cristovao, the **Feira do Nordeste** (market of northeastern Brazil) takes place every Sunday. Here the people of northern Brazil sell their various wares at low prices. It's hot and dirty, but fascinating.

Another interesting place in this area is the **Estadio Maracana** (Maracana Stadium) known locally as Mario Filho. Built for the 1950 World Cup Finals in Rio, it is the world's biggest stadium with seating for 200,000. It is also very well planned, so that even the last rows are not too far from the playing field. (Open to visitors Mon.-Fri., 9am-5pm.) Climb to the dignitaries' section and visit the modest sports museum. Nearby is another stadium, the **Maracanazinho** or "Little Maracana", which can seat 20,000 spectators, it accommodates basketball, volleyball, and other entertainment events.

Centro

This is Rio's large, important business and commercial hub. During the day it bustles with workers and business people, but it empties out after working hours. Once that happens, it is best not to wander about its dark and lonely streets.

The first landmark in the Centro is to the right of the freeway leading in from the south. On the northern edge of Flamengo Park is a monument to the fallen of World War II (Brazil fought alongside the Allies in the Italian campaign, in which 467 soldiers lost their lives). Close to the memorial is a small museum which commemorates the Brazilian soldiers' contribution to the war effort.

A little past the monument is the **Museu de Arte Moderna** (MAM), (Open Tues.-Sun., 1-5:30pm). This was one of the most important museums in Brazil until 1978, when a disastrous fire destroyed almost all of its very fine collection. The museum has not succeeded in rehabilitating itself, and its value as an artistic institution has declined.

Not far from the Museu de Arte Moderna, on Praca Marchal Ancora, is the **Museu Historico Nacional**. The building is one of the oldest in Rio, erected in the early 17th century as the Sao Diego Fortress. The museum was established in 1922, as part of the celebrations for 100 years of Brazilian independence. Brazil's most important historical museum, it presents the country's history since its discovery. (Open Tues.-Fri., 9am-6pm, Sat.-Sun. 2-6pm, closed Mon.)

Not far from the Museum is **Praca Quince de Novembro**, a site where a number of historical events took place. Here King Dom

BRAZIL

RIO DE JANEIRO – CENTRO

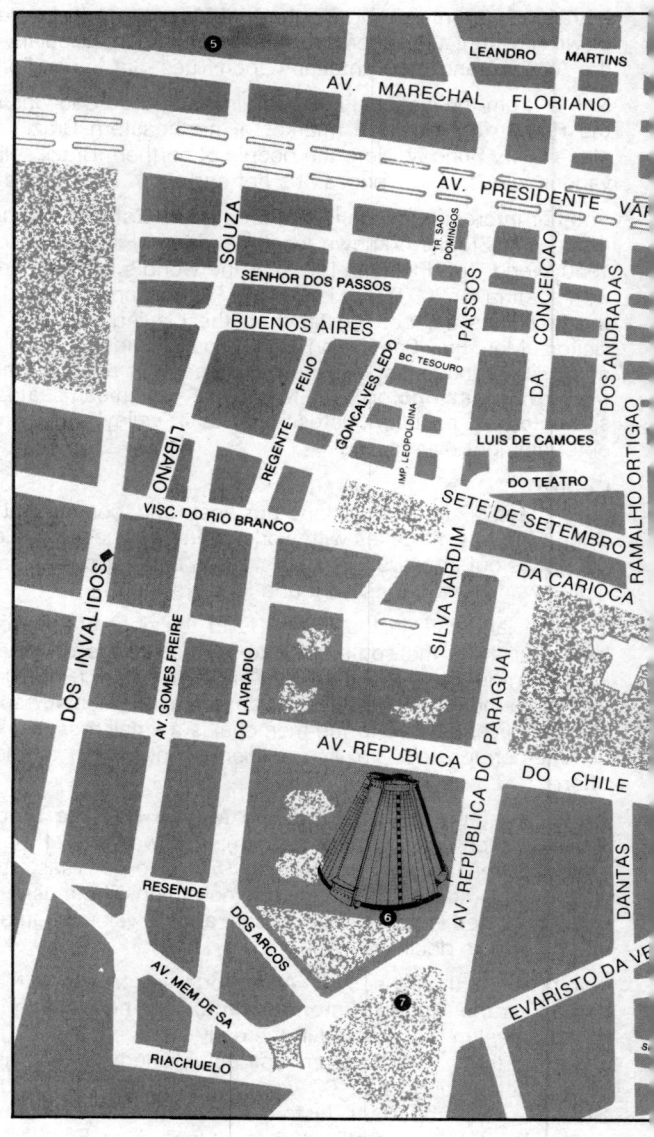

Index
1. Museu Historico Nacional
2. Praca Quince de Novembro
3. Catedral Metropolitana
4. Igreja de Candelaria
5. Museu Itamarati

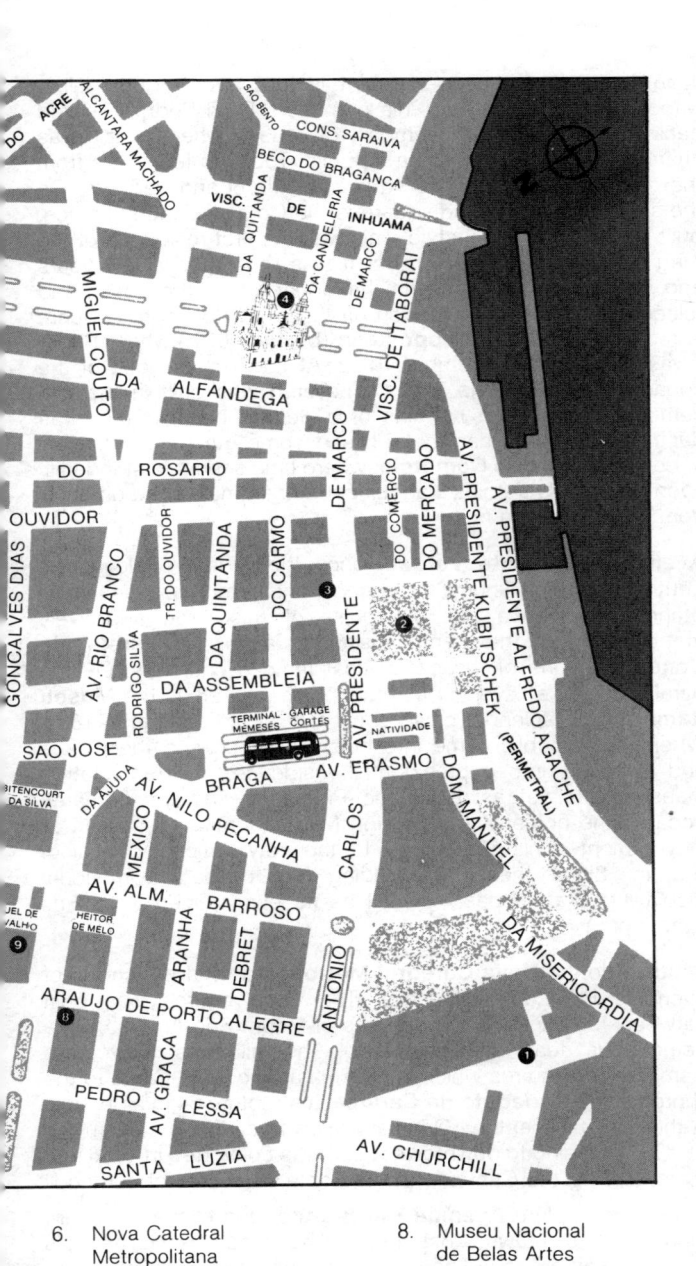

BRAZIL

6. Nova Catedral Metropolitana
7. Aqueduto da Carioca
8. Museu Nacional de Belas Artes
9. Teatro Municipal

BRAZIL

Joao VI of Portugal stepped ashore in 1808 after Portugal fell to Napoleon. From here, too, his grandson, Dom Pedro II, sailed back to Europe on November 15, 1891, when Brazil was changed from an empire to a republic. Today, a ferry sails from the dock at the end of the square to Niteroi and Paqueta. On the southern edge of the square is the Commissioners' Palace, built in 1743 in colonial style. This was the first residence of the King of Portugal in Brazil. After it was renovated a few years ago, the building became the headquarters of the postal and telegraph services. The church on the west side of the square is the old **Catedral Metropolitana** (built in 1671), where Pedro I was crowned in December, 1822. At the northern end of the square is the **Arco de Teles**. The arch was built in the l8th century. It is all that remains of a Senate building that was destroyed by fire. Pass through and come out on a little side street, **Travessa do Comercio**, where time seems to stand still. Even today, it is a quiet, tranquil pedestrian mall, quite different from the rest of the area.

Avenida Presidente Vargas, once the widest boulevard in South America, still hums with people and commercial activities. Standing here, we feel the pulse of this large and lively metropolis. On the central island stands the **Igreja de Candelaria**, one of the city's most famous churches. On the parallel street, at Avenida Marechal Floriano 196, is the **Museu Itamarati** – a splendid palace built by Baron Itamarati in 1852. When the Republic came into being, it purchased the palace and turned it into a presidential residence. In 1897 another mansion was set aside for the President, and the Itamarati became the home of the Foreign Ministry until 1970, when all Government ministries moved to the new national capital of Brasilia. Since then, the building has housed a museum displaying Brazil's past as well as its own. (Open Tues.-Fri., 11am-5pm.)

Continue to the **Nova Catedral Metropolitana** at the corner of Avenidas Paraguai and Chile. The huge church was built between 1964 and 1976 at the site of Mount Sao Antonio. By a tremendous feat of engineering, the hill was moved to Flamengo, to an area which is now Flamengo Park. Close to the church is the **Aqueduto da Carioca**, a structure 64 m high, built in the mid-18th century. Originally used to carry water from the Rio Cosme Velho to downtown Rio, it was converted in 1986 into a road linking the Centro with the Santa Terese neighborhood.

Finally, we explore **Avenida Rio Branco**, one of the important thoroughfares in town. Most of the airline offices, as well as Rio's black market, are found here. In 1904, hundreds of houses were destroyed in order to built the broad, busy boulevard, and until a few years ago, when a special route was built for the purpose, the Samba parade thundered down this artery, too. At Rio Branco 199 is the **Museu Nacional de Belas Artes** (Museum of Fine Arts). Founded in 1837 it houses one of the best and most important collections of Brazilian art. (Open Tues.-Fri. 12:30-6:30pm, and Sat., Sun., and holidays 3-6pm.)

Near the museum stands the magnificent **Teatro Municipal**, built in 1905 on the model of the Paris Opera, it is the venue of symphony concerts, ballet and opera.

Flamengo and Botafogo

Until the 1940s, Flamengo and Botafogo (the southern extension of Flamengo) were considered the most prestigious neighborhoods of Rio. Today, Copacabana has somewhat eclipsed them, and they have become rather drab residential districts. Flamengo regained some of its prestige, through the artificial expansion of the Flamengo beach. Along the wide beach is a pleasant green park which is used by locals for sports. The park extends from the Santos Dumont airport in the north to Botafogo in the south. In 1960, over a million cubic meters of earth were moved here from Mount Sao Antonio to create this stretch of land. Do not walk around here at night, as it is dark and dangerous.

North of the park are the **Museum of Modern Art** and the **World War II Memorial**, which are included in the description of downtown because of their proximity to other sites there.

The beaches of Flamengo and Botafogo are among the least attractive in Rio. The bay water is polluted, and most of the people who use the facility are from the city's poor northern neighborhoods. All the area can offer is a few museums, the most interesting of which is the **Museu da Republica**, at Rua Do Catete 179 in Flamengo. It is housed in the Palacio do Catete, built in 1866 in neoclassical style for use as a residence by the Brazilian aristocracy. It was purchased in 1896 by the Republic for the President. The museum exhibits the history of Brazil from the founding of the Republic to 1960, when the Presidential residence moved to the new capital, Brasilia. (Open Tues.-Fri. 9am-6pm, Sat.-Sun. 2-6pm.)

The **Museu do Indio** is at Rua Das Palmeiras 55 in Botafogo. April 19 is Indians Day in Brazil, and the museum opened on that date in 1953. It displays artifacts of Indian tribes from Brazil's various areas, including the culture and folklore that developed in each region. It's an interesting museum, although the explanations are only given in Portuguese. (Open Mon.-Fri. 10am-5pm, Sun. 1-5pm.)

BRAZIL

Zona Sul
Zona Sul, the south of Rio, is a prestigious residential area interspersed with many commercial centers. In the 1940s and 1950s, **Copacabana** was the most exclusive area of the city, but today even the charms of the famous 4 km Copacabana Beach have palled in the eyes of the *Carioca*, who now prefer new seashore haunts.

The northern neighborhood of this part of town, from Morro do Leme to Avenida Princesa Isabel, is called Leme. Along Avenida Atlantica, parallel to the beach, are many classy hotels, homes and places of entertainment in high-rises which form a kind of wall against the sea. This lovely beach is not natural; it was transformed in part by human hand into the attractive, broad stretch of sand we see today.

Ipanema and **Leblon** are presently the most exclusive residential areas of the city, with magnificent apartment houses, luxurious shops, and boutiques lining the main boulevard. Superb restaurants and bars are located on the side streets.

On Sundays, the **Hippie Fair** is held at Praca General Osorio in Ipanema. This is a delightful market where objets d'art, musical instruments, leather goods, and much more are on sale. Prices are high, and the bargaining is tough. Some of these typical offerings are available elsewhere in Brazil at much lower prices. Nevertheless, the market is worth a visit, if only to enjoy the pleasant atmosphere and inspect the handicrafts.

Avenida Visconde de Piraja is the main shopping center of Ipanema. Here, at the corner of Garcia d'Avila, is the H. Stern building, headquarters of the H. Stern jewelry chain, one of the world's largest. Brazil's ample natural resources include gems of many kinds, and the Stern company controls over 60 percent of this trade. It is a fascinating place to visit. Watch the stones being polished, and inspect the company's best wares in its elegant showroom.

The beaches of Ipanema and Leblon are actually one stretch of very fine beach about 2 km long and only slightly narrower than the Copacabana beach. This is where Rio's upper classes and, of course, its beauties come to bathe. The boulevard along the beach is lined with homes and a few prestigious hotels. Unlike Copacabana, most hotels and all the nightspots here are on the side streets.

The Jardim de Ala canal separates Ipanema from Leblon and leads from the sea to Lagoa Rodrigo de Freitas, called **Lagoa** (Lake) for short. The lake covers 4500 sq/m is situated at the foot of soaring cliffs covered with tropical foliage. West of Lagoa is the **Joquei Club Brasiliero**, the Jockey Club, which has a

BRAZIL

particularly fine race-track (see "Sports"). Beyond it is the **Jardim Botanico**, with a fantastic collection of plants and trees from all over the world. One can spend hours strolling through the gardens and enjoying their delights. (Open daily, 7am-5pm.)

Sao Conrado: Leblon is separated from Sao Conrado on the west by a mountainous ridge. This ridge is crossed by two roads; one along the coast and the other heading through a tunnel. The Sao Conrado quarter is another wealthy and prestigious residential area, with three excellent hotels. The beach here is known as Praia do Pepino – Cucumber Beach.

Floresta da Tijuca

This forest is the largest park in Rio, covering more than 120 sq/km in the Corcovado area and the hills to its west. It is an area of luxuriant jungle foliage, steep granite cliffs, rivers, and waterfalls. The hills range in height from 100 to 1020 m above sea level, giving the park a cooler and more pleasant climate than that of the city itself.

There are some wonderful observation points in the park, the best of which is Alto da Boa Vista. There are many ways to reach this point; the nicest is the ascent from the Botanical Gardens. This route passes another two attractions: **Vista Chinesa**, and **Mesa do Imperador**. They are so called because of unsuccessful attempts by Chinese to grow tea here in the days of Dom Pedro II. Walk along the park's paths and enjoy the tranquil atmosphere. The park is open 7am-7pm. There are two restaurants within the park. Don't stay after dark.

Nightlife

In planning your daily schedule, bear in mind that entertainment does not end at sunset. Rio offers a varied and rich assortment of activities, from all kinds of light amusement to opera and chamber music.

Theater, Concerts, Opera: Despite the prevailing impression that Rio's night life is nothing but nightclubbing and discos, the city has no shortage of more classical forms of entertainment. Ballet fans will find a very good dance company that performs at the luxurious Teatro Municipal downtown. This venue is also used by the city opera, an excellent company which hosts international guest singers, from time to time. Symphony concerts take place at the Teatro, while chamber concerts and recitals are held in the smaller Sala Cecilia on Largo da Lapa, also in the center of town. Local theater, though of great variety, is not a good idea for those who do not understand Portuguese.

Cinema: Films are shown in their original languages with

RIO DE JANEIRO – ZONA SUL

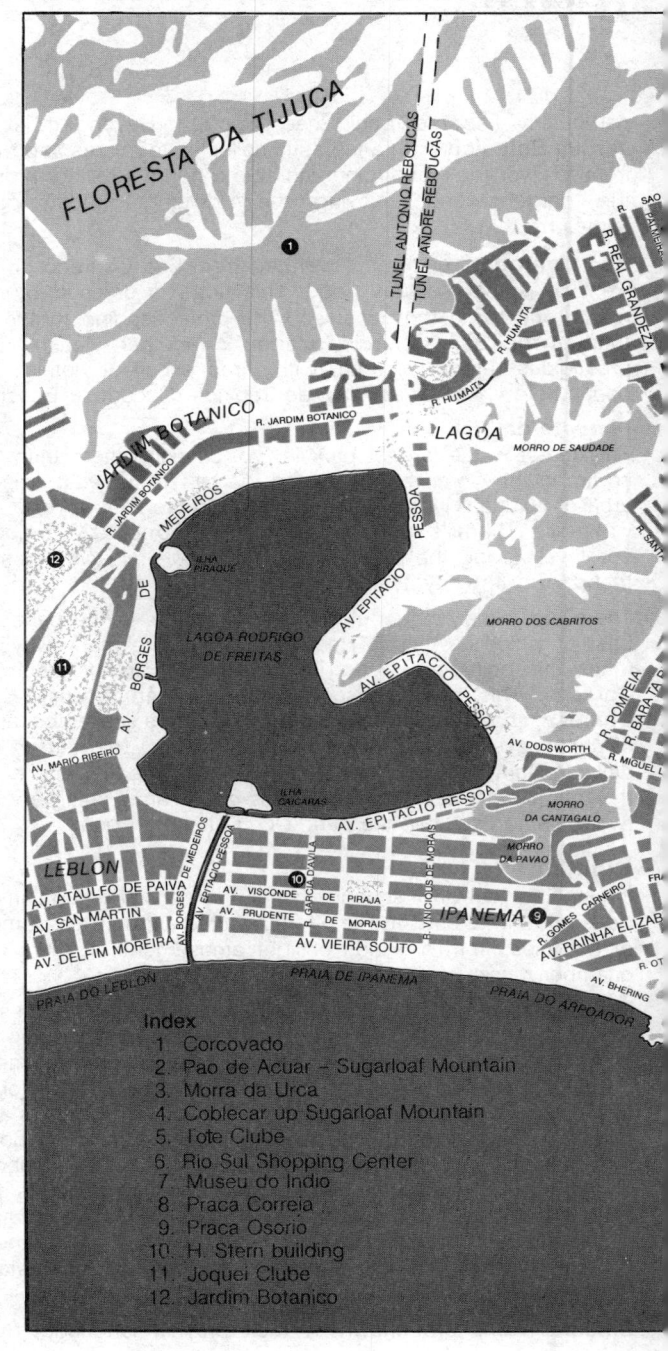

Index
1. Corcovado
2. Pao de Acuar – Sugarloaf Mountain
3. Morra da Urca
4. Coblecar up Sugarloaf Mountain
5. Iote Clube
6. Rio Sul Shopping Center
7. Museu do Indio
8. Praca Correia
9. Praca Osorio
10. H. Stern building
11. Joquei Clube
12. Jardim Botanico

Map

BOTAFOGO BAY

AV. NAÇÕES UNIDOS
AV. LUIS ALVES
AV. PORTUGAL
AV. PASTEUR
AV. VENCESLAU BRAZ
PRINCESA ISABEL
LADEIRO DO LEME
RIBEIRO
LEME
R. GUSTAVO SAMPAIO
R. TONELEROS
R. BARATA
AV. N. S. DE COPACABANA
AV. ATLANTICA
PRAIA DO LEME

PRAIA VERMELHA
MORRO DA BABILONIA
MORRO DO URUBU
MORRO DO LEME

PRAIA DE COPACABANA

ATLANTIC OCEAN

N

Scale
1:40,000

0   400   800   1200 M.

231

BRAZIL

Portuguese subtitles, and popular European and American movies reach Rio shortly after their original release. Movie theaters proliferate in all parts of Rio, and most are very satisfactory. Tickets cannot be bought in advance, and on weekends there are long lines at box offices.

Samba: This is the kind of entertainment for which most tourists really come to Rio. The excellent *Scala Rio* nightclub at Avenida Afranio de Melo Franco 296 in Leblon – one of the largest clubs in town – stages samba shows. Enjoy the mulatto dancers in their glittering carnival costumes. Another major samba performance is that of the group Oba-Oba. These mulatto dancers appear at Rua Humaita 110 in Botafogo.

If you have never seen a samba school parade during a carnival, you can get some sense of the atmosphere in a weekly performance by the small group from Beija Flor. This is one of Brazil's best samba schools, and is famous for its colorful parades. The performance takes place at the Morro da Urca, halfway up Sugarloaf Mountain. The performance against the backdrop of the spectacular view is an experience not to be missed.

Nightclubs: Rio has a number of excellent clubs, although the very best are for members only and are very expensive. The *Hippopotamus* in Ipanema, on Praca Nossa Senhora da Paz, is a three-story building with an excellent discotheque, a bar, and a very good restaurant.

Castel in the Rio Palace Hotel is another excellent and exclusive nightclub. The *Biblos Bar* in Lagua, Avenida Epitacio Pessoa 1484, is a small, crowded place frequented mainly by singles. Samba shows are held here during the week, and there is dancing on weekends.

One of the most popular discotheques is *Help*, at Avenida Atlantica 3432 in Copacabana. This is an enormous club with a reasonable entrance fee that includes the first drink. The entrance fee is lower on weekends. Brazililan and Western music is played, and the crowd is made up of singles and tourists. On weekends another good discotheque, *Noites Cariocas*, opens its doors at Morro da Urca. Its clientele is mostly young, and the music is mostly Brazilian.

Bars: *Cariocas* love to sit in bars, some of which have modest musical shows. Bars proliferate throughout the city, especially in Ipanema, Leblon and Barra.

Performances: The best Brazilian musicians often perform in Rio; check the local press for details about forthcoming attractions. These shows are usually very enjoyable experiences: great music, fantastic atmosphere. One of the

BRAZIL

major performance spots is the *Canecao*, opposite the Rio Sul shopping center. This is a prestige location with prices to match, and the atmosphere is formal and restrained. Things are more lively and open at the *Circo Voador* on Larga da Lapa, downtown.

Sports

Obviously, the most popular sport in Rio, as in all Brazil, is **soccer**. Every Sunday tens of thousands of fans stream to the Maracana stadium for the big game. Soccer fans and others should not pass this up, whether for the game itself or for the atmosphere generated by the crowd. This is particularly true of city derby matches or contests between the best league teams, when the standard of football and the spectator fervor are high.

Another "must" sport while visiting Rio is ocean bathing (see "Beaches" below for details). Rio offers a variety of activities for the sports-minded. Exercise is almost an obsession with the *Carioca*, for whom physical fitness and beauty are extremely important. The best of the many sports clubs are at the *Sheraton* and the *Inter-Continental* hotels.

There are horse races at the Jockey Club four times a week throughout the year. The Grand Prix is held on the first weekend in August. Horses from all over South America take part, urged on by thousands of spectators.

Golf fans will find two clubs in town. Both are private, but they welcome visitors on weekdays: the Gavea Club in Sao Conrado, opposite the *Inter-Continental Hotel*, and one in Barra da Tijuca.

Hang gliding is a well developed sport in Rio, which has one of the best locations in the world for it. Many gliders take off from Pedra Benita at the top of the Tijuca Forest, and land on the Pepino Beach at the foot of the cliffs. Drive to the launching site by car and enjoy the view, or watch the landing from the beach.

Motor-racing is a popular Brazilian sport, and many of the world's leading racing drivers are Brazilian. Each year Rio hosts a Grand Prix race for Formula 1 cars.

For **sailing enthusiasts**, almost all kinds of vessels – from wind-surfers to large yachts – are available for hire at the Gloria Marina. The Rio Yacht Club has a marina of its own, but it is reserved for club members. If you plan to bring your own yacht to Rio, write to the Yacht Club in advance.

Finally, Rio has several ideal surfing beaches (see below).

BRAZIL

Beaches

One of the things everyone does in Rio is visit one of the wonderful bathing beaches which stretch for almost 90 km along the shore. This is the place to which to escape in summer, to enjoy the sun, the cool water, and the crowd. For *Cariocas* the beach is almost a second home, and here their good looks are clearly revealed: tanned, lithe men and beautiful, shapely, women whose famous bikinis, reveal much more than they conceal.

On weekends, especially in the summer, the beaches are packed, and it's hard to find a patch of sand. Watching the crowds is fascinating, but this is not the time for a relaxing swim.

The beaches along the bay, at Botafogo and Flamengo, are not particularly clean, and they are used mainly by people living in the poor northern neighborhoods. The famous **Copacabana beach**, too, has passed its days of glory. The most popular beaches today are **Ipanema** and **Leblon**. This is where anyone who's anyone turns out to see, and be seen. The eastern end of the Ipanema Beach, the **Praia do Arpoador**, is a good place for surfers or surfer-watchers.

The western end of the **Praia do Pepino**, the end furthest from town, offers several spectator and participant sports; this is the haunt of Rio's motorcyclists, young lovelies, beachcombers, and hang-gliders. The atmosphere is young and easygoing. Beyond is the longest beach in Rio, **Praia Barra da Tijuca**, 15 km long. The highway to this beach is impressive – a double-decker road on pillars that runs parallel to the ocean. Nearer town the beach faces a residential area, and it is, therefore, very crowded on weekends. The further one goes, however, the more deserted the beach becomes. A huge granite boulder marks the end of the long Barra beach and the beginning of another strip 2 km long. After that is a short stretch of beach, only some 150 m in length, called **Prainha**. This lovely place is Rio's best surfing beach, which on weekends attracts many surfers and their companions.

About a half hour drive from Ipanema is the beautiful **Praia Grumari**. On weekdays it is completely deserted, with not a hint of the nearby metropolis. On weekends, *Cariocas* flock here for a change of air and scenery.

Warning: The sun is very intense during the summer, and those unaccustomed to being out of doors won't manage to adjust during a short visit. Use liberal amounts of protection cream and refrain from extended exposure to the sun. As for swimming in the sea, treat stormy water with caution, even if the surfers

BRAZIL

make riding the huge waves look like a lot of fun. The great breakers are perilous, and there are lots of whirlpools that cannot be seen from the shore. The human hazards are just as serious. The beaches, particularly the city beaches, crawl with thieves just waiting for an opportunity! Leave your belongings in the hotel, and bring only the minimum amount of money necessary. Leave your cameras behind at the hotel, since these are highly prized loot.

Weather

Rio is a tropical city. The summer (October-March) is very hot and rainy, with temperatures varying from 32-40°C (90-104°F) with high humidity. Average annual rainfall is over 1000 mm. The Atlantic coast enjoys cooling winds from the ocean, but from Botafogo northwards the heat and humidity are particularly oppressive since this area is on the bay, where the cliffs surrounding the city keep the ocean breezes out. Winter (April-September) is much more pleasant; there are only a few rainy days, and temperatures vary from 20-30°C. (68-88°F).

Photography

Photo supplies of all kinds are available in Rio, though prices here are high, as they are throughout South America. However, it is possible to find all kinds of film and batteries for cameras. At the lower gallery at Avenida N.S. de Copacabana 581, there is a good, moderately priced selection of photo gear. If you are in the middle of a long trip and have used a lot of film, have it developed in Rio, where the quality of development is high. The best agencies are Colorcenter and Curt, with branches around town and in the large commercial centers.

Shopping

In Brazil, only Sao Paulo surpasses Rio as a place to shop. Apart from the many shops and boutiques throughout town, several large, modern shopping centers have been built in recent years. Rio offers a wide selection of varied products, and it is particularly worthwhile to buy clothing and jewelry here.

Rio is considered to be one of the world's leading cities for jewelry. The country's natural resources of gems and precious stones are fully exploited. Jewelers' shops, large and small, are found everywhere. The leader in this field, as previously mentioned, is the international H. Stern chain, with its headquarters in Ipanema at Rua Garcia d'Avila 113. The Natan chain also has an excellent selection of jewelry and precious stones at reasonable prices, with stores all over the city. Gems are used also in other forms of design such as statuettes and ashtrays.

Rio also has a good selection of clothing. The casual summer

BRAZIL

fashions come in a great variety of styles and colors, and prices are low. Footwear and women's handbags are excellent buys, too.

For a wide selection of almost all wares, try the large new shopping centers. The best of these is the Rio Sul at Avenida Lauro Muller 116, near the Coelho Cintra tunnel in Botafogo. The center consists of four stories of boutiques, shops, restaurants and snack-bars. On the fourth floor is a record store with a good selection of Brazilian music. Other centers are Barra Shopping in Barra (with a skating rink on its lower floor), Sao Conrado in the neighborhood of the same name, and Gavea Shopping Center on Rua Marquez de Sao Vicente.

There are other large concentrations of shops and stores all over Rio. For an abundance of exclusive stores with goods of particularly high quality, head for Rua Visconde de Pirajai in Ipanema. Another less expensive shopping area is along Avenida N.S. de Copacabana. Here too the quality of the shops and their goods is high.

Banks and Currency Exchange

Most Rio banks handle foreign currency exchange (at the official rate) and international transactions of all kinds, including cashing travelers' cheques in local currency, for a very small fee. When exchanging currency at the official rate, keep the receipt because you reconvert, on departure, up to one-third of the dollars originally exchanged. While the difference between the official and the "parallel" (black market) rate fluctuates according to the state of the economy, the black market rate is almost always significantly higher. Casa Piano on Praca de Paz in Ipanema offers the highest rate of exchange. Exprinter is also reliable, and offers good rates at branches throughout the city.

The dollar rate is higher in Rio than anywhere else in Brazil, except for Sao Paulo. Keep this in mind when changing currency before leaving the city.

Postal and telephone services

Postal and telephone services in Rio are efficient, and there are many post office branches and telephone offices throughout the city. The branch at Avenida NS de Copacabana 540 handles international parcel service. Air mail is recommended; it is more expensive but more reliable than surface mail. This branch also has a telex office. Not far away, at N.S. de Copacabana 642, is a 24-hour telephone office. There's another at Rua Visconde de Piraja 111 in Ipanema, open 6:30am-midnight. There are many other post offices throughout the city. The International Airport

BRAZIL

also offers postal, telephone and telex services. Telegrams may be sent from any post office.

English-language reading material

Brazil has a number of local travel guides in the *Guia Quatro Rodas* series. *Guia Rio* providest important and up-to-date information, and is available at newspaper stands and book stores.

Quite a few good book stores in Rio carry a wide variety of foreign literature, especially in English. Most major hotels also sell English books and newspapers, so finding reading material should not be much of a problem.

The local English daily, *The Latin America Daily Post*, is sold throughout Brazil. The major local journals in Portuguese are *O Globo* and *Jornal do Brasil*.

Personal security

Social gaps are especially acute in Rio, making the city one of Brazil's major centers of crime. Suffice it to say that for fear of being attacked, local drivers never stop at night, even for a red light. The police are apparently unable to stop crime, even though tourist areas are heavily patrolled. Thus refer to our introduction (see "Personal security") and take all the precautions suggested there. If you nevertheless meet with trouble, do not hesitate to approach the nearest police station or any policeman in the area.

Important addresses

British Consulate: Praia do Flamengo 284, 2nd Floor, Flamengo. Tel. 225-7252.

American Consulate: Avenida Presidente Wilson 147, Centro. Tel. 292-7117.

Immigration Office: Avenida Venezuelo 1, Centro.

Tourist Police: Avenida Humberto de Campos 315, Leblon. Tel. 259-7048.

Tourist Bureaus: Embratur, Rua Mariz e Barros 13, Praca da Bandeira. Tel. 273-9592.

Riotur: Rua Sao Jose 90, Centro. Tel. 232-4320.

24-hour Tourist Information: 580-8000.

The Rio de Janeiro Carnival

Spectacular carnivals take place throughout Brazil, but the one in Rio is the most famous. The carnival takes place on Shrove Tuesday (usually in February) and the three preceding days. Saturday and Sunday are the days for the procession of the

BRAZIL

main samba. The samba school parade, the highlight of the carnival, with its thousands of dancers, is an unequalled spectacle, with its electrifying atmosphere and indescribably exotic and fantastic costumes and decorations. All the clubs in the city hold special carnival festivities, while passers-by in the street are drawn into the passing crowds of dancers. All this, and more, makes Carnival in Rio an unforgettable experience.

The Samba School Parade

The schools begin preparing for the parade months before the carnival itself. As the great competition approaches, tension mounts, preparations become more intensive, and everyone is absorbed in preparing the stunning decorations and costumes. During this period, a visit to one of these schools – to watch the rehearsals and even to take part in the dancing – is fascinating.

Most samba schools are in the distant northern part of town; the only one in the south is Beija Flor, close to the Botafogo beach. This is one of the largest schools, with a glorious and successful record in these competitions. Mangueira, another large school, is housed in Palacio do Samba on Rua Visconde de Niteroi, close to the Maracana Stadium.

Tickets for the Parade: Purchasing tickets for the parade is no simple matter. Officially, tickets are dispensed at Banerj, the Rio de Janeiro State Bank, or at travel agents. However, the supply runs out within a few days of issue, and then the only way to obtain tickets is from black market dealers who charge several times the official price. Seats are not marked; only the grandstand number appears on the card. The best and most expensive of these is No. 11, from which you can see the boulevard itself and the square where the groups finish and disperse. From here one gets a sense of the whole parade. Opposite is Stand No. 4, which is also considered good, although the sun will be in your eyes at dawn. Stands 6 and 13 are cheaper, but one sees only the dispersion square, not the boulevard. Heads of state and V.I.P.s sit in special boxes.

The Parade: The major attraction of the Rio Carnival, as we have said, is the competitive parade between the samba schools. A panel of judges grades each school by fixed criteria. The competition lasts two nights, Saturday and Sunday, starting at 7pm and finishing the next day around noon. The first to set out each night are the less well known schools, so there's no need to be overly punctual. Ask locals or inquire at your hotel which are the best groups and in what order they appear. Although the parade is impressive and fascinating, you'll get tired of it sooner or later, so it's worth finding out the best time to attend.

BRAZIL

The winning schools are announced at the Maracanazinho Stadium, with the great festivity and exciting atmosphere so characteristic of the carnival as a whole.

On the first Saturday after the carnival, a "Victors' Parade" is held for the four winning groups from each of the two days of competition. Although some of the exuberance and tension of the competition are missing, this, too, will be etched in your memory as an unforgettable event.

Balls and Parties
Parties abound in nightclubs and private homes. Private parties are, of course, by personal invitation only, but the nightclubs offer a good alternative. There is an entrance fee to the nightclubs which is often steep. Nevertheless, a carnival party should not be missed: crowded, electric, everyone dancing with everyone to nonstop samba music played on wind instruments and drums. The women's costumes leave little to the imagination, and there's no end to the fun.

All nightclubs and discotheques hold these parties; we mention only the largest and most recommended of them. About a week before the start of the carnival there is a Hawaiian ball in the *Iate Club do Rio de Janeiro* (Rio Yacht Club) in Botafogo. Two days before the carnival, one of the most famous annual events takes place: the Red and Black Ball of the renowned Flamengo soccer team, held at their club, where the revelers dress in the team colors.

Two famous clubs, the *Scala Club* at Avenida Afranio de Melo Franco 292, and *Monte Lebano* on the banks of the Lagua at Avenida Borges de Medeiros 701, have parties throughout the carnival period. The latter has a particularly magnificent celebration on the last night, called Baghdad Night.

The Street Carnival
As if the Samba school parade and the parties were not enough, carnival festivities spill into the city streets and beaches. You will meet groups of dancers and musicians celebrating for hours on end. Particularly busy are Avenida Rio Branco downtown, and Avenida Atlantica on the Copacabana beach. Music blares from loudspeakers throughout the evening hours, and thousands are drawn into the whirling throng of merry dancers.

BRAZIL

Around Rio

As if the delights of Rio itself were not enough, the vicinity also has its share of lovely and fascinating places to visit, such as Buzios beach, Itatiaia park with its mountainous jungles and cliffs, colonial-style towns like Angre dos Reis (a memorial to the days of Portuguese rule), and imperial cities established by the l9th-century Brazilian monarchy.

Our tour of the area around Rio is divided into three parts: east along the shore, north to the mountains and the imperial cities, and west along the beautiful coastline between Rio and Sao Paulo.

The Coast East of Rio

Ilha Paqueta

Paqueta is about an hour and a half by boat from the center of Rio. It is one of the most beautiful islands in Guanabara Bay. There are no motor vehicles on the island, which does much for its tranquil atmosphere. The beaches are marvelous, and strange and varied rocks are strewn in the sand. Few people visit on weekdays, but it is crowded on weekends. To get around, hire a horse or bike. The ferry to Paqueta leaves every few hours from the quay on Praca 15 de Novembro downtown.

Niteroi

Niteroi is on the other side of Guanabara Bay, facing Rio. Founded in 1573, the town has always lived in its big sister's shadow. The 14 km Rio-Niteroi bridge was built to connect the two cities.

Niteroi is a rather nondescript city with a population of around 400,000. Nevertheless, there are some lovely beaches in the vicinity, particularly those facing the ocean. The most beautiful of these are Piratininga, about 20 km away, and Itacoatiara, close by. However, the beaches downtown and those facing the bay are no more beautiful than those on the bay in Rio. Note the beautiful **Igreja Boa Viagem**, built in the l7th century on a small island close to the shore, and **Forte Santa Cruz**, built in 1555, which commands the approaches to the bay.

BRAZIL

SOUTH EASTERN BRAZIL

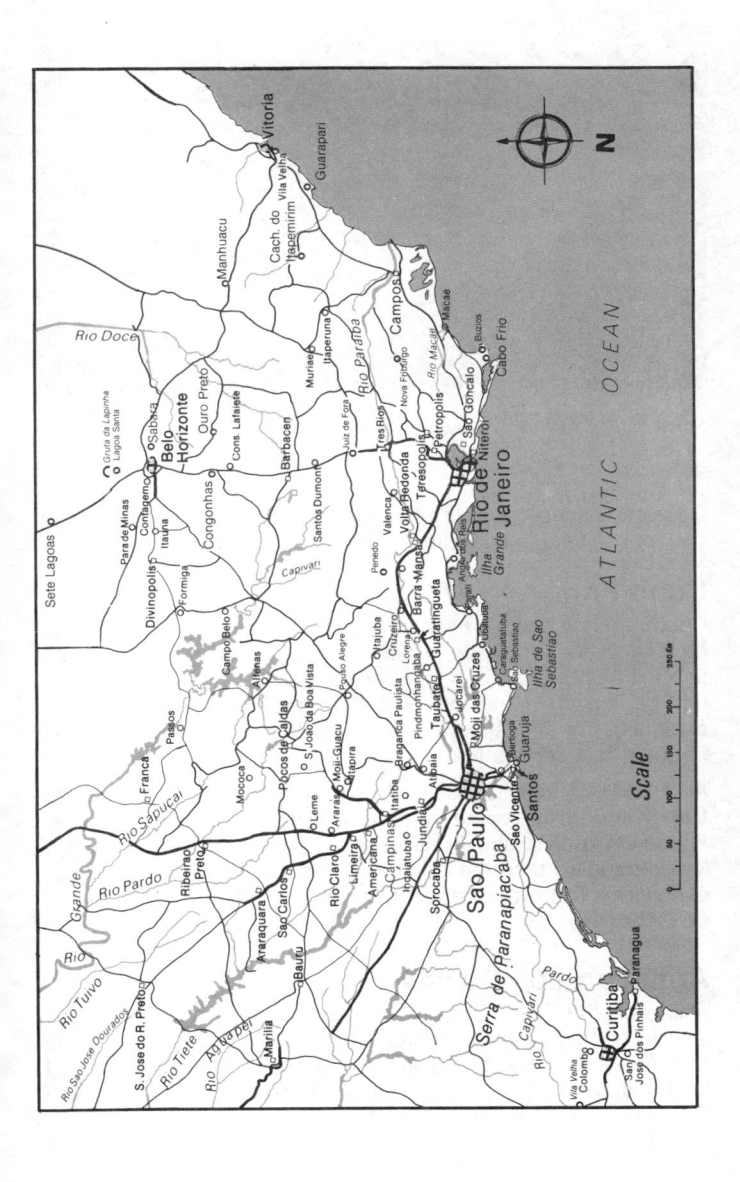

BRAZIL

Surroundings of Buzios – beaches, bays and sparkling water

Buses for Niteroi leave the Rio *rodoviaria* every few minutes all day long. There is no point in staying in Niteroi overnight.

Cabo Frio

Cabo Frio is a coastal town of 50,000. It is about 3 hours' travel time by bus east of Rio. Thanks to its beaches of pure white sand, it has become a popular holiday resort. The town itself is not particularly pleasant, and the hotels are usually rather expensive for the standard and facilities they offer. There is frequent bus service from Rio.

About 18 km from Cabo Frio, is the small town of **Arraial do Cabo**, and in the vicinity are some nice beaches – especially Pontal do Atalaia and Praia Grande. The hotels here are of a lower standard than those in Cabo Frio, but they are much less expensive. There are frequent buses from Cabo Frio to Arraial do Cabo.

Armacao dos Buzios

This delightful little village, 23 km east of Cabo Frio, is surrounded by many beautiful beaches and rocky, green hills that meet the blue sea along a jagged coastline with sandy beaches. This is a popular holiday resort, particularly for rich Brazilians and Europeans, and most of the locals earn a living from tourism. Buzios became very popular with the jet-set after Brigitte Bardot spent a holiday here in the 1960s.

BRAZIL

A rather rough dirt road connects Buzios with Cabo Frio. Bus service between the two towns (a one-hour trip) is frequent nevertheless.

Food and lodging
Buzios is a rich man's vacation resort, and its many hotels and restaurants are priced accordingly. The best and most expensive hotel is the *Auberge de l'Hermitage* on the splendid Formosa beach, about 6 km from the village (Tel. 2118). It includes a bar, a restaurant, sports facilities, and a club. For reservations, call the hotel's agents in Rio at Tel. 233-0822. Two other hotels are the *Pousada dos Buzios* (Tel. 2155) and *Pousada Byblos* (Tel. 2151). Like *Auberge de l'Hermitage*, they are small and rather expensive.

Two good restaurants are the Italian *Le Streghe* and the French *Au Cheval Blanc*. Another good place to eat is *do David*, which is inexpensive, and serves generous portions of delicious fish.

The Mountain Area

Itatiaia Park
Some 170 km west of Rio, a little to the north of the highway to Sao Paulo, is Itatiaia Park with its towering green mountains, rivers, and waterfalls. The highest of its peaks is Agulhas Negras, 2797 m above sea level. Many trails lead to various attractions in the park, through thick foliage and along streams. The most beautiful waterfalls (*cachoeira* in Portuguese) are the Moromba and the Veu Noiva. For trail and campground information and maps, stop at the office at the entrance. There is also an interesting museum with specimens of indigenous plants and wildlife.

Near the park is a town of the same name, with several hotels – all rather expensive.

Petropolis
The most interesting of the mountain towns is Petropolis, some 840 m above sea level. Founded in 1857, it is named after the Emperor of Brazil, Dom Pedro II, who moved the royal residence here and made it the local capital. Today, despite a population of almost 200,000, Petropolis maintains its tranquil, small-town atmosphere. The climate is pleasant, and the views across the verdant hills and mountains are spectacular.

Transportation
Petropolis, 66 km from Rio de Janeiro, is reached by a

BRAZIL

breathtakingly beautiful route which winds up the hillsides through enchanting forests and along the edges of steep cliffs. The trip takes about an hour and a half, and bus service is frequent throughout the day. Buses from Sao Paulo reach the downtown terminal.

Food and lodging

The best hotel in town is the *Casa do Sol*, a few kilometers outside Petropolis on the road to Rio. The view is sublime, and the hotel has a restaurant, a cinema, two bars, a sauna, and tennis courts (Tel. 435-062). The *Margaridas* is a moderately priced hotel at Rua Jose Pereira Alves 235, in a quiet, pleasant neighborhood. The *Retiro* is very inexpensive and pleasant (Tel. 420-434).

Le Candelabre restaurant, downtown at Rua Joao Pessoa 35, has a good continental menu but is very expensive. *Mauricio* is a good fish restaurant on Rua 16 de Marco. All along the main street, Rua do Imperador, there are plenty of restaurants and snack-bars where tourists on any budget can eat well.

Tourist services

The Petrotur office is on Praca Rui Barbosa.

What to see

An obelisk on Rua do Imperador marks the center of town. As we have said, Dom Pedro II moved the royal residence here in 1845, and had a magnificent royal palace built. Today, it houses the **Museu Imperial**. The museum, on Avenida 7 de Septembro near the obelisk, displays the royal jewels, weapons, clothing, and furniture. One of the most interesting exhibits is the royal crown – with its 639 diamonds and 77 pearls, it weighs 1,720 grams!

The palace is well preserved, and in order to prevent damage to the delicate wooden flooring visitors are asked to exchange their footwear for special sandals provided at the entrance. The palace is surrounded by a beautiful and well tended garden. (Open Tues.-Sun. noon-5pm, closed Mon.)

Return to the boulevard, turn right, and continue until **Catedral Sao Pedro**, a magnificent Gothic church. Dom Pedro II, his wife Teresa-Christina, and Princess Isabel are interred in magnificent tombs in a room to the right of the entrance.

The front end of the church faces a broad, green boulevard, Avenida Koeller. A stream flows through the center of the boulevard, and on either side are the splendid homes of the local aristocracy. The first house on the right was used by Princess Isabel just before the turn of the century. The beautiful boulevard ends at Praca Rui Barbosa, where Petrotur has its

BRAZIL

offices. Close by is Casa Santos Dumont, which was the summer home of the famous aviation pioneer. Today it houses a modest museum with documents, awards, and other milestones of his life. Avenida Silveira branches off from Praca Barbosa; we follow it to its end and turn right. To the left of the stream, which we have followed all the way from the obelisk, is the Palacio de Cristal. This unusual building was erected in 1884 as a pavilion for an international flower show.

The city is surrounded by green hills. You can reach the summit of one of the peaks by cablecar, and here you can enjoy a lovely view and some good mountain air. A long slide provides a novel and exciting way of descending to the foot of the hill.

Several kilometers out of town is a well tended golf course, beautifully situated, with a fine view.

Teresopolis

In the first half of the 19th century, a wealthy Englishman bought a huge area of land in the mountains, and established a house and farm there. In 1855 the government of Brazil bought the farm, divided the land into small estates, and sold it very cheaply to encourage settlement in the region. This place, Empress Teresa Christina's favorite summer resort, gained momentum and rapidly grew into a town which today has a population of some 90,000. At 910 m above sea level, it is the highest of the mountain towns, and many of Rio's wealthy citizens have weekend or summer homes here.

Teresopolis is close to the Serra dos Oragaos (Organ Mountains), so called because the peaks are reminiscent of organ pipes. The range has been declared a national park, and many visitors come here on weekends to stroll along lovely trails through luxuriant vegetation, rivers, waterfalls, and tall cliffs, which are scaled by rock climbers. The most famous of these peaks is called **Dedo de Deus** (the Finger of God), a high and mighty cliff pointing towards heaven. Its peak, some 1650 m above sea level, is visible from several miles away, as one approaches the town.

The road connecting Rio to Petropolis and Teresopolis is stunningly beautiful. The trip takes two hours, and there is frequent bus service.

Food and lodging
There are no 5-star hotels in Teresopolis. The best accommodation is at the *Sao Moritz* (Tel. 742-4360), about 36 km away on the road to Novo Friburgo. The hotel has sports facilities, swimming pools, a sauna, a restaurant, and two bars. The *Alpina* (Tel. 742-5252), a good establishment, is about 3 km

BRAZIL

from the center of town. In the center itself are other intermediate-class hotels. The Teresopolis area is well provided with campgrounds, including two in the Serra dos Orgaos park.

Nova Friburgo

This city, in a green and pleasant valley some 850 m above sea level, was founded in 1918 by Swiss immigrants from the town of Fribourg. The population today stands at 100,000, and the main sources of income are light industry and tourism.

From Praca dos Suspiros a cablecar climbs to the top of the Morro da Cruz, providing a spectacular view of the town and its environs. The cable car runs on weekends from 9am-6pm, and during the week from 1pm. The Olifas park, with its opulent gardens and natural pools, is also well worth visiting.

There are regular buses to Nova Friburgo from Rio (about 140 km) and from nearby Petropolis and Teresopolis.

From Rio to Sao Paulo Along the Coast

Two roads link Rio to Sao Paulo. One is the main highway, on which the trip takes 6 hours. It is a wide, convenient freeway running between green mountains near Park Itatiaia. The second route runs along the coast to Santos, near Sao Paulo, and is splendidly beautiful – soaring mountains covered in vegetation, slopes spilling into the blue sea, and beaches hidden in sparkling bays. A good road was recently built from Rio to the town of Sao Sebastiao. From Sao Sebastiao to Bertioga, further west, there is still no paved road, but the scenery is extremely beautiful.

The route is lined with little picturesque towns; some are tourist centers for people in the two large cities and outsiders in search of recreation.

Transportation
Rio and Santos are linked by direct buses which use the local road and take longer to make the trip than they would on the freeway. Many buses link the coastal towns along the way

Angra dos Reis
This small, placid town of 25,000 is 154 km west of Rio. Founded in 1502, it is one of Brazil's oldest settlements. Its little port handles cargoes and serves the fishing boats, while its lovely

BRAZIL

lagoon and gorgeous beaches make it a popular resort. Boats set out from here several times a week for the 90-minute cruise to Ilha Grande (see below).

Food and lodging
The two good hotels in the Angra dos Reis vicinity are the *do Prade*, on the beach of the same name, 36 km from town toward Ubatuba (Tel. 651-212), and *Portogalo*, 26 km away in the direction of Rio (Tel. 651-022). Both hotels have bars, restaurants, a swimming pool, and sports facilities. Make reservations before leaving Rio (Tel. 267-7375). The town itself has two medium-quality hotels: *Londres* at Rua Pompeia 75 (Tel. 650-044), and the *Palace* at Rua Carvalho 275 (Tel. 650-032).

In Paria Grande, 6 km from Angra, is the Italian restaurant *Le Streghe*, the best in the area. Restaurant *Jacques*, Rua do Comercio 144, has a menu of fish and seafood.

Ilha Grande

Ilha Grande is an island within the bay of Angra dos Reis. On the sizable island there are lovely beaches, luxuriant tropical vegetation, streams and many waterfalls. Most of the people on the island are either fishermen, who live in little villages, or prisoners – one of Brazil's largest penitentiaries is found on the island.

Boats set out for the island several times a week from Angra dos Reis. A daily boat travels from Mangaratiba, a little town on the road from Rio to Angra dos Reis. The cruise to the island takes about an hour and a half. The island has two rather expensive hotels and an abundance of campgrounds. There are also several little restaurants which, of course, serve seafood.

Parati

This town is about halfway between Rio and Sao Paulo, 100 km from Angra dos Reis. In the 17th century it was an important port, from which much of the gold discovered in Minas Gerais was shipped out. Seven forts defended the city approaches against pirates. In the 18th century, Parati turned into a center of the slave trade. The Turks and Lebanese who had settled here helped in its development. In the middle of this century, the town center was declared a national monument. Closed to vehicular traffic, it has been preserved as a museum of Portuguese colonial architecture.

The churches in Parati were built with racial segregation in mind – separate facilities for Blacks, Indians and Whites. Only one church was set aside for them all, so as to signify the equality

BRAZIL

of all people before God... Today, Parati is a popular tourist destination, and many young people come here to spend their vacations on the lovely beaches around the town by day, and in the bars by night.

Food and lodging
The best and most expensive hotel is *Pousada Pardieiro*, Rua Francisco Antonio 74 (Tel. 711-370). At No. 362 on the same street is *Hotel Coxixo*, a small, pleasant establishment with lower prices (Tel. 711-568). There are several low cost hostels on Rua Santos Dias.

Seafood is the most common restaurant fare, of course. The best restaurant is *Sancho Panca* on Praca Helio Pires. *Hiltinho*, Rua Deodoro 233, is also good. The *Galeria do Engenho*, Rua Franscisco Antonio 40, is low priced and serves good portions of fish and seafood delicacies.

Ubatuba
The lovely seaside town of Ubatuba is 75 km from Parati. The little town has a population of about 25,000, of whom many make a living by tourism. Thanks to the many gorgeous beaches in its immediate vicinity, Ubatuba has become a very popular resort, frequented by throngs of the wealthy citizens of Rio and Sao Paulo.

Especially beautiful beaches are Itamambuca, 12 km north of Ubatuba; Promirim, 23 km away (with natural water pools); the adjacent Vermelha do Sul and Tenorio, a few kilometers south of town; and Enseade and Toninhas, about 10 km south.

Tourists can take to the skies in a light plane for a flight over the jagged green coastline of the area. For details, contact the aviation club (Aeroclube, Tel. 322-737).

Food and lodging
Of the many hotels in and around Ubatuba, most are expensive and some are medium priced. Two of the best are on the Enseada beach, 9 km south of Ubatuba: *Sol e Vida* (Tel. 420-188) and *Mediteraneo* (420-112). Both have swimming pools, restaurants and bars. A third hotel, *Le Pastis*, is much cheaper. On this beach you will also find the *Beija Flor* restaurant, which serves delicious pancakes.

The expensive *Ubatuba Palace* is downtown at Rua Domiciano 500 (Tel. 321-500). Another beach with a cluster of hotels is Lazaro, 13 km south of town. The best hotel there is *Saveiros* (Tel. 420-172). There are no inexpensive hotels in the Ubatuba area, but several tourists can rent a house or an apartment

BRAZIL

together, at lower cost than hotel accommodations. Another option is camping at one of the many local campgrounds.

Restaurants in Ubatuba are mediocre; expect no culinary surprises. Most of the restaurants specialize in seafood, but there is one good Italian restaurant, *La Mama*, at Avenida Iperoig 332.

Sao Sebastiao

This is the last stop on the new coastal highway from Rio; the next stretch to the southwest, toward Santos, is in bad condition. Around this little resort town are beautiful beaches, from which ferries set out very often to the island of Sao Sebastiao, better known as Ilhabela.

Ilhabela

This is also the name of the major town on this lovely island, which is settled only on its western or mainland side. Its origin is volcanic; it is covered with thick tropical vegetation and criss-crossed by streams and waterfalls. Hike into the gorgeous scenery, on paths that wind through the thicket and open on to observation points in the soaring mountains, which reach 1300m in elevation. There are gushing waterfalls, and you can of course swim on one of the beautiful beaches on the island. The beaches on the side facing the mainland are easily accessible by a coastal bus. Another road on the island heads east, to the enchanting Baia de Castelhanos.

The island is accessible by frequent ferries from Sao Sebastiao (a 15-minute cruise). The ferries also carry cars. The town of Ilhabela has some rather expensive hotels, and a few others that are less expensive. The best of these is *Itapemar*, Avenida Morais 341 (Tel. 721-329). Next door is another good hotel, the *Ilhabela* (Tel. 721-084). Less expensive are the *da Praia*, the *Sao Paulo*, and the *Ibel*.

The next stretch of the way, west to Santos, is extremely beautiful. A considerable section of the road as far as the town of Bertioga is unpaved. After Bertioga, one crosses a river by ferry to the island of Guaruja.

Guaruja

The road from Rio to Santos ends at the resort town of Guaruja (the trip is completed by ferry). The town is situated on an island of the same name, and has a population of 70,000. Its economy is based on tourism and recreaction, and the beaches and streets are well tended and sparkling clean. Many Paulistas have summer homes here, and there are plenty of hotels on the

BRAZIL

shore. On weekends the town is packed with recreationers, mainly from Sao Paulo, who fill the Guaruja and Pitangueiras beaches downtown. Many young people spend their days on the beach and their nights at the bars and other entertainment spots. Bear in mind that the roads back to Sao Paulo are packed at the end of the weekend. North of the town are many beaches, of which the most beautiful are Pernambuco, Iporanga, and Enseada. Some of Guaruja's best hotels are found at Enseada.

Transportation

Buses from Sao Paulo reach the Guaruja terminal very frequently, covering the 87 km at a rapid pace. Buses also arrive from Rio, Sao Sabastiao, and Ubatuba. Santos and the island of Guaruja are linked by many ferries. The ferries, like the road to Sao Paulo, are packed on weekends; even though they set out every few minutes, drivers waiting in line for a place aboard need a great deal of patience. Take a local bus to the ferry and spare yourself this ordeal.

Food and lodging

Guaruja has plenty of hotels that serve its many visiting vacationers, but there are very few for those on a limited budget. *Hotel Casa Grande* on the Enseada beach at Avenida Miguel Stefano 999 (Tel. 862-223) is the best, and it has a swimming pool and a good restaurant. Tel. 282-3833 to make reservations from Sao Paulo. Not far from there, on the same avenue at No. 1295, is *Hotel Delphin* – slightly less expensive than the Casa Grande (Tel. 862-111). *Hotel Gavea*, on Rua Floriano 311, moderate in quality but pleasant, is downtown, overlooking the beach (Tel. 862-212).

The coastal boulevard, Avenida Miguel Stefano, is lined with many restaurants, all rather expensive. Here, too, are most of the bars and entertainment spots. They are packed, especially on summer weekends.

Santos

Almost half of all Brazil's imports and exports pass through Santos (pop. 400,000), Sao Paulo's port city. Its buildings are large, and its avenues wide and verdant. The city does not have any sites of particular interest to tourists, and the beaches are crowded and dirty. The city is built on an island, linked to the mainland by a number of bridges.

The seaside hotel district, where Santos' night life is concentrated, is called Gonzaga. A bus terminal near the city center provides very frequent service to Sao Paulo. The road

BRAZIL

between the two cities is an excellent dual carriage road, winding between green mountains, and parts of it are double decker. On weekends, it is congested with traffic from Sao Paulo heading for the beaches of Santos and Gonzaga.

From the *rodoviaria*, several buses set out every day on the beautiful coastal highway heading for Rio de Janeiro. There are very frequent buses to Sao Paulo and there is also an inexpensive, rapid taxi service.

BRAZIL

Sao Paulo

This city – the largest in Latin America, with more than 8 million inhabitants – is Brazil's most important industrial and commercial center, and supplies some 40% of the republic's total production.

Sao Paulo was founded in 1554 by two Jesuit priests. The mission they set up was just a small and peaceful town. But since the second half of the last century, it started to develop at an astonishing rate, as its energetic inhabitants built up flourishing industries. In 1920, the population was half a million, but it grew to more than three million by 1960! In the last quarter century, another five million residents have been added, and the influx from all over Brazil continues unabated. Today Sao Paulo is a cosmopolitan city, home to immigrants from many different countries and cultures: Japanese, Italians, Jews, Arabs, and others. Each group clusters in its own neighborhoods and preserves its characteristic lifestyle.

Sao Paulo does not have any special attractions for the visiting tourist. The view from the air is beautiful and impressive, with the city stretching from horizon to horizon, traversed by boulevards and expressways. On the ground, however, the city is gray, graceless, noisy and crowded. Despite its size, Sao Paulo has hardly any impressive tourist sites. It does, however, have a fairly rich cultural life, and an exciting nightlife. Sao Paulo is a major business center, and its residents – *Paulistas* – are known for their seriousness and practicality.

Sao Paulo has a fine geographical location. The city lies on a plateau 760 m above sea level, and enjoys a relatively pleasant and temperate climate for Brazil: temperatures are lower than usual for the coast, and the humidity is not high.

There is no city center as such in Sao Paulo. Since all parts of the city are bustling and developing rapidly, new centers make their appearance from time to time, with office buildings, banks, and shopping centers. The old center is the area between Praca da Republica and Praca da Se, where the major offices, banks, and stores are concentrated. The Avenida Paulista and its environs, formerly a prestigious residential neighborhood, has also become a dynamic business center. Most foreign consulates are located here. Another fast developing center is Avenida Brigadeiro Faria Lima.

BRAZIL

How to get there

By air: As befits a city of its size, Sao Paulo has two airports: **Viracopos**, situated 97 km from the center of town, has flights to all parts of the world, as well as domestic flights to Rio and Vitoria; **Congonhas** (only 14 km from downtown), is the busier airport. It too has international flights from all the capitals of South America, the important European capitals, and from Miami, New York, and Los Angeles. It also handles most domestic flights, including the Rio de Janeiro shuttle.

By land: Buses – there are two *rodoviarias* (bus depots) in the city. The more important and modern one is Tiete, the terminal for service to all parts of Brazil, as well as for international lines to Montevideo (Uruguay), Asuncion (Paraguay), Buenos Aires (Argentina) and Santiago de Chile. A bridge connects a spacious terminal to the Metro station, on a line to downtown Sao Paulo. The other bus terminal is in Jabaguara, at the southern end of the Metro line. It has very frequent bus service to Santos and to the coast.

The **train** station, Luz, has service to Campo Grande and Corumba, and even Brasilia, via Campinas.

Urban transportation

Taking into account its size, public transportation within Sao Paulo is reasonably good.

Taxis – The meter reading has to be translated into the fare according to the driver's charts. Sao Paulo has three types of taxis: regular taxis; roomy, air-conditioned taxis, which cruise near the major hotels and airports; and radio-linked cabs, which can be ordered by telephone round the clock (Tel. 251-1733).

Only one **Metro line** has been completed. A number of other lines are open only over certain stretches. Despite this limitation, the Metro certainly helps ease traffic congestion. All the lines pass through downtown, meet at Praca da Se, and extend to the interurban bus and train terminals. City buses stop at all the Metro stations.

City buses serve all parts of the city. But given the distance involved, a bus trip is liable to take a long time.

Whichever means of transportation you use to get around the city, try not to travel during the rush hours – around 8am, noon, and 6pm – when traffic is heavy, slow, and congested.

Food and lodging

Sao Paulo has about 600 hotels. Some of them meet the highest international standards, with correspondingly high prices. The best hotel is the luxury *Maksoud Plaza*, at Alameda Campinas 150, Bela Vista (Tel. 251-2233). Among the hotel's three

BRAZIL

restaurants, the French *La Cuisine du Soleil* is the best. Two other expensive hotels are located downtown: the *Hilton*, at Avenida Ipiranga 165 (Tel. 256-0033), and the *Grand Hotel Ca'd'Oro*, at Rua Augusta 129 (Tel. 256-8011). The latter has a superb Italian restaurant, one of the best in the city. The *Othon Palace*, at Rua Libero Badaro 190 (Tel. 239- 3277), has a high standard, and is slightly less expensive than the above mentioned hotels, although still expensive. Good, moderately priced hotels are the *Excelsior*, at Avenida Ipiranga 770 (Tel. 222-7377), the nearby *Plaza Maraba*, at Avenida Ipiranga 757 (Tel. 220-7811), and the *Samambaia*, on Rua 7 de Abril, near the Praca da Republica (Tel. 231-1333). All three have central and convenient locations. Fairly inexpensive hotels downtown include the *Lider*, at Avenida Ipiranga 908 (Tel. 223-5455), and the *Itamarati*, at Avenida Vieira de Carvalho 150 (Tel. 222-4133).

Young tourists, especially those with limited budgets, will find many moderately priced hotels around the Luz terminal, especially along Rua Santa Ifigenia. Most of the hotels here are cheap, although some are slightly more expensive. Check a number of these hotels before selecting one that suits your budget and requirements.

Sao Paulo has many superb restaurants. One of the most popular is the *Terraco Italia*, on the 41st and 42nd floor of *Edificio Italia* (Italy Building) on Praca da Republica. The view is spectacular, particularly at night, but the food is nothing special. *Le Coq Hardy* is an exquisite French restaurant at Avenida Adolfo Pinheiro 2518, some distance from downtown. *Marcel*, near the Praca da Rupublica, is another excellent French restaurant. The *Jardim de Napoli* at Rua Martinico Prado 463, is not far from downtown. Despite its deceptive facade, its Italian cuisine is among the best in the city. An excellent but fairly inexpensive restaurant is the *Bassi*, at Rua 13 de Maio 334. The restaurant is extremely popular, and there is almost always a long line of people waiting for a table.

Liberdade is the Japanese quarter of the city, and has many Japanese restaurants, conspicuous for their traditional decor. Some have no tables, and diners sit on mats. One of the best, the *Sushi-Yassu*, at Rua Tomas Gouzaga 110, is not particularly expensive. The *Suntory*, in the Jardim Paulista quarter, is also excellent. There are many low-priced eateries throughout the city, and American hamburger fans will be relieved to know that there are many *McDonald's* franchises in the city.

BRAZIL

Tourist services
The **Sao Paulo Tourist Office**, *Paulistur*, has set up tourist information booths throughout the city. There is a booth at Praca da Republica (Open Mon.-Fri. 9am-6pm, Sat. noon-4pm, Sun. 9am-1pm). Another such booth is found at the Liberdade Metro station, and keeps the same hours. There are also booths at the Se Metro station (Open Mon.-Fri. 9am-6pm, and weekends 9am-1pm), on Praca Dom Jose Gaspar, on Avenida Paulista, and on Avenida Ipiranga.

All the airlines that fly to Brazil have offices downtown. Varig has branch offices throughout the city, and at Congonhas airport.

Car rental: There are many rent-a-car companies in Sao Paulo. A number of companies, such as AFM and Crasso, can provide chauffeured cars. Black-Tie has a fleet of Cadillacs, for those intent upon leaving plenty of dollars in Brazil. The large rent-a-car companies are Nobre, Hertz, VIP's, and Locabraz-Avis. But be warned: city traffic is unbearable, and driving around town will turn you into a nervous wreck. Don't rent a car unless you plan on using it for excursions out of town.

Tourist sites
Sao Paulo's densely packed old center spreads between Praca da Republica and Praca da Se. **Praca da Republica** is a spacious green square, the site of a beautiful handicraft market on Sundays. The **Edificio Italia** rises skyward at the corner of Avenida Sao Luiz, and the observation deck at the top affords a fabulous view of the giant city. Most of the adjacent streets are closed to automotive traffic, and have an enormous number of stores and inexpensive restaurants.

There are guided tours of the **Municipal Theater**, on Praca Ramos Azevedo, on Wednesdays and Fridays, noon-1pm and 2-3pm. Work on this magnificent building began in 1903. It was enlarged, in the 1950s, its main auditorium can hold almost 2000 spectators. **Praca da Se** is a large square, with a row of fountains that are illuminated at night. The large Gothic-style **Catedral Metropolitana** (Municipal Cathedral) faces on to this square.

Time has transformed the **Avenida Paulista**, formerly the city's prestigious residential sector, into a bustling commercial district. Most of the foreign consulates are located here. Southwest of the avenue is the pleasant and peaceful **Jardim America** neighborhood. Sao Paulo's most important art museum, the **Museu de Arte de Sao Paulo** (MASP),is situated at Avenida Paulista 1578 (Open Tues.-Fri. 1pm-5pm; weekends 2pm-6pm; closed on Mondays). The modern building holds a permanent

BRAZIL

SAO PAULO

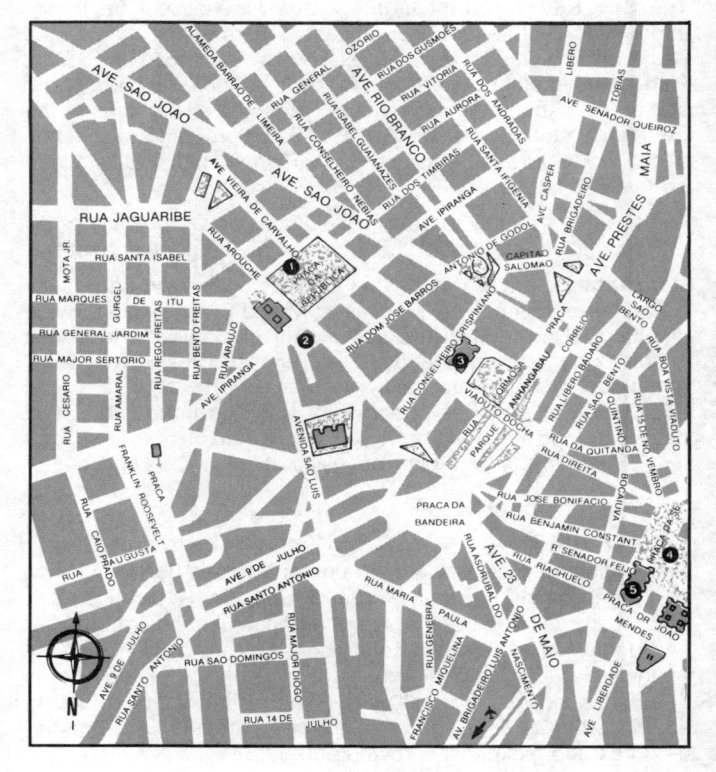

Index
1. Praca da Republica
2. Edificio Italia
3. Teatro Muncipal
4. Praca da Se
5. Catedral Metropolitana

exhibit of the works of European artists, and Brazilian art is somewhat scarce. This situation is redressed by the two museums of modern art – the **Museu de Arte Contemporanea**, and the **Museu de Arte Moderna**, both situated in the **Parque do Ibirapuera**. This large park has other museums, of which the most noteworthy are the **Museum of Folklore**, with exhibits of traditional costumes, household implements, and musical instruments (Open Tues.-Sun. 2pm-5pm); and the **Museu Aeronautica** (Aeronautical Museum), housed in the same building, which commemorates the work of aviation pioneers (Open Tues.-Fri. 2pm-5pm; weekends 10am-5pm). A large

BRAZIL

Milking a snake for venom at Instituto Butantan

sculpture in honor of the city's pioneers graces the entrance to the park.

One of Sao Paulo's most popular sites is the **Instituto Butantan** (Butantan Institute), at Avenida Vital Brasil 1500. The institute, founded in 1898 and affiliated with the Ministry of Health of Sao Paulo State, carries out various research projects in health and biology. It gained fame by specializing in snakes and poisonous animals. The institute has one of the largest and most impressive collections of snakes in the entire world – tens of thousands of snakes, both poisonous and non-poisonous. Several times a day you can watch the venom being milked from the snakes. Be sure to visit the museum, near the entrance to the institute, where there is an exhibit of several poisonous creatures, and methods of protection against them (Open daily, 8am-5pm). Of further interest to animal lovers are the **Zoological Gardens**, about half an hour's trip from the center of town, with a very large and interesting collection of animals from all over the world. Another interesting visit for animal lovers is the **Simba Safari**, not far from the zoo.

Entertainment
Sao Paulo offers a wide variety of entertainmment, not concentrated in a single district, but spread throughout the

BRAZIL

giant city. The magnificent **Teatro Municipal** (Municipal Theater), located downtown, stages concerts, shows, and operas. Movie theaters – usually modern and comfortable – are scattered all over town. Sao Paulo has many night clubs, such as the *Ta Matate*, in the Itaim neighborhood, and the *Pool Music House*, a dance club, usually jammed with throngs of gyrating youths. The southern end of Rua Augusta and its cross-streets have many bars, frequented mainly by young people and students. These places are especially crowded at weekends.

For children, young people, and the young in spirit, Sao Paulo's amusement park, the **Playcenter**, will provide a happy diversion. The most exciting attraction is the huge roller coaster. Another attraction is *Cine 2000*, which shows 3-D movies that give the spectator the sensation of being right in the middle of the action. The Playcenter is on Avenida Marginal do Tiete (Open Tues.-Fri. 2pm-10pm, Sat. 2pm-11pm, Sun. 10am-10pm.)

Shopping

Since it is Brazil's largest commercial center, Sao Paulo is undoubtedly the place to do your shopping. In recent years a number of large and modern shopping centers have been built. The most impressive and highly recommended of these (not just to visit) is *Eldorado*, located rather far out in Pinheiros, and noted for its interesting, modern architecture. This gigantic shopping center has cafes, restaurants, stores, fun arcades, and very expensive boutiques. The *Iguatemi* shopping center is not far away. Another large shopping center is *Ibirapuera*, near the park of the same name. Here, too, there are numerous stores and boutiques, where prices are lower than in the other shopping centers. Along Rua Augusta, particularly in the garden district, the *Jardims*, there are many luxury shops and boutiques. Many clothing stores and shops selling imported goods are concentrated downtown, and their prices are usually low.

Postal and telephone services

The Sao Paulo telephone company, Telesp, provides good and efficient service. You will have no trouble calling anywhere in the world. A telephone office at Avenida 7 de Abril 295, downtown, is open round the clock. Other downtown telephone offices are found at: Praca Dom Jose Gaspar 22, Rua Benjamin Constante 200, and Rua Martins Foate 150, (all three open daily, 6:30am-10:30pm). There are also telephone offices throughout the city, including one at the Luz terminal and one at Congonhas airport.

Numerous post offices are scattered throughout the city. There

BRAZIL

is one at Congonhas airport, another downtown, at Praca da Republica 390, and another in the Ibirapuera shopping center.

Banks and currency exchange

Most Brazilian banks have offices downtown, and most bank branches buy foreign currency. If you want to buy local currency on the black market, there are quite a few *casas-de-cambio* (money exchanges) downtown, especially near Praca da Republica. Exprinter, at Rua Itapetininga 243, is good and reliable.

Important addresses

American Consulate: Jardim America, Rua Presidente Joao Manuel 933 (Tel. 881-6511).

British Consulate: Cerqueira Cesar, Avenida Paulista 1938, 17th floor (Tel. 287-7722).

Tourist Office (Paulistur): Avenida Olavo Fontoura 1209 (Tel. 26-2122).

Emergency Numbers:

Ambulance: Tel. 136.

Police emergency: Tel. 190.

Police downtown station: Tel. 222-8386.

BRAZIL

Southern Brazil

Southern Brazil has a different character from the rest of the republic. This is the most developed part of the country, where European influence is particularly strong. The population is mainly made up of descendants of immigrants, chiefly German and Italian. This area has the lowest illiteracy rate in the entire country. Agriculture is developed, the land is rich and fertile, and yields are good. The local wine industry, especially that of the southernmost province state of Rio Grande do Sul is justly famous. The other two southern states are Santa Catarina and Parana.

The green mountain range known as Serra do Mar, which never exceeds 1000 m above sea level, runs parallel to the coast. Its western slopes gradually become a broad and rolling plateau, which extends to the western borders of southern Brazil. The climate is fairly pleasant, but chilly in winter. One of Brazil's most important tourist sites is the Iguacu Falls, which are at the western edge of this region.

Curitiba

Curitiba, founded at the end of the 17th century, is the capital of Parana state. The town lies in an area of green hills, 900 m above sea level. The climate is pleasant and temperate. Curitiba has a population of approximately one million, and is a modern industrial and commercial center, but has no places of special interest. The train ride from Curitiba to Paranagua is, however, a breathtaking trip.

Transportation

The airport, 17 km from the town, is served by many flights from all of Brazil's important towns. The modern new terminal, for buses and trains, *Rodoferroviaria*, is not far from the center of town. From here, a number of buses leave daily for Rio de Janeiro (about 12 hours), Sao Paulo (6 hours), Florianopolis (6 hours), Porto Alegre (about 11 hours), and Foz do Iguacu (about 12 hours), to which there are also night coaches. The Graciosa bus company runs frequent buses throughout the day to Paranagua, which is also accessible by train. If you want to travel from Curitiba to Iguacu, be sure to buy your bus ticket early in order to guarantee yourself a seat.

BRAZIL

Food and lodging
The town's best hotel, the *Iguacu Campestre*, is actually outside of town (Tel. 262-5313). There are several fairly classy hotels with correspondingly high prices downtown. The best and most expensive of these is the *Del Rei*, at Rua Ermelino de Leao 18 (Tel. 224-3033). An intermediate class hotel is the *Ouro Verde*, downtown at Rua Dr. Murici 419. Very moderately priced hotels can be found opposite the bus and train terminal, on Avenida Afonso de Camargo, and on the small streets that radiate from it.

One of the town's best restaurants is the *Swiss Matterhorn*, situated at Rua Mateus Leme 575. Try their excellent meat fondue. The *Ile de France* restaurant at Praca 19 de Dezembro 538 serves excellent French cuisine. There are lots of inexpensive restaurants around the train station.

Tourist sites
Curitiba's modern center teems with life. **Rua 15 de Novembro**, the town's main street, has the most important banks and office buildings. A section of the street, from Rua Praca Osorio to Praca Generoso Marques, is closed to vehicular traffic. The old Town Hall, built in 1916 in ornate art-nouveau style, is located in this square. Today the building houses the **Museu Paranaense** (Parana Museum) which displays interesting archeological and anthropological exhibits, as well as artifacts of the Guarani Indians (Open Tues.-Fri. 9am-6pm; weekends noon-5pm). Nearby is **Praca Tiradente**, with its impressive cathedral. A lovely **handicrafts market** is held in Praca Rui Barbosa on Saturdays, where artifacts and handicrafts – especially in ceramics and wood – are sold.

Vila Velha
Vila Velha is a beautiful national park, some 97 km from Curitiba. Here you can see interesting rock formations, carved by wind and rain. Daily buses reach Vila Velha from Curitiba and Sao Paulo.

The train from Curitiba to Paranagua
Brazil's most beautiful rail route is the one linking Curitiba to the port of Paranagua. The tracks cross the verdant Serra do Mar range, pass through tunnels, climb mountains, and traverse canyons. All along the route you will see luxurious vegetation, streams, and waterfalls. There are two daily trains. One, intended for tourists, has particularly comfortable cars and stops en route at especially scenic spots. This train leaves the Curitiba station slightly after 8am, and returns from Paranagua at 3pm. The regular train, which costs about a third of the tourist train, leaves Curitiba at 7am and returns at 4:30pm. The trip takes

BRAZIL

about three hours. You can travel one way by train, and return by bus. Buses are much quicker than the train, and also much more frequent.

Paranagua
This port town of 70,000 lies on Paranagua Bay. The harbor mainly serves landlocked Paraguay. Visit the quays to watch the bustling activity in the spacious port. In the town itself, stroll through the area near the coast and the fish market. Apart from these, there are no other places of interest. If you want to go for a swim, you will have to go to Pontal do Sul, about 45 km away. Buses there leave the small bus station frequently.

Ilha do Mel is a particularly beautiful island, with enchanting beaches and small fishing villages. You can take an enjoyable hike along the beaches and coves, and sleep in the fishermen's houses. The boat from Pontal do Sul to the island takes about half an hour, and there is no regular departure time.

Florianopolis

Florianopolis, the capital of Santa Catarina state, has about 150,000 residents. The town is named after Floriano Peixoto, the leader of the federal revolution of 1893. The town has two parts – one on the island of Santa Catarina, and the other on the mainland. Two large bridges span the 250 m wide strait. The island is lovely, with green hills, blue lakes, and splendid beaches. The place is a popular tourist site, and swarms with foreign tourists and Brazilian vacationers from December to February.

Transportation
Florianopolis' small airport is on the island, about 11 km from the center of town. A number of daily flights link it with Rio de Janeiro, Sao Paulo, Porto Alegre, and all the other state capitals. There is a daily flight from Foz do Iguacu. Especially beautiful is the flight from Sao Paulo, which flies low over the magnificent coastline.

The modern and spacious bus terminal is also on the island, at the foot of the Colombo Sales bridge, the southernmost of the two bridges. Scheduled buses leave for Porto Alegre (about 8 hours), Curitiba (about 6 hours), and Sao Paulo (about 12 hours). Daily buses also leave for Foz do Iguacu; Ascuncion (Paraguay), and Buenos Aires.

Food and lodging
The best of the town's hotels is the *Florianopolis Palace*, at Rua Artista Bittencourt 2, near the central square (Tel. 229-8633). The *Faial Palace Hotel*, at Rua Felipe Schmidt 87 (Tel. 232-766),

BRAZIL

is much more reasonably priced than the former, and offers good service. The inexpensive *Querencia Palace* is centrally located, at Rua Jeronimo Coelho 1. The *Majestic*, at Rua Trajano 4, is an inexpensive and good hotel. The *City Hotel*, extremely good, clean, and reasonable, is near the bus terminal. All these hotels are downtown, on the island, and are preferable to those on the mainland, since access to the various parts of the island and its beautiful beaches is harder from the mainland.

If you are vacationing in Florianopolis, stay in a beach hotel, away from the town itself. The *Jurere Praia Hotel* (Tel. 660-108) has the same name as the beach on which it is situated; it is an excellent if expensive hotel, and has a beautiful view. There are several hotels on Canasvieiras beach, of which the best is the *Canasvieiras* (Tel. 660-106), but the place is crowded and noisy during the tourist season. Around Lake Conceicao are several fairly inexpensive hotels: among them the *Saveiros* (Tel. 320-3656) is moderately priced and has a beautiful view. There are also numerous camping sites all along the island.

Bars and restaurants can be found up and down Avenida Arruda Ramos, which runs along the north coast of the city, where most of the nightlife is centered.

Seafood is the most popular fare in Florianopolis, and for good reason! Throughout the island, and especially along the beaches, lakes, and tourist sites, there is an incredible number of restaurants serving all sorts of fish, crab, shrimp, and other delicacies. Avenida Rendeiras, south of Lake Conceicao (see below) has "wall-to-wall" fish restaurants. Noteworthy here is *Alice Maria Vieira*, which serves large and satisfying portions at low prices – the shrimp is excellent.

Tourist services

The town has a number of **tourist information bureaus**, of which the best and most efficient is on the mainland, near Colombo Sales bridge (Open daily 8am-6pm), in front of a small handicrafts shop. Another tourist office is located in the main square, Praca 15 de Novembro (Open daily 8am-10pm during the tourist season; open Tues.-Fri. 8am-8pm out of season). There are also information bureaus at the airport and the bus terminal, but they are not always helpful.

The Scuna-Sul company (Tel. 221-860) organizes boat trips in the bays between the island and the mainland. There are two trips – in the northern and southern bays. The cruise in the southern bay, which lasts 8 hours, is particularly recommended.

Car rental: Rent-a-car services can be found along Avenida Rio

BRAZIL

Florianopolis – old folks in the shade of an old tree

Branco. The largest is Nobre, at 110 Rio Branco. Coelho's offices are at the airport.

Tourist sites

Florianopolis' old section has narrow streets and colonial

BRAZIL

buildings. In the middle of **Praca 15 de Novembro** stands a huge Ficus tree more than a hundred years old. The cathedral, built in 1750, is on the same square. To the left of the square is **Palacio do Governo** (the State Capitol). On the edge of downtown rises Morro da Cruz hill, which offers a panoramic view of the town and its surroundings. A short bus ride from the center of town takes you to the top.

Santa Catarina Island

Santa Catarina is an enchanting island, with 42 beaches, green mountains, and gorgeous lakes. In the middle of the island is a large, beautiful lake, Lagoa da Conceicao. The most beautiful beaches are the eastern ones, which are less developed and wilder than the northern beaches. Praia da Joaquim is one of the most popular beaches, and is packed and noisy during the tourist season. Other good beaches are Campeche and Armacao, south of Praia de Joaquim, and Mocambique and Praia dos Ingleses, to the north.

Among the northern beaches Canasvieiras deserves mention – it is another beautiful beach which is jammed during the tourist season. You can reach the eastern part of the island from Florianopolis – local buses cover the distance in about half an hour. The road crosses a narrow bridge, below which anglers cast their lines into the water. Two roads lead to the northern end of the island, one on the west coast and the other on the east coast.

Rio Grande do Sul

Brazil's southernmost state, Rio Grande do Sul borders on Uruguay to the south and Argentina to the west. The dominant landscape is pastoral and hilly. The land is extremely fertile, and provides excellent grazing for cattle. The millions of heads of cattle and pigs raised here serve the extensive meat and leather industry. Viniculture has also developed in the area, and about 75% of all Brazilian wine is produced here. The center of the wine industry is **Caxias do Sul**, a modern town of about 200,000 residents, many of whom are the descendants of Italian immigrants. Visit the wine cellars and taste their quality wines.

Many residents of Rio Grande do Sul raise cattle on their carefully tended ranches. These cowboys are known as "gauchos," and the name has spread and stuck to all the inhabitants of the state. The locals are friendly and hospitable, and will be happy to help out whenever required. Their easy-going manner is apparently influenced by the local climate, which is pleasant and temperate. Only a few summer days are uncomfortably hot, and the winters are no more than cool, while in the mountains snow falls only for a few days a year.

BRAZIL

Porto Alegre

Porto Alegre, the capital of Rio Grande do Sul, has about a million residents. The town is developing at a rapid pace. Even though it is modern and fairly busy, it still preserves the charm of bygone years. The city is on the banks of the Rio Guaibo, where the river empties into the largest freshwater lake in South America – Lagoa dos Patos. The lake, which has an outlet to the ocean, is the site of Porto Alegre's main harbor. This serves as the point of export for many goods manufactured in the south – in particular leather, meat, and tobacco products.

Porto Alegre is thus the most important commercial center south of Sao Paulo. All the same, there's not much to interest tourists here.

The main street – 7 de Setembro, flanked by modern skyscrapers, crosses Rua Canabarro, which has a daily **handicrafts market** famous for its leather goods. The **Mercado Publico** (central market) – built in 1869 – is on Praca 15 de Novembro.

Several public buildings are situated on Praca Deodoro, of which the most important is **Palacio Piratimi** (Piratimi Palace), which serves as the seat of government. The cathedral is next door. Across from these two buildings is the **Sao Pedro Theater**, constructed 1858 in baroque style, and renovated in 1984. Near the square, at 1231 Duque de Caxias street, is an interesting historical museum, the **Museu Julho de Castelhos** (Open Tues.-Fri. 9am-6pm; weekends 9am-noon and 2-5:30pm). Close by is a spacious park, with lots of greenery and ponds.

A number of good and expensive hotels can be found downtown. The best is the *Plaza Sao Rafael* at Avenida Alberto Bins 514 (Tel. 216-100). The hotel has two very good restaurants: the continental *Le Bon Gourmet*, and the *Capitao Rodrigo*, which serves marvelous steaks. Moderately priced hotels can be found near the bus terminal.

Transportation

Porto Alegre's sprawling airport, 10 km from the center of town, has service to all parts of Brazil. Varig flies daily to Foz do Iguacu, Montevideo, and Buenos Aires.

The modern and well-planned bus terminal is not far from downtown. There are many daily buses to Rio (over 24 hours), Sao Paulo, and Florianopolis (about 8 hours). There is one bus a day to Foz (about 18 hours), and regular service to Montevideo and Buenos Aires (24 hours).

On to Uruguay and Argentina

The Brazilian border town on the coastal road from Porto Alegre

BRAZIL

to Montevideo is **Chuy**. Two buses a day make the 8-hour trip. Remember to get your passport stamped when leaving Brazil, and again at Chuy, on the Uruguayan side of the border.

Some 650 km west of Porto Alegre is Uruguaiana, on the Argentinian border. A bus leaves there every half hour for Paso de los Libres on the Argentinian side, crossing the bridge over the Rio Uruguay, which forms the border between the two countries.

The Iguacu Falls

When you see the torrents of water thundering down on all sides, you cannot help being stirred by that feeling of awe one experiences when in the presence of Nature in all her sublimity. The Iguacu Falls, among the largest and most impressive in the world, are an enthralling experience, an amazing sight of overwhelming height, which gives the abstract words "natural wonder" a real and unforgettable meaning.

Of all the natural wonders and landscapes that South America has to offer the tourist, these gigantic falls, located on the border of Brazil and Argentina, near the common border with Paraguay, are surely the most impressive.

As the falls can, and preferably should, be visited from the Argentinian as well as the Brazilian side there is a chapter on Iguacu in the two relevant countries. Some of the information, applicable to Argentina and Brazil, has been repeated while material specific to only one side is mentioned only once. It is advisable to read both chapters.

It is not surprising that they draw more than two million visitors annually. Every second, nearly 450,000 gallons of water come crashing down over a distance of 4 km, in hundreds of subsidiary waterfalls that are 60 to 80 meters high. This magnificent sight, together with the clouds of spray that envelop the area and the incessant roar of the cascading waters, recreates primeval nature in all her glory. And as if to complete the legendary quality of the place, the whole area is covered by a luxuriant tangle of tropical growth, a study in bright green, a feast for the eye.

Travel to and from the Falls
From within Brazil: There is daily bus service to Foz do Iguacu (the town on the Brazilian side of the falls) from Rio de Janeiro (travel time: 24 hours), Sao Paulo (17 hours), and

BRAZIL

Breathtaking Iguacu Falls

BRAZIL

Curitiba (12 hours). The buses are luxurious and the roads are good. The buses leave from the central bus station at all hours of the day and night. You must buy your ticket **at least** one day in advance! Cruzeiro do Sul and Varig fly daily from Rio via Sao Paulo to Foz, and back.

From Argentina: Expreso Singer has a direct bus several times a day from Retiro Station to Posadas (20 hours) and on to Iguacu (4 more hours).

Aerolineas runs regular and frequent flights from Buenos Aires to Posadas, from which buses leave frequently for Iguacu Falls. Direct flights to the falls, and especially return flights, are heavily booked. This is, of course, the fastest and most convenient way of traveling and if you have bought a "Visit Argentina" ticket in Brazil, you can begin your tour of Argentina from here. A direct flight to the Brazilian side of the falls (Foz do Iguacu) is far more expensive than a domestic flight to Puerto Iguazu.

From Paraguay: Buses from Asuncion cover the distance to Foz in about seven hours, along Paraguay's only paved highway. The Nuestra Senora, Rapido Iguazu, and Pluma companies run several buses a day to the Brazilian side (Foz) and back. The buses are comfortable and the journey pleasant, usually with one intermediate stop.

Food and lodging

You have three options: to stay in Puerto Iguazu (Argentina), to stay in Foz do Iguacu (Brazil), or to stay in Puerto Stroessner (Paraguay). Your best bet is Brazil, since it offers the best tourist facilities. So, if you're coming from Brazil, stay there until you continue your journey. If you're coming from Argentina on the way to Brazil, cross the border and stay in Foz. And if you're coming from Asuncion, the same advice holds: cross the bridge to the Brazilian side (see Argentina chapter).

Foz do Iguacu

This city of more than 100,000 people is geared entirely to cater to the local and foreign tourists who come to visit the famous falls. Its long avenues and adjacent streets are packed with dozens of hotels of varying quality. Here, too, the most luxurious and expensive hotel – the *Hotel das Cataratas* – is situated directly opposite the falls and many high-priced motels can be found between the city and the entrance to the park. The hotels in the town itself are far cheaper. The most comfortable and pleasant of these is undoubtedly the large and

BRAZIL

THE IGUACU FALLS

BRAZIL

luxurious *Diplomat*, which has a swimming pool and other facilities and is within walking distance of downtown. The *Foz do Iguacu Hotel*, on Avenida Brazil, is cheaper, and has air-conditioning. Many plainer and cheaper hotels surround the bus station (the *Brazil Hotel* is **not** recommended). There is a wide choice of restaurants: in the large hotels, along Brazil Avenue, and around the bus station.

How to tour and what to see

Although Iguacu Falls are basically on the Argentinian side of the border, it is from the Brazilian side that you get the best and most impressive overall view of the falls. Every hour, buses marked Cataratas or Parque Nacional leave the central bus station in Foz for the falls. The journey lasts about 30 minutes; after you have paid you will be let off in front of the luxurious Hotel das Cataratas. From here you follow a long, winding path through the dense undergrowth to the heart of the waterfall area, where you can look out over the whole region — a truly breathtaking sight. The most exciting part of the hike is crossing the narrow bridge that leads almost into the heart of the great **Floviano Falls** — and being soaked to the skin by the flying spray. At the bottom of the cliffs is a small elevator to take you back up to the top, from where you can return to the hotel (lunch at its excellent restaurant is highly recommended), and back to town (buses leave once every hour). Before returning to town you may wish to turn right, into the beautiful park, and enjoy the thousands of magnificent butterflies. On the Brazilian side, a helicopter ride to the site is available for approximately U.S.$25.

The Argentinian and Brazilian waterfalls are situated on either side of the Iguacu River (raging waters in Guarani — the language of the Paraguayan Indians). In order to travel from one side to the other you must cross the border and the river. Crossing from Argentina to Brazil is a simple matter — all you have to do is walk to the river bank and take the ferry over. (Cars are also allowed on the ferry although not at all seasons). Once in Brazil your passport will be stamped, and then you can board any bus for Foz itself, and go on to the falls.

If you want to cross from Brazil to Argentina, take the bus marked Porto Meira from the central bus station to the river, and then the ferry over to Argentina. If you plan to return to your initial side of the border the same day, you don't have to have your passport stamped. Just tell the immigrations official what you're planning — if you're coming from Brazil, you can obtain a visa from the Argentinian consulate in Foz.

When you visit the falls, wear comfortable walking shoes with skid-proof soles, and take along a plastic bag in which to put your camera and papers so they won't get wet.

BRAZIL

Itaipu

Twenty kilometers upstream from Foz, at Itaipu, Brazil and Paraguay are erecting on the Parana River a giant hydroelectric plant, the largest in the world which, when completed, will supply 12,000 megawatts of power. This bi-national venture puts a heavy economic burden on both countries, but it has become a matter of national prestige. The plant was originally intended primarily to meet Brazil's power needs. Paraguay undertook to sell Brazil the surplus energy generated by the dam, and anticipates revenues of hundreds of millions of dollars a year from the sale.

Travel agents in Foz organize trips to the plant, which include slide shows and explanations of the construction of the huge dam. These trips require a special permit from the company. Although you will only be allowed to visit certain sections of the site, the experience is very interesting. The construction of this immense dam caused the destruction of a wonderful nature spot — the Sete Quedas waterfalls, the volume of whose waters was double that of the Niagara Falls. The project caused the flooding of vast areas upstream, and no trace is left of the waterfalls, which are now buried under the lake which was created when the dam was built.

BRAZIL

Minas Gerais

The landscape of Minas Gerais state is mountainous and verdant. The mountain range in the south reaches a height of 2800 m above sea level. The northern sector is mainly rolling hills. Minas Gerais, which has a flourishing cattle industry, is one of Brazil's most fertile states and one of its largest producers of corn, beans, rice, and bananas. However, Minas is most famous for its mines, whence its name (*minas* – mines). The region has large quantities of various natural resources – from iron, gold, manganese and beryllium to precious stones. Minas is the source of the Sao Francisco river, which empties into the Atlantic Ocean in Bahia State, north of Salvador.

The discovery of gold in the 18th century put Minas Gerais on the map, and the state still bears the mark of the fevered gold rush that ensued. Many cities and towns were founded then by immigrants from the coast. Mining became an established industry, and Minas' many natural resources were sent abroad through the ports of Santos, Angra dos Reis, Rio, and Vitoria.

Belo Horizonte

The capital of Minas Gerais, Belo Horizonte, with one and a half million residents, is the third largest city in Brazil. Founded in 1897, it was originally intended to serve as a large and central regional capital. Today Belo Horizonte is endowed with spacious avenues, green squares adorned with statues, and multi-story buildings downtown. The city is an important center for business and industry, and keeps growing at a rapid pace.

Belo Horizonte is not a "tourist town" in the full sense of the word. Although pleasant, cultured, and tranquil, it has few places of interest. On the other hand, there are a number of colonial towns nearby – some of the most famous and beautiful in Brazil – and Belo Horizonte can serve as the starting point for a visit to these places.

How to get there
By air: The **Confins Airport**, 39 km from the city, was opened at the start of 1984. The passenger terminal is very large and modern, and far exceeds the city's requirements. The airport handles only internal flights. You can reach the center of town quickly by taxi, or by special buses, which leave throughout the day for the bus terminal downtown. There are also a number of

BRAZIL

rent-a-car companies at the airport, whose prices vary significantly. If you plan on touring the area, a rented car is certainly the most convenient way to do so – although it is a fairly expensive option.

By land: The city's bus terminal, on Praca Rio Branco, serves all the interurban bus lines – those from nearby towns such as Ouro-Preto, as well as those from more remote places such as Rio, Sao Paulo, Salvador, Recife, Vitoria, Brasilia, and Campo Grande. The best bus companies operating here are Penha, Itapemirim, and Util. If you want to travel north toward Salvador, along the coast south of Salvador, first head east to Vitoria, as many buses continue north from there.

A train runs twice a week between Belo Horizonte and Rio. You can continue by train from Rio to Sao Paulo.

Food and lodging

From Confins airport, you can make a direct call to one of the hotels that have a special line to the terminal. The best hotel is the *Othon Palace*, at Avenida Afonso Pena 1050 (Tel. 226-7844) – conveniently situated in the center of town. The hotel has an excellent restaurant, the *Tacho de Ouro*, which serves continental cuisine. A good, moderately priced hotel is the *Cecilia*, at Rua Carijos 454. The *Casa dos Municipios*, at Rio Grande do Norte 1017 (Tel. 226-0171), a former private residence converted into a hotel, is both comfortable and reasonably inexpensive. The *Vitoria Hotel*, near the bus terminal, at Rua Curitiba 224, is quite inexpensive.

There are a number of good restaurants scattered throughout the city. The Savassi and Funcionarios quarters contain most of the good restaurants. Savassi is especially popular among young people and students, and is full of bustling cafes and bars. Funcionarios has many good restaurants, such as the French *Cafe Ideal*, the Italian *La Greppia*, and *La Taverna* which is extremely popular among the young. In the Savassi quarter, we can recommend the *Buona Tavola*, which serves good Italian food, and the *Arroz Con Feijao*, which serves traditional Brazilian fare. One of the best and most popular restaurants in the city is the *Tavares*, at Rua Santa Catarina 64, downtown. The restaurant is not known for its interior decor, but rather for its excellent game and fish.

Tourist sites
Downtown
Praca da Liberdade is a green square in the city center, which accommodates Belo Horizonte's main attraction – the wonderful **handicraft market**, held every Thursday evening and Sunday morning, where jewellery, leather goods, pottery, paintings, and

BRAZIL

local foods are sold. The market has a particularly pleasant ambience, and the items on display are unique, very beautiful and attractively priced. You should definitely not miss it. On Saturday afternoons a smaller market is held in the square, where you can find mainly antiques and paintings.

Opposite the square is the **Palacio do Governo**, the Minas Gerais state capitol. The spacious building is stunning, and every evening there is the changing of the guards and the lowering of the flag. Visits must be arranged in advance.

At Rua Bahia 1149, is the beautiful Gothic **Museum of Mineralogy** with a collection of minerals and precious stones (Open Tues.-Fri. 8:30am-6pm; weekends 8am-5pm). Nearby is the large **Municipal Park**. The cultural center known as the **Palacio das Artes**, at the south edge of the park, is used for plays and concerts, various exhibitions, and an expensive and high-quality handicrafts fair.

The **Mangabeiras** quarter, which spreads over the lower slope of the green mountain range south of the city, is the city's most prestigious neighborhood, worth touring for its beautiful buildings and individual character. On the outskirts of the neighborhood, further up on the mountain, is **Mangabeiras Park**, which offers a breathtaking view of the city. The park itself has many sporting facilities, and rich and well-tended vegetation. There is an entrance fee.

Pampulha

Some 10 km from town, in the direction of the airport, is Belo Horizonte's most prestigious suburb, almost a separate city. Pampulha extends around a large artificial lake, surrounded by private homes and impressive estates. This is where the wealthy of the district reside. Close by is Pampulha airport, which, since the opening of the new Confins airport, serves only the locals' private planes. On the southern shore of the lake stands the **Church of Sao Francisco**, built in 1943. The architect was the well-known Oscar Niemeyer, who designed many of Brasilia's buildings. The church is small and not particularly impressive, but is noteworthy for its style, and its beautiful view of the lakeside. East of the Church of Sao Francisco is the **Mineirao Stadium** – the second largest in the world – built in 1965. The stadium can hold 130,000 spectators (Open to visitors daily, 8am-5pm). On the other side of the lake is the **Museu de Arte** (Art Museum), housed in an impressive building surrounded by a lovely garden, also designed by Niemeyer. However, the facade of the museum belies its interior – the collection is poor and unimpressive (Open daily, 8am-6pm).

At the western end of the lake is Belo Horizonte's **Jardim Zoologico** (zoo). This spacious and meticulously designed park

BRAZIL

Gorilla in the Belo Horizonte Zoo – waiting for better days

accommodates over a thousand species of animals in large, pleasant enclosures designed to recreate the natural environment appropriate to each animal. The zoo grounds abound in greenery, and can be toured by car (Open daily, 7am-5pm). Recommended.

Stalactite Caves
The Belo Horizonte area boasts two stalactite caves, which, although a source of regional pride, are not particularly impressive.

The more beautiful of the two is Gruta do Maquine, about 125 km from the city, in Cordisburgo. Gruta da Lapinha, 40 km from town, in Lagoa Santa, is less impressive, but nearer. A small museum nearby displays local antiquities, fossils, and stuffed animals.

The Colonial Towns
The main tourist attractions in the Belo Horizonte area are the picturesque colonial towns spread over the mountain slopes southeast of the city. These towns have preserved their colonial character, with their many churches, unique architecture, and cobblestone streets. Here you can see the work of Brazil's greatest sculptor, Antonio Francisco Lisboa, better known as Aleijandinho. Aleijandinho (1738-1814) suffered from leprosy, as a result of which his body was deformed and his fingers fell off. In spite of this he continued sculpting – indeed his most beautiful and famous works were created after he became handicapped.

Sabara is 27 km from Belo Horizonte. The town's **Museum of Gold**, housed in a building erected by the governor of Minas Gerais in 1732, has a collection of furniture and the tools used by gold miners. Also worth visiting is the **Church of Nossa Senhora do Carmo**, built in 1763. Its facade is the creation of Aleijandinho.

The town of **Congonhas** contains Aleijandinho's masterpiece – his statues of the twelve apostles in the Bomjesus church (which also offers a breathtaking view). Congonhas is 80 km from Belo Horizonte, with frequent daily bus service between them.

Ouro-Preto
Ouro-Preto – "Black Gold" in Portuguese – is one of the most enchanting colonial towns in the world, one of Brazil's tourist gems, and without doubt the crowning glory of a visit to Minas Gerais. It is not suprising that the entire town has been declared

BRAZIL

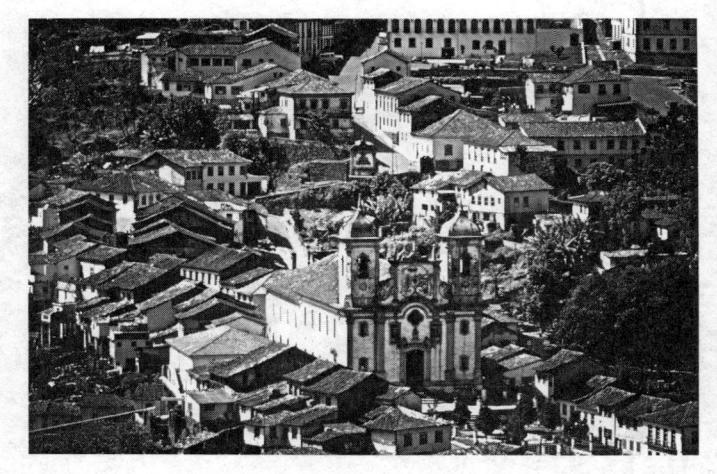

Rooftops of Ouro Preto

a national monument – an architectural preserve that may not be altered or added to. Ouro-Preto was founded in 1698. About 25,000 people live in the town itself, and a similar number in its suburbs. The town is famous for its many churches, each with its own particular charm and grace. Some contain statues by Aleijandinho. The town's streets are narrow, winding, and cobbled. The houses are generally two-story whitewashed buildings with red-tile roofs and wooden verandas – characteristic of the Portuguese-colonial style.

Ouro-Preto lies some 1100 m above sea level, and enjoys excellent weather all year round. Green hills surround the town on all sides. The most prominent is Pico do Itacolomi, a huge bluff south of the town that rises to 1753 m above sea level. Don't miss the impressive view from its summit, of the surrounding district and especially of the enchanting town at its base.

Many young people come from all over Brazil to study mine engineering at Ouro-Preto's famous university. This institution has turned Ouro-Preto into a campus town, full of youthful effervescence: every corner has its small bars and clubs, which are packed in the evenings with students.

Transportation

Ouro-Preto is 98 km from Belo Horizonte over a good road that passes through a mountainous landscape covered in greenery.

BRAZIL

OURO-PRETO

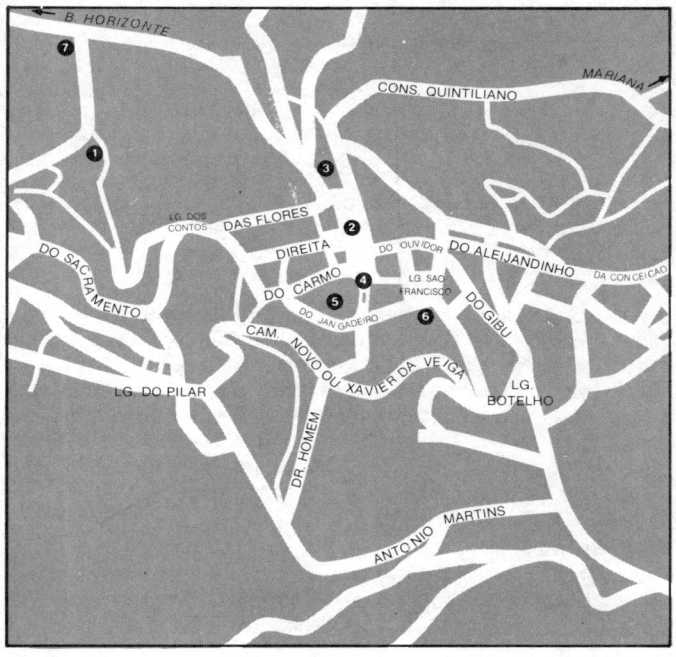

Index
1. Church of Sao Francisco de Paula
2. Praca Tirandentes
3. Museu de Mineralogia
4. Museu de Inconfidencia
5. Igreja do Carmo
6. Igreja Sao Francisco de Assis
7. Rodoviaria

The small bus terminal handles many daily buses from Belo Horizonte (less than two hours away), as well as direct buses from Rio de Janeiro, Sao Paulo, and Vitoria. The Util bus company, which runs most of the bus lines to Ouro-Preto, is good and reliable.

Food and lodging

Ouro-Preto has many hotels with varied levels of service and price, and there is usually no problem in getting a room. The *Grande Hotel*, at Rua Rocha Lagoa 164, is comfortable, spacious, and has a good view of the beautiful town. If you want to combine a vacation with a tour of the place, stay at the *Estrada Real Hotel*, situated 3.5 km from Ouro-Preto and far off the main road. The hotel offers its guests a sauna, pool, and

BRAZIL

bungalows. The *Colonial*, near the central square, is a moderate hotel – in terms of both quality and price.

Young tourists will have no trouble in finding an inexpensive place to spend the night. The town has plenty of student residences, known as *republicas*, whose tenants – students at the local university – are usually quite happy to put up tourists for a paltry sum, and sometimes for free. Make the rounds of the *republicas* until you find one that suits you.

The town has several restaurants. Although conventional restaurants can be found in the large hotels, there are many local gastronomical institutions tucked away on the narrow streets, which are well worth trying.

A good but expensive restaurant, serving the traditional fare of Minas Gerais, is the *Casa do Ouvidor*, at Rua Direita 42. Around the main square, **Praca Tiradentes**, there are a number of snack bars and fast food restaurants – which are small and inexpensive. You should definitely stroll through the streets and lanes of the town. At nightfall music can be heard emanating from many places, including discotheques, bars, clubs and restaurants, which makes for a very pleasant stroll.

What to see

The best way to appreciate Ouro-Preto's beauty and charm is simply to wander through its small streets. Along the way, visit some of the churches you pass, and experience the youthful atmosphere created by the local students. It is worth visiting the beautiful **Church of Sao Francisco de Paula**, which lies atop a hill at the entrance to the town. From here you have a bird's-eye view of the area. The souvenir and handicraft sellers, who congregate outside the church, will try to tempt you with their wares.

Many shops selling tourist souvenirs – especially precious stones and jewellery – are scattered around Praca Tiradentes in the center of town. There are also two interesting museums on the square. The **Museu de Mineralogia** (Museum of Minerology) is affiliated with the local university. Although small, it has a wonderful collection of minerals and gemstones. Don't miss it! (Open Tues.-Fri. noon-5pm; Sat. 8am-10am; closed on Sundays.) The other museum is the **Museu de Inconfidencia**, which was once a prison. Today, the building houses exhibitions of Christian religious art, statues by Aleijandinho, and documents and exhibits that recount the history of Ouro-Preto (Open Tues.-Sun. 11:30am-5pm).

There are only two cruises each month. Details and dates of departure can be obtained from the **Companhia Navagacao do Sao Francisco** boat company in Pirapora. The company's

BRAZIL

offices are at Avenida Sao Francisco 1396. The company also has offices in Juazeiro, at Rua Coronel Aprigio Duarte 3.

Some 10 km from Ouro-Preto, near the town of Mariana, is the goldmine known as Minas da Passagem. The chambers and tunnels in this mine, which dates back to the start of the 18th century, stretch to an overall length of 1140 m. The daily output of the mine is now around one kilogram of gold. You can take an organized tour of the quarry, which includes a descent in a miner's cage to an inactive sector of the mine. Later you will see how the gold is extracted from the silt (Open daily, 9am-6pm). A bus that leaves Ouro-Preto every half hour for Mariana stops at the mine. Recommended.

Not far from the town is an underground waterfall – **Cachoeira das Andorinhas** – hidden inside a cave carved out of the green, rocky landscape. Access to the cave is extremely complicated, since it is visible only after one reaches the edge of a bluff. Be sure to get precise directions before setting out. You can get there by car, or walk from Ouro-Preto (about an hour's walk).

Shopping

The typical handicrafts of Ouro-Preto are figures of stone, wood, or clay, jewelry, and of course precious stones, which are plentiful in the area. There are many souvenir shops scattered around the central square. All have a large, fairly similar selection, at a variety of prices. In Batia, one of the shops in the square, you will find a large selection of high-quality and inexpensive articles. At several "strategic points" in town, youngsters will spread cheap souvenirs at your feet. You can usually bargain down the price.

A boat trip down the Sao Francisco river

The **Rio Sao Francisco**, which originates in the mountain range of Minas Gerais, flows north and then east, before emptying into the Atlantic Ocean between Salvador and Maceio, in the north-east. Two steam boats cruise the river on a regular basis, connecting Pirapora in Minas Gerais with the twin towns of Juazeiro and Petrolina, located on opposite sides of the river, the first in Bahia and the second in Pernambuco. The river is navigable for some 1300 km, and a trip all the way down the river by steamboat takes about a week.

The average width of the river is about 500 m, and the surrounding landscape is monotonous and boring. Along its level banks you will see the occasional house and remote town. The boats make short stops at some of these towns – during which you can snatch a hurried tour. The local population is

BRAZIL

miserably poor, and the illiteracy rate is high. This is the other Brazil, worlds apart from the large cities and the developed south. Here you will discover a simple, primitive world, untouched by the Western pace of life.

There are only two cruises each month. Details and dates of departure can be obtained from the **Companhia Navagacao do Sao Francisco** boat company in Pirapora. The company's offices are at Avenida Sao Francisco 1396. The company also has offices in Juazeiro, at Rua Coronel Aprigio 3.

BRAZIL

Along the Coast from Rio to Salvador

Vitoria

Vitoria, the capital of Espirito Santo state, lies some 500 km north of Rio de Janeiro, and numbers some 150,000 inhabitants. The city lies at the junction of three important routes: north to Bahia, south to Rio, and west to Belo Horizonte and Brasilia. Some of the mineral resources of Minas Gerais are exported through the city's harbor. Vitoria is situated on an island, and is connected to the mainland by two bridges. The sandy beaches are suitable for bathing.

Near Vitoria, on the mainland, is the small colonial town of **Vila Velha**, founded in the 16th century. You can get there on a local bus marked Vila Velha, or on a ferry which leaves downtown every 20 minutes. At the top of the hill are the remains of the monastery of Nossa Senhora da Penha, and a beautiful view of the bay. The beaches of Vila Velha are among the most beautiful in the area, so take along bathing suits.

Guarapari

The summer resort of Guarapari (30,000 residents) is 54 km south of Vitoria. Most of the inhabitants live off tourism. The majority of tourists are Minas Gerais residents who come to spend their vacation by the sea. There is ample accommodation and many places of entertainment along the beach, but they are expensive, and fairly crowded during the summer. Guarapari offers its visitors peace and quiet. The town has pleasant beaches and good restaurants, and it has a quiet, agreeable atmosphere. If you are looking for a simple, relaxing vacation without much excitement, this is the place for you.

Porto Seguro

Porto Seguro, in south Bahia, is one of the oldest towns in Brazil. Little has changed here over the centuries. The small and quiet town has a mere 5000 inhabitants – the majority make their living from tourism, but some rely on fishing. The beautiful local beaches attract many Brazilian vacationers, as well as young tourists from all over the world.

BRAZIL

Transportation
Porto Seguro is about a 20-hour trip from Rio. Take any of the frequent buses from Rio or Vitoria to Salvador. Get off at Eunapolis, on the main road. There is frequent bus service from Eunapolis to Porto Seguro. The trip takes about an hour. The Sulba company operates direct buses from Salvador to Porto Seguro (about 10 hours). There is a small airport near the town, which serves only light planes. The Brazilian government, which in recent years has been attempting to develop the tourist industry in the area, has plans to improve the airport.

Food and lodging
Porto Seguro and the nearby villages, have only small hotels. Due to local conditions, they are of only moderate standard, or even less, but meet the requirements of most tourists to the area who are usually youngsters and backpackers. The same holds true of the restaurants, most of which specialize in seafood. In Porto Seguro you will have no trouble finding a place at an inexpensive hostel, *pousada*, but most tourists prefer to stay in the nearby villages of Ajuda and Trancoso.

The beaches
Porto Seguro and its environs are famous mainly for their beautiful beaches. On your way there, though, you should look around the town itself. There are no places of particular interest, but the town has a tranquil atmosphere, and it is pleasant to wander along the small streets. There is a tiny fishermen's port here. To the north and south stretch long sandy beaches, which border on coconut palms and thick vegetation. The small bus terminal is situated near the mouth of the little Rio Buranhem, where there is a small jetty used by the ferries that cross the river. A yacht leaves this jetty daily for a coastal cruise lasting several hours. The yacht anchors en route at several spots, to enable passengers to visit the beaches and go swimming.

Arraial de Ajuda
Arraial de Ajuda lies some 5 km south of Porto Seguro. To get there you must cross the river by ferry, and then take one of the jeeps or vans, *camionetas*, that leave frequently for Ajuda, or one of the several daily buses that continue to Trancoso. Ajuda is situated on a hilltop overlooking the coast. During the Brazilian tourist season – the summer vacation – the village is packed with crowds of young people. The pleasant beach at the foot of the hill has many bars, *barzinhos*, some of which also serve fish dishes. The town itself has plenty of inexpensive hostels (*pousadas*), as well as bars and small restaurants.

BRAZIL

The beach at the foothills of Trancoso

Trancoso

Trancoso, about 12 km south of Ajuda, is smaller than the latter and less popular with tourists. It has an enchanting beach – a wide, clean stretch of sand, coconut palms and vegetation, and clear, clean water. If you need a break from the vanities of the world, this is the place. Several buses a day from Ajuda to Trancoso follow a road through banana plantations and palm trees. The village itself has a number of small, inexpensive hostels, as well as fish restaurants and bars. You can reach Trancoso by foot from Ajuda along the coast – a beautiful hike that takes about 4 hours.

Morro de Sao Paulo

Morro de Sao Paulo is a small fishing village, on Ilha do Tinhare, an island near the town of **Valenca**. The village itself, whose houses are scattered on the upper slopes of the hill, lacks distinction, but the beaches below it are among Bahia's most beautiful. Since relatively few tourists come here, the tranquil and isolated character of the place has remained unspoilt.

A ferry leaves Valenca daily, arriving at Morro de Sao Paulo in the afternoon, and returning to Valenca early the following morning (the trip takes about an hour and a half). You can reach Valenca on the direct bus from Salvador or from the island of Itaparica. At Morro de Sao Paulo it's hard to find anything to eat except for fish, so take along fruit and vegetables from Valenca.

BRAZIL

There are no hotels, but you can rent rooms from the local inhabitants. Many visitors simply put up tents on the beach.

The splendid tropical landscape is endowed with thick vegetation and palm trees right up to the beach itself. Take a walk along the various hillside paths and along the beaches. If you climb beyond the village, you are sure to encounter small monkeys playing among the trees, and you can enjoy a magnificent view.

BRAZIL

Nordeste: Northeast Brazil

The demography of this region presents some particularly difficult problems. Illiteracy stands at 50 percent, the birth rate is Brazil's highest, and the infant mortality rate is one of the highest in the world. Nordeste is home to one-third of Brazil's population, but its contribution to the Gross National Product is only 12 percent. The region's interior hinterland is one of the few places on earth where the feudal system still persists: rich landowners live in large cities, while laborers live on the sugar and cocoa plantations, destitute and totally out of touch with the outside world. Drought is another problem that frequently plagues the region, especially the northern part. Droughts sometimes last several years in succession, followed by a period of especially heavy rains. In 1985, this phenomenon caused disastrous floods, in which many thousands lost their homes.

This notwithstanding, the tourist sees a very different picture: a pastoral scene of pleasant towns, small tranquil fishing villages, wonderful beaches that rank among the world's most beautiful, and an almost perpetual summer. The people are simple, friendly and warm. The *jangada*, a raft equipped with a large sail, is the symbol of the area.

The large cities of Nordeste are Recife and Salvador. Blacks comprise much of the population here – descendants of slaves brought from Africa, and mulattos of mixed African and Portuguese extraction. The language spoken here is different in accent from that of the south, and so is the music. The samba is less popular; the characteristic dances are the *forro* and the *frevo*, highly rhythmic and extremely fast dances with accordion accompaniment.

The government of Brazil has decided to exploit the tourist potential of the region and its wonderful beaches, and is investing heavily in developing tourism along the Nordeste coastline. Thus far the coastal area is inhabited mainly by fishermen and by young travelers on vacation, looking to let themselves go in a free atmosphere.

Salvador-Bahia

Salvador, capital of the state of Bahia, was founded in 1549 and served as Brazil's capital until the mid-18th century. With a population of 1,500,000, it is the fifth largest city in Brazil. Blacks

NORDESTE

BRAZIL

predominate here, and many live in grinding poverty. It is thanks to them that the local folklore developed, based on the African culture of the Black slaves. Salvador offers a combination of simplicity, poverty and mysticism, combined with Western sophistication. The well-known Brazilian writer Jorge Amado excelled in describing this strange world. The city's location on the edge of Baia de Todos os Santos (the Bay of Saints) and its famous beaches, have been an inspiration for writers and musicians. The city's many churches reflect the development of a special Christian sect which combines the beliefs and customs of the Africans with those of the Portuguese.

Salvador weather is about the same most of the year – hot, humid, and rainy. April is the rainiest and stormiest month, and the least suitable time to visit.

How to get there

The **2 de Julho Airport**, 28 km out of town, is served by several flights from Brazil's major cities each day, as well as by daily flights from provincial towns. Taxi fare into town is a little steep because of the distance. A special tourist bus goes to Praca da Se in the center of town. The regular bus follows the same route, and the trip lasts about one hour. In addition, microbuses set out at irregular intervals from the airport for the hotel district at Barra. They stop at the various hotels on request, and are considerably less costly than taxis.

The large bus terminal is quite far from downtown. Two good major bus companies, Penha and Itapemirim, link Salvador with all the large coastal towns to the north and south. Outside the terminal building there are bus stops for the many bus lines that serve all parts of town. Taxis are plentiful too. The buses are marked with route number and destination; taxis are white or red.

Tourist services

There are several information bureaus in Salvador. The tourist information bureau at the airport is open whenever the airport is, and has up-to-date information on hotels, restaurants, and tourist sites. The staff is happy to help you make hotel reservations. The main tourist bureau is between Praca Municipal and Praca de Se. There are smaller offices at Porto da Barra beach and the bus terminal.

Brazil's major airlines have offices in Salvador, most are downtown. Many countries have consulates here.

Food and lodging

Downtown is very lively during the day but becomes unpleasant and dangerous at night. *Pousado do Carmo*, a 5-star hotel,

SALVADOR

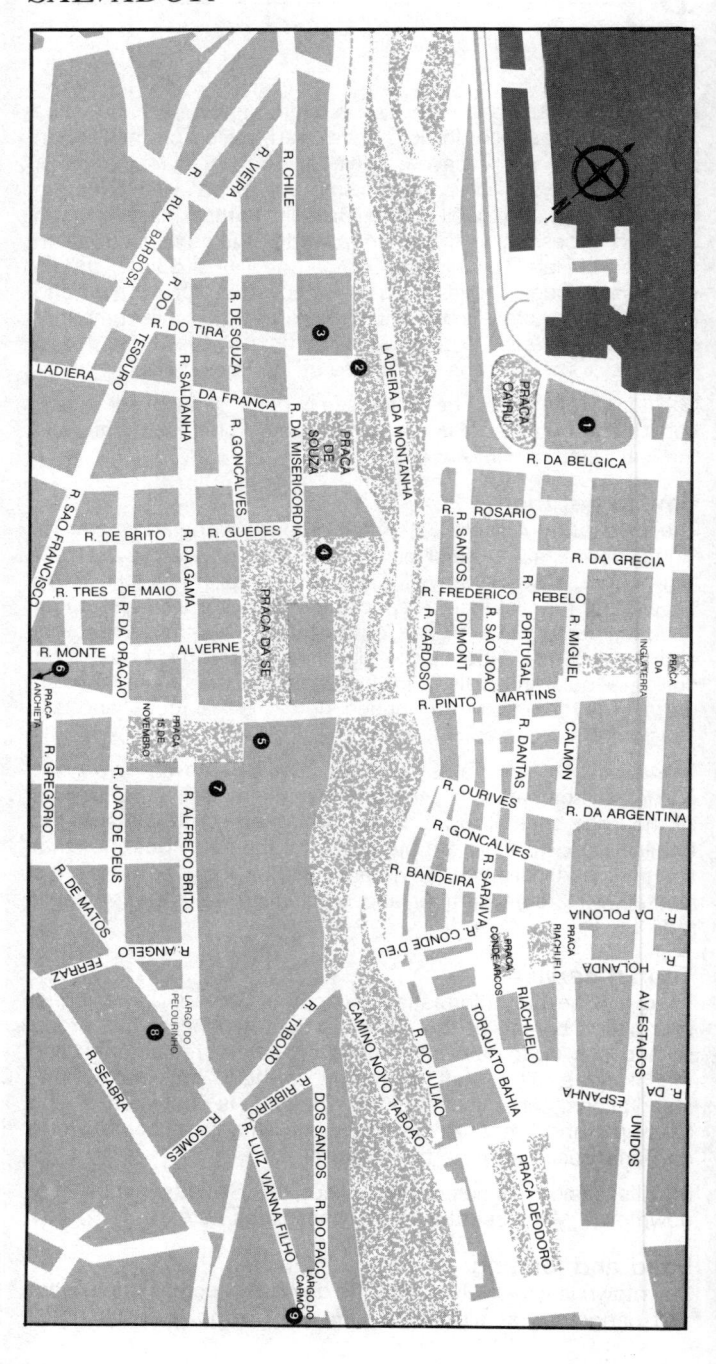

BRAZIL

notable for its pleasant atmosphere, is in the heart of this area at Largo do Carmo 1 (Tel. 242-3111). The *Pelourinho Hotel* at Rua Alfredo Brito 20 (Tel. 242-4144) is modestly priced and pleasant, but, once again, its interesting location is also its greatest drawback. The recommended hotel district is Barra, some 15 minutes away from the center of town. The *Quatro Rodas Hotel* is Salvador's finest. It has two excellent restaurants, and the French restaurant is especially superb. Although this hotel is far from the city, it is close to the airport and Itapoa Beach (Tel. 249-9611). The *Bahia Meridien Hotel* at Fonte do Boi 216, on the beach near Barra, is also highly recommended. It also has an excellent French restaurant (Tel. 248-8011).

Among the best medium price hotels is *Ondina Praia*, Avenida Presidente Vargas 2275. It is in a convenient location and has good service. *Barra Turismo*, Avenida 7 Septembro 3691, is less expensive and still good. The cheapest hotels are downtown around Praca da Se. These hotels are rundown, and the neighborhood is unpleasant, especially at night. One possibility is the *Vigo Hotel* at Rua 3 de Maio, about 100 m away from the square. Don't be in any hurry to book a room in one of these hotels; young travelers at least can choose an excellent hostel in a good neighborhood at a similar rate. Dona Carmen's house at Rua 8 Dezembro 326, in the Graca neighborhood close to Barra is recommended. The atmosphere is warm and homey, and the price includes an excellent Brazilian breakfast.

Bahia cuisine is perhaps the most interesting in Brazil. It is highly varied, relying largely on seafood cooked in many different, sometimes unusual, ways. *Moqueca*, fish cooked in coconut oil, is definitely worth trying. As in all Nordeste, there is an abundance of excellent tropical fruit. The best place for Bahai food is *Senac Restaurant*, on Largo do Pelourinho in the Pelourinho Quarter. This is a buffet-restaurant with some 40 main courses and 15 desserts on the menu. Open for lunch and dinner daily, except for Sunday. The best place for an informal dinner is the Barra Quarter, which has many bars and restaurants.

Downtown is packed with places to eat. The Bahia women sell local foods at colorful sidewalk stands. The aromas are appetizing, but conditions are not very hygienic.

Index
1. Mercado Modelo
2. Elevator Lacerda
3. Palacio Rio Branco
4. Tourist Information Bureau
5. Catedral Basilica
6. Igreja Sao Francisco
7. Museu Afro-Brasileiro
8. Senac Restaurant
9. Museu do Carmo

BRAZIL

The lift connecting upper and lower Salvador

What to see
Downtown
Central Salvador is divided into two: upper and lower downtown. The two sections are connected by the famous elevator, Elevador Lacerda, built in 1930. At its base is a large square, **Praca Cairu**. Across the way is the large building that accommodates the renowned Salvador market, called **Mercado Modelo**. The building was restored after a serious fire in 1984. Although the market is very touristy, it is lively and colorful. Souvenirs, Brazilian musical instruments, wood crafts, leather goods, lace, and clothing are on sale. Spirited bargaining will bring down the high prices quoted by the vendors. In the square behind the building, *capoeira* dances are sometimes held (see "Folklore"). The market is near a marina where boats depart for for the island of Itaparica. Opposite the marina is the round **Sao Marcelo Castle**, built in the l7th century.

On Praca de Souza in the Upper City, to the right of the elevator is **Palacio Rio Branco**, seat of the Governor of Bahia. Across the way is City Hall. To the left of the elevator, a wide platform overlooks the Lower City and Todos os Santos (Bay of All Saints). The street on the left leads to the **Praca de Se**, a small and neglected square surrounded by small shops. The monument in the center was erected in memory of Fernandez, the first bishop of Brazil (l6th century). This square links up with another, **Terreiro de Jesus**. Here there are no fewer than three churches. That closest to Praca da Se is **Catedral Basilica**, one of the most beautiful of the city's 135 churches. Built in 1672, it

BRAZIL

Bahian woman selling typical foodstuff

is an enormous place with gilded interior decorations. In the center of the square a fine *artesania* market is held every day with Bahian women selling local delicacies from stands.

On the far side of the square is **Igreja Sao Francisco**, constructed in the l6th century. The exterior facade of this church is not impressive, but the interior is decorated with paintings and gilded decorations. (Open Mon.-Sat. 8-11am, and 2-5:30pm.) To its left is a small church with an impressive Spanish-Baroque facade.

A narrow street, Rua Alfredo Brito, leads away from Terreiro de Jesus Square. The building on the left was formerly a medical school and today houses the **Museu Afro-Brasileiro**. (Open Tues.-Sat. 9:30-11:30am, and 1:30-5:30pm.) At the end of the street are some small *artesania* shops. Alfredo Brito leads into Largo Pelourinho, the neighborhood's central quarter, where the Black slaves once lived. Public floggings, intended as a deterrent to others, took place here. The quarter still retains its colonial atmosphere: the streets are narrow and cobblestoned, and each house is painted in a different color. On this square is the municipal museum and the excellent *Senac* restaurant.

We follow the street directly opposite. This is Ladeira do Carmo, also called Luiz Vianna. This street ends at another square, **Largo do Carmo**, where you will see a church and the **Santo**

BRAZIL

Antonio Fortress. The fortress played an important role in the Portuguese resistance to the Dutch occupation in the mid-17th century.

Retrace your steps and pass the Church and **Museu do Carmo**. The church has a painted wooden ceiling, and the museum displays religious art, a collection of coins, and an assortment of precious stones. Opposite the museum is a large souvenir store, Gerson, selling gems, jewelry, silvercrafts, and Bahian dolls.

Monte Serrat

The quiet, peaceful Monte Serrat Quarter is north of downtown on a peninsula. Buses bearing this name leave the Franca bus terminal in the Lower City. In the center of the neighborhood is the magnificent **Igreja Bonfim**, built in the mid-18th century. Note the huge altar, frescoes, high painted wooden ceiling, and dark wooden pews. Across from the church is a lovely square planted with date palms.

Next to the church is Rua Plinio de Lima, which we follow for several hundred metres. At its far end is the **Forte de Monte Serrat**, from which there is a nice view of the city of Salvador and of the bay as far as the beaches of Barra. Close by are two churches: Monte Serrat and Boa Viagem.

The Beaches

Of the bay's short, narrow beaches, the most pleasant is **Barra**, which has a 17th-century fortress, at either end: Santa-Maria and Sao-Diego. Beyond the stately lighthouse is **Faro da Barra**, a quieter beach.

The beaches on the Atlantic are better, with long, wide stretches of sand and soaring coconut palms. The most famous beach is also the farthest away: **Itapoa**, the inspiration for many a song. Buses marked Aeroporto or Itapoa reach this beach after traveling the length of all the other beaches. Two other good beaches along the way are Jardim de Ala and Piata. The great Iemanja festival, in honor of the Kandomela sea-goddess takes place at Vermelho beach each year (see "Folklore").

Itaparica

Thirty four islands are found in Todos os Santos Bay, and several are easily accessible by ferry. The most popular with tourists is Itaparica, which is served by a ferry which leaves from Sao Joaquim Terminal and docks at Bom Despacho. The ferry leaves once an hour from 6am-10pm, and the trip takes about 40 minutes. Buses go from the pier to the towns of Mar Grande and Itaparica. There is also a boat from the port near Marcado Modelo to Vera Cruz on Itaparica; from there the only means of transportation is by taxi

BRAZIL

Itapoa beach

The beaches of Itaparica are beautiful, even though they are not the cleanest. The vegetation is lush and tropical. The houses in these small and very tranquil towns are of simple colonial style. A Club Mediterranee has been established, and many Brazilians and foreigners spend vacations there.

Feira de Santana

This city of 225,000, about 115 km northwest of Salvador, is the center of a cattle raising district. One of Brazil's finest markets is held here on Mondays, when locals stream to town and peddle their wares, mainly leather products.

A great carnival, the **Micarete**, takes place here about two weeks before Easter. It is much smaller than the one in Salvador, but it's just as lively and noisy. The streets are packed with dancers and revelers. There is frequent bus service between Feira de Santana and Salvador, and the trip takes about 2 hours. The town has several hotels and restaurants, most rather modest.

The Salvador Carnival

The Carnival in Salvador is unquestionably the wildest and most exciting affair of its kind in Brazil. The festivities continue almost nonstop from beginning to end. Fleets of vehicles called *trios electricos* slowly cruise the city streets, with loudspeakers broadcasting music. Thousands of revelers follow them, dancing and singing for hours on end. The merrymaking dies down for a few hours in the morning, but at noon a parade of dance groups takes to the streets. In the afternoon, the *trios electricos*

BRAZIL

resume their rounds. This goes on for four solid days. The great dancing processions move mainly through the area between Graca and Praca da Se, via Praca Campo Grande. The crowd then heads back along parallel streets.

All the nightclubs and discotheques hold special dances for the Carnival, and some of them are really spectacular. The town's elite shows up, and tourists, too, will find this side of the Carnival worth visiting.

Warning: Exuberant and exciting as it is, the Salvador Carnival is also very violent. Muggings and robberies increase during this period, so don't carry any valuables. Try to stay on main streets, and avoid dark alleyways. Keep away from fights, which can develop very quickly.

Folklore

Bahian folklore is the most rich and interesting in Brazil, thanks to African customs and traditions brought by the slaves. Some of these customs are well integrated into Salvador's daily life. One example is the traditional attire of the Bahian women: beautiful, large white dresses, and special hats. *Figa*, the famous statuette of a clenched fist, is a symbol of luck. *Figas* in various sizes are for sale in every souvenir shop and stall.

In some places in town, including the Marcado Modelo building, there are street performances of the *capoeira* dance. In this African war dance, two participants kick at each other without making contact. It is fast paced, and the slightest lapse of coordination on the part of either participant is likely to end in injury. The accompanying music is monotonous and simple, played on a drum and a special string instrument called a *berimbao*. Several schools in Salvador teach *capoeira*; visit them and try your skills at this art. One of the best schools is the Associacao do Capoeira Mestre Bimba, on Praca Terreiro do Jesus at Rua Francisco Muniz Barreto 1, 1st floor. (Open Mon.-Sat., 7-9pm.)

Candomble is a pagan cult originating in Africa. The women handle the rituals while the men deal with secular matters. In the *Candomble* rite, the women dance for so long and at such a pace that they reach a trance-like state. Visitors may attend these ceremonies. One *candomble* center is Terreiro do Oxum Apara, at Ministro Carlos Coquiejo 44 in Itapoea. Children peddle *Fitinha do Senhor do Bonfim* – a bracelet which, according to *candomble* tradition, brings luck to its wearer.

The greatest and most famous *candomble* festival is *Iemanja*, which is held each summer about one month before the carnival. Iemanja is the goddess of the sea, who protects the fishermen and sailors. During this affair, thousands go down to the shore

BRAZIL

Capoeira battle dance

with flowers, incense and other gifts likely to please the goddess. These offerings are handed with great ceremony to the fishermen, who take to sea in their heavily laden vessels. Once they are at a distance from the shore, they toss everything overboard, where Iemanja awaits. This is followed by carnival-like festivities, with dancing in the street until the early morning. The scene recurs all over Brazil, but the one at Praia do Vermelho in Salvador is the biggest and most interesting.

Maceio

The largest town between Salvador and Recife is Maceio (pop. 400,000) – capital of Alagaos, industrial center of the whole region, and a major port, particularly for the export of sugar and tobacco. Downtown is a noisy place of no interest to the tourist. On the north end of town, along the beautiful Pajucara beach, there is a green and pleasant promenade with hotels, restaurants and places of entertainment. An *artesania* market takes place here on Sunday evenings.

Transportation

The airport of Maceio, about 20 km out of town, is served by daily flights from all major Brazilian cities and Natal, Belem, Manaus, Foz do Iguacu, and Florianapolis. The bus terminal on

BRAZIL

the outskirts of town is spacious and modern. Several buses leave daily for Salvador, Recife, and other large cities.

Two roads lead from Maceio to Recife. One is the main highway, which crosses the interior. The other is the slow, scenic route, passing small and picturesque villages, workers in the sugar fields, and along the beautiful coast with its sand dunes and palms.

Food and lodging
The best hotel on the promenade is the *Jatiuca*, Lagoa da Anta 220 (Tel. 231-2555), with a good restaurant which serves local cuisine. Another good hotel on the promenade is the *Luxor*, Avenida Caxias de Duque 2076. *Pousada Pajussare*, inexpensive and good, is on Praia Pajucara at Rua Jangadeiro Alagoas 1163. At Pontal da Barra there are small, simple restaurants serving excellent seafood.

Beaches
The Maceio area has some excellent beaches. About 3 km north of downtown is **Praia Pajucara** with fishing *jangadas*. At low tide, small natural pools form in the rocks all along the shore. **Praia Jatica**, about 10 km north of town, is another fine beach. Beyond it is one of the best beaches in the region, **Praia Graca Torta**, and a little further is **Praia Pratagi**, which also has hidden pools among its rocks. About 18 km south of town is **Praia Frances**, a broad, beautiful beach with palms. It is deserted on weekdays, but packed with local residents on weekends.

Pontal da Barra
This little village, about 3 km south of Maceio, is situated on a narrow stretch of sand dunes between the sea and a large lake called Lagoa Mundao. It is bedecked in greenery and palm trees. The houses are small and simple. Most people earn a living by fishing or making *artesania*. This is the place to buy lace, which is famous for its beauty and quality.

While visiting, rent a canoe and go out on the beautiful lake. The scenery is particularly gorgeous at twilight.

Recife

Recife is the capital of Pernambuco, and one of the largest cities in Brazil. Blacks constitute the majority of its population of 1,200,000. The city is situated on Brazil's Atlantic coast and is crossed by several rivers. The meaning of the Portuguese word *recife* is "reef," and the city takes its name from the many reefs along the coast.

Recife was established in 1709, although this is not evident from

BRAZIL

Serene beauty at Pontal da Barra

its modern boulevards, buildings, and the many bridges connecting its various sections. Not far from Recife is the town of Olinda, where the colonial ambience lingers on.

Recife is a major industrial and commercial center, whose development was accelerated by the growing sugar industry.

Transportation
For many tourists, Recife is the gateway to Brazil and to South America. Its international airport is about 10 km south of town, near Boa Viagem. Cheap flights are available from most European capitals, Miami, and places throughout Brazil. Taxis are available at the airport. The white taxis charge special fixed rates to take you directly to a hotel. Across the plaza there are regular orange taxis, which charge according to the meter. Buses marked "Aeroporto" leave the terminal every 10 minutes until midnight, traveling via Boa Viagem to the center of town.

Recife's central bus and train stations are situated near downtown. Trains to Maceio and Natal are slow and the bus is better.

Tourist Services
There are tourist information bureaus at the airport, the bus terminal, and the Casa da Cultura de Pernambuco on Rua

BRAZIL

Floriano Peixoto. All are are efficient, and provide information on the whole State of Pernambuco.

Tourists may also make use of a telephone information service. Dial 139 for all relevant information, in English, between 7am-10pm. The Pernambuco Ministry of Tourism, Empetur, is at the corner of Avenida Cruz Cabuga and Rua Artur Coufinho. Most airline offices are on St. Antonio, downtown. Most countries maintain consulates in the city.

Food and lodging

The luxury hotels are on the Boa Viagem promenade; the best are the *Miramar* at Rua Dos Navegantes 363 (Tel. 326-7422), and the *Othon Palace* at Avenida Boa Viagem 3722 (Tel. 255-1208). The *Savaroni* hotel, less expensive but recommended, is nearby at Avenida Boa Viagem 3727. Just two blocks from the beach is the *Casa Grande e Senzala*, Avenida Aguiar 5000 (Tel. 326-0260) – pleasant, moderately priced, and with a good restaurant. The *Albergue Arrecifes* hostel is one block from the shore at Rua Padre Carapuceiro 132 (Tel. 326-7549). With its rock-bottom rates, it is a favorite of young Brazilian and foreign travelers.

A few more hotels are available in Olinda, just north of Recife. The luxury *Quatro Rodas* is the best in town. It has an excellent restaurant, and is close to the beach at Avenida Moreira 2200 (Tel. 431-2955). Olinda also has some fairly inexpensive hostels, such as the *Hospedaria do Turismo* at Avenida Beira Mar 989. It's a very old establishment with lots of character, and the range of prices varies according to the standard of the room. *Pousada Barlavento*, Avenida Moreira 1745, is for the genuine bargain hunter.

The least costly places to stay in Recife are the hotels downtown, especially around the *Rodoviaria*. *Ysa Hotel*, Praca 17 287, has basic services but is very noisy. *Central Hotel* in Boa Vista, Avenida Manuel Borba 209, is only slightly more expensive than the former, but considerably better.

Recife has many good restaurants. Avenida Boa Viagem is lined with good restaurants and bars, most fairly expensive. The area is crowded at night, and is one of the recommended entertainment spots. The *Lobster* restaurant is at Boa Viagem 2612, and serves excellent seafood. At No. 4780 is the *Rodeio*, renowned for its meat dishes. Order *rodiseio* – all you can eat for a moderate price. *Costa Brava*, Rua Barao Leao 698, excels at local cuisine. For inexpensive eating, try downtown. *Gregorio* is one of the most popular establishments. There are also good restaurants, in this area, such as *Galo d'Ouro* which serves local dishes. *O Tocheiro*, near the Museu do Homen do

BRAZIL

Nordeste, is recommended for its continental food.

Olinda also has good restaurants. The *Mourisco*, Praca Joao Alfredo 7, is the best restaurant in town for local offerings. *L'Atelier*, Rua De Melo 9l, is outstanding for its food and service. *Rei da Lagosta*, on the beach at Beira Mar 1255, serves good fish and seafood. There is a Chinese restaurant on the same boulevard: the *Tai-Pei*, very good and relatively inexpensive.

What to see

As stated, Recife is crossed by several rivers. The commercial and business center is situated on a sort of peninsula called Santo Antonio. It is a combination of old and new: wide boulevards and skyscrapers alongside narrow alleyways and old houses, crowded markets and ancient churches. At the edge of the peninsula is a broad green square bordered by several important public buildings. To the north is the **Palacio do Goberno**, the seat of government of the State of Pernambuco. Opposite is the **Palacio da Justica**, the magnificent courthouse built in a rich neoclassical style. On the west of the square is **Teatro Santa Isabel**, the municipal theater.

On nearby Rua do Imperador, branching off the square, is **Igreja Santo-Antonia** and its abbey. The building's plain facade conceals an opulent interior: an embellished ceiling, an altar of impressive dimensions, and a lovely gilded room to the left of the entrance.

A little further on is a triangular plaza, Praca da Republica. South of this plaza the streets are narrow, and many are closed to vehicular traffic. The whole area, in fact, is a large and noisy market. Its heart is Mercado Sao Jose, where typical Nordeste products and handicrafts are sold. The lively and interesting market is open Mon.-Sat. 6am-5pm, Sun. 6am-noon.

There are several churches in the market vicinity. The loveliest is **Igreja Sao Pedro**, a fine example of Brazilian church architecture. The ceiling is made of wood and adorned with paintings; there are some magnificent altars on the sides, also made of wood and embellished with reliefs. Behind the church is a small abbey, and in front of it is a square surrounded by restaurants and *artesania* shops.

Cross the broad Avenida Dantos Barreto, close to the church of Sao Pedro, and continue a few blocks until reaching the **Casa da Cultura**, on the banks of the Rio Capibaribe. The building, erected in the mid-19th century, was the city jail until it became a cultural center in 1975. The prison cells have been converted into *artesania* shops, and folklore performances take place almost every afternoon in the courtyard. Across the river is the

BRAZIL

Boa Vista Quarter, more modern than Santo Antonio. This district contains bustling commercial areas alongside quiet residential quarters and spacious, green squares.

A short distance from downtown at Avenida de Agosto 2187 is the **Museu do Homen do Nordeste** – the Anthropological Museum of Northeast Brazil. Here is a tasteful display of Nordeste anthropology: dress, tools, housewares, furniture, and more. The explanations alongside each exhibit are in Portuguese only, but one may request a guided tour in English. (Open Tues., Wed., and Fri. 11am-5pm; Thurs. 8am-5pm, weekends 1-5pm.)

Boa Viagem, Recife's prestige neighborhood, is south of downtown. It extends along a fine stretch of coast, and has a promenade with luxurious hotels and restaurants. In vacation season, the beach is packed all day long. There is a reef of rocks parallel to the coast which at low tide is exposed, creating little pools of water. On Praca de Boa Viagem, an attractive *artesania* fair is held on weekend afternoons, with music, dancing and refreshments.

Olinda

About 7 km from Recife is Olinda. It's a delightful little town, founded in 1536 and stubbornly maintaining its colonial profile. Olinda is famous for cobblestone lanes that wind up the hillside to a lighthouse.

We begin our tour of Olinda at Praca do Carmo, close to the beach. Take the local bus from Avenida Guararapes in Santo-Antonio. The square is named for the old church located there, the **Igreja do Carmo**, built at the end of the l6th century. Although it is not particularly impressive, it is the main church of Olinda. From the square, head up Rua do Bonfim. It is typical of Olinda's streets, lined with one and two-story colonial houses with facades of different colors.

A right turn on the second street off the square, leads uphill to another square with a fine view of Olinda – small houses surrounded by greenery and coconut palms, with church spires protruding here and there. On the right of the square is another church, **Igreja da Se**, and the square itself is well appointed with bars and *artesania* shops. There is also a small market selling lace, shirts, and wood carvings. Watch the woodcarvers as they work with admirable speed and skill. At night, especially on weekends, the square bustles with young people. They crowd into the bars, some of which play dance music.

Continuing left, we reach the **Museu de Arte Sacre** not far away. The museum is small and not particularly interesting. (Open Tues.-Fri. 8am-noon and 2-6pm; Sat.-Sun. 2-6pm.) Farther up the street, where it turns left, is the **Igreja da Misericordia**,

BRAZIL

Olinda surrounded by greenery

which was built in 1540. It affords another beautiful view of Olinda. Follow the street to the foot of the hill, to **Mercado Ribeiro**, with its *artesania* shops. At the end of the street is the **Sao Bento monastery** with a beautiful church alongside.

The Olinda Carnival
Olinda has one of the most exciting carnivals in Brazil. It is marked with virtually nonstop merrymaking and festivities in the streets; the locals set aside only the morning hours to recharge their batteries for the day and the night ahead. Even then, the more zealous revellers do not stop. Unlike Salvador, where the *trios electricos* lead the dancing parade, Olinda has central platforms where music is played. Music can be clearly heard all along the routes taken by the dancers, as the parades whirl through the streets.

As with every carnival in Brazil, visitors should be wary of violence. Gangs of muggers roam the streets during the carnival period, so stay off dark side streets, leave valuables behind, and do not carry large sums of money.

Shopping
Recife Shopping Center in Boa Viagem is large and modern. It has shops, boutiques, department stores belonging to large chains, cafes, and restaurants.

The characteristic *artesania* of Recife and Pernambuco are carvings and engravings, lace, and ceramics. Of special interest

BRAZIL

are ceramic figurines of various characters – lovely but very fragile. The best places to buy them are Praca da Se in Olinda and Mercado Sao Jose. Prices are lower there than at the Casa da Cultura, and the selection is much wider.

The Caruaru Market

Caruaru, about 135 km west of Recife, is noteworthy for its market. (Open Wed. and Sat. 5am-7pm.) It is one of the finest and most interesting in Brazil, and the prices are particularly low. Various local products are sold, especially ceramics, leather and wickerwork. Bus service from Recife is frequent, and the trip takes about two hours.

Nova Jerusalem

This site is an approximate reconstruction of Roman Jersualem. During Holy Week (Semana Santa), an open theater is held here presenting the story of Jesus and his crucifixion. Stages are set up in "Jerusalem", and a different scene is depicted on each as the visitors and actors move from one stage to the next. The drama is interesting even for those who do not speak Portuguese, and the pyrotechnics are impressive. The site is really only worth visiting when there is a performance to see.

The easiest way of reaching Nova Jerusalem from Recife is by organized tour, which takes you to and from the performance in a comfortable bus. The second possibility is less expensive: take a bus from Recife to Caruaru and change for Fazenda Nova, which is within walking distance of Nova Jerusalem. If there is no bus back to Caruaru at the end of the show, hitch a ride in one of the jeeps leaving Fazenda Nova.

Guaibu

One of the most beautiful beaches in the Recife area is Calheta, within walking distance of the village of Guaibu. The beautiful beach borders a small, deep bay with clear blue water, and its narrow strip of sand is edged with hills and greenery. The village is lively and many young people come here on holiday to enjoy the beautiful beaches. Guaibu is reached from the town of Cabo, not far from Recife.

Joao Pessoa

Some 120 km north of Recife on the shores of the Rio Paraibam, is Joao Pessoa (pop. 200,000), capital of the State of Paraiba. It is a grey industrial town, with nothing of interest to tourists apart from the impressive, 18th-century **Igreja Sao Francisco**.

About 7km away is the beautiful beach and fishing village of **Tambau**, with a very expensive hotel and a good restaurant. Approximately 11 km to the south is Cabo Branco, the

BRAZIL

Natal – Genipabu beach

easternmost point in the Americas. The view is beautiful, and there is a good restaurant.

The airport is about 11 km from downtown, and planes land every day from all over Brazil. The bus terminal is a little far out from downtown. It is served by several buses every hour from Recife, and others from Natal and Fortaleza.

Natal

Natal (pop. 380,000) is the capital of Rio Grande do Norte. The city, located on the eastern bank of the Rio Potengi, is the region's industrial and commercial center. While it does have several interesting sites, the real attraction here is the proximity of some marvelous beaches.

Transportation

The airport is about 15 km out of town and is served by flights from all major Brazilian cities. The bus terminal is at Cidade Esperanca, quite far from downtown. Traveling time to Recife is about five hours, to Fortaleza about seven hours.

Food and lodging

The best hotel in town is the *Ducal*, downtown at Avenida Rio Branco 634, which also has a good restaurant. Another good hotel facing the beach is *Reis Magos*, at Avenida Cafe Filho 822. Less expensive is the *Sambura*, at Rua Professor Zusa 263 downtown. A highly recommended economy-class hotel is *Pousada Meu Canto*, at Rua Manuel Dantas 424 in the

BRAZIL

Patropolis Quarter.

Case de Mae, Rua Pedro Afonso 153, serves excellent local cuisine at reasonable prices. *Do Marinho*, not far away in the downtown area at Rua Areial 267, is also very good and reasonably priced. *Xique-Xique*, Avenida Afonso Pena 444, is an elegant restaurant.

What to see

Stop at the municipal tourist bureau at Avenida Hermes da Fonseca 970 for information on the various sites and how to reach them. The main street in town is Avenida Rio Branco. At the central square, **Praca Joao Maria**, there are two churches: one old and traditional, the other modern. Natal's oldest structure (16th century) is **Forte dos Reis Magos** – the bastion on the Praia do Forte. **Mercado do Alecrim** is an *artesania* market which is worth visiting.

About 20 kilometers from Natal is a missile installation known as the Barreira do Inferno (Devil's Barrier). One can visit here, but only in organized groups. Make reservations 48 hours in advance at one of the travel agencies that organize these outings.

Beaches

There are several marvelous beaches in the immediate vicinity of Natal. One of the most beautiful is **Genipabu**, about 30 kilometers north of town. There is a large sand dune, with many palms, which slopes steeply into the blue sea. Another excellent beach is **Ponta Negra**, 14 kilometers south of town, and farther away is another beautiful beach, **Piranji**.

Fortaleza

Fortaleza (pop. 650,000) is the capital of the State of Ceara. It is a pleasant city which enjoys the natural amenities of Nordeste: almost year-round summer, lovely beaches, and friendly people. The *artesania* in this city is famous throughout Brazil for its beauty and quality. The superb lobster delicacies are also outstanding.

Transportation

The Fortaleza airport, about 9 km from town, is reached by daily flights from almost all the large cities of Brazil, as well as Manaus, Natal, Florianopolis, and Foz do Iguacu. The airport is not noted for its services. The passenger terminal is old and has no air-conditioning, and the tourist office is inefficient. The special airport taxis are white, and the regular ones are orange.

BRAZIL

Fishermen hauling in their catch

The spacious, efficient bus terminal is outside the city center. Several buses arrive every day from Recife after a 13-hour trip. The bus ride to Belem takes about 24 hours, as does the trip to Brazilia. From the bus terminal, bus 502 heads for downtown, reaching Praca Jose de Alencar, the municipal central bus station.

Food and lodging

Luxury hotels are concentrated in Beira Mar, and the most conspicuous are those along the coast on Avenida Presidente Kennedy. The two very best are *Esplanada Praia* at Avenida Kennedy 2000, and the *Imperial Othon Palace* at Avenida Kennedy 2500. In the same area, on Avenida Kennedy 1696, is *Hotel da Praia* – with an excellent location, basic services, and rather low rates. The truly inexpensive hotels are downtown in the Praca da Se area, mainly along Rua Pompeu. By day this is a bustling business area, but at night it becomes an unpleasant red-light district.

Beira Mar is also the area for good restaurants and bars. *Trapiche* is an excellent fish restaurant with unsurpassed and renowned lobster delicacies. It is situated at the far end of Avenida Kennedy at No. 3956. Another restaurant which serves very good seafood is the adjacent *Aquarius*. *Sandra's*, on Praia do Futuro, is one of the best restaurants in town. *Mikado*, next to the Museum of History, serves good steak.

BRAZIL

Setting sail in a jangada

What to see

Downtown bustles during the day, and traffic inches along. At Avenida Pompeu 350 is the **Centro de Turismo**, built in the mid-19th century as the city jail. Today it houses an *artesania* market, a restaurant, and a tourist office (on the first floor). The second floor accommodates **Museu de Arte e Cultura Populares**. (Open Mon.-Fri. 8am-noon and 2-6pm; Sat. 8am-noon.) The museum has a large model of a *jangada*, the typical raft of Nordeste fishermen, and displays various artifacts of daily life.

Not far from the tourist center is a large fortress, **Fortaleza Nossa Senhora da Assuncao**, which lent the city its name. It was built by the Dutch, and renovated in 1810. On Praca da Se is the large, strange **Catedral de Se**, which from the outside looks like a fortress. In the center of the square stands a statue of Emperor Dom Pedro II. The covered city market is next to the square. The *artesania* here is fantastic; don't hesitate to haggle.

The wealthy section of Fortaleza is in the west. Three beaches – Meireles, Iracema, and Mucuripe – are really one stretch of shore, with Avenida Kennedy and its lovely promenade alongside. Most of the town's prestigious hotels and restaurants are found here. Every evening between 6-8:30pm a pleasant, well-stocked *artesania* market opens along the promenade, and everyday around 3pm the *jangada* return to the beach at the

BRAZIL

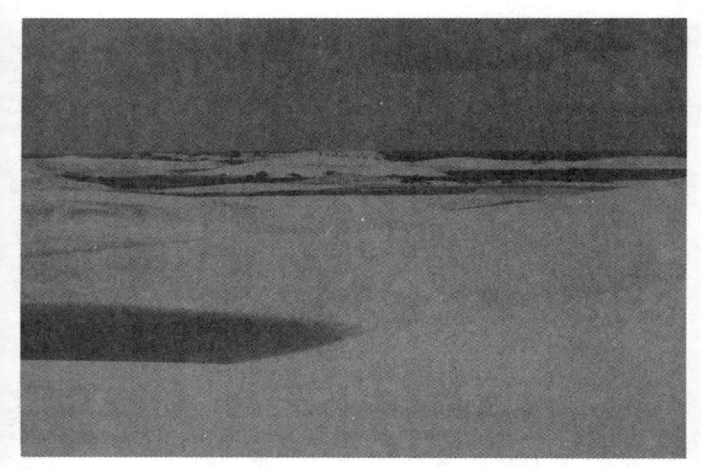

Paracuru – pools of fresh water in the dunes

end of Avenida Kennedy. One can watch the fishermen bring in their catch, and buy some fresh fish at the same time.

The **Museum of History and Anthropology** is at Avenida Barao de Studart 410, but it does not have very interesting exhibits. Across the way is the modern government building; next to it is the mausoleum of Castelo Branco and his wife. He was a president of Brazil, who died in an aviation accident.

Shopping
Fortaleza offers a wide variety of interesting and beautiful *artesania*, at some of the lowest prices in Brazil. The hammocks for sale here are renowned for beauty, quality, and low price. Bottles of multicolored sand, superb embroidery, and marvelous ceramics are typical local *artesania*.

At Central de Artesanato, Avenida Santos Dumont 1500, one can watch the artists at work. If you are buying, bargain over the prices. Another good place to buy *artesania* is Mercado Central. Several shops sell hammocks along the streets just west of Praca da Se. Prices are low, the selection is large, and quality is good. Dozens of fine shops on Avenida Monsenhor Tabosa stock *artesania*. (Open Mon.-Sat. 8am-4:30pm.)

The Beaches of Ceara
The State of Ceara has about 600 kilometers of beaches, and they are undoubtedly Brazil's loveliest: golden sand, white

BRAZIL

dunes, palms, and kilometer after kilometer free of human presence. Several beaches attract throngs of young people from Brazil and elsewhere. The most famous and popular is **Canoa Quebrada**, just outside the city of **Aracati**. Buses reach Aracati from Natal and Fortaleza, and Aracati itself is a point of departure for vehicles heading for Canoa Quebrada. This village bustles with life and offers an abundance of bars and simple little restaurants.

Closer to Fortaleza, 78 km to the southeast, is the lovely **Morro Branco** beach with its multicoloured sand. If you prefer an excellent beach in the city's immediate vicinity, try **Praia do Futuro**.

The village of **Paracuru** is a three-hour bus ride west of Fortaleza. The entire coastal area here consists of splendid dunes, which descend steeply into the ocean. After heavy rains, fresh water gathers in pits carved into the dunes. On weekends the place is packed with young people from Fortaleza. The surfers who spring into action when the sea picks up are well worth watching. Weekend *forro* parties at the oceanside bar attract crowds of young people from Fortaleza and the vicinity.

Sao Luis

Sao Luis, founded by the French in 1612, is between Fortaleza and Belem. This city, the capital of Maranhao, is situated between two bays on an island linked to the mainland by a bridge. Although its downtown area is bustling, a 17th-century ambience lingers on. The colonial architecture is lovely, but most of the buildings are rundown. On the northern side of the channel is the Sao Francisco neighborhood, the "New City" of Sao Luis, with well kept residences. Sao Luis is known for the great extremes of its tides. In the afternoon, at low tide, vast areas of the sea bed become visible.

Transportation

The airport of Sao Luis, which is small but efficient, is situated about 10 km out of town, and has many connections every day from all parts of Brazil. Taxis wait at the airport's exit, and buses set out for town every hour. The Sao Luis bus terminal is about 5 km from downtown. The trip from here to Fortaleza takes about 16 hours, and there are direct buses to Recife as well. The trip from here to Belem is very difficult, and parts of the road are unpaved. Two buses cover the route every day, and the trip takes about 13 hours.

Food and lodging

Quatro Rodas, 8 km out of town on the Calhau beach, is an

BRAZIL

excellent hotel, with a lovely landscape, good recreation, tennis court, fine restaurant, and two bars (Tel. 227-0244). *Hotel Vila Rica* on Praca Dom Pedro is good, centrally located, and has a fine restaurant. Next to it on the square are another two hotels: *Lord* and *Central*. Both are inexpensive. One can spend the night for a nominal fee at *Casa do Estudante* (the student hostel), just outside the city center on Rua do Passeio.

What to see
The historical center of Sao Luis is along Avenida Dom Pedro II. On this lovely boulevard stands the government palace, **Palacio dos Leoes** (Palace of Lions), built in 1776. (Open Tues. and Thurs. 4-6pm.) Continue up the avenue to the place where it turns into **Praca Dom Pedro**. On this square is **Palacio Arquiepiscopal**, the bishop's residence, and next door is **Catedral da Se**. Built in 1763, it is one of the most beautiful churches in town. Dom Pedro is linked to another square – Praca Benedito Leite, where there are several little bars as well as some shops and hotels. The cobblestone streets around this square are very old and most of the houses date from the 18th and 19th centuries.

From here, turn onto Rue do Sol and follow the street to a three-sided plaza, **Praca Joao Lisboa**. Another two blocks and we reach Teatro Artur Azevedo, constructed in 1817. A little further is the **Museu Historico e Artistico do Maranhao**, (Open Tues.-Fri. 2-6:30pm, weekends 3-6pm). Further along the road is another square, **Praca do Panteon**, where the municipal library stands. Next to this square is **Quinta do Barao**, which is a good example of the colonial estates of Nordeste.

Again, don't miss the tides. Go down to the beach at Avenida Beira Mar early in the morning, when high tide is at its peak, and come back in the afternoon to see how far the ocean has receded.

A local festival, Bumba Meu Boi, is held here in the second half of June. Its official date is June 24, but the festivities begin several days earlier. Watch dance parades in the streets and note the traditional costumes.

Alcantara
Alcantara is opposite Sao Luis on the western side of Sao Marcos Bay. It's an interesting small town, which served in the distant past as the capital of Maranhao. All that remains of its golden years in the 17th and 18th centuries are ruins, a few miserable streets, dilapidated colonial houses, and a handful of rundown churches. The ruins of **Casa do Imperador** are overgrown with vegetation, as are the remains of **Forte de**

BRAZIL

Sao-Sebastiao (mid-17th century). The **museum of Alcantara** is open Tues.-Sun. 9am-1pm.

A week of traditional local festivities begins on May 15. A "prince" and "princess" for the week are elected each year, and a carnival atmosphere prevails.

Boats from Sao Luis set out for Alcantara every morning at 8am from the marina at Praca Pinto Martinez, opposite Avenida Dom Pedro II. The trip takes about an hour and a half. The boat returns to Sao Luis between 1-2pm, depending on how low the tides are that day. Once you arrive, find out the time of the return trip. Alcantara itself has a couple of little hostels and a few simple seafood restaurants.

BRAZIL

The Amazon Basin

The Amazon River and the jungle covering the immense Amazon basin fire the imagination as few other sites can. The river's tremendous dimensions are beyond human conception, and the endless jungle, with its innumerable species of animals – for whom this is the last stronghold – is one of nature's most incredible wonders.

The Amazon, the world's second longest river, originates in the Andes of western South America and spills into the Atlantic Ocean after a journey of 6280 km. Its volume is the world's largest by far – 15 times that of the Mississippi. In certain areas it is tens of kilometers wide. Hundreds of tributaries drain into the huge Amazon basin. Many of the tributary rivers which feed into the Amazon and flow through Brazil have their origins in Bolivia, Peru, Equador, Colombia and Venezuela.

Brazil began developing the Amazon region, which comprises a major portion of its territory, in the 1950s. This development included the large-scale project of building the Trans-Amazon Highway. The project was a failure, and it was severely detrimental to the environment and to the tribal Indian population. Once the road was finished, it proved passable by motor vehicle during the dry season only, and the fortune taken from Brazil's impoverished national coffers had gone down the drain.

Belem

Belem is situated on the southern bank of the Amazon delta. This city, capital of the state of Para, has a population of about 750,000. Until the 1960s, when a road was built from Belem to Brasilia in the country's interior, the city was accessible only via river and air routes. Founded in 1616, Belem today serves as a commercial and industrial center, mainly for wood and textiles. Its port is the largest and most important on the Amazon.

Situated slightly south of the equator, Belem has a tropical climate – very warm and muggy. All year round at the stroke of 3pm, they say, heavy downpours wash the city, and certainly during our brief stay there, that's exactly what happened.

How to get there
Belem's international airport serves regular flights from all over

BRAZIL

THE AMAZON BASIN

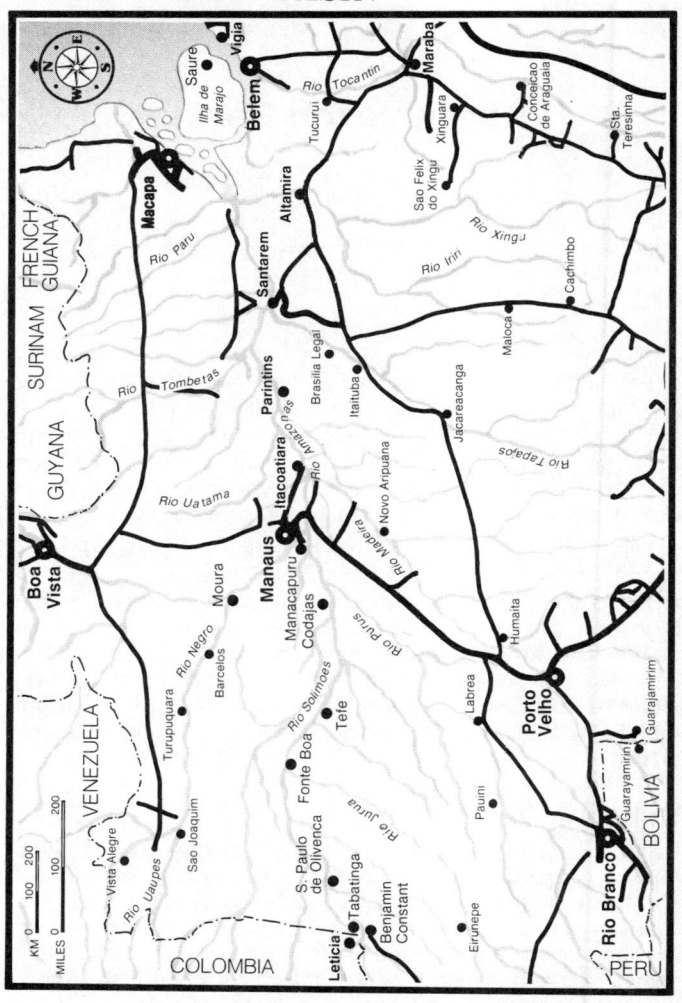

Brazil, daily flights from Buenos Aires, and weekly flights from Miami and Spain.

Belem can be a point of departure or final destination for a cruise on the Amazon. Most passenger boats sail to Santarem and Manaus, with occasional voyages to Porto Velho. The

BRAZIL

journey upriver to Manaus takes about 5-6 days, and the ships are packed with passengers. The river is very wide in this area, so don't expect to see breathtaking tropical jungle scenes from the middle of the river. There are three passenger classes: cabins (the most expensive), first class (on deck in the fresh air), and second class, in the ship's interior (hot, crowded, and noisy because of the engine). Never mind the low price; pass up second class! You would have to come equipped with hammocks, mosquito netting, and bug-repellent. All tickets include meals, but they are far from filling; it is a good idea to bring fruit. Cruises are organized by the government-owned Enasa company, and the ships set sail from Porto de Enasa on Avenida Castilhos Franca.

The local bus terminal is located 5 km from the center of town. A few buses leave daily for Brazilia. There is a bus to Santarem once a week, which travels along the Trans-Amazon Highway. Service is more frequent to Maraba, from which Santarem is easily accessible. Two buses a day depart for Sao Luis, traversing a difficult road, and two others go to Fortaleza and Recife. There is a direct bus every day to Rio de Janeiro.

The flight from Belem to Manaus deserves special mention because of the gorgeous scenery it flies over. The flight crosses the Amazon where it is at its widest – so that one sees one bank only, the other is hidden somewhere beyond the horizon!

Food and lodging

The *Hilton Internacional Belem* is excellent and centrally located at Avenida Presidente Vargas 822 (Tel. 223-6500). Another good hotel is the *Novotel*, on Avenida Bernardo Sayao 4804 (Tel. 226-8011). This hotel is far from downtown, but has a shuttle service of its own that runs several times a day. Both hotels have good restaurants with continental cuisine. *Vanja*, at Rua Benjamin Constant 1164 (Tel. 222-6457) is easier on the budget and more centrally located. *Hotel Avenida*, at Presidente Vargas 404, is very inexpensive. In the Old City area near the harbor there are a few low-cost hotels which offer basic services.

Near the Castello fortress is a good fish restaurant, *Circulo Militar*. Its specialty is a typical Belem fish dish called *pirarucu*. *O Outro*, at Avenida Jose Malcher 982, serves good local cuisine. *Hotel Equatorial*, downtown at Avenida Braz de Aguiar 612, has two good restaurants: the continental *1900*, and the *Terrace Grill*, which specializes in meat dishes.

Tourist services

The municipal tourist office is at Avenida Nazare 231. Several

BRAZIL

countries, including the United States, Great Britain, Venezuela, and Colombia, have consulates in the city.

International phone calls can be made at the bus terminal and the airport. An additional phone exchange is located downtown at Praca de Republica, at the corner of Vargas and Riachuelo. The phone company is called Telepara.

A recommended travel agency is Ciatur, with offices at Avenida Presidente Varga 645.

What to see

Belem's commercial center is situated at **Praca de Republica**, a spacious and green square. In the center of the square stands the splendid **Teatro de Paz**, built in 1874 in neoclassical style. Worth a visit (Open Mon.-Fri, 8am-noon and 2-6pm).

Close to the river's edge is the triangular Praca Castilhos Franca, the heart of the city's old district. A little beyond it is the harbor for fishing boats, and a colorful, crowded market – **Mercado Ver O Peso**. We continue along the riverside until reaching **Forte de Castelo**, a bastion dating from the nineteenth century, close to the landing place of the city's Portuguese founders. Across the way, still at the square, is Belem's oldest church built in the early 17th century.

Across town on Avenida Nazare is the enchanting **Basilica da Nazare**, its interior lined with gilded ornamentation and frescoes. Somewhat further, at Avenida Magelhaes Barata 518, is **Museu Emilio Goeldi**. (Open Tues.-Fri. 8am-noon, 2-6pm; Sat. 8am-1pm.) This large museum encompasses a zoo and a botanical garden, which exhibit a selection of jungle flora and fauna. There is also an interesting anthropological museum.

Ilha do Marajo

From Belem, this island is reached by a 5-hour river cruise or a 30-minute flight in a light plane. Large areas of this enormous island are almost uninhabited; its population of 90,000 is concentrated in 7 different towns, the main one being **Soure**. Marajo island is unique for its many buffalo herds. There are a number of farms (*fazendas*) on the island where tourists can stay, and from which one can set out on wildlife observation safaris. Several travel agencies in Belem organize excursions to the island, which set out from the city itself. They are good, and recommended, but expensive.

Mosqueiro

The town of Mosqueiro is located on an island of the same name. It is reached by an excellent road from Belem 86 km away, and a bridge connects the island with the mainland. The island is covered in tropical jungle, and the beaches are sandy

BRAZIL

Alligators at Museu Emilio Goeldi in Belem

and pretty – especially **Baia do Sol**, 26 km north of town. There are other lovely beaches west of the town. In Mosqueiro there are several hotels and restaurants.

Santarem

Halfway between Belem and Manaus, on the Amazon's south bank near its confluence with the Tapajos, is the city of Santarem (pop. 100,000) which serves as a center of the lumber and textile industries. The convergence of the two rivers is an impressive sight, as the rivers maintain their different colors even after they merge. Passenger boats set out from Santarem for the confluence. Beautiful, sandy beaches are close at hand. Worthy of special mention are those along the Tapajos. In the rainy season, however, the river submerges every strip of beach.

It's about a two-day boat trip from Belem or Manaus to Santarem, and flights between Belem and Manaus stop over in Santarem. Most of the hotels and restaurants here are, at best, mediocre.

Manaus

Manaus is on the Amazon's northern bank, about 1700 km upriver. With a population of about 650,000, it is the largest of

BRAZIL

Opera house at Manaus

the river cities. Manaus is the capital of Amazonas, Brazil's largest state. Until just a few years ago, there was no land access to Manaus; the city could only be reached by air or river. It has a large harbor, and because the river is so wide and deep, even large ships can sail as far as Manaus.

Today there are roads to Manaus from Porto Velho in the south and Boa Vista in the north. Just a few kilometers out of town is the confluence of the Amazon's two largest tributaries: the Rio Negro and the Rio Salimoes. Manaus itself lies on the bank of the Rio Negro, aptly named for its black water.

At the end of last century, Manaus became a boom town after rubber was discovered nearby. The Amazon area was the world's only source of this commodity at the time, and rubber accounted for 25% of Brazil's exports in 1880. The famous opera house, built at the time, mirrors that prosperity. As suddenly as prosperity came, however, so did it end. Malaysia also began growing rubber trees, and Manaus lost its monopoly and its mad attraction for investors. Today it is a city like any other – busy, crowded, and dull – and the opera house stands like a monument to the days of glory. In 1967, in an attempt to revive Manaus' economy, the city was declared a duty-free zone. This turned it into a bustling shopping center. Tourists arriving in Manaus are asked to declare all valuables in their possession upon arrival, and all purchases upon departure.

BRAZIL

The lively floating port at Manaus

Transportation

Eduardo Gomes International Airport, about 14 km from downtown, is modern and spacious. Connections to and from the airport are handled by fixed-rate taxis and by buses that run every 30 minutes. There are many flights between here and destinations throughout Brazil, and there are other regular connecting flights with most South American capitals, Mexico City, and Miami.

The harbor where the passenger boats dock is close to downtown and hums with people and activity. Schedules are irregular. There are frequent trips to Belem (a 4-day journey) and other vessels travel to Benjamin Constant or Tabatinga, both situated where the borders of Brazil, Peru, and Colombia converge (about 8 days journey). There is occasional direct boat service to Leticia on the Colombian border, and Iquitos in Peru. Boats traveling between Porto Velho and Manaus leave more frequently.

Even today, despite the Trans-Amazon Highway and the clearing of a road to Porto Velho, most traffic is still handled by river and air transport. The bus terminal, called *Rodoviaria*, is located out of town, on the way to the airport. It is reached from downtown by buses marked "Aeroporto" or "Praca 14". From the terminal, buses leave several times a day for Porto Velho, and there is a daily bus to Boa Vista, en route to Venezuela. Buy

BRAZIL

tickets several days in advance, because the buses are usually full.

Food and lodging
The *Tropical Manaus* hotel, about 18 km out of town on the Ponta Negra beach, is the best and most expensive in town (Tel. 238-5757). The best accommodation downtown is at the *Amazonas* on Praca Adalberto Vale (Tel. 234-7679). It has a restaurant, a coffee-shop, and a sauna. There are four hotels on Rua Dr. Morreira, including the moderately priced *Internacional* and the inexpensive *Nacional*. Genuinely cheap hostels and hotels are concentrated on Rua Joaquim Nabuco. Manaus does not specialize in good restaurants. The best belong to the large hotels, particularly the *Tropical Manaus* and the *Amazonas*.

Tourist services
The spacious airport has an efficient tourist information office. Call direct from there to the city's major hotels. Additional tourist offices are located downtown at Praca 24 de Otubro, at the floating harbor, and in the main Post Office at Marechal Deodoro 117. Several travel agencies in town organize jungle tours. Selvatur (offices on Praca Adalberto Vale, in the *Amazonas* hotel) is recommended.

Most South American countries, and some European countries, station diplomatic representations in Manaus. The United States Consulate is at Maceio 62.

What to see
The first stop is the fabulous opera house, **Teatro Amazonas**. This magnificent building, built in 1896 and renovated in 1974, reflects the affluence and prosperity of that earlier period. Its facade is decorated with columns and statues, and crowned with a gilded dome. The interior is divided into several halls. The largest is the playhouse, with seating for 700. The ceiling is adorned with four paintings, each depicting a different type of art: music, dance, drama, and opera. Worthy of particular attention is the ballroom, which is the loveliest hall of all. Note the floor, made of 12,000 wooden strips. The walls are covered with paintings depicting Amazon jungle scenes, and the ceiling is also decorated. The marble was imported from Italy. The opera house, (open Tues.-Sun. 9am-6pm), is situated on Praca Sao Sebastiao. There is a beautiful fountain in the square, and on the right is the **Igreja Sao Sebastiao** (Sao Sebastiao Church). Not far from the square is the neoclassical **Palacio da Justica** (courthouse).

The tax-free shopping district lines the narrow, crowded downtown streets. Along the river is the **Porto Flutuante**, the floating harbor. Owing to major fluctuations in the river's water

BRAZIL

level, the piers are not fixed but are left to float. River boats drop anchor here, and there is a continuous bustle of loading and unloading. Close to the harbor is the crowded **Mercado Municipal** (municipal market), with the fishing boat jetty across the way. If you want to explore the Amazon on your own, find a guide here, and remember to haggle over the price.

Museu do Indio (the Indian Museum) is at the corner of Avenidas 7 de Setembro and Duque de Caxias. The museum depicts the life of Rio Negro's Indian tribes – clothing, handicrafts, and ritual implements. (Open Mon.-Sat. 8-11am and 2-5pm.) **Palacio Rio Negro** at Avenida 7 de Setembro currently serves as the governor's residence. Formerly it was the splendid home of a rich German merchant.

Jungle excursions

Manaus is a good point of departure for tours of the Amazon and the jungle. The river is immensely wide in this area, with a proliferation of islands, narrow channels, and lovely lagoons.

Remember, however, that this is a settled area, and do not expect a voyage into the unknown, or fascinating encounters with wildlife. Only an expensive trek lasting many days can provide such an adventure.

There are two ways to explore the jungle. The first is to join a travel agency's organized tour, and the other is to hire a guide with a canoe, and negotiate with him the duration, route, and price of the trip. The guides can be found in the marketplace and the adjacent fishermen's jetty. Always bargain, and never pay more than half the sum in advance! In any event, these excursions are very expensive – generally more expensive than tours elsewhere along the Amazon.

Most tours probe little channels bursting with tropical vegetation. One may also fish for pirhanas, and trap crocodiles. Here one can see the huge water plant called *Vitoria Regia* which grows up to 3 meters in diameter. There are also rubber trees and, if you are fortunate, you may see some wildlife. An impressive sight is the confluence of the Rio Negro and Rio Salimoes. The waters of the Rio Negro really are black, and the waters of Rio Salimoes are grey. There is no doubt about where the convergence occurs. If you set out with a guide, make sure to include this in the itinerary.

It requires several days' travel to penetrate deep into the jungle. We recommend spending only two or three days there. After this

*B*RAZIL

Wonders of the jungle, tamed

the sights become routine, and an additional few days of trekking will not produce anything really new.

Shopping
The tax-free shopping center, as mentioned, is downtown between Rua 7 de Setembro and the river. Dozens of shops offer imports from clothing to photo and electronics equipment. Prices are low by South American standards, but tourists from the United States and most European countries will not find bargains. There is a legal limit as to how much one can buy. Typical *artesania* of this region include Indian art, woodcraft, and ceramics.

Boa Vista
Boa Vista (pop. 50,000), capital of the Roraima area, is 800 km north of Manaus in the middle of a vast, monotonous savannah. Two roads continue from there: one to Santa Elena on the Venezuelan border 200 km to the north, and the other to

BRAZIL

Enormous leaves of the Vitoria Regia plant

Normandia on the border with Guyana, 140 km away. Daily flights arrive from Manaus, and a few flights a week touch down from other cities. There is also a daily bus from Manaus. The city has a few hotels; most are basic in price and services. The same holds true for the restaurants.

On to Venezuela
Trucks set out for Venezuela from Rua Benjamin Constant, and one can try to catch a ride with them. A regular jeep service runs between Boa Vista and Ciudad Bolivar in Venezuela, and a bus sets out for Santa Elena every other day. Upon entering Venezuela, have your passport stamped at the border. Inquire at the Boa Vista police station where passports are stamped upon leaving Brazil.

Benjamin Constant
This little town abuts the Colombian border and is a center of the drug trade. It is not a pleasant place to visit, and should be avoided if possible. It can be reached by boat from Manaus, and is a stopover point en route to Colombia or Peru via Leticia. Two ferries a day travel between Benjamin Constant and Leticia (about a two-hour ride).

If you do decide to come here, take an excursion to the area of the rubber trees which produced an incredible economic boom in the Amazon at the end of the last century.

BRAZIL

On to Colombia and Peru
Tabatinga is the Brazilian border town, lying close to Leticia in Colombia. Have your passport stamped in Tabatinga when leaving Brazil and again on your entry into Colombia at Leticia. Brazil's Varig Airlines flies twice weekly from Manaus to Iquitos in Peru, passing through Tabatinga on the way back. Entry visas into Peru are best obtained in Iquitos.

Porto Velho
Porto Velho (pop. 100,000) is the capital of the State of Rodonia in the southern Amazon basin. It is the hub of an agricultural region whose main crops are rice, cocoa, and coffee. There are a number of Indian reservations in this area, where the tribes maintain a completely primitive way of life. Visiting these reservations is allowed only by special authorization from Funai, the agency reponsible for protecting and aiding the Indians.

Porto Velho is on the banks of Rio Madeira, and boats from Manaus reach its little port at irregular intervals. The town itself is not particularly interesting; it is a mere stopover station on the way to the Bolivian border.

Porto Velho offers a few mediocre hotels and a number of lower quality establishments. Of the restaurants, the *Almanara*, at Jose de Alencar 2624 is recommended. It is good, inexpensive and serves generous portions.

The airport, 7 km out of town, is served by regular flights from all over Brazil. Buses arrive from Manuas by a long and difficult road, passable only in the dry season. There is also bus service from Cuiaba and Campo Grande to Porto Velho, and from Rio Branco in the west.

On to Bolivia
Two buses a day leave Porto Velho for Guajaramirim, on the bank of the Rio Mamore. Upon reaching this town on the Bolivian border be sure to get a Brazilian departure stamp in your passport. Ferries cross the river to Guayaramerin, on the Bolivian side, where you will receive an entry stamp, valid for a 30-day stay. Buses head from Guayaramerin to Riveralta, on the Rio Beni. Riveralta has air connections to Cochabamba and La Paz. Those who want to can continue upriver; riverboats proceed as far as Rurrenabaque.

*B*RAZIL

The Midwest

The Brazilian Midwest includes the states of Goias, Mato Grosso, and Mato Grosso do Sul, as well as the federal district set aside for the new capital, Brasilia.

This is one of Brazil's most remote, isolated regions. Until the end of the previous century, the journey from the Atlantic coast to Cuiaba entailed a long, arduous trek through Uruguay and northward up the Rio de la Plata! With the establishment of the new inland capital, the overland connections with the coastal region were greatly improved. New roads were paved, railroads were built, and cities were developed and modernized. The weather in the area is hot the year round.

The Pantanal Swamps

The vast Pantanal area covers 230,000 sq/km of the Brazilian Midwest, in the area of the border with Bolivia and Uruguay. *Pantanal* is Spanish for "large swamp", and the whole area is indeed covered from horizon to horizon with endless swamps – a garden of Eden for water plants and animals. The Pantanal is the catchment area of Rio Paraguay and is crossed by many tributaries. Between June and September the water level in the marshes and rivers is low, and this is the best time to visit here. Much of the region is accessible by jeep during this season, permitting a close-up look at the abundant wildlife. Between October and March the rivers flood their banks, the water in the marshes rises, and access to animals becomes difficult. It is, however, the right time of year for botany lovers.

The diversity of wildlife in the area is immense and many rare species are found here in abundance: hundreds of species of birds and parrots in huge flocks, innumerable crocodiles (*jacare*), herds of *kapibra* (the largest member of the rodent family), communities of monkeys, anacondas, and more. These creatures share a tangle of marsh vegetation, bushes, and giant trees. Fish abound here too, making Pantanal one of the world's best spots for amateur fishing. The law permits catches of up to 30 kg per person.

The Pantanal is not "touristy" and is often left off itineraries to Brazil. Nevertheless, nature lovers will find it one of the most fascinating places in Brazil.

One can reach the Pantanal from several points of departure:

BRAZIL

THE PANTANAL

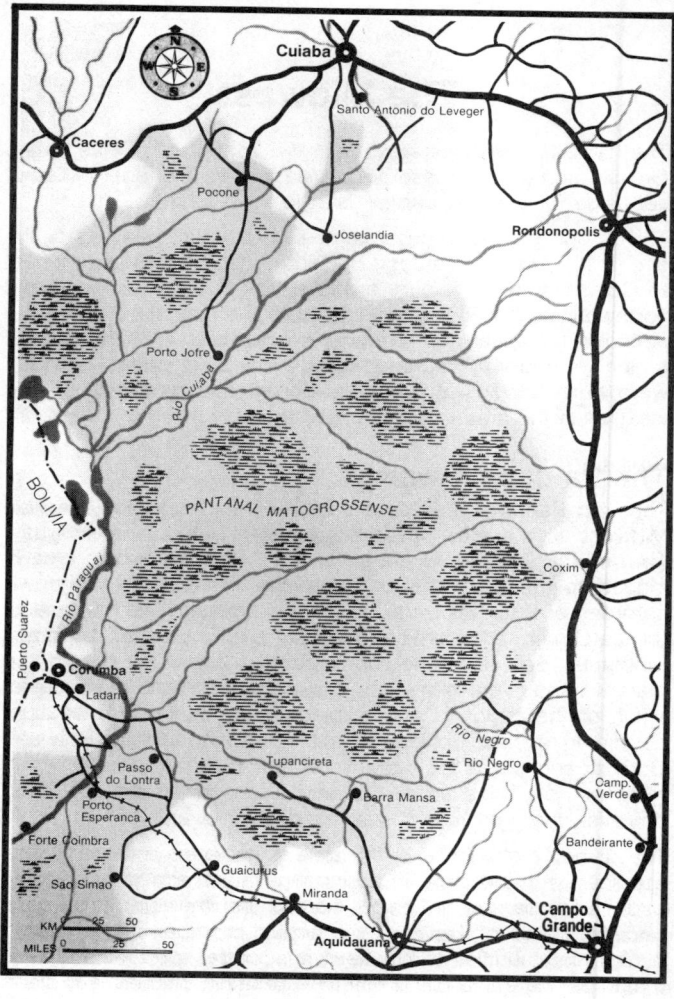

from Corumba (see "Corumba") to the southwest, at the border crossing with Bolivia; from Campo Grande (see "Campo Grande"), and from Coxim, halfway between Campo Grande and Cuiaba. The most suitable section of Pantanal for touring is the northern region, which is easily reached from Cuiaba (see "Cuiaba").

BRAZIL

Cuiaba

Cuiaba (pop. 170,000) is the capital of the state of Mato Grosso. Rapid development in recent years has turned it into a modern, busy city, serving Western Brazil as a large commercial and industrial center. The vicinity of Cuiaba has several nature sites, rich in wildlife, of which the Pantanal is considered to be the most important and fascinating. In town, visit the large Gothic-style church known as **Igreja Bom Despache**.

Transportation

The airport is 12 km from downtown Cuaiba and is served regularly by Varig, VASP, and Trans-Brazil.

The bus terminal is 3 km from the city center. Many buses set out every day for Campo Grande, Brasilia, Sao Paulo, and Rio de Janeiro. There are direct buses to Manaus and the journey takes several days, depending on the season and the condition of the road.

Food and lodging

Hotel Aurea Palace at Avenida General Mello 63 (Tel. 322-3377) is Cuiaba's best, with a pool, bar, and good restaurant. *Hotel Excelsior*, just off central Praca de Republica at Avenida Getulio Vargas 246 (Tel. 322-6322), also has a good restaurant. *Hotel Mato Grosso* at Rua Comandante Costa 2522 is small and good. *Hotel Lord*, at Avenida Getulio Vargas 1406, is more moderate and the rooms are air conditioned. *Hotel Samara* at Rua Joaquim Murtinho 2376 is extremely inexpensive.

Internacional, at Praca Antonio Correia 40, is a good fish restaurant. For good Oriental food, try *Baalbek* at Avenida Vargas 600. Both are quite expensive. On Avenida Izaque Povoas there are several inexpensive restaurants and bars. *Patotinha* is a very popular bar with the young, who throng there on weekends.

Tourist services

The local tourist office, Turimat, is on the city's central square, Praca da Republica. The staff is very friendly and efficient. Apart from its other activities, Turimat runs a telephone information service (Tel. 139). Another information office is located at the airport.

Car rental: The Nobre company (main office at Avenida Vargas 600; branch office at the airport) provides good service.

Several travel agencies in Cuiaba arrange tours of the Pantanal for one day or several days. Make sure that the tours do not leave a free day on the schedule. Without a vehicle and a guide, you will simply be marooned there, and the heat and mosquitoes

BRAZIL

The Pantanal – a Garden of Eden for animals

will rule out any possibility of enjoyable leisure.

One guide we recommend is Vinicius Maranhao, a young man who organizes trips to the Pantanal by jeep and motorboat. He speaks English, is pleasant, and knows the area well. Look him up at the airport (everyone there knows him), or call Tel. 341-1753.

Exploring the Pantanal

The northern section of the Pantanal is the best for touring. Set out from Cuiaba by bus to Pocone, 100 km away. There are two very inexpensive hotels here which provide good basic services. From Pocone a road heads south to Porto Jofre; a cluster of houses and an anchorage for riverboats. A compressed dirt road, 145 km long, crosses the marshes. The road crosses 128 wooden bridges on route, and from every bridge one can see dozens of crocodiles. In the dry season the road is passable for all types of cars. Pixaim lies 66 km south of Pocone, and has a relatively expensive hostel, a restaurant and a gas station.

There are no buses south of Pocone, which means that one must either rent a car in Cuiaba or try one's luck at hitchhiking. There isn't much traffic, but the drivers are generally helpful. Equip yourself with food, and be prepared for long hours of waiting.

BRAZIL

The trans-Pantanal road ends at Porto Jofra, on the Rio Cuiaba. Close by is Fazenda Santa Rosa, which is an expensive place to stay. One can travel upriver to Corumba on a cargo boat. The journey takes three days, but the boats do not have a frequent or regular departure schedule. Alternatively, one can return the way one came.

Santo Antonio de Leverger

This is the beach of the Rio Cuiaba, an hour's ride from the city. Buses leave frequently for the beach from the *Rodoviaria* in Cuiaba. It is a lovely beach; the water is clean and good for swimming, and fishing enthusiasts are attracted by the abundant fish. Santo Antonio is, however, best known as a Garden of Eden for bird watchers and nature lovers. The variety of birds nesting here is incredible – multitudes of birds of prey, parrots, toucans, and many other species.

Campo Grande

Campo Grande (pop. 300,000) is the capital of the State of Mato Grosso do Sul. The overland route from the Brazilian coast to Corumba and Bolivia passes through this city. The city, modern and quite pleasant, is the commercial hub of a bountiful agricultural hinterland, where the major crops are wheat and rice.

Downtown, at Rua Barao do Rio Branca 1843, is **Museu Dom Bosco**, the Indian Museum, a truly worthwhile place to visit. It exhibits a rich collection of Indian implements from Mato Grosso, *artesania*, musical instruments, and a large collection of stuffed animals of the species inhabiting the Pantanal.

Campo Grande is a suitable point of departure for tours of the Pantanal area, although this entails a long ride to the periphery of the marshes. Tourists continuing onwards to Bolivia are better advised to set out from Corumba.

Transportation

Campo Grande has regular air connections with Brazil's major cities, and VASP flies from here to Corumba. A few buses a day arrive from Sao Paulo (a 14-hour ride), Rio de Janeiro, Brasilia, and Cuiaba. Buses travel to Corumba only in the dry season, because the road crosses a marshy area. Two trains make the trip between Sao Paulo and Corumba daily, passing through Campo Grande at 8am and at 8:30pm. The night train is expensive, because it consists of sleeping cars only. The beautiful ride to Corumba lasts 11 hours. It is better to make the trip from Sao Paulo by bus as it is much faster than by train.

BRAZIL

Corumba

Corumba (pop. 70,000) is situated on the banks of the Rio Paraguay, close to the Bolivian border, on the edge of the Pantanal marshes. Because of its location, it is a good launching place for exploring the marshes. The town itself is quite placid, with mostly one or two story houses. A small port on the river caters mostly for fishing boats.

Of the several hotels in Corumba, the best is the *Santa Monica*, an average quality establishment at Rua Coelho 345 (Tel. 231-2481). The rest of the hotels provide basic services only, at low prices. Particularly low cost hotels are found on Rua Delamare.

The **tourist office**, MS Tur at Rua Dom Acuim 405, is efficient and helpful.

Transportation

Corumba's small airport is very close to the city, and VASP has daily flights to and from Campo Grande and Cuiaba. Two trains a day reach Corumba from Sao Paulo (a 35-hour trip) and from Campo Grande (about 12 hours). In the rainy season, the Pantanal marshes flood the road to Campo Grande, and only the train can get through.

Cargo boats ply the Rio Paraguay, crossing the Pantanal while heading north upriver to destinations close to Cuiaba. The cruise takes up to ten days, and in the dry season one can see abundant wildlife on the riverbanks.

Excursions to the Pantanal

In the dry season, a short excursion in the Corumba area will suffice to reach concentrations of wildlife. Access is far more difficult during the rainy season, when the rivers spill over their banks and flood the marshes.

All travel agencies in the city offer boat trips to the Pantanal. The Pantanal Express, at Avenida General Rondon 1355, is recommended. Another possibility is to find a private guide in the small fishermen's harbor.

There are several hostels in the heart of the marsh area around Corumba, and they can be used as points of departure for short outings. The best of them is *Fazenda Santa Clara*, about 120 km from Corumba. Make inquiries in Corumba (Tel. 231-5797).

On to Bolivia

When leaving Brazil be sure to have your passport stamped. Do this in Corumba, at the police station in the train depot. Buses set out for the border from Praca da Republica every day, every half hour, 6am-6pm. Travelers with heavy loads are usually

BRAZIL

requested to ride in a special bus, which departs from the end of the adjacent Rua Antonio Mario.

On entering Bolivia, have your passport stamped at the border. The stamp allows for a 30-day stay. From the border, taxis set out for nearby Puerto Suarez, a Bolivian border town. From there, the famous "death train" leaves daily, making its way to Santa Cruz in about 20 hours. The train is so called because of the many delays on the way, sometimes hours long, and the stories told about its going off the tracks... There are twice-weekly flights to Santa Cruz and La Paz.

Although by Brazilian standards, the Brazilian side of the border zone is not a particularly well developed or orderly area, the change between it and Bolivia is nevertheless dramatic. One feels it in the Puerto Suarez train station and on the train, which is packed with Indians and their belongings.

Currency exchange

Because the exchange rates for Bolivian currency are better in Corumba than over the border in Bolivia itself, change at least enough money to last until Santa Cruz or La Paz. For buying Brazilian currency, however, this area is at a disadvantage. Moneychangers congregate on Rua Antonio Maria, and there is a branch of Banco de Brasil at Rua De Jungo 13.

Brasilia

The city of Brasilia was established and proclaimed the Republic's formal and political capital on April 21, 1960, by the then-President of Brazil Juscelino Kubitschek. Brasilia, unlike other cities which grow naturally with their populations, was developed in an artificial way. Built in the middle of nowhere, it was meant to attract the population of the crowded coastal strip to Brazil's interior. Brasilia has an ultra-modern urban layout designed by Lucio Costa. Many of Brasilia's buildings were designed by the famous architect Oscar Niemeyer.

The city was well planned and was built systematically. From overhead, it has a shape like an airplane. Its "wings" are the residential neighborhoods. Each of them, called a Super-Quadra, provides complete public services – schools, medical centers, churches, gas stations etc. The Super-Quadras are linked by boulevards. A superhighway traverses the length of the "fuselage", with the city's major public buildings arrayed alongside. The "tail" contains the national theater, sports stadium, and a shared train and bus terminal (*Rodoferroviaria*). In the "cockpit" are the government buildings and Parliament. The city's "nose cone" abuts an artificial lake. There are also two diplomatic sectors (see "What to see") and two hotel districts

BRAZIL

BRASILIA

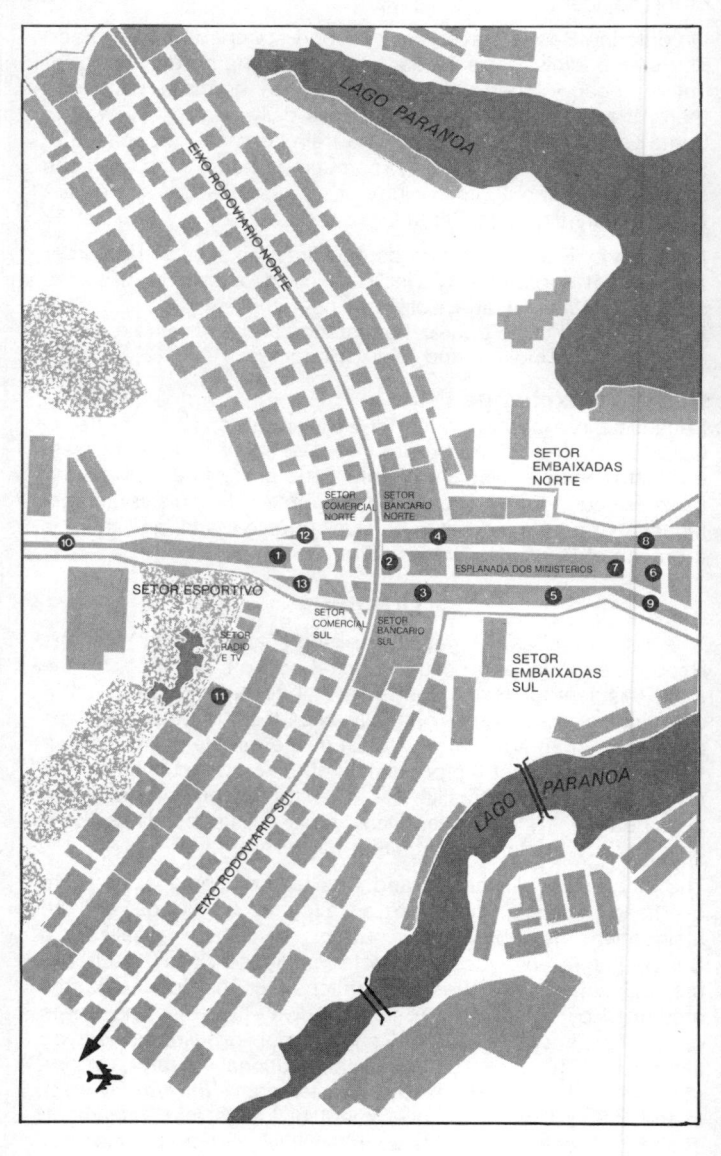

BRAZIL

Brazil's House of Representatives – twin towers and hemispheres

(see "Food and lodging"). Roads and neighborhoods are marked by numbers, not names.

Brasilia lies 1200 m above sea level on a hot, dry plain covered in savannah vegetation. The population currently stands at 400,000. The idea of transforming Brazil's desolate central and western provinces into a center of culture and settlement has, in the main, been a failure. Morever, Brasilia itself, meant to be the lodestone, has not lived up to expectations.

Transportation
Brasilia's modern and convenient international airport is 12 km out of town. It has connections with all South American capitals plus New York, Miami, Los Angeles, and several European capitals. A shuttle service connects Brasilia and Rio, and there are many daily flights to all of Brazil's major cities. Taxis run from the airport to town (rates are determined by meter), and a convenient bus reaches the *Rodoviaria* in the city center.

Index
1. Torre de TV
2. Rodoviaria
3. City Cathedral
4. Teatro Nacional
5. Palacio do Itamarati
6. Praca dos Tres Poderes
7. House of Representatives
8. Palacio do Planto
9. Supremo Tribunal Federal
10. Monumento Juscelino Kubitschek
11. Igreja Dom Bosco
12. Setor Hoteleiro Norte
13. Setor Hoteleiro Sul

BRAZIL

The combined bus terminal and train depot (called the *Rodoferroviaria*) is not to be confused with the *Rodoviaria* downtown, which accommodates the local and regional buses.

Buses leave from the *Rodoferroviaria* for all parts of Brazil: to Rio (20 hours or more), Sao Paulo (about 15 hours), and Belem (about 40 hours). There is also bus service to Porto Velho, Cuiaba, and Campo Grande.

The railroad to Brasilia was completed in 1981, and there is a line to Sao Paulo. The train ride is quite comfortable and very inexpensive.

Food and lodging
Almost all of Brasilia's hotels are in two districts: Setor Hoteleiro Norte (the northern sector) and Setor Hoteleiro Sul (the southern sector). Hotel rates are 20% lower on weekends. The best hotel is the *Nacional*, at 1 Lote in the southern sector (Tel. 225-8180). The *Carlton Hotel*, in the same sector at 5 Quadra, Bloco G (Tel. 226-7320) is also very good. Less expensive but still good is the *Bristol Hotel*, also in the southern district. Hotels of medium cost and standards are the *Diplomat* and the *Pilar* in the northern sector, and the *Brasilia Imperial* and the *Planalto* in the southern sector.

There are several hotels outside the major districts, all mediocre. The least expensive of them is the *Paranoa*.

Brasilia itself has no cheap hotels. However, in Taguatinga, 30 minutes away, there are many such hotels.

All the large hotels have restaurants, most serving continental cuisine. *Chez Malin*, Comercio Local Sul 216, Bloco A, is very good. Close by at no. 202 is another good restaurant, *Tarantella*. One of the best in town is the *Gaf*, at Seto Habitacoes Individuais Sul, Bloco B.

Tourist services
There are tourist offices in the airport and at the *Rodoferroviaria*. Many travel agencies (including several with offices at the airport) offer organized tours of Brasilia. This is a good, convenient way of getting to know the city.

Rent-a-car: The two largest companies are Avis (Tel. 225-3975) and Nobre (Tel. 246-6728).

What to see
Start with an overview of the city from the **Torre de TV** (TV Tower), situated in the middle of the broad boulevard between the two wings of the "airplane". From here we see the city's basic structure, some of its important and modern buildings, and its layout of wide boulevards and highways.

BRAZIL

Brasilia's cathedral

Now head south, toward the front of the "airplane". Pass the *Rodoviaria* en route to downtown and stop at the **City Cathedral**, a modern structure and a famous Brasilia landmark. From the outside the cathedral looks small. Upon entering, however, we find that most of it is underground. Statues of angels "soar" over the worshippers' heads in the cavernous hall.

On the eastern side of the broad boulevard is the **Teatro Nacional** (National Theater). Continuing along the boulevard, notice a series of rectangular buildings along the two sides. Each houses a government ministry. The last building on the right is the home of the Ministry of Foreign Affairs, the **Palacio do Itamarati**. It bears the name of the Ministry's former residence in Rio de Janeiro. This magnificent building is one of the most impressive and beautiful in Brasilia, with artificial waterfalls and pools. (Open Tues.-Fri. 10am-4pm. Be sure to ask the guards for permission to enter.)

The cross-town boulevard ends at **Praca dos Tres Poderes**, a large, open square. Here you can see the complex which houses the country's three governmental authorities. The first structure is the **House of Representatives** – twin towers housing the offices of congressmen and senators. Semispherical buildings appear on either side of the towers; these are the assembly halls of the Senate and the Congress. (Open to visitors Tues.-Fri. 9am-noon, 2-5pm; weekends 2-5pm). The second edifice is the

BRAZIL

Angels soaring on high

Palacio do Planalto (Presidential Palace) where the President has his offices (Open Fri. 9-11am, 2-5pm). The third building is the **Supremo Tribunal Federal** (Supreme Court), and the statue opposite symbolizes blind Justice. To enter, one needs permission from the guards and one has to be properly dressed. In the center of the square is the city museum of Brasilia, and

BRAZIL

at the far end a large Brazilian national flag flutters in the breeze.

The street branching off the square in the direction from which we came leads to the grand **Palacio do Alvorador** (presidential residence) on the lake.

The two districts beyond the government ministries accommodate the **Setores Embaixadas** (diplomatic corps). Each country with diplomatic representation in Brazil was apportioned a parcel of land and was asked to build an embassy in its best architectural tradition. In a few cases, the results are interesting and beautiful. The bridges crossing the lake at the front of the "airplane" lead to a quarter of luxurious villas where the city's wealthy class and the government ministers live. By observing how luxuriously the government ministers and officials live, one gets an impression of the enormous gap between rich and poor, which lies at the root of Brazil's serious social and economic predicament.

North of the main boulevard, in the rear part of the "body of the plane", is **Monumento Juscelino Kubitschek**, commemorating Brazil's late president and the founder of its new capital. The site includes a museum marking events in his life. (Open Tues.-Fri, 9am-noon and 1-6pm; weekends and holidays 9am-7pm.)

Continue a little further north along the boulevard until you reach a cross which marks the cornerstone of the city. To the right is the **Quartel General do Exercito** (army headquarters). Opposite it is a large statue shaped like an upside-down trigger. The statue's acoustic design is such that a rapidly repeated echo is heard at its center.

In the southern residential area, Quadra 702, is **Igreja Dom Bosco**. The church's blue glass creates a wonderful light effects, and there is an immense chandelier hanging from the ceiling.

Important Addresses
U.S. Embassy: SES, Avenida das Nacoes, Lote 3 (Tel. 223-0120).

British Embassy: SES, Avenida das Nacoes, Lote 8 (Tel. 225-2710).

Post Office: SCS, Edificio Nordeste.

Goiana
This youthful modern city, capital of the State of Goiana, is 210 km southeast of Brasilia. Founded in October, 1933, it has a

BRAZIL

population of 700,000. The well-planned city is crisscrossed by wide, green boulevards. The buildings downtown, tall and modern, accommodate most of the commercial life in the state of Goiana.

In the center of the city is a spacious square called **Centro Civico**. The governor's mansion, **Palaicio do Governo**, is situated here, and on Sunday mornings an artesania market takes place here. Avenida Araguaia, branching off the square, leads to **Parque Mutirama**, a spacious, green, park with a modest zoo and playgounds.

The airport is close to town, and regular flights land from all of Brazil's major cities. Buses reach the city terminal from Brasilia, Cuiaba, Rio de Janeiro, and Sao Paulo.

CHILE

Chile, a narrow strip of land between the western slopes of the Andes and the Pacific Ocean, is a land with a serene and pleasant folk tradition. Its variegated scenery – from desert in the north to glaciers in the south – offers numerous places to visit and routes to travel. The Chileans are friendly people, tolerant and always willing to help. Getting to know them – in the large cities and even more so in outlying areas – will undoubtedly be the highlight of your stay. All this, along with the clean, invigorating air, varied climate and well run tourist infrastructure, make a visit to Chile an enjoyable and unforgettable experience.

History

The Indian tribes, who populated Chile before the first Spaniards arrived in 1536, retained control of the country's southern region for many decades thereafter, leaving only the northern and central areas to the newly arrived conquerors. The Spanish attributed no great importance to Chile; for some time they refrained from moving south and clashing with the natives, who continued to maintain their ancient tradition without interference.

Eventually, however, Pedro de Valdivia (founder of Santiago) and the Spanish under his leadership did attempt to expand southward and lay claim to more territory, a move that met with fierce Indian resistance. Chilean history in the seventeenth and eighteenth centuries is a tale of the Indians' struggle to delay the inevitable and keep the Spanish out. A number of the important characteristics that typify Chile to this day took shape in that period – chiefly those pertaining to the country's demographic makeup and class structure. The Spanish immigrants excelled at winning the local women's hearts, and intermarriage between the two groups became a common occurance. Consequently, the mixed European-Indian *mestizos* quickly became the largest population group. In due course, most *mestizos* fell into the underprivileged working class which, until recent years, had almost no rights at all. Since the Spanish generously apportioned Chile's land among themselves, a privileged class of wealthy landed gentry came into being. This stratum grew even more important when, after Chile declared

CHILE

its independence, it took the reins of government into its own collective hands.

Chile's first independent government was established in 1810, but was ousted two years later by Spanish loyalists. Bernardo O'Higgins, Chile's national hero, and later its first President, left for Argentina, where he raised a joint Chilean-Argentinian army. This force, led by the Argentinian General Jose de San Martin, succeeded in expelling the Spanish and re-establishing Chilean independence. Though O'Higgins was appointed head of state in 1817, his liberal policies did not please the local population, and he resigned in 1823.

Seven years of social, political, and economic chaos set in and only when a military junta seized power, supported by broad groups in the army and the general population, did things calm down. The constitution of 1833 guaranteed control of Parliament to the landed gentry. A period of domestic tranquility and economic wellbeing ensued.

The discovery of natural resources and mineral deposits in northern Chile – which contributed to the development of trade with England, the United States, and even distant Australia – filled the coffers of the state, and led to an accelerated process of modernization. Roads were paved, railways laid, ports dredged, and the infrastructure of an educational system (even if restricted to the children of the rich) was set up. As trade and cultural relations with Europe broadened, the new winds blowing there also influenced many members of the ruling aristocracy and liberal tendencies critical of the conservative regime began to gain strength in social and political circles.

The momentum of industrial development produced a balance-of-payments deficit, and the Chilean Government went to war with Peru and Bolivia – which controlled a fertile region rich in mineral deposits – with the intention of taking over the mines and enjoying their proceeds. Chile, it is true, won the War of the Pacific (1879-1884), taking Antofagasta from Bolivia and Arica from Peru, and even reaching the outskirts of Lima. These conquests, however, sent the country into a severe internal and political tailspin, which culminated in a short civil war.

During the same period, important social changes were taking place. At the end of the nineteenth century, political parties began to organize and the government began to require their support in Parliament. In the early twentieth century, the lower and middle classes also began to accumulate power, and the regime's inability to satisfy them and offer solutions to pressing problems caused the social ferment to spill over into the military. The army seized power in 1924, held it for one year, and then

CHILE

returned it to President Arturo Alessandri who, despite all his efforts, could not restore tranquility.

Political parties gained and lost political influence rapidly, chiefly because of the economic woes that became worse during the Great Depression of the 1930s. The recovery that took place during World War II (in which Chile joined the Allies in declaring war on Germany) marked a turning point of sorts, along with closer relations with the United States and encouragement of American capital investments. Nevertheless, inflation and unemployment persisted, and magnified yearnings for reform of the unfair social structure, in which the bulk of economic power rested in the hands of the traditional minority. As a result, Chilean regimes changed frequently.

In 1967, President Eduardo Frei introduced a far-reaching agrarian reform, including land expropriations from the estate owners, and improvements in the living and working conditions and wages of agricultural laborers. Numerous difficulties, however, impeded its fulfilment. The same period witnessed a rise in the power of the Left when leftist representatives of various parties combined forces to found a National Unity Party. Led by Salvador Allende, they won a plurality in the 1970 elections. An economic policy calling for nationalization of mines, among other tenets, damaged American economic interests and led the United States to impose sanctions. Allende reacted by drawing close to the Soviet Union and its allies.

In the 1973 elections, Allende was again victorious but was deposed and killed in a military coup in September of that year. A military junta headed by General Augusto Pinochet has run the country with unconcerned ruthlessness ever since. A new constitution, adopted in 1981, declares that Pinochet will remain in power until 1989, when the Junta will decide on his successor. The Government's efforts notwithstanding, the economic recession has continued, and social discontent erupts periodically. Organized opposition to the Government began to develop in the early 1980s and during 1983 and 1986 resistance to Pinochet was accompanied by scores of strikes, protests and mass demonstrations.

In 1985, despite strong measures used to suppress it, the resistance to Pinochet's Government strengthened. Practically in all parts of Chile one can feel the tension, which sometimes explodes into acts of violence. The army shows no mercy, using much force against the opposition, hoping if not to stop it, at least to minimize its activity in the streets. Although public order is generally maintained, curfews, arrests, searches and other signs of a harsh military regime can occasionally be seen and

CHILE

felt. In certain areas, particularly the suburbs of Santiago, where unrest prevails, one can see increased military presence. Clashes occur from time to time between protestors and soldiers, occasionally claiming lives among the former. The internal situation in Chile receives much public attention and censure, internally and abroad, and it seems that Pinochet's Government is not as sound as it was in the past.

Geography and Climate

Though it is the longest of the South American countries – extending more than 4300 kilometes from north to south – Chile's average width does not exceed 200 km, so that it is only the fourth largest country on the continent in terms of area (757,000 sq/km). Though Chile is divided for historical reasons into seven regions from north to south, a rough geographic reckoning may view the country as having three main sections: the desert in the north, the temperate center, and the cold, rainy south.

The Andes delimit the three regions to the east, with the Pacific Ocean on the west. In the north the mountains are very broad and have plateau-like summits; in the center they become narrower and higher (with peaks reaching some 7000 m); and in the south they are lower – "only" 2500 meters. The Pacific Ocean washes a straight coastline in the north and center while in the south, the coast is broken up, ending in a far flung archipelago.

This unusual geography is accompanied by additional phenomena: The mountains have a high level of seismic activity, and earthquakes and volcanic eruptions have brought disaster with them more than once. The ocean too has destructive power and surging floods occasionally wash over the coastal cities and villages.

The northern region: Though it is a dry, rainless desert, temperatures here are moderate, and the weather is pleasant and comfortable even in summer. The average temperature (23 degrees Celsius, or 74 degrees Fahrenheit) and relatively low humidity make staying or working in this desert zone easier than in other deserts. Beneath it lie most of the natural resources and mineral deposits that serve as the central pillars of the Chilean economy.

The central region: This zone, extending southward to Puerto Montt, is home to about 90% of Chile's population and serves as the country's economic and social hub. Here the climate is comfortable and temperate; rainfall increases as one goes southward. Temperatures are moderate the year round, and only

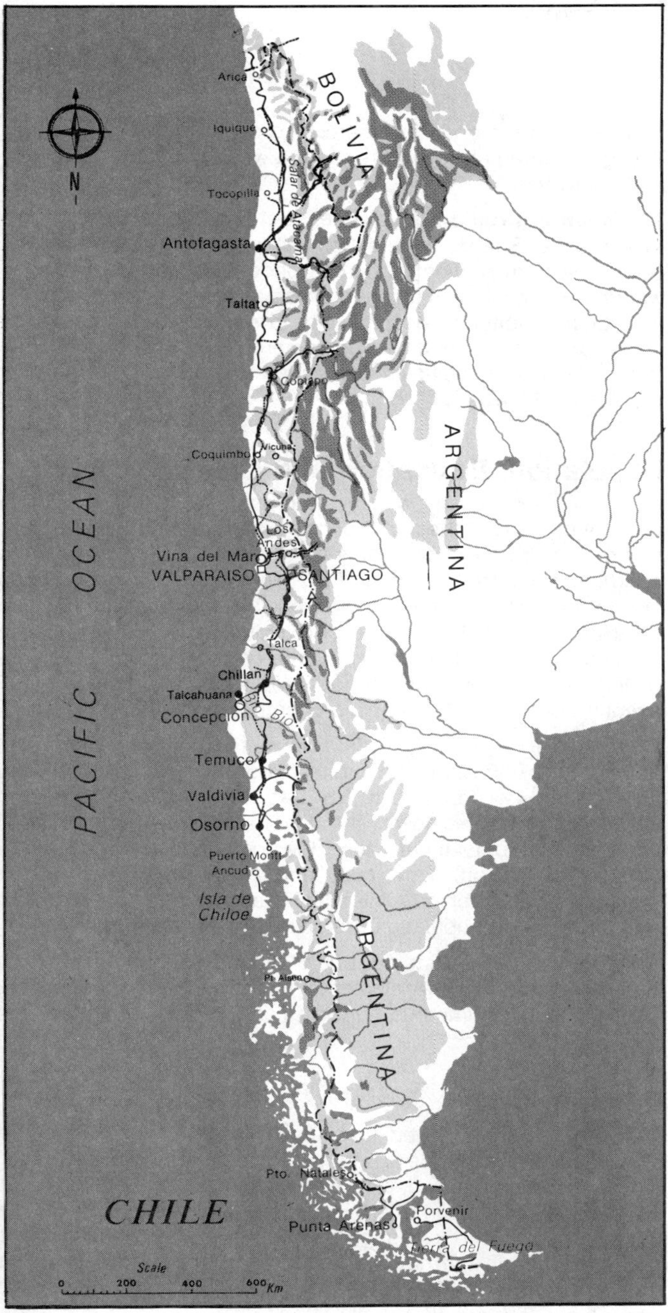

BOLIVIA
Arica
Iquique
Salar de Atacama
Tocopilla
Antofagasta
Taltal
Copiapo
Coquimbo
Vicuna
ARGENTINA
PACIFIC OCEAN
Los Andes
Vina del Mar
VALPARAISO
SANTIAGO
Talca
Chillan
Talcahuana
Bio Bio
Concepcion
Temuco
Valdivia
Osorno
Puerto Montt
Ancud
Isla de Chiloe
Pt. Aisen
ARGENTINA
Pto. Natales
Porvenir
Punta Arenas
Tierra del Fuego
CHILE
Scale
0
200
400
600 Km
N

CHILE

on mountaintops does the mercury drop to the freezing point. This is an extremely fertile area with a wealth of flora – both wild and cultivated.

The southern region: This zone, stretching from Puerto Montt to Tierra del Fuego, suffers from an extremely harsh climate. Given the combination of fierce winds, rain and cold, it's no wonder that the area is uninhabited save for a few cities. Despite the harsh conditions and proximity to Antarctica, temperatures do not drop below freezing. The numerous glaciers found chiefly in the southernmost tip of the region are mute survivors of a bygone geological epoch.

Population, Education and Culture

About 300,000 Indians with no European blood still survive in Chile. Almost all of these are concentrated around the southern city of Temuco. Most of Chile's other eleven million citizens are *mestizos* – of mixed Indian and Spanish descent. The European immigrants, who left their imprint on the demographic makeup of Argentina and Uruguay, never reached Chile, either because of the country's distance from Europe or because of the barriers posed by the towering Andes. Whatever the reason, they account for a mere 1.5% of the country's population.

More than 90% of all Chileans live in the central region, with about a third of these in the capital of Santiago, which is growing at a rate of 4% per annum. Nor has the trend of accelerated urbanization passed over the less attractive northern and southern sectors; there, too, the population is essentially city-based. A drop in mortality and a high birth-rate are the principal factors behind Chile's 2.5% annual population growth rate; 40% of the population are children below the age of 10.

Chile's educational system is one of the most advanced in South America. In addition to elementary and secondary education, Chile boasts numerous universities, which offer diverse curricula.

Economy

Chile's economy is based first and foremost on exploiting the numerous mineral deposits and natural resources with which the nation has been blessed. Copper, of which Chile supplies about 10% of world consumption, accounts for about half of the nation's total exports. Though its price has fallen, it still retains pride of place in the national economy. Other metals found in the rich veins of northern Chile – mainly iron, and some gold and silver – are mined in smaller quantities. Another important

CHILE

export industry involves lumber and wood products (paper, etc.), which are derived from Chile's vast forests. Deep-sea fishing is another important sector, and places Chile among the world's leading fish-exporting countries.

Agriculture, the second-ranking industry, employs more than 20% of Chile's manpower. Even so, local farms do not manage to meet the domestic demand and Chile must import great quantities of foodstuffs from other countries. Three million head of cattle and about seven million sheep make up a significant portion of the agricultural field with most meat and meat products earmarked for export.

In recent decades, Chilean governments have implemented a policy to encourage accelerated industrial development. This is concentrated around the large cities, and employs close to 25% of the workforce. Because of the low technological level and the lack of capital, most industrial plants are labor-intensive, producing textiles, food products and simple, low-quality consumer goods. Recent years have seen a trend towards technological expansion and development and more sophisticated factories, producing machinery, motor vehicles, and even petrochemicals and so forth are being constructed at a steady pace. From its own reserves Chile produces less than half of its national consumption of oil, natural gas and coal.

When General Pinochet seized power, he introduced the economic system championed by the well-known economist Professor Milton Friedman, stressing freedom of capital, free competition and reduced import duties. Credit was granted with great flexibility by non-governmental agencies and foreign investments received special assistance and encouragement. Though inflation, which reached 341% in 1975, was halted for a time, unemployment swelled and violent social ferment was reawakened. The government has struggled desperately to stifle the resulting unrest.

In 1979, Pinochet began trying to maintain a fixed dollar exchange rate for the peso. Economic pressures, however, forced him to desist. In 1982 he devalued the Chilean peso and adopted a series of economic measures which in effect ended the Milton Friedman era. Today, Chile is struggling with the ruinous consequences of the Friedman approach and the tottering economy it left behind.

The economic crisis has only intensified over the years. Unemployment has risen, reaching up to 25% of the local work force in some areas. Many Chileans emigrate to other countries, particularly Argentina, searching for work. Inflation levels which are causing much dissent and resentment in business and

CHILE

public circles, also burden the Government, crippling its attempts to repay outside loans, and to continue internal development. Their inability to raise foreign capital or to receive international credit adds further to Chile's economic difficulties.

General Information

How to get there
By air: Close to twenty airlines link Santiago with the important cities of Europe, the United States and the Far East, as well as the other countries of South America. Some flights include stopovers in Brazil, Argentina, Peru, etc.

Lan Chile, Air France, Iberia, Sabena, KLM, Lufthansa, SAS, Swissair and other airlines fly from Europe, while Eastern and Lan fly from New York and Miami. All the South American flag carriers maintain regular routes between their respective capitals and Santiago.

By land: The Pan-American Highway (*Carretera Panamerica*) traverses the length of Chile and links it with Peru. Numerous roads cut across the mountains to Argentina and Bolivia (details concerning each road and border crossing will be provided as we proceed). Buses connect Chilean frontier towns with their counterparts across the borders, and Santiago with the capitals of the neighboring countries. Trains travel from Antofagasta to La Paz, Bolivia.

Documents
Passport holders from the U.S. and Western Europian countries (excluding France) require no visas for a 90-day visit to Chile, with an additional 90-day extension issued with no problem at the Immigration offices in Santiago. Arriving in Chile you will need a tourist card, issued by the air line or obtainable at the border point. The immigration officers will attach the tourist card to your passport, and you must carry it at all times and surrender it when leaving the country.

There is a tourist tax on visitors from various countries, to be paid when entering Chile. It changes from one country of origin to another, but is generally not more then a few dollars.

Where to Stay
Chile has many hotels of all categories. Their overall quality is satisfactory and the cheaper ones, too, are usually clean and honest. A number of cities have youth hostels, but most of these are open only during the tourist season. An ever-growing number of campsites are being set up throughout Chile, most

CHILE

providing convenient facilities. Hotel rates, posted in every room by law, include a 10% service fee and a 20% tax. It's important to check if the tax is also added to the tab for meals when the bill isn't paid on the spot. If so, it's better to pay there and then and avoid the tax.

Wining and Dining

The superb flavor of Chilean cuisine undoubtedly stems from its basis in succulent seafood. Most restaurants serve the standard fare of meat and its familiar side-dishes (beware of raw fruit and vegetables, which may not have been washed!), but the seafood overshadows them. Fish, crabs, oysters and their numerous cousins from the briny deep are served in various forms: roasted, boiled, fried, etc.

Chile's excellent wines, unquestionably the best in Latin America, complement these dishes admirably. Chile's three hundred wineries produce some one thousand varieties of wine, an inexhaustible selection. Some are ranked by quality: *vino reservado* is the best of all, followed by *vino especial*.

Most restaurants customarily offer a four-course table d'hote menu: appetizer (usually salad or vegetables), soup, entree and dessert. This is much less expensive than ordering each course separately (a la carte), and the quality of the food is definitely adequate. Chileans eat lunch between noon and 3pm, and dinner after 9pm. It is customary to leave a 10% tip.

When to come; National Holidays

Summer – from October to April – is the best time to visit Chile, both the cities and the countryside. During the winter – July through October – the excellent ski areas near and south of Santiago are open.

The major holidays are January 1, May 1, September 18 (Independence Day), and December 25.

Currency

The local currency is the peso. Lately restrictions have been placed on the foreign exchange market, but there is no black market. Cashing travelers'checks is slightly more complicated than dealing in cash, especially outside of Santiago, but no significant difference in exchange rates is involved. Bank drafts are paid in local currency only, as are cash withdrawals against credit cards. American Express and Diners Club cards are widespread and accepted in most of the exclusive hotels and restaurants.

CHILE

Domestic transportation

Buses run between all the major cities, from Arica in the north to Puerto Montt in the south. If you have a student card you're entitled to a sizable discount, though you may have to demand it forcefully (though politely) at times, since drivers are not too eager to give it.

Passenger trains currently operate only in the Santiago region, on a line between the capital and Puerto Montt. The trip is fast and pleasant, though tickets must be purchased in advance. Second class is crowded and uncomfortable. Lan Chile Airlines provides frequent air service between all major cities.

You can continue south of Puerto Montt in three ways: via Argentina, by air, or by ship (see "Puerto Montt"). It is easy to find your way in a rented or private car, for the roads are good and, with the help of the up-to-date maps supplied by the local Auto Club, you can go almost anywhere without difficulty.

The Chileans' friendliness is expressed on the highways, too. Hitchhiking is more commomplace here than anywhere else in South America. Drivers will often volunteer to take hitchhikers to their destination, even if they have to make a detour to do so. It usually won't take you long to flag someone down, and the overall experience is a pleasure!

Measurements, electricity, time

The metric system is standard. Electrical current: 220V. The Chilean hour is GMT-4 (GMT-3 in summer)

A Suggested Itinerary for Touring Chile

Due to Chile's length, there is no point in covering the country from end to end. It is better to combine your visit to this interesting country with trips to nearby sites in the countries to the east. In accordance with your general route, you can cross the Andes in various places, "pop in" at adjacent sites, and head back. Tourist sites in Chile are concentrated in the following regions:

North: between Arica and Antofagasta

Center: Santiago de Chile and its vicinity

South-central: the area between Temuco and Isla Chiloe, including the lake area

South: Patagonia and Tierra del Fuego; Puerto Natales, Puerto Arenas, and surroundings.

CHILE

Central Chile

Santiago de Chile

Chile's capital was founded by Pedro de Valdivia in 1541 when he arrived at the site with a group of Spanish settlers. The city developed slowly, evolving gradually into an economic, social and political center of great importance and, in due course became the national capital.

Its location in the geographical center of Chile, between north and south, close to the ocean (100 km) on the one side and to the Andes (50 km) on the other, also aided Santiago's development and helped turn it into the bustling nerve center of the entire country. Alongside the splendid scenery and exceptional design, Santiago's altitude – 556 m above sea level – gives the city an ideal climate both summer and winter.

Close to one third of all Chileans – 3.8 million all told – have chosen to live in Santiago and its environs and with good reason: The region is in a state of constant expansion and development. Santiago's elegant upper-class east side is home to the rich elite. The poorest citizens – who have migrated from the countryside in search of fortune in the big city – live in the overcrowded and depressed south side, which is also the industrial and commercial zone (about 60% of Chile's industry is concentrated here). The city's commercial, political and cultural heart flaunts an untidy melange of building styles, with grand Colonial-style facades from the sixteenth to nineteenth centuries standing alongside modern office buildings, shopping centers and the like. But the promising exterior cannot hide the economic depression afflicting Chile: streets and avenues abound with peddlers, hawking their wares on every corner.

Its rare scenery, tourist sites, comfortable climate and hospitable citizens combine to make Santiago an interesting and pleasant city to visit. It is no wonder that tens of thousands of tourists come here every year.

How to get there
By air: The modern Arturo Benitez Airport is 24 km from Santiago. A fast, comfortable Aerobus Tours Express bus sets out for the city every hour, with other buses plying the route at irregular intervals. Taxi fare to the city is fixed, irrespective of the number of passengers.

CHILE

By land: Numerous bus lines link Santiago with the north and south. Most of these arrive at and depart from the Alameda Bus Terminal, on Alameda O'Higgins. Buses arriving from Argentina also stop at this station. From here the subway takes you downtown in a matter of minutes. Buses from Uruguay, Peru, Brazil, Ecuador, Colombia and Venezuela operate from the offices of their respective companies, all located downtown.

The central train station, too, is situated on Alameda O'Higgins. Several trains set out daily, all headed south, stopping at the large cities until they reach Puerto Montt (an eighteen-hour trip). Though a second-class ticket is cheaper than bus fare, second-class cabins are crowded, uncomfortable and not recommended for long trips. To ensure a place, you must buy your ticket in advance at the railway offices (not at the station), at Alameda O'Higgins 853 (Tel. 30746, 391-848), open Mon.-Fri. from 9am-12:45pm and from 2:30-5:30pm.

Accommodations

Santiago's most expensive and luxurious hotels, excluding the *Sheraton*, are located downtown. The most important and prestigious of these, the *Carrera* (Tel. 82011), is right on Plaza Constitucion, next to the Finance Ministry. The *Pan-American* is two blocks away – at Calle Teatinos 320 (Tel. 82911). This is an excellent hotel, slightly less expensive than the Carrera. Next down the list are the *Hotel City* at Calle Compania 1063 (Tel. 69161), next to the centrally located Plaza de Armas, and the *Hotel Santa Lucia* at Calle Huerfanos 779 (Tel. 398-201). The *Santa Lucia* is recommended for its excellent location and professional, courteous service. The hotel occupies the upper floors of an office building, with the reception desk on the fourth floor.

Very close to the Santa Lucia, on the upper floors of Huerfanos 801, is the *Hotel Victoria* (Tel. 30742, 31380). Moderately priced, it is recommended. A good medium range hotel is the *Espana* at Calle Morande 510 (Tel. 85245).

Really cheap hotels are located some distance from the city center, mainly in the vicinity of the train station and Alameda O'Higgins. Most are reasonably clean and provide very basic services (though it's a very good idea to check for hot water – its availability should not be taken for granted). One such hotel is the *Souvenir* at Calle Amunategui 850, near the Mapucho Station.

What to eat, where and when

Breakfast, lunch, and *once* (pronounced "on-tsei") – rather like afternoon tea, taken between 5 and 7pm – can be had at any

CHILE

of Santiago's many restaurants. Most offer standard Continental fare during the day. These restaurants-cafes open in the early morning hours and are packed at meal time. In the vicinity of the train station, the markets and the city center, there are many such restaurants, most rather inexpensive. In places where you eat at the counter, prices are about 25% lower.

As for dinner, the picture is altogether different. It's customarily not eaten before 9pm and is served in restaurants of various sorts, with regard both to menu and to prices. Supper is a quick, informal affair in popular restaurants, but can easily turn into a sumptuous feast in the excellent luxury restaurants, which you'll find downtown and in the big hotels. Most such establishments serve superb seafood, along with meat and poultry. The seafood is of rare quality; washed down with the excellent local wines, it is a pleasure you must not miss. We'll mention only one of the most special restaurants, *Los Adobes de Argomedo*, on the corner of Argomedo and Lira (Tel. 229-794), which serves excellent meals at reasonable prices. The large restaurant is decorated in ranch-style, and the waiters are dressed accordingly. Each evening at 10 o'clock there's a rousing folklore performance with songs and dancing. Los Adobes specializes in steaks, seafood and popular Chilean dishes.

Transportation

Santiago's modern subway makes getting around downtown much easier. And although the lines are short (the longest is 11 km), it saves a great deal of travel time since it passes under the congested city center. It operates from 6:30am till 10pm. Buses and minibuses also run with great frequency, but are usually jammed. Taxis – a very large fleet – are painted black and have yellow tops. They charge by the meter, adding a 50% surcharge after 9pm and on Sundays.

The Sinatur company at Avenida Santa Maria 1742 (Tel. 236-815), and Carrera Taxis in the Hotel Carrera (Tel. 84097), can provide tourists with chauffeured cars. If you want to do your own driving, there's Hertz (Tel. 237-937, 495-321) or Avis in the Hotel Carrera (Tel. 86267). The Auto Club (Tel. 749-516, ext. 254) is always ready to help.

Tourist services

The Government Tourist Bureau, at Calle Catedral 1165 (Tel. 82151) can provide a wealth of information about Santiago and the entire country. The office is located opposite the Congress building and is open from 9am-6pm (half-day on Saturday). Explanatory material is available at the Auto Club, Calle Pedro de Valdibia 195. Topographic maps may be obtained at the *Instituto Geografico Militar*, at Alameda 240.

CHILE

Airline offices are located downtown on Agostinas, Monda and Huerfanos. The office of the national airline, Lan Chile, is at Calle Bandera 172 (Tel. 65201).

Tourist sites

Anyone wishing to get to know Santiago should begin at the beautiful central square, **Plaza de Armas**. This marks the edge of the downtown area which stretches from it to the Alameda – Avenida O'Higgins. The lovely plaza, the heart of the entire city, is the site of some of the most important municipal institutions: the **Post and Telegraph Office** at its northern end, the **City Hall** and **Municipal Cathedral** to its west. The main commercial streets branch off from here, as does the handsome **Ahumada** pedestrian mall, which extends as far as Alameda O'Higgins. East of the plaza, on the corner of Merced and San Antonio, we find the **Casa Colorada** ("Red House"), built in 1769 to serve as the governor's official residence. Later it became the Presidential mansion, and today is a museum (open Mon.-Sat., 10am-1pm).

The **Congress Building** is located two blocks west of the plaza on the corner of Compania and Moranda. A left turn onto Calle Moranda takes us to **Plaza de la Constitucion**, where we find the **Hotel Carrera** and the Chilean Finance Ministry. On the plaza's southern side, the official Government Palace – **La Moneda**, built in 1805 – stands in all its splendor, and in front of it stands a statue of former President Arturo Palma. The magnificent palace was damaged during the 1973 military coup; repairs have only recently been completed. The building currently houses several Government ministries and is used for official receptions.

From here it's only a short hop to Santiago's main avenue, **Avenida Bernardo O'Higgins**, called the **Alameda** by the local citizens. This boulevard, about a hundred meters wide and more than three kilometers long, is in fact the southern border of the commercial district. It is adorned with gardens, statues, fountains and scores of public institutions. Hundreds of peddlers hawk their wares – highly varied and inexpensive – up and down its sidewalks. Turning right, westward, we head toward the train station and unremarkable residential quarters. A left turn, eastward, will bring us to some of the most beautiful and impressive sites in town.

As we walk down the Alameda, we first discover on our right the grand structure which houses the **University of Chile**, founded in 1842, and the largest and most important of the country's seven universities. Powerful spotlights illuminate the

CHILE

SANTIAGO

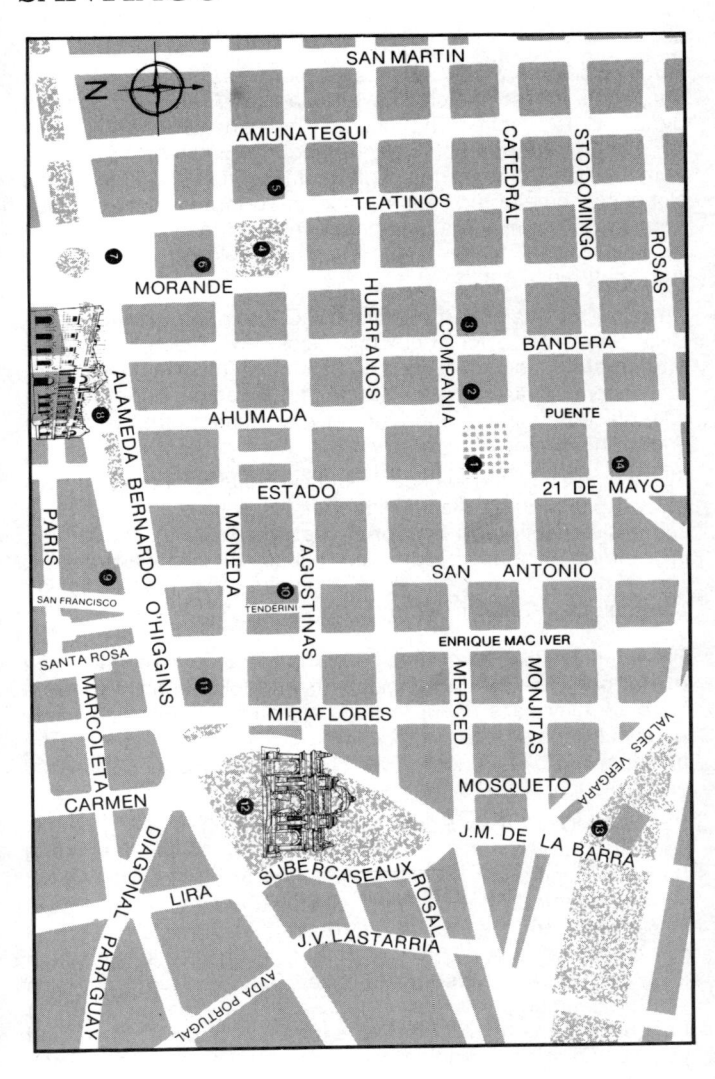

index
1. Plaza de Armas 2. Santiago's Cathedral 3. National Congress 4. Plaza de la Constitucion 5. Carrera Hotel 6. La Moneda Government Palace 7. Plaza de la Libertad 8. University of Chile 9. San cisco Church 10. Municipal Theater 11. National Library 12. Santa Lucia Hill 13. Museum of Fine Arts

CHILE

magnificant structure by night, and the vicinity pulses with life until very late.

Three blocks onward, on the same side of the street, is Santiago's oldest church, the **Iglesia San Francisco**, topped by a tall red spire. The church, built in 1618, houses an interesting **museum** of Colonial and Religious Art; paintings from the seventeenth and eighteenth centuries are displayed alongside some of the nation's most important national-religious treasures. The museum is arranged in good taste and certainly merits a visit: open Sun. 10am-1pm; closed Mon. Open Tues.-Sat. 3-6:30pm.

Crossing the Alameda opposite the Church and walking down Calle San Antonio for about two blocks, we reach the **Teatro Muncipal** (Muncipal Theater), Chile's most important center for the performing arts. Major musical and theatrical performances take place here often, and I strongly recommend that you go to one of them.

Continuing down the Alameda, but now on its northern side, two blocks past Iglesia San Francisco, we find on our left the impressive **Biblioteca Nacional** (National Library), the largest in South America; the building also houses the national archives. The National Library is open Mon.-Fri., 9am-8pm, and on Saturday, 9am-12 and 3-6pm.

Behind it, at Calle Mira Flores 50, is the entrance to the **Museum of History**, where Indian implements and folk art are displayed. Here we may gaze upon portraits of national leaders and their personal effects, along with a large collection of firearms. The museum is open Sunday, 10am-12, and Tues.-Sat., 10am-1pm and 2-5:30pm. Closed Monday.

Past the Library rises **Santa Lucia Hill** (69 m). It was near this spot that the Spanish seafarer Pedro de Valdibia founded Santiago nearly four hundred fifty years ago. The well tended hill is undoubtedly one of the loveliest and most pleasant places in Santiago, and the view it affords is unforgettable. Trails and numerous flights of steps lead to its top, where a small church and modest **art museum** repose. Benches and fountains scattered among the flower beds and trees add a touch of tranquility to the hill. A visit here is unquestionably a "must," and you can time it to coincide with a restorative afternoon *siesta*, with the bustling city at your feet.

North of Santa Lucia Hill, on the bank of the Rio Mapucho, lies one of the most beautiful and best kept of Santiago's parks – *Parque* Forestal, des*igned in* its present form in 1901. The **Museum of Fine Arts** is situtated here, an impressive

CHILE

institution with an extensive permanent collection of paintings and sculptures by Chilean artists. Undoubtedly the most important of its kind in Chile, the museum is well arranged and properly maintained and a visit here is highly recommended. It is open on Sunday, 2-5pm; Tues.-Sat., 10am-1pm and 2-6pm; closed on Monday.

Another central site not to be overlooked is the park on **San Cristobal Hill**. The steep hill (228 m) stands out against the backdrop of the city, and its summit is Santiago's highest point. The hill is north of the Rio Mapucho, within walking distance (about 1.5 km) from downtown, not far from Santa Lucia Hill, Parque Forestal and the Art Museum. The cablecar will take you to the hill's summit, where an enormous **statue of the Virgin Mary** looks out over the splendid view below. The statue is illuminated in the evening, and the panorama of Santiago's lights is most impressive.

The well tended **park** on the hill offers a wealth of amusement and recreation facilities, including restaurants and a swimming pool. Halfway up the hill is the **Municipal Zoo**, with more than one thousand animals (open 9am-6pm). The cablecar has a station at the zoo entrance. In the park's upper section the statue of the Virgin is kept company by an interesting **observatory** (run by the Catholic University), restaurants, and park benches. These are dispersed among lawns and shrubbery, groves of shade trees, fountains and other graceful attractions which lend the park its special charm.

While in the park, be sure to see the **Enoteca** (Wine Museum). This handsome Colonial building has been lovingly restored and displays many of the wonderful Chilean wines. A visit here is no substitute for visiting one of Chile's wineries, where one can see the wine-making process; however, the Enoteca is interesting for its own sake. What's more, the friendly waiters will invite you for a little drink, on the house, at the end of your visit!

Parque O'Higgins, another special place, is located between Avenida Tupper and Avenida Rondizzoni (buses 19 and 20 from downtown, or subway line 2 to the *El Parque* station). A small, Colonial-style village – *El Pueblito* – has been built within the park. Among its eighteen houses are restaurants that specialize in the cuisine of Chile's different regions. Alongside the restaurants are displays of local crafts, and you can see artists at work. The park is open Tues.-Sat., 8am-8pm. Here you'll also find South America's largest amusement park, with modern and exciting rides laid out with great care amid rich greenery and small pools. The facilities at Fantasilandia are open Wed.-Fri. from 3:30pm, and on Saturdays and Sundays from 10:30am.

CHILE

Not far from the park, on Avenida Blanco Encalada, is the **Club Hipico**, Santiago's major sports club, founded in 1869. Its swimming pool and recreational facilities are for members only, but the racetrack, where races are held on Sunday and holiday afternoons, attracts crowds of spectators.

Finally, we should also mention the interesting **National History Museum**, located in Parque Quinta Normal (bus 5) with its entrance behind the church. This museum is open Tues.-Sat. 10am-1pm and 2-6pm; Sunday 2:30-6pm; closed Mondays. The museum has a collection of mummies, fossils from all over Chile including a small dinosaur, displays from Easter Island, and more. The most famous exhibit is the frozen body of a child who lived more than five hundred years ago, found in the early 1950s at an elevation of 5000 m above sea level on the peak of El Plomo. The corpse, amazingly well-preserved, is the subject of many studies and theories as to its origin, the culture to which the child belonged, and the circumstances of his death. Some scholars claim that the boy did not die a natural death, but was rather frozen in the ice after having been offered as a human sacrifice to the local gods.

Entertainment, culture, and nightclubs

What with two symphony orchestras, a ballet company, fifteen theaters, scores of cinemas, and more, there's no doubt that Santiago is an important cultural center.

Major cultural events generally take place in the *Teatro Municipal*, Calle San Antonio 149 (Tel. 32804, 35689). These include operas, concerts, ballet, and plays. Try to attend a performance if you can. Most of Santiago's other theaters are also located downtown, and so are the many cinemas, which show the latest American releases. Naturally, we shall not overlook nightclubs and discotheques. These are active chiefly on the weekends, when the various **cafe-concerts**, too, burst into action. In the latter you may spend an enjoyable evening listening to the strains of a small and colorful ensemble, *muy simpatico*.

Clubs put on folklore shows including the *cueca* – Chile's national dance – for the general public. The most famous and prestigious of these is *El Pollo Dorado* at Calle Agostinas 881 (Tel. 32619), where the excellent show comes with an equally excellent dinner – and at an even higher price! All in all, El Pollo Dorado provides an enjoyable and interesting experience. The show starts after 10pm and it is best to make reservations.

Currency exchange

Foreign currency can be changed at banks and through

CHILE

moneychangers (*cambio*). Banks customarily charge a commission, especially for cashing travelers' checks. Many moneychangers will cash travelers' checks into dollars, and you should avail yourself of their services if you are continuing on to countries where a black market operates and cashing these checks can be a sticky and complicated affair. Most moneychangers are located downtown, on Huerfanos and Agostinas. They are closed in the afternoons, and for most Saturday is a half-day. Luxury hotels have in-house moneychangers; be sure to deal with them and not with hotel cashiers! Compare rates before changing currency, for the differences may amount to several percent.

Postal and telephone services
The central Post Office is situated in a large building on the Plaza de Armas. Here you can mail letters, send packages, and make international phone calls.

Shopping
Santiago's largest and most important shopping district is along the streets that border the Plaza de Armas, and those leading from it toward Alameda O'Higgins. Two streets in this area – Huerfanos and Ahumada – are pedestrian malls, lined with stores that offer merchandise ranging from miscellaneous souvenirs to the latest in consumer goods. Speaking of souvenirs, the government shop (CEMA) at Avenida Portugal 351, undoubtedly offers the broadest selection. This store, housed in an impressive colonial-era building, is the main branch of a specialty chain set up by the Government aimed at providing tourists with one central "address" for most types of souvenirs and products typical of Chile. Bear in mind, of course, that prices here are higher than elsewhere; if you're exploring the entire country, you'll do well to buy your souvenirs outside the capital.

Nevertheless it's certainly worth your while to pay the government store a visit for a first impression – it's got everything.

Chile is especially noted for metal crafts. Since mining is so important to the economy, it's only natural that Chilean artists and craftsmen make use of a variety of metals as their raw material. Accordingly, you can find silver, copper and bronze artwork of many types and tastes, from decorative housewares, ashtrays and candlesticks to coffee tables and other furniture. The silver jewelry, studded with locally produced gems, is truly special.

CHILE

Embroidery, ponchos, rugs, clothing and various leather goods are produced outside of Santiago, primarily in southern Chile, and are likely to be much cheaper there. The lovely pottery prominently displayed in shop windows is also "imported" – from a small town named Pamaire, located some 60 km from Santiago in the heart of a region rich in clay. Those with a taste for the potter's craft will certainly wish to visit Pamaire and watch the craftsmen at work in their homes.

Chilean wines are excellent and inexpensive. I certainly recommend trying them at every opportunity – as the saying goes – wine is proof that God loves men!

The area surrounding the Hotel Carrera is packed with stores that offer a variety of souvenirs, handicrafts and jewelry. This is certainly the place for you to do your shopping. For one, it's where the locals go; for another, prices are reasonable (there's probably a connection here!). For clothing and footwear go back to the city center, where the large stores sell the latest fashions – at appropriate up-to-date prices. High quality shoes, purses and leather briefcases are relatively inexpensive.

A new and modern shopping center is located in Providencia, ten minutes from downtown. Here you'll find dozens of boutiques and nice little shops that offer a huge selection of merchandise of all kinds, at various prices.

Weather
The Santiago area enjoys a Mediterranean-type climate. Summer is hot and dry, with the afternoons and evenings particularly pleasant. Winter is cold, though temperatures rarely fall below freezing. Most of the rain falls in winter, though scattered showers may occur in spring and autumn as well.

Important addresses
U.S. Embassy: Edeficio Cordina, Agustinas 1343 (Tel. 710-133).

British Embassy: Ave. La Concepcion 177, 4th floor, Casilla 72-D, Providencia (Tel. 223-9166).

Immigration Department (for extending your visa): Bandera 46 (Tel. 80378).

First Aid : Tel. 224-422 for an ambulance.

Central Hospital: Portugal 125 (Tel. 382-354).

National Airline: Lan Chile, Bandera 172 (Tel. 65201).

On to Argentina
In addition to the air service described above, many companies provide overland service between Santiago and Argentina – chiefly to Mendoza. For details, see the chapter on Argentina

CHILE

(Mendoza). The most reliable companies, as far as schedules and service are concerned, are Nueva O'Higgins San Martin (recommended), Calle San Francisco 30 (Tel. 380-410), and Cata, Calle Huerfanos 1147 (Tel. 65845, 69502).

Short trips from Santiago

Since Santiago is halfway between the mountains and the sea, it's only natural that vacation and getaway sites of various sorts are relatively close by – the seashore to the west and ski resorts to the east. Vina del Mar, the western resort town, is Chile's most popular summer vacation spot, while the various ski slopes in the soaring Andes have achieved international fame, and are equal in quality to similar resorts in Europe or the United States.

Vina del Mar

Vina del Mar (pop. 260,000) is one of the most beautiful and picturesque of South American cities; it has become Chile's most popular vacation resort for good reason. With its broad avenues and their rows of towering palm trees, its well tended plazas full of shrubbery and flowers, its bustling promenade, open air cafes and white beaches, Vina del Mar welcomes the visitor to its relaxed, carefree atmosphere. Add the excellent climate and a wealth of hotels and restaurants, and you've got all the ingredients for a successful resort town.

When to come and how to get there

Vina del Mar is only a few kilometers from Valparaiso, Chile's second largest city. Buses from Santiago leave the Mapucho station frequently; the 135-km trip takes about two hours. The official season at Vina del Mar runs from September 15 until March 15. However, the city is buzzing from late August through the end of April. During this period it is almost impossible to find a room unless you book well in advance.

Where to stay

Vina del Mar has countless hotels and guest houses at various levels of price and service – from luxury hotels to cheap hostels to campgrounds. The leading hotels are the *O'Higgins* in Plaza Vergara (highly recommended), the *San Martin* – located out of town – and the *Miramar*. In the intermediate price range are the *Espanol* and the *Chalet Suisse*. A great many cheap hotels and pensions (*residencials*) are dispersed throughout the town; most are reasonably clean. The youth hostel, near the Sausalito stadium, admits only card-carrying members of the Youth Hostel Association.

CHILE

What to see

The Chilean Tourism Ministry has an Information Bureau at Avenida Valparaiso 507, third floor, suite 303 (Tel. 882-285).

Vina del Mar makes no pretenses of offering anything beyond rest and recreation, and has no special "tourist sites". Wander through town – on foot, by car, or in a horse-drawn carriage – and pass the luxury hotels, fancy villas, and handsome residences built around the plazas, and surrounding Laguna Marga Marga in the town center; keep going until you reach the floral clock at the seashore. A tour such as this will afford you a basic familiarity with Vina del Mar, and thereafter you'll probably prefer to spend your daylight hours stretched out on the soft, clean sand at the beach. The well-maintained public beaches run the full length of the city, and are packed with thousands of bathers in a colorful, merry tumult. On the beaches and in the city itself you will find abundant opportunities for recreation activities such as golf, tennis and water sports.

In the afternoons and evenings, nothing beats the promenade for a relaxing stroll, during which you can comtemplate the sun as it sinks bewitchingly into the western sea. Here you can also enjoy the enticing aromas that waft from dozens of restaurants and cafes, and savor the ice cream, fruit juices and the like – high-calorie pleasures to be sure (beware – you'll have to reappear in swimwear the next day...). You can, of course, choose one of the superb seafood restaurants and enjoy an evening feast in the fresh sea air. Afterwards, Vina del Mar offers you its multifaceted nightlife: cinemas, discotheques (the most famous is Topsy Topsy, one of the most beautiful in South America), concerts and ballet (intermittently), and, of course, the municipal casino, housed in a large building approached by a bridge over Laguna Marga Marga.

Vina del Mar is surrounded by small resort towns that benefit from the large city's tourist "spillover." The most attractive and interesting of these is **Renaca**, five km north of Vina del Mar, with hotels, restaurants and beautiful beaches. If you find that Vina del Mar is booked up – or, alternatively, if you want to rest in a quieter place – go to Renaca; a totally enjoyable experience is guaranteed.

Ski resorts

Several dozen kilometers east of Santiago, a number of the most interesting and beautiful ski areas in South America are hidden away among the snow-cappped peaks of the Andes. Taking advantage of the topography and comfortable climate of the region, the Chileans have built resort towns that provide skiers

CHILE

with service of international caliber. This, along with excellent slopes for skiers of all levels, from beginner to world champion, has proven a powerful magnet for the skiing set.

When to come and how to get there

Because the seasons are "reversed" in South America, winter, the best ski season, runs from June through October, when the ridges are covered with more than six feet of gleaming snow that makes for superb skiing. Accommodations are hard to find during the ski season, though possibilities abound in the various towns. It is best, of course, to make reservations, but a little patience and perseverance will probably find you a place to lay your head even at the height of the season. The farther south you go, the longer the ski season lasts, and in southern Chile you can usually go skiing even in late November.

Ski slopes can be reached by rented car (depending on the conditions of the road on snowy days), bus and train. Buses of the Grez company (Calle Ahumada 312, suite 315, Tel. 83997) leave Santiago several times a day. The trip lasts up to four hours each way. Several companies specialize in package excursions to the ski slopes, supplying transportation, lodging, meals, and lift tickets. These deals are rather expensive; if you can reach the Andes on your own you'll probably save quite a bit. Reservations can be made at the Chile Ski Club in Santiago Calle Compania 1068, suite 1009 (Tel. 81247).

Special shops and ski clubs on the slopes rent out all kinds of ski equipment. You must remember to bring warm clothing, a woolen cap, gloves and, of course, sunglasses to prevent snow-blindness.

Portillo

Chile's most famous and best developed ski area is Portillo, site of the 1966 world ice-skating championships. It's a nice little town, 144 km from Santiago and 2865 m above sea level. Picturesque Portillo, surrounded by snow-covered and treeless mountains, is the primary ski area and one of the most popular resorts in all of South America. Here many ski lifts will carry you to the slopes, which are well-appointed both quantitatively and qualitatively. Skiing instruction and other services are at your disposal as well. Portillo's snow is smooth; even beginners will find it easy to ski here. Even so, be careful to choose the course which best suits your proficiency. On the village edge is a long, narrow lake – *Laguna del Inca*. Frozen over during the winter, its glassy surface serves as a skating rink and playground. The *Hotel Portillo* is the town's largest and grandest, but its prices

CHILE

appear to stand in direct proportion to its altitude. There are, to be sure, other hotels, but these are rather expensive as well.

Farellones

The resort area of Farellones (elevation 2300 m), which has grown more popular in recent years, is a mere fifty kilometers from Santiago. Only ninety minutes from the capital, Farellones is surrounded by a number of small resort villages (the most famous are *La Parva* and *El Colorado*). Taken all together they offer vacationers a broad range of winter sports. The hotels and restaurants here are less expensive than those in Portillo and are in ample supply. The weather is great; the sun beams down and the ski runs are clearly marked and well designated. Many lifts, a skiing school and equipment rental shops are at your service, making it easy for you to get organized. Many young skiers prefer Farellones because of its relaxed, informal atmosphere, reasonable prices and rare beauty. Santiago's two universities – the General and the Catholic – operate inexpensive hostels for those of limited means. Although they are situated slightly out of town, you will find their atmosphere pleasant. Recommended.

The Northern Deserts

Chile's northern third is a vast, arid, and desolate desert which, apart from a few medium sized cities and small oases, shows absolutely no sign of life. The sun, which beats down mercilessly 365 days a year, and the nearly total absence of rain, prevent the existence of any sort of flora, and because of the lack of water there is no wild life. Settlement here is therefore based on a continual supply of water and food from central Chile, and the inhabitants derive their income mainly from the abundant mineral resources with which this part of Chile has been blessed.

Arica

Chile's northern border town, 2336 km north of Santiago, lies on the Pacific coast near the border with Peru, and serves as a transit point for those arriving overland from Peru and also from Bolivia. Arica's 100,000 residents engage in commerce and services, for most of the exports and imports of neighboring landlocked Bolivia pass through the town. Arica, Chile's "city of perpetual spring" with an annual mean temperature of 22 degrees Centigrade (72 degrees Fahrenheit), is steadily gaining in popularity as a resort. Its wonderful beaches and excellent location, the desert scenery with sand dunes stretching as far

CHILE

as the eye can see, the blue ocean to the west, and the Andes delimiting the eastern horizon, provide sufficient reason for this.

How to get there
Arica's airport links the city with Santiago and Antofagasta (from where you can reach the rest of the country), and with La Paz, capital of Bolivia. The Pan-American Highway, running the length of South America, passes through Arica and links it with Peru to the north and Antofagasta and Santiago to the south. Traffic on this road is rather sparse, gasoline stations are few, and settlements are separated by many long hours of travel. From Arica, regular bus routes run north to Peru and south to Santiago. The southern route is traveled by several companies – some provide meals on the way – and the fare is high. It is twelve hours from Arica to Antofagasta, and twenty-eight to Santiago. Hitchhiking on this road is rather difficult, due to the light traffic. But if you've decided to try anyway, be sure to keep your head covered and bring plenty of water, as you're liable to spend long hours waiting in the hot sun. If you plan to drive, check with the Tourist Bureau as to whether you'll need special permits at checkposts along the highway; furthermore, be sure to take along enough fuel and an extra container of water.

On to Bolivia
A train runs between Arica and La Paz only twice a month, but buses set out daily for Charana, the Bolivian border town. The road climbs to heights of 4000 m above sea level, and crosses *Parque Lauca*. From Charana there is a train twice weekly to La Paz, and the line is full and crowded. One must take warm clothes for the trip because even on clear days it is cold at these high altitudes.

An entrance permit for 30 days is issued at the Bolivian border, and can be extended, if necessary, in La Paz.

Food and lodging
Since Arica became a popular resort town, hotels, pensions and restaurants have sprouted like weeds. The rustic Hotel *El Paso* is delightful, and moderately priced. The *Hotel King* and *Hotel Saxamar* are slightly cheaper, and provide good service. There are numerous pensions (*residencials*) in Arica – clean, comfortable and very inexpensive – along with a simple campground at the southern end of town, along the seashore.

Arica's restaurants and cafes are mostly located around the beaches and provide tasty, inexpensive fare. *Residencials* serve especially inexpensive three-course meals. The prestigious restaurants are open in the evening; most specialize in fish and

CHILE

seafood. You'll find an expensive and very good restaurant in the casino building.

What to see

Arica's **Tourist Bureau**, at Calle Prat 375 (second floor), will provide you with up-to-date information about events in town and places to visit in the area.

The wonderful beaches are Arica's main drawing card. Along the many miles of clean golden beach you can get a tan, frolic in the cool water the year round, and enjoy the company of other vacationers. The prominent attraction downtown is **St. Marcos Church** in **Plaza de Armas**, built on an iron frame to the design of the French engineer Gustav Eiffel, designer of the Parisian tower bearing his name.

Fresh fish is sold near the pleasant **fishing port**, where flocks of pelicans rest on the breakwater and feast on the abundance of fish. From the cliff which extends south of the city, there is a good view of the city, the shoreline and the desert inland, and one can also see birds of prey gliding above.

There is a **history museum** built on the cliff which commemorates the glorious battle of the Chilean conquest of Arica from the Peruvians at the end of the 19th century, during the Pacific War.

Of night life there isn't much; the most bustling and exclusive place is the **municipal casino**.

As for shopping, Arica offers a choice selection at low prices, since many items are duty-free as part of Government policy to encourage people to live in the region. Photographic equipment and supplies are cheaper here than in Santiago.

Excursions

Arica is the starting point for two interesting places: the town of Tacna on the Peruvian border and Lauca National Park on the road to Bolivia. Each is a short trip from Arica, and you can either return to Arica or keep going to the neighboring countries.

Tacna

The Pan-American Highway out of Arica passes through Tacna on its way to Ariquipa, in Peru. You'll cross the border a little before you enter town; if you're going to return to Chile after visiting Tacna, tell the immigration officials before you cross over. There are several buses each day on the 55-kilometer route between Arica and Tacna; the trip takes about an hour and a half. The town is not particularly special but it does have a tax

CHILE

free market for electronic and photographic equipment, and it is worth comparing prices with those in Arica.

Parque Nacional Lauca

On a plateau among the snow capped Andes, 140 kilometers east of Arica and about 4000 meters higher, a large area has been set aside for a unique national park.

In this region, administered and supervised by Chile's National Parks Authority (*CONAF: Corporacion Nacional Forestal*) lives one of the largest concentrations of *vicunas* in the world. This member of the llama family was hunted nearly to the point of extinction for its soft wool and delectable meat. The United Nations intervened and the *vicuna* was declared a protected species. In the countries where they live in relatively large numbers (chiefly Chile and Bolivia), their habitats were declared nature reserves, and off-limits to hunters. Another rare animal which exists in large numbers in the park is the *vizcacha*, a creature which resembles a rock rabbit.

Parque Lauca, however, offers more than lots of *vicunas* and hundreds of species of birds and animals. Its wonderful location, exquisite scenery, and lovely blend of blue, lakes, green plants and snowy white peaks will make your visit there a special experience.

There aren't too many ways to get there, however, since transportation to Lauca is not well organized. Tour companies in Arica offer one-day outings to the park, but these are naturally rather expensive. Those with time on their hands will be interested in hiking Lauca's wonderful trails for a few days and then going on to Bolivia. Ask about transportation at the CONAF offices, since CONAF sends a supply truck to Lauca several times a week, and you can often hitch a ride. There are several *refugias* – little wooden cabins for tourists who need a place to sleep – scattered about the park. **Be sure to keep in mind that you may encounter difficulties in breathing because of the high altitude**. Walk slowly, refrain from undue exertion and avoid foods that are hard to digest. (Additional guidelines for coping with high altitudes are given in the Introduction.) Don't forget to pack enough food for your entire stay in the park, as supplies there are rather limited.

Antofagasta

The port city of Antofagasta (pop. 200,000) is the largest town in northern Chile. Life here is centered around the harbor, where a massive breakwater protects the anchorage from ocean storms. This port, from which most Chilean copper is exported,

CHILE

is the most important one to the national economy and Antofaqastans are proud of the fact. Along with an excellent climate, Antofagasta boasts broad beaches studded with stones carved into wondrous forms by the pounding surf. Because of its industrial nature, however, Antofagasta is not known as a resort town or tourist attraction. Its great economic importance notwithstanding, the city actually has no substantial economic base of its own, and even drinking water is piped in from streams in the foothills of the Andes.
climate, Antofagasta boasts broad beaches studded with stones carved into wondrous forms by the pounding surf. Because of its industrial nature, however, Antofagasta is not known as a resort town or tourist attraction. Its great economic importance notwithstanding, the city actually has no substantial economic base of its own, and even drinking water is piped in from streams in the foothills of the Andes.

How to get there

Antofagasta's airport links the city with all parts of Chile, plus Argentina, Bolivia, Peru, and even the United States. The most frequent service is to Santiago.

Buses, too, connect Antofagasta with Santiago, Arica, La Paz and Argentina. The Pan-American Highway passes through the city and is its main street. The train runs from Antofagasta to La Paz, the capital of Bolivia. The difficult trip takes more than a day and half, with the train climbing to elevations where the thin air makes breathing difficult. The nights are extremely cold, so if you're planning a night trip, **bring along a sleeping bag in addition to warm clothing!**

Food and lodging

Inasmuch as Antofagasta is an industrial city, it's only natural that most hotels there are intended for business travelers. The best is *Turismo Antofagasta* on Calle Part, which offers its guests a broad range of services and rest and recreation facilities. The *Prince* and the *San Martin* are intermediate-class hotels. Inexpensive hotels are located near the bus terminal, around the train station, and along Calle San Martin.

Restaurant menus are reasonably varied, but the seafood is especially good. In the large hotels, at the Automobile Club at the edge of town, and at the seafront restaurants you can eat well without too great a financial outlay. Fish and seafood are cheaper than meat which, along with most of the merchandise in Antofagasta's shops, must be brought in from Santiago, and is therefore somewhat more expensive.

CHILE

What to see

The city itself is rather slim pickings from a tourist's viewpoint. If you find yourself here on business (unlikely), or en route to somewhere else (far more likely), take advantage of your brief stay to take a walk downtown. Visit the **Clock Tower** in the central plaza (a gift of the British community in Chile), and the beautiful **University** and adjacent **Museum**; see the bustling **port** and go out to the seashore. The most popular beach is **La Portada** where, in addition to swimming and sunbathing, you can contemplate the effect of seawater on the rocks. Restaurants abound near the waterfront and nearly all of them specialize in fish and seafood. Their atmosphere is pleasant and their prices affordable; we can recommend them. For evening hours you'll find cinemas, discotheques, and a theater downtown.

The Tourist Ministry is located in the old Customs building, on the corner of Bolivar and Balmaceda.

Excursions

Chiquicamata

Some 220 kilometers northeast of Antofagasta, at an elevation of 3011 meters above sea level, is the largest open-pit copper mine in the world. Until the Allende Government nationalized such industries in the early 1970s, this mine (like many mines and factories) was American-owned. Now it is run by government representatives and the workers, and in the heart of an arid and desolate region, thousands of laborers dig out immense quantities of copper, which is transported first to Antofagasta and then to all corners of the world. Most of the 34,000 residents of the town of Chiquicamata earn their living from mine-related activities.

The guided tour of the enormous pit and the equipment used for excavating and transporting the ore is fascinating. These excursions set out from Antofagasta, but tourists who reach the site by themselves – by public transportation or by hitchhiking – are received at the Tourists' Center at the mine entrance and can join a group there. Lodging possibilities are limited. There are inexpensive workers' restaurants in the mine area and in town.

San Pedro de Atacama

One of the most interesting places in northern Chile is the little village of San Pedro de Atacama, in the heart of the Atacama

CHILE

Desert. This remote hamlet, home to fewer than two thousand people, was a God-forsaken oasis until not many years ago, when fascinating archeological relics were discovered here, dating from the early Stone Age (the Paleolithic period, 10,000 BC) until the period immediately preceding the Spanish conquest (sixteenth century), and today many visitors travel the difficult route to San Pedro de Atacama.

To reach the village, you must go via the city of Calama, 116 kilometers northwest. Buses make the trip several times each week in approximately two and a half hours. On days when there's no bus, you can go by truck or by hitchhiking. There are several hotels and inexpensive pensions in the village, and you can proceed directly – though it's complicated – to Argentina.

The road to San Pedro de Atacama passes through unique "badlands." Here, unlike other such valleys, the strange giant shapes are formed, not of stone, but of salt. Geological changes in this area caused an uplifting of the mountains, which consist of a large quantity of salt; these, once hardened, created a unique and dazzling sight.

On the slopes of the mountains surrounding the village you can make out strange stone formations. These appear to have been ancient redoubts; troves of tools, fabrics, ceramics, jewelery and other artifacts have been found in them. All of these, together with dozens of mummies, skeletons, and skulls, have been put on display in a fascinating **Archeological Museum** on the site. Here you may behold the relics of a bygone culture, preserved in exceptionally good condition by the dry climate. The pride of this museum is its collection of mummies of women, whose clothes – and even their hairstyles – have been preserved in an almost perfect state.

Within hiking distance of the village you'll find the remains of what has been called "the lost world." This site, with thousands of ancient graves, strongholds, and settlements, is rich in artifacts more than fifteen centuries old. Here, in addition to mummies and skulls, an abundance of weapons, wood carvings, tools, and various other types of interesting finds have been discovered.

Once you've completed your visit to these sites and seen the museum and its exhibits, there are additional possibilities for short outings in this area, to remote oases populated by Indians, ancient cities of stone, and the volcanic geysers of **El Tatio**, which erupt each morning.

CHILE

The South-Central Region – Land of Lakes and Volcanoes

Of all the exquisite natural treasures on Earth, I doubt that many surpass those of southern Chile's lake district in beauty, grandeur and charm. The rich blend of lakes, dense greenery, small villages, picturesque houses, grazing cattle and volcanoes billowing forth white smoke, creates a wonderful landscape of sublime tranquility.

A trip to southern Chile is one of the most exhilarating experiences a traveler can look forward to while touring South America. Though you must take care to choose the right season (winters here are rainy and unpleasant) it is hard to imagine a more interesting and enchanting place. To absorb the spirit of the area, it's not enough to organize a hasty scramble from site to site. If you mean to cultivate a real affection for this region, you must blend into it at a natural, somewhat slow pace, and conduct yourself with patience, tolerance, attention and sensitivity.

It is only natural that if you concentrate on the major sites, the ones tourists always frequent, you'll find that the character of the place has been somewhat blunted. If, however, you explore further, even a little – you'll uncover a different world. Here, perhaps more than anywhere else, it is contact with people that counts. The enchanting scenery is splendid in its own right, but the experience of getting to know the local people, their goodheartedness, generosity, and willingness to help, is in my opinion, incomparable.

The superb cherries which grow here are another feature of this splendid area, and anglers will enjoy the good fishing in the lakes.

Temuco

The commercial center of this fertile region is Temuco (pop. 190,000), 672 km south of Santiago. Founded only in the 1880s, Temuco is one of Chile's "young" cities, which is evident in its commercial nature, its architecture, and its people. Temuco is located in the heart of the area where most of Chile's surviving Indians dwell, and it serves them as a marketing center for the wares they produce in the surrounding villages and small towns.

CHILE

Temuco's immediate surroundings are rich in interesting sights and enchanting scenery and it is, therefore, not surprising that there are seven national parks here.

How to get there
Temuco, too, is situated on the Pan-American Highway, and many buses run north to Santiago and as far south as Puerto Montt. The train, running parallel to the highway, is very comfortable (especially in Pullman class) and we recommend that you take advantage of it. The trip to Santiago takes about ten hours. Buses set out for Argentina very early every morning, traveling by way of San Martin de los Andes to Bariloche (concerning this lovely route, see "Argentina – the Lake Region"). Two companies, one Chilean and the other Argentinian, take turns to travel the route each day. In winter, when the snow builds up at higher elevations, the pass is blocked and the only way to reach Argentina is via Puerto Montt (see below).

Food and lodging
The *Hotel Turismo*, off the central Plaza, is Temuco's best, and is moderately priced. The *Hotel Continental* is slightly cheaper. Lots of inexpensive pensions are located near the market and the train station. As for food, there's nothing exceptional about Temuco, and the city's many restaurants serve typical Chilean fare. Like the other cities in the south, Temuco offers a wealth of fish and seafood, in addition to the meat and vegetables that grow in this region.

What to see
Temuco's rather narrow main streets are lined with houses, most two stories high, fronted with shops, shops and more shops. The city center has no special attractions apart from Indian men and women in their multicolored dress. With no special sites that one "must" visit, all we can do is amble quietly along the streets, at Temuco's relaxed tempo and make friends with the locals. In order to meet the natives, especially the Indians from the surrounding villages, it's worth your while to visit the large, covered **market**, located downtown on the corner of Rodrigues and Aldunata. Here you'll find foodstuffs, vegetables and meat, along with artifacts, jewelry, handicrafts, weaving, etc. – all made by the Indians. Many of these items are more beautiful and of higher quality than those offered in most South American markets though prices are in accordance. The beautiful ponchos, wall hangings, sweaters, woodcrafts and metalcrafts, all reflect the unique style of this region, though if you're on your way to the Andean countries (Bolivia, Peru, Ecuador) bear in mind the tremendous variety which awaits you there, at much lower prices.

THE LAKES

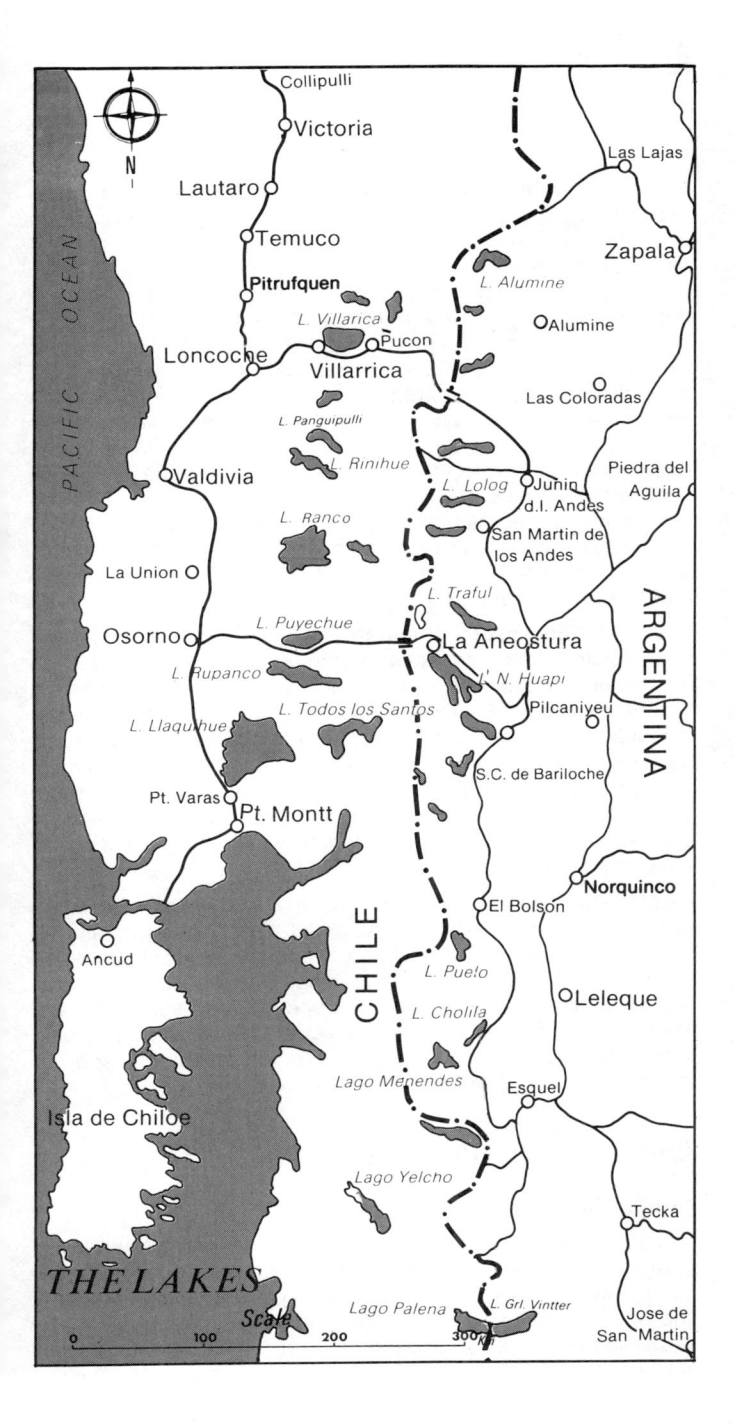

CHILE

Speaking of marketplaces, we should mention Temuco's **cattle market**, one of the most famous in South America, which operates on Thursdays and Fridays between 1 and 4pm. Dozens of ranchers come into town, bringing hundreds of head of cattle for sale. Cattle merchants and other interested parties congregate on a special platform, and the cattle are put up for auction one by one. Hundreds of cattle are jammed into corrals next to the train station, and the *huasos* (Chilean cowboys) then drive them into a small arena where the buyers observe them and set a price. The prices shouted out by the caller are per kilogram of meat; once an animal's price is so determined, the beast is led into a pen to be weighed and have its final price set. The traders, usually dressed in the traditional ponchos and wide-brimmed hats, sit as if frozen to their seats and their bids are indicated by slight gestures apparent only to the auctioneer. Visitors can watch the proceedings from a roofless terrace (bothersome on rainy days).

A stop at the **Museo Araucano** will reward you with further acquaintance with the Indian community. Here you'll find an interesting collection of Indian handicrafts from various periods and of various types. The second floor houses a library on the subject and the staff will be delighted to answer your questions and tell you about the local population, their history, customs, and so forth. After visiting this museum, you can learn more about the Indian's ways of life by personal experience, and go out to tour the neaby villages, where you'll see the Indians in their daily routine.

If you favor a panoramic view, you'll certainly want to climb **Nielol**, a hill which affords a splendid view of the city and its surroundings. A peace treaty between the Spanish from the north and the Araucano Indians, who controlled the area until then, was signed on this hill about one hundred years ago and Temuco was founded in the wake of the accord. A round Indian-style house has been reconstructed on the hill, and not far away, there is an exhibition of the local flora.

Excursions in the area

Indian villages

Several dozen kilometers west of Temuco are a number of villages populated by Indian tribes. Anyone who expects to see war-painted Indians is in for a disappointment, since nothing of the sort is at hand. The local residents may perhaps be descendants of such Indians and at times one may even observe traditional ceremonies that have been preserved – but

CHILE

on normal days they listen to the radio, wear sneakers and accept dollars. Nevertheless, their handicrafts, behavior and way of life is extremely interesting.

To reach the villages, either take a taxi or hitchhike about sixty kilometers through lovely scenery (on a far less lovely road) to the coastal town of Carahue. The route passes through small settlements, but only from Carahue onwards, both to the south and up the Rio Imperial, will you encounter communities where life still goes on in a pattern that is slowly vanishing.

Skiing

The Andes rise east of Temuco and their peaks are lower here than they are in the Santiago area. Abundant rainfall and cold climate join forces, with the result that some of Chile's most beautiful and pleasant ski areas are located here. As if to add charm to the idea, some of these ski centers are spread over the snow covered slopes of volcanoes – including some active ones.

Villarica (see below) and Llaima are the most important ski areas. Llaima, 185 km east of Temuco, is at the foot of the volcano bearing the same name. The mountain soars to an elevation of 3060 m, though the highest point in the ski area itself is about a thousand meters lower.

Llaima is located in the center of the Conguillio National Park. This wonderful park abounds in forests, lakes and snow capped peaks. A dirt road passes through the park and one can tour by car or do some of the walks and hikes. One recommended possibility is the climb to the summit of Llaima, whose crater continuously gives off white smoke. This is a full day's climb, and demands suitable preparation. Another much easier route, which is also enchanting, is the hike along the Sierra Nevada trail, which takes only a few hours.

In both cases, one must begin the hike at the camping area in the center of the park, on the shores of the beautiful Lake Conguillio. Those who wish to visit the park without a car can catch a bus which travels the route from Temuco to Melipeucio, a quiet and remote Indian village. From here it is a day and a half of pleasant walking to reach the central camping area, but it is not difficult to hitch a ride along the way.

Villarica

Villarica is a charming and tranquil town seventy-five kilometers southeast of Temuco. Many buses travel from Villarica to Temuco on a daily basis. The trip – south on the Pan-American Highway.

CHILE

to the town of Freire, and from there east to Villarrica – takes almost two hours. (The journey is longer and more complicated by train, and is not recommended.) The bus from Temuco to Argentina picks up passengers in Villarrica and Pucon. Villarrica, with a population of 24,000, lies on the southwestern shore of Lake Villarrica and serves as a popular resort and ski center. The lake – twenty kilometers long and eight wide – is one of the most beautiful in the area, and its shore, rich in greenery, provides recreation and resort sites that both tourists and locals love. In summer, throngs of visitors pass their time at water sports – sailing, swimming, fishing – while skiing takes over in the winter.

Villarrica has restaurants and a number of hotels, of which the best is the *Yacht Club*, housed in a handsome building surrounded by small houses. The *Hotel Parque*, like the Yacht Club, is located on the lakefront, but is less expensive. In the town itself you'll find cheaper hotels and pensions, though as a rule you must remember that it's a resort town and that prices are quite high, especially during the tourist season.

Pucon

The pleasant town of Pucon (pop. 18,000) hugs the southeastern shore of the lake some twenty-four kilometers east of Villarica. The wonderful climate, the gorgeous scenery and the giant Villarrica volcano, which looms behind the town, have helped make Pucon an exclusive and ever-in-demand resort – a fact reflected in its prices. While it's true that the people who live here should be grateful for the natural delights that have turned their town into such a sought-after place, they also should also thank the Queen of England for their prosperity. Since Elizabeth II stayed here during a state visit to Chile in 1968, Pucon's reputation has spread far and wide, and hordes of visitors flock to it. The subject of Pucon's prices is like the question of which came first, the chicken or the egg: I don't know whether the Queen's visit caused prices to skyrocket, or whether the prices are so high that one must be the Queen of England to vacation here ...

But we mustn't panic. Anyone who doesn't insist on staying at the lakeshore *Gran Hotel Pucon* or the *Antumalal* (where the Queen stayed) has a reasonable chance of finding cheaper accommodations. Two possibilities are the *Residencial Araucarias* and *Hotel Suiza* and there are a number of others. City dwellers will certainly be delighted to spend the night in one of the comfortable and inexpensive campgrounds between Villarrica and Pucon. As for food, apart from the restaurants in

CHILE

town you can try your luck at fishing. Lake Villarrica is packed with fish, and even the inexperienced fisherman can expect to land a satisfactory lunch. Happy fishing!

The Volcano

Behind Pucon, Mt. Villarrica rises to an elevation of 2940 m above sea level. Its lovely crater, which erupted most recently in 1985, gives off a constant stream of white smoke and lava particles, and on a clear day can be seen from great distances. The mountain's upper portion is perpetually snow clad; the black stains on it are actually scattered patches of lava. The ski area, thirteen kilometers from Pucon, is reached by a charming dirt road. Before you reach the mountain you'll pass a park rangers' station; the rangers can inform you about the weather, as well as climbing and skiing conditions. During the skiing season a bus leaves from Pucon each morning, though you can always hire a taxi if you so desire (it's also an easy, enjoyable four-hour walk). At the foot of the mountain, near the lower end of the lift, there's a *hosteria* that provides accommodations for skiers, but it's quite expensive and open only during the ski season. About one kilometer before you reach it are two *refugias* (cabins) where you can stay for nothing, though these lack water and beds.

Of all the experiences that came my way as I toured South America, that of climbing the active volcano at Pucon is engraved in my memory as one of the most stunning. It took more than six exhausting hours to reach the rim of the crater, from which we beheld the awesome sight of molten lava bubbling out of the bowels of the earth.

In order to climb the mountain you've got to get there the day before and spend the night in one of the *refugias*. Bear in mind that the weather is quite treacherous and that the climb is out of the question in winter because of the snow pack covering the mountain. During the rest of the year the weather swings between extremes from one day to the next and it's hard to predict when climbing will be possible. We reached the *hosteria* on a rainy day, so cloudy and foggy that we could not even tell in which direction the mountain lay. The next day the weather cleared and we set out under a cloudless, sunny sky.

The mountain's innocent appearance is highly misleading and it doesn't take too long to find this out. You should climb up the left side, which isn't as steep as the right; it's easier though longer. Tremendous lava flows cleave the path leading to the slope, and you must cross them one by one. To add to your burden, the basalt rock is not solid, as in some other sites, but

CHILE

consists of layer upon layer of volcanic sand and particles of tuff (porous sedimentary rock). For every twenty centimeters you climb, you're liable to slide back eighteen, as if you're climbing sand dunes. The climb itself is difficult and complicated. The slope may have appeared moderate, but reveals itself to your legs as quite steep. If you want to go straight up, you'll have to stop every few minutes to catch your breath. The right way to progress, therefore, is on a "switchback course", zig-zagging from side to side. This makes the slope more moderate, but it also lengthens the hike and tires your legs. All of this happens in the first four or five hours of the climb. Then you reach the ice belt, a glacial strip that surrounds the crater like a collar. It is very difficult to cross and you should avail yourself of special climbing gear. The glacier is steep and slippery. With no rocks to grab hold of and no obstacles to break your fall, a slip is liable to end in disaster! **Be very careful!** Once across the glacier, you come to the rim of the crater, which is three hundred meters in diameter and fifty meters deep. Here you'll behold a breathtaking sight. As you stand there, look straight down into the center of the crater, into the gaping green, red and yellow hole in the ground, from which globs of molten lava and grey-white clouds of smoke pour continually. It should be noted that this crater disgorged millions of tons of lava little more than ten years ago, changing the appearance of the entire area.

The terrible cold and gusting winds notwithstanding, try to wait here until you hear a dull roar out of the depths of the earth, followed by a loud blowing sound. These phenomena herald the eruption of a large cloud of smoke, in which glowing particles of molten lava are suspended.

The way down is also hard. Be careful not to step on broken chips of ice and don't slide between them; treat lava rocks and downhill slopes with similar caution. Try to go down on exactly the same path you used to go up, and remember to do so by daylight. If you take too long to climb up or spend too much time at the top, you won't have enough time to come down by daylight – an extremely dangerous proposition.

Note
It is true that climbing to the crater of an active volcano is an unparalleled experience, but it involves considerable effort and great danger. Accordingly, if you're considering it, you should give the matter careful thought; don't rush your decision. To have enough time to reach the crater and return before dark you must set out by 6am and be prepared for twelve hours of non-stop, exhausting, complicated climbing with neither trail nor path, on porous tuff and slippery, extremely dangerous patches

CHILE

The Villarica volcano

of ice. Dress warmly, for the mountain gusts are bone-chilling despite the exertion of the climb. You **must** wear strong hiking shoes and take along food and water. Ropes and climbing pitons will make it easier to cross the glacier, and greatly reduce the danger of slipping on the ice.

Finally, one of the most impressive experiences that man can enjoy is to witness nature in its full grandeur and power. Mt. Villarrica offers the visitor such an experience. Of all the active volcanoes on the South American continent, this appears to be the easiest to climb, and a single day suffices for the round trip. It is also one of the most beautiful of mountains and its classic shape, in addition to the splendid view from its summit and slopes, make the climb an experience you'll never forget. So be careful – and go.

Osorno

The town of Osorno (pop. 106,000), 260 km south of Temuco, was founded by German immigrants as an agricultural colony. Despite struggles with the Indians who controlled the area – which resulted in the town's abandonment for a short time – the immigrants managed to build a settlement that, over the years, became a large regional agricultural center, where the German influence is evident to this day. Many of the numerous hotels, restaurants, shops and clubs in Osorno bear German names, and German is still spoken in many places.

CHILE

How to get there

That lengthy thoroughfare, the Pan-American Highway, reaches Osorno, too, on its way from Temuca via Valdibia to Puerto Montt. Daily Lan Chile flights link Osorno with Santiago, as do many bus lines. Buses for neighbouring cities set out frequently from the market area. The Santiago-Puerto Montt train stops in Osorno and the trip, in Pullman or first class, is very comfortable.

There are two major ways of going to and from Argentina: the highway from San Carlos de Bariloche, and the bus-ferry route across *Lago Todos Los Santos* ("All Saints' Lake"). The bus (several times weekly in winter, daily in summer) passes through beautiful countryside, though during winter one should expect to be delayed due to snow. The lake route takes a full day, and some bus companies include in a night's lakeshore accommodation (in this case, the trip takes two days). Crossing the lake, one of the loveliest in the region, is a very impressive experience. If you've got time on your hands, don't miss it.

Food and lodging

The *Gran Hotel* on the central plaza is excellently located and moderately priced. The *Centro Juvenil* on Avenida Gral MacKenna is an inexpensive youth center-hostel. Inexpensive pensions are located near the train station. There are two clean campgrounds with good facilities on the outskirts of the town.

In the culinary field, the local products are prominent, though the residents' German ancestry contributes its influence as well. Many restaurants specialize in German food: lots of meat, marinated in oil and roasted, are served alongside seafood and typical Chilean dishes. The best restaurant is the *Plaza* on the central square, which serves German food at rather high prices. The *Bahia* on Calle Ramirez is far less expensive and its food is excellent. The less expensive restaurants are located in the vicinity of the bus and train stations.

What to see

Osorno generally serves only as a transit point for people going to the lake region and I can't imagine any other reason for staying there. Except for the Spanish Maria Luisa fortress and two small museums, Osorno, although a pleasant city, has little to interest the tourist. Even the **Tourist Bureau**, next to the Provincial Government building on the central plaza, finds it hard to provide information about city attractions, and the staff will generally content themselves with talking about the town's surroundings, where there's lots to see.

CHILE

Lakes: In summer the lakes in the region are popular with vacationers, though there's no feeling of crowding. From Osorno, many buses head each day for the lakeshore, where you can get away from it all, spend several days hiking, and visit small towns and picturesque villages still not connected to the national power grid, where wooden ox-drawn plows remain the norm. Lakes *Rupanco* (sixty kilometers from Osorno) and *Todos Los Santos* are the most famous and popular in the area.

Parks: Puyehue National Park is situated eighty-one kilometers east of Osorno in the heart of a forested area. The park centers around hot springs – the *Termas de Puyehue* – and the adjacent massive, old Gran Hotel. A swimming pool and hot baths are situated next to the hotel, near mineral water springs whose output is bottled and sent into town. One bus a day makes the two-hour trip from Osorno. The *Antillanca* ski area, which has become popular in recent years, is located within the park's confines, a circumstance which has spurred development of the region. Hotels, hostels and restaurants have been built (such as the Osorno Andes Club which has opened a hostel at the base of the ski area with accommodations for two hundred). The park itself is drenched in greenery, interspersed among small lakes. You can camp out for days, just resting up, or hiking through the serene and undisturbed countryside.

The volcano: Mt. Osorno soars to a height of 2600 m above sea level on the shore of *Lake Llanguihue*, the largest of the southern lakes. On clear days a splendid view, one of the most beautiful imaginable, can be had from the slopes of this volcano. If you're a good hiker, we recommend that you make the climb. Getting all the way to the summit is a difficult and complicated undertaking; one has to climb through thick forest and the mountaintop itself is snow covered even in summer. During the winter, the entire mountain is enveloped in deep snow and its slopes turn into an active, bustling ski area.

A hike: Apart from the normal route from Osorno to the charming town of Puerto Varas ninety-nine kilometers further south, good hikers have the fascinating option of making their way on foot through one of the most beautiful hiking areas in the world. Head east from Osorno in the direction of Puyehue Park, and from there make your way southward from village to village toward *Lake Rupanco* and from there to *Lake Todos Los Santos*. There's a pleasant little town called Petrohue on the lake's western shore and from there you can go sailing on the limpid waters. If you wish, you can take a ferry from here straight to Argentina. If you stay in Chile, you can continue westward to the town of Ensenada on the shore of *Lake Llanguihue* and then on to Puerto Varas. This area abounds in trails and paths

CHILE

that pass through lovely towns and villages. For part of the way, of course, you can use public transportation or hitch. Elsewhere you can use a boat or walk. Almost any particular route you choose will meet your expectations and provide an extraordinary experience. Plan for a week on the road and take along suitable camping equipment and plenty of food. You'll have no trouble finding water along the way.

Puerto Varas

The town of Puerto Varas (pop. 31,000) lies on the western shore of *Lake Llanguihue*, the largest of Chile's lakes, nineteen kilometers north of Puerto Montt. The town is called the "City of Roses" for the rosebushes that adorn its short street. Across the lake you'll see Mt. Osorno in all its glory, the white crown stunning in its perfection. Near the town, unique archeological remains have been found, which testify to human habitation from very early days. These are the most ancient archeological finds anywhere in the Americas and scholars claim that they provide proof of human settlement here, in periods far earlier than had been commonly supposed. Excavations have gone on for a number of years. Though final conclusions have yet to be drawn, the "dig" is undoubtedly interesting. A road from Puerto Varas circles the lake along which there are places to relax, fish and enjoy the vivid greenery. Buses make the trip from Puerto Montt several times a week on the Pan-American Highway.

On to Argentina through Lake Todos Los Santos

A few kilometers before Lake Todos Los Santos are the beautiful and turbulent **Petrohe Falls**. From Petrohe there is a ferry which crosses the lake to the village Peulla. The cruise, which takes two and a half hours, is exceptionally beautiful. From Peulla one reaches the Argentinian border, 18 km away, by dirt road, and from there another cruise crosses *Lake Frias*, whose enchanting scenery is reminiscent of Norwegian fjords. Tourist buses travel daily along the road between the two lakes. They are expensive, but one has no hope of hitching here. Those who wish to do the route on foot are advised to do so in the reverse direction – from Argentina to Chile – because then most of the way is downhill. The start of the route on the Argentinian side is at Puerto Blest on *Lake Nahuel Huapi*.

The main route from Puerto Montt to Argentina passes through Puerto Varas and continues on to Lake Todos Los Santos and the lakeshore town of Petrohue.

CHILE

Puerto Montt

The Pan-American Highway reaches its southern terminus 1057 km south of Santiago de Chile, at the lovely port city of Puerto Montt, on the northern edge of the Gulf of Ancud.

Puerto Montt was founded in 1852 by a group of German immigrants whose descendants still live there. As time passed, the city developed and became a center for agriculture, fishing and tourism, which has achieved ever-growing popularity in recent years. The more than 97,000 people who live here make their living from the sea, from tourism and from services they provide to the small towns of the region. The city effectively constitutes the southern extremity of Chile's unbroken settled area; south of here stretch more than a thousand kilometers of a sparsely populated archipelago which suffers from a harsh, rainy, wintry climate most of the year.

Transportation

Like the Pan American Highway, the railroad from Santiago reaches its terminus here at a noteworthy station, if only because it is the southernmost train station in the world. Trains from Santiago reach here eighteen to twenty hours after setting out, with many intermediate stops. A daily express sets out for Santiago, while a "milk-run" follows the same route at a more leisurely pace, stopping at every village and city along the way. A timetable is posted at the train station, which also offers baggage-checking service and a restaurant. The modern bus terminal is some distance from the city center. There is bus service to Santiago (several times a day), to cities in the area – Puerto Varas, Osorno and northward (approximately once an hour), to Isla Chiloe (every two hours) and to Argentina. Buses to the latter destination depart every morning and go either directly to Bariloche or via Puerto Varas and Lake Todos Los Santos (including overnight accommodations). Students are eligible for a considerable discount on bus travel, but sometimes one must insist on getting it. A Student Card isn't always enough and one who requests a discount must stand up for his or her rights firmly – though politely. It helps. Lan Chile flies daily to and from Santiago and Punta Arenas.

South to Patagonia

Many tourists who wish to continue to the continent's southern tip come to a "dead end" in Puerto Montt for lack of a conventional land route southward. There are, however, a number of ways to proceed, some very expensive and others not so; the matter requires lots of luck and perseverance.

CHILE

During the summer, passenger ships ply the route from Puerto Montt to Punta Arenas – a captivating voyage through exceptional scenery of fjords and icebergs. A tourist boat makes the trip in four days or more, while a cargo ship may take up to ten days. Passenger ships have three classes; third class is definitely satisfactory for young tourists. In addition to the passenger ships, many cargo ships operate on this route and their captains will often agree to carry passengers for pay. This is an interesting and inexpensive way to make the trip, which we can recommend highly. Its only drawback is that you may be delayed in Puerto Montt for quite some time until you find a suitable ship. Should you find it hard to locate one in the Puerto Montt harbor, try your luck at the port in Chiloe.

Another way, of course, is by plane. Lan Chile flies south and back several times each week. The Chilean Air Force also flies southern routes. Though these flights are cheaper, it is quite difficult to obtain a ticket and their frequency and timetables change constantly.

The only possibility of reaching Patagonia by land is via Argentina. You must cross the mountains and proceed south from San Carlos de Bariloche. The fastest (though lengthy) route is from Bariloche to Commodoro-Rivadavia, then to Rio Gallegos and westward to Rio Turbio and the adjacent border crossing to Puerto Natales.

Food and lodging

The best and most expensive of Puerto Montt's hotels is the *Vincente Perez Rosales*. The *Hotel Montt* and *Hotel Angelmo* (the latter right downtown) are cheaper. There are many hotels, some quite expensive, on the main street next to the train station. On the side streets, the pensions and hotels get less expensive the farther you get from the shore. Many residents will accommodate guests in their homes for a small fee. Negotiations with some pension-owners may result in permission to sleep on a mattress in the attic – very cheap. The rate in some pensions includes use of the kitchen. A small youth hostel is open during the summer.

Puerto Montt is famous for its superb seafood. Even experienced and knowledgeable gourmets will find themselves surprised at the abundance and quality of Puerto Montt's fare. In the city's numerous restaurants – especially those in the Anjalmo area – strange looking monsters of the deep are laid on your plate, and you'll need a stiff upper lip and a broad mind to overcome your instinctive horror and get the fork into your mouth. Anyone who can't take it, of course, can choose from fish, crabs and other offerings that are easier to digest, if only in the psychological sense ...

CHILE

Beef, *empanadas*, rice and the other familiar Chilean dishes are also served in plentiful portions and good quality, so there's no need to bring along canned food and even those who can't work up the courage to take a chance on the seafood will not die of hunger.

What to see

The **Tourist Bureau** is next to the **Municipal Theater**, close to the train station, at Calle Quillota 124. The staff will be delighted to assist you with maps and information and will help you in matters of accommodation and transportation.

Puerto Montt is a quiet, pleasant town, and its residents are kindly disposed toward tourists. The tranquil landscape, the small wooden houses, the clean sea and the surrounding greenery create a relaxing atmosphere. You'll enjoy wandering along the streets and observing the wonderful, slow paced life they lead here. The little fishing port Angelmo, about a kilometer out of town, is a colorful jewel of a place, bustling in its own way with small fishing boats, lots of fishermen, tourists and – in their wake – simple fish restaurants, stands with handicrafts for sale, and more. One of the finest times to visit Angelmo is at low tide, for in these high southern latitudes the water ebbs considerably, leaving scores of meters of moist sand on which the lovely fishing boats are calmly beached. The local market offers a selection of superb, reasonably-priced local *artesania*. (handicrafts). This is one of the best places in Chile for purchases of this sort.

Apart from being a lively tourist spot, Puerto Montt also serves as a point of departure for many sites in the vicinity:

Fjords, lagoons and icebergs: The entire region south of Puerto Montt, especially south of Isla Chiloe, is a beautiful uninhabited area where primeval nature reigns undisturbed. Travel here is possible only by sea, and the weather is usually harsh, greyish, rainy and cold – factors that make the experience doubly moving.

Laguna San Rafael: This is considered the most beautiful of South Chile's lakes. Far to the south of Puerto Montt, amidst islands and fjords, it can be reached only by boat. Tourist itineraries which include Laguna San Rafael are very expensive, so it's worth your while to make inquiries among the fishermen in the port (though it won't be much cheaper even then). The lagoon is exquisitely beautiful, with giant icebergs hemming it from every direction. Parts of these sometimes fall into the lake, making a tremendous noise.

CHILE

High-rise' lakefront houses

Small towns: We highly recommend that you wander around the port area and try to hitch a ride on one of the little supply ships that make their way among the settlements in the area. If you succeed, you can expect the marvelous and unique experience of a visit to remote places reached by few outsiders, where the natural beauty has not yet been marred by the tourist plague.

Chiloe Island

Isla Chiloe, one of the most charming jewels in all of South America, lies a short distance south of Puerto Montt. This enchanting island bursts with greenery. Its houses are tiny and picturesque and its atmosphere pastoral and serene. The whole scene, calm and relaxing, appears to have been taken out of a beautiful Impressionist oil painting. There are two major towns

CHILE

on the island – Castro and Ancud – plus fishing villages spread up and down the coast.

Buses set out for Chiloe from Puerto Montt every two hours or so and, after about an hour's ride on Route 5 as far as Pargua, a ferry takes the bus across the narrow strait separating Chiloe from the mainland. Then you continue, first to Ancud and then on to Castro. Ancud, the smaller of the two towns, is located on the shore of a bay which is left half-dry at the evening low tide. The small and colorful houses of the town nestle in a valley situated between two green slopes.

Possibilities for accommodations in Ancud are numerous and inexpensive and the town is an interesting place in its own right. The central square, the little port, the handsome streets and lovely houses undoubtedly merit a visit. At the same time, I

CHILE

personally find Castro far more fascinating. This pleasant town (linked to Ancud by a concrete highway that winds through forest and meadow, between bay and village) has a strange character all its own. Since Chiloe was low on the Spaniards' list of objectives and was subsequently the last district to join the call for independence from Spain, the remnants of past cultures have yet to disappear and the residents of Chiloe in general and Castro in particular, are known for their tendency toward superstitions – as expressed in their somewhat odd behavior ...

The houses on Chiloe are built of wood, and only in recent years have they been connected to a power grid and water system. Most locals dress 1930s-style; the men generally wear dark plastic hats while the women are clothed in bulky and graceless woolen attire.

On the waterfront, the buildings are erected on wooden piles so as not to be flooded; their images reflect in the clear, montionless water. This is one of the most interesting sights of human settlement in all of South America. Places that deserve a visit include the **seaside market,** the friendly **Tourist Bureau** on Plaza de Armas, and the tiny **museum** adjacent to it. The **cemetery** on the hill overlooking town is colorful and rather special; you should visit it, too.

Castro offers a number of inexpensive little hotels, most near the Plaza de Armas. The *Residencial Miraso*, at Calle San Marin 815, is very nice and recommended.

From Castro you'll find it worthwhile to take an excursion through the little fishing villages in the vicinity. It's best to go off the main road and penetrate the rural areas, if only a little way. If you do so, an unforgettable experience of visiting a "living museum" – the last remnants of a vanishing way of life – awaits you.

On Sundays, the little fishing village of Dalcahue, 20 km north of Castro holds a special kind of market. A bus sets out from Castro before daybreak, and the trip is an entertaining experience in its own right. Castro residents load goods and food on to the bus, in quantities that would normally require three buses or more. These goods are put on sale at the market, where you will find various foodstuffs, a large selection of wool products, sweaters, wall hangings and much more. Recommended.

Given all the wonders of this vicinity and its attractions, it seems to me that one shouldn't miss the opportunity to visit Chiloe Island. I warmly recommend it!

CHILE

The Far South – Patagonia and Tierra del Fuego

At South America's southernmost extremity, where dry land comes to an end, you'll find some of the wildest, most astounding and stunning regions on earth. Among the icebergs, fjords, lakes, lagoons, ice fields and gigantic mountains that make up nearly one third of Chile's total area you'll find less than 3% of its population. This is an open area of primeval nature, where the works of man are hardly discernible. Chilean Patagonia is a land enchanting in its beauty, stunning in its virgin glory.

Most of the region's tourism and commercial activity is concentrated around its two major cities – Punta Arenas and Puerto Natales. The two towns also serve as points of departure for wonderful trips into the countryside. Words cannot describe the scope and power of the experience that awaits you here: the sensitive visitor cannot help being moved by everything and everyone he encounters. While plant life is almost totally lacking, Patagonia abounds in wildlife. Llamas, foxes, pumas and many more species inhabit Patagonia's vast expanses while innumerable birds, including the condor, fly above.

Patagonia's climate is harsh most of the year; not many plants, as we've noted, can grow here. Fishing and sheep-herding are the main activities. Rain falls the year round, and the driving winds can reach speeds of 100 kph and more!

In summer, the sun shines twenty hours a day – because of Patagonia's proximity to the South Pole – and the high and low tides, characterized by extreme differences in the water level, are something to behold. The normal tourist season is summer, between November and February. Few visitors come to Patagonia the rest of the year, especially between April and September, and most forms of transportation to the various sites of interest are unavailable. You must bring along warm clothing at any time of year. Furthermore, if you intend to sleep under the stars in parks, pack an excellent sleeping bag and a strong, reliable tent!

Since it's harder to change money here than elsewhere, you should bring pesos from the north and as for foreign currency, stick to cash dollars. Travelers' checks can be cashed only after some effort on your part and at a poor rate. Since Patagonia is remote and isolated and almost everything has to be brought in from the north, goods usually cost about 50% more than they do elsewhere in Chile; a fact you must take into account.

CHILE

Punta Arenas

Punta Arenas is not only Chile's southernmost city, but also one of its nicest. This city of 110,000 people, located 2200 km south of Santiago, has served as an important regional center since 1584, when the first settlers arrived. Due to its strategic location – on the northern shore of the Strait of Magellan – settlement here has always been regarded as vital, even more so in recent years following the discovery of significant quantities of oil. This has added impetus to urban development: many homes have been built and new streets paved, and new settlers have arrived in droves. The area currently supplies much of Chile's consumption of oil, natural gas and coal.

How to get there

Punta Arenas is connected by land to neighboring Argentina and by air and sea to northern Chile. Lan Chile, Aerolineas, and other commercial airlines, as well as the Chilean Air Force, provide excellent air service to and from Santiago, Puerto Montt and Buenos Aires. In summer tickets must be reserved well in advance. As for reaching Punta Arenas from the lake region, see "Puerto Montt".

Two good roads link Punta Arenas with Rio Gallegos in Argentina. The shorter and more convenient runs along the coast of the Strait of Magellan, provide a beautiful and interesting trip that takes from five to seven hours, depending on border-crossing difficulties. Buses run several times a day in summer and several times a week in winter. Buses leave Puerto Natales several times a day for the four-hour trip along a new concrete highway. A ferry provides daily service to and from Puerto Porvenir in Tierra del Fuego, setting out from a harbor about five kilometers from downtown Punta Arenas (take the bus to Zona Franca and then walk about a kilometer). Tickets can be purchased on the ferry itself for the three-hour trip across the Strait of Magellan. Departure times vary according to the time of year and day of the week. Check at the Tourist Bureau in Punta Arenas as to the exact schedule on the day you want to sail.

Food and lodging

Hotels and restaurants of various standards are scattered throughout Punta Arenas, especially downtown along the streets around the Plaza de Armas. On the plaza itself you'll find the largest and grandest of Punta Arenas' hotels – the *Cabo de Hornos*. The *Miramar* and *Turismo Plaza* are less expensive and are recommended. A very inexpensive hotel is located above the *American Service Restaurant* at Calle Roca 953.

CHILE

Senor Abelardo, owner of the restaurant, lets out little rooms on the second floor. Though they're rather miserable, they've got everything you need: a bed, a closet and a gas heater. The price is very reasonable, and in a town where accommodations are so expensive this option is quite satisfactory. The Tourist Bureau can provide you with information about accommodation in private homes.

There is no shortage of restaurants in Punta Arenas. Though the accent is on seafood, lamb is no less commonplace. Vegetables, eggs and the like are expensive, for most such foods are brought in from the north. The downtown area has a number of sandwich-and-hamburger places, which serve the fastest and cheapest fare available.

What to see

The municipal **Tourist Bureau** is in the **Provincial Government Building** at Calle Waldo Seguel 689. The friendly staff will give you a map of Punta Arenas, background material and explanations concerning the city, its attractions, outings in the area, transportation and hotels.

Punta Arenas has been favoured with a great many interesting sites that deserve a visit. The streets are laid out in a grid pattern, making it easy to find you way around. The **Plaza de Armas**, with its **statue of Magellan** (the European discoverer of the area), is the heart of town and most activity in Punta Arenas is concentrated in its vicinity. If you want to assure yourself good luck, try kissing Magellan's enormous foot; local tradition attributes wondrous powers to this act. In the plaza you'll also find a small and interesting **museum** with displays of local history, animal life and natural resources.

The city lies on the shore of the broad strait through which the famous Portuguese navigator Fernando Magellan made the first passage in November, 1520, thereby confirming Columbus' hypotheses about the way to the Indies, by finding a direct route from Europe to East Asia. The coastline essentially serves as Punta Arenas' eastern border, with the city spread out along it. From the shore there is a lovely view of the island across the strait – Tierra del Fuego (Land of Fire).

On the eastern side of town there's a unique graveyard which is certainly worth a visit. The carefully tended **cemetery**, enclosed within a high stone wall, abounds in greenery and trees that have been pruned with exemplary precision into a variety of interesting shapes. The numerous house-like structures are in fact family mausoleums, where each member of the family is entombed in an individual sarcophagus, around which many ornaments and religious icons have been scattered.

CHILE

Some of these graves possess especially weird shapes – such as one tomb shaped like a ship with the "upper-deck" on ground level leading down directly into the "hold", where family members are buried in the walls.

North of the cemetery, and 2.5 km from downtown, you'll find the **Patagonia Institute** on the left hand side of road, with its museum of work tools, handicrafts, textiles, wool products and pottery typical of the Patagonia area. The Institute also offers a shop in which lovely, charactistically Patagonian ornaments are sold (but at very high prices!). A small **zoo** housing animals native to the region is located in the Institute's courtyard. Of interest are the *guanaco* (wild llama), the terrifying puma, and the condor, impressive for its size and wingspan. In front of the Institute, on the lawn between it and the main highway linking Punta Arenas with the ferry terminal, there is an **exhibit** of railway locomotives and rolling stock, and old agricultural machinery, for which there was probably no other place anywhere in Chile.

Across from the Patagonia Insititute is a bustling modern **shopping center.** As one of the Government incentives to encourage settlement in Patagonia, a free-trade zone was established in Punta Arenas. Here you can buy a wide variety of luxury items – from exclusive clothing, to all sorts of photographic equipment, liquor and imported chocolate, to state-of-the art electronics. The *Zona Franca* was set up here, a short distance from the center of town, and it contains a long row of modern shopping centers, built with care and filled with dozens of shops. Even if you have no intention of buying a stereo system or a color TV, you'll certainly be interested in visiting this fascinating place, which is reached from town by taxi or numerous bus lines. If you want to stock up on film, lenses and other photographic equipment, or to treat youself to some Swiss chocolate, this is certainly the place. Prices are similar to those in New York, and the variety is adequate. The self-service restaurant on the premises is expensive and not very good.

Excursions in the area
Isla Magdalena and sea cruises

A two-and-a-half-hour cruise south from Punta Arenas in the Strait of Magellan brings you to Isla Magdalena, home to tens of thousands of penguins, seals and sea lions, and an abundance of birds and animals that depend on the region's icy waters for their sustenance. In the waters around the boat you'll easily spot

CHILE

dolphins and, at times, even small whales splashing innocently around the island. Sailing to Isla Magdalena is but one facet of a broad and generally expensive variety of cruises offered by agencies in Punta Arenas. Some organized excursions go as far as Antarctica, in an area where the marine scenery, rich in fjords, lagoons and massive icebergs, is among the world's most fascinating.

Tierra del Fuego

A ferry sails every day between Punta Arenas and Puerto Porvenir, the Chilean town in Tierra del Fuego (see also "Argentina"). The western, Chilean half, of the island is slim pickings for tourists and is liable to be disappointing and your main interest is in passing through to get to Argentina. The bus from Puerto Porvenir to Rio Grande, Argentina, runs several times a week, crossing the border at the San Sebastian checkpoint. Here you may encounter problems with the authorities and you must be patient and careful.

Puerto Natales

Puerto Natales (pop. 20,000) is 254 km north of Punta Arenas. This quiet town, situated on the shore of an enchanting lagoon amidst splendid pastoral scenery, is frequented by tourists mainly during the summer on their way to the natural attractions in the vicinity. The border crossing to Rio Turbio, Argentina (see Argentina – "Rio Turbio") is close by, a 30-minute bus ride away.

Small boats set out from Puerto Natales' little port for nearby bays, and a cruise on one of these is recommended. On less frequent occasions, and with no fixed schedule, a ship on its way north (to Puerto Montt) pulls into port and here it's easier than in Punta Arenas to persuade the captain to be so kind as to let you aboard.

In and around town you'll find many hotels and small pensions, but their prices are high. With a little initiative you can pitch a tent in a corner of town and spend the night there. At the *Secretaria de la Juventud* (Youth Secretariat), next to the plaza, you can sleep cheaply – in a sleeping bag on the floor. There's no shower, and you must get permission from the person in charge if you want to shower in the adjacent school. Those setting out for a trip in the vicinity would do well to leave all spare gear here, for unnecessary weight is liable to be an unbearable nuisance – in both senses of the word!

To and from Punta Arenas there is fast, comfortable bus service several times daily. A student card gives you a discount, though

CHILE

Paine - an enchanting view untouched by time

some persuasion may be required. Hitchhiking opportunities abound and this form of transportation should present no problems.

The main attraction that has put Puerto Natales on the tourism map is the *Torres del Paine* National Park, 130 kilometers northeast of the town.

Parque Nacional Torres del Paine

To the west of Argentina's Calafate Glacier Park a number of strange mountain ridges with sharp peaks look like gigantic towers touching the sky. These are the *Torres* (Towers) *del Paine*. Although they soar to "only" 2670 m, the sharp uplift is impressive because the region from which they rise is not much above sea level. As if this did not suffice, the mountains are blessed with a number of lakes, glaciers and unspoilt countryside to which an abundance of animal and bird life and

CHILE

a tempestuous climate are added, creating one of the most amazing places in the whole world.

The *Paine* has become a powerful attraction in recent years due to its beauty and fascinating hiking trails. To visit the park you must come well-equipped – with rain-proof tent, warm sleeping bag, cooking gear and, of course, food.

When you stock up on food, pack a 50% reserve to allow for unplanned delays. Bring along light items that will satisfy your hunger but are quick and easy to prepare. True, food is available in the park itself at a shop in the administrative center – at high prices – but since you'll probably be miles from there, except for the first and the last day, you won't want to rely on this, so come equipped. The weather is very pleasant during the summer but terribly cold during the rest of the year. In summer, the wind blows with unbelievable force and exhausts anyone who gets in its way. Temperatures plunge at night, and there's

CHILE

nothing unusual about sleeping in heavy clothing inside your heavy sleeping bag. For the daylight hours, be sure to bring along a jacket, gloves, a good woolen cap, a scarf and, of course, a rainproof poncho (which you'll need frequently).

Reaching the park is no simple matter. Since it is far from Puerto Natales, with only one village between it and the town (Costelo, about seventy kilometers away), transportation is meant mainly for tourists. During the summer, when most of the visitors come, a bus runs several times a week and goes as far as the Park Office. Hiring a taxi is expensive, but in the transitional seasons – before October and after February, when the park is almost devoid of visitors – it's almost the only way to get there and back. You must make arrangements with the driver about the return trip, otherwise you're liable to be stranded for days after your hike in the park. *Torres del Paine* is cut off in the winter and there's no way of reaching and exploring it. Trucks do set out for the park from the CONAF (Parks Authority) office in Puerto Natales at irregular intervals and, at times, especially during the off-season, they are be willing to pick up hitchhikers.

A hike around the park's periphery, encompassing the "towers," takes from six to ten days at six to eight hours' walking per day, and this is the most popular route. If you like, of course, you can stay in the park for weeks on end and hike the approximately two hundred kilometers of marked trails that penertrate every corner of the immense park.

You'll have to pay an admission fee and register at the entrance, and you'll be given a map on which the hiking trails have been marked. The perimeter hike itself may begin in a *refugio* (a hut set aside as a shelter for hikers) about fifteen kilometers from the entrance, or at the *Administracion*, several kilometers farther down the path along the southern shore of Lake *Pehoe*. At the *Administracion* compound you'll find a **visitor's center** with a relief map of the park and information concerning its history, geology, flora and fauna, etc. – all very interesting, arranged in good taste and worth a visit. The somewhat "dry" scenery of the route leading here changes suddenly, the moment you actually begin to hike amidst the wild foliage, past gorgeous lakes, around steep mountains, alongside glaciers and beside churning streams. Numerous wild animals – llamas, *guanacos*, foxes, hares and many more – will cross your path. With special luck, you may get a close-up view of a giant condor hovering in the air, or some pumas – which, though not dangerous (at least that's what the park rangers say) should be treated with great caution

The hiking trails will lead you between colorful lakes, each at a different elevation. These came into existence as a result of the

CHILE

melting glaciers from the last Ice Age, several million years ago. But if you stick your hand into the water, you'll discover that it does not appear to have had time to heat up much since then... The waters are cold, pure and good to drink, and each lake is of a different hue.

The greatest experience of all is your encounter with the massive mountains of ice, especially the Grey and Dickson Glaciers – an unforgetable sight. As you approach these giant glaciers, you hear a dull groaning sound emanating from beneath them, caused by the movement of water seeping underneath and melting them. The great weight of the ice gives the glaciers a sharp blue coloration and generates tremendous pressure which changes the crystalline structure of the glaciers, an astonishing and incredibly beautiful sight to behold. These glaciers are in a state of continuous melting and are only a "little" behind schedule, when compared with the many other glaciers that once covered the region. You're lucky to have arrived now. Had you put off your visit for a few million years, I don't think anything would have remained of them ...

There are a number of *refugias* (log cabins for visitors) along the route. In a *refugia* you should try to sleep on the upper bunk, and to hang your gear in the air – because of the mice. These too have discovered the pleasures of the *refugia*, and many of them make their homes there, so that you must keep all equipment and food out of their reach. *Refugias* have large wood-burning stoves. The custom is that the first to arrive goes out to gather wood. The wood you find in the *refugia* should not be used, since it's meant for visitors who may be delayed on the way and therefore arrive after nightfall. Given the length of the trail and the chances that the number of hikers will exceed the facilities offered by a *refugia*, be prepared to sleep under the stars. Also consider the possibility of rain, in any season. Charming wooden houses are located throughout the park. The experienced and polite park rangers (*Guarda Parque*) who live there will be delighted to offer reliable and up-to-date advice concerning hiking possibilities on the various trails, the condition of bridges, etc. Let them be of assistance to you.

A visit to *Parque del Paine*, one of South America's largest and most beautiful, has become a status symbol for young travelers who tour the continent and few are willing to forego it. What's more, they're right. This is perhaps the finest trip I can recall of all those I've taken the world over! Now that you're well-equipped, fit and raring to go, all that remains is to set out – on one of the most beautiful excursions anyone could ever hope to make.

COLOMBIA

Gorgeous scenery, towering mountains, pristine beaches, dense jungles, fascinating archeological sites, large cities, and little villages – all these and more await the tourist who has come to discover the hidden treasures of Colombia, South America's northernmost country. Just south of Central America, lying between the Pacific and the Atlantic, is one of the continent's most exceptional countries and perhaps the most dangerous.

Colombia is a mass of contradictions. At one time, it was one of the most important countries in South America and its capital the site of crucial decisions. Simon Bolivar established it in the center of "Greater Colombia", his lofty dream of South American unity, which proved hollow even before his death. Today's Colombia lies on the fringe of the political map in South America. Perhaps due to the acute poverty and deprivation that plague the country, Colombia has become notorious as a world center for the production and export of cocaine and marijuana. Tourists are not warmly welcomed here and in no other South American country are they as prone to theft as in Colombia. While enjoying Colombia's splendid mountain and river landscapes, visiting its cities and villages, landing or departing at the airport, or reclining in the taxi that brings you into town, behave as if on a battlefield – alert, cautious, and ready to fend off any kind of attack.

Bandit gangs terrorize the country, and seem to have an affinity for vulnerable tourists. The local authorities often collaborate with the bandits, and, when they do not, are either unable or unwilling to help luckless tourists. Before deciding to visit Colombia, take this state of affairs into account.

Just the same, throngs of visitors have reached, seen and enjoyed Colombia, and left unscathed. The country offers a wide variety of possibilities for touring, rest, and recreation – whether in the extraordinary capital of Bogota, on the Caribbean coast, in the Amazon jungles, or in the archeological village of San Agustin in the south. Colombia is the gateway to the continent for those who arrive from Central America, and serves as a convenient departure point for the Caribbean or the United States.

History

Colombia was claimed for Spain in 1500 by Rodrigo de Bastidas, an early explorer who reached the area in pursuit of legendary treasures of gold. The first half of the 16th century was a period

COLOMBIA

of exploration and conquest, which intensified in response to rumors that *El Dorado*, the legendary Inca city of gold, was sited on the plateau where Bogota rests today.

The conquistadors encountered Indians of the *Chibcha* tribe, whose fondness for gold and treasure encouraged speculation concerning *El Dorado*. The Chibchas had a rich and well developed culture, with a strong central monarchy. Their major pursuit was agriculture, which they usually practiced in settled communities. Unlike the Incas and the Aztecs, they were not noted for monumental architecture, and their sphere of influence was restricted to the mountainous regions of Colombia.

The Chibchas yielded to Spanish domination without a fight, rapidly assimilating and giving rise to the major ethnic element in modern Colombia – the ***mestizos***. The Indian character was gradually lost over the years, and today Spanish domination in language, religion, and way of life is more perceptible in Colombia than anywhere else in the Andes.

In Bogota, the Spanish established a magnificent education system, including institutions of higher learning (the first university was founded in 1573) and highly-developed cultural and community life. During the 17th and 18th centuries cultural and colonial influences peaked and Bogota was known as "the Athens of South America".

In Colombia, as in the other Latin American crown colonies, the ambitions of the Creoles, descendants of the Spanish settlers, began to grow. They were instrumental in the struggle for independence from Spain, and supported Bolivar's efforts to establish "Greater Colombia" as a sovereign state free of Spanish control. "Greater Colombia" declared its independence in 1810. At first, called "Nueva Granada", it embraced Ecuador, Venezuela, and Panama, as well as modern Colombia.

Spain was not about to give up these territories without a struggle, and its troops spent the next decade trying to maintain Spanish dominion over the rebellious colonies. It was only in 1819, after Bolivar's famous victory in the battle of Boyaca, that Spain's colonialist dream finally ended and that the independence of the region was assured. At the time, Spain was facing difficulties as a result of Napoleonic conquests in Europe.

Bolivar's vision of unity faded swiftly. Ecuador and Venezuela left the Federation in 1832, and two opposing blocs, liberal and conservative, began squabbling for power in Colombia, a struggle which persists to this day. This internal strife has come at the expense of national development and has severely damaged the country's economy and social order.

COLOMBIA

A two-year civil war broke out in Colombia in 1840, each side seeking total defeat of the other. Toward the turn of the century in 1899, a harsher and more grievous period of internal fighting erupted, which claimed more than 100,000 casualties in the ensuing four years.

One of the most bitter results of this war was Panama's withdrawal from the Federation. The Panamanians took advantage of the anarchy in Colombia, and, with the support of the United States, declared their independence. The act was of far-reaching consequence regarding subsequent U.S. relations with the states of South America. Colombia refused to recognize Panamanian independence and objected to the Panama Canal project. This brought about the protracted dispute between Colombia and the United States which was resolved only after World War I. The United States agreed to generously compensate Colombia in return for Colombian agreement to waive its canal-based claims. This paved the way for the affluent 1920's and the emergence of a Colombian *nouveau riche*, which benefitted from American compensation together with soaring prices in the world coffee market.

The world-wide economic crisis provoked by the crash of 1929 put an end to the boom. Colombia once again sank into domestic difficulties and power struggles, with the Liberals finally coming out on top. The country's social and political contradictions radicalized both camps. Extremist factions emerged on both sides. Jorge Gaitan set up a leftist bloc in the Liberal Party, while, on the right, positions were influenced by European Fascism.

In the 1946 elections, the Conservatives defeated a factionalized Liberal party against the backdrop of an unprecendented recession. Domestic unrest grew and violent demonstrations rocked the country. Gaitan's assassination in April, 1948 unleashed the full fury of the embittered villagers, who streamed into Bogota *en masse* and vented their rage on property and people, as the authorities stood by helplessly.

For 20 years Colombia was caught in a web of violence known as **La Violencia**, costing the country a quarter of a million casualties. The national economy was paralyzed, and polarization and hatred reached new extremes.

A military coup in 1953 brought General Pinilla Rojas to power, at the head of a repressive regime bent on quelling the violence. The imperatives of the times brought the Liberals and Conservatives together in an unprecedented accord: a united "national front" devoted to ending Rojas' tyranny. The general was forced to resign in 1958.

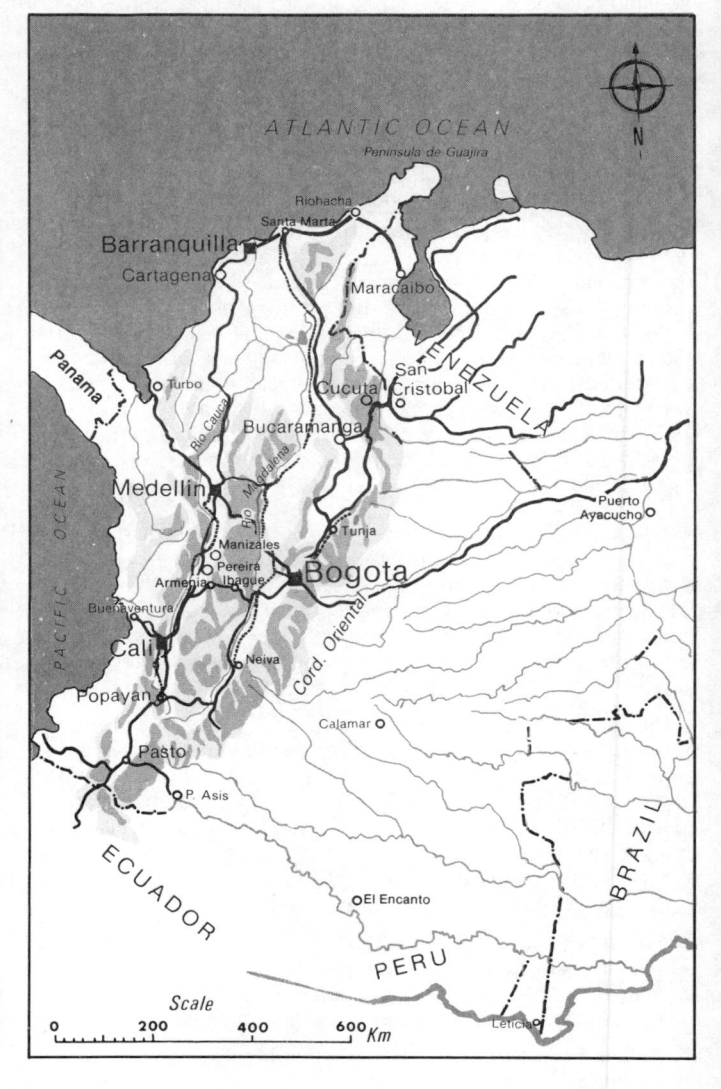

COLOMBIA

COLOMBIA

COLOMBIA

The United States government met Colombia's ongoing crisis with grants and long-term loans that helped stabilize the economy and restore tranquillity. In 1966 Lleras Restrepo was elected President and his tenure is considered one of the most successful. Rising coffee prices helped Restrepo stabilize the country's economy and political scene – but not for long.

Leftist guerrilla movements began operating in Colombia in the early 1970s, countered by a new right-wing party led by the former-dictator Rojas. Domestic ferment continues today, though the Government is making a tremendous effort to stabilize the country and restore order. By endeavoring to narrow economic and social inequities and by diverting resources to programs for the poor and disadvantaged, the Colombian government is attempting to reduce the frustration and rage that underlie crime and violence. In 1985, Colombia made world head lines due to two tragic events: the volcanic eruption of El Ruiz which buried an entire village, claiming 25,000 lives and the terrorist attack on the Supreme Court building in Bogota and the unsuccessful rescue attempt of the hostages.

Geography and climate

Colombia is the fourth-largest country in South America and covers 1,138,000 sq/km. The country has a varied topography and climate. Colombian landscapes range from beaches to plains and mountains and the climatic zones range from tropical in the jungles and along the coast, to temperate in the mountains and valleys. In addition, the differences in population and culture are especially prominent.

The Andes jut into Colombia, splitting into three ranges (*cordilleras*) – eastern, central and western. In between and almost parallel to them flow the Magdalena and Cauca Rivers, which originate in the south of the country and converge before emptying into the Caribbean Sea. The rivers serve as convenient transportation routes from the seacoast to the interior.

The central *cordillera* is the highest of the Colombian Andes, with peaks soaring to 5750 m. The central and western ranges are composed chiefly of granite, while the eastern range (*Cordillera Oriental*), which continues into Venezuela, consists of volcanic rock and limestone. Colombia is known for volcanic activity, and some of its many volcanoes remain active. The river valleys are filled with volcanic ash – the remains of eruptions in former geological epochs.

Lower mountain ranges run along the coast. The most important of these is the *Sierra Nevada de Santa Maria*. Its loftiest summit, at 5775 m, is the highest point in Colombia.

COLOMBIA

The mountain plateaus break down into several types: volcanic plateaus in the southwest at the foot of the central *cordillera*, and basins covered with ancient sediment in the central and northern highlands.

The jungles (*selva*) and **the plains** (*llanos*) run along Colombia's Caribbean coast, where the climate is hot and muggy. The eastern plains stretch across the upper watersheds of the Orinoco and the Amazon. These regions, which account for more than half the country's territory, are nearly uninhabited: fewer than two per cent of Colombia's people live there, in harsh climatic conditions and cultural isolation.

A humid equatorial climate dominates the lowlands, where temperatures remain the same throughout the year. Precipitation rates are among the world's highest, with about 3000 mm of rain per year along the Pacific coast and in the Amazon basin. The Venezuelan border area in northern and northeastern Colombia enjoys a relatively dry savannah climate, with an average of 600 mm annual rainfall.

The climate in the mountain areas changes gradually, in keeping with elevation, from tropical in the low-lying zones to chilly and temperate above 3000 m. The high humidity causes clouds to form on the *cordillera* slopes, which are usually shrouded in fog.

Colombia lies on the migration route of more than 1500 species of birds, who nest or pass through on their way to and from North and South America.

Population

About half of Colombia's 27 million people, and the dominant social and political group, are *mestizos* of mixed Spanish-Indian descent. About 25% of the population is *mulatto*, 20% is Caucasian of European ancestry, 4% Black and only 1% are Indian, descendants of the *Chibcha* tribe who refused to intermarry with the Spanish colonists.

About 80% of Colombia's population lives in the mountainous central region, the heart of economic and political activity. Another 15% dwell along the Caribbean coast. The Amazon and Orinoco plains, which account for 60% of Colombia's land area, are home to only 2% of its people.

The Spanish colonial tradition is most jealously preserved in Colombia. Spanish is the national language, though 180 different Indian dialects are spoken in various areas. Catholicism is the state faith, and the Church enjoys a special social status and broad influence in the country's education system.

Though Colombia boasts 35 functioning universities and compulsory, free elementary education, 25% of its citizens are illiterate.

COLOMBIA

Economy

The Colombian economy can draw on many natural resources some of which only began to attract attention in recent years. The 1960s marked the turning point in Colombia's economy. Until then, 90% of the country's income derived from the export of one crop, coffee. Industry has since been developed extensively, mineral deposits have been exploited and other economic activity has been increased. Although Colombia's superb coffee still accounts for half of its export income, the country also exports gold, emeralds, uranium, and various metals – in addition to consumer goods, chiefly textiles and paper.

Colombian oil, coal, and natural gas reserves are being exploited at an ever-accelerating pace. The country is nearly self-sufficient in oil and natural gas and many industries have relocated so as to use gas as an energy source. Colombian coal mines produce more than 60% of all the coal in South America, and vast amounts of equipment have been purchased in recent years to lay the infrastructure for further expansion of the mining industry.

About 30% of Colombia's labor force is agrarian, and the country is agriculturally self-sufficient. Apart from coffee, Colombia exports cocoa beans and bananas. According to unofficial estimates, however, all these together fail to equal even half of Colombia's income from the export of drugs.

Colombia needs a tremendous energy system to power its industrial development and technological progress, and huge sums have been invested in the project. A high priority for the government is the exploitation of the country's hydroelectric potential. Construction (industrial and residential) and road building have also enjoyed massive government aid, and local authorities take advantage of such projects to solve severe social problems and reduce unemployment.

Colombia's external debt did not begin to trouble the world banking system until 1984, when the country sought to exploit the financial situations of Brazil, Argentina, and other Latin American states by assembling a debtors' cartel which would negotiate interest and repayment terms with the creditors. Colombia's own foreign debt amounts to some $7 billion, a sum which the country's economy is well equipped to handle. The inflation rate is one of South America's lowest, and the government labors aggressively to keep it that way.

COLOMBIA

General Information

How to get there
By air: From Europe, Air France, British Caledonian, Lufthansa, and Iberia all fly from their respective capitals. Viasa and Avianca also reach Colombia from Europe. Avianca, Colombia's national airline, offers low-cost flights from Rome, Frankfurt, and Paris to Colombia, with connections to other destinations through its local agents. This may be the least expensive way to fly. Avianca, Eastern, Aero Peru, and Varig fly from the United States (the latter from the West Coast). The lowest airfares are available via Panama or the Miami-San Andres lines. San Andres is a Caribbean island that belongs to Colombia, and from it one can fly to the mainland at little cost.

Colombia has four international airports, – Bogota, Barranquilla, Cali, and Medellin. Each is served by several airlines. All South and Central American countries have air service to and from Bogota.

By land: Colombia is linked by highway with Venezuela and Ecuador. Cross into Ecuador at a point south of Pasto. Venezuela has two border crossings: the little town of Maicao on the Guajira Peninsula in the north, and the town of Cucuta in the mountain region. Maicao and Cucuta are unpleasant as border towns. From Brazil it is possible to take the river as far as Leticia and continue by air (see "Leticia"). Regular bus service links Bogota and the Andean countries.

Documents
A passport and tourist card are usually enough for Colombian immigration officers, though they sometimes ask for a departure ticket or proof that you can afford one. Under new immigration laws, visits to Colombia are restricted to 30 days and a visa is required to extend the stay. A transit visa, together with a passport and a ticket for the next leg of the trip, is good for 15 days. In addition, U.S. citizens must obtain a visa from the Colombian consulate prior to departure. Tourist cards are issued on the plane or at border checkpoints.

A $15 departure tax is levied when leaving Colombia by air, except for stopover visits less than 24 hours long. Tickets purchased in Colombia are subject to an 11% excise tax, as are tickets bought elsewhere for journeys originating in Colombia.

When to come: national holidays
The climate in Colombia is the same through most of the year, with variations according to elevation. The rainiest months are April-May and October-November; the dry season runs from December through February.

COLOMBIA

The coastal zones, the plains, and the eastern jungles are hot and muggy the year round, while nights in the mountains may be rather chilly. The weather changes rapidly in southern Colombia: days that start out like spring and end up wintry are not uncommon.

Much of Colombia goes on vacation from early December through mid-January, and many businesses are closed. Peak seasons along the Caribbean coast are December-April and June-August.

Colombia's national holidays are January 1, May 1, July 20 (Independence Day), August 7 (Battle of Boyaca Day), October 12 (Columbus Day), November 1 (All Saints' Day), and December 25.

Accommodation

A National Tourism Company ranks Colombian hotels on a star system according to quality, sets each hotel's maximum rates, and handles complaints of overcharging. A 5% tax – but no service charge – is added to hotel bills. As for tipping, 10% is certainly sufficient.

The big-city hotels and seaside resorts are up-to-date and modern. Hotels in small cities, towns, and villages are much humbler, though most are clean and tidy. **Pensiones**, modest guest houses where prices generally include meals, can be found in the villages and on the outskirts of most cities. Colombia's few **campgrounds** are located in parks. Most come without service facilities, showers, and the like, and one dare not leave anything unattended there.

Note: Some inexpensive hotels, especially in outlying areas, have an electric device over the water tap with which one heats water for a shower. **Be very careful** in operating it; one false move can lead to disaster.

Food and drink

Hotel restaurants in Colombia's major cities serve high quality international fare. Restaurants in every city specialize in local foods. Menus vary from one region to the next, reflecting the country's wide variety of cuisine. Popular-class restaurants are not noted for their hygiene. Prices are rather low; even in better restaurants one can eat for no more than the cost of a moderate meal in Europe or the United States.

The national drink of course, is coffee, black strong and invigorating, served with lots of sugar in a little cup. When ordering it, ask for *tinto*, because *cafe* means instant coffee. Colombia, like several of its Caribbean neighbors, produces several types of rum, (the most popular is *Aguardiente*), which

COLOMBIA

are served both straight and mixed. *Canelazo*, a popular cocktail, consists of rum with lemon, sugar, water, and cinnamon. The local wines are rather poor, so treat yourself instead to Chilean or Argentinian wines, which certainly lend support to the dictum: "Who loves not wine, women, and song, remains a fool his whole life long." Carbonated soft drinks are called *gaseosa*. Stick to bottled water, especially outside the large cities. In jungle zones, water must be purified with chlorine tablets.

As for the national cuisine, all the varieties are delicious. Soups, *empanadas*, *arepas* (cornflour rolls), and fruit can be purchased for next to nothing on every streetcorner. Restaurant menus are based on beef, chicken, and seafood. Common dishes include chicken with rice (the popular *arroz con pollo*, tasty enough for any connoisseur); *ajiaco*, a chicken-and-potato ragout; and *sancocho de gallina*, a thick vegetable chicken soup. Seafood in great variety is most easily available along the coast and in Bogota. Recommended are *arroz con chipichipi* – rice with crabs – and *criolla*, smoked fish with salad. Popular beef dishes are *bistec a caballo*, steak topped with a fried egg, with a side dish of bananas; *muchacho relleno*, beef with rice and vegetables; *puchero santaferneo*, a delectable stew with several kinds of meat and vegetables; and *chicharrones con frijoles*, deep-fried pork served with red beans. Most restaurants served fixed-price menu, called *comida* which includes soup and a main dish, inexpensive and satisfying.

Currency

The currency of Columbia is the peso, divided into a hundred centavos. Its symbol is "$". Coins go up to 5 pesos, while the largest banknote is 1000 pesos.

Cashing traveler's checks is complicated and requires documented proof of identity. Many moneychangers and banks do not cash traveler's checks, but the national bank, *Banco de la Republica*, does honor them. It is hard to convert currencies other than the U.S. dollar. Hotels cash traveler's checks only for their guests and even then at a low rate. When traveling outside the large cities, take enough local currency to meet requirements, since it is difficult to cash checks in outlying towns, and the rates offered in those locales, especially in the jungle and coastal areas, are lower. An official receipt affirming that you have converted foreign currency in Colombia entitles one to buy dollars back before leaving the country, though only after completing an exhausting bureaucratic runaround. Credit cards, especially Diners Club and Visa, are very common.

COLOMBIA

Business hours
Stores open before 9am, close for *siesta* 12:30-2:30pm, and reopen until 6:30pm (7pm in city centers). Companies and offices are open for business 8am-noon and 2:30-5pm. Banks in Bogota are open Mon.-Thurs. 9am-3pm, Fri. till 3:30pm, and half day on Sat. (though not all). Banks in other cities open at 8am but close for *siesta*. Government offices in Bogota are open 8am-3pm.

Domestic transportation
Air service: The fastest and most convenient way to cover Colombia's tremendous distances is, of course, by air. Avianca, SAM, and more than a dozen other airlines provide regular service on a scale rarely equalled in South America, to almost all Colombia's cities and towns.

Though Avianca charges more than the other airlines, it provides the most reliable, convenient and frequent service to any destination. Avianca offers a 25% discount on many of its routes and takes stand-by passengers on flights between major cities. It also offers a "Get-to-know-Colombia" (*Conozca a Colombia*) ticket for $224, good for unlimited air travel anywhere in the country except to Leticia and San Andres Island for thirty days. A ticket which includes both these places costs $325. The ticket must be purchased outside of Colombia, and no place can be visited twice.

Satena, the army airline, provides inexpensive air service to Leticia. SAM and other small companies have low cost flights to San Andres.

Bear in mind that every flight in Colombia is subject to an airport tax of about $5.

Buses: The quality of bus service in Colombia varies from place to place. In and between the large cities, the vehicles are modern and comfortable. Off the main routes, however, the service deteriorates severely. Most roads are not paved, and the buses are old and prone to breakdowns. Stops are far apart, and terminal employees and just about everyone else have access to the unlocked luggage compartment. The best thing by far is to take one's gear on the bus. Even if most drivers object, insist on it. Be firm!

For long-distance trips, bus travel usually costs nearly as much as airfare. Both possibilities are worth investigation. Buses are frequently stopped for police inspection; passengers must open their bags and, at times, submit to body searches.

Train: Though the large cities are linked by rail, passenger trains run only between Bogota and Santa Marta. Most of the trains are antiquated and slow, though some relatively modern

COLOMBIA

carriages have been introduced in recent years. Buy tickets in advance, and keep an eagle eye and a tight grip on your gear.

Car: Driving is no more complicated in Colombia than elsewhere in South America, though road service is hard to obtain, and highway conditions invite breakdowns. Try to stay off the road at night, and always carry essential spare parts.

The international car rental companies have branches throughout Colombia and provide well maintained, late model vehicles. An ordinary or international driver's license suffices for the local police, as long as a Spanish translation is attached.

Taxi: Most taxis in Colombia are equipped with meters; be sure they are turned on. If there is no meter, always negotiate the fare in advance! When you get out of a cab at your destination, or if the taxi breaks down, always have your bags in hand. Cab drivers have been known to ask passengers to help fix something, push the car, or get out at the journey's end ... while they take off with the luggage.

Hitchhiking: Thumbing it is no problem along major highways, which are used mostly by trucks. Hitchhike from police inspection points, and refrain from getting into cars occupied by several men. Make sure your would-be benefactor is not driving an unmarked taxi; if he is, he may charge for the trip at the end. Do not hitchhike at night. Young women must not travel alone.

Photography:
In comparison to other South American countries, Colombia is relatively advanced in the sphere of photography. In most parts of the country there is no difficult in finding film at reasonable prices. It is more difficult to get film for slides. In Bogota there are many places which develop films very adequately.

Measurements, electricity, and time
The metric system is used. Electricity is usually 110V though in some places it is 220V, therefore it is advisable to enquire before using electrical instruments. Colombian time is 5 hours behind GMT.

Personal security
Colombia has acquired a reputation in recent years for harassing and harrying tourists. Thousands of innocent visitors have paid for their trips the hard way – getting robbed on the one hand, and undergoing humiliating police inspections on the other. It is hard to describe every hardship a visitor may encounter here. It suffices to mention several episodes where passengers on Colombian buses treated tourists to food laced with sleeping drugs and robbed them the moment they dozed off. Other visitors have been mugged under threat of machetes (long

COLOMBIA

jungle knives) while enjoying a quiet stroll in the San Agustin archeological park. It is important to stress the severity of the problem.

Unlike Peru, where banditry is a sophisticated but non-violent sport, Colombian thugs have no qualms about how they obtain their loot. Be vigilant at all times! Trust no one; deal correctly but suspiciously with even the most respectable looking people. Sad as that attitude is, the alternative could be much worse. Never agree to carry parcels for strangers, and never let people on the bus place their baggage near your seat! When the police get on board for an inspection, your neighbors might claim it is yours.

Look out for your gear everywhere and at all times. Be sure to keep bags, packs, and suitcases locked, and **never** leave them unattended. Get off at every bus stop, and make sure that no fellow passengers or bus company employees have taken your belongings "by mistake".

Never wear jewelry, cameras, watches, and the like. They serve only to attract thieves. Keep your money and documents in inner pockets.

The local police, too, are a nuisance. Routine highway inspections are known to develop into destructive forays through tourists' luggage. Airport customs inspections and drug searches in hotel rooms are much the same story. All too often, police plant drugs in a tourist's personal belongings and then threaten the frightened foreigner with arrest unless he hands over hundreds of dollars in bribes.

When being searched, never let the policemen touch your belongings; instead, remove and display the contents yourself. It is important to behave politely and patiently, never picking a fight. If complications develop, notify your country's embassy **immediately** and ask for help.

In case of theft, the police are likely to make trouble when you apply for a form to show the insurance company in order to prove your loss. Victimized tourists often have to bribe the police to be so kind as to fill out the forms properly.

A suggested itinerary for your visit to Colombia

Visitors to Colombia coming to or from South America will most likely follow a south-to-north route (or the reverse), with detours east and west. One can then visit southern Colombia – San Agustin, Cali and the surrounding area (perhaps even the jungles), Bogota and north to the Carribean coast (Cartagena). From there one can continue on to Panama, Venezuela or to the Islands of San Andres.

COLOMBIA

This long route is recommended as it covers most of Colombia and offers a wide range of special sites – from the captivating south, to the industrial heartland, to the pleasant Caribbean coast.

Those arriving in Bogota and making excursions from there to other parts of Colombia, would be best advised to take a circular route – to the south (San Agustin), to the jungles (Leticia) and to the north (Carribean coast).

Trips to the area of *Cordillera Oriental* (towards Venezuela) and the Pacific coast are not essential.

Bogota

An interesting story of conquest preceded the establishment of Bogota in 1538. Upon hearing of legendary treasures of gold owned by the *Chibcha* or *Muchica* tribes that populated the lovely plain where the Colombian capital now stands, no few Spanish adventurers got the urge to set out in search of the mysterious place. *El Dorado*, "the Golden City", was every Spaniard's dream from the day America was discovered, and a quite a few fortune hunters penetrated the unexplored recesses of the continent in search of it. Together with various localities in Peru, Venezuela, and elsewhere, the Bogota plateau was considered one possible location of the hidden treasure. Gonzalo Jimenez de Quesada reached the area from Santa Marta on the Atlantic coast in 1538, beating his competitors by only a few days after a grueling and bloody march. He came from Santa Marta along the shores of the Atlantic ocean and he founded Santa Fe de Bogota, on the lovely mountain ringed plain, 2640 m above sea level.

Bogota developed and expanded quickly. The Spaniards looted every speck of gold they found among the *Muchica* Indians, and herded the natives into a restricted areas. Some Indians opposed the Spaniards; they were ultimately annihilated or driven east into the jungle. Most, however, submitted to the new regime and assimilated into the Spanish community, laying the foundations of the *mestizo* society that still exists.

Today Bogota and its suburbs are home to a population of more than five million, engaging in business and industry. Northern Bogota boasts exclusive residential neighborhoods and elegant office buildings along wide boulevards. In the south, by contrast, are *barrios* where hundreds of thousands live in shameful poverty, a miserable mix of want and deprivation, rage, frustration, and daily insecurity. Western Bogota is the industrial zone. In the city center, near Plaza Bolivar, Colonial and modern

COLOMBIA

architecture converge in a rare harmony, as 17th century edifices coexist side by side with modern high-rises.

Bogota is an interesting, effervescent, rather tempestuous city. It is a topsy-turvy metropolis, where a facade of serene grandeur overlays social unrest and unspeakable poverty – a breeding ground for crime and violence. Its temperate climate (average temperature 14 degrees Centigrade or 57 degrees Fahrenheit) and special geographic location lends it a pleasant, charming ambience, and a grandeur and grace which few cities enjoy.

How to get there

By air: Bogota's El Dorado Airport, about 10 km from the center of Bogota, provides tourist police service, car rental companies, services for hotel reservations, elegant duty-free shops, and currency exchange (the rates are better in town).

Taxis ply the route from the airport to town. A fixed sum is added to the meter reading, depending on the time of day and day of the week. Verify this information before getting into the cab. Buses and *colectivos* (shared taxis) are much cheaper and are recommended. When they set out for the airport (from Calle 19), they are marked *Aeropuerto*.

By land: Buses from everywhere in Colombia and from Ecuador, Peru, and Venezuela arrive at the big and modern bus terminal situated between the airport and the city center, on Av. Boyaca. Buses set out for Medellin, Cartagena, Cali, Popayan, and San Agustin many times each day. The train station is at Carrera 18, and Calle 16. Passenger trains arrive from Santa Marta only.

Where to stay

Bogota boasts not only some of South America's most modern and luxurious hotels but hundreds of less expensive ones, including some which literally charge pennies. Most hotels are clean and tidy. The Ministry of Tourism ranks them and fixes their maximum rates (to which one adds a 5% tax). Don't leave valuables in your room; lock the door when you are inside. Here, more than in many other countries, it is important to leave money and jewelry in the hotel safe.

The top of the range is the 41-story *Hilton Bogota* on Carrera 7 (Tel. 285-6020) – hundreds of rooms, swimming pool, posh lobby, restaurants, and convention rooms. Very expensive. The *Tequendama* (Calle 26 corner Carrera 10, Tel. 282-9066), *Bacata* (Calle 19, Tel. 283-8300), *Dann* (Calle 19, Tel. 284-0100) and *Continental* (Avenida Jimenez, Tel. 282-1100) are several further examples of Bogota's best and most expensive hotels. All are located in the city center, near the business, shopping and entertainment districts.

COLOMBIA

The *San Diego* (centrally located: Carrera 13, Tel. 284-2100) and the *Cordillera* (Carrera 8, Tel. 234-0506) are less costly. Truly inexpensive lodgings abound in the area of Calles 14-17 between Carreras 14-17, near the bus and train terminals. Two recommended cheap hotels are *Aragon* (Carrera 3, No. 13-14) in the heart of the tranquil colonial area and *Italia* (Carrera 7, corner calle 20).

What to eat, when and where

Bogota's business district and northern areas have hundreds of eating establishments, where Colombians fill themselves to satiation. Bogota offers a tremendous selection of restaurants for every taste and pocket. Every streetcorner has a creole restaurant (indigenous food), or something of French, Italian, Chinese, and more. Recent years have witnessed a proliferation of pizzerias, ice-cream shops (*heladerias*), and little pubs with inexpensive meals in an informal atmosphere. These places where young people and students congregate, are near the University area.

With the wealth of possibilities, only the best known restaurants can be mentioned here, together with some which deserve special mention for their special decor, location and the like. This is not meant as a slur to the others; visitors are sure to quickly find the restaurants most amenable to their tastes.

Elegant hotel restaurants present a combined menu of indigenous and continental dishes. The *Hilton* and the *Tequendama* have opulent rooftop restaurants with splendid views of the city. Another restaurant at the Tequendama serves a relatively inexpensive, top quality buffet lunch. Excellent Swiss restaurants are on hand as well: *Refugio Alpin* next to Hotel Monaco, and *El Chalet Suizo* at 21-51 Carrera 7.

One of Bogota's best and oldest French restaurants is *Le Grand Vatel* at Calle 24, corner Carrera 7. *Ramses*, a superb Oriental restaurant, is situated at the corner of Calle 19 and Carrera 7.

The prime attraction, of course, is typical Colombian food and the restaurants that specialize in it. Few visitors, after all, cross oceans and continents in order to eat American style pizza or steak. Try the national delicacies mentioned in the introduction at *Casa Vieja*, 3-73 Jimenez Av. This is one of Bogota's classic restaurants and, though it is a bit old, it treats its customers to delicious food at reasonable prices, with folk music in the background. Other possibilities are *Casa Vieja de San Diego* (across from Hotel Tequendama), and *Zaguan de los Aguas* at 5-61 Calle 19.

A more expensive and festive place to eat is *Los Sauces*, which

COLOMBIA

offers a full evening of Colombian folklore and delicacies: excellent service, superb cuisine, and a folk music performance – certainly one of Bogota's most pleasurable Creole restaurants; it is worth visiting for lunch or dinner.

Transportation

In Bogota, taxis are recommended. Bus service is fast and frequent, but one is at the mercy of thieves. If you choose public transportation anyway, the best choice is a *buseta*, a minibus which charges twice the regular bus fare and does not take on standing passengers, or a *colectivo*, a fixed-route taxi for six to eight passengers.

The green and beige taxis at special stands beside the major hotels are meant exclusively for tourists. They charge more than regular taxis, but the drivers speak basic English and are relatively reliable. Taxi fares are determined by meter; drivers are allowed to add a surcharge for night, holiday, and Sunday trips. Should you find a taxi without a meter, be sure to negotiate the price before you set out.

For vehicle rental, try Hertz at Hotel Tequendama (Tel. 284-2696) or Avis on Carrera 10 (Tel. 241-9742). Renting a car for in-town driving is not recommended. Never leave valuables in the car, and park only in supervised parking losts.

Tourist services

The Government Tourist Bureau is at 13a-15 Calle 28, ground floor. There is a Municipal Toruist Bureau opposite San Diego Church. The National Parks Authority has offices at 138-47 Calle 26, 3rd floor. The Auto Club, at 46-72 Carrera 14, has road maps. For hiking maps, go to the Instituto Geografico. *DAS*, the immigration service, is at 18-42 Carrera 28.

Foreign airlines have modern offices downtown; most are computerized. For local companies, try Avianca at Carrera 7 16-36 (Tel. 266-9700); SAM, Carrera 52 52-11; and Stena, Carrera 7.

Guia de Bogota, a tourist publication that covers events and places to visit in town, is distributed free at the hotels. More detailed maps and a weekly, up to date brochure are available at almost any newsstand.

Tourist sites

For the tourist, most places of interest in Bogota are near the city center or in the colonial district to its south. To the east, the city is flanked by a green mountain range. The south is a slum district, as is the eastern district, which also has industrial zones. Since these areas are not only uninteresting but also dangerous, we concentrate rather on the more pleasant sides

COLOMBIA

BOGOTA

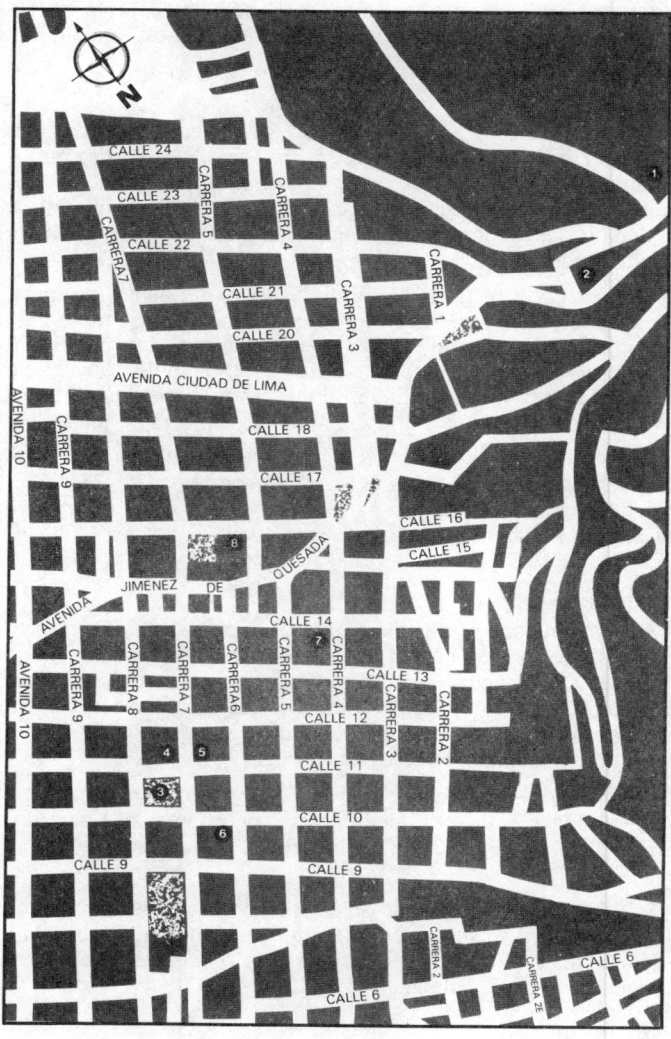

Index
1) Cable car station to Monserrate
2) La Quinta de Bolivar
3) Plaza Bolivar
4) Palacio de la Justicia
5) July 20th Museum
6) Church of San Ignacio
7) Archaelogoical Museum
8) Museo del Cro

COLOMBIA

of Bogota, a city that becomes more modern as one heads north.

First, a brief outline of the street numbering system. Here, as in all other cities of Colombia, streets have numbers only, not names. East-west arteries are called *calles* (streets), while north-south thoroughfares are *carreras* (avenues). The roads are numbered in ascending order from south to north, and from east to west. Buildings have two numbers, the first being the number of the nearest street, and the second indicating the number of the building on that street. Thus, for example, 24-45 Calle 13 is the equivalent of 13th St., No. 45, between Carreras 24 and 25.

The tour starts with a visit to the observation point atop the **Monserrate**, the mountain bordering the eastern part of town. Use the cablecar, which runs daily, 9am-6pm. Try to avoid Sundays if possible, since you will have to wait in line for the cablecar for a long time. Do not attempt the ascent or descent on foot as the place swarms with tourists – and, therefore, with muggers who do not hesitate to waylay pedestrians at knife or gun point. The foot of the mountain, near the cablecar station, is also dangerous. The summit itself is safe, due to a heavy police presence. On top are a small church, souvenir shops, a cafe and a restaurant. At 3153 m above sea level, the mountain peak provides a breathtaking bird's eye panorama of the entire city. The transition from old to new, highlighted by the modern skyscrapers downtown, is easily discerned from this vantage point.

Down at the bottom, near the cablecar station, is **La Quinta de Bolivar** (Bolivar's House), built in 1793 by a Spanish merchant who presented it to the liberator, Simon Bolivar, in 1820. Bolivar lived here until leaving Bogota shortly before his death. The estate has been preserved in its original condition, including the furniture and *objets d'art*. The gardens, too, have been well maintained, with a wealth of flowers and trees. Some of Bolivar's personal possessions and arms, as well as numerous documents preserved from that era, are kept in the back of the house. Open Tues.-Sun. 10am-5pm.

The next stop is the colonial district, with **Plaza Bolivar** in its center. (Since traffic is always heavy here, it is best to arrive by public transportation or on foot.) A statue of Simon Bolivar stands in the middle of the square, which is surrounded by public buildings. To the south is the **Capitol**, or the National Treasury; facing it is **Palacio de la Justicia**, Colombia's renowned Supreme Court of Justice. It was here in October 1985, that a band of guerrillas seized a large group of hostages, including the President of the Supreme Court. The government, true to its iron fist policy in dealings with guerrillas, refused to negotiate. Instead, they sent in the armed forces with tanks and mortars. The guerrillas and their hostages (about 150 people all told) were massacred.

To the west of the square is **City Hall.** The house in the northeast corner is the spot where Colombia's independence was declared on July 20, 1810. Today the edifice houses the **Museo 20 de Julio** (July 20 Museum) with a collection of documents and paintings relating to that historic event. On the southeast corner is the **Church of San Ignacio**, the most impressive of Bogota's colonial churches. Its sophisticated, progressive architecture contrasts with the simple design of the other churches. The interior houses a rich collection of paintings and sculptures by Bogota's principal 17th century artists.

Plaza Bolivar is in the **Candelaria** Quarter, formerly known as **Barrio de los Principes** (the Princes' District) because the Spanish nobility made its home here. A stroll through its narrow streets between the colonial houses, provides a picture of how Santa Fe de Bogota developed socially, culturally, and architecturally under the Spanish between 1550 and 1810. The **Archeological Museum** off Plaza Bolivar (7-43 Carrera 6), open Tues.-Sat. 10am-5pm, was once the home of the renowned Marquis San Jorge. The building gives one a glimpse of the life style of its former occupants. It is a beautiful example of colonial architecture with its large windows, balconies and spacious patios. Today it exhibits a fine collection of ceramics found in the ruins of various pre-Columbian civilizations.

Another recommended stop in this vicinity is the **Arts and Crafts Museum**, on the corner of Carrera 8 and Calle 9, with its splendid collection of handicrafts from all parts of the country. The whole quarter is highly congested with traffic, so it is preferable to use public transport or to walk.

Slightly north of Candelaria, at 5-41 Calle 16, is Colombia's most important museum, the best known institution of its type in the country, an establishment renowned throughout the Americas, and a "must" for any visitor – the **Museo del Oro** (Museum of Gold).

The museum contains one of the world's largest collections of gold objects – approximately 25,000 items! Most of these are relics of pre-Columbian civilizations, which attributed divine properties to gold. The artifacts on display, salvaged by the *conquistadores*, represent but a tiny fraction of the original treasure. The museum was founded by the Central Bank in 1939 in order to avert the mislaying of such treasures as could still be found. Most were purchased from antiquity looters, and only a small percentage from archeologists.

COLOMBIA

Miniature raft from the remains of the Mochica culture in the Gold Museum

The gold itself, as well as most of the processing techniques, reached the pre-Columbians from Central America. Since pure gold is difficult to shape, most artists worked in a gold and copper alloy with a gold content of no more than 80%.

Of the museum's three floors, the first houses temporary exhibitions of gold items, the second exhibits a representative sample of pre-Columbian gold relics in various styles, and the third is devoted exclusively to safes, arrayed up and down long corridors, in which most of the museum's collection is kept. Here, too, the items are classified by different cultures. Note the great delicacy of the workmanship. Some of the exhibits are placed behind a magnifying lens, to enable the viewer to appreciate the finer details. Open Tues.-Sat. 9am-4pm, Sun. 9am-noon.

Bogota's business hub is between Calles 19 and 34 and Carreras 7 and 13. This area has the best selection of top hotels and stores, and the largest number of travel agencies and embassies in town.

On the corner of Calle 28 and Carrera 7, in a building that once served as the city jail, is one of Colombia's most important museums: **Museo Nacional** (The National Museum). It houses a wide variety of exhibits of Columbian and pre-Columbian ethnography and history. Open Tues.-Sat. 9:30am-6pm.

Aficionados of the avant-garde will certainly want to visit the

COLOMBIA

permanent and seasonal exhibitions of contemporary art at the **Museum of Modern Art**, 6-05 Calle 26.

Northern Bogota
Northern Bogota, though hardly "touristy", is worth visiting if only to sense the vast disparities among the various sections of town. This is an area of modern neighborhoods, luxury homes, and shaded avenues. Bogota's wealthy citizens, diplomats, and foreign dignitaries live here. However, in spite of – or rather because of – the high standard of living, the residents of northern Bogota live in constant fear of robbers and burglars. One who has visited the slums of Bogota should not find it hard to understand why.

Zipaquira
This town (pop. app. 40,000), a short ride from Bogota, is the capital of cattle country. Of special interest to us, however, is the magnificent **Salt Cathedral**. The region has vast salt deposits, which were discovered and first exploited by early Indians. Over time, a large salt mine was built into a rocky hill in the area, and the church was hewn out of the center of this hill.

One approaches the church by walking 120 m through the mine tunnel. Its nave can accommodate up to 8000 worshippers, and the central altar is made of a block of salt weighing 18 tons!

Bus service to Zipaquira (from Avenida Caracas) is very frequent. The trip takes over an hour. Travel agents also organize guided tours.

Entertainment and Culture
Bogota is not famous for its exciting night life; the locals seem to prefer staying home rather than braving the city's outlaws. Movie fans will find plenty of good, modern cinemas. The local cinematheque, for one, is at 22-79 Carrera 17.

The major nightclub and discotheque district is the north side of the town. The most popular nightclub, however, is actually in the city center at *Hotel Tequendama*.

While local concert halls offer symphony and chamber music, there is no municipal orchestra as such. *Teatro Arte de la Musica*, 10-65 Calle 62, invites the best Colombian and foreign orchestras, as well as staging ballet and opera.

Shopping
Bogota's several shopping centers are best for leather goods, gold items, and handicrafts. Colombia has been blessed with large deposits of emeralds, which are therefore relatively inexpensive. Beware of street peddlars who may approach you furtively and offer you stones for sale; most are fake.

COLOMBIA

Many shops with large stocks of high quality merchandise are situated on Avenida 15. The area between Calles 50 and 65, known as **Chapinero**, abounds in cut rate leather and textile stores. The lobbies of the Hilton and Tequendama have shops with souvenirs, gold items, and superb leather goods – prices are sky-high!

Stores belonging to the **Artesanias de Colombia** chain, situated around town, sell handicrafts (*artesania*). The main outlet is at 26-50 Carrera 10. On the corner of Calle 127 and Carrera 15 is **Unicentro**, a modern shopping center and one of South America's largest. Apart from stores, Unicentro has movie theaters, restaurants, and nightclubs.

Banks and currency exchanges

Colombia's national bank, *Banco de la Republica*, has branches around town, where one can exchange dollars (cash or travelers' checks) for local currency without any problem. Here, one can also perform all standard business banking transactions – international currency transfers, obtaining letters of credit, etc.

Postal and telephone service

Try to send letters and parcels by air mail only. Parcel postage is not costly at all. Poste restante service is available at the post office in Edificio Avianca, 16-36 Carrera 7, open Tues.-Sat. 7am.-10pm. Sun. and holidays 8am-1pm.

The local phone company, *Telecom*, has its central office at 13-49 Carrera 23 and a branch office in the commercial center of Hotel Tequendama. International collect calls cannot be made from the Telecom offices, though private phones permit this.

Climate

At 2600 m above sea level, Bogota can be a little chilly, with an average temperature of 14 degrees Centigrade or 57 degrees Fahrenheit. Because of its proximity to the equator, there is little seasonal variation in the weather, and the plentiful rainfall is distributed throughout the year.

Beware: thieves

Pickpocketing and mugging are rife in Bogota. Keep constant watch on your possessions. Never put a purse or wallet in a back pocket, and never wear jewelry. Steer clear of any group, since it is liable to be a set up. Aggravated armed robbery is a routine occurrence, and the bandits are not reluctant to use their weapons.

Tourists are best advised to confine their movements to city center and northern Bogota. Be careful around the foot of the Monserrate. To ascend or descend the mountain on foot is to

COLOMBIA

tempt fate! The area around the lower terminus of the cablecar, too, teems with muggers.

The Bogota police are worse than ineffective: they often work hand in hand with the bandits by turning a blind eye to their forays. Just the same, report any case of robbery or theft to the tourist police, at 27-50 Carrera 7. Tel. 283-4930 or 284-5047.

Important addresses
Corporacion Nacional de Turismo (The National Tourism Corporation): 15-134 Calle 28, 16th floor. Tel. 283-9466.

DAS offices: 18-42 Carrera 28. Tel. 277-9211.

Avianca: 16-36 Carrera 7. Tel. 282-0100, and 266-9700.

Automovil Club de Colombia (Auto Club): 46-64 Carrera 14.

American Embassy: 8-40 Calle 37. Tel. 285-1300.

British Embassy: 13-37 Calle 38. Tel. 287-8100.

Immigration Office: at *DAS* Division de Extranjeria, 17-85 Carrera 27.

Tourist police: 27-50 Carrera 7. Tel. 283-4930 or 284-5047.

From Bogota to Cucuta

The road to Cucuta forks at Tunja into two alternate routes, both of which pass through spectacular mountain scenery: a smooth paved road via Bucaramanga, and an especially scenic, but largely unpaved and difficult route through Paitama and Malaga. The latter road passes through little towns and villages, where one can enjoy a convivial and relaxing visit and spend the night. The two routes converge at Pamplona, forming a single paved road that leads directly to Cucuta.

Transportation
A number of direct buses travel the Bogota-Cucuta route daily, along with several flights per week. The buses are comfortable, and the journey takes about 24 hours. Regular bus service links the towns en route. A direct road connects Bucaramanga with Santa Marta on the Caribbean coast.

Tunja

Tunja, the capital of Boyaca province and one of Colombia's oldest towns (founded in 1539 by Gonzalo Suarez Rendon), is about a two hour ride from Bogota. Its old quarter still preserves its grand Spanish colonial character, but the new areas are rather undistinguished. At 2800 m above sea level, Tunja is fairly cold.

COLOMBIA

The most important surviving colonial buildings are the **Church of Santo Domingo** (const. 1594), **Santa Clara Monastery**, today a hospital, and **La Casa del Fundador** (Founder's House). The latter, built in 1540, was the residence of the town's founder and houses some of the most interesting relics left by the Spanish conquerors.

Food and lodging

The old part of town has a small selection of hotels and restaurants which, though of average quality at best, project a relaxed and friendly ambience. *Hotel San Francisco*, on the central plaza, is moderately priced and definitely recommended. The hotel restaurant offers good, fairly inexpensive meals. *Residencias Fundadas*, at the corner of Plaza Bolivar, is an inexpensive, good and safe place to stay. For satisfying, reasonably priced meals, try *La Fonda* or *El Cumbre*. A slightly more expensive alternative is *Bodejon de los Frailes*.

The Boyaca Bridge

About 16 km south of Tunja is the site of the famous Battle of Boyaca, the decisive campaign in Colombia's War of Independence. Tunja fell to Bolivar on August 6, 1819. The following morning, he led his troops with reinforcements to the marshy banks of Rio Boyaca, where they challenged British battalions which had come to the aid of the Spanish army. Through audacity and good strategy, Bolivar's army overcame the Spanish forces despite their superior numbers, inflicted numerous casualties, and got away almost unscathed. The handful of Spanish who managed to escape reported to the Spanish governor in Bogota, who fled the town and left his royal treasures behind. This, in effect, marked the end of Spanish rule and paved the way for Colombia's independence.

The Boyaca Bridge on the Bogota-Tunja highway is graced with a large statue of Bolivar, a monument to that glorious triumph. Its anniversary, August 7, is a national holiday.

Villa de Leyva

This small town, founded in 1572, is so well preserved architecturally that progress seems not to have been allowed in.

This town was home to some of Colombia's most famous patriots, such as Antonio Narino, who translated Thomas Jefferson's *The Rights of Man* into Spanish in 1794. Narino's house is a museum today. Open Tues.-Sat. 8am-noon and 2pm-6pm.

Stroll through the town's pleasant plazas and peaceful streets, and visit the house where the first joint committee of the States of "Greater Colombia" met in 1812. The **Luis Alberto Acuna**

COLOMBIA

Museum, on the central plaza, is named after the famous Colombian painter and houses a collection of his works. The stores along the plaza stock the usual selection of handicrafts, and a market is held here on Saturdays.

Just out of town is the **Monastery of Santo Ecce Homo**, a stone and clay edifice built by the Dominicans in 1620.

When planning your visit, bear in mind that most museums and places of interest here are closed on Mondays.

Food and lodging
El Molino La Mesopotamia, on Calle del Silencio, is a good, pleasant hotel in an old building with beautiful, well-tended gardens and a pool. *Convento de San Francisco*, on Plaza San Francisco, also has a pool and is recommended for its high quality service. For low budget accommodations, try *Los Olivos*.

There are several good restaurants on the central plaza. One of the best restaurants in town, *Los Balcones*, is just off the plaza.

Bucaramanga

Bucaramanga, the capital of Santander province, was founded in 1622. Until the second half of the 19th century, Bucaramanga was simply a small town, but has since developed at a fantastic pace, and now has a population of half a million. Its burgeoning growth is due largely to the success of its coffee plantations, which export their produce worldwide. Reminders of the past are easily discerned in the modern city, with its spacious parks and squares. Parque Santander graces the heart of the modern section, while Garcia Romero Plaza marks the center of the colonial district. Near this plaza is **Casa de Bolivar** (Bolivar's House), where he stayed for two months in 1813. The mansion is an archeological museum today, with a collection of pre-Columbian pottery. Opposite Bolivar's House is **Casa Cultura** (House of Culture).

Transportation
Bucaramanga lies about 10 hours' travel from Bogota, on the junction of three main highways – to Venezuela, north to Santa Marta and the Caribbean Sea, and south to Bogota. *Berlinas del Fonce* (offices at 31-06 Carerra 18) provides good bus service to and from Bogota. The trip to Cucuta takes about 6 hours. Because the buses to Cucuta are often full (the routes begin in Bogota), it may be best to travel by *colectivo*, which, though slightly more expensive than the bus, is faster and more comfortable. The trip to Santa Marta takes about 15 hours, or

COLOMBIA

even more in the rainy season. Copetran provides bus service on this route.

Food and lodging
All hotels here are on the modest side. The best is *Bucarica*, on the main plaza – moderate prices, swimming pool, and a good restaurant. *Hotel El Pilar* (Calle 34 at Carrera 25) is lower priced, clean, and friendly. Truly low budget hotels that are nonetheless good and clean are *San Pablo* and *Amparo*.

For restaurants, *La Carreta* is good, famous for its meat dishes, but expensive. *El Maizal*, Calle 31 at Carrera 20, serves good local fare. The specialty of the house is *hormigas* (large fried black ants)!

Cucuta

This town, with a population of over half a million, is the capital of Santander del Norte province. Founded in 1734 and leveled by an earthquake in 1875, Cucuta was rebuilt as a modern city with wide avenues and parks. The climate is hot with an average daily temperature of 28 degrees Centigrade or 82 degrees Fahrenheit. Coffee and tobacco are grown extensively. Due to Cucuta's proximity to the Venezuelan border, however, many of the locals deal in smuggling. Its location also affected its role in the War of Independence. After capturing Cucuta in 1813, Bolivar set out from here for Caracas at the head of his forces. A modest statue marks the spot where Bolivar billeted his troops before the campaign.

The small town of **El Rosario de Cucuta**, some 14 km from Cucuta en route to the border, is the place where representatives of the Confederation of "Greater Colombia" first convened. They ratified the unification of Colombia, Venezuela, Ecuador and Panama, elected Bolivar president, and selected Santander (who was born nearby) as his deputy.

Shopping
Cucuta is recommended for inexpensive leather goods, such as boots and wallets.

Transportation
The bus ride from Cucuta to Bogota takes about 20 hours, or more in the rainy season. Berlinas del Fonce and Bolivariano buses leave Bogota almost every hour. Berlinas also provides frequent bus service to Bucaramanga, on the way to the Caribbean coast. The bus station is on Avenida 7.

Avianca provides air service to Bogota several times per week from Cucuta's airport, located just out of town.

COLOMBIA

Changing currency
Cucuta offers a good exchange rate for both Colombian *pesos* and *bolivares* (Venezuelan currency). Street moneychangers, who wander around the main square, usually outbid Banco de la Republica (Calle 11 at Av. 5). Convert all leftover pesos in Cucuta, since this is hard to do in Venezuela. Travelers' checks can be cashed at the bank.

Food and lodging
Hotel Tonchala has a fine restaurant, a swimming pool, air conditioned rooms, and high prices. A good, inexpensive hotel with a pool is *Casa Blanca*. *Residencias Gomez* provides basic services for low budget travelers.

For restaurants, the *Bahia* (near the main plaza) is good, pleasant, and affordable. *Chez Estevan*, with its continental cuisine, is recommended.

On to Venezuela
From Cucuta, take a taxi or a bus to San Antonio, the Venezuelan border town. Because the border itself has no immigration offices, passports must be stamped for exit at the DAS office in Cucuta at 2-60 Calle 17. Open daily 8am-noon and 2-5:30pm. Closed Sun. To enter Venezuela, one must also obtain a tourist pass at the Venezuelan consulate in Cucuta, on Calle 8. Open Mon.-Fri. 8am-1pm. It is always best to obtain entry visas, where required, in one's country of origin. Failing this, visit the Venezuelan Embassy in Bogota.

Upon entering Venezuela, passports are stamped at the immigration office in San Antonio. Expreso Occidente buses leave San Antonio twice daily for Caracas – a 14 hour journey.

The Caribbean Coast

Colombia's northern coast, on the Caribbean Sea, offers history, sun and lots of fun. Here the Spanish colonists founded their first cities on Colombian soil, as bridgeheads for the numerous explorers sent from the Old World to the South American interior. The coastal towns were also used as ports for the huge cargos of gold that left for Spain. As such, they attracted hordes of pirates, and the numerous fortresses erected to guard the approaches to the cities stand as silent witnesses to the cruel battles that raged along this beautiful coast.

The Santa Marta mountains, with their snow capped peaks, loom in the distance and extend as far as the tropical, sun drenched beaches. The climate, consistently hot, seems to have produced people of similar nature. The *costenos* (coastal

COLOMBIA

people) are descendants of intermarriage between Whites, Indians, and Blacks. On the whole they are warm and outgoing people.

Note: All previous warnings about pickpockets and thieves are even more relevant here. The coastal area is even more prone to violence than the interior. Guard your possessions, and try not to tour alone.

Bearing this in mind, we now explore the coastal area – from Cartagena east to Venezuela, including San Andres Island.

Cartagena

History

The first Spaniards to reach the many inlets of the Northern Colombia shore found a local population of *Calamari* Indians, a nation of warrior tribes with enormous quantities of gold and a fairly sophisticated culture.

Rodrigo de Bastidas of Spain discovered Cartagena Bay in 1501, and large numbers of Spaniards followed. The great influx of conquerors and explorers who reached Cartagena on their way inland made it necessary to establish a port. Thus, in 1533, Pedro de Heredia founded the city of Cartagena at a well chosen location – an indented, flat coastline, with two precipitous hills that provided a good view of the maritime approaches to the city.

The exploration parties, heading inland, soon encountered the indigenous Indian populations with their spectacular treasures of gold. Entire Indian villages were devastated, the gold was plundered, and melted down into ingots which were then shipped back to Spain. Ships returning from Spain were loaded with goods for sale. Cartagena became a rich town, and one of the most important ports of the Spanish Empire. This, however, proved to be a mixed blessing. Its wealth attracted many enemies, including the legendary Sir Francis Drake who attacked the city in 1586. Only a ransom of ten million gold coins dissuaded him from razing the city to the ground. Consequently, the Spaniards built a system of fortresses along Cartagena Bay, blocking all approaches to the city, which was itself surrounded by a wall. The construction work spanned the late 16th century and the first half of the 17th. As for the cost of this endeavor, the story goes that the King of Spain, gazing from his palace window in Madrid and musing on the enormity of his expenses, was surprised not to see the outcome of his investment on the horizon...

The long arm of the Spanish Inquisition reached this area as well, and set up its regional courts in Cartagena, in a beautiful

COLOMBIA

Cartagena and its fortresses

palace built for this purpose. Until the city declared its independence, putting the Inquisition to an end, almost a thousand people fell prey to its *autos-da-fe*.

A large French force under Baron de Pointis attacked Cartagena in 1697. De Pointis mounted a siege and attacked the fortress of Bocachica, which blocked the approaches to the Bay. Once Bocachica fell, after a hard and bloody battle, the other fortresses fell more easily until the entire city was conquered. After methodically plundering the city and destroying most of its defenses, de Pointis was forced to retreat due to epidemics which were decimating his forces.

England's decision early in the 18th century to deploy troops in the Caribbean area caused a rupture in Anglo-Hispanic relations. When the Spaniards launched a provocative attack on an English ship in the area, the English reacted harshly. In March 1741, 186 English warships – the largest naval force ever employed in the region – appeared off Cartagena. The commander of this armada, Admiral Vernon, spent an entire week deploying his forces around the city, and only then ordered an attack on Bocachica. The fortress fell, and the English ships entered the Bay. After bombarding the city for a week, the English attacked the mighty fortress of San-Felipe de Barajas. After a short and fierce battle, the tables were turned: the English were routed with heavy casualties, and were forced to hoist anchor and flee.

COLOMBIA

Cartagena flourished during the second half of the 18th century. The defenses were repaired and renovated, and the great markets (*ferias*) in the area attracted thousands of merchants from the interior. Trade in **Black** slaves, too, was a booming business. The victims were the forebears of the large Black population that resides in the Caribbean to this day.

Cartagena played a decisive role in Colombia's struggle for independence. On November 11, 1811, the city declared itself free of Spanish rule. It spent several years thereafter fighting off relentless attacks by opponents of independence and Spanish royalists. In 1815, for example, a Spanish expeditionary force under Pablo Morillo managed to subdue the rebellious city and control it. A third of the population was killed in this cruel battle, for which Cartagena came to be known as *La Ciudad Heroica* (the Heroic City). Only in 1821, after Simon Bolivar's final victory, was Cartagena completely liberated from the Spanish yoke.

Today, Cartagena is a large, modern city of 500,000, the capital of Bolivar province, and an important port. Various monuments – palaces, colonial houses, fortresses – testify to its glorious past. The town also boasts bustling tourist facilities, shopping centers, and beaches alive with color and action.

When to visit

During December and January, the peak of Colombia's tourist season, Cartagena swarms with tourists. It is essential to make advance hotel reservations. Hotel prices are 25% higher at this time.

Cartagena's 4-day Independence Day festivities begin on Nov. 11th. The locals turn out in their best clothes, don masks, and dance in the streets to the sound of folk music.

How to get there

Cartagena's Crespo International Airport has regular flights from all of Colombia's major cities and San Andres Island in the Caribbean. One of the most economical ways to fly to Colombia from Central America is to fly first to San Andres and then to Cartagena on a domestic flight. Another low-cost way is by boat from Panama.

Expreso Brasilia buses run between Cartagena and Medellin (17 hours) and Bogota. Comfortable and regular bus service links Cartagena with other towns on the Caribbean coast. There is also a direct bus to Maicao on the Venezuelan border.

Food and lodging

As a tourist town, Cartagena has plenty of hotels. Again, however, reservations are essential during peak season.

COLOMBIA

Luxury hotels are congregated along the Bocagrande beach, about a 10-minute ride form downtown. The best hotel is the *Cartagena Hilton*, overlooking the sea at the edge of El Leguito (Tel. 50666). The *Capilla del Mar Hotel* on Calle 8 and Carrera 1 (Tel. 47140) is also excellent, and has a good French restaurant. *El Dorado*, 4-41 Av. San Martin (Tel. 80211) is an intermediate class hotel with good service.

The hotels near the city center are more modest. The best of them is *Plaza Bolivar* at 3-98 Plaza Bolivar; its restaurant, too, is excellent. Several low budget hotels are available on Calle Media Luna. But beware: not all are safe; do not leave valuables in the rooms. Neither are they the cleanest of places.

To give Old Cartagena a new profile, its alleyways have been renovated and quite a few good restaurants have opened along them. One of these is *Nautilus*, located at the city wall across from the statue of La India Catalina. Nautilus is noted for its excellent seafood and good service. Another excellent but slightly expensive restaurant in the Old City is *Bodejon de la Candelaria*, on Calle de las Damas. *Club de Pesca*, at the Pastelillo Fortress, is an outdoor restaurant with a splendid view. Though it is expensive and a bit far from downtown, its superb seafare earns a recommendation. For good low budget restaurants, try the Plaza Independencia area.

Tourist services

The official **Tourist Office** is at Casa de Marques de Valdehoyos House on Calle de la Factoria. There is another information office at Crespo Airport. The **tourist police** station and a **Telecom** office are situated at La Maluna, in the city center.

Car Rental: Try Hertz (Hotel Capilla del Mar) or Avis (Bocagrande, 6-91 Carrera 2).

Tourist sites

The Old City is partitioned by a wall into inner and outer sectors. Both comprise houses no taller than one or two stories, done in Spanish colonial style. The narrow, winding streets were built this way on purpose, to provide shade from the searing sun.

The inner section consists of two neighborhoods: **El Centro**, home to the city's nobility, governors and Inquisitors, and **San Diego**, which housed the middle class, merchants, priests and the military. The outer section is known as **Getsemani**. The best way to get to know the town is to take a leisurely walk along the narrow lanes and to imbibe the atmosphere. In this manner one cannot help but encounter places of interest.

The tour starts at **Plaza de los Coches**, where the inner and outer sections meet. It was once the site of the huge slave

COLOMBIA

market, and has a clock tower dating from the mid-19th century. Cross into the inner section via **Plaza de la Aduana** (Customs Square) with its stone statue of Christopher Columbus. Here *El Centro* begins, with its narrow lanes and elegant 2-storey homes. Near Plaza de la Aduana is another plaza, graced with a monastery and church built by Jesuits in 1603. It is named after San Pedro Claver, a Spanish monk, who dedicated himself to the cause of the Black slaves brought from Africa. He was canonized more than two hundred years after his death, and his body is preserved in a glass coffin inside the church.

Turning north towards **Plaza Bolivar** (a statue of Bolivar stands in its center), you will see the **Palace of the Inquisition** – a splendid example of colonial architecture, which served as the Inquisition's Court of Justice. The first floor of the palace has a display of torture machinery used on heretics. The second floor houses two small museums: a **Museum of Anthropology** with archeological exhibits from local pre-Columbian civilizations, and a **Colonial Museum** with an exhibit of documents, weapons and other items in daily use. Open Tues.-Sat. 10am-5pm, and Sun. 9am-1pm. Also on Plaza Bolivar is a branch of Banco de la Republica's **Museo del Oro** (Museum of Gold) – smaller than the main branch in Bogota, but worth visiting nonetheless.

The Church and Monastery of **Santo Domingo**, on the street of the same name, was built in the late 1500s and is Cartagena's oldest church. At 36-57 Calle de la Factoria, is **Casa de Marques de Valdehoyos**. This magnificent colonial residence, used today as a tourist bureau, was built in the early 1600s by Don Fernando de Hoyos, a slave trade tycoon.

Further north is the **San Diego** quarter. There, on the grounds of San Diego Park, is the **Church and Monastery of Santa Clara**, originally built in the early 17th century. The monastery was subsequently converted into a hospital. Not far from here is **Plaza de las Bovedas**. From this spot, one may assess the grand dimensions of the city walls – 12 m high, 16 m wide! The niches, once prison cells, now serve as souvenir shops.

We cross into **Getsemani**, the outer section of Old Cartagena, built of low houses and streets so narrow that a person standing in the middle can sometimes touch the walls on either side. At the end of Calle Media Luna is a huge sculpture of a pair of shoes. It is a monument to a native son, poet Luis Carlos Lopez, who once described the city as being as inspiring as an old pair of shoes.

Nearby is the most important of Cartagena's fortresses – **San Felipe de Barajas**, completed in 1657. Though it fell to Baron de Pointis of France, it bravely withstood the onslaught of Admiral Vernon of England (see "History" above). The defenders'

COLOMBIA

homes and offices, as well as a system of secret subterranean passageways, lie under the walls and fortifications. A sound-and-light show on the glorious history of the fortress and the city is staged here on Saturdays at 9pm.

Another link in the port's defenses is **San Sebastian de Pastelillo**. An earlier fort (16th century) built here to ward off pirate attacks was completely destroyed in one of those assaults. The current fort, built in its place, is equipped with a dock used by the *Club de Pesca* (Fishing Club) and an excellent seafood restaurant.

Excursions in the area

About 20 minutes east of Cartagena is the fishing village of **La Boguilla**. Its weekend evening dance parties, powered by the lively rhythm of local music, are recommended. The mangrove swamps around the village are excellent bird-watching territory.

Lovely indigenous handicrafts are available at the village of **San Jacinto,** 1 1/2 hour's ride from Cartagena.

The Rosario Islands

The lovely Rosario Islands, outside Cartagena Bay, are reached by a pleasurable but expensive 8-hour boat ride from Cartagena (departures every morning). The trip offers a good view of the fortifications that formerly guarded the city's approaches. Once ashore, note the palms, the dazzling white sands, and the color of the water – which changes from the lightest turquoise to dark blue as it gets deeper. Spend the night in one of the islands' picturesque houses, and enjoy the area's typical seafood.

Barranquilla

On the west bank of Rio Magdalena, several km from the river's mouth, is Barranquilla. The city began as a small rural settlement populated first by livestock breeders and later by fishermen. Over time however, it has become a large industrial center and Colombia's largest and most important port. Of its population of more than one million, most are employed in the sophisticated industries typical of a modern, progressive city.

Barranquilla is no tourist attraction, but as a major sea and air port it is the place most tourists reach first when approaching Colombia from the north.

Once a year the city shakes off the humdrum of its daily existence for **Carnaval Joselito**, a 4-day festival held in January. Everyone in town – together with throngs from the

COLOMBIA

entire Caribbean coastal area and even inland – pours into the street in fancy dress to watch the parades, and to dance and sing to the local music. Hence a nickname that has stuck to Barranquilla – *La Ciudad Loca*, or Crazy City.

How to get there

Corfisso International Airport is a modern, spacious facility about 10 km out of town; local buses, airport buses and taxis serve the airport. Air service to and from Corfisso is available from all Colombia's main cities, as well as from Mexico City and Caracas.

Ships from all over the world dock at Barranquilla's huge port. Tourists wishing to head north by sea have a variety of options. To sail for Panama, however, it is best to embark from Cartagena. To take a car on board, be prepared to spend up to two days clearing through red tape.

Regular bus service links Barranquilla with Santa-Marta (about a 2-hour journey) and Cartagena (about 3 hours). It's about 16 hours to Medellin, and approximately 20 to Bogota. Direct buses also set out for Maicao, on the Venezuelan border.

Food and lodging

The best hotel in town is *El Prado* at 70-10 Carrera 54 (Tel. 456-533). *Cadebia*, 41-79 Calle 75, Tel. 456-144 has a swimming pool, sauna, and casino. A slightly more modest hotel which offers good service is the *Caribana*, 40-02 Carrera 41. Another possibility, recommended, although a bit far from downtown, is the *Majestic*, 54-41 Carrera 53. *Hotel Zhivago* on Plaza Bolivar is good for those on a tight budget. Hotel rates skyrocket at carnival time, and rooms are hard to get.

An excellent seafood restaurant is *El Pez que Fuma*. In the Alto Prado quarter, the *Sorrento* serves very good South-American dishes. *La Colonia* is recommended for less expensive fare.

Tourist services

The **Tourist Office** has a main office at 43-57 Carrera 72, and a branch in the Municipal Library.

Various countries have consulates in Barranquilla, including the United States (46-63 Calle 34, 10th floor) and Great Britain (45-57 Carrera 44).

Tourist sites

Barranquilla is not exactly a major tourist attraction, but there are some things worth seeing. The main street, **Paseo Bolivar**, is a pedestrian mall, and the city's shopping district is along Calle 72. Plaza San Nicolas is graced with a beautiful church which is guarded by a statue of Columbus. An attractive,

COLOMBIA

colorful market is held daily along a channel of the Rio Magdalena known as the Cano de las Campanias. **Parque 11 de Noviembre** and the port area are pleasant to visit. The port was originally intended to serve river barges plying the Magdalena. Over time, the need arose for a large sea port and the harbor was deepened and widened. Today it serves enormous ocean-going vessels.

Barranquilla's residential quarters are in the hilly area north of downtown. One of them, **Alto Prado**, still retains the town's original architecture.

During the annual 4-day carnival, each neighborhood organizes its own parades and celebrations, so there is no shortage of amusement. Nightclubs provide a variety of evening entertainment and dances, and it is advisable to inquire as to the current year's favorite.

On to Santa Marta

The coastal road heads east from Barranquilla, crosses a bridge over the Rio Magdalena, and continues through marshland rich in marine vegetation, birds, and wildlife. The route passes through the town of **Cienaga** (pop. 70,000) and its backdrop of cotton, banana and cocoa farms. Another 100 km brings us to Santa Marta.

Santa Marta

Santa Marta, Colombia's first city, was established in 1525 by Rodrigo de Bastidas. It was the territory of the *Tairona* Indians, a tribe famous for its gold handicrafts. In the 16th and 17th centuries, the city became a center of the pearl industry and repeatedly suffered attacks by pirates, notwithstanding the two fortresses on the island off shore. Simon Bolivar spent his last days here.

Today, Santa Marta (pop. 350,000) is the capital of Magdalena province. Its scenery includes the deep harbor, the snowy peaks of the Sierra Nevada de Santa Marta in the distance, and beautiful "sandscapes" on the road from the airport to *El Rodadero Beach*. These make Santa Marta a popular resort for lovers of sea and sun.

How to get there

Simon Bolivar Airport, some 20 km from the city, has flights to and from all of Colombia's major cities.

An express passenger train with only one class makes the 30-hour trip from Bogota to Santa Marta once a week. It leaves Bogota on Saturdays, and returns on Sundays.

The bus terminal is at Calle 24 on Carrera 8. Service to

COLOMBIA

Surf, sand and fun at Rodadero Beach

Barranquilla, Cartagena and Riohacha is frequent. The road south to Bucaramanga is long and difficult; from Bucaramanga, however, there is frequent bus service to Bogota. Buses also leave Santa Marta for the Venezuelan border and Maracaibo.

Food and lodging
There are two hotel districts: Rodadero Beach, and in town. Rodadero is the place for luxury hotels. The best and most expensive of these is the *Irotama*, at kilometer 14 on the road to the airport. It has good service, and a beautiful private beach (Tel. 27642). For moderate to inexpensive hotels, try in town. The *Miramar*, 1C-59 Calle 10, is recommended; easy on the budget, well situated (near the beach and the train station), clean, and safe.

Santa Marta has plenty of good restaurants, most specializing in seafood. Like the hotels, the restaurants at Rodadero are more expensive than those in town.

Tourist sites
Avenida Bastidas is the long thoroughfare along the shore, with well-tended gardens alongside the beaches. **Punta de Betin,** the bluff that closes off Santa Marta Bay, affords a marvelous view of the city.

The **Customs House** (*Casa de la Aduana*) in Parque Bolivar presently houses a branch of Banco de la Republica's **Museum of Gold**. Its rich collection of archeological findings includes

433

COLOMBIA

gold handcrafts discovered in the Parque Tairona and Sierra Nevada area. Open Tues.-Sun. during tourist season and Mon.-Fri. the rest of the year.

About 15 km from downtown is *El Rodadero Beach*, tourist country. The best hotels, restaurants, and shops are situated here, as is the best of local nightlife. The nearby **Aquarium** has interesting specimens of the underwater life of the Caribbean coast.

Another museum worth visiting is the **Hacienda de San Pedro Alejandrino**, a colonial estate about 5 km southeast of the city. Here Simon Bolivar spent his last weary, destitute days, before he died at the age of 47. Though he was buried in Santa Marta, his remains were later reinterred in the Pantheon in Caracas, Venezuela. The estate is surrounded by beautiful, well kept gardens, and the house still contains some of Bolivar's personal effects. Open daily except Tues. (open Tues. during tourist season.)

Parque Tairona

About 35 km north-east of Santa Marta, along the slopes of the Sierra Nevada de Santa Marta, is Parque Tairona, named for the Indians who predated the Spaniards in Colombia. The scenery is gorgeous – golden beaches, abundant tropical flora, five enchanting lagoons and indented coastlines. There is also an archeological site in the area: a former Tairona village called *Pueblito*.

There are several ways to visit the park, including an organized tour that lasts a few hours, or a trip by taxi. Hikers with plenty of time can take a bus to the park entrance, walk the 5 km or so to the park's major beach – Canaveral – and spend the night at its parking area. The beaches and the lovely lagoons are just right for a leisurely stroll or a lazy afternoon in a hammock.

Note: The thieves find this area attractive, too. Do not walk around alone, and try to sleep only in official campgrounds.

Sierra Nevada de Santa Marta

This great mountain range plunges into the Caribbean from a height of 5775 m, over a distance of only 50 km as the crow flies! The lower slopes, covered with tropical flora, are the habitat of natural wildlife and the home of Indians who retain and live by their cultural heritage. Higher up, the slopes become rocky and icy, and the peaks are snow capped.

A major archeological discovery was made in the depths of the mountain forest; large terraces which served as the foundations of stone houses, together with interconnecting steps and paths.

COLOMBIA

The site, covering 2 sq/km, is known as **La Ciudad Perdida** – (the Lost City).

Taking the mountains of Santa Marta on foot is an arduous and complicated venture. One way to do so is to travel to Valledupar via Riohacha, where jeeps continue to the Indian village of Pueblo Bello.

Riohacha

The capital of the Guajira district, Riohacha (pop. 100,000), is 160 km east of Santa Marta. Founded in 1545 by Nicolas Federmann at the mouth of the Rio Cesar, the city first flourished because of its pearl industry – which motivated Sir Francis Drake to attack the city in 1596.

Today's main industry in Riohacha is smuggling. Thus it is no surprise that the locals are not too friendly to strangers.

Riohacha is the place of origin of the legendary Macondo, about whom the celebrated Colombian author, Gabriel Garcia Marquez, wrote in his famous book *One Hundred Years of Solitude*.

The **Indian market** held every day in Riohacha is well worth visiting. The main highway out of Riohacha leads straight to Venezuela. Before leaving, however, it is worth visiting the **Guajira Peninsula**. This is an arid zone, sparsely populated by *Guajiro* Indians who fish and raise sheep for a living. To get there, find a place in the car that sets out twice a day for Manaure from the Riohacha Indian market. The trip lasts about 3 hours. Occasionally someone with a car continues on to Cabo de la Vela, with its marvelous, untouched beaches, and lagoons with flocks of flamingos. From Manaure, one can reach Maicao via Uribia.

On to Venezuela

The Colombian border town of Maicao is the capital of the smuggling industry between Colombia and Venezuela, and much of the trade involves drugs. It's obviously a dangerous place. **Do not linger here!** Proceed straight to the nearest large town in Venezuela, Maracaibo.

If you need an entry permit, try to obtain one in your country of origin, or failing that, in Bogota. The Venezuelan Consulate in Riohacha (9-85 Calle 3) is infuriatingly slow and inefficient.

There are flights to Maicao from Barranquilla, and buses to Maicao from all cities along the Caribbean coast.

COLOMBIA

San Andres Island

This enchanting Caribbean island has a lot to offer: white beaches, palms, clear water, sun all year round, places to dive, and reggae. The island, 3 km wide and 14 km long, was discovered in 1527 by Spanish navigators on the eve of the Festival of San Andres, whence its name. Since 1827, the island, like its neighbor Providencia, has belonged to Colombia. Most of the local population, some 25,000, are Black. San Andres Island is a duty-free zone, so it is usually packed with Colombians combining a vacation with a shopping spree on imported goods.

How to get there

By sea: Freighters make the 3-day cruise from Cartagena twice a month (the trip takes 72 hours); ships from Colon, Panama, make the trip in 48 hours.

By air: Avianca, Sam, Sahsa, and Satena airlines fly to and from San Andres and all major Colombian cities. The more expensive version of the *Conozca a Colombia* air ticket, offered by Avianca, includes a flight to San Andres (see "Colombia – Domestic transportation"). There are international flights to San Andres from Miami, Guatemala, Costa Rica and Panama.

Fleets of taxis wait at the airport to take travelers into town. The fare is fixed, and the rates are on display at the airport tourist office. Make sure you are not being overcharged.

Food and lodging

Hotel Aquarium, in Punta Hansa on Colombia Avenue, is an excellent establishment, with air conditioned rooms, a fine restaurant and a beautiful view of the Caribbean. The **Casa Blanca**, 53 Av. La Playa across from the beach, is a very good Spanish-style hotel with air conditioned rooms.

The *Morgan*, 1A-59 Av. Nicaragua, is less expensive but has a swimming pool and a reasonable restaurant. The *Residencia Restrepo*, near the airport, is for truly tight budgets. Though noisy, it is clean.

The characteristic cuisine here, of course, is seafood. An excellent local dish is crab soup (*sopa de congrejo*). As for restaurants, *El Aquario* has an excellent selection of seafoods, *La Tortuga* serves Italian cuisine at moderate prices, and *San Andres* is both affordable and good.

Local women set up stands along Av. La Playa in the evenings; the selection of local home-made dishes they offer is well worth trying.

COLOMBIA

The city of San Andres

Tourist services

The main **Tourist Office** is on Av. Colombia, with a branch at the airport.

Currency exchange: Obtain local currency at Banco de la Republica. Open Tues.-Fri. 8am-1pm.

Car Rental: Rental cars are available for 2 hours or more at the Morgan or the Abacoa Hotel. A pleasant alternative is a bicycle, which can be rented at the seashore.

Tourist sites

As the capital of a duty-free zone, the town of San Andres has become a noisy and drab shopping center packed with Colombians on their shopping sprees. Av La Playa, parallel to the beach, is lined with hotels, restaurants and bars. Concerts of local reggae music have become popular recently. The beaches, too, are crowded – and not particularly clean.

From a vantage point on the beach, a tiny island crowned with palm trees comes into view. Known as **Johnny Key**, it can be reached by a motorboat which sets out from the beach opposite the Abacoa Hotel. Johnny Key is an enchanting spot: white, pristine sand, clear, clean water, and leafy palms which provide shade from the burning sun. In the center of this tiny island is an outdoor bar. The ambience is young and friendly, and the bar turns into an instant discotheque as the music moves the vacationers.

COLOMBIA

Beach on Providencia Island

Motorboats setting out from the same place on the San Andres beach drop anchor at **Aquarium**, another tiny island. This is a diver's paradise, where the marvels of underwater life come into view. Other lovely beaches are yours at San Luis and nearby Bahia Sonora. At *Hoyo Soplador*, the pounding of waves against the face of a cliff has created subterranean tunnels. The end of the tunnel has openings where the water bursts out. When the wind is blowing in the right direction, the place looks like a geyser field.

Shopping
Coral ornaments are the most typical of local handicrafts. Shops stock a variety of imported goods: photo and electronic equipment, decorative items and fabrics. Though the prices are low in South American terms, they are lower still, naturally, in Western countries.

Providencia
This little, hilly island (17 sq/km, pop. 4000) lies about 70 km north of San Andres and is linked to it by daily flights. Again, the beaches are breath-taking, the water clean and clear, and there are a variety of marine sports to enjoy. Providencia is much less "touristy" than San Andres. The locals make use of the fertile soil for cultivating crops, especially fruit. The island offers a few campgrounds and two hotels: El Paraiso, and Las Cabanas.

COLOMBIA

Darien Gap

Colombia and Panama are linked by a marshy, sparsely populated, and completely undeveloped strip of land. Nearly half of eastern Panama consists of such territory, and is known as the Darien Gap. The region has no land transport, and the few Indian villages are reached only by air, boat, or foot. The area has therefore become something of a challenge for an ever growing number of adventurers. The trek takes from one week to two, and it costs more than the airfare from Colombia to Panama. The amount the Indians charge for their various services, increases in relation to the number of travelers who need them, with a corresponding decrease in the friendliness.

Special guidelines

The trip is easiest to take during the dry season, between mid-December and mid-April; the paths are not marshy then, and the mosquitos are scarcer. Nevertheless, bring mosquito-repellent ointment, a mosquito net, chlorine tablets for water, and malaria pills. Pack enough food for at least 5 days (although one can usually find some along the way).

Do not overpack. Bear in mind that everything has to be carried and borne, along with the heat, humidity, and mosquitos. Unnecessary equipment can be mailed to the next station en route. Send everything by air mail only, and use the postal services only between major towns. Remember, too, that a return flight ticket must be presented to the Panamanian immigration authorities in order to get an entry permit for the country.

The route

The route begins at the port town of **Turbo**, on the coast of Uraba Bay. Daily buses reach Turbo from Medellin (about 15 hours away) and Cartagena. Turbo has several hotels, of which the best and most expensive is *Playa Mar. Residencias Sandra* is both affordable and good. Banks are closed on Mondays and Tuesdays, and travelers' checks cannot be cashed. Be sure, too, to stop at the DAS office for an exit stamp from Colombia, since this is the last Colombian immigration office on the route.

Further progress is made by cargo boat, canoe and on foot. The route traverses remote areas and interesting Indian villages. The Indians in several of them greet visitors warmly and may even offer you hospitality for a few days. The *Choco* Indians, who live along the last stretch of the route, are noted for their hearty hospitality. On the first part of the tour, you will get to know the

COLOMBIA

Cuna Indians, survivors of a superbly constituted pre-Columbian empire which dominated all of Panama.

Entry stamps to Panama are obtained in the village of Boca de Cupe. The route ends in the town of Yaviza, where a daily bus leaves for Panama City.

For further details, see *Backpacking in Mexico and Central America*, by Hilary Bradt and Rob Rachowiecki.

The Cordillera Central

The Cordillera Central range is flanked by the Rio Cauca on the west and the Magdalena valley on the east. This is Colombia's most developed region, both highly industrialized, containing two of Colombia's largest cities, and a fertile agricultural zone.

Before the arrival of the Spanish conquerors, the area was inhabited by Indians who practiced subsistence agriculture and mined silver and gold.

The Spanish arrived in 1539; and two years later, founded the city of Antioquia. At the beginning of the 17th century a wave of Spanish immigrants founded the city of Medellin. Strongly opposed to slavery, they refused to use Black or Indian labor. Their lands were therefore divided into small farms, which each family worked individually. Besides farming, the immigrants mined gold for export.

Later, during the second half of the 19th century, the settlers started growing coffee. By the beginning of this century coffee production had begun to play an important role in the economy of the Antioquia and Caldas provinces. Today these regions supply about half of Colombia's total coffee production. The success of the coffee industry led to rapid economic development and the establishment of other industries, particularly textiles.

Medellin

Medellin, the capital of Antioquia province, is Colombia's second largest city, with a population of approximately two million. The city lies in a valley, 1540 m above sea level, and is surrounded by lofty mountain peaks. The weather is springlike year round, but there is a certain industrial haze in the air. Medellin was founded in 1616 by European immigrants, most of them Jewish. The old colonial structures have almost entirely disappeared, replaced by modern buildings. Only a few churches remain from days gone by. The city has become an important industrial center: about 80% of the Colombian textile industry is concentrated here, and this accounts for only half of the total local industrial production! The climate lends itself to

COLOMBIA

horticulture, and Medellin is one of the world's orchid-growing centers. There are four large universities, and other institutes of higher education as well. Medellin's citizens are justifiably proud of their town.

How to get there

Medellin's international airport operates only by day, since the mountainous terrain makes it dangerous to land or take off by night. Numerous daily flights link the city to Bogota – a 45-minute flight. There are also scheduled flights to all of Colombia's other main cities. The Copa company flies to Panama several times a week.

The train runs from Medellin to Barrancabermeja. Those wishing to reach the Caribbean coast can pick up the Bogota-Santa Marta train at Puerto Berrio. If you reach Medellin by rail late at night, you might decide to spend the night in nearby Barbosa, at one of the two modest hotels in the central plaza.

The Flota Magdalena company operates an efficient bus service between Bogota and Medellin. There are several buses a day; the trip takes about 15 hours. There is a very frequent bus service to Cali (a 12-hour ride) and likewise to Manizales (a 7-hour ride).

The Brasilia and Pullman Ocha companies run buses to Cartagena. The second company is slightly more expensive, but its buses are also faster and more comfortable. The trip to Cartagena takes 14 hours.

Note: All the bus company offices are located in the Caribe quarter – a very dangerous area. Avoid lingering there, especially if you have luggage with you. Take a taxi to the bus station of the company you will be traveling with.

Food and lodging

Medellin has a number of excellent hotels. The best is the *Intercontinental-Medellin*, on Variante Las Palmas (Tel: 266-0680), which has a magnificent view. Its two restaurants provide excellent service. Its only drawback is its location – rather far from the center of town. Another excellent hotel is the *Amaru*, located downtown at 53-45 Carrera 50A (Tel: 231-1155); its restaurant is excellent. A slightly less expensive hotel is the *Veracruz*, at 18-54 Carrera 50; this one has a swimming pool. Among the low-budget hotels, we can recommend the *San Francisco*, at 44-48 Carrera 54.

Medellin also has its share of good restaurants. We will mention just a few: *La Posada de la Montana* offers exquisite local fare, in a beautiful colonial-style building, surrounded by gardens with

COLOMBIA

a fountain. The place is expensive, and rather far from downtown. *Las Lomas* serves delicious fish and sea food. Meat lovers should definitely try *La Res*. An excellent, if somewhat expensive, French restaurant is *La Bella Epoca*. A very inexpensive and good restaurant is *La Vida*, near the San Francisco hotel.

Tourist services

The main **Tourist Office** is at 46-66 Calle 54; there is a branch office at the airport.

Currency exchange: Money can be changed at the Banco de la Republica, whose main branch is at 21-51 Calle 50.

Car rental: Hertz has an office at 23-50 Carrera 43A, and another office at the airport.

Telephone: The Telecom office is at 49-73 Calle 49.

Tourist sites

Although Medellin is a busy industrial town, its spacious avenues, green parks, quiet residential neighborhoods, and cleanliness belie its industrial nature. The buildings are modern, especially downtown; ancient monuments are virtually nonexistent. Only a few old churches have escaped the relentless march of progress. The oldest is the **Church of San Jose**, built in 1646, at the corner of Calle 49 and Carrera 46. **La Catedral Metropolitana,** at the corner of Carrera 48 and Calle 56, is one of the world's largest brick buildings. The cathedral's impressive steps lead down to **Parque Bolivar**, with its statue of the Liberator. A market – known as the **Mercado San Alejo** – is held here on the first Saturday of each month when craftsmen sell their wares.

Medellin has been the home of many of Colombia's famous artists, as can be seen by the numerous statues and fountains that adorn the city. The most famous of the city's sculptures – Rodrigo Betancur's *The Fountain of Life* (La Fuente de la Vida) – stands opposite the Centro Residencial Sudamericana Building.

Medellin has a fair selection of museums. The **Museum of Anthropology**, located on the new campus of Antioquia University, has a collection of pre-Columbian pottery. Open Mon.-Fri., 10am-12 noon and 2pm-6pm. Closed on Sat. and Sun. The **Museo de Zea**, at the corner of Calle 52 and Carrera 53, has an important collection of the works of contemporary Colombian artists. Open Tues.-Sat., 9am-1pm and 3pm-6pm. **El Castillo**, in the El Poblado quarter, was formerly the residence of one of the town's wealthy notables. Today its imposing rooms house art objects from all over the world. Chamber music

COLOMBIA

concerts are sometimes held here. Open Mon.-Sat., 1pm-3pm. Closed Sun. The **Museum of Modern Art** is at 51-64 Carrera 64B. Stamp collectors will be interested in the **Museo Philatelico**, in the Banco de la Republica building. It has a large collection of Colombian stamps, as well as stamps from other countries.

The beautifully tended **Joaquin Antonio Uribe Botanical Gardens**, near the new campus of Antioquia University, are well worth a visit. The gardens, which are open daily between 9am-5.30pm, have a rich collection of flora. South of the city, the **Santa Fe Zoo** has a collection of South American animals and birds.

Shopping

Most of Medellin's business and commercial life is concentrated downtown. Several roads have been closed to traffic and converted into shopping malls, with shops and boutiques selling various goods of very high quality and price. The town also has several modern shopping centers; the largest is the Almacentro.

Locally produced textile and leather goods are especially inexpensive. Silver products are less costly here than in the rest of Colombia.

The Medellin area

Santa Fe de Antioquia, north-east of Medellin, was founded in 1541 by Spanish gold miners. Until 1826, when Medellin assumed this coveted position, it was the capital of the Antioquia province. The city's colonial character and atmosphere survive together with its cobbled streets. Of special interest are the **Catedral Basilica** and the **Church of Santa Barbara**. The **City Hall** building (*Palacio Municipal*) was the seat of the colonial government during Spanish rule. The road to Santa Fe crosses the Rio Cauca over a wide bridge that is 350 m long.

The trip from Medellin to Santa Fe takes about 2 1/2 hours. The town has two hotels.

There are several places worth visiting east of Medellin. The area is pastoral and picturesque, dotted with villages and hamlets that still preserve their ancient lifestyle. The road from Medellin to El Retiro passes by the **Hacienda Fizebad**, an old estate whose interior has been preserved exactly as it was two hundred years ago. Its beautiful gardens feature a marvelous display of orchids.

The town of **Rionegro**, named after the river on whose banks it lies, was founded in 1663. Rionegro was the birthplace of Jose

COLOMBIA

Maria Cordoba, one of Bolivar's generals, and a hero of the War of Independence. The town has a monument to his memory, and the local bank preserves the triumphal crown bestowed on him after the Battle of Ayacucho.

The surrounding villages are famous for their ceramic and leather products. Most of the work is done by hand – sophisticated technology is almost unknown here. Two villages of special interest are **La Ceja** and **Carmen de Viboral**. The inhabitants of both villages are used to tourists, so don't expect to find any bargains. The road to La Ceja passes near the **Tequendamita Falls**. We recommend a stop at the **Parador Tequendamita** restaurant, near the falls. The little town of **Marinilla** should be visited for its cathedral, its Town Hall, its museum, and the Church of Jesus Nazareno. A little further on is **El Penol**, famous for the nearby bluff – 200 m high!

Manizales

This town, the capital of Caldas province, was founded in 1848. The area is known as the "Coffee Zone" (*La Region Cafetera*), since about 30% of Colombia's coffee crop is grown here. Manizales was twice the victim of huge fires. Today its multistorey buildings are constructed of modern, fireproof materials. Textile and leather industries provide employment for Manizales 400,000 inhabitants.

The city lies 2153 m above sea level, and has a very humid climate. The average temperature is 17 degrees Centigrade or 63 degrees Fahrenheit. Rainfall is plentiful. The most pleasant season begins in mid-December and continues until March. January is the month of the traditional coffee carnival, with its parades, folk dancing, and bullfights.

How to get there

The local airline Aces provides good service from Manizales' small airport to Bogota, Medellin, and other major cities. An alternative is to fly Avianca to Pereira in the Cauca valley, and then travel the remaining 50 km along an excellent road that passes by breathtaking scenery. Good bus service links the town to Bogota (a 9-hour trip), Cali, Medellin and Pereira. Local roads are good, and the scenery spectacular.

Tourist sites

The most famous building in the city is the modern **Teatro de los Fundadores**, which supposedly has the largest stage in all of Latin America. There is also a large Gothic style cathedral. The **Museum of Gold,** located in the Banco de la Republica, has a display of locally discovered gold artifacts. The **Museum of Anthropology** has an interesting collection of pre-Columbian

COLOMBIA

finds, discovered near Mt. El Ruiz (*Nevado El Ruiz*) The museum offers a fantastic view of the mountain.

The El Ruiz volcano erupted in November 1985, causing heavy casualties. The immediate effect of the explosion caused the snow to melt on the volcano's peak, resulting in floods which carried away entire villages with their inhabitants. The town of Armero was particularly hard-hit. About 25,000 people lost their lives in the disaster. Massive international assistance was required to help save and rehabilitate thousands of victims.

Southwest Colombia

Southwest Colombia is an enchanting area, one that combines the natural beauty of fertile mountain ranges with varied and interesting man-made attractions. The Andes divide here into three sections, and the scenery keeps changing as you travel east: from the temperate plains of the Pacific coast, across high, verdant mountains with snow capped peaks and volcanos, to the hot and humid tropical jungle in the east.

The terrain makes many areas isolated and difficult to reach. This inaccessibility is exploited by guerrilla fighters, as well as coca growers and cocaine smugglers. Consequently, the army is deployed in greater numbers here – especially in the towns and along roads – than anywhere else in Colombia. Roadblocks and thorough searches are extremely common. Be patient during such searches, and obey the soldiers' instructions.

This chapter surveys various places along the Cauca Valley, occasionally branching off the west-east axis to outlying areas. Most travelers, in fact, use this axis as their baseline. The area is full of beautiful landscapes and places of interest.

Cali

Belalcazar, one of Francisco Pizarro's officers, founded Cali in 1537, in the Cauca Valley. During its first years, Cali experienced numerous Indian attacks, prompting the eventual removal of the entire town to its present location. It was only at the beginning of this century that Cali changed from a small provincial town into an important and modern one – the agricultural, industrial, and cultural center of the Cauca Valley. This revolution, once begun, continued at an amazing pace. Today Cali is Colombia's third largest city, with some 1,800,000 inhabitants.

The city enjoys a pleasant climate: eternal summer, with rainfall year round. The inhabitants are very friendly; the beauty of Cali women (*Las Calenas*) is legendary. This combination of human

COLOMBIA

SOUTHWEST COLOMBIA

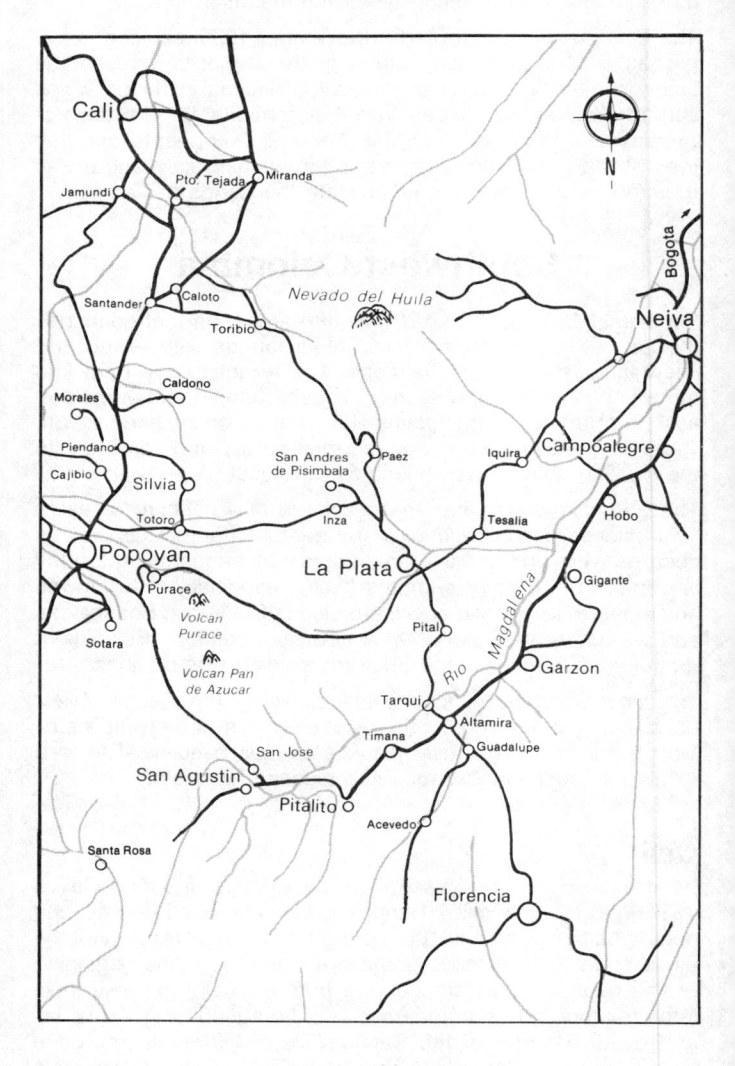

COLOMBIA

and climatic factors makes Cali a pleasant place to visit, although it lacks places of particular interest.

Note that violence is rampant in the poorer neighborhoods. Each morning the inhabitants of Cali count the previous night's victims. So avoid outlying areas, and stick to the center of town. **The Tourist Office**, 3N-28 Calle 12N, provides information on dangerous areas.

Transportation

There are a number of flights each day from Bogota and other large Colombian cities to the international airport of Palaseco, near Cali. The Avianca offices in Cali are situated at 13-52 Carrera 7. The Satena airline office is on the same street, at 8-20.

Cali's modern and spacious bus terminal is situated near the center of town. Frequent bus service links the city with Bogota (a 10-hour trip). The Expreso Bolivariano company is recommended. It also runs buses to the south – to Popayan and Pasto (10 hours). Other companies run buses on these routes daily. The Empresa Arauca company runs buses to Medellin. All these roads are good, paved roads, and the buses are fairly modern and comfortable.

Food and lodging

The best hotel is the *Interncontinental-Cali*, at 2-72 Av. Colombia, near the center of town (Tel. 823-225). A less expensive hotel with an excellent location – in the heart of Cali's shopping and entertainment district – is the *Don Jaime* at 15N-25 Av. 6 Norte (Tel. 825-521).

The famous Avenida 6 has a number of restaurants, most of them both good and expensive, although it is possible to find some cheaper ones. For a good meal with a beautiful view, try **La Torre de Cali** on Calle 18N. The restaurant, which features international cuisine, is located on the 41st floor of the tower. Expensive.

Nightlife

Unlike other Colombian towns, which are generally closed as soon as the working day is over, Cali has a flourishing nightlife. In Avenida Sexta (Sixth Avenue) there is activity all night long. There are two modern comfortable cinemas, an abundance of restaurants, coffee shops and bars. In the streets near this avenue you will find exclusive restaurants and nightclubs. The nightclubs in Cali are called *griles*.

The Juanchito quarter is another center for nightlife. Here there are many discotheques, which are packed over the weekends, playing popular *Salsa* music as well as Western music.

COLOMBIA

Tourist sites
The **Plaza de Caycedo**, a green square with numerous palm trees, lies in the heart of the business district. On its western side stands the Banco de la Republica, the first modern building erected in Cali.

Two blocks away is the Rio Cali, bordered by the tree-lined Avenida Colombia. Beware of thieves in the area! On that street, at No. 5 East-105, is the **Museum of Modern Art**, which has seasonal exhibits. The municipal cinematheque is next to it.

Also worth visiting is the **Archeological Museum**, whose modest collection of ceramics offers a chronological survey of pre-Columbian civilizations. The museum is situated on Carrera 5, between Calles 8 and 9. Open Tues.-Sat., 9am-12:30pm and 2-6pm. Closed Sundays and Mondays. Nearby is the Museum of Religious Art, **La Merced**.

Not far from Plaza de Caycedo, near the river, stands the ornate Gothic church, **La Hermita.** Looking east from this church, you will see a 43-story skyscraper, the **La Torre de Cali** (Cali Tower). There is an observation deck on the top of this building, which is the tallest building in town.

The town's modern shopping and entertainment district runs along the **Avenida Sexta,** on the other side of the Rio Cali. The avenue has numerous boutiques and luxury shops, cafes, restaurants, and two movie houses. Mingle with the pedestrians during evening hours, or sit in one of the many cafes and feast your eyes on the town's beautiful women.

Buenaventura
This town lies some 130 km west of Cali. It is Colombia's most important Pacific port, with a hot and humid climate. It has no particular attractions, apart from a number of attractive beaches. (Be on the look out for thieves!). This is a duty-free zone.

Popayan

This town predates the arrival of the Spanish conquerors, and owes its name to a local Indian ruler. The Spanish town was founded by Belalcazar in 1537. Over the years the town grew and prospered, largely due to its role as a link between the northern and southern parts of the "New World". It also became a center for the gold, silver, and other metals that were mined in the area. Although an important cultural center today, Popayan preserves its pleasant and modest character.

In March 1983, a considerable portion of the town was destroyed by an earthquake. The town's 200,000 residents embarked on a

COLOMBIA

campaign to restore and renovate many of the ancient buildings that had been damaged. Thanks to widespread international assistance, new attractive residential neighborhoods were built around the town to accommodate the many citizens left homeless by the earthquake.

Each year, the city holds celebrations during Holy Week (*Semana Santa*) before Easter. This festival, a 400 year old tradition, includes the festival of religious music, which fills Popayan's churches with enthusiastic audiences.

Transportation

A new and spacious bus terminal has been erected within walking distance of downtown. Buses leave for Cali every 20 minutes; the trip takes 2 hours. There is also regular bus service to Pasto, about 8 hours' ride away. The small airport, near the bus terminal, serves scheduled flights from Bogota, Cali and Pasto.

There is a daily bus to San Agustin from the bus terminal. This trip, which passes Parque Purace and the village of La Plata, takes about 11 hours. Jeeps for La Plata leave from the avenue near the terminal. These take a difficult, tortuous route, but the journey takes only 5 hours. Both routes cross the *Cordillera Central*, so take warm clothes.

Tourist services

The municipal **Tourist Office** at 3-69 Carrera 6, provides good service, up-to-date information, and collect dialing service.

There is a telephone office of Telecom at the corner of Calle 4 and Carrera 4. Putting through an international call involves a lengthy wait.

Food and lodging

Hotel Monasterio, 10-50 Calle 4, was formerly a monastery – whence the name. Today it is a good hotel with a swimming pool. *Residencias Camino Real*, at 5-59 Calle 5, is another good hotel, with a fine restaurant. A recommended budget hotel is the *Viajero*, which has clean rooms and a friendly atmosphere.

A good but fairly expensive restaurant is the *Herreria*, at 5-88 Calle 2. Fish-lovers should definitely try the *Fantasia Marina*, at the corner of Carrera 8 and Calle 6. Another restaurant which is good for both stomach and wallet is *El Faisan*, on Calle 4.

Tourist sites

Although Popayan is a bustling center for the Cauca Valley, one would never know it from its slow, peaceful atmosphere. The locals are friendly, and the narrow downtown streets are not

COLOMBIA

jammed with traffic. The pleasant weather throughout the year, with an average temperature of 18 degrees Centigrade or 64 degrees Fahrenheit, contributes significantly to this ambience.

Downtown, around the central plaza, you can still see the ravages caused by the earthquake. Not all the damage has been repaired, and most of the ancient buildings are still surrounded by scaffolding. The modern Banco de la Republica stands out from most other buildings in the area, which were built in the colonial style. At the beginning of Calle 6, near the central bank, is Rio Molino, spanned by a bridge that dates back to 1868. The bridge, known as *Puente del Humilladero*, is built on eleven stone arches, and is about 250 m long.

Silvia

For centuries, the Cordillera Central was the home of various Indian tribes. The only tribe to preserve its traditions is the *Guambianos*. They are dispersed among several villages in the mountains northeast of Popayan.

The friendly *Guambianos* are peaceful farmers who live in a communal society based on cooperation in work and production. They preserve their language and dress: the men wear long blue skirts, and the women wrap themselves in a sari-like dress of the same material. The women wear an impressive amount of jewelry around their necks, like the Indians of northern Ecuador. Both sexes wear identical hats and have similar hairstyles, except that the women's hair is slightly longer.

On Tuesdays, the *Guambianos* gather in their main village, Silvia, situated in the valley, between the green mountains. They travel in vans laden to bursting point, in order to sell their produce – mainly potatoes of various kinds. Their handicrafts are quite similar to those of the Otavals of Ecuador. At their colorful market you can see the *Guambianos* in their traditional costume. Eavesdrop on their conversation and catch snatches of their ancient Guambiano tongue. The market opens at dawn, and closes at 1pm.

Behind the vegetable and handicrafts market is the smaller livestock market. This market is run by the men, whereas at the other market women are in charge. You can see them discussing at length the value of a cow or pig.

Those with strong stomachs should not miss tasting the excellent *empanadas*. After enjoying the market, its smells and colours, take a short walk in the town and its outskirts.

The village outskirts make a pleasant contrast to the sights, sounds, and smells of the market. The road to the village of Guambia meanders through captivating scenery. After a short distance you will come across villagers working in the fields.

COLOMBIA

Try and reach Silvia as early as possible on market day. You may spend the night at one of its modest hotels, the best of which is the *Hotel de Turismo*. Those who stay the night in Popayan can take the 6am bus to Piendamo (it takes about half an hour). Plenty of jeeps travel the lovely and verdant road to Silvia, which is only another half an hour away. A direct bus from Popayan to Silvia leaves every day at noon.

To proceed to Tierradentro, take the bus which leaves Silvia for Totoro at noon on market days. Catch the Popayan-La Plata bus at Totoro (see "Tierradentro – Transportation").

Parque Purace

The road from Popayan to Tierradentro and Neiva passes through *Parque Purace*. This park stretches over the highest section of the Cordillera Central. The view is breathtaking: rivers, cliffs, large waterfalls, snow capped volcanos, and hot sulfur springs.

The 7am Popayan-La Plata bus passes through the park. Detailed information on recommended sites is available in Pilimbala, although it's better to obtain this information at the tourist office in Popayan.

To brave the snow capped peaks of the **Purace Volcano**, take the 4am Popayan-La Plata bus and get off at Pilimbala. Note the stone pools of sulfur water from the sulfur springs (closed Tuesdays). The path to the summit of the 4700 m high volcano begins here.

Another recommended spot is the **San-Juan Springs**. Here 112 hot sulfur springs combine with melted snow to form a multicolor mixture of volcanic rock and moss. A restaurant is located nearby and one can spend the night in the park ranger's hut for a small fee.

Tierradentro

Near the village of **San Andres de Pisimbala** is an important and interesting archeological park, **Tierradentro**, which means "territory within territory". This strip of land was so named by the Spanish conquerors, who met with stubborn resistance on the part of the local Indians. The name reflects the fact that the Spanish infiltration was slow and painful – for conquerors and conquered alike.

The area is a valley high within the *Cordillera Central*. The mountains are steep and green, criss-crossed by many rivers. This fertile agricultural zone is currently inhabited by Whites, mestizos and Indians – members of the *Paez* tribe. They are descendants of the Indians who lived here before the Spaniards

COLOMBIA

arrived. The 25,000 Paez make their living from agriculture, in particular corn and vegetable crops. They have retained their ancient language and original social structure, headed by a ruling council, which is elected annually. This council is responsible for the functioning of an organized hierarchical body that governs cooperative labor. On Wednesday mornings, many Paez congregate in San Andres to participate in the colorful market.

The archeological findings discovered here testify to the existence of a number of civilizations, each with its own economic and cultural development, although very little is known about them. Clay and gold handicrafts were fairly advanced, but most remains had been plundered by the beginning of the Spanish conquest. The few relics that remain are exhibited in the small local museum, and in the Museum of Gold in Bogota.

The most interesting of the local relics are the subterranean burial shrines, hewn out of soft rock by means of a hard flint. Spiral stairs lead down into the burial caves, whose roofs are supported by pillars. The dead were cremated; the burial chambers have niches where the urns containing the ashes of the dead were placed. The walls, roof, and pillars are decorated with various shapes, the most common motif being the rhombus, colored red and black against a white background. About one hundred burial caves of various sizes have been discovered in the area. Their depth varies from 3 to 9 m below ground level. Researchers do not know who built these caves, but there is no doubt that they were members of a developed and wealthy civilization, since considerable planning and manpower must have been required for such work.

Transportation

A number of buses leave Popayan daily on their way to La Plata, via Inza. The trip takes about 6 hours. Get off at the San Andres junction, then walk about 2 km to the park administrative offices, and another half hour to the village itself. After visiting San Andres, get back on the Popayan bus and continue to La Plata. From La Plata there are buses to San Agustin and Neiva.

Food and lodging

Simple and inexpensive *pensions* can be found along the road leading from the park's administrative offices to the village of San Andres. Of these, the best is *El Bosque*, a clean, good *pension*, with friendly owners. There are no really good hotels or restaurants in the area. Some of the houses near the administrative office serve as restaurants. The nearby *Nelli Parra de Jovar* is recomended, but meals have to be ordered in advance.

COLOMBIA

The archeological park
The park at Tierradentro has several sites worth visiting, most within a short walk from the adminsitrative offices. The small museum, housed in the administrative office itself, exhibits some locally discovered pottery. Most of the archeological treasures were plundered long before the arrival of archeologists. Furthermore, many local finds are displayed in museums in Bogota.

The most important area of the park is known as **Segovia**. Fifteen burial caves of various sizes were discovered here. The decorations on some of them survive. The area is about a 15 minute walk from the museum. At **El Duende** (a 10 minute walk from Segovia) four more burial caves were discovered. On the way to El Duende you will pass the houses of the Paez Indians.

The next place to visit is **El Aguacate**, about an hour and a half's walk from the museum. Here the whole of Tierradentro spreads out around you. The place also has a number of ornate burial caves.

El Tablon, near the museum, has eight statues with features similar to those of the San Agustin statues. This indicates that there was some connection between these different cultures.

For those wishing to tour the park and its environs on horseback, horses can be rented at San Andres.

One of the more famous sites in Colombia is the village of San Agustin, with its archeological treasures. Here you can see remnants of an ancient culture which has long since vanished, the art and sculpture are of rare quality. In order to appreciate these puzzling relics and the people who produced them, we have included a short introduction, which briefly describes the story of the Agustin culture.

The San Agustin Civilization

For more than two hundred years scholars have been trying to shed some light on one of the most interesting Andean civilizations, the San Agustin, so-called because of the proximity of its remains to the town of that name. This civilization, which flourished for 1500 years, still remains largely a mystery.

A Spanish priest visiting the area in 1758 was the first to report the existence of ancient relics in the area. The site began to attract researchers, but only in 1913 was the first comprehensive scientific study undertaken, by the German archeologist Theodor Preuss. Further investigations have since been carried out by various official expeditions, and excavations

COLOMBIA

continued intensively until the 1970s. About 500 statues were unearthed, as well as many graves and some gold and pottery. The most ancient statue discovered dates back to the 6th century BC.

From their various findings, the researchers concluded that the San Agustin civilization reached its peak between the 2nd and 8th centuries AD, a period they termed its "classical period". Nevertheless, the place was clearly inhabited centuries before this period, and settlement continued to exist until approximately the 10th century.

The origins of the San Agustin people are not clear, but they apparently came here from the jungles of southern Colombia. This deduction is based on the fact that Indian tribes living there still celebrate spiritual rites using masks (made out of tree bark), which are identical to the faces of the San Agustin statues.

The San Agustin economy was based mainly on agriculture. They cultivated corn, peanuts, and yucca, and gathered wild fruits and vegetables. They were also hunters, and to a lesser extent, fishermen (since the strong current of the rivers prevented large scale fishing). Stoneworking was fairly developed, as one can see from their many stone tools, the most significant of which were those used for quarrying. The San Agustins were familiar with metalworking processes even before the Christian era. Their widespread use of gold-copper alloys testifies to the influence of central American cultures. This is also evident in the various motifs prominent in the sculptures. Little is known about the structure of Agustin houses, since significant remains of buildings have not been found. Nevertheless, various traces indicate that their houses were round, with bamboo walls and straw roofs.

The family was the basic social unit of the Agustins. The various family groups were connected by economic and religious ties. From the end of the 5th century AD, the growing power and influence of the tribal leaders on the social stucture becomes apparent. The dead were buried in chambers covered by a large stone slab. Sometimes a statue would be erected at the entrance to the chamber, its size varied according with the importance of the deceased. It was customary to place the deceased's personal effects next to him, including jewelry, and clay, metal, and stone implements that he used in his lifetime. Religious rites were held near water sources, and many of the Agustin divinities were water or rain gods.

No one really knows why the San Agustin culture vanished. One theory suggests that the area was attacked by other Indian tribes – possibly even the Tierradentro Indians. Just as little is known of the life of this civilization as of the reasons for its

COLOMBIA

Monolithic masterpieces of the Agustin culture

disappearance hundreds of years before the arrival of the Spanish conquerors. The Agustins left behind only graves, daily work tools, and a wealth of statues. All the rest has disappeared.

Agustin sculpture

The quantity and quality of the sculptures discovered, testify to the high social status of the Agustin sculptor. It is clear that the sculptor was allowed to devote most of his time and energy to his craft.

Stylistically, the statues can be divided into various levels of sophistication. While some are rough and simple, others are so intricate and detailed that it becomes possible to discern individual features. The Central American influence can be seen in the various motifs, such as large facial features. In most cases, only the front is carved, while the back of the statue is smooth stone. Very few sculptures depart from this rule.

Religious significance was attached to the figures. The eagle, for example, was a symbol of power and light, and the serpent symbolized the god of rain. Feline figures, such as the jaguar, symbolized the dark underworld. Monkey figures were used in fertility rites. Frogs, lizards, and salamanders were used in water ceremonies. Some of the statues consist of two overlaid human figures. The lower figure represents man's ego, and the top figure his spirit.

By studying the statues, something of the Agustine culture and life can be learned: the male figures generally hold tools or skulls

COLOMBIA

in their hands, while the female statues hold their children. The heads are out of proportion to the rest of the body. Paint residues have been discovered on some of the statues. Most of the statues served as gravemarkers.

The quality of Agustin sculpture indicates an advanced and developed civilization, to which researchers attribute considerable influence over other Andean cultures.

San Agustin

The town lies in southern Huila province, an area of rolling green hills. Rio Magdalena, Colombia's largest river, has its source in this area, and flows through a deep canyon near the village. San Agustin has some 18,000 inhabitants. The weather is very pleasant all year round, with an average temperature of 18 degrees Centigrade or 64 degrees Fahrenheit. From November to February, the weather is particularly temperate, but this is also the height of the tourist season. Since San Agustin is one of Colombia's most important tourist attractions, many local residents depend on the tourist industry for a livelihood. There is a fairly large number of restaurants and hotels, and people are generally friendly. Nevertheless, the many tourists attract thieves and pickpockets to the area: guard your possessions well!

Transportation

The Pitalito airport, about half an hour's journey from San Agustin, is served by Satena and Aeres flights. Beware of thieves in Pitalito. This is one of the most dangerous places in a dangerous country!

The town of Neiva is about 5 hours away. Aeropesca and Satena airlines fly there.

The daily bus from Bogota to San Agustin passes through Neiva. The trip, on a fairly good road, takes 11 hours.

From Popayan there are two ways to reach San Agustin. The bus leaves Popayan bus terminal every morning and travels via La Plata; the trip takes about 11 hours. One may also travel by jeep-taxi, direct to San Agustin. This route is difficult and tiring, but takes only about 5 hours. There are no fixed departure times for the jeeps – they simply leave when they are full. The jeep fare is only slightly higher than the bus fare. Both routes are beautiful and cross the Cordillera Central. High up it gets extremely cold.

Food and lodging

San Agustin has a large number of hotels and pensions, but no luxury hotels. The best hotel is the *Yalconia*, which is perfectly

COLOMBIA

adequate and has a swimming pool. It lies outside the town, about 2 km from the archeological park. Another adequate hotel is the *Motel Osoguaico*, which also has a swimming pool. This hotel is slightly farther from downtown and nearer the park. Make advance reservations for these hotels.

Low-budget hotels abound. Always bargain about the prices since the number of *pensions* greatly exceeds demand. This category includes the *Residencias Colonial* on the main street, adjoining the plaza. This establishment is highly recommended: located in a renovated colonial building, it is clean and comfortable. The *Residencias Luis Tello*, at 15-33 Calle 4A, is also recommended. The owners of this private house, who let a number of rooms to tourists, are extremely friendly and pleasant. **Camping** is possible in San Agustin, but for obvious security reasons, it is inadvisable!

As for restaurants, do not expect an outstanding gastronomical experience here. The local diet is based on vegetables, eggs, meat, and, of course, rice. The better restaurants are situated in the two good hotels mentioned above, the Yalconia and the Osoguaico. The *Brahma*, offering low cost vegetarian fare, is located near the tourist office. Another fair restaurant that provides a satisfying meal (*comida*) is in *Hotel Colonial*.

Tourist services
The **Tourist Office**, at 14-45 Calle 5A, provides excellent service. Open Tues.-Sat., 8:30am-12:30pm and 2:30-6:30pm; in tourist season only, also Sun. 8am-noon and 2-6pm. The personnel are friendly and helpful, speak English, and are eager to help in whatever way they can. Excellent regional maps, and up to date lists of hotels and restaurants are available.

Attractions in the San Agustin area, such as the archeological park, are best toured on foot. Places further out can be reached by rented jeep or on horseback. Jeeps can take up to eight passengers. The rentals are fixed, and depend on where you want to go. The price list can be obtained at the tourist office. If you want a guide for the park, the tourist office can provide one who will be happy to offer you a comprehensive survey of the archeological sites.

Tourist sites
The Archeological park
The most important of the many tourist sites around San Agustin is the archeological park, where most of the Agustin graves and statues are found, is about 3 km from town. Open daily 8am-6pm. A thorough visit takes about three hours.

The administrative offices at the entrance to the park house a small museum with an exhibit of local archeological findings.

COLOMBIA

Most of the pottery and gold artifacts found in the area are on display at the National Museum and in the Museum of Gold, both in Bogota. The admission fee for the museum includes entrance to the park.

The archeological finds are grouped in *mesitas*, or "tables". These are mounds that the Agustins raised over the graves of the most eminent members of the community. There are four *mesitas* in the park; one of them houses the museum at the entrance. On these mounds are the sarcophagi and statues that served as gravemarkers.

The largest tomb of all is in *Mesita B*, which also has two other tombs and a sarcophagus. *Mesita C* has two statues with carved backs – a rare phenomenon among the statues in the park. A little beyond Mesita C is the large rocky area known as *Fuente de Lavapatas*. Here many figures of monkeys, salamanders, lizards, and human figures were carved into the rockface. The figures are surrounded by tiny channels and many small pools. The water that used to flow through these channels created a picture of total harmony. Today, in order to preserve the rockface, the channels are kept dry. Just the same, these splendid remains – once the Agustins' most important local shrine – are still extremely impressive.

Further up the hill is the area known as **Alto de Lavapatas**. A number of large statues stand at the top of the hill, enjoying, as it were, the fantastic view. It encompasses two mountain ranges (the central and the eastern), the entire archeological park, and the valley in which San Agustin nestles.

After leaving the park, visit the **Bosque de las Estatuas** (Forest of Statues), a beautiful area set in an enchanting natural forest. Along the path that winds through the thick vegetation, 35 statues – transported here from their original setting – have been erected. They represent the various motifs of the San Agustin statues.

Alto de los Idolos

The second most important place in San Agustin is known as the *Alto de los Idolos* (the Heights of the Idols). There are three ways of getting there: by jeep, approximately an hour's journey along a terrible road; two and a half hours on horseback along a beautiful route that crosses the Magdalena canyon; or a half day hike which includes a visit to the site. The *colectivo* from Pitalito to San Jose de Isnos picks up passengers at the San Agustin junction (San Jose has an interesting market on Saturdays). Alto de los Idolos is about a two hour walk from San Jose. Return to San Agustin by continuing along the same route – a three hour hike leads through a landscape of green mountains and waterfalls plunging into the Magdalena canyon.

COLOMBIA

Alto de los Idolos was discovered and studied only in the 1970s. Many tombs, sarcophagi and statues were found here, as well as San Agustin's largest statue, about 7 m high and only partially uncovered. The structure of the burial chambers here is clear – statues guard the entrance to the tombs. Open daily 8am-6pm.

Those traveling by rented jeep can stop en route at **Salto del Mortino** – a large waterfall on the Mortino River. Also worth visiting is **Alto de las Piedras**, which has a number of statues, and **Salto de los Borbones**, Colombia's highest and most impressive waterfall.

El Estrecho

El Estrecho is an impressive, natural narrow channel 2.2 m wide, through which the waters of the Rio Magdalena flow. The best way to reach the area is on horseback, which takes about two hours. On the way, one can turn on to the path leading to **El Tablon**, with its five statues of moon gods. Also worth visiting is **La Chaquira**, where more statues crown the bluff that rises from the Magdalena canyon.

Pasto

The capital of Narino province bordering Ecuador, Pasto lies 2534 m above sea level.

The city was one of the first Spanish settlements in Colombia, but it has long since lost its colonial character. During the War of Independence, Pasto served as a stronghold for supporters of the Spanish crown, and was the last town to fall to the patriots. The inhabitants of Narino province wanted to become part of Ecuador when it seceded in 1830 from the confederation of "Greater Colombia", but their wish was thwarted by Colombian troops in a bloody struggle.

Today Pasto is the center of the area's agricultural industry. With a population of about 350,000, it is the last major city before Ecuador.

West of Pasto, the Galeras Volcano towers to a height of 4276 m above sea level. It last erupted in the 1950s. Make the ascent by car (app. 30 minutes) for a fantastic view of the city and its environs.

In the town itself, visit the **Church of San Juan**, on Calle 18 between Carreras 25 and 26. The inside of the church is richly decorated. Although rebuilt in 1969, the colonial building, one of the oldest in the town, has been repeatedly damaged in earthquakes.

A two day carnival is held here at the beginning of January. The first day (January 5) is known as the *Dia de los Negros* (black

COLOMBIA

Las Lajas - one of Colombia's most famous churches

day), for then the celebrants paint each other's faces with black grease. The next day is the *Dia de los Blancos* (white day), when the revelers throw flour at each other. Sometimes the merriment gets out of hand and takes a violent turn.

Even here, beware of the local thieves!

On to Ecuador

The usual crossing to Ecuador is near the border town of Ipiales, about two hours south of Pasto. But there are two other alternative routes; both are jungle trails, difficult and off the beaten track. The first is via the road that turns southeast from Pasto, to the lower reaches of the Amazon basin and Putumayo province; the second runs west of Tumaco, on the Pacific coast. Both routes are described below.

Via Ipiales

The road from Pasto to Ipiales (pop. 30,000) is paved and comfortable; and the trip through beautiful scenery takes about two hours. A colorful market is held in Ipiales on Saturdays. Change dollars and travelers' checks into pesos and sucres (Ecuadoran currency) in the modern Banco de la Republica. In the same building is a small branch of the Museum of Gold, with a modest collection of gold artifacts and archeological finds from Narino province.

Be sure to visit the famous **Santuario de las Lajas**, an ornate Gothic church atop a bridge spanning the canyon. On Sundays, the church is visited by Quechuan Indians from Ecuador, who

COLOMBIA

believe the canyon waters have special properties. Las Lajas is about a ten minute ride from Ipiales. Taxis to Las Lajas leave Ipiales frequently from the station near the main square.

Many inexpensive hotels are situated near the central plaza of Ipiales. Of these, we recommend the *New York*. There are no first-class hotels; the closest approximation is the *Alcala*, also near the central plaza.

The Ecuadoran border, only a few kilometers from Ipiales, runs along the canyon of the Rio Carchi. A natural bridge links the two sides of the border. Taxis, which reach the border in a few minutes, set out frequently from the market in Ipiales. The crossing is open daily 8am-6pm, though it may be closed during *siesta*. Have your passport stamped at the DAS office in Colombia, and at the Ecuadoran border police office. You may have to prove to the Ecuadoran immigration officials that you have sufficient means to finance your stay. A tourist visa is valid for 30 days. Vehicles must be fumigated against diseases affecting coffee trees. This is done at the border itself.

Via Putumayo province

Trans Ipiales runs several buses a day from Pasto to the town of **Puerto Asis**, in Putumayo province, on the edges of the tropical Amazon jungle. The trip takes about 11 hours. The road first passes through green, pastoral scenery, near *Laguna Cocha*. It then climbs a steep mountain range, and crosses it to the east. The eastern slopes of this range are covered with exotic mountainous jungle. The narrow, tortuous road winds through thick vegetation, and crosses many rivers and waterfalls, and terrifying abysses, before descending to the extremely hot and humid jungle plains.

Cargo boats sail down the Rio Putumayo from Puerto Asis on their way to Puerto Leguizamo (two days' journey) and Leticia (a week). The cruise begins on a fairly narrow channel of the river, which winds through beautiful thick jungle vegetation. Although this is jungle territory, do not expect to encounter a wide variety of wildlife en route.

Although the Ecuadoran border is not far from Puerto Asis, it is a 5 hour journey. Local transportation is typically a truck that has been converted to carry passengers, packed to bursting point with people and goods. The Colombian border village is called San Miguel. From there, travel by canoe down the Rio San Miguel, half an hour from the Ecuadoran border, from which a vehicle leaves every hour for the town of **Lago Agrio**. This can be a convenient starting point for a jungle safari of several days through the eastern part of Ecuador (see "El Oriente – Ecuador").

COLOMBIA

Remember to have your passport stamped before leaving Colombia at the DAS office in Puerto Asis! Entry stamps for Ecuador are arranged at the police station in Lago Agrio.

Warning
Putumayo province is full of coca plantations; in fact, it is the starting point of the cocaine smuggling route to the West. The residents of Puerto Asis are active in the drug trade, making this a particularly violent area! Frequent and thorough checks are carried out by the army and police. Think carefully before undertaking this route. Consider, too, that the area is infested with malaria; take the appropriate medication.

Via Tumaco
About 250 km west of Pasto lies the city of Tumaco. The road to Tumaco is unpaved and extremely difficult to negotiate; the trip takes about 12 hours. Part of the road runs along the trans-Andean oil pipeline, which starts in Putumayo. Cattle ranches and rice and cocoa plantations are frequent sights along the road. Most of the people here are black, and they live in two-storey wood houses. The remains of the pre-Columbian civilization which lent the province its name have been discovered in the Tumaco area.

Tumaco (pop. 100,000 inhabitants) is rife with unemployment and poverty. It's nonetheless an interesting place to visit. Houses are built on piles over the water. A nocturnal visit is bound to be dangerous and is not advised! Neither should one drink water which is polluted. The coastal area is marshy, with lots of mangroves. Many streams cross the marshes, and it is worth renting a boat at Tumaco to cruise through the area.

Ecuador is reached by water only – partly along beautiful streams, and partly by sea, which is usually fairly stormy. A canoe leaves Tumaco each day for *San Lorenzo*, Ecuador. Passports are stamped on the Colombian side at the DAS offices in Pasto or Cali. The Ecuadoran entry visa is affixed in the Ecuadoran coastal town (see "San Lorenzo – Ecuador").

The Amazon Jungle

Though most of the mighty Amazon basin is in Brazil, it also extends into the neighboring Andean countries, including Colombia. All of southeast Colombia is one vast green plain, of which little has been explored by white men. The primeval nature of this zone has therefore been preserved, and both the thick tropical vegetation and wildlife continue to exist here undisturbed. The climate is of course tropical, and extremely hot. Annual rainfall is about 4000 mm (4 m!) . The area is almost

COLOMBIA

Rio Putumayo - life in the heart of the jungle

entirely unpopulated, and the handful of isolated houses are scattered along the rivers. There are no overland roads, and the only means of transport are boat, ship or plane. The two tributaries that carry most of the river traffic are the Putumayo and the Caqueta. Most of the local population are Indians or *mestizos*.

The best starting point for a jungle safari is **Leticia**, the southernmost point in Colombia. There are organized tourist services here, and one should have no trouble finding a travel agent or local guide. After a short boat ride, the local guides will lead you into the heart of the fascinating tropical jungle.

Much less touristy is the area around **Mitu**, a village on the banks of the Rio Vaupes near the Brazilian border. It is a good base for visiting interesting Indian villages, which are a subject of anthropological research.

The options for interesting treks through the unexplored jungle are almost infinite. All one needs is an adventurous spirit, and plenty of time and patience. There is no regular transport, since the local population lives at a very leisurely pace.

Special instructions

Leticia has a good exchange rate for dollars; buy enough local currency here for the entire jungle trip. Elsewhere in the jungle, the dollar rate is extremely low, if foreign currency is accepted at all.

COLOMBIA

Bring anti-malaria pills, and purify drinking water with chlorine tablets. Important, too, are mosquito repellents and mosquito netting. When setting off down the river, remember to include enough food and fuel, and, of course, a first aid kit.

Leticia

Leticia was founded in 1867 by the Peruvian Captain Bustamante. It is situated 3200 km from the mouth of the Amazon River, at the border point shared by Colombia, Brazil, and Peru. An agreement among the three countries in 1922 awarded a narrow strip of jungle to Colombia. Leticia lies at the southern tip of this strip, on the northern bank of the Amazon.

The 20,000 inhabitants are of mixed Indian, Asian, and European descent; their language is a blend of Spanish and Portuguese. The old wooden houses are increasingly giving way to modern buildings, and the town is expanding and developing all the time. The harbor, on the main trade route with neighboring Brazil and Peru, teems with life.

Leticia is the starting point for many tourists who take the lengthy cruise down the Amazon River. The cruise ends in Brazil, at Manaus or Belem, where the Amazon empties into the Atlantic Ocean. But Leticia is also a tourist attraction in its own right. Many tourists prefer to take short and relatively uncomplicated trips into the country around the city. These can provide a good idea of the nature of the jungle, and a glimpse of the secrets of the fascinating Amazon world.

When to visit

It's always hot in Leticia, with an average temperature of 30 degrees Centigrade or 86 degrees Fahrenheit. Getting around is hard during the rainy season (December-March) and when the rivers rise several meters (May-June). The best time for a visit is during the dry season – from July to November.

Transportation (to Colombia and other countries)

By air: Avianca has five flights a week to Bogota and Satena has only one. Aeropesca has three or four cargo flights a week, and Aerotal only two. Try to get on to these flights by speaking to the pilot at the airport.

The Brazilian airline Cruzeiro has three weekly return flights along the route Manaus-Tabatinga-Iquitos (in Peru). (Tabatinga is Leticia's Brazilian neighbor). One of these flights continues from Iquitos to Pucallpa.

By boat: Puerto Asis is the furthest departure point upstream for boats to Leticia. The trip takes about a week. Boats leave Puerto Asis fairly infrequently, but one can sail to Puerto Leguizamo, where boats sail more frequently to Leticia.

COLOMBIA

There are only a few boats from Leticia to Manaus (Brazil), but boat service from adjacent Tabatinga is more frequent. The trip takes about five days. Private cabins are available on the boat, but this is quite expensive. First class (upper deck) is easier on the budget. Second class is not recommended, since it is in the cargo hold below deck. The price of the cruise includes meals. It is advisable to bring your own food (at least fruit) since meals are awful. Buy provisions in Leticia, which has a larger selection than Tabatinga.

Boats leave Ramon Castilla, on the Peruvian side of the river, for Iquitos and Pucallpa. These boats have no fixed timetables. At each border point, remember to request an exit and entry stamp in your passport. The Brazilian immigration office is located at Tabatinga, the Peruvian one in Ramon Castilla, and the Colombian one in Leticia.

Food and lodging

Generally speaking, a stay in the jungle towns is far more expensive than one in the center of the country, because most goods have to be freighted in.

The *Parador Ticuna*, 6-03 Av. Libertador, is a first class hotel with a swimming pool, bar, and restaurant. The *Anaconda*, popular and fairly expensive, has air conditioned rooms, a bar and a restaurant. The *Pension Leticia* is moderately priced and clean. The service is friendly, and the meals are good and affordable.

Rio Grande restaurant offers superb meat dishes. The main restaurant fare, however, is excellent fresh water fish. Inexpensive local food, such as fried bananas or yucca, is sold in the market near the port, but hygienic conditions are not the best. Good tropical fruit can also be bought here at low prices.

Tourist services

The **Tourist Office** is situated at 9-86 Calle 10. Various tourist agencies organize jungle trips. The most highly recommended of these agencies is Turamazonas, on Plaza Orellana. The agency offers a variety of tours; service is good, and the staff are reliable professionals. It is the most expensive agency, but the service justifies the price. Another good company is Amazonia Tours, near the Hotel Anaconda. Other agencies are not reliable; tourists are forced to haggle, and to make sure the necessary equipment is really available. The least costly way of touring is on one's own, hiring a local guide with a canoe.

Always make sure the guide is reliable and responsible, since anyone who is not totally familiar with the area is liable to cause a disaster.

COLOMBIA

Change money at the cambio opposite the Hotel Anaconda, where the rates are better than at the banks.

Tourist sites

Isla de los Micos (Monkey Island) is one of the most popular tourist attractions. The island is about 90 minutes out of town, upriver by canoe. It was purchased in the early 1950s by an American who established a monkey reserve there. Today, the monkey community is very large; don't be suprised if the bolder specimens welcome you ashore. Walk through the forest to the center of the island, and imbibe the jungle atmosphere. The pools hidden beneath the undergrowth are the habitat of the *victoria regia*, a gigantic water plant with a circumference of 2 m! The island has a hostel.

Another 90 minutes upstream is Taraporto, the lake district. Here, too, the gigantic water plant flourishes, as do a myriad of fish.

You may come across a few Indian villages here and there.

The Indians are used to tourists, indeed, it is somewhat sad to think that they have turned into tourist attractions.

Ticuna Indians live in the village of Arara, on the river of the same name, only a few kilometers from Leticia. The cruise to the village is extremely enjoyable and passes through dense, luxuriant jungle. The *Yaguas* live on the Rio Atucuari. They are isolated and inaccessible, which makes this trip more expensive. The *Caciques* of Peru can be visited as well.

Crossing to the Brazilian side of the border one reaches **Benjamin Constante**, where one can see rubber trees. When the bark is punctured this tree secretes a white liquid, which hardens after a few seconds, and is latter processed into rubber.

The Savanna – Los Llanos

The savanna stretches between the slopes of the Cordillera Oriental and the Orinoco jungle. Here the population is very sparse, and there are few roads. Until the Spaniash arrived in 1531, the area was inhabited by primitive Indian tribes. Over the years, they intermingled with the Spanish settlers; most of the current population of 500,000 are *mestizos*. They raise livestock on the grassy plains, and fish in the Orinoco tributaries that cross the area.

To tour the savanna, one must first get to **Villavicencio,** at the foot of the Cordillera Oriental. Frequent buses travel the lovely route from Bogota in about 3 1/2 hours. From here, the

COLOMBIA

possibilities are almost endless. Continue along a paved road to **San Martin,** or visit **Sierra de la Macarena**, a park with a huge variety of wildlife. Take a canoe trip from Puerto Lopez, or drive across the endless stretches of plains extending east and south. The best time for this is December-March, when the dirt trails are passable by jeep. Remember to bring food, water, anti-malaria pills, and plenty of spare fuel. Thus equipped, one can enter this wasteland and escape from civilization for a while.

Maps and further details about road conditions and attractions can be obtained in Bogota, at the offices of the Gobernacion del Departamento de Meta, Calle 34 at Carrera 14, or at the National Tourist Office (see "Important Addresses").

*E*CUADOR

Ecuador, among the smallest and most unspoilt of South American nations, owes its name to its geographic location – astride the equator. The country is divided into three regions: the western coastal strip, the central Andes and the jungles to the east.

Though not large in area or population, Ecuador's charm and national character lend it a special grace. The Ecuadorians' easygoing, nature, a relaxed political atmosphere and the gorgeous scenery, impart to Ecuador a splendor that captivates the hearts of multitudes. A visit to Ecuador may be nothing more than a flying tour of the capital, Quito – a quiet and pleasant city in its own right – or it can last many weeks, allowing time to really discover and get to know the people and places of this special land.

In my opinion, Ecuador is one of those countries which shouldn't be missed. Trapped between Peru to the south and Colombia to the north, Ecuador exudes an unmistakable atmosphere of calm and tranquility – so different from the tension which reigns across its borders. In Ecuador there are few thieves; robbery is truly rare.

The Ecuadorians are hearty, unprejudiced, generous and guileless. Given these national traits, a visit here is everything a tourist could wish. Those who spend their vacations here, or simply traverse the country, are bound to leave with feelings of pleasure and affection.

History

Because of its particular geographic situation – sandwiched between two huge neighbors – Ecuador has been pushed aside in the Latin American political game. Even before the Spanish came, when quiet and unassuming Indian tribes peopled its territory, Ecuador aroused little interest. The Incas from Peru bestirred themselves to conquer its central mountain region only during the fifteenth century; they did not enjoy a very long stay. The war between the two brothers Atahuallpa and Huascar, heirs to the Incan ruler Huayna Capac, weakened the empire. When Francisco Pizarro reached Peru in 1527, he had little more than a mopping-up operation to perform.

Ecuador was a bone of contention between the Spanish territories of Peru and Colombia. Eventually it fell under Peruvian control. For almost three hundred years its people enjoyed quiet

*E*CUADOR

and serenity. This period witnessed the development of agriculture in the coastal region and the consolidation of social classes, whose internal conflicts continue to be an issue to this day. With Bogota and Lima the great centers of Colonial activity, Ecuador was considered to be an insignificant backwater.

Only at the beginning of the nineteenth century, when the tide of nationalism washed over Spain's South American colonies, did significant political developments take place in Ecuador as well.

An unsuccessful revolt was mounted in 1809, while the Napoleonic Wars raged in Europe and King Ferdinand of Spain's power was wavering. But it was only thirteen years later (May 24, 1822) that General Antonio Jose de Sucre, supported by the forces of the Venezuelan Simon Bolivar, drew Ecuador out of the Spanish orbit for good.

The newly-liberated country was annexed into "Greater Colombia", the federation of Colombia, Venezuela and Ecuador that was Bolivar's dream. However, once Venezuela seceded from the forced union in 1829, Ecuador's ties unravelled as well and on August 10, 1830 Ecuadorian independence was declared

It took Ecuador another hundred years to achieve political stability. This era of domestic and external strife, some of it violent, ruined any chance of economic development.

A border dispute with Colombia (Ecuador regarded that country's southern region as a natural extension of its own north) ended in compromise only in the early years of this century, while disagreements with Peru over extensive jungle areas in eastern Ecuador have lasted to this very day, turning violent at times. The fiercest struggle, however, was the domestic one between the *Flores* of Quito and the Andes, and the *Rocafuerte* of Guayaquil and the coastal strip.

Quito has served as Ecuador's administrative hub – the seat of government bureaucracy and home of the conservative landholding aristocracy – since the Spanish conquest. Guayaquil, by contrast, developed into a cosmopolitan port city subject to the influence of well-to-do merchants with a liberal world view. The two groups clashed ideologically and fought for control of the state, with the army alternating in its allegiance between the rival blocs.

At the peak of the strife, between 1830 and 1845, Ecuador was plunged into political chaos. Only in 1861, when Garcia Moreno rose to power, did the situation change. Though a liberal, Moreno ruled dictatorially, restricting freedom of speech and assembly, exiling opponents and strengthening the status of the

ECUADOR

Catholic Church. Economic development began during his years in power: major highways were paved, the foundations of a Quito-Guayaquil railway were laid, schools and hospitals were built and steps were taken to promote agriculture and expand cultivated land.

In 1875, fifteen years after taking power, Moreno was assassinated. His death sparked renewed Liberal-Conservative strife and the period of relative calm ended. The Liberals, led by General Alfaro, seized power once again at the end of the nineteenth century. Among the legal reforms they introduced, the most important was the removal of public education from Church control. Alfaro's regime, however, was not substantially different from his predecessors: Ecuador was run by a handful of plutocrats and special-interest groups. Alfaro was deposed and jailed in 1911 and was lynched several months later by a mob in the streets of Quito.

The world economic crisis of the 1920s hit Ecuador grievously, for its cocoa exports fell as food prices rose. The economic hardship and social unrest it entailed brought a military junta to power; this regime, however, was no more successful than the previous one at relieving the distress. Between 1925 and 1948, Ecuador suffered slow economic development, political anarchy resulting in sporadic outbreaks of violence and continued social tension.

In 1941, in the midst of this period, Peru exploited Ecuador's weakness and sent its army into large sections of the uninhabited Amazon Basin in eastern Ecuador. Though a temporary arrangement – reached under United States mediation – left most of the disputed territory in Peruvian hands, Ecuador has never accepted the decision and continues to consider those regions as occupied territories which must be returned. The border areas remain tense to this day. Armed clashes between the two countries erupt from time to time, with the Government using the controversy to divert public attention from sensitive domestic problems.

Post-World War II Ecuador has enjoyed relative stability, founded on reforms instigating a constitutional government which is elected every five years. Though the army has aborted the democratic process on several occasions by seizing power, the takeovers have been short-lived and have ended with the return of power to an elected civilian president. Until 1972 the charismatic President Dr. Jose Maria Ibarra left his imprint on affairs, and despite his own involvement in recurrent scandals, contributed greatly to stabilizing the rule of law and order.

A new constitution was approved by plebiscite in 1978. Among its provisions are the guarantee of civil rights, extension of

ECUADOR

suffrage to all literate adults, expanded presidential powers and a one-term limit for presidents.

Excluding temporary aberrations, the spirit of this constitution has been preserved; today Ecuador is experiencing a political tranquility it has rarely known. The main thrust is now directed at developing agriculture and the economy, expanding the educational system and introducing moderate social reforms.

Geography and climate

Ecuador has a diverse geographic structure, with wide variations in scenery and climate. Its estimated area of 284,000 sq/km can be divided into a western coastal strip, a central mountain range and the eastern jungles. The country is bounded by the Pacific Ocean in the west, Colombia in the north and Peru to the east and south.

Since Ecuador straddles the equator, we would expect its climate to be tropical. Due to its diverse topography, however, the decisive climatic factors are elevation and terrain. Certain regions, especially the mountain strip, enjoy a temperate and pleasant climate. Ecuador's location on the equator has an interesting advantage: sovereignty over the Galapagos Islands, a unique archipelago that lies about 1000 km west of the Ecuadorian coast. Here biological time appears to have frozen, leaving behind flora and fauna which seem to have undergone no change since Creation.

Most of Ecuador's soil is volcanic; earthquakes and eruptions have always been part of the country's life. Dozens of volcanoes, some of them active, jut above and constitute a constant threat to their placid surroundings. The tallest of these is Chimborazo (6310 m), but it hasn't given cause for alarm in many years.

The coastal strip (*costa*) between the Pacific Ocean to the west and the Andes to the east (with a maximum width of 100 km) is the nation's traditional breadbasket and a number of cities have sprouted there. The most important of these, Guayaquil, serves as Ecuador's major port and the commercial and economic center of the country.

The coastal strip itself is not uniform. Its northern section, bordering Colombia, is very wet and covered with thick vegetation and forest. In the south, close to Peru, the land is arid and requires irrigation if agriculture is to be at all possible. The inhabitants of the northern coastal strip are black or mulatto, descended mainly from African slaves brought there to work the plantations, while descendants of the Indians dwell in the south. In Guayaquil and environs you'll find mostly *mestizos* of mixed white/Indian blood, who deal mainly in commerce and in transporting produce from the farm to the major harbors.

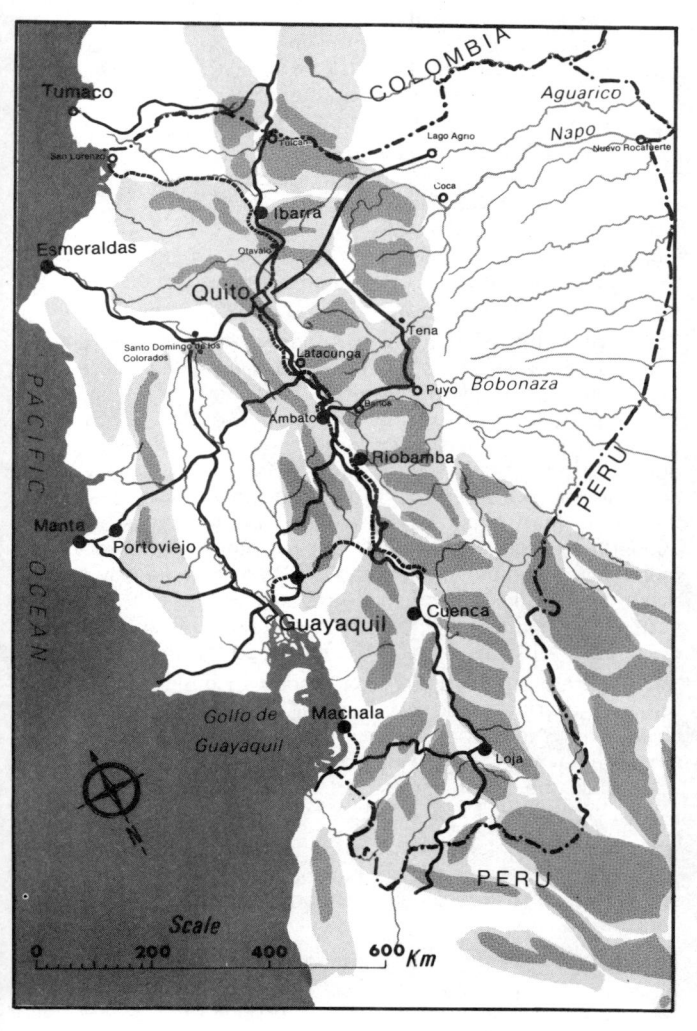

ECUADOR

ECUADOR

ECUADOR

The climate here is tropical, though the chilly Humboldt Current holds temperatures down to 23-24 degrees Centigrade or 73 degrees Fahrenheit. Day-night temperature differences are considerable, though there are no extremes between seasons. From December until April it is warmer and from late May to late November it's really quite pleasant.

Nearly half of Ecuador's population lives in the coastal area and produces most of the country's agricultural yield. Bananas, cocoa, sugar, rice and even cotton, familiar crops in this vicinity, amount to about half the country's exports. The lowlands near Guayaquil consist mostly of very fertile sedimentary soil. The region enjoys abundant rainfall, high humidity and plentiful river water. The yields have improved progressively in recent years.

The mountains (*Sierra*): The Andes divide into two parallel chains in Ecuador – the western (*Cordillera Occidental*) and the eastern (*Cordillera Oriental*), which run like twin spinal columns from north to south. The valley in which most Ecuadorians live, and where most of the mountain area's agricultural produce is grown, runs for about four hundred kilometers in between. Some thirty volcanos serve to fence in the valley from either side, thrusting proudly to a height of 6000 m and more. Some peaks are perpetually snow-clad and extremely beautiful. The mountain chains are broken by several rivers, each with its own isolated arable valley. The deep river valleys (*hoyas*) are home to agricultural communities whose way of life seems to have remained unchanged for centuries.

The climate of the mountain zone varies according to elevation, but is comfortable and pleasant for the most part. Rain falls chiefly from November to May, mostly in the evening and at night. The highlands are wintry and cold throughout most of the year, while the lower parts are tropically hot and humid. The valleys are noted for a comfortable, healthy climate and the Indian population for its longevity.

Most sierra-dwellers are of Indian descent and engage in agriculture and traditional vocations such as a variety of handicrafts.

The eastern region (*Oriente*) includes the lower, eastern Andes and the upper Amazon Basin. Its elevation is about 1500 m and its climate is tropical: hot, humid (up to 90%) and rainy (as much as 5000 mm (5m!) or more annually). The region is densely forested and carved by rivers great and small; most of its territory is uninhabited and unexplored.

Though it accounts for about one-half of Ecuador's land area, only 30% of the population lives here, mostly in towns and villages. In recent years oil fields have been found in the area and economic development has accelerated with the urge to

ECUADOR

exploit them and find new drilling sites. This is taking a rapid toll on the region's special character: obscure Indian tribes are becoming more exposed to westernization with each passing year.

The Galapagos Islands undoubtedly belong to a separate geographic category by virtue of both their nature and their location. We'll discuss them in a separate section.

Population

Ecuador has about eight million inhabitants, of whom more than a third are Indians, another third are *mestizos* and the remainder are Caucasions, Blacks and Orientals. The population density is the highest in South America – twenty-nine people per square kilometer. Though most of the population is agrarian and rural, the accelerated organization process typical of the Third World in recent decades has not skipped over Ecuador and its major cities are steadily growing. Today, 56% of Ecuador's people live in agricultural regions, while the urban sector is engaged in commerce and industry.

While the eastern jungle area is almost uninhabited, the population is divided almost equally between the mountain region and the coastal strip. Though the school system is constantly expanding in those areas, more than one fourth of all Ecuadorians are still illiterate.

Most Ecuadorians speak Spanish, the national language, but the Indians often continue to use their original tongue, Quechua; for some, it's their only language. An overwhelming majority of Ecuadorians – 95% – are Catholic.

Economy

Though only 15% of Ecuador's territory is used for agriculture, the national economy is based first and foremost on the fruit of the land. Until the early 1970s, when oil revenues from the east began to swell the national treasury, farm produce accounted for 90% of export income. Ecuador, fourth in the world in banana production, and sixth in cocoa beans, was subject to sharp economic fluctuations as world market prices for these commodities rose and fell.

Though agricultural produce is still a highly important factor in the national economy, oil has taken over the first place; and despite the fall in oil consumption and price, petroleum revenues are still the mainstay of the economy. About half the workforce is agrarian, but primitive agricultural methods, plus the geographic and transportational obstacles, cause Ecuadorian produce to sell at high prices which nevertheless return low profits. An agricultural reform that the Government sought to

ECUADOR

introduce during the 1970s enjoyed no conspicuous success. Its main contribution lay in its development efforts and the attempt to diversify the agricultural economy and expand it into previously unexploited areas.

Only 18% of Ecuador's working population engages in industry. This activity, mostly small scale, is concentrated mainly around the large cities, Guayaquil and Quito, and is not sufficient to supply the growing demand in the national economy. As a result of rising oil revenues, the government invested considerable sums in extensive development programs which were nipped in the bud, however, when prices and sales volume fell sharply. Per capita income has risen significantly: among South America's lowest ten years ago, today it amounts to around $900 annually.

Ecuador has run up a foreign debt of $7 billion and has lately begun to encounter difficulty in repaying it. The government has slowed the pace of investments and devalued the currency, but symptoms that arouse the concern of the world financial community are still discernable. Ecuador's membership in the Organization of Andean States, whose aim is free trade among all Andean nations, helped establish a number of industrial plants, which, together with a revitalized oil market, are expected to extricate Ecuador from its woes.

As for minerals, there are indications of some progress in the exploitation of existing mines and the development of new ones, though not at a pace that can guarantee significant momentum in the near future. Traces of gold, copper, silver and sulfur have been found in various locations, but they do not yet amount to anything significant at a national level.

General Information
How to get there
By air: Ecuador has convenient plane connections with the rest of South America, Europe and the United States. Iberia, Air France, KLM and Lufthansa fly from Europe to Quito and Guayaquil, while Avianca, Viasa and other South American airlines provide connecting flights to their respective countries. Young tourists who wish to hold down costs may find it best to fly to Lima, Peru, to which service is cheaper and more frequent; and from there, continue by bus to Ecuador. Ecuatoriana, the national airline, flies from Mexico City, Miami and New York, as do Eastern, AeroPeru, Air Panama and others. South American countries – apart from Chile, Uruguay and Paraguay – enjoy regular air service to and from Ecuador.

By land: Since no railroad links Ecuador to its neighbors, the only means of reaching it overland is by bus or private car. The

ECUADOR

Pan-Amercian Highway passes through Ecuador, from its northern border with Colombia to the Peruvian border in the south. A number of bus companies provide service between Ecuador and the cities of Bogota and Lima and to even more remote destinations. However, we recommend that you do not rely on them. Rather, take the trip in stages: first to the border; then cross over by yourself and continue on a local company's bus or minibus. Doing your own driving isn't hard as long as you stay on the main roads. On the lesser-traveled tracks you may find the going difficult. The unpaved roads are regularly damaged by floods and natural disasters. The authorities, unfortunately, don't always get around to repairing them. Hitchhiking is convenient and safe almost everywhere in Ecuador.

Documents and taxes

A passport valid for at least six months is a prerequisite for entering Ecuador. Tourist cards are distributed free-of-charge, either aboard the airplane or at frontier stations for overland travelers. Fill them out carefully and make sure they are properly stamped. Such a card is good for a ninety day stay, on condition that the immigration clerk has indeed approved this period of time. Tourists have often been called upon to present a departure ticket or, alternatively, to prove they have means of support sufficient for the duration of their stay. The border police will usually be satisfied if you display an MCO and several hundred dollars.

Only visitors who wish to remain in Ecuador for more than ninety days during a single year require a visa. If a stay of less than ninety days' duration was approved for you at the border station and you wish to extend it, you can do so without difficulty at any of the immigration offices located in the large cities.

Airline tickets purchased in Ecuador are subject to a 10% excise tax.

A final warning: carry identification at all times! Police and army checkposts demand I.D. regularly – even within the cities – and react harshly against those who can't produce the required documents.

When to Visit, National Holidays

The best time to visit Ecuador is between June and September, the dry season. The weather is comfortable the rest of the year too, though the nearly daily rains between December and March are a nuisance. The coastal area swelters in heat and humidity between December and April-May.

Important holidays: January 1, May 1, May 24 (Battle of Pichincha Day), July 24 (Simon Bolivar's Birthday), August 10

ECUADOR

(Independence Day), October 12 (Columbus Day), November 1 (All Saints' Day) and December 25.

Accommodation

Hotels, hostels and pensions are rather inexpensive; most are clean and tidy. First-class hotels are located only in the major cities; add 10-15% in taxes and service charges to their rates. Reservations are needed generally only at holiday time or for a short, rushed business visit. The smaller cities have very low-priced pensions and hostels *(residenciales)*, most of which are clean and pleasant. Guest homes – some with attached showers, fans and other "luxuries" – have come into being in recent years.

Food and drink

Ecuador abounds with clean, reasonably priced restaurants that serve diverse types of cuisine. In the large cities you'll find a wide variety – Chinese, French, Middle Eastern, etc. – and the large hotel restaurants will satiate you on Continental fare. Menus in smaller cities and villages are characterized by the popular local dishes, and along the coast by a wealth of fish and seafood.

Breakfast in Ecuador is a light meal taken before 8am. The main meal is lunch, eaten at about 1pm, while supper may be as early as 7:30 pm. In the cities, five o'clock is tea-time.

The national dishes are similar to those of Peru and Colombia, Ecuador's neighbors. Among them: *cebiche* (fish and seafood marinated in tomato sauce with lemon, orange juice and sugar), a corn bread called *tostado*, cream of potato soup *(locro)* and others. Main courses: *churrasco* and *fritada*, chunks of pork fried in oil and served with corn bread and fried bananas *(maquenos fritos)*.

Currency

Ecuador's currency, the sucre, is linked to the dollar at a rate set by the government. Ecuador has neither a black market nor any restrictions on the import and export of foreign currency. Dollar travelers' checks can be cashed almost anywhere for a small commission; this is recommended, especially for those heading for countries where there is a black market for hard American currency. Money sent to an Ecuadorian bank in dollars is paid out in dollars as well, an undoubtedly refreshing service in comparison with most South American countries, where you're given local currency, which devalues almost from one hour to the next.

Credit cards, especially Visa and Diners Club, are very common; you can also use them to withdraw funds in U.S. dollars. Before leaving the major cities though, it's worthwhile to obtain enough

ECUADOR

local currency, as it is difficult to exchange dollars in remote villages and towns. Even when you can do so, the rate you'll get for them there will be significantly lower. Before you leave Ecuador, buy the currency of the countries to which you're heading, or convert your remaining sucres into dollars.

Moneychanging is handled in banks or by moneychangers, without delay or hassle.

Business hours

Most offices and businesses open every morning at 8:30, close for a two-hour *siesta* at 12:30pm. and then reopen on weekdays until 6:30pm. On Saturdays they're open only in the mornings and are closed Sundays.

Government offices and quite a few private offices are closed Saturdays. The banks are open on weekdays between 9am and 1:30pm.

Domestic transportation

Buses: The most convenient way of touring Ecuador, apart from airplane, is by bus. Many companies operate bus and minibus lines throughout the country: most are reliable, frequent, fast, inexpensive and quite comfortable. Almost all cities and villages are served by several companies that link them to their neighbors and it's worth your while to use them.

Trains: Travel by rail, by contrast, is miserable, slow and uncomfortable. There is really only one major line in Ecuador, between Guayaquil and Quito. Still, the route between coast and mountains is interesting and quite exceptional.

Airplane: The military airline Tame provides frequent air service between important cities in all parts of Ecuador, together with small airlines that serve local destinations. Tame has a monopoly on flights to the Galapagos Islands and flies there several times a week (see "Galapagos"). Air service between Quito and Guayaquil is frequent; the flight takes about forty-five minutes. It's important to note that you must reach the airport early, for the airlines have a strange tendency to issue more boarding cards than there are seats and to leave them unmarked.

In-town-travel: Buses and minibuses are very inexpensive, though most are rather crowded and do not run as frequently as one would like. Taxis abound and fares are not high. Hertz, Budget and Avis rent out cars in the major cities.

Measurements, electricity, time

The metric system is customary in commerce and obligatory for official documents. Electricity is 110V. Time is 5 hours behind GMT in Ecuador and 6 hours behind GMT in the Galapagos Islands.

ECUADOR

A suggested itinerary for your visit to Ecuador

The route we're about to present aims at taking in most of the areas worth visiting in Ecuador; it would take at least several weeks to cover in its entirety. Accordingly, visitors must select the route most suitable to their taste, based on fields of interest, time, budget and general direction of their trips. Quito will serve as a departure point for most of the excursions; you can reach it either from Peru via Guayaquil, or from Colombia via Tulcan. Sites are noted in a northbound direction, as follows:

From the Peruvian border to Guayaquil.

From Guayaquil to the Galapagos Islands and back.

Up the mountains to Quito via Riobamba and Banos.

From Quito to the eastern jungles and back.

From Quito to Esmeraldas (on the northern coastal strip) and back.

North to Otavalo, San Antonio de Ibarra, Tulcan and Colombia.

One can, of course, combine routes so as to eliminate the need to double back on any single section. One example: combining routes 3 and 4 and continuing from Banos to the eastern jungles, returning to Quito. Another possibility: combining routes 5 and 6 and going on to Colombia along the coast (less recommended).

Quito

Ecuador's capital and its immediate surroundings rest a few kilometers from the equator at 2860 m above sea level. Its population (app. 900,000) enjoys crisp air, and a comfortable climate, and the ambience is serene, tranquil and slow-paced. Quito is altogether different from most South American capitals: smaller, cleaner and infused with a pervasive inner peace. Its residents are pleasant and forthcoming, their manners simple and honest. Their way of life seems to have been created with the express purpose of blending in with the surrounding green and placid mountains.

Quito is ensconced in a long, narrow valley running from north to south. A range of hills runs to the east, and Pichincha, an active volcano, casts it shadow to the west, its distant cone belching clouds of white smoke.

ECUADOR

A bird's-eye view of Quito

Quito was founded in 1534 by Sebastian de Benalcazar, who came to South America with Pizzaro, conqueror of Peru. The original quarter is in the southwest part of town. The northern section is newer and there we find elegant residential quarters, parks and public institutions. Tranquility and security reign in both parts of town. Quito is not a violent city and has been spared the all too common blights of most South American cities – poverty, hunger, illiteracy, drugs and crime.

Everything moves slowly here – no one is in a rush. The city closes down at night; only a few people wander the streets or frequent the entertainment spots. Most folks in Quito prefer to spend their nights at home with their families.

Quito is the ideal starting point for the tourist who wants to get to know Ecuador. From here its easy to go just about anywhere, whether eastward to the jungles, northward toward Colombia, or westward to the lovely coastal areas. For tourists, Quito is bound to be a case of love at first sight and the feeling will grow stronger the longer they stay there and come to know its sites and attractions.

How to get there
By air: Quito's Sucre Airport, a somewhat antiquated facility situated not far from downtown, is a very busy place. Planes arrive from many points in South America and from other cities in Ecuador itself. The airport is rather small, the service courteous and efficient. You'll find a bank for changing money, several shops and a small restaurant. You can reach town from

ECUADOR

the airport by taxi or by bus. It's customary to modestly tip the blue-uniformed skycaps.

By land: Buses and minibuses are Ecuador's most common means of getting around. They are run by many companies, each serving different destinations, and set out from the various company offices scattered around town. Fares are low; the service is reliable. Buy your tickets two or three days in advance, get to the terminal somewhat early and be sure to lock and secure your gear before stowing it in the luggage compartment. The bus ride to Peru and Colombia is best done in stages: take one bus to the border point, cross over yourself and continue on a Peruvian or Colombian bus. This is bound to save you money, and often time as well. Buses that stop in Quito let passengers off in various places throughout town and from there you can continue by city bus or taxi.

The **train** runs between Quito and Guayaquil, stopping on the way in Riobamba, Ambato and other cities. It's considered one of South America's most beautiful and interesting train rides; I recommend it. The train passes through breathtaking scenery, climbing over 3500 m on its 460 km course. There's nothing like it for bringing Ecuador's scenery and variety to life. The climb from Guayaquil up the mountains to Quito is slow and somewhat fatiguing, but the downhill trip is quite nice. The trains are generally packed; tickets must be purchased several days in advance. The railroad station is on Calle Maldonado, not far from the city center. The cars are not modern and nighttime trips can be very chilly.

Where to stay

Quito's hotels are numerous and varied – some luxurious and expensive, but most are reasonably priced. Even the latter, however, are clean, tidy and pleasant. The *Hotel Colon* (Tel. 521-300) at the end of Avenida Amazonas (corner of Patria) is one of the grandest and best in town. Its restaurants, coffee shop, casino and discotheque enhance its pleasant atmosphere, courteous service and excellent location. In my opinion, it is the most recommended choice for anyone who doesn't quake at the thought of spending tens of dollars per day on accommodations. If you're in this class, make reservations: this hotel, like its competitor and peer, the *Quito Intercontinental* (Tel. 230-300), enjoys high occupancy throughout most of the year and is occasionally booked out.

Businesspeople will undoubtedly find these two hotels suitable for their needs. Less-expensive hotels, will also meet every requirement of tourists who need a place to rest their weary feet. Among these, we can recommend the *Inca-Imperial* adjacent to the old part of town (Calle Bogota 219, Tel. 230-600),

ECUADOR

the *Embassy* (Calle Wilson 441, Tel. 525-555), the *Zumag* (Avenida 10 de Agosto, Tel. 247-802) and the *Savoy* (Tel. 247-222).

For thrifty cheap lodgings, try one of the many pensions around town. We can recommend the *Residencial Italia* on Avenida 9 de Octubre and the *Pension Americana* on Avenida 6 de Diciembre.

The *Gran Casino Hotel* has become the center for young travelers who come to Quito. Most of them stay here, while for others it is the place to meet traveling companions for different trips. The cafeteria here is crowded almost the whole day. The standard is low, it is dirty, unreliable and the rooms miserable. The hotel is located on Calle Garcia Morena (near Ambato), walking distance from Plaza Santo Domingo in the Old City.

The *Hotel Republica*, a modern, comfortable establishment, is located next to the airport.

What, when and where to eat

Have a light breakfast at one of the cafes, diners, or kiosks situated around town, especially along major streets. For lunch and supper it's best to look elsewhere for a place to satisfy your appetite. The Old City abounds in small, inexpensive restaurants that usually serve tasty and fresh Ecuadorian foods which I certainly recommend. The restaurants, like the entire area, empty after nightfall: come early for supper, for it's hard to find anything open after 9:30pm.

Quito's streets present you with a large selection of eateries of diverse type and quality. In the markets and along major streets you can eat simply and well. Hotel and luxury restaurant menus, by contrast, are far more sophisticated, though not necessarily expensive.

Some of the best restaurants in town are situated in the hotels. On the Intercontinental's roof, *El Techo del Mundo* ("Roof of the World") specializes in a Continental menu served against a background of music and a gorgeous view of the city and the valley. The *Hotel Colon* too, serves excellent food in its cafeteria, coffee shop and elegant *El Conquistador Grille*. *Chalet Suisse* (Calle Calama 312, Tel. 230-686) serves excellent, expensive steaks, and *Moby Dick* (Ave. Amazonas 272) offers superb fish and seafood. The excellent French restaurant *Rincon de Francia* (Calle Roca, corner of 9 de Octubre, Tel. 232-053) offers its patrons the finest French cuisine; *Costa Vasca* (Calle Reina Victoria 836, Tel. 234-846) specializes in Spanish food.

We recommend *Casa China* (Ave. Amazonas, corner of Mariana de Jesus) for Chinese food, and *Pizza Nostra* for its fare (Calle

*E*CUADOR

Reina Victoria, corner of 18 de Septiembre, Tel. 239-170). A Lebanese restaurant specializing in excellent Middle Eastern food is located next to the airport.

If you'd like to sample local delicacies, we can recommend *La Choza* (12 de Octubre corner of Cordero, Tel. 230-839). There you'll dine in a pleasant atmosphere at reasonable prices, enjoying some of the finest Ecuadorian dishes.

Transportation

Getting around Quito and its suburbs is simple and easy. The streets in residential areas are broad enough to handle traffic; congestion is rare. On the other hand, downtown streets – especially in the Old City – are narrow, allowing little if any room for parking. Add mediocre street signs and the chances of losing your way and you'll find yourself refraining from driving and favoring public transit whenever possible. A great many buses and minibuses rumble up and down the streets, taking everyone everywhere. You'll hardly ever have to change buses to reach your destination and the journey will usually not involve prolonged waiting or inconvenience of any kind. At the same time, remember that public transit leaves one vulnerable to pickpockets: keep an eye on your handbags.

You can, of course, avail yourself of taxis if you so wish and have loose change to spare. Hundreds of them cruise the town and are easy to hail even in relatively distant suburbs. Drivers set fares in advance (bargaining with them is definitely acceptable) according to the destination and time of day. Expect higher fares at night and on weekends.

Rental cars are available from Avis and Hertz at the airport, or from Expo on Avenida America, corner of Bolivia (Tel. 233-269). The latter also provides drivers. When renting a car, be sure to ascertain that the insurance is comprehensive; otherwise, breakdowns and minor accidents are liable to be expensive. It's important to compare prices and to check the car's condition from top to bottom.

Tourist service

There's a Ministry of Tourism branch office in the arrival hall at the airport. If luck is with you and you haven't found the place closed, it will equip you with maps and pamphlets about the city and its attractions. The Ministry also has two offices downtown, one on Calle Reina Victora, corner of Roca (Tel. 239-044) and the other at City Hall – *Palacio Municipal* – on Plaza Independencia (Tel. 527-002). In the first you can view video movies on various tourist sites in Ecuador, produced by the Ministry of Tourism. In order to do this come with at least 5 people to the branch office.

ECUADOR

Additional maps, especially of distant sites, mountain hikes, jungle excursions and the like, are available at the **Instituto Geografico Militar** (Calle Paz corner of Nino), or at the Libri Mundi bookstore, about which we'll have more to say as we proceed (see "Literature").

Almost all Quito travel agencies are somehow involved in organizing tours to the Galapagos Islands; check on various possibilities concerning types and prices of excursions (see "Galapagos").

Tourist sites
In addition to a comfortable, hospitable climate, nature has graced the Ecuadorian capital with an enchantingly beautiful location. It also enjoys a rare combination of Colonial grace and urban modernization. Quito lies in a long, narrow valley stretching from north to south between the green slopes of the soaring Andes. At almost every turn you will be greeted by a view of the mountains, which seem to shelter the city from the surrounding world. Quito has always been an isolated, cut-off city: expansion east or west is difficult, due to the obstacles posed by the mountain ridges. Thus the city developed lengthwise, chiefly northward, leaving its flanks uninhabited. Today's visitor to Quito will discern the substantial difference between north and south, which expresses centuries of social development, architectural perspective and a multifaceted national identity. It seems to me that a walk through Quito from south to north is a journey through both space and time: the sixteenth and seventeenth centuries in the south, the eighteenth and nineteenth centuries in the middle and the twentieth century in the north.

Visitors to Quito should take their time. Amble along the broad boulevards in the city's north; stroll through the alleys in its south; dine and shop along Avenida Amazonas, visit the museums and linger in the gardens and plazas, etc. Pleasant excursions await you close to town: mountain hikes, interesting lookout points, an enjoyable picnic. The most famous site is *La Mitad del Mundo* (Center of the World), a monument sitting precisely "on" the equator.

As is our custom, we shall survey Quito geographically, from north to south, focusing on the more unusual and interesting sites. We will conclude with a survey of the sites located outside the town. Avenida 10 de Agosto, which runs spine-like through the entire city (apart from the southern extremity) will serve us as a main artery.

North Quito
Though the Old Quarter in South Quito is conventionally thought

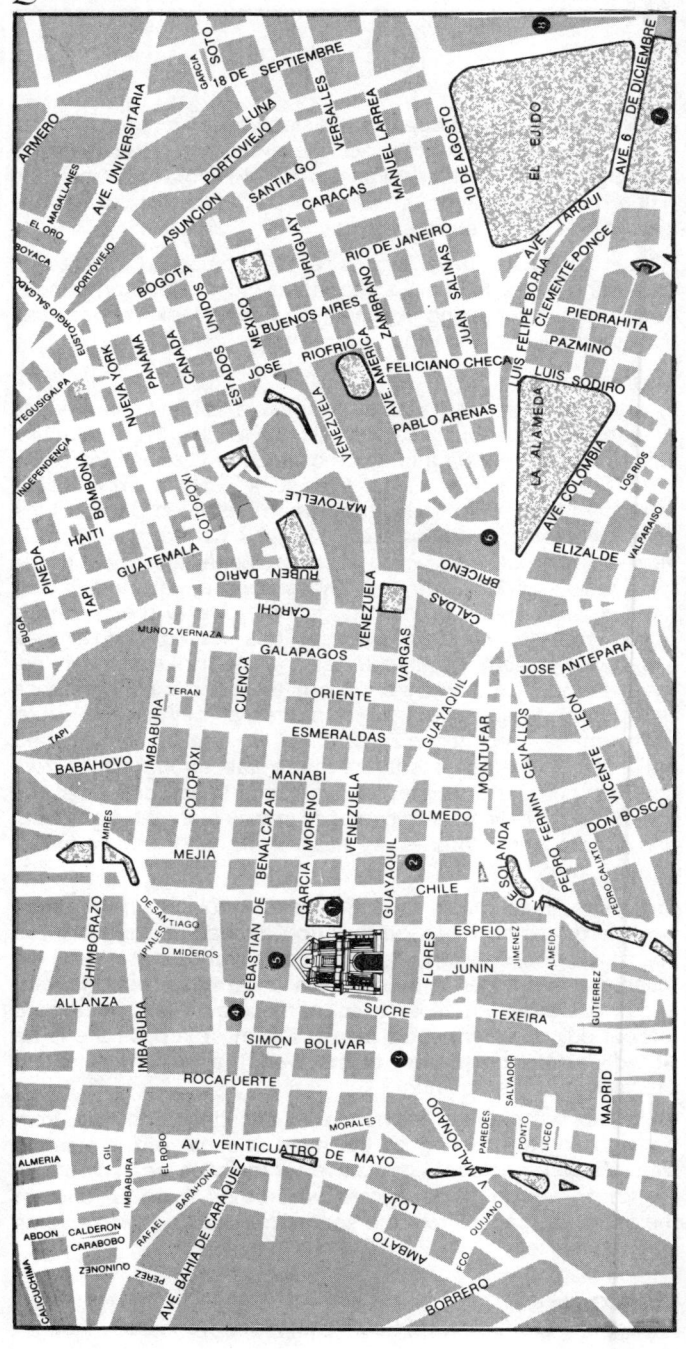

QUITO

ECUADOR

of as the city's most ancient section, it was actually in the north – the Cotocollao area – that human settlement in Quito began, five millenia ago. Here, in what today is a wholly modern area, was the Cotocollao Kingdom, one of the most advanced of that period's civilizations. Its survivors intermarried with the Indian invaders who, in turn, were subsequently annihilated by the *conquistadores*.

Nothing of that bygone era has survived in this area, now an exclusive residential neighborhood. The whole north end of Quito has been built up and is constantly developing; new buildings, streets and neighborhoods spring up year after year.

Even the Sucre International Airport, which seemed so far from town only a short time ago, is trapped today in the heart of well-tended residential quarters and constitutes a nuisance to their residents.

This rapid expansion has led to the development of a special Quito building style, which allows wealthy residents – those who populate the northern quarters – ample room, spacious apartments, public parks, streets, boulevards and so on. Some diplomatic missions and prestigious estates are situated here today, as are a number of modern office buildings and important shopping centers.

North Quito has no "tourist sites" in the conventional sense of the term, but those seeking to form an impression of today's Quito should nonetheless visit it.

The New City

While the north is Quito's prestigious residential district, the center – between those exclusive neighborhoods and the Old City – is a most interesting part of town, where traces of the past century mingle with the beginning of the current one in a graceful manner. Here are many of the city's offices, shops, entertainment spots, restaurants and so on.

We shall tour the area between Parque El Alameda in the south

---

Index
1) Plaza Independencia
2) San Agustin Church
3) Plaza Santo Domingo
4) Plaza San Francisco
5) La Compania Church
6) Central Bank Museum
7) Casa de la Cultura
8) Hotel Colon

ECUADOR

and Avenida Naciones Unidas, bordering Parque Carolina, to the north.

Before entering Parque El Alameda, you should be sure to visit the **Museo del Banco Central** (Central Bank Museum), located on the fifth and sixth floors of the Bank building at Avenida 10 de Agosto, corner of Brinceno – right across from Bolivar's statue at the park entrance. It's open Tues.-Fri. 9am-8pm; Sat.-Sun. 10am-5pm; closed Mon. (Tel 510-302). It's one of South America's most interesting and important museums; don't miss it. The fifth floor is devoted to a display of thousands of archeological finds from all over Ecuador, while the sixth floor presents a selection of paintings and furniture dating from the Golden Age of Spanish rule. The museum, through well thought out and tasteful displays, thoroughly and extensively covers the history of human settlement in Ecuador, beginning thousands of years before the Spanish arrived. Though the exhibits are documented in detail, we recommend that you join one of the English-language guided tours offered several times daily. In the late afternoon and on Sundays, admission to the museum is free of charge.

El Alameda Park stretches opposite the Bank. Here you can rest on a park bench, contemplate passers-by, or visit the small planetarium located in the center. El Alameda Park is, in fact, a transition point between New and Old Quito. North of here, the streets become wider and the building style and types of businesses change. Continuing along Avenida 10 de Agosto, we arrive shortly at one of the best-known parks in Quito – **Parque El Ejido**.

This large park is divided into two sections by Avenida 6 de Deciembre. Its eastern part has lawns, trees and benches; its west is home to Quito's cultural center, Casa de la Cultura, with a display of paintings, works of art, books and musical instruments. It also has a movie theater that screens quality films.

The area around the park contains some of Ecuador's important institutions. The most important are the **Palacio Legislativo**, (Legislature) and **Placio de Justica** (Hall of Justice), both on Avenida 6 de Deciembre between El Alameda and El Ejido Parks. On the other side, in the northwestern corner, the **American Embassy** overlooks the park and Plaza Mantilla. A few blocks down Avenida 12 de Octubre, continuing from the American Embassy, we reach the **Catholic University**, one of Ecuador's most esteemed academic institutions. The University Library houses an interesting archeological collection from the estate of the late researcher Caamano. The artifacts included in this display thoroughly and comprehensively analyze and

ECUADOR

Avenida Amazonas

explain ancient Ecuadorian cultures. The University's museum houses a rather mediocre display of uniforms and paintings. Open Mon.-Fri. 9am-noon and 3-6pm.

On the other side of Ejido Park, several blocks farther along Avenida 10 de Agosto, we pass the Treasury and the Foreign Ministry, and plunge into quiet residential areas. Therefore we will continue our tour from Ejido Park northward along Avenida Amazonas, Quito's most popular shopping and entertainment street.

Avenida Amazonas is one of Quito's longest, extending from Ejido Park to Plaza Olmedo behind the airport. Its bustling, famous section runs from Avenida Patria, on the edge of Ejido Park, as far as Carolina Park. At its beginning is the grand *Hotel Colon*, which is not only a shelter for affluent tourists, but also an exclusive social institution in town. From here we'll head north along the attractive boulevard, peer into the shop windows, review the cars creeping along, pass tourist agencies and airline offices, restaurants, boutiques with some lovely leather goods and more. Avenida Amazonas is surrounded by small streets lined with hundreds of attractive businesses offering the best Ecuadorian wares – from typical *artesania* (handicrafts) of the Indians in Otavalo (see "North of Quito"), to office services, banking, art galleries and the like. It's a lovely area, bound to capture any tourist's heart. Here, on the pedestrian section of Avenida Amazonas and in the small buildings crowded along the adjacent streets, you can find

ECUADOR

shops in line with your budget, restaurants for your palate, or bars in which to "let your hair down".

The boulevard is busy and noisy as far as Avenida Cristobal Colon (that's Christopher Columbus in Spanish). From here onward we may either continue northward to **Carolina Park**, where we'll find Quito's largest **Hippodrome** (race track), or turn left toward the University. If we go straight, to the north, we'll first pass the park and then encounter the Inaquito commercial center – a shopping complex – along Avenida Amazonas. Past Inaquito, a right turn from Avenida Amazonas onto Avenida Naciones Unidas brings us to **Atahuallpa Stadium**, one of the city's most active sports centers. Almost every Sunday, many thousands of spectators attend the soccer matches (the official season runs from June to November).

Turn left onto Avenida Colon from Avenida Amazonas and walk several blocks (crossing Avenida 10 de Agosto as well) to reach **Ciudadela Universitaria** (University City) – site of the city's general university. The modern campus serves more than 15,000 students, with a stadium, cinema, and more. It's an interesting place to encounter the active and lively Ecuadorian youth.

The Old City

Quito's southern section, bounded by Alameda Park and Panecillo Hill, which juts 180 m above the city, is undoubtedly the most charming and interesting in town. Almost every house along the alleyways has a fascinating story to tell, from the expeditions of the Spanish founding fathers to the efforts today's city leaders are making to preserve the antiquities for posterity.

At the center of the Old City is **Plaza Independencia**, considered the heart of San Francisco de Quito since its founding. Were they able to talk, the surrounding buildings would relate stories of most of the important happenings in the annals of the town. The well-tended, tree-adorned plaza preserves the charm of bygone days with a rare grace; it continues to cast a spell of pleasant serenity on all its visitors. On its southern side stands the well-known Cathedral of Quito, one of more than eighty churches and chapels throughout the city. The **White Cathedral**, which has clearly known better days, houses an important art collection including the masterpieces of the most famous Ecuadorian artists, as well as the tomb of Sucre, the famous military leader.

Opposite the cathedral is the **Archbishop's Palace**, once the prelate's home and today packed with little shops offering a range of goods. The old **City Hall** building is also located on the

ECUADOR

square, at its northeastern corner. The handsome colonial **Government Palace**, on the plaza's northwestern side, serves the President (his office is on the second floor) and the highest functionaries of the Government. A splendid mosaic graces its first floor. To its left is a small lane running between the **Municipal Library** and the **Central Post Office**.

From here onward, a casual stroll through the alleys and a visit to some of the lovely sites is recommended. All the streets are narrow, paved with timeworn cobblestones and lined on both sides with little two-story houses in which people still live and work. Within the radius of a few blocks down, you'll find a concentration of churches and monasteries, which display an architectural beauty rarely seen with art collections to match.

We'll set out on a circular route from Plaza Independencia, passing the Quarter's important and famous sites. First we'll turn east onto Calle Chile and cross Calles Venezuela and Guayaquil, Quito's busiest commercial streets. This is where the locals do most of their shopping, as the piles of merchandise and crowds of people along the sidewalks attest.

Between Calles Venezuela and Guayaquil there is a conspicuous concrete structure to our right. It's the new **City Hall**, built in the late 1970s to replace the old Municipality Building on Plaza Independencia. After Calle Guayaquil we come to our first stop: the **San Agustin Monastery**. Here many heroes of the War of Independence are buried, and here Ecuador's Declaration of Independence (from Spain) was signed.

Now we turn right onto Calle Flores. Crossing Calle Espejo, we notice the Church of Santa Catalina to our left. Another two blocks brings us to **Plaza Santo Domingo**, where a monastery and church of the same name are located. The center of the square features a statue of General Sucre, who appears to be gesturing proudly toward the slopes of Pichincha where he defeated the Spanish Royalists in battle. The monastery and church are decorated with unique woodcarvings and there is an art collection inside.

From here we turn left onto Calle Guayaquil and take a right a few meters later onto Calle Morales, known as **La Ronda**. The quarter's oldest street, it is lined with little houses renowned for their beauty. Walk down the narrow street until it ends at Avenida 24 de Mayo. This boulevard was once known as the gathering place for Indian traders, who sold and marketed innumerable products of diverse types. Severe restrictions have been placed on commerce along the boulevard in recent years and many of the traders have relocated to a covered market built especially for them. Though others still continue in their forefathers'

ECUADOR

footsteps along the boulevard, its special character has undoubtedly changed beyond recognition.

We may now head south, toward **Panecillo Hill**. Its summit affords us an enchanting view of all of Quito and especially the Old City. The climb, on paths and steps, is not difficult at all and takes no longer than half an hour. For a rather low fare, a taxi will whisk you in a few seconds to the picnic area at the top. The hilltop has a good restaurant where you can eat to your heart's content. A statue of The Virgin can be seen nearby.

A right turn from Avenida 24 de Mayo onto Calle Benalcazar and about two blocks' walking, will bring us to **Plaza San Francisco**. The church and monastery of that name – South America's most ancient Christian institutions – are on its western side. The **Church of San Francisco** was founded in 1535 by the Belgian Jaboco Ricke and is Quito's largest church. Its beautiful towers are not the original ones, having been reconstructed after the earthquake of 1868. Inside we find an altar of gold and a unique wooden ceiling, the epitome of human creativity. On the site is a **museum** with a large and important collection of religious art. The church and museum are open to visitors from 6am till noon and from 2:30 till 7:30 pm.

Two blocks east of Plaza San Francisco, on Calle Sucre at the corner of Moreno, stands the **La Compania Church** – undoubtedly Quito's most beautiful and one of the most impressive in all of Latin America. Its magnificent facade gives only a foretaste of its rich interior, covered with superb carvings in wood and gold. The beauty here will certainly excite even those who don't normally enjoy churches and religious art. It is open 10-11am and 1-6pm; unfortunately women are not allowed inside.

A short walk from here takes us to **General Sucre's Home**, at the corner of Venezuela and Sucre. The building has been reconstructed with great authenticity regarding its appearance in colonial times. Open 9am-noon and 3-6pm.

If you want an additional glimpse of the colonial art treasures with which Quito has been blessed, you'll certainly be delighted by a visit to the **Museum of Colonial Art** on Calle Cuenca, corner of Mejia, behind the La Merced Church.

Excursions
La Mitad del Mundo (Center of the World)
The equator – 0 degrees latitude – runs 23 km north of Quito. Since it gives the country its name, we should not wonder that the Ecuadorians attribute great significance to this imaginary line – greater than if it were real. Most tourists to Quito take the trouble to visit the spot where the imaginary line splits the world

ECUADOR

in half, and where an attractive monument, a restaurant and souvenir stands are also located. **La Mitad del Mundo** is reached by a half-hour ride on a bus, marked with its name, through lovely mountain scenery. All told, crossing from the Southern into the Northern Hemisphere is an entertaining experience, definitely worth the effort. Though globe-shaped markers grace a number of sites in Ecuador, La Mitad del Mundo is the most famous, most beautiful and best displayed of them all.

Mt. Pichincha
West of Quito, volcanic Pichincha towers to 4735 m above sea level, and the city is built along its green slopes. Local residents love to wander about on the mountainside; many spend their weekends there when weather permits. Splendid sunsets can be seen from the mountain, whose distant peak often wears a mantle of gleaming snow. The view of Quito spread out below it is quite exquisite.

Mt. Cotopaxi
A trip to the Nature Reserve on Cotopaxi, the world's highest active volcano, is a "must" for nature-lovers. The Pan-American Highway leading south of Quito will take you to the park entrance, where there is a Nature Reserve to protect rare animals, whose continued existence is endangered because "civilization" is encroaching on their natural habitats. One day suffices for the excursion, during which you'll encounter wild animals which roam freely through an alternating landscape of forest and lava.

Many meet the challenge of climbing to the snow-capped peak of Mt. Cotopaxi which looms 5896 m above sea level. The trip takes about 3 days. On the first day one must reach the *Refugio* (hut), which is also accessible by car. The second day is the climb to the summit which takes about 6 hours. One must leave at daybreak, not later than 4am, in order to complete the climb before the snow, which hardens overnight, softens. The climb is exhausting with prolonged walking through snow and icy patches. One must be equipped with accurate route information and basic climbing gear. On the third day one makes the descent to the main base and from there back to Quito.

Entertainment and culture
Quito is no entertainment "hot-spot". It's a city where nightfall brings quiet and tranquility, inducing the locals to head home for supper, conversation, television and sleep. The people of Quito are early-to-bed types, rarely seen about the streets after

ECUADOR

10pm. Nightlife – if so exciting a term can be used in Quito's case – heats up somewhat on weekends and holidays, while on weekdays you'll hardly find an open discotheque, not to speak of a genuine nightclub. Weekday-evening entertainment for those who wish it consists of movies, occasional concerts, or folklore shows. The *Sucre National Theater* on Calle Flores, between Guayaquil and Manabi (Tel. 216-668), and *Casa de la Cultura* on Avenida 6 de Deciembre in El Ejido Park (Tel. 231-142) offer symphony concerts and ballet; admission to some of these is free. Folklore shows are presented several times weekly at clubs known as *penas* as well as in the large hotels. A visit to at least one is recommended. Even those arriving from Bolivia and Peru will find that the music, rhythm and dance of Ecuador are different from those of its neighbors to the south, and are definitely worth a try. *Pena Pachamama*, Calle Washington 530 (Tel. 234-855; closed Sun. and Mon.) is justly considered the best in town. *El Chucaro*, Reina Victoria 1335, is also recommended. *Nuca Canchi*, very close to "University City," attracts students. There's also *Pena Quito Libra* in the Old City. Though most *penas* open as early as 9pm for drinks, performances hardly ever begin before 10pm, or even later on weekends.

Those who want to dance the night away will enjoy an evening in some of Quito's better discotheques. Heading the list is *La Licorna*, the Hotel Colon's prestigious disco club, where the elite of Quito's society – mostly sons and daughters of the city's well-to-do and dignitaries – move to the beat. Those of them who wish to save the carfare from North Quito downtown, choose *Discotheque Faces* in the north, just across from the municipal tennis and golf center. You'll find more conservative nightclubs in the *Hotel Humboldt* and *Le Club*; the former has a casino as well, while the latter, one of Quito's finest entertainment spots, is a combination restaurant and club which offers enjoyable shows each and every night. A number of hotels, in addition to the Humboldt, have casinos for the gamblers among us. The nicest, at least in my opinion, is in the basement of the *Hotel Colon*. Here activity comes into life late at night (late in Quito terms, of course), when the cream of Quito's citizens and guests, dressed in their finest, try their luck – some at cards, others at roulette – at the gaming tables. The hall is lined with slot machines, which will happily swallow your coins to the accompaniment of whistles and shrieks. These should certainly be enough for the "poorer" visiting gamblers.

Sports
The men and women of Quito are known for their love of sports of every kind; many participate while others prefer watching the

ECUADOR

pros fight it out. Soccer is undoubtedly the most popular of all; the Olympic Atahuallpa Stadium is packed every Saturday and Sunday, when the matches are held.

Quito has several tennis clubs, most rather high-priced. The large tennis and golf center on Avenida Brazil near the airport (Tel. 241-918) features tennis courts, a well-kept golf course and a swimming pool. Expensive. If you've got swimming in mind, head for Hotel Colon, or the Intercontinental.

Mountain climbing has become quite popular in recent years; many Ecuadorians, along with many tourists, are great enthusiasts. Though the towering mountains around Quito guarantee ample opportunity for this sport, you would do well to remember the effort and the risks involved. Quito has a number of climbers' clubs, which will be glad to advise, organize outings and even to sell, buy, or rent professional climbing gear. Make inquiries at one of these before you set out.

Horse racing fans can visit the racetrack on Sundays, at the Hippodrome in La Carolina Park, and join the many spectators who follow their favorite thoroughbreds – on whom they have bet their hard-earned cash. Interesting.

Entertainment of a different kind – perhaps the most popular variety of all – is bullfighting. This unique Latin tradition, played down in its home-base Spain, is enjoying a renaissance in Quito. It arouses mixed emotions: some fervor and enthusiasm, some discomfort and revulsion. Quito's most important bullfights take place in early December, featuring some of the finest matadors from Spain and Mexico. Though the bullfights in the preceding months are less grand, almost all of them lead to the same outcome: the bull's demise before the eyes of a multitude who roar "oles" with no inhibitions. This warfare of man and beast is generally held on Sundays at **Plaza de Toros**, at the junction of Avenidas Amazonas and Cojanes. Tickets are rather expensive and are best procured in advance. Also, it is best to come early. A visit to the *corrida* (bullring) is a unique experience. All told, it is a noble combination of rhythmic music, picturesque dress, a stylized struggle waged according to a rigid ritual and an uninhibited reaction of an audience including women and children. All these elements justify a visit to this special event, which will surely not leave you unmoved.

Festivals

Quito celebrates a variety of holidays between November and January, of which the greatest and most important marks the anniversary of its founding.

The merrymaking begins with a city-wide cleanup campaign (an enviable tradition in its own right) on a single day during

*E*CUADOR

Bullfighting in Plaza de Toros

November. On this day, called *Minga* after the ancient custom it preserves, everyone in Quito labors at cleaning, renovating, painting, washing and so on. Nothing – buildings, streets, parks, plazas – is overlooked. This marks the beginning of the carnival period, which compensates the populace for its trouble.

Quito's own celebration takes place during the first week of December (the city was founded on December 6) with a series of colorful events. Throughout the entire week there are bullfights by day and balls, shows and the like by night. The carnival reaches its peak with parades of marching bands and dance troupes, some local and others from the surrounding Indian villages. The dancers cavort down the packed streets with inexhaustible fervor, with spectators pulled along in their wake.

An all-night parade of celebrants, most of them costumed, takes place along Avenida Amazonas to the accompaniment of fireworks and tempestuous music.

The great party resumes the week of New Year's Day. Quito's citizens and entertainers take to the streets once again, as if to use up energy left over from the festivities of the previous three weeks. If you find yourself in Ecuador during that time of the year, a fascinating experience awaits you.

Banks and currency exchange
Changing foreign currency in Ecuador is unrestricted, involves no difficulty and is done at any bank branch or through official

ECUADOR

moneychangers (*cambio*). Rodrigo Paz's moneychangers' network has a good reputation and branches all over town, but the exchange rates are not always the highest. The conversion procedures are simple and speedy, the hours convenient. The large American (Citibank, Bank of America), British and European banks have branches in town. At the airport bank branch (open on weekends too) you can reconvert leftover sucres into dollars.

Postal service and telephones

We highly recommend sending all postal items to and from Ecuador by air mail only; even so, expect delays. The Central Post Office is behind the Government Palace on Plaza Independencia, with the IETEL offices (international calls) next door. International calls are rather expensive and involve a lengthy wait. Service at IETEL's north Quito office (on Avenida Colon near Avenida Amazonas) is sometimes a little faster.

Shopping

Quito and its environs offer an inexhaustible selection of souvenirs, knickknacks, clothing, and so on. The combination of quality, beauty and reasonable prices makes Quito a bargain-hunters' paradise, as proven by the many visitors who've thrown economy to the winds in the face of such attractive buys. Always remember that any purchase, anywhere – marketplace, shop, plaza, or boulevard – should begin with stubborn bargaining, it's the local custom, accepted and in good spirit.

Most of the Indian crafts produced in the Quito area are brought into the city. If you have no way of going out and exploring the Indian villages and towns by yourself, you can buy their wares – at slightly higher prices, of course – in town. Beyond the monetary gain, it seems to me that the artists' villages (especially Otavalo, San Antonio de Ibarra and their neighbors) deserve a visit, and we shall explore them as we proceed (see "North of Quito"), even though their goods, as said, may be purchased in town as well. In Quito you will find a wealth of wool products – sweaters, wall hangings, blankets – in addition to colorful ceramics, carved wood sculpture, silver jewelry, leather clothing and more. These can be purchased at any of the many stores along Avenida Amazonas and the adjacent streets, or in the less-elegant, lower-priced parts of town a short walk away. Some of the best shops are in Quito's new section. Of them, the best-known is Folklore at Avenida Colon 260, owned by Olga Fisch. She has opened branches in the Hotel Colon and the Intercontinental as well, where you will also find the well-known H. Stern jewelry chain, which does business in most Latin American capitals. In the same area you will also find the large

ECUADOR

La Bodega *artesania* shop, at Calle Mera 641 (Tel. 232-844), opposite the Libri Mundi Bookstore. It has everything from wooden statuettes to furniture. The OCEPA government *artesania* store is at Calle Carrion 13.

The areas closer to the Old City, especially around Calles Guayaquil and Venezuela, are noted for a large selection – displayed in conspicuous disarray and distressing density, though at prices much lower than those in the places we have listed so far. Here – obviously – is where the locals shop. The Plaza Independencia area has a number of souvenir shops offering an exhaustive selection at convenient prices. The sidewalks of Avenida 24 de Mayo and in El Ejido Park are covered with seated Indians proudly offering their wares – fertile hunting grounds for genuine bargains.

Quito also has shops that sell various types of antiques, some of them genuine. Be careful to verify that what you have bought is authentic and – no less important – that the dealer is licensed. To be caught leaving Ecuador with an archeological artifact for which you have no permit is an altogether unpleasant experience.

Foreign-language literature
One of South America's best bookstores is in Quito: Libri Mundi on Calle Mera (Tel. 234-791), a venerable institution in the town. Here you will find almost every book ever written about Ecuador, alongside an impressive selection of works on nature, science, economics and the like – in English, French, German and Spanish. Libri Mundi is near the Hotel Colon; we recommend a visit, if only to browse. English-language newspapers are available in the large hotel shops and at kiosks along Avenida Amazonas.

Weather
Quito enjoys wonderful weather. Its proximity to the equator and its elevation give it a magnificent climate with enviable seasonal stability. Rains fall throughout most of the year and usually at the same hour every day. The driest months are from May until November, when much less rain falls. Quito's air is pure and pristine; the sun's rays burst through the thin mantle of clouds that frequently shades the city in a manner which can be troublesome for the sun-sensitive. Shield your head and face from radiation and use sunscreen. Contact lenses are liable to prove painful, because of the dryness and the high altitiude.

Days in Quito are warm; temperatures generally hover around 22 degrees Centigrade or 72 degrees Fahrenheit. At night, however, the mercury plunges considerably. Warm clothing is necessary; a raincoat and umbrella will also prove most useful.

ECUADOR

Important addresses
Police: Tel. 247-500.

Ministry of Tourism: Dituris: Reina Victoria y Roca. Tel. 239-044.

Ministry of Immigration (for extending your stay): Avenida Amazonas 2639.

U.S. Embassy: 120 Avenida Patria. Tel. 548-000.

British Embassy: Calle Gonzalez Suarez 111. Tel. 230-070 / 1 / 2 / 3, 523-124, 521-755.

Guayaquil

Guayaquil is Ecuador's largest city, home to about one and a half million people. It is Ecuador's major coastal city, and is also the country's industrial and commercial metropolis and the traditional home of most of its economic institutions. It is undoubtedly Ecuador's most "western" city, which tourists will notice immediately.

Guayaquil, founded as part of the Spanish campaign of conquest and settlement, established industrial, commercial and agricultural elites from its earliest days. The fertile areas that encompass it have made Guayaquil very important indeed, in determining patterns of national development in many spheres. The city is highly influential in determining the size and composition of the national foodbasket, the scope of the country's foreign trade and its economic strength.

With regard to tourism, Guayaquil is hardly one of the Seven Wonders of the World; if you are not passing through on the way to somewhere else, you probably would not miss much by skipping the city. Most people who come as far as Guayaquil do so on business; others take advantage of its convenient location en route from Peru to the mountains or as a point of departure for the Galapagos Islands. The city lies on the western side of Rio Guayas along the innermost reaches of the Gulf of Guayaquil, about fifty kilometers east of the Pacific coast. The city boasts the modern Bolivar Airport and a gigantic commercial harbor. The latter, known as **Puerto Nuevo** (New Port), provides exceptionally convenient and secure anchorage for enormous ships. The well developed port, which handles about 80% of Ecuador's import and export freight, is always bustling. At the same time, it is kept clean and almost never appears disorderly or chaotic.

Guayaquil was the arena for political conflict during the struggles for independence waged by the Latin American

E CUADOR

people against the Spanish monarchy. The most important encounter that took place here was in August 1822, when the Venezuelan general Simon Bolivar met his Argentine counterpart Jose de San Martin, to discuss the city's future. Bolivar, engrossed at the time in his dream of "Greater Colombia", sought to annex the city to the northern confederation, while San Martin, one of Peru's liberators, wished to attach it to that country. The conclusion of the secret meeting is shrouded in fog, but its results were to have long-term consequences: Guayaquil was included in "Greater Colombia", while an embittered San Martin went off to self imposed exile in France, where he remained till his dying day. His remains were brought to Buenos Aires and interred in the cathedral on Plaza de Mayo.

Transportation

Guayaquil has many and various transportation connections with most Ecuadorian cities, with Peru and the other Latin American countries, and with Europe and the United States. Many airplanes from Quito and elsewhere in Ecuador land every day in its modern, centrally located airport, along with others which stop over en route to and from neighboring countries. The daily flight from Quito to the Galapagos and back stops here as well (see "Galapagos").

Guayaquil is also easily accessible by bus. The trip from Quito takes about eight hours (about ten hours for the return – uphill – trip), passing through lovely mountain scenery. Transandina and Empresa provide convenient and reliable daily service. Local companies also run buses along this line, using more antiquated vehicles, though fares are adjusted accordingly. Transportation to Cuenca (five hours), Esmeraldas (seven), Riobamba (five) and elsewhere is also frequent.

The most enjoyable way to go from Quito to Guayaquil is by train (see "Quito – Transportation"). The railway station is in Duran, across the river; from there, take a ferry or taxi (the latter crossing the impressive bridge) into town.

A number of bus companies provide service between Guayaquil and the border city of Machala, with several departures every hour (see below: "Onward to Peru").

You can get around in Guayaquil itself by means of buses, minibuses and *colectivos* (fixed-route taxis) – all cheap and fast, but crowded and noisy. Regular taxis are in abundance; be sure to agree on a fare with the driver **before** you climb in. The international car-rental companies have branch offices at the airport and in town.

ECUADOR

Food and lodging
As an important economic center, Guayaquil has been blessed with a wide range of places to eat and sleep. The best hotels are the *Oro Verde* at the corner of 9 de Octubre and Garcia Moreno (Tel. 510-201) and the *Continental*, at the corner of Calle Chile and 10 de Agosto. The latter has a beautiful old wing and superb restaurants. The *Hotel Palace*, Calle Chile 216, is less expensive and recommended. Also high on our list are the affordable *Hotel Plaza* (Chile and Ballen) and the nearby Rizzo.

Thrifty accommodation is available north of Avenida 9 de Octubre, along Calles Junin and Urdaneta and south of Avenida 10 de Agosto, on Sucre, Boyaca and nearby streets. Among these, the *Hotel Imperial* (Urdaneta 707) is recommended.

You'll find excellent restaurants in the luxury hotels. We recommend the ones in the *Continental* and *Oro Verde* hotels, along with the *1822 Restaurant* in the grand *Hotel Guayaquil*. Guayaquil also offers many Chinese restaurants, mostly downtown. *Chifa Mandarin* on Avenida 9 de Octubre is recommended. On that boulevard you'll also find a familiar American *Burger King*. The restaurant on the corner of Chimborazo and Huancavilca serves Middle Eastern food. For a host of restaurants specializing in fish and seafood, head for Urdesa.

Tourist services
Maps and printed material are available at the Dituris office, the Central Tourist Bureau, located on the corner of Malecon and Avenida Olmedo (Tel. 518-926); open until 4pm.

Though many tourist companies organize excursions in Guayaquil and its surroundings, their main expertise is in cruises to the Galapagos Islands (see below). Flights to Galapagos are run by TAME airlines (Tel. 305-800).

Tourist sites
Though Guayaquil is not noted for fascinating sites, there are a number of places worth seeing. The **Malecon**, a sort of promenade, runs along the riverfront, bustling with people and cars on one side and a procession of boats on the other. The Government and Municipality buildings are along the Malecon, as are many public buildings. The entire area is crowded during most hours of the day and the evening. At sunset, many locals take their evening constitutional, ending at the **Clock Tower** at the end of Avenida 10 de Agosto. This nineteenth-century Oriental clock serves as a familiar landmark for locals and visitors alike. Heading northward along the Malecon, we come to Avenida 9 de Octubre, Guayaquil's main street, which runs

*E*CUADOR

GUAYAQUIL

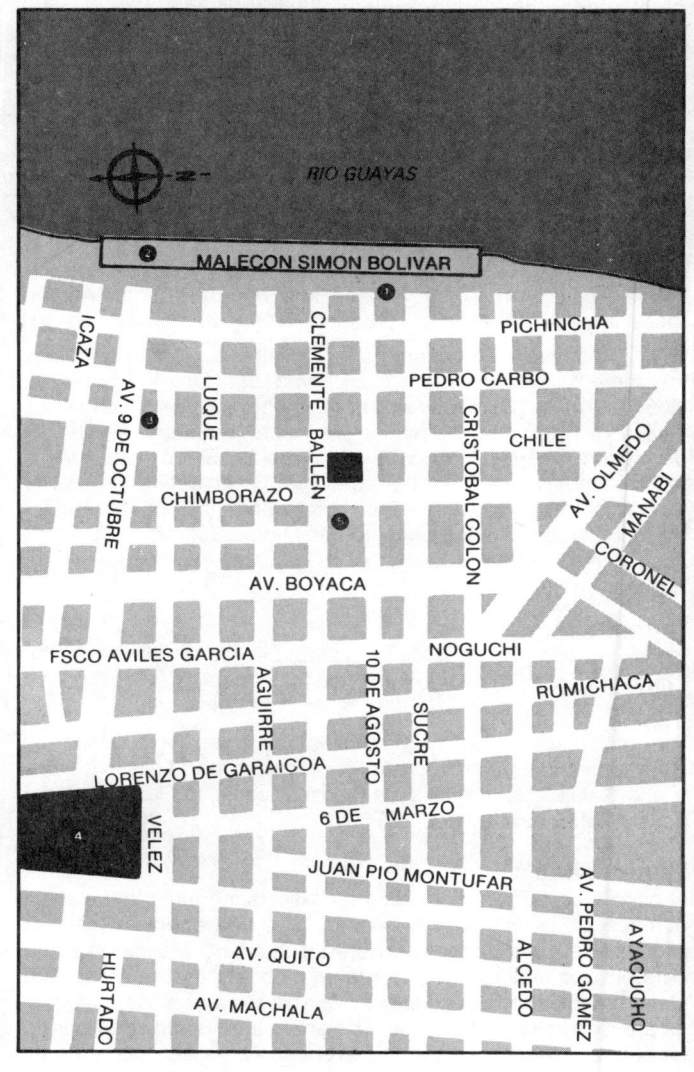

Index
1) Clock Tower
2) La Rotonda
3) San Francisco Church
4) Plaza Centenario
5) Cathedral

ECUADOR

perpendicular to the northernmost quay. Opposite the intersection of this boulevard and the Malecon is **La Rotonda**, a monument commemorating the fateful meeting of Bolivar and San Martin. One block north of here, at the intersection of the Malecon and Calle Icaza, Banco de Pacifico displays a collection of regional art. Recommended.

We now turn left – westward – up Avenida 9 de Octubre, passing the shops and restaurants that line this humming business street. Three blocks later we reach the Church of San Francisco. This church, one of the city's loveliest, is noteworthy for its interior decor, a well-preserved survivor from the colonial era. Beside the church, on Calle Chile, are a number of stalls which comprise a sort of small market. To visit another beautiful church, **La Merced**, cross the street opposite San Francisco, turn onto Calle Cordova and continue for a few meters.

Proceeding up Avenida 9 de Octubre, we arrive at **Plaza Centenario**, Guayaquil's main square. The monument to the heroes of national independence dates from 1920. A **Museum of Pre-Columbian Art**, run by the Ministry of Culture, is at 1260 Avenida 9 de Octubre. Here you can feast your eyes on antique handicrafts, gold jewelry and more. Open daily (except for *siesta* time). Recommended.

From here we'll head back, southward, toward the intersection of Avenida 10 de Agosto and Calle Chimborazo. Here we come upon a small park named for Simon Bolivar, and across the way, a relatively modern cathedral with white towers and broad dimensions, which may be visited during mass. We continue toward the river, passing the Municipal Library and reaching Calle Pedro Carbo.

Turning right, we arrive at the corner of Calle Sucre. Here we find the **Municipal Museum**, with its impressive display of gold implements and archeological findings, alongside shrunken heads ... a reminder of the customs of the wild Indian tribes. Though the ground floor is occasionally used for exhibitions of modern art, most of it is set aside to display archeological collections and colonial art objects. On the upper floor you'll find collections of handicrafts, folklore and the like. Visiting hours: Tues.-Fri. 9am-noon and 3-7pm; Saturday 9am-2pm.

From here it's but a short walk to the Malecon, near the Clock Tower. Once we've come to know the city center, I think it worthwhile to venture a bit farther. From La Rotonda you can keep going straight – northward along the Malecon – to **Las Penas**, Guayaquil's Old Quarter. Though it is not a long walk, we do not recommend it, for it goes through a poor and dangerous neighborhood. It is best to let a taxi take you there. In this rickety neighborhood, at the foot of Santa Ana Hill, you

ECUADOR

can roam the cobblestoned streets between squat houses, centuries old. Here you will find **The Santo Domingo Church**, Guayaquil's first, dating from the mid-sixteenth century. For a bird's-eye view of the area, climb a little way up the hill until you come to two ancient cannons, and contemplate the scene around you. The cannons were installed here centuries ago to defend Guayaquil against attackers from the sea and have remained ever since.

The prestigious suburb of Urdesa, with its many cinemas, fine restaurants, clubs, sports facilities and more, is northeast of the city center.

Night life

Guayaquil's status as Ecuador's most active city finds expression in entertainment, as well. Unlike Quito, Guayaquil does not excel in folklore activity though this too is available – but rather in more Western entertainment: discotheques, cinemas and nightclubs the like. The first two can be found in the large hotels, the city center and Urdesa. Most are open every night, though they are mainly active on weekends. The cinemas show first-rate films. A number of resort towns and recreation centers around Guayaquil offer a broader range of leisure-time pursuits.

Banks and moneychanging

Several foreign banks have branches in Guayaquil, which deal in matters of trade between Ecuador and their respective countries while handling all conventional monetary transactions. Citibank, Banco Holandes and Bank of America branches also handle the transfer of money to or from Ecuador. For changing currency it is best to turn to the moneychangers (*cambio*), most congregating along Avenidas 9 de Octubre and Pichincha. The airport *cambio* is open on weekends as well. For buying Peruvian intis it is best to wait until you reach Peru, though the exchange rate is sometimes better in Guayaquil. Check first.

Postal service and phones

The Central Post Office is downtown on Calle Carbo. The IETEL office for international phone calls is nearby.

Resorts

Guayaquil is surrounded by several popular resorts where the locals spend their weekends and holidays. The most popular ones, Playas and Salinas, have frequent bus service to town. Both of them have nice hotels, pleasant restaurants, sports and entertainment clubs and a casino.

The tourist office in Guayaguil will provide you with transportation details. If you are planning to visit during the

ECUADOR

holiday season, you would do well to make reservations in advance.

South of Guayaquil

The main highway south of Guayaquil skirts the Gulf, and connects Puerto Bolivar and Machala, Ecuador's fourth-largest city (pop. 130,000). Machala is the largest town near the Peruvian border. This rapidly developing city is the center of a large agricultural area – the main product grown here is bananas. Frequent bus connections link Machala with Ecuador's other cities and with Peru.

Onward to Peru – border-crossing procedures

Border crossing formalities between Peru and Ecuador are handled in the frontier town of Huaquillas, with all the standard immigration procedures carried out nearby. The checkpoint is open daily from 9am until 5pm with a two-hour afternoon *siesta*. Tourists entering Peru are sometimes required to present departure tickets from that country, and an MCO is not always enough. (If that is the case, buy an inexpensive bus ticket from any border town to some destination in a neighboring country). You must cross the border on foot. After completing departure procedures, you will have to submit to the bureaucracy of immigration regulations of the country you are entering. You can go to street moneychangers who congregate at the border area to change currency. It is worth remembering, however, that exchange rates here are lower than those prevailing in the nearby cities, so change only enough money for your immediate needs. On weekends and while the banks are closed, the rate of exchange is even poorer. Be sure to compare a number of moneychangers' rates – and check the amount handed to you.

Direct bus service from Huaquillas brings you to Quito and to other large cities. From the Peruvian side, *colectivos* (fixed-route taxis) will take you to Tumbes, where you can get express service to Lima and other cities in northern Peru.

The Galapagos Islands

Though many places on earth are called "unique" or "exceptional", the Galapagos Islands, a thousand kilometers west of the Ecuadorian coast, are exclusive in their ability to actually back up the claim with statistics. Dozens of animal and hundreds of plant species flourish here, and a considerable

ECUADOR

number of the sea animals, about half the flora and almost all the reptiles exist nowhere else on earth

The Galapagos Islands – *Archipelago de Colon* in Spanish – were discovered in 1535, and ever since have aroused the wonder and admiration of zoologists and botanists the world over. The archipelago, named after the giant sea turtle (Sp. *Galapago*) consists of several dozen islands of various sizes at varying distances from one another. Noticeable differences in flora and fauna types can be discerned even between one island and the next.

Of the five thousand people in Galapagos, about half dwell on San Cristobal Island (the administrative center) and many others live on the major island of Santa Cruz. Ships link the islands and also transport tourists from the island of Baltra, where the flights from the mainland touch down, to Santa Cruz where most island cruises begin.

The Galapagos Islands are home to hundreds of animal species. Among them: giant sea turtles, marine and terrestrial iguanas (huge lizards), sea lions, penguins and birds by the tens of thousands. The most famous animals are the large iguanas, which resemble prehistoric dinosaurs, and the huge turtles, which served for years as easy prey for pirates who feasted on their tasty meat. Since, historically, they have had little contact with man, the beasts lack an instinctive fear of people. For the visitor, this is perhaps the most astounding phenomenon of all. Not only do the animals not flee from one; they actually swim up to one and give one a friendly greeting. The prophecy in Isaiah 11:6 – "And the wolf shall dwell with the lamb ..." appears to come true before our very eyes.

The Government of Ecuador and the Darwin Foundation, with assistance from UNESCO, set up a research station on Santa Cruz in 1959. Most scientific research in Galapagos is concentrated here, along with a very interesting exhibit of the local flora and fauna. We highly recommend that you stop here **before** cruising among the islands. Thus you will acquire a basic familiarity with what you will see and increase your enjoyment of this strange world where time seems to have stood still since Creation.

The development of Galapagos

The Galapagos Islands were never part of any continent and are in fact the peaks of volcanoes that reach as high as 3000 m above sea level. Though actual eruptions are extremely rare, some of the volcanoes are still active; you can sometimes see smoke wafting from distant cones. The islands, commonly

ECUADOR

assumed to be three million years old, consist chiefly of volcanic basalt. Only limited areas are covered with top soil which supports the dense tropical vegetation appropriate to their geographic location. The equator runs nearby; so does the Antarctic Humboldt current, which meets the warm El Nino Current not far from here. Some regard this singular geographic combination as the key to the wondrous phenomenon of the Galapagos.

According to the accepted hypothesis, the animal and plant life on the Galapagos Islands developed over hundreds of thousands of years, during which various biological families were transported here by sea and wind, each finding its own niche in this odd environment. This theory underlay the conclusions of the British scholar Charles Darwin, who visited the Galapagos in 1835 as a crewman aboard the *Beagle* and came to know at first hand the archipelago's unique natural phenomena. Darwin's Galapagos observations laid the foundations for his famous work *The Origin of Species*, in which he presented his view of the evolutionary process. Its essence: animal and plant life undergoes a process of development influenced by environmental changes in such a way as to make possible their survival in the new conditions.

The theory of evolution

Basing his theory on observation and research, Darwin concluded that all life originated from a single source. In search of support for his ideas, the British scholar turned to a variety of complementary theories, widely-held in his day, and integrated them into his own. Darwin's evolutionary hypothesis is based on the fact that animals and plants produce offspring in quantities far greater than those necessary for maintaining the species at its current population level, while those levels have remained stable over extremely long periods of time. At the same time, each generation is somewhat different from its precursors. The first two arguments led Darwin to conclude that every generation's mortality rate is high, the third led him to infer that some individuals have better chances of survival than others. The survivors, claimed Darwin, are those who are better able to adapt to changes – and these will subsequently become dominant.

The theory of evolution made a big splash the moment it was published. Today, more than a century later, it is widely recognized. New discoveries and scientific experiments tend to confirm the idea of change and the thesis that all creatures derive from a single primeval source. Humans, land animals, sea animals and even birds have many common traits. Genetics, the biological frontier of our age, explains how the process of

ECUADOR

evolution actually takes place; its description of the mutation of genes tends to confirm Darwin's most important arguments.

Visiting the Islands

Tourists with the Galapagos Islands on their itineraries may choose between two possibilities, both "organized". Because there is a quota of 1500 visitors per month and because transportation among the islands is possible only by rented boat, we haven't many alternatives. The first option is a package tour which includes a flight to the islands and a cruise among them. The second possibility is to get there yourself and haggle with some local captain over renting his vessel. Though the first way is usually more expensive, it guarantees full utilization of your time, reliability and a comprehenisve pre-planned route. The second option, though liable to involve a lengthy wait until a boat becomes available – with the possibility of prolonged delay and waste of precious time – is sure to end up considerably cheaper than the "packaged" way.

A number of factors should be taken into account when you select a tour and determine the type of excursion best for you. First of all you must choose between a real ship and a bouncing boat. The former has a number of advantages, the most important being stability (especially since the sea around the Galapagos is rather stormy) and optimum use of time (since a ship can continue traveling throughout the night as well). The great drawback: you will be in a large group, with no possibility of a "one-on-one" contact with the animals. When you go ashore, you will march along in a tight little queue with an even tighter timetable. A small boat, by contrast, offers a significant advantage in this respect, for a group of eight to ten people is far more flexible about how it behaves on shore and how much time it spends on a given island. At the same time, the waves will rock your boat and you will waste precious daylight hours sailing between islands, since small boats are incapable of night time navigation. If you are young or young-at-heart – and if you do not suffer too grievously from seasickness – I would recommend a boat. The pleasant atmosphere, excellent food which the crew hauls out of the sea each day, plus the flexibility en route will definitely compensate you for the inconvenience.

When you rent a boat yourself, generally in Santa Cruz, it is essential to bargain with the boat owner over the rate and route, stipulating the precise route the boat will follow, the time to be spent on each island and the overall duration of your trip. Rates fluctuate between $15-$30 per day per passenger, depending on the type of vessel, speed, comfort and the like. Remember that the cheapest option is not necessarily the best, and be sure to ascertain that the crew has equipped itself sufficiently for the

ECUADOR

THE GALAPAGOS ISLANDS

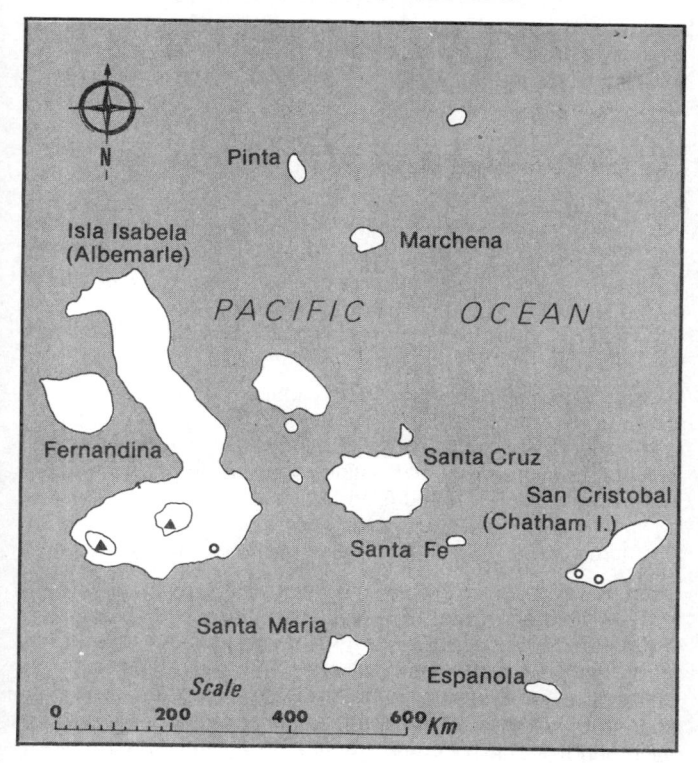

duration of your trip, otherwise you will waste valuable time restocking.

If you are on an organized excursion, the crew of your boat will meet you at the airport to take you to the vessel on which you will spend the coming week. Many travel companies organize Galapagos tours – some from Quito, others from Guayaquil – and their rates vary considerably. It is important to verify the quality, reliability and condition of the ship or boat and, of course, the duration of the cruise and its route. Among the reliable firms, we can mention Metropolitan Tours in Quito, which offers many tours either by ship or by boat.

Though TAME Airlines flies to the Galapagos from Quito and Guayaquil every day, you have to buy tickets in advance, for the planes are always packed. If you are on your own, take a boat

ECUADOR

from the airport on Baltra to Santa Cruz, where you will start organizing your outing. Be prepared to wait a long time for a boat. Concluding an agreement with a boat owner is likely to take a week during the "hot" tourist season. Individual tourists will easily find potential partners on Santa Cruz with whom to team up to rent a boat

The ideal Galapagos excursion itinerary runs from seven to ten days and the following islands are recommended:

Santa Cruz – the major island, with more than one thousand inhabitants. Here you will find the most important attraction: the Darwin Center for Galapagos Island Research, with its fascinating exhibit of various aspects of life and its development on the Islands, and the giant sea turtles cared for under special conditions to prevent their extinction. Visiting hours: 9am-4pm weekdays. A "must".

Lodging possibilities in the island's main village, Puerto Ayora, are limited and generally rather basic. Reservations are important between June and September and in December and January. Bear in mind, that eating, drinking and moving about freely are forbidden on the islands except in specified areas or by special permit. The restrictions are intended to guarantee a minimum of damage to the natural environment that the animals require.

On Santa Cruz you can hike to Tortuga Bay or Mount Crocker. Another recommended outing takes you to the turtle preserve, accessible by car from Santa Rosa (about 20 km from Puerto Ayora).

Espaniola – one of the most beautiful islands, favorite playground of sea lions and frequented by tremendous flocks of birds, among them the albatross, masked boobies amd blue-footed boobies.

Isabela – the largest island, populated by a great number of birds, as well as iguanas, penguins and more. If you are in shape and willing to make the effort, we recommend a climb to the top of volcanic Mt. Alcedo, with its splendid view.

Floriana – an island full of stunningly beautiful birds.

Plaza – covered with dense vegetation and populated by iguanas, birds and assorted marine creatures.

Santiago – a gorgeous island with thousands of iguanas, birds, sea lions and other marine species, who will gladly join you in a swim along Espumuilla beach. Games Bay is an exquisite bay with a basalt coastline where sea lions and birds bask in the many pools which have been formed in the rock surface. An exceptionally beautiful part of Santiago Island is that opposite

ECUADOR

the adjacent Bartolome island (enchanting in itself). In this area the lava has solidified into strange and varied forms.

Daphne – on this island two types of boobies nest – the blue-footed and the masked booby.

Seymore – this is the nesting ground of the frigate. During the mating season one can observe the incredible breast of the male which inflates into a big red sack – protruding below its head – part of his attempt to court the female.

Other recommended islands – the more remote Tower and Fernandina Islands (a visit there requires an extra day or two). Tower Island is the only nesting place of the red-footed boobies.

Miscellaneous comments

1) For more information, consult the many books available on the Galapagos Islands. They are available in Quito, Guayaquil and on the Islands, as well.

2) Take along enough local currency. Prices are higher in the Galapagos than on the mainland, since almost everything must be flown in. Moneychanging possibilities are limited. Those places – banks and other institutions – that are willing to change dollars will do so at a lower rate and a higher commission.

From Guayaquil to Quito – up the Andes

One of the most beautiful and interesting routes that ascend the heights of the Andes, is that from Guayaquil to Quito. Though we have mentioned the railroad which plies this route, in our sections on Quito and Guayaquil, it is hard to refrain from taking it up again and recommending it.

A trip along this route is certainly unforgettable. Though two trains set out from Guayaquil up the mountain each day, only one, the *Autoferro*, reaches Quito. This train, with its comfortable, spacious cars (some designed especially for tourists) and relatively low fares, starts out a bit after 6am every morning and climbs towards the capital. This railroad, completed in 1908, reaches an elevation of 3609 m above sea level at Urbina (275 km from Guayaquil). The second train, *tren mixto*, hauls passengers and freight only as far as Riobamba; from there you will have to take a bus to Quito. It also departs each morning and takes about ten hours to reach Riobamba, after stopping in every village and hamlet along the way to take on and unload passengers and freight. It is a lively ride, full of peddlers – an experience in itself.

E CUADOR

Remember that the trains do not run on Sundays and that it is advisable to buy tickets in advance at the office in Guayaquil (no need to go as far as the terminal, located across the river in Duran). Though the trains make a number of stops and the platforms en route are swarming with peddlers, we recommend packing food for the trip. First, you will not always have time to wait in line; secondly, the peddlers' "bargains" will not always favorably strike your palate.

Plenty of buses ply this route every day as well, using the Guayaquil-Quito highway. Most of the bus companies that serve this line are low-priced and reliable (see also "Quito – Transportation").

Some of Ecuador's most interesting towns lie along this route and we will visit them while traveling between the country's two largest cities. At one point we will detour to visit the city of Cuenca, where a number of delights justify our attention.

The route heads northeast from Guayaquil and we spend four hours crossing fertile, heavily farmed plains. The last stop before climbing the Andes is Bucay, a small provincial town 87 km from Guayaquil at the foot of the mountains (you can also reach Bucay from Guayaquil by bus, covering a route no less beautiful in half the time). Then the train begins its steep climb, the most captivating part of the trip and the reason for its fame. The first important stop is the town of Sibambe, 130 km from Guayaquil. The route to Cuenca branches off here. Past Sibambe the tracks make some astounding switchbacks up **Noris del Diablo** (The Devil's Nose) – an utterly fascinating stretch – and continue toward the mountain cities. But, as promised, we will detour to Cuenca, about six hours south of Sibambe.

Cuenca

Cuenca (pop. 150,000; elev. 2600 m) is Ecuador's third-largest city and the center of the Ecuadorian handicrafts "industry", whose reputation has spread far and wide. This convivial town was founded in 1557, and its old homes and cobblestoned streets do not seem to have changed much since. Its climate is spring-like the year round, its Indian population forthcoming and friendly.

The lovely *artesania* market held on Thursdays (on Calles 9 de Octubre and San Francisco) offers a wide selection of the best local handicrafts. Try to arrange things so as to reach town on market day (there is a city market on Sunday as well, but it is much smaller and less impressive). For shopping, we can also recommend the Productos Andinos Cooperative, with its variety of wares at reasonable prices, or any of the shops throughout town, mainly along Avenida Gran Colombia.

ECUADOR

Transportation
Many buses from Guayaquil, Quito, Ambato, Machala and elsewhere reach Cuenca. Two trains arrive every day from Sibambe, one leaving it in the morning and the other in the afternoon (the trip takes about six hours). The trip from Sibambe is a little faster by bus, but less impressive and not as interesting. Take the bus only if you have missed the train. SAM has daily flights to and from Quito and Guayaquil.

Where to stay
Cuenca has a number of restaurants and hotels. The best hotel is *El Dorado* on Gran Colombia. The *Hotel Crespo* on Calle Larga (Tel. 827857, 829989) is less expensive and recommended. The *Hotel Milan* is reasonably priced and convenient.

What to see
The **Tourist Bureau** is in the Carmelo Building, at the corner of Calles Malo and Sucre.

Cuenca is renowned for its many churches, whose steeples dominate the skyline. We recommend a visit to the El Carmen Church on Calle Sucre, the cathedral in the central plaza and the San Francisco and San Blas Churches.

No visitor to Cuenca should miss visiting the museums. The **Municipal Museum** displays impressive Indian ornaments, Incan and other pre-Columbian archeological relics. The **Banco Central Museum** houses a highly interesting, unquestionably unique collection of antiquities, the Padre Crespi collection. The priest, who died in 1982, amassed the collection to support his contention that the first settlers in this part of the world were Phoenicians, who had crossed the Atlantic Ocean in their small boats and penetrated the continent along the Amazon and its tributaries. The museum, in the Banco Central building on Calle Gran Colombia, displays artifacts which, in Father Crespi's view, attest to their owners' Mediterranean origin. Interesting.

Excursions in the vicinity
Las Lajas Park is located not far from town. The park is rather hard to reach and has no facilities. Nevertheless, the area, more than 4000 m above sea level, is lovely, with lakes, lagoons and small streams. You could spend several enjoyable days hiking here. Bring food and excellent camping gear.

Ingapirca, Ecuador's only Incan ruin, is located two hours out of Cuenca by train, bus, taxi or thumb. Though deserted on weekdays, it is full of visitors on weekends when transportation is easier to arrange. For lodging, you can pitch a tent nearby or

E CUADOR

camp in a *refugio* (hut). The purpose Ingapirca served is not certain, but it appears to have been used, among other things, for sun worship.

After exploring Cuenca and its environs, we will return to the Guayaquil-Quito route and continue the climb from Simbote to Riobamba.

Riobamba

Riobamba was founded by refugees from Cajabamba, a town about thirty kilometers away that was abandoned after being levelled by an earthquake in 1797. Riobamba, an attractive city 2750 m above sea level, is home to a population of 75,000, who engage mostly in business, agriculture and the manufacture of decorative items. A delightful market held every Saturday offers local *artesania* and a view of the citizens in their traditional attire.

The Guayaquil-Quito *Autoferro* train stops in Riobamba and continues on to Quito, while this is the end of the line for the *Tren Mixto* from Guayaquil. Many buses travel to Riobamba from Quito (three hours), Guayaquil and the other mountain and coastal plain cities.

Riobamba is full of restaurants. Among the city's many hotels, the best is the Galpon (far from downtown). We recommend the Humboldt (on Avenida Borja). You'll find very reasonable hostelries along the streets near the train station.

The Tourist Bureau (Calle 5 de Junio, corner of Primera Constituyente) will advise you concerning accommodations, transportation and outings in and about town. In Riobamba itself, we recommend a visit to the churches and the religious museum in the Concepcion Monastery. You should then head 10 km north to the village of Guano, renowned for the wonderful fabrics woven by the local residents.

From Riobamba we continue toward Quito, either by train or by bus, passing between soaring mountain peaks and broad plains. Our next stop: Ambato.

Ambato

Ambato (pop. 110,000), 150 km from Quito, is largely a new city built atop the ruins of its predecessor, devastated in the terrible earthquake of 1949. Today's reconstructed Ambato, with its handsome streets and buildings, is a quiet, rather sleepy town, which bursts into life in February when its **Fruit and Flowers Festival** attracts crowds of participants.

The city center is graced with a lovely plaza, where you will find the cathedral and a small museum displaying stuffed local birds

E *CUADOR*

and animals (closed weekends). Nearby are a number of *artesania* shops where you can acquire a selection of souvenirs.

Many buses from Quito, Guayaquil, Cuenca, Banos (see below), and other cities pull into Ambato.

The city is the starting point for the ascent to volcanic Mount Chimborazo. If this is for you, make inquiries beforehand at the Tourist Bureau (located in City Hall at the corner of Calles Castillo and Bolivar) about climbing conditions, weather, transportation, necessary equipment, etc.

It should be noted that mountain climbing, a stormy adventure in its own right, requires experience, superb physical condition and appropriate equipment. Because of the high elevation you **must** be doubly cautious, spending several days in the area before setting out, to allow your body to acclimatize to the rarified atmosphere (see "Introduction – Altitude").

Climbing Chimborazo

The most propitious time of year to climb this volcano (summit: 6272 m) is from June through August or December and January. The weather then is favorable, with almost no extreme changes. The most popular route up is via Pogyos (elev. 4000 m), an hour and a half from Ambato by bus. Rent mules to haul your gear the rest of the way. From Pogyos it is about a four-hour climb to Refugio Zurita, a hikers' shelter at 4950 m; spend the night there. The next day – **very early** – begin your final assault on the peak, a nine-to-ten-hour trek. The descent is far easier, usually taking about five hours. Be sure to wear comfortable hiking shoes and warm clothing; bring top-grade climbing and camping gear.

Banos

This resort town takes its name from the hot springs in the vicinity, which account for much of its popularity as well. The town lies 1800 m above sea level in the middle of a fertile tropical zone. It attracts tourists in its own right and by being on the road to the eastern jungles, as well as serving as a crossroad of the hiking and mountain-climbing routes. Try not to come here on the weekends because this is when throngs of locals arrive. The hotels are fully booked and the warm water pools are packed with bathers.

Transportation

The city enjoys frequent bus service with Ambato, continuing to other destinations on the Quito-Guayaquil route. Buses leave for the eastern jungles several times a week, reaching the jungle

*E*CUADOR

towns. Tena and Misahualli. The road is rough, but passes through gorgeous, tropical landscape (see "El Oriente"). Buses leave from the terminal located near the city center.

Where to stay
Banos is full of hotels of various grades and price levels. The *Hotel Sangay* is the best in town; apart from sleeping accommodations, it has a delightful restaurant and sports facilities. *Pension Patty* (near the marketplace) is cheaper, as is *Residencial La Delicia* on the central plaza. Santa Carla, located near the central plaza, is where most young travelers stay. The atmosphere is intimate and congenial and it is inexpensive. One also has access to the kitchen. There is a nice campground opposite the *Hotel Sangay*. You will find plenty of cheap hotels and pensions downtown, but since Banos is a resort town, occupancy is high: you will have to move fast – even faster on weekends – to find a vacancy.

What to see
Hot Springs are located in Banos itself and slightly out of town. The most distant of them, **Salado**, is about one kilometer west of Banos, with frequent bus service to bring you there. It is much less crowded and the experience of bathing in the pleasant water justifies the trip.

The gorgeous **Agoyan Falls** are about 9 km out of town. Daily buses set out from Banos passing the Falls. Walk back to town along Rio Pastaza.

The Zoological Gardens: At the eastern approaches to Banos there is quite an interesting zoo, and among the many jungle animals there, one may also see the gigantic Galapagos turtles.

Mountain hikes can be pursued along numerous routes around town. Some of the most beautiful ones are in the area between Banos and Puyo. A hike along the streams winding between the towns will expose you to pristine views, lush foliage and gentle falls. Hiking is not difficult and the pleasant climate permits hiking almost all year round. Bring along food and camping gear and spend a few days exploring the area.

You can continue from Puyo to the jungles of The Oriente.

Climbing Tungurahua
This active volcano looms 5016 m above sea level and it takes 2-3 days to climb. Don't worry; the volcanic activity of the mountain is restricted to emitting small amounts of sulphuric steam from the crater. The view from above is breathtaking; slopes covered in snow, and way below stretch green valleys. On the horizon more snow capped peaks can be seen, such as

ECUADOR

those of Chimborazo and Cotopaxi. About a 2 hour climb below the snow line is the *Refugio*, a mountain hut where one can sleep and use the stove for a few pennies. It's about a 5-10 hour climb to reach here from Banos, but it is best to do most of the trip with a car which leaves every morning from the Santa Carla and Patty Hotels. These hotels also have climbing gear. On the day of the climb one must get up very early and leave the *Refugio* at dawn – an incredible sight in itself. The climb to the crater takes about 3 hours with an additional hour to the summit. It is worthwhile to make the descent from the *Refugio* to Banos by foot and to enjoy the beautiful green pathway. The descent takes about 3 hours.

El Oriente

Few journeys are engraved deep in my memory as more exciting, stirring and interesting than the one I took in the *selva* (jungle) of Ecuador's east (*Oriente*). Here nature has offered man a rare opportunity to observe a primeval, almost unexplored corner of the world. The enchanting scenery, dense vegetation, animal life, Indian tribes, fearsome rivers, little towns ... even the derricks which pump out the oil discovered here recently – all exude a unique essence. The wild jungle atmosphere accompanies the visitor's every step, and the feeling of Creation acquires a dimension of rare power.

Even though El Oriente accounts for about half Ecuador's territory, no more than 100,000 people live there – just a little over one percent of all Ecuadorians. The predominant population is Indian, consisting essentially of three tribes: the tranquil Yumbos, the Jivaros (once known as head-shrinkers) and the wild Aucas. In addition, a community of Catholic missionaries has dwelled here for many years, engaging in linguistics and religious activity.

The climate here is hot and humid. Though temperatures usually do not exceed 32 degrees Centigrade or 89 degrees Fahrenheit, humidity can reach 97%. Rain – lots of rain – falls almost every day. The greatest precipitation falls in the western section of El Oriente, along the eastern slopes of the Andes (5000 mm per year!). As one heads eastward toward the upper Amazon Basin, the amount drops to "only" 2000 mm. This is one of the world's rainiest areas, a fact which leaves its imprint both on the river-sliced topography and on the composition and amount of vegetation. The latter is dense and features hundreds of different species, with a considerable number belonging to the palm family.

The thick tropical growth, which imbues everything with a bold

ECUADOR

green hue, gives the observer a misleading sensation of inexhaustible fertility. In fact, it appears that the jungle soil is not rich at all; the very tangle of vegetation actually accounts for itself. This is the reason that most attempts to deforest the jungle and plant domesticated crops there have, at best, been modestly successful. Bananas, yucca and other typical Indian crops rapidly drain the soil of its nutrients. The growers have no choice but to abandon their holdings and migrate every few seasons.

The first white man to visit here was Francisco de Orellana. Sent into the thicket in 1541 to hunt for gold, he succeeded in coming down Rio Napo and reaching the Amazon intact after an exhausting and perilous campaign. He was the first to succeed in returning from the wild and unexplored region in one piece. Though he came back with no gold, he was greatly esteemed and respected. Orellana set out again for the jungle in 1546 – and never returned.

Not much has changed since. Only in the twentieth century did the area begin to reflect signs of genuine change. The missionaries began to establish little settlement points, schools, hospitals and religious institutions. With the help of boats and light planes they began penetrating the depths of the *selva* intending to convert the natives. Their energetic activity first encountered the Indians' intuitive opposition, for the indigenous people were "culture-shocked" by the foreign agent who had penetrated their territory. This sentiment later turned into an almost ideological hostility: the missionaries, the tribesmen claimed, were disrupting their ways of life and damaging their ability to preserve their tradition. The Indians demanded that the invading missionaries be ousted. The Ecuadorian Government, concurring, issued directives during the 1970s calling for downscaled religious activity in El Oriente. In so doing, the Government found it necessary to enter into confrontation with religious bodies of tremendous worldwide influence. The missionary institutions are funded directly by the Vatican (though not all the missionaries are Catholic). Their work is done on a voluntary basis, the priests receiving only their food and clothing needs. Almost all the priests own nothing and spend decades in the jungle without commitment to family, people, or country, save their religion and mission in life.

Only in recent decades has non-religious development also begun to take place in El Oriente. Growing numbers of whites have discovered the dormant potential of the jungle and have relocated there, establishing a number of villages and towns. The year 1967, when top-quality petroleum was discovered in commercial quantities, marked a dramatic turning point in Oriente history. A large-scale development boom followed.

ECUADOR

American oil companies and the Ecuador Government have joined forces to exploit the fields, investing enormous sums to push through roads, build settlements and erect derricks. In 1972, a 500 km oil pipeline as far as Esmeraldas on the Pacific coast began conveying the local produce to the port where it is loaded on tankers for export all over the world.

The American companies, chiefly Gulf and Texaco, invested $1 billion in building a suitable oil production infrastructure. Their contribution was decisive in turning El Oriente into an area of utmost economic importance. The discovery of oil caused an upheaval in Ecuadorian economic thinking and its financial possibilities, and petroleum sales are still a decisive input in the country's income despite falling prices and demand.

Transportation

In El Oriente you will surely notice a beefed-up military presence – a consequence of Ecuador's prolonged border disputes with Peru. If you wish to explore the area in depth, you will need to obtain special permits for the purpose. Daily flights serve the major towns, as do buses. Though dirt roads (some covered with asphalt) link some of the settlements and allow antiquated buses to bounce along them, riverboats appear to constitute the chief method of getting around. They reach most settlement points, including the most remote little hamlets.

TAME flies from Quito to Lago Agrio every day and to Puerto Orellana (better known as Coca) several times per week. Fares are low and flights are usually packed. Buses from Quito set out for Lago Agrio several times daily, making the difficult trip in about fourteen hours depending on weather and the quality of the vehicle.

The main highway heads eastward from Quito to the town of Baeza. There it forks – one leg south toward Tena, the other north to Lago Agrio. From Tena the road continues to Misahualli and from Lago Agrio to Coca. The latter two – typical jungle towns – are points of departure for adventurous outings into the *selva* thicket, about which we will have more to say as we proceed.

Another route from Ambato to Tena passes through Banos and Puyoso. This, however, is much less convenient and entire stretches are washed out at times by flash floods.

The Ecuador Air Force operates non-scheduled flights to El Oriente cities. You can sometimes get on board. Texaco flies several times per week to Coca and Lago Agrio and tourists occasionally get special boarding permits at the company offices.

ECUADOR

How to get around

A tour to El Oriente, in my view, is not the kind of experience you should pass up. Nevertheless, it is important to emphasize that the matter involves no few difficulties and obliges visitors to be willing and prepared to bear considerable hardships – primitive roads, harsh climate, mosquitos, irregular food and lodging conditions, two-legged "transportation" and so on. Older tourists who wish to get a taste of the jungle with minimal effort, cruise aboard the *Flotel* the floating hotel on Rio Napo. *Flotel* excursions are organized by the **Metropolitan Tours** in Quito (Avenida Amazonas 239, POB 2542, Tel. 524-400). *Flotel* fares are rather steep ($300-$500 per person) for the three to five day trip. Fares include the flight to El Oriente, a comfortable room aboard ship, meals and outings. As *Flotel*, sails down the broad river, passengers can avail themselves of small boats to explore side rivers and reach more remote villages. Those wishing to tour in this manner should be sure to make reservations and synchronize their itineraries with Flotel's departure dates.

Young and daring tourists can set out on more lengthy voyages and wander deep into the thicket to extremely remote, interesting and unique primitive Indian villages. If you have this in mind, your first requirement will be a rudimentary command of Spanish. You will need to rent a boat and hire a crew for such an outing and this requires negotiating skills and ability to communicate continuously.

Another way to explore the jungle – in fact the most popular of all – is to reach Misahualli, Tena, Coca or Lago Agrio on your own and hire a local guide to take you into the jungle. This is a convenient compromise between the previous alternatives. It is also interesting, relatively convenient, safe and unquestionably much cheaper than the others. (Misahualli, though somewhat commercialized, is known as a popular point of departure for such outings. See below).

Where to visit

The route covered below is a fascinating one incorporating most of what is worth seeing in El Oriente and delving into the remotest points of the *selva*. The means of transportation are varied, as is the amount of time required. Its a circular route beginning and ending in Quito. To carry it out in full you would need several weeks and lots of money. I am presenting the matter this way so as to meet every visitor's needs, with no intention of having everyone go through it all. I mean to cover select sites in a logical, geographic sequence. I suggest that you read the entire route meticulously and then determine which of the sites you would like to see. A number of alternatives for integrating other routes are given for each of the places

ECUADOR

surveyed here. In this way, you can combine a visit to various sites according to your personal preferences and possibilities.

Start out in Quito. From here, take a bus or plane to **Lago Agrio** Ecuador's oil capital. The overland route to this town starts out paved, though once you have crossed the mountains it deteriorates as it progresses eastward. Baeza, the missionaries' town on the eastern side of the mountains, is the last important point of settlement on this route. Once you have passed it, the road narrows and crumbles as it winds through enchantingly beautiful tropical scenery. We recommend that you make a brief stop at **San Rafael Falls** (150 m high). Once you have reached Lago Agrio, the attractive lagoons in the vicinity (especially Quiarenos) also deserve a visit. In Lago Agrio you can rent a canoe for an excursion along the nearby rivers, relying on its owner to take you far enough for an impression of the bird and plant life. There are buses from this town to nearby hamlets which, however, are graceless places of no special interest.

Lago Agrio's tiny airport (far from town) is served by frequent flights from Quito. Open trucks equipped with seats await arrivals at the airport. These will take you either into town or straight to Coca past wooden houses with straw roofs, oil pipelines and other features of jungle life. If you're coming by plane, an enjoyable shock awaits you upon arrival – for the change in scene is extreme and stunningly powerful.

In town you will find small, basic hotels along with bars, restaurants, shops and a small market. The bus company serving Quito and the surrounding area has its offices "downtown".

A main road out of Lago Agrio heads toward **Coca**, passing oil derricks, oilfield workers' camps, little concentrations of houses and more. A number of rivers cross our path; the bus mounts ferries to traverse them. Though bridges have actually been erected over some of the rivers, they are damaged at regular intervals by flash floods in which the rivers surge over their bank and wash away anything in their path.

Coca, situated at the confluence of Rios Coca and Napo, is the organizational center for the river communities. It is a faraway, rather desolate little place where the locals stick to their own affairs. There are several rather basic hotels and a number of convivial restaurants which serve good, plain fare. It is my opinion that Coca, in the heart of the jungle, is a window opening onto a wonderful, unknown world. From here you can set out on the *Flotel* for a cruise on Rio Napo or rent a boat for a voyage far up its tributary streams. Boats also head upstream to Tena and Misahualli.

ECUADOR

Along Rio Napo

The most recommended outing takes us down Rio Napo for somewhere from two days to two weeks, depending on interest and budget. At the **Capitania**, the riverside boat office, you can inquire into departure times or take off on your own by renting a canoe. Regular transportation down Rio Napo consists of boats which take passengers and missionaries to their villages, plus cargo and mail vessels which go as far as the town of Puerto Rocafuerto. By regular transport you can reach the riverside settlements only. If you are interested in penetrating deeper into the jungle, you will require the services of a boat owner who's willing to take you. Negotiate persistently with these boat or canoe owners, and give them no more than an advance before you set out so they can purchase fuel and food. It is very important to bring along sufficient food, water-purification tablets, mosquito repellent, camping gear and lots of patience, for as the cruise goes on day after day, the distant coast and the scenery become monotonous and exhausting.

The cruise to Puerto Rocafuerte takes about two days, though it isn't complicated. If you wish to head inland from this town (up Rios Tiputini and Yasuni) into the territory of the wild Aucas Indians, you will have to rent a canoe and equip yourself with a special army permit at the Defense Ministry in Quito. Before setting out, be sure to register at the army base across the river in Coca (cross the bridge and ask for Headquarters). Otherwise, military inspection stations downstream are liable to make you turn around and head back.

The first leg of the cruise down Rio Napo passes quickly and tranquilly. Along the banks of the broad river you'll notice isolated houses surrounded by gardens. They belong to placid Indians who engage in fishing and agriculture. About two hours out of Coca, you'll reach Primavera, a convivial little jungle hamlet where you can stop for rest and a light meal. A little later, you'll come upon the missionaries' village of **Pompeya** with its mission school and museum which you may visit. The latter houses an interesting display of ornaments, musical instruments, hunting tools and burial caskets belonging to the Indians who live along the banks of Rio Napo; nuns will instruct you about all these fascinating exhibits. Back on the water, you'll float past **Monkey Island**, so-called because of the numerous monkeys climbing its trees (they are seen chiefly in the early morning or late afternoon hours). A river channel off the Napo leads to **Limon Cocha**, a missionary town where you can meet a distinguished cross-section of the churchmen who have spent many years here in an attempt to bring the natives into the fold.

E CUADOR

Indians in the heart of the jungle

Their activity arouses controversy, and their movements have been subject to restriction more than once. The mission's light plane is sometimes available for hire when remote places must be reached, though this is a costly undertaking. The village also has a number of canoes for rent, enabling you to tour the surrounding jungle with the help of a local guide. If you've arrived here on the freight ship, you can "hitchhike" back to Coca on one of the many boats which head there every week.

If you are continuing down Rio Napo you will reach **Pana Cocha**, a tiny village on the river's left bank where you can spend the night – in a sleeping bag. Pana Cocha has a sort of half-kiosk, half-restaurant which serves ample portions of local delicacies. The tastiest of these, to my mind, are the *platanos* (sweet fried plantains), whose flavor brings to mind fried potatoes.

From here, the watercourse becomes more monotonous. Apart from the military inspection point in Tiputini, where you will have to present army transit permits, no towns or villages are to be found – until **Nuevo Rocafuerte** (also known as Puerto Rocafuerte), a collection of several houses, a couple of tiny shops and only a few dozen inhabitants. This, if memory serves, is the only town I have visited in South America which does not have even a single restaurant ... though lodging can be arranged in a local resident's home or at the boathouse.

Your genuine jungle campaign begins at Nuevo Rocafuerte. From here onward there are no more points of settlment, no more boat traffic: the mighty jungle simply keeps on rolling silently and undisturbed as it has since the begining of time.

*E*CUADOR

Even if you have reached the town by "public transit", you have no choice but to rent a small boat if you intend to continue on. Make very sure that the boat owner knows his way around; bargain ... for even so the pleasure is unlikely to be cheap. At the same time, people who sail up Rios Tiputini and Yasuni into the heart of Aucas Indian territory can expect a trek of unequalled fascination, during which they will have the privilege of observing a multitude of animals and coming upon Indian tribes which live exactly as their forebears did hundreds of years ago. This is undoubtedly an emotional and aesthetic experience.

From Nuevo Rocafuerte you can return to Lago Argrio by heading upstream on Rio Aguarico, traversing pulsatingly beautiful jungle areas, parts of which have been declared nature reserves. If you have come this far on your own resources, you can try to continue toward Lago Agrio on the mail boat which puts into Puerto Rocafuerte several times each month. This is certainly an interesting and enjoyable possibility. The only alternative return route is Rio Napo, by which we have come.

Up Rio Yasuni

Rios Tiputini and Yasuni – both narrower than Rio Napo and both utterly desolate – wind into the depths of the *selva*. The motionless water in their tributaries is a comfortable environment for crocodiles, water tortoises, giant Anaconda snakes (up to twenty meters in length, dangerous though not poisonous) and a host of other terrifying creatures. Monkeys clamber in the trees, while at ground level huge wild boars roam about, and birds soar above. It is a nature-lover's Paradise, a golden opportunity to explore one of the few places in the world which has not been ruined by the white man and the civilization which accompanies him.

The crowning point of our trip must certainly be a visit to the Aucas Indian villages. The tribe's name in Quechua (the dominant Indian tongue in this region) means "wild", and not without reason. The Aucas were the last to come into contact with the white man and submit to his sovereignty. Until a few years ago they were wont to attack and murder visitors. During the 1960s, the tribesmen were in the habit of coming up to the bank of the Napo (considered the border of their hunting grounds) to shoot arrows and other weapons at the settlers who had attempted to settle there. During the 1970s, an expanded search for oil in **El Oriente** led to increased friction with the native Indians. Only after violent confrontations, some fatal, did a few missionaries find a way to bridge the gaps and make initial contact with the natives. As a result of this understanding,

ECUADOR

"exchange visits" between priests and the indigenous people commenced, with a few of the Indians reaching Puerto Rocafuerte in early 1982 (here we are speaking of the Aucas in this region). The tribes at the western end of the vast territory, closer to the town of Tena, have maintained relations with the whites for many years and have long since abandoned their forefathers' ways. Accelerated exposure to Western civilization has brought in tow changed behavior patterns: most of the Indians have stopped going about naked and have begun using aluminium tools and fire. They even vary their diets now including rice, sugar, salt and candy in addition to the traditional monkeys, fish and yucca.

When I visited this region in late 1982, I still had the privilege of finding an "unspoilt" population. The tribesmen went about naked, hunting with the aid of long, well-maintained blowguns, fished with harpoons and plied the river in boats they had carved out of tree trunks. It was like falling into a time tunnel and emerging several millenia in the past. I had come across primeval creatures whose development had seemingly been halted in a manner difficult to describe. The encounter was an agitating one. Few such meetings could equal it in power and significance. Given the pace of events as we know it, we may easily assume that most of these Indians presently wear clothes and that their customs have changed beyond recognition. I am nonetheless quite sure that inasmuch as they were the last to be "discovered", a certain measure of that distant civilization, a rare ingredient of a vanishing world, is still preserved.

The Aucas and their culture

Little is known of the Aucas. They cast fear over the entire area by being known as a dangerous community from whom it was best to keep a healthy distance. When I first encountered them, I found it hard to overcome the fears instilled by their fierce reputation. We were not sure if we would be received pleasantly or rejected until the moment we arrived. To our great delight, the natives proved forthcoming, pleased to host us with warmth and in friendship.

The language barrier is difficult and burdensome. The Aucas speak neither Spanish nor Quechua, but rather their own unique tongue consisting of sharp guttural consonants and dissonances, which rarely exceed two syllables in length. The Aucas' violent image notwithstanding, their language is gentle. For example it has no command form.

The Aucas are primitive in appearance, going about the jungle totally naked and barefoot (they did once, at any rate), armed with primitive weapons of their own making. They live in little

*E*CUADOR

Mother and child of the Aucas tribe

thatched shelters and sleep in hammocks. The Aucas tribe and family structure has no "chief" in the accepted sense and decisions are reached freely among family heads. This is how settlement territories are determined and land distributed. The latter is worked according to the cycle of the yucca, the Aucas' staple crop. When the land loses its nutrients at the end of a

ECUADOR

lengthy nine to ten months' cycle, the tribe relocates five or six kilometers away and repeats the process. The calendar is determined by agricultural events: the monkeys' birthing season, for example, or by the growth cycles of the trees.

Their loyalty is to a single god, Uynuny, creator of all. The Aucas offer him no sacrifices of any kind; they have no symbols, gestures of honor, no prayers, no rituals.

Family celebrations are handled modestly, usually with quiet song, dance and *chiche* (a fermented yucca beverage). Burial of the dead is also handled in a special way: the body is left in the family's shelter while its occupants go somewhere else, never to return.

Especially interesting is the fact that despite their total isolation and unknown origins, their concepts of good and evil are very close to our own: no murder, no theft, no incest. Though Aucas youth are taught to be highly independent and tough, no ceremony or test of masculinity or femininity upon attainment of adulthood has been discovered.

In recent years, as the trend of Aucas integration into modern civilization gathers strength, the attitude towards them is changing as well. Things have reached such a state that these amiable, forthcoming Indians (today!) even wish to change their tribal name ... from Aucas – "wild" – to **Uarany** – "people".

From Coca to Misahualli, Tena and Ambato

Regular boat traffic links Coca to **Tena**, capital of Napo Province, a quiet town populated mainly by Spanish-speaking Indians of the Yumbos tribe. The Yumbos have long been in touch with Western civilization and are subject to strong missionary influence. Tena offers a few hotels, small eateries and bars. There are daily buses to Puerto Napo, Puyo, Banos and Ambato, while less-frequent buses head for Quito via Baeza (the trip takes about ten hours).

From Puerto Napo, about ten kilometers from Tena, you can cross the river and go downstream another fifteen kilometers to **Misahualli**. This town, at the confluence of Rios Napo and Misahualli, is a popular departure point for jungle tours which are interesting though a far cry from those you can enjoy farther downstream.

Misahualli is easy to reach from Quito by bus via Tena, from Ambato via Puyo or by boat from Coca (the latter a twelve-hour crawl upstream). Many boats to and from Coca make the journey every other day and some are designated for passengers.

ECUADOR

If your visit to **El Oriente** has begun here, and if you intend to go on from Coca toward Puerto Rocafuerte, you will need a rented canoe to get there. It is worth your while to make inquiries about rentals as early as Misahualli. This will save you time and considerable effort while it will not involve any significantly higher expenses.

The town has a number of basic and intermediate-level hotels, along with little restaurants whose standard fare will probably not go over well with fussy eaters. A popular tourist spot, it has got a well-developed and flourishing tour industry with many guides eagerly waiting to be hired, each promising to take you into wholly unexplored sections of forest. Choose your guide carefully; check the route he has planned for you (it may include a lengthy hike) and bargain over the price. It is important to recall that Misahualli and its immediate environs (i.e. anything within a one or two-day radius) are rather touristy and the local Indians have long since grown accustomed to Western faces which smile at them from behind Japanese lenses. Though this holds true for the animals as well, you cannot hope to encounter many of them during your outing here.

If you are interested in more authentic experiences and are prepared to expend the necessary effort and time, you will need to go hundreds of kilometers downstream (see "Coca" above). This notwithstanding, Misahualli unquestionably provides a relatively convenient and very interesting opportunity to explore the jungle from up close, getting to know its vegetation, life and ways. It would be a shame to pass it up.

Special instruction

Your number-one requirement when visiting **El Oriente** is willingness to tolerate tremendous lack of comfort, to cope with difficult sleeping, diet, hygiene and sanitation conditions, to put up with the humid climate ...and more. Though it is undoubtedly an exciting experience, take into account the fact that it is recommended only for healthy, resourceful tourists with camping experience and an ability to improvise. Even these tourists would do well to conduct themselves with redoubled caution in light of the hazards to be expected here. You must obey safety rules and the authorities' instructions down to the last letter. First of all, obtain the appropriate military permits from the Defense Ministry in Quito and register at every inspection post. This way your movements will be traceable, something to be made use of should the need arise.

It is important to insist on a **reliable guide** with a river-worthy boat. Sudden storms, cloudbursts and floods are common

ECUADOR

occurrences and you would do well to minimize the unavoidable dangers by being equipped with the very best. Check and recheck before you decide, for the money you save is liable to prove a mistake which you cannot always correct.

Stock up on food, mosquito repellent, a first-aid kit, anti-malaria pills, water purification tablets, camping gear, a mosquito net and hammock. These will prove indispensable in this harsh problematic environment; their absence may lead to unpleasant situations and needless suffering.

El Oriente is a wild, undeveloped area, and as a result malaria is rife; infectious and intestinal diseases doubly so. Again, be especially careful and prepare for the possibility of sickness. Since medical services here are rather basic, we recommend that you bring along medicines in sufficient quantity for an emergency. You **must** boil water before drinking it; if it is river water, add disinfectant.

The local population will warmly accept modest gifts. People you visit in their homes will greatly appreciate something simple such as chewing gum, picture postcards, simple metal crosses and the like. In certain places the value of hunting bullets for rifles is higher than that of money, and sometimes they will be welcomed in lieu of payment.

Moneychanging is no simple matter in El Oriente, for banks in this area are almost nonexistent and dollars go for low rates and high commission. Have enough local currency on hand before you get here, and remember that "enough" means a considerable sum. For one, prices here are higher than elsewhere in Ecuador (transportation expenses inflate the price of almost everything); for another, your expenses seem to multiply as you go along.

Warning: Be Careful! One cannot minimize the dangers of a trek through the jungle and every precaution must be taken. Apply wise, level-headed thought to every aspect of the decisions you make on your trip and use every strategy to lower risks. Even if most hazards are of nature and therefore unavoidable, many others are subject to our control.

From Quito to the northern coast

Another interesting area lies northwest of Quito and descends to the northern section of the Ecuadorian coast. The entire region is covered with dense jungles wholly different from those in the eastern sector. Here you will find a number of picturesque

ECUADOR

towns, Indian villages, concentrations of black Ecuadorians, white settlers' farms and more – which together form a unique and complex social matrix.

To reach this area, take the bus from Quito toward Santo Domingo de Los Colorados (from where you can continue in various directions). The route will then take you to the coast and to the largest of its cities, Esmeraldas. A visit here will last several days, during which you can combine hikes, cruises and trips to remote settlements – remote in both the geographic and the cultural senses.

Santo Domingo de los Colorados

The provincial town of Santo Domingo de los Colorados (pop. 65,000) is a rather worn-out tourist attraction. In the middle of Ecuador's western jungle, the town is on the road to Quito, Esmeraldas, Manta and Quevedo. Its fame derives mainly from the Colorado Indians, whose villages are scattered in the surrounding forests and who frequent the town on Sundays – when they bring their wares for sale in the local market.

Transportation
It takes three or four hours to cover the 123 km from Quito to Santo Domingo; the difficult highway becomes even more so on rainy days.

Transportes Esmeraldas and Transportes Occidental operate buses that pass through Santo Domingo several times daily on the Quito-Esmeraldas route. The offices of both companies in Quito are next door to one another, in Calle Ambato. Other buses reach Santo Domingo from Guayaquil (six hours), Ambato, Manta and the other towns in the vicinity.

Food and lodging
Santo Domingo has a rather large selection of cheap pensions, but only a few hotels worthy of the name. You will easily find pensions downtown, though on weekends you may well have to try a number of them before you find a vacancy. The *Hotel Zaracay* which is located far from downtown, is one of the best and most expensive hostelries, with a swimming pool and a good restaurant. The *Hotel Tinalandia*, with a golf course and swimming pool, is located in a quiet area about ten kilometers out of town.

Treat yourself to the local delicacies in any of the many restaurants in the center of town.

What to see
Though the Indian market held every Sunday has brought fame to Santo Domingo, its charm has faded in recent years. The

ECUADOR

crowds of visitors and the commercialization of its traditonal "Indian-ness" have left their imprint on the entire event. Today, it is not much more than a tourist showcase. Much of the merchandise is made especially to serve as decoration and conversation pieces in European or American living rooms and the same holds true for the Indians' colorful attire, hairstyles and body paint.

The Colorado tribe is noteworthy for its unique style and mode of dress. The men used to smear a bright red paint – made from a local plant – over their bodies and short hair, in order to ward off evil spirits. The women too, painted themselves red and walked about their villages topless. Today's Colorados (1500 in number) are well-adjusted to the new reality, having been baptized and having adopted modern ways of life. Most engage in fishing and agriculture. Though they still dwell in straw huts open to the elements, little seems to have survived of their ancient traditions.

While in the Santo Domingo vicinity you should venture into the jungle for a close-up of the Indians' way of life. A number of tour companies organize guided excursions from Quito to Santo Domingo, with a visit to the jungle villages on the itinerary. It is best to reach the town independently and to use it as a base for short trips on your own.

The road south of Santo Domingo leads to Quevedo, a town whose population of 80,000 includes quite a few of Chinese origin. The roads out of Quevedo (to Manta and Guayaquil on the coast and to Latacunga up the mountains) pass among fertile plantations, where you can see how the people of tropical highlands live.

If you wish to go on from here to Guayaquil, you may choose between the busy main road via Daule, or a quieter byway via the town of Babahoyo. Many buses set out every day from Santo Domingo to the port town of Manta (pop. 90,000). Here coffee and bananas are loaded for shipment, a fishing industry thrives and the commercial needs of the district are taken care of. Flights from Guayaquil and Quito land here several times a week.

Esmeraldas

The coastal city of Esmeraldas, Ecuador's fifth-largest (pop. 120,000), is the hub of most commercial and industrial activity along the northern coastal plain. Its port handles the local produce – tobacco, cocoa and timber. The oil pipeline from El

ECUADOR

Oriente terminates nearby, and the precious liquid it has conveyed is loaded onto tankers in Balao for export all over the world.

Esmeraldas' special ambience is a combination of geographic location, tropical environment and isolation. Restaurants and bars are packed – higher prices notwithstanding – and both locals and visitors seem to be in perpetual motion. Refinery and port workers, along with gold miners and villagers who visit the city, contribute to its unique atmosphere.

Transportation
Buses operated by Transportes Esmeraldas and Transportes Occidental make the trip from Quito to Esmeraldas in about six hours, travelling via Santo Domingo. To reach Guayaquil, Ambato, or Manta, you must also go via Santo Domingo.

Esmeraldas is served by daily flights from Quito and Guayaquil, which land at the small airport across the river.

What to see
The **Tourist Bureau** is located at Calle Bolivar 541, and will be able to supply you with information and maps of sites in the vicinity. Wander through the city and observe how it lives. The main street is closed to vehicular traffic between 7:30 and 9:30pm, when the locals may stroll along it to their hearts' content. Most people in Esmeraldas are descendents of black slaves whom the Spanish brought here in the sixteenth and seventeenth centuries to work the banana plantations. They've preserved some of their traditions, mainly in the music and dance; African rhythms and the *marimba* dance are very common here, and you can enjoy them in dancing clubs and schools, especially on weekends and holidays.

Many Ecuadorians come to Esmeraldas for a pleasant seaside vacation. A thirty-minute trip south of town brings you to two popular resorts, **Atacames** and **Sua**, which offer little hotels and palm=spangled beaches. It is best to stay in these places, as it is cheaper and more pleasant than staying in Esmereldas. Here the beaches are suited to days of relaxing and tranquility. **Las Palmas**, north of Esmereldas, is also developing as resort area its pristine beach attracts many enchanted visitors.

The northern coastal strip swarms with mosquitos. Be prepared by bringing a repellent and some netting to put over your bed.

The route to San Lorenzo
The trip to San Lorenzo involves bus and boat and takes eight hours or more. The bus part is difficult and exhausting, for the road is mostly unpaved and the vehicles are antiquated. You will

ECUADOR

go through the village of Rio Verde and the town of Rocafuerte (where you can enjoy excellent seafood) before you reach Limones. From this town, located at the confluence of two rivers, you can take a side trip to the delightful Cayapa Indian villages of Borbon and Zapallo Grande. To proceed north to San Lorenzo, go by boat from La Tola for a cruise of several hours along a lovely seashore, rich in plant and bird life.

San Lorenzo

San Lorenzo, Ecuador's northernmost coastal town (situated next to the Colombian border) is especially famous for the local *marimba* bands which you can hear rehearsing practically every night.

It also offers a number of rudimentary hotels and an intolerable plague of mosquitoes (remember to bring netting and repellent).

From San Lorenzo you can either set out on short jungle trips to local villages or sail southward to the coastal towns. Between San Lorenzo and the city of Ibarra there is a decrepit railroad on which the *Autoferro* runs twice daily. The 193 km journey sometimes lasts many hours longer than planned as a result of technical delays and track problems.

North of Quito

The Pan American Highway north of Quito runs for 250 km to the Colombian border, crossing a serene mountain region of enchanting beauty and grandeur. Green mountain landscapes and volcanic peaks grace the road from either side and towns and villages come into view at every turn. Some of these villages are among Ecuador's most interesting. They are in the "musts" category, whether you visit them on an outing from Quito or drop in en route northward to Colombia.

The route is well traveled by buses and minibuses, allowing you great flexibility and mobility. Though reserved seats are recommended, it is hard to imagine that you will run into trouble, for service is frequent, efficient and provided by a number of companies.

This pleasurable region of Ecuador is noted for its handicrafts and art. Each of the places we are about to visit has been graced with its own special character and is known for its particular wares.

Otavalo

The Indian market in Otavalo (pop. 20,000) is one of South America's most famous, a magnet which attracts hordes of

ECUADOR

Saturday's morning market in Otavalo

tourist year after year. Otavalo, 110 km north of Quito, is laid out pleasantly with small, somewhat squat buildings, lining its handsome streets. The myriad shops in those structures offer an impressive selection of wool and textile clothing, the finest handiwork of the Indians who live in the surrounding villages. They have been long famous for the beauty of their wares, which suits the blazing color of their attire, their characteristic hairstyle and the manner of their speech and behavior. It is this successful combination which serves as the basis of the lovely market held in the central plaza every Saturday morning and afternoon. As early as 6am the main square is flooded from end to end, with an abundance of colors and pleasantries emanating from dozens of stands, offering enchanting wall carpets, ponchos, sweaters, dresses, shirts, leather handbags, sandals, ornaments – and so on.

Truth be told, the market's great popularity has slightly damaged its traditional character. At the same time, however, there is absolutely no doubt that this is **the place** to visit and shop. The

ECUADOR

prices are attractive – not before bargaining, of course – and the display is worthy of a king.

Because the market opens at the crack of dawn, most tourists prefer to reach Otavalo the day before, exploring the area and spending the night in one of the town's modest, clean, well-kept and inexpensive hotels. It is best to make reservations. Alternately, arrive early on Friday before the tourist rush begins. *Hotels Central, Sucre* and *Sami Huasi* (near the market) along with pensions *Otavalo* and *Vaca No. 2* are recommended.

You can explore the Otavalo vicinity – especially the area between the town and Lake San Pedro – on foot, enjoying two or three hours of pleasurable country hiking, wonderful scenery and crisp mountain air.

Cockfighting, accepted practice in Otavalo, is pursued every Saturday afternoon. Bullfights take place in June.

San Antonio de Ibarra

San Antonio de Ibarra, the "Village of Wood", is situated beside the main road between Otavalo and Ibarra. Many of its residents engage in woodcarving, their goods gracing marketplaces throughout the country. You will find a number of shops packed with statuettes around the central plaza. These, however, charge higher prices than those you will find farther away. Quite a few of these creations are true "kitsch", but many others are definitely estimable. Roam through the village and try to visit the workshops. Avoid visiting on Saturday afternoon, for then most of the shops are closed and your possibilities narrow down to a choice among those on the square.

Ibarra

The largest town in the region (pop. 60,000), Ibarra is a tranquil, pleasant place whose light-colored buildings give it a clean, calm hue. Here you will find an *artensania* market, hotels and restaurants. Many tourists prefer to stay the night here rather than in congested Otavalo.

The train to San Lorenzo on the Pacific coast sets out from Ibarra twice daily. Though the route (*Autoferro*) is beautiful and interesting, frequent breakdowns tend to reduce some of the enjoyment.

Tulcan

This is Ecuador's northern border town, 250 km north of Quito and 3000 m above sea level. Its main and only attraction is ... a visit to the cemetery, a gloriously well-maintained place with greenery pruned so painstakingly it is hard to describe. Trees and bushes have been shaped meticulously into images of animals, faces, buildings and the like.

ECUADOR

'State of the art' in the Tulcan Cemetery

Tulcan's 30,000 people host most of the travelers between Ecuador and Colombia and vice versa. Flights from Quito arrive here, as do buses and minibuses. You will also find a number of simple hotels and a few restaurants.

Onward to Colombia – border crossing procedures

The international border runs four kilometers north of Tulcan. Ecuadorian immigration procedures must be completed as you leave town. From there, take a taxi or bus to the checkpoint itself, where the Colombian immigration procedures are implemented. There is a Colombian consulate in Tulcan which will issue visas to citizens of those states which require them.

Rumichaca, a natural bridge, serves as the border between the two countries. Here you will easily find transportation either to Tulcan or Ipiales, the Colombian border town.

The crossing station is open 8am to 6pm, but closes for a one-hour *siesta* around noon. Dozens of buses and trucks cross the border each and every day, frequently causing lengthy delays. Crossing procedures are simple and speedy; on the whole, they involve no special difficulties.

Dispose of all your remaining local currency before leaving Ecuador; the same applies if you are arriving from Colombia. Except in Bogota, where there is a black market, all currency changes into Colombian currency is done at the Banco de la Republica – a branch of which is found in most cities, including Ipiales. Remember, on your arrival in Ecuador to exchange the minimum of money until you reach Quito, because you get a higher dollar exchange rate there.

PARAGUAY

When you enter this South American state, it may seem that you have reached a forsaken country where ignorance and economic backwardness prevail. This first impression, even if not totally incorrect, is rather superficial. Anyone who spends some time here will discover a unique country. Paraguay's name comes from the *Guarani* language, and means "a place with a great river". The reference is to the confluence of the Paraguay and Pilcomayo rivers, where the capital city of Ascuncion stands.

Paraguay has known many wars, whose destructive results are evident to this day. The country has been ruled tyrannically by a president who has been in office for some thirty years. The economy has been devastated by financial power brokers from within and without the country. It is conventional to think of this land, where the percentage of surviving Indians is the highest in South America, as a giant "farm" run by the president as if it were his personal estate. Paraguay is home to an international business community which has taken shelter there because of the country's flexible and unconstricting economic laws. In recent years a process of accelerated development has evinced itself in many fields, funded by outside capital channeled into Paraguay in recognition of its increasing importance, and this obviously has social and political consequences. For the tourist, Paraguay is one of the few countries where one is impressed by a simple way of life, a tough regime, and the influence of modernization on a primitive, tranquil and friendly population.

History

Paraguay was initially populated by the Guarani tribe, extending from Brazil in the east, to the slopes of the Andes in the west. When the first Spaniards arrived in 1525, the Indians refrained from fighting them. The lack of hostility, led the Spanish to begin frequenting the area and laying foundations for settlements. In 1537, Juan de Salazar founded the capital city of Asuncion. This was the start of a nation building process exceptional in Latin America, in which the native Indians integrated harmoniously with the Spanish newcomers. The slight importance which the

PARAGUAY

Paraguay and Pilcomayo Rivers had in relation to the gold and silver centers of Bolivia and Peru, and the obstacles the Indians in northern Argentina set in the path of those navigating these waterways, led to the isolation of Asuncion's Spanish community. The colonists quickly assimilated into the local population, and the community that developed was but slightly influenced by its subjugation to the Spanish viceroy in Peru. In 1776, when a viceroy based in Buenos Aires was appointed for the La Plata region, Paraguay was attached to the new jurisdiction. In May 1811, Captain Pedro Caballero led a rebellion against Spanish rule. He and his men routed General Belgrano, who had been sent from Argentina to Paraguay to ensure the latter country's continued ties with Buenos Aires. About a month later, a junta was formed which headed the young state. Paraguay, in contrast to its neighbors, won its independence with almost no struggle and nearly no casualties. In 1814, Jose Rodriguez Francia declared himself sole ruler

Jose Francia, known as El Supremo, led Paraguay for 26 years, until his death in September 1840. His rule was rigid and unbending; employing terror against his opponents and isolating Paraguay from the outside world. No one was allowed to enter Paraguay or to leave it, and trade with other countries was banned altogether. Only when he was replaced by Carlos Antonio Lopez, a professor of philosophy, were the borders opened, and Paraguay's relations with its neighbors allowed to develop. Various disputes soured relations with Brazil, Argentina, and even the United States, Great Britain and France. However, the momentum of accelerated development – and Carlos Lopez's political tolerance – ushered in a period of growth and prosperity that lasted until Lopez's death in 1862. He was succeeded as dictator by his son, General Francisco Solano Lopez. Three years later, Paraguay became entangled in a terrible, destructive war – the war of the Triple Alliance.

This conflict, which began in a dispute with Brazil, and a subsequent invasion of Uruguay in pursuit of the Brazilian Army, became more and more of an entanglement, lasting five full years. Argentina, Brazil, and Uruguay formed an alliance devoted to destroying Lopez's army. When it ended, Paraguay was utterly routed, and casualties amounted to one million men! As the war drew to an end, Solano Lopez seized often with attacks of madness and rage, was killed in the battle of Cerro Cora on March 1, 1870. Even so, he is still regarded as one of the greatest national heroes.

At war's end, Paraguay tried to rise from the ashes, but a prolonged border conflict with Bolivia over control of the Chaco

PARAGUAY

(Paraguay's western section) led to another war, which broke out in 1932 and lasted three years. In its course, the Bolivian army was repelled and Paraguay secured control of the entire area. A cease-fire and peace treaty between the two combatants were achieved with the mediation of the neighboring countries and the United States. An arbitration panel consisting of the presidents of these countries awarded three-fourths of the Chaco to Paraguay.

During the following two decades, Paraguay knew a series of tyrants who created social, economic, and political havoc. In 1954, backed by the army and the *Colorado* party, General Alfredo Stroessner seized power, which he has held tenaciously to this day.

In the course of his rule, Paraguay's isolation has slightly lessened – its currency has stabilized, roads have been paved, air routes developed, and accelerated industrial and economic development has begun to manifest itself. In 1967 the regime loosened its grip somewhat, and a new constitution, slightly more liberal than the previous one, went into effect. General Stroessner has been continually re-elected to additional five-year terms, for a total of more than thirty years.

Geography and Climate

Paraguay, 407,000 sq/km in area, is divided by the Paraguay River into the "Eastern Region", about one third of the country, and the "Western Region", the Gran Chaco.

More than half of Paraguay is forested, and the remainder serves chiefly for cattle grazing. Only 6% of the land is devoted to agriculture, and almost all of it is concentrated along the Paraguay River.

Massive rivers surround Paraguay, and their tributaries spread a network of veins throughout the country. The harsh tropical climate places great obstacles in the path of orderly and organized agricultural development. The immense Chaco region remains desolate, as if waiting for a redeemer. Apart from cattle grazing, it is of little value to the country's economy. The Eastern Region, geographically an extension of the Brazilian lowland, is home to about 90% of Paraguay's population, who engage mainly in agriculture under almost feudal conditions. Several hundred immigrant families hold close to 300,000 sq/km of land, some three-fourths of Paraguay's total area, whereas more than 100,000 native families must share only another 30,000 sq/km amongst themselves. Most of the latter have neither title deeds nor permanent rights to their land.

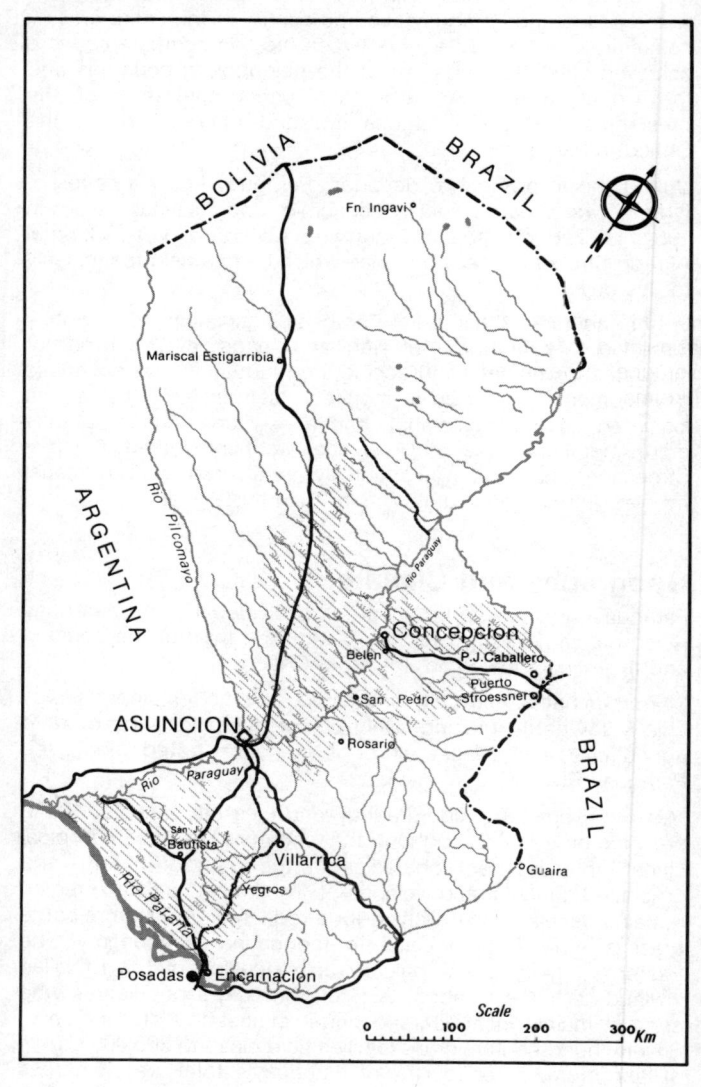

PARAGUAY

PARAGUAY

PARAGUAY

The subtropical climate in Paraguay is harsh and uncomfortable. Little rain falls in the Chaco region, though humidity is very high. Summer in the Eastern Sector and Asuncion is very hot; temperatures soar as high as 40 degrees Celsius (104 degrees Farenheit). Rain falls an average of eighty days, spread throughout the whole year. Winter temperatures are significantly lower, but the humidity is high and really cold weather is rare.

Population, Education and Culture

The proportion of native Indians in the local population is higher in Paraguay than in any other South American nation. Although only 60,000 "pure" Indians have survived, some 75% of Paraguay's 2,700,000 inhabitants have Indian blood, so that even the the relatively small European immigrant community has assimilated into them. Paraguayans are noted for their mutual tolerance, as evinced in the areas of religion, language, and customs.

Most of Paraguay's population lives off the land, chiefly in the country's Eastern Region. Asuncion (pop. 750,000) is the only large city. The high proportion of Paraguayans of Indian descent who preserve the ways of their ancestors has caused the Guarani language to remain the country's primary spoken tongue. The use of Spanish is common mainly in Asuncion, and serves mostly for official requirements.

The slaughter of men in Paraguay's wars has left its imprint to this day: the rate of out-of-wedlock births is the highest in Latin America. It is accepted practice for a man to have a number of "wives" in addition to his lawful spouse. Their number is determined by his ability to support them and their children.

Although elementary education is ostensibly compulsory and free, Paraguay's illiteracy rate approaches 25%. The educational system has expanded in recent years, and about 75% of school-age children are enrolled. Higher education is offered mainly in Asuncion, home to the country's two universities. The variety of subjects taught there is rather restricted, and many Paraguayans go abroad for higher education.

Economy

Since his rise to power, Stroessner has striven to stabilize the local currency, to calm economic conditions, and to bring about growth. The government appreciates the economic importance of industrialization, as well as the massive initial investment and high cost of the energy required to run an industrial system. With these factors in mind, the government has undertaken a

PARAGUAY

variety of activities to encourage capital investment from abroad, mainly from the U.S., Europe, and Japan, which have lately discovered Paraguay's latent potential. In recent years investment has been concentrated in mammoth power plants that Paraguay is constructing along its river borders with Brazil and Argentina. In due course these will produce several times as much electricity as is required for domestic consumption and the surplus will be sold to Paraguay's neighbors for hundreds of millions of dollars annually. These construction projects on the Parana River place great pressure on the local economy and cause fluctuations and shifts in its make-up but the government is making efforts to prevent any negative impact. Industrial development has accelerated in directions other than the traditional branches such as meat and meat products. (The meat industry has seriously deteriorated in recent years and is no longer a prominent factor in the national economy.) Large plants are now being built for essential products as well as for consumer and export goods. Export of wood and wood products, for example, accounts for a healthy slice of the national income. Nevertheless, Paraguay still lives by working the land. About half of Paraguay's population engages in agriculture, working only 6% of the country's land! Yet the agricultural sector accounts for most of Paraguay's export revenue.

Folklore

Paraguay preserves ancient and undisturbed Indian folklore. The relative scarcity of tourists and outside visitors helps to preserve the native culture, which remains authentic.

Handicrafts, chiefly weaving and embroidery, are highly original, as is the local woodwork. As for music, the characteristic Paraguayan instrument is the lyre; the folk songs are wistful and quiet.

Asuncion

Paraguay's capital, more than an interesting tourist city, is a genuine reflection of this unique and strange country, whose population congregates around Asuncion. As you walk about the downtown section, through Plaza Uruguaya and the narrow streets nearby, you will find it hard to believe that this is the center of a city with 750,000 inhabitants. The relative tranquility and the absence of typical urban phenomena such as cramped quarters and overcrowding are perhaps the best expressions of the easy-going and placid nature of the Paraguayan, as well as

PARAGUAY

his special grace and charm. The city is marked by low houses that seem to have known better days. The serene face this city presents casts a calming spell on the visitor. This, to a great extent, compensates for the city's lack of special tourist sites, the harsh and humid climate, the plague of mosquitoes (described by Gerald Durrell in his book *The Drunken Forest*) and the poverty of the natives.

Transportation

By air: The President Stroessner Airport is 16 km from downtown. Transportation into town, by bus, minibus or taxi, is fast and comfortable.

The national airline, LAP, flies weekly to Madrid, Frankfurt, and Miami, and offers numerous daily flights to neighboring countries – Argentina, Uruguay, Brazil, Peru, Chile, Bolivia, and Ecuador.

Iberia flies from Madrid via Brazil, and Eastern Airlines reaches Asuncion by way of Peru and Bolivia. Most South American airlines fly to Asuncion several times a week.

By land: The train ride between Buenos Aires and Asuncion is rather exhausting, the trip takes more than two days. Asuncion's train station is in Plaza Uruguaya. Buses make the trip several times weekly in half the time. The *La Internacional* and *Nuestra Senora de la Asuncion* companies operate buses to and from Brazil several times each day via the Iguacu Falls (see "Iguacu" in the chapter devoted to Argentina). The COIT company runs buses to Montevideo twice weekly (office in Plaza Uruguaya, corner of Antiquera Street, Tel. 48274, 47290) – a 26-hour trip in modern buses. The enjoyable ride takes you past the scenery of the Chaco through Argentina. There is no bus service to Bolivia; one must go by way of Argentina. Asuncion's central bus terminal is located on the eastern side of Plaza Uruguaya.

Automobiles and hitchhiking: One can get to Asuncion from Brazil with no difficulty via the Iguacu Falls on Route 7 (Ruta 7) as far as Coronel, and then taking Route 2 to Asuncion. From Argentina, one crosses the river from Posadas to Encarnacion; from there it is 730 km on Route 1 to Asuncion. The desolate and rather difficult Trans-Chaco Highway leads to Bolivia. Hitchhikers should bring along enough food for prolonged waiting, and twice as much patience. Crossing the border here is also more complicated than usual. In the absence of an official and orderly transit point, the Bolivian soldiers may well require you to report to the immigration offices in La Paz to obtain a

PARAGUAY

visa. Travel along this route, through extremely monotonous landscape, is nonetheless a singular, unusual experience.

Food and lodging

The *Chaco Hotel*, on the corner of Caballero and Mariscal Estigarribia Streets, one block from Plaza Uruguaya, is among the best in Asuncion. The same may be said of *Hotel Guarani* – on the southeastern side of Plaza de la Independencia – a modern facility with air-conditioning (important!), telephones in the rooms, restaurant, and a swimming pool. This hotel is very popular with businessmen. As for somewhat less expensive hotels, the *Sahara* on Oliva Street and the *India* on General Diaz Street are safe.

With Asuncion's hotels, even those defined as "inexpensive", are still expensive. It's very difficult to find one which is clean and centrally located and not expensive. One such place, though, is *Residencial Rufi*, at 660 Cerro Cora Street, corner of Antiquera, (Tel. 47751). Its location is excellent and its rooms large and clean – recommended! Small, cheap hotels, near the train station and Plaza Uruguaya, are called *residencial*, distinguishing them from the more expensive hotels.

As for food, Paraguay, too, is noteworthy for its superb meat, served in a variety of styles in the many restaurants situated throughout Asuncion. It's important to choose a place that looks clean, since various diseases caused mainly by poor sanitary conditions are still widespread in Paraguay (though less so in Asuncion).

The large hotels offer good restaurants; others can be found on the city's main thoroughfares. Prices are usually high and do not include taxes and service charges.

Empanadas, pastries filled with cheese, meat, vegetables, etc. are sold on the street. The local specialty is the *chipas*, a small tasty cake made of cornmeal dough mixed with cheese and egg. Don't eat one unless it's fresh! Although the flavor is usually excellent, the hygienic conditions under which they're made are not the best. ... Paraguayans love soup, and it's served in every restaurant, stand, bar, and wherever. Fruit is excellent but expensive, and is usually sold by peddlars along downtown Asuncion's main streets.

Cafes/restaurants are also found downtown, and are especially suitable for breakfast and for taking breaks while touring the city.

There's a *Kentucky Fried Chicken* in Plaza de la Independencia for those of you who've had enough of the local food.

PARAGUAY

Asuncion's public transportation

Urban transportation

The small, colorful buses that drive along the narrow streets are the most popular way of getting around Ascuncion. For me, the buses here were a never-failing source of entertainment: even the old U.S. school buses, with the protruding, front-mounted engines, are glorious specimens in comparison to the noisy crates of Asuncion. These buses are apparently powered by the residual inertia of a push given them in the thirties... that is, the 1830s, when they marked their hundredth birthday! It's hard to describe the situation any other way. The bus drivers, too, make a living in an unusual fashion. On some lines there are no tickets, and the driver reports the number of passengers as he wishes and pockets the rest of the money, whereas drivers on lines for which tickets are provided receive a certain percentage of the proceeds. It follows logically then that the bus spends most of its time just waiting for passengers. You don't have to stand at a bus stop, since the driver stops for anyone who waves. It may also happen that someone flags down a bus from 200 meters away, and the driver may simply park and wait until the would be passenger covers the distance at his own leisurely pace. An Asuncion bus has not only a driver but also a conductor, whose function is to pull people aboard and push them inside to make room for more. The buses have rather low roofs, and anyone of average or above average height cannot stand erect. Riding these buses, in sardine can conditions and with bent head, is therefore an unforgettable experience...

PARAGUAY

Tramcars have been returned to service, but they operate only along short lines in the city center. Taxis, too, are mostly found downtown. Their prices are moderate, and it is customary to add a 10% tip.

Tourist services
The Government Tourist Ministry is located on Oliva Street corner Alberdi (Tel. 49521), and is closed during the afternoon *siesta*. The office offers the tourist explanatory material, maps (better maps in stores), etc. – in Spanish.

Tourist sites
Most of the sites of particular interest to the tourist are found within walking distance of one another, in the vicinity of the central plazas. **Plaza Uruguaya** is the transportation center; the bus and train terminals are located there. It is only natural that the inexpensive hotels are nearby as well. The plaza, square in shape and sheltered by large shade trees, is almost always swarming with children, senior citizens, soldiers and peddlars. During the afternoon *siesta* one can hardly find a place to sit down. The long streets leading away from the plaza are lined with closely built two-story buildings housing innumerable shops. Next to the plaza, at the very beginning of Mariscal Estigarribia Street, is the **Museum of Fine Art**, which houses a disappointing and neglected collection of works of art.

Five blocks northwest of the plaza is another square, no less important: the beautiful and well kept **Plaza de la Independencia**. At its northern end is the impressive **Pantheon**, where the nation's heroes are buried. An honor guard of Paraguayan soldiers is stationed here. Buried here are the remains of dictator Francisco Solano Lopez, of Estigarribia (a hero of the Chaco war of the 1930s), and of two "unknown soldiers".

A right turn on Chile Street brings us to **Plaza Constitucion**. It is bounded on its eastern side by the **National Cathedral**, whose grand, impressive facade belies its plain interior. Across the plaza is the **Congressional Palace**, the seat of delegates whose authority is limited mainly to speechifying (and restrained speechifying at that...)

Continuing down El Paraguayo Independiente Street, which leads away from the plaza, we reach the **Government Palace**, a sort of imitation of the Louvre in Paris. In front of this building, guarded on all sides by armed soldiers, is a well kept garden and large floral clock. Here the President of Paraguay oversees all affairs of state. Visitors are not permitted to enter it, nor can they come too close.

PARAGUAY

Plaza Uruguay - human scenery

Close by, on the corner of 14 de Mayo and President Franco Streets, is the **Casa de la Independencia**, which houses displays from the annals of Paraguay's history.

Palma, **Estrella** and **Oliva** Streets are Asuncion's main arteries; along them you will find respectable businesses, banks, restaurants, and the like. A stroll here during rush hour is an interesting experience, although it is crowded then.

The impressive **Botanical Gardens** are located 7 km from downtown, along the Paraguay River on grounds that were formerly the private estate of the Lopez family. The gardens are very well kept, and offer an impressive variety of flora and a small zoo. The Lopez mansion itself, not far from the Gardens, has been converted into a museum of Paraguay's history and of its Indian population. From downtown, take bus 40, 36 or 2, and be sure to ask which way the bus is going when you get on.

From the Botanical Gardens, a dirt road about 2 km long leads to the river. Crossing the river in a small boat, we reach the **Indian reservation**, home to members of the *Maca* tribe who were brought here from the Chaco to serve as a tourist attraction. Apart from the plague of mosquitos, it's hard to say that we're dealing with an especially fascinating site. True, the aging Indians are adorned with massive feather headdresses, but they also wear sneakers. From their straw huts – protected from the rain, of course, with sheets of plastic – we hear Western music blaring from state-of-the-art radio sets... Pretty

PARAGUAY

ASUNCION

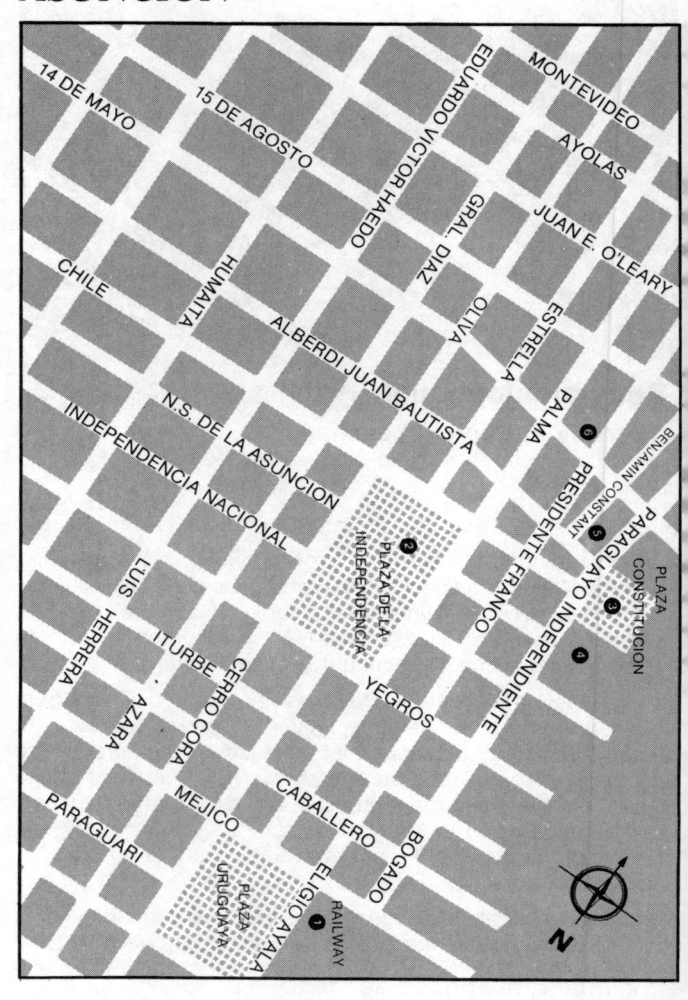

1. Train Station
2. Pantheon
3. Congressional Palace
4. National Cathedral
5. Central Post Office
6. Independence House

PARAGUAY

girls and wrinkled old women will approach you, more than willing to be photographed topless, for a fee of course. In short: skip it.

Entertainment
Asuncion is not much for nightlife. Shortly after dark, the streets fall silent and people vanish into their homes. Only in a few places is there any late hour entertainment, and these are meant chiefly for tourists and the young generation, mainly local students.

The downtown offers several rather antiquated cinemas. A number of nightclubs and discotheques – some located in the large hotels – are also in operation, but they are generally empty on weekdays.

General information

Currency and foreign exchange
The national currency is the *guarani*; its dollar exchange rate is set by the government. Bank notes are easier to exchange than travelers' checks, for which the banks charge a high commission. Bank transfers are paid out only in local currency and according to the official rate. Moneychangers offer a higher rate than do the banks, but be very cautious and count your money carefully! Moneychangers at border points offer a lower exchange rate than in Asuncion, so try to exchange only the amount required for your immediate needs until you reach the capital.

In Asuncion the best place to change currency is the area of Palma and Alberdi Streets, where most of the moneychangers *(Casa de Cambio)* are located. Not only do they offer slightly more than the bank rate, there is less bureaucracy.

The guarani is considered a stable currency and wide fluctuations in its rate are rather uncommon. Outside Asuncion – even in hotels and restaurants – it is hard to change dollars. Stability notwithstanding, guaranis are not sought after, and it's best to get rid of them before leaving Paraguay.

Postal and telephone services
Telephone service links Paraguay to most countries of the world, though collect calls are not always available. Postal service is very slow and letters take a long time in transit. The central post office is on Alberdi Street, corner of Benjamin Constant Street. A branch is located in the Hotel Guarani (Plaza de la Independencia) and provides most services.

PARAGUAY

Itaguan handicraft - the pride of the local people

Business Hours and Holidays
Most shops, businesses, banks, and government offices open early, and close for the *siesta* as early as 11am. The major public holidays, when everything is closed, are May 1, May 14-15 (Independence Day), and December 25.

Measurements; electricity and time
The metric system is used throughout the country. Paraguayan electricity is 220V. Paraguayan time is GMT-4 (GMT-3 in summer).

Weather
Hot and muggy. The summer is particularly harsh and an extended stay in this subtropical climate is highly unpleasant. The temperature difference between day and night is not great; the nights, too, are very hot and humid. Winter is slightly cooler, but still not pleasant. During the afternoon hours the temperature drops and fresh breezes blow, making these hours the most pleasant. Cotton clothing is the most suitable, since synthetics become distinctly uncomfortable.

PARAGUAY

Personal documents
Every tourist entering Paraguay is required to pay a $1.50 tourist tax. American and Western European citizens will be asked to present valid passports, and will be given a tourist card upon arrival, which allows a 90 day stay in the country.

Important Addresses
U.S. Embassy: Mariscal Lopez 1776 (Tel: 21041/9).

British Embassy: President Franco 706 (Tel: 49146).

The Paraguay Auto Club is located on 14 de Mayo Street, corner of Brazil Street.

Excursions

San Bernardino
This resort town on Lake Ypacarai, 55 km from Asuncion, is frequented during the summer by Paraguay's rich. It offers a variety of vacation services including hotels, restaurants, and sports facilities. As in Asuncion, mosquitoes thrive here. Those planning a lakeside vacation should take them into account and equip themselves accordingly. You can reach San Bernardino quickly by bus from Asuncion, or by driving down Route 2.

Itaugua
A visit to Itaugua, 30 km east of Asuncion, is highly recommended. This picturesque little town, more than two hundred fifty years old, is the center of an embroidery and weaving industry that produces unique fabrics which greatly resemble spiders' webs. Some handcrafted specimens are of stunning beauty and complexity, the result of years of work. They may be seen on public display in stores and workshops along the road through town. The unique tablecloths, blouses, dresses, ornaments, and so forth are impressive and their high price is justified. These embroidery works are known as *nanduti*.

In the center of town is a neglected square bounded on one side by an ancient church. The entire plaza, with its white houses and red shingled roofs, has a special charm.

The bus trip from Asuncion to Itaugua takes less than an hour, and a visit here requires no more than another two. Accordingly, Itaugua is just right for a short day trip from the capital.

*P*ERU

Ever since the first Spaniards landed on its shores more than 450 years ago, Peru has been known as a fascinating country, and its charm has increased over the years. Apart from having so much to offer – fabulous scenery, rare archaeological sites, a wonderful culture – Peru bewitches visitors with her mystery, which is unlike that of any other country. Peru is a unique blend of sights and sounds, a treasure trove of experiences that words cannot easily express. It's an exotic, strange land, a land of yesterday and today, and to a certain extent of tomorrow, too.

It would take a tourist several months to really get to know Peru, to take in the numerous sites, even if only the most important and famous among them. However, in a short time – about a week or two – one can form deep impressions and get a taste of one of the world's most interesting countries, a "must" on the itinerary of anyone who wants to experience excitement and fascination. Since Peru's tourist infrastructure is rather limited (especially outside the major cities) visitors are forced to improvise tour routes, transportation – everything, in fact – and herein, perhaps, lies the secret of Peru's special charm, which attracts hundreds of thousands of tourists each year.

History

Peru was the cradle of enlightened civilizations centuries before the Spaniards arrived. Remains discovered in Chavin, Paracas and Nazca date to 1000 BC and earlier. At the time of the Spanish conquest, until Francisco Pizarro overthrew their empire in 1531, the Incas dominated the entire region from Ecuador in the north to central Chile in the south (see "The Incas").

In the wake of Pizarro's takeover, Peru served as the principal foothold for the newly arrived Spaniards. In addition to the use of its ports, through which the treasures of South America were shipped to Spain, Peru became the starting point for the conquest and settlement parties who set out for neighboring lands. The Spanish viceroy established his seat in Lima and from there oversaw Imperial outposts throughout the continent. As the years passed and the other colonies developed and grew in strength, the viceroy's influence weakened until another viceroy had to be appointed for the Buenos Aires region.

As the King of Spain's largest and most important stronghold, Peru was one of the last colonies to respond when the call for independence rang throughout South America. Not only did Peru not declare its own independence, but it even dispatched

PERU

armies to repress the revolutionaries in Argentina, Uruguay, Chile and Bolivia. Only when General Sucre defeated the Spanish forces at Ayacucho in 1824 was the struggle for independence brought to an effective resolution, and Peru, like neighboring Bolivia, won its freedom. Much of the credit was due to the intervention of the Argentinian General San Martin and Simon Bolivar of Venezuela, who led their armies to Peru's aid.

The Republic's first years were marked by power struggles between military and civilian forces for the leadership of the young country. Though a rather liberal constitution was adopted in 1828, General Augustin Gamarra seized power less than a year later, becoming, in effect, Peru's first military ruler. Economic and national interests led Peru to enter into a confederation with Bolivia, led by the Bolivian General Santa Cruz. But before the success of this pact could be tested, the two countries were forced into a war against Chile, who feared the consequences of such a union and therefore forced the partnership to disband. Spain, too, found it hard to accept the loss of Peru and only in 1869 did it officially recognize Peruvian independence, after a large Spanish naval force encountered spirited resistance and was forced to withdraw. Around this time Peru began to develop its transportation and industrial infrastructure in order to fill the state coffers. But within ten years, in 1879, the war of the Pacific broke out with Chile fighting Bolivia and Peru over exploitation of the natural resources of the Atacama Desert, which was then Bolivian and Peruvian. The five-year conflict resulted in great losses of life and property. Chile's well-trained army won and took over the desert. Its soldiers reached the Peruvian capital of Lima, more than a thousand kilometers north of the battlefield, and imposed a humiliating treaty of capitulation.

The war's end found Peru on the verge of bankruptcy, but European economic aid, given in exchange for control of mines and other Peruvian production facilities, prevented a complete collapse and helped pull the nation out of its dire economic straits. This European involvement lasted into the 1920s, when the old problems again arose, chiefly concerning land ownership and the status of the Indian population. In the wake of the growing turmoil, the army again seized power. Social tension and economic pressures were greatly aggravated during the early 1930s, as a result of the Great Depression in the United States. Only some ten years later did a certain calm return, due to American economic aid, which must be understood in the context of Peru's unreserved support of the American policies during World War II. Democracy was restored in 1945, but the hoped for stability did not come in its wake. The 1950s and 1960s were characterized by political and economic unrest, with

PERU

a rapid succession of presidents. Even so, much was done during these years to quiet the country, and attempts were made to solve painful fundamental problems. These included far-reaching reforms: land was allocated to the Indians, the irrigation system was improved, roads were paved, new schools were built, and more. Peru was plunged, however, into another economic crisis during the 1960s; the army rebelled in 1968, seized power once again, and implemented a tough nationalization policy involving not only domestic banks and financial institutions but foreign-owned – chiefly American – companies as well.

The military regime enacted far-reaching decrees with clear socialist overtones in the agricultural, mining and industrial fields. At the same time, Peru forged diplomatic ties with the Eastern Bloc and in 1974 became the first Latin American state to have Soviet advisors.

A severe earthquake struck Peru's coastal area in 1970, leaving fifty thousand dead and causing hundreds of millions of dollars of damage to the tottering economy. Only $500 million in credit received from the World Bank prevented total collapse. The quake and its consequences, in addition to the nation's economic straits, led the Army to apply sharp austerity measures in the mid-1970s. Leftist elements and students then initiated spirited anti-government activity, which was of decisive importance in restoring Peruvian democracy in 1980. In the middle of that year, free elections were held for President and Congress, and tranquility and order have since prevailed. A policy of economic restraint, along with encouragement of moderate social forces, has permitted orderly governmental procedures, though extreme leftist groups have been conducting a guerilla war, particularly in the mountain region, disrupting transportation and social life. Clashes between these forces and the army and police increased in 1983 and 1984, though not of an extent to undermine the overall stability of the democratic regime.

In 1985, Alan Garcia Perez – aged 35 – was elected president of the Republic. His election constituted a substantial change in Peruvian politics by virtue of his having moderate communist tendencies, unlike his predecessors who were influenced by the West.

For the first time in a long while a Peruvian president enjoys extensive public support. In addition, the young energetic president intensified his struggle against the underground extremists. In 1986 a rebellion of security prisoners was quelled with much cruelty when the army burst in and killed most of the prison inmates – more than 300 men.

PERU

Geography and Climate

Peru, the third-largest country in South America, covers nearly 1.3 million square kilometers. Though its climate is generally tropical, its range of geographical zones leads to variations from region to region. Peru can be divided into three geographical and climatic strips, each with its own characteristics.

The coastal strip: Peru's western section, between the Andes and the Pacific shore – covers about 10% of the country's total area. This fertile region is home to almost 50% of the population and is the center of most of Peru's political and economic activity. The cold Humboldt Current keeps rainfall scant and the climate arid, though temperatures are quite comfortable. The cool waters carry a wealth of fish, so that Peru ranks among the world's leaders in this important industry. The soil along the coast is fertile, and agriculture has blossomed as the irrigation system has expanded. All this, however, is disrupted every few years, when a hot current from Ecuador, *El Nino* – "The Boy", upsets the fragile desert equilibrium, bringing rain and flooding, and the death of fish, birds and other local wildlife. This rather rare natural disaster usually occurs in September.

The Andes strip runs through central Peru, with a rather arid western slope (affected by the coastal region's desert climate) and a lush, wet eastern side. This area contains most of Peru's natural resources, and its mineral deposits account for about half of Peru's exports. The mountain range towers to more than 3000 meters above sea level, with many individual peaks reaching 6000 m or more. The northern peaks of the ridge have a tropical influence from neighboring Ecuador, but further south the weather turns cooler, more temperate. The Cuzco area is rather chilly, with noticeable day-night temperature differences. This region accounts for about one-fourth of Peru, as well as for some of its most splendid scenery. It has a comfortable climate, land suitable for agriculture and livestock and is home to more than 40% of Peru's population.

The remaining Peruvians are dispersed over the enormous **Amazon Basin**, which stretches over more than half the country's territory. The Andes' eastern slopes are, as said, blessed with lush vegetation, which grows more variegated and profuse as one journeys eastward, descending from the mountains into the broad valley. This vast region is covered throughout with thick tropical jungle carved by hundreds of rivers and streams – transportation arteries for local produce, which is comprised chiefly of wood products and the spoils of hunting. The region's economic potential has yet to be exploited. This is due to financing and development difficulties on the one hand, and to its geographical isolation from the rest

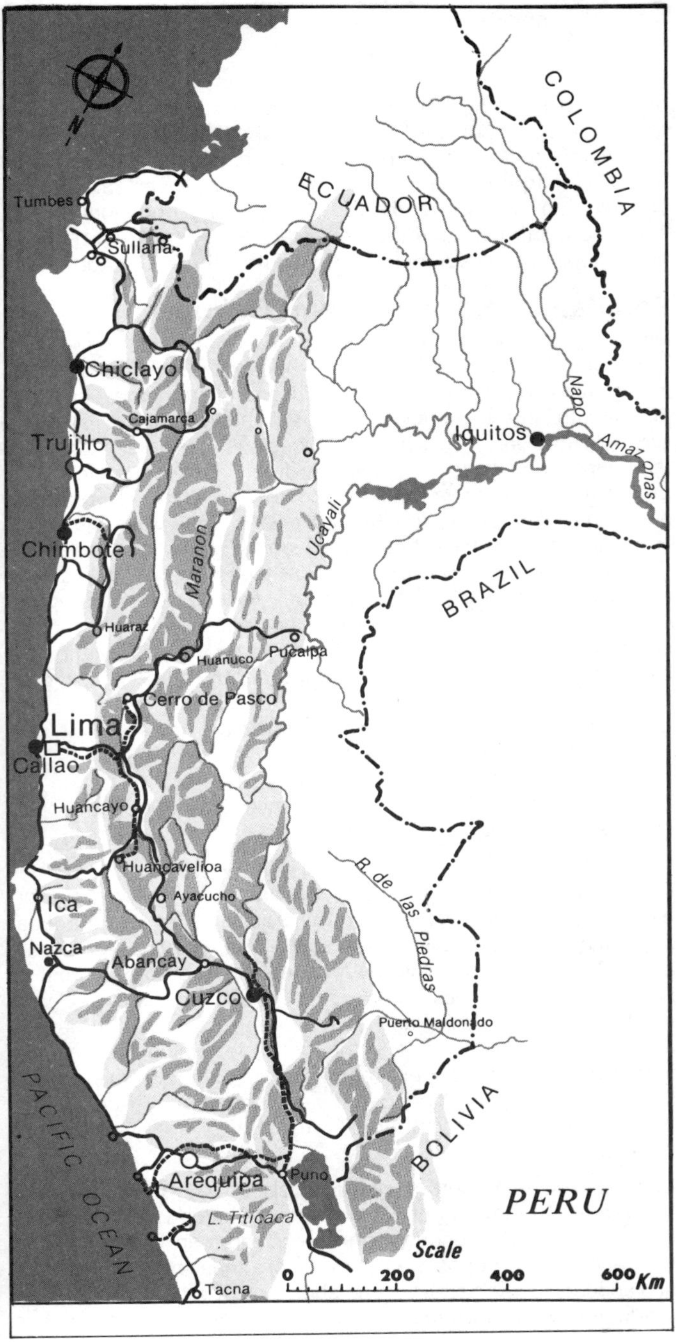
N
COLOMBIA
ECUADOR
Tumbes
Sullana
Chiclayo
Cajamarca
Trujillo
Chimbote
Maranon
Ucayali
Napo
Iquitos
Amazonas
BRAZIL
Huaraz
Huanuco
Pucalpa
Cerro de Pasco
Lima
Callao
Huancayo
Huancavelica
Ayacucho
Ica
Nazca
Abancay
Cuzco
R. de las Piedras
Puerto Maldonado
PACIFIC OCEAN
BOLIVIA
Arequipa
Puno
L. Titicaca
Tacna
PERU
Scale
0
200
400
600 Km

PERU

of Peru on the other (almost no convenient land routes lead to the region's populated zones). Oil, however, has been discovered in commercial quantities in its northern sector, near the city of **Iquitos**, and an oil pipeline has been laid to the coastal region. As a result, the region's economic and settlement infrastructure is expected to expand which, it is hoped, will accelerate the development of the entire country.

Population, Education and Culture

Historical developments peculiar to Peru have given its population of 17.5 million a mixed and varied ancestry. Massive immigration, both from Europe, Africa and from the Far East, along with the tolerance shown the newcomers, created a colorful mixture in which Caucasians, Blacks, Chinese, Japanese and Indians intermarried freely. Descendants of the pre-Columbian Indians account for about half of all Peruvians and some 70% of the mountain-dwellers. They have managed to preserve their traditions, dress and way of life, and even though most are baptized Catholics their religious practice is mixed with beliefs and rites from their remote politheistic past. The Indians generally speak their ancient languages, though some speak Spanish. They live in poverty and deprivation, in climatic zones where raising livestock-agriculture is difficult. The day-to-day struggle for mere existence has thus far prevented their educational and technological development, and their way of life remains as primitive as ever. Illiteracy rates among the Indians exceed 60%; though education is compulsory from the age of six, the government finds it hard to enforce such regulations among the Indians, due to the prevailing situation.

People of mixed Spanish-Indian descent called *mestizos* – the descendants of Spanish settlers who assimilated into the local population – constitute Peru's "nobility". The *mestizos* live chiefly along the coast and in the mountain cities, and control most of Peru's resources, industry, and economic and political institutions. Most senior army officers and government leaders are *mestizos*, and since it is they who determine the nation's mores and character, their imprint is discernible in everything. Most of them are well-educated and the illiteracy rate among them is low when compared with that of the rest of the population.

Children and teenagers account for about half of all Peruvians and many of them do not attend school. Nationwide illiteracy is about 28%, and in recent years the government has accorded education special priority. Peru has more than thirty universities of various types, but a severe shortage of jobs for university graduates, along with the low pay and low living standards, has

PERU

caused a "brain drain". Migration from village to city has increased in recent decades, and the high rate of natural increase, by which the population doubles every twenty-five years, also creates severe problems in housing, jobs and education, problems especially fierce because only one-fourth of the population contribute to the productive sector of the economy.

Economy

Latin America's major affliction – deficits in the balance of payments and massive external debt – has not spared Peru, though it is better off than most of its neighbors due to its rigid economic system and low standard of living. The army, when it seized power in the late 1960s, introduced an economic policy based on socialist principles, by which national treasures would be exploited for the betterment of all. Accordingly, the government began nationalizing natural resources and production facilities on a slow and limited basis, while providing massive investments to encourage agricultural, industrial and power projects, giving export subsidies and enforcing severe restrictions on imports. At the same time, Peru strengthened its political and economic relations with the nations of the Eastern Bloc, thereby receiving easy credit while opening broad new export markets.

Peru's cultivated areas do not succeed in meeting the rising demand for agricultural products, because half the country is covered with forest. Though new areas are constantly being opened to cultivation, Peru must import basic foodstuffs – a heavy economic burden. Most agricultural activity takes place along the coast, with sugar, rice, cotton and coffee among its chief crops.

Fishing is undoubtedly Peru's most important agricultural sector. Until several years ago, Peru ranked first in the world in fish production but this industry has declined significantly due to crises and natural disasters that have afflicted it. Nevertheless, the government has expanded its investments in fisheries, which continue to occupy first place in Peruvian industry. About 2.5 million tons of fish products are produced in Peru each year, of which a large portion is exported.

Mountain agriculture is still rather primitive, with cultivation generally carried out using hand implements and with the aid of animals. Most of the produce is consumed locally and sold in regional markets. It has no importance in terms of the national economy. By contrast, wool shorn from mountain beasts, chiefly alpaca and vicuna, contributes to national production, with some being reserved for export.

PERU

Natural resources undoubtedly constitute Peru's major export. In recent years, since oil from the northern jungles near Iquitos has become Peru's most important export, the entire jungle has enjoyed tremendous development. The oil fields, once controlled by American companies, were nationalized in 1968 and the Peruvian National Oil Company has operated them since, pumping tens of millions of barrels each year from Iquitos to the coast, and from there abroad. The oil pipeline running from Iquitos to the coast, along with the roads pushed through the jungle, suggests that the tremendous potential of the Amazon jungle is about to be fulfilled.

The coastal and mountain regions yield more than one million tons of various minerals per year, including ores of zinc, copper, lead and silver. The mines, too, have been nationalized gradually since 1968, and their income flows into the national treasury. The mines were damaged in the 1970 earthquake, but were re-opened with assistance from the World Bank, and today produce more than ever.

About one-fourth of the gross national product is derived from the industry, centered primarily around the large coastal cities, with 50% in the vicinity of Lima. Accelerated urbanization has brought about extremely rapid development in industrial production, and chemical, petrochemical, steel, heavy and light industry and textile factories have been set up in the suburbs with funds supplied by the government and foreign investors. Most industrial production is intended for domestic consumption, and its main contribution to the national economy lies in reducing the need to import equivalent goods. Today there is a growing tendency to expand industry for export purposes as well, especially of fish products. The great concentration of industry in urban areas has led to ecological problems, but at present it appears that its supreme economic importance outweighs all other considerations. Peru has been suffering from a spiraling inflation for a number of years. As a result the Peruvian currency was changed in early 1986 when 3 zeroes were taken off the *sol* and it was replaced by the *inti*. The mean per capita income is $700 a year, which is among the lowest in the world.

General Information

How to get there
By air: Peru is one of the cheapest destinations in South America. The visitor from Europe or the United States who wishes to take in the entire continent and has no special preference regarding the first stop, will undoubtedly find Peru the most suitable starting point price-wise. Aero Peru flies

PERU

between Lima, Iquitos, Cuzco and other cities, and to many destinations in neighboring countries, as well as to the United States and Europe. The London-Lima and Miami-Lima routes are known for their low fares. There are daily flights from the United States – from New York, Miami and the large West Coast cities – operated by Aero Peru and Eastern. Faucett Airlines, too, has very cheap flights from Miami. Most European airlines fly to Lima, including Lufthansa, British Caledonian, Air France, Iberia and KLM. The Russian Aeroflot also offers a cheap flight from Germany to Peru, with a stopover in Cuba. All the South American national airlines maintain daily service between their respective capitals and Peru's major cities, from where one can continue to other destinations the world over.

By land: Convenient bus lines link Peru with its neighbors. Direct lines run from the national capitals to Lima and Cuzco (details in our discussion of these cities). If you have a private car you'll need to obtain customs documents from the Auto Club, along with an International Driver's License.

Documents

When crossing into Peru, citizens of the United States and Western Europe (excluding France) must present a valid passport and fill out a tourist card, which must be carried at all times. Tourist cards are either issued by your airline or can be obtained at the border check-point. Visitors from certain countries need a visa, which is issued by a Peruvian consulate. A visa is good for one entry within one year of the date of issue. Both a visa and a tourist card allow a ninety-day stay. You can request a 30-day extension at the Ministry of the Interior in Lima. When you enter Peru you will rarely be asked for proof of sufficient funds. However, the immigration clerks of frontier points usually demand to see your return ticket. A $150 MCO usually satisfies them, otherwise you would be well advised to buy and display a cheap bus ticket from a Peruvian border city to a neighboring town outside the country.

A valid Student Card, **bearing your picture,** will prove useful and cut expenses throughout Peru – in museums, institutions, public transportation, and elsewhere.

When to come; National Holidays

Peru's weather is especially agreeable in winter, May through October, when only a little rain falls in the mountains and in the Cuzco area, where the Inca antiquities are situated. The rest of the year is rainier, though temperatures remain comfortable. Only in the mountains do temperatures fall below freezing point. The coastal area is very humid, especially between June and November.

PERU

The *Inti Raimi* Sun Festival, celebrated in accordance with ancient Inca traditions and considered one of the largest and most important of South American festivals, takes place in Cuzco at the end of June every year. Between June and September, Peru is swamped with European tourists who, exploring its treasures, create an overcrowded feeling at tourist sites, hotels, restaurants, transportation facilities – in fact, just about everywhere. You should take this into account, though it certainly should not put you off entirely.

National holidays during which Peru shuts down are January 1, May 1, June 29, July 28 (Independence Day), and December 25. In addition, a great many local festivals take place every month, offering a variety of folklore shows. For details about each month's events, consult *Peru – Where, When, How,* a tourist magazine distributed by the Tourist Office in Lima.

Where to Stay

There are plenty of good hotels, particularly in the large cities. Hotels are divided into four ranks: hotel, hostel, *residencial* and *pension*. The first two offer better service, higher prices and 20% taxes, plus 10% service on top of that. In *residenciales* and *pensions* the rate already includes the tax, but the level of cleanliness and service are not of the highest. Camping is convenient and has become widespread, particularly outside the cities; but while it is a pleasant experience in the coastal region, mountain campers must consider the possibility of rain and equip themselves with extremely warm gear.

Wining and Dining

Peruvians customarily eat a light breakfast and a moderate lunch (1-2:30pm), followed by a 5 o'clock break for tea, coffee, or alcoholic beverages. Only between 8 and 9pm do they sit down for the day's large meal, which usually includes soup, seafood and meat, and dessert, accompanied in elegant and intermediate restaurants by local wine.

Breakfast and lunch can be had almost anywhere. Marketplaces and city streets are strewn with countless kiosks serving various kinds of Chinese food, fruit juices, seafood, *empanadas*, and more, at very low prices. The national sweet tooth is satisfied by *chorisos* – a sort of doughnut filled with sweet cream and dipped in sugar; these too are sold in kiosks and are excellent when served hot. Try them! As a rule, one must be very careful where one eats, for the level of hygiene is extremely low and visitors quite often suffer from intestinal upsets. The problem is especially acute in places where people are not strict about refrigeration, cleanliness in their tiny kitchens, washing their dishes, taking out the trash, etc.

PERU

Peru abounds in Chinese restaurants, which serve good food at low prices, and they are cleaner than the markets. These, like the *confiterias* (cafes) which serve cheap light meals – sandwiches and the like – are packed at lunchtime and during the late-afternoon tea break. Many Peruvian restaurants, called *chicherias* or *picanterias*, specialize in good and inexpensive national dishes. The hundreds of Criolla restaurants, found everywhere, specialize in mixed Spanish and Indian cooking. You'll find lots of fish and seafood on this menu, for Peru's proximity to the coast and the well developed fishing industry are naturally reflected in the local diet. One famous dish is a combination of raw fish, lemon and onion called *cebiche de corvina*. Grilled chicken, another popular offering, is called *chicharrones de pollo*. Try it. Restrictions are occasionally placed on serving meat in restaurants because of the country's economic difficulties, and temporary regulations set dates on which beef may neither be purchased nor ordered in restaurants. If you've arrived during such a period, you will have to settle for chicken and fish. Take care to eat salads only in clean places, for raw vegetables are liable to cause disease. The soups are popular and extremely tasty. Large cities offer an abundance of exclusive and intermediate restaurants, located in the large hotels, along the main streets, and around the central plazas. Here you will be served *menu fijo* (business lunch) according to a fixed menu; the tab will be lower than for a similar meal served at night, so that even a visitor on a tight budget can enjoy one. Taxes add 15%-20% to the bill.

One of the typical features of Peru are the outstanding cream cakes. In all the big cities there are lots of coffee houses which serve such cakes which you certainly will not be able to resist.

Peru's "national drink" is *pisco*, a sort of brandy which is produced along the coast and serves as the basis for the *pisco sour*, served everywhere and downed with pleasure at any time. Tea, coffee and soft drinks are also found everywhere.

Health

Sanitation and hygiene standards in Peru do not begin to meet the expectations of a Western tourist. Visitors can contract various diseases – most involving the digestive tract. We therefore recommend extreme caution concerning where and what you eat, especially in markets. In addition, it is imperative to be particularly careful about drinking water. As a rule, you should drink only bottled water, especially outside the cities. Water purification tablets will help, particularly on trips into the country where all sources of water will need them. You should also bring a sufficient supply of medicines of various kinds, for those sold in Peru are costly and not always fresh and suitable

PERU

for use. Anti-malaria pills are necessary only in the eastern jungles; take them for a week before entering the region and continue for six weeks after leaving. Elevation sickness becomes a problem in mountain regions; go slowly there (see "Introduction – Altitude – how to cope with thin air").

Currency

Peru's national currency is the *inti* and its exchange rate varies due to inflation. Accordingly, change dollars only as you need to. Stock up on local currency before leaving the large cities for remote areas. Exchange rates are generally lower at border crossings; change only the minimum necessary to get into town. Occasionally it's best to buy intis in neighboring capitals (La Paz, Quito) where preferential rates sometimes prevail. Dispose of leftover intis before leaving Peru.

Official currency exchange takes place at banks and through moneychangers and travel agents. The latter also sell dollars, though not always. *Casa de Cambio* (exchange offices) and moneychangers in the street will change your dollars according to the black market rate which is sometimes identical to the official rate at banks, but which can sometimes be much higher. When this happens the rate for travelers' checks is lower than for cash dollars. In any event, it is best to keep at least part of one's money in traveler's checks for fear of thieves. International credit cards, too, are commonly used in the cities. Diners' Club, Visa and American Express are accepted in many shops, restaurants and hotels. Note, however, that cash advances against a credit card can be drawn in local currency only, therefore make every effort to cash only as much money as you will need during your stay in Peru.

Business Hours

Shops and offices are open from 9am until 7pm, with an afternoon *siesta*. Banks and government offices are usually open in the mornings only. Most shops operate half day on Saturdays and are closed on Sundays. Restaurants are open from early morning hours until past midnight.

Domestic Transportation

Buses and trucks reach almost every settlement accessible by any sort of land route. Most roads, especially outside the coastal region, are unpaved, and driving them is both difficult and tiring. Roads in the mountain region ascend to heights at which internal-combustion engines do not run smoothly and drivers would do well to seek out professional advice about suitable engine tuning. Rain or snow occasionally block roads, cutting off many places. The large bus companies run modern, comfortable buses between major cities, although most other

PERU

Peruvian buses are antiquated, noisy, uncomfortable, crowded and – above all – poorly maintained. Trucks operate mainly in the mountain region and link various places off the beaten path if they are close (at times a 20-hour trip is considered "close" ...). Travel at night requires **very** warm clothing (!!), a sleeping bag, and other means of protection from the cold. The trucks are crowded and their frequency unpredictable, but they are cheaper than the bus.

Trains operate in southern Peru, from the coast, via Arequipa and Puno, on the shore of Lake Titicaca, to Cuzco. From there a train sets out northward to Machu-Picchu. Another line links Lima to the nearby mountain cities. The trains are old, slow, very crowded and do not run on Sundays. Second-class is much cheaper, but finding a seat is difficult and your baggage is liable to be stolen (see "Note: personal security").

Aero Peru and Fawcett provide daily air service between all of Peru's large cities, and even to the remote jungle towns to which there is no overland access. Fares are moderate, but a 10% surtax is imposed on them. Because the planes, too, are very crowded, you must make reservations as early as possible and confirm them 24 hours before your flight. Take into account the possibility that your flight may be canceled, delayed, or disrupted in some other way, due to various breakdowns and unstable weather in the mountains and jungles. You should check that your flight is taking off as scheduled before you set out for the airport. Get to the airport early, since these airlines usually overbook! Keep a very watchful eye on your luggage during domestic flights, for the airlines generally treat it with great contempt, and their workers have a way of losing some en route. Once you reached town, buses or taxis will take you to a hotel or anywhere else. Taxi fares are determined between driver and passenger at the start of the trip, and one can (and should) bargain. Tipping is not customary.

Measurements, electricity, and time
The metric system is used for weights and measures. Clothing is marked in European sizes.

Electricity: 220V. Peruvian time: GMT-5.

Shopping
Artesania – the range of artifacts and handicrafts is rich and varied. The southern region – Cuzco and Lake Titicaca – excel in woolen goods and sweaters, and this is also by far the cheapest place for these things. In the Huaraz region, too, the woolen goods are plentiful and are characteristically different from those in the south. Huancayo, situated on the mountains east of Lima, is famous for its painted gourds. These are gourds

PERU

which are dried out in the sun or over a fire, and on which local artists engrave pictures depicting their daily lives. In the north, particularly in the vicinity of Trujillo, you will find jewelry, which is usually made with torquoise stones. One must not forget, of course, the popular wall carpets found here, as in other Andean countries.

A Suggested Itinerary for Touring Peru

Peru is rich in fascinating sites and you would need months to see them all. This chapter divides the country into three broad areas: the northern region, the central region and the southern region. These can of course be connected into one long trip or you can settle for a visit to parts of each separately, as your departure point and individual objectives dictate.

The northern region takes in the area north of Lima to the border with Ecuador in three strips: coastal, mountain and Amazon Basin.

The central region consists of the city of Lima and its immediate surroundings.

The southern region encompasses the areas south of the capital – the coast, the mountain ridge, Lake Titicaca and its surroundings, the jungles and, of course, the Incan capital of Cuzco and the nearby ruins.

The sites described in the sections on the northern and southern regions are surveyed in order of their distance from Lima, though the material is arranged so that it can also be useful to those coming from other directions. Possibilities for combining and merging touring routes are noted in every case. The two sections first survey attractions close to Lima which may be visited either on the way to or from the capital, or as a day trip from it.

Note: personal security

The problem of security in Peru has become much more serious in recent years, with a Maoist underground that calls itself *Sendero Luminoso* ("The Glittering Path"). They operate in Lima and the mountains – laying explosive charges, clashing with the army and engaging in other forms of terrorism. Police in these areas act with great force and little manners, vis-a-vis tourists as well. Numerous roadblocks are scattered along the highways and searches are a common occurrence.

The number one problem, however, is undoubtedly thieves. Daring and sophisticated, they have bestowed upon almost everyone the "favor" of their attentions, sometimes successfully and sometimes not. The profusion of tourists on the one hand

PERU

and the helplessness of the police on the other, have created a convenient scene for their operation. Those who cross into Peru should consider the possibility of eventually leaving it without part of their gear. If you wish, you can add it to your calculation of the total cost of the trip ...

Be doubly cautious in any public place, especially if it's crowded. A moving crowd is one of the best hunting-grounds for a thief. A wallet, camera, or even the contents of the inside pocket of your pants can vanish without your noticing it. The predators carry sharp knives and do not hesitate to cut open briefcases or trousers to get at the loot. You should therefore carry only the minimum of essentials and a little well-concealed money (an ordinary moneybelt isn't enough), and leave everything else in a closed bag which you **never carry on your back, but only in front of you and at chest height.** It's highly advisable to walk in groups, especially at night or upon reaching a new place with all your gear. Under no circumstances should you sport any sort of jewelry, or carry a camera openly. Attach metal chains to your camera and hook it to your belt, so that if someone cuts a strap you'll sense it immediately. The thieves generally operate in groups; while several divert your attention by conversing with you or by "accidentally" knocking into you, their friends will finish the job. When you're on the train, secure your baggage to the shelf with a locked chain and hold all hand baggage firmly. Don't drowse or nod off, and try to bring along a flashlight which you'll turn on the moment your train enters an unlit tunnel. Unsupervised bags are liable to disappear in a few seconds of darkness! Both on the train and in the station, you should not move around alone; organize into the largest groups possible, walk as a group, and carry all equipment in front of you. Those who really want to do it right will wrap their gear (especially backpacks) in sacks or even metal netting to keep it from being cut open: the method may be cumbersome, but it works. Before getting off the train, wait until the platform is cleared of passengers. Crowds, as mentioned, are the natural habitat of thieves. When traveling by bus, be sure to check at each and every stop that the baggage you placed on the roof or in the luggage compartment does not inadvertently "fall off" before you reached your destination. In taxis, too, remove your gear first and then get out; one often hears of drivers who take off immediately after their passengers have alighted, giving them no opportunity to remove their belongings.

Though all of this must sound odd if you haven't yet visited Peru, it won't take long to see that things are just so. Many visitors, of course, emerge unscathed, but many do fall victim to thieves (including myself, who contributed two cameras, a lens and various and sundry extras to the Peruvian economy). Remember that the thieves' great skill and brazen gall, and the minimal risk they face, have resulted in an "open season" on attractive tourist gear. The most extreme precautionary measures you can take are not excessive!

Those with the misfortune to have lost money or baggage to thieves must navigate an obstacle course in order to recover it (from the insurance company, that is). Go to the Tourist Police or to PIP – *Policia de Investigaciones del Peru* – after buying (!) the police documents necessary for filling out the report in the kiosk-like structures next to the police stations.

Lima

Since 18th January 1535 – when Francisco Pizarro laid the cornerstone of Lima – and throughout the intervening four hundred fifty years, Peru's capital has been a major center for all of South America. In this foggy coastal city, covered on most days by a mantle of clouds, many of the historical processes that shaped the development of the entire continent were set in motion. Besides being the Spanish monarch's most established and reliable colony in South America, Lima was and remains an important focus of political, economic and social power. Then as now, it presents a blend of severe contradictions – wealth and poverty, beauty and ugliness. Only in recent decades, roughly from the end of World War II, has Lima undergone far-reaching changes, which have driven the city rapidly – sometimes too rapidly – into the 1980s. Its population has grown tenfold, and now approaches five million – about one-third of the total population of Peru. With the growing trend of migration from rural and provincial areas to the city, a great many poor suburbs known as *pueblos jovenes* (young villages) have grown up, where "greeners" live in harsh conditions that are a hothouse for social unrest – expressed in criminal activity and extreme revolutionary politics.

Lima, built on the banks of Rio Rimac, takes its name from the mispronunciation of the river's Indian name. The eye-catching peaks of the Andes, only one hundred fifty kilometers away, loom to the east and the long beautiful seashore lies to its west. The port of Callao, one of South America's largest, was far from the new city when built, but the expansion of Peruvian industry (of which almost three-fourths are located in this area) has blurred the urban boundaries, creating a busy and crowded industrial zone. Downtown Lima is a mosaic of Colonial and modern architecture, centered about the Plaza de Armas. The suburbs, particularly the exclusive southern ones – Miraflores, San Isidro and Barranco – are no less effervescent, especially after dark.

PERU

Few tourists to South America skip a visit to Lima – either because it is the continent's major port of entry, with inexpensive flights from all over the world, or because it is a convenient starting point for all the captivating sites that Peru offers. Indeed, for all that it lacks beauty, charm and grace, and for all its squalor and problems, Lima is among South America's most popular cities. Those who understand its spirit and come to know its ways, will find that it offers many interesting and extraordinary experiences.

How to get there

By air: Lima's modern Jorge Chaves Airport is located in Callao, fifteen kilometers from downtown. Flights arrive here from the four corners of the earth – Europe, the United States, the Far East, and all South American countries. From the airport one can take a taxi, bus, or a minibus downtown; the latter is rather inexpensive and very convenient. Tickets are bought in the air terminal and you must specify your destination.

To get to the airport from the city, take a taxi, special minibus, or bus starting out from various locations downtown. Hotel Trans at Camana 828 in the center of the city (Tel. 275-697) runs a frequent airport shuttle service around the clock. Opposite Galeria Internacional, at N. de Pierola 733, *colectivos* provide service to the airport from 6am-6pm. From Miraflores, a bus sets out from Palma 280 (Tel. 469-872). The trip takes thirty minutes. Those leaving Peru are subject to a $10 port tax – payable only in American dollars. The airport duty-free shop is one of Latin America's largest.

By land: Buses reach Lima from all parts of Peru and from neighboring capitals. Each bus company has its own terminal, from which you continue by taxi or local bus. The interurban and international service is convenient and dependable.

Accommodations

Lima has many hotels at a wide variety of levels. Most are decent and clean, but even here you must watch your luggage carefully and not leave valuables in the rooms. Service charges and tax add 15%-21% to the hotel's base rate; check carefully whether the prices you are quoted include this supplement.

If you want to spend a long time in Lima or want to keep down expenses without foregoing clean lodgings, you'll do well to stay at one of the many suburban *pensions*. These are usually private homes in which several rooms – immaculate, tidy and simply furnished – have been set aside for guests. *Pension* rates are far lower than those in hotels and sometimes include a Continental breakfast.

PERU

You'll find a great many hotels – some new – in Lima's central and southern areas (especially in Miraflores).

The *Gran Hotel Bolivar* – Peru's classiest and most famous – is undoubtedly unique. Its 350 rooms, furnished in colonial style, are impressive and comfortable. It excels in superb service and an elegant atmosphere, and contains excellent restaurants and a bar which serves as a prestigious rendezvous for Lima society. The hotel, ideal for tourists and businessmen alike, is located on Plaza San Martin (Tel. 276-400).

You'll find the twenty-story *Lima Sheraton*, a new and luxurious hotel, at Paseo de la Republica 170 (Tel. 328-676). It has 400 rooms, along with a variety of sports facilities, shops, restaurants and other facilities, including a nightclub and reserved parking.

The new *Cesar's Hotel* is located in central Miraflores on Avenida La Paz at the corner of Avenida Dies Canseco (Tel. 465-099). It has seventeen floors of rooms, tastefully furnished in a functional, comfortable, modern style. Guests are invited to enjoy the sports facilities, shops, restaurants and more.

The *Hotel Crillon*, among Lima's best-known, is centrally located and convenient on Avenida Nicolas de Pierola 589 (Tel. 283-290). The 22-story, 550-room hotel is crowned by a rooftop restaurant, where you can enjoy wonderful food along with a splendid view and entertainment.

The following hotels, though still high-priced, are less expensive:

Hotel Savoy, Cailloma 224 (Tel. 283-520) – central, clean and comfortable, with rooftop bar and restaurant. Ideal location, reasonably priced. Recommended.

Hotel Riviera, Avenida Garcilaso de la Vega 981 (Tel. 289-460) – another central hotel, clean and comfortable.

El Plaza Hotel, Nicolas de Pierola 850 (Tel. 286-270) – a modern hotel, not large.

Hostal Miraflores, Avenida Petit Thouars 5444 (Tel. 458-745) – located in central Miraflores, spacious, pleasant and very comfortable; moderately priced.

Hostal San Francisco, across from Plaza San Francisco, Jr. Ancash 340 (Tel. 283-643) – modern.

It's highly recommended to make reservations for most hotels and *pensions*, especially if you are planning to come during the tourist season.

Young travelers will find several cheap hotels in the vicinity of Plaza de Armas. Among these *Hotel Damasco*, located one

PERU

street away from the plaza at 199 Calle Ucagali, is recommended. *Hotel Europa* is popular among travelers, and is frequently fully booked during the high season. It is opposite the San Francisco Church on Calle Ancash in the San Francisco neighborhood. *Hotel Union*, although not recommended, is the cheapest and is situated near Plaza de Armas on the Union Pedestrian Mall.

What to eat, where and when

Lima has thousands of restaurants offering a vast array of different cuisines. Though the tens of thousands of tourists who visit Lima each year appear to prefer the several dozen best-known restaurants, it seems to me that you would do well to let yourself experiment with gastronomic experiences at precisely those restaurants which do not generally appear in tourist guides or advertise extensively. The result will be much better and the food more interesting and much less expensive. In the Introduction to Peru there is a general survey of the various types of restaurants, along with details concerning their service and we will only mention them here in the context of Lima. You'll find a profusion of kiosks and stands around Plaza 2 de Mayo and along Calle Nicolas de Pierola, which links that square with Plaza San Martin. As you approach Plaza San Martin, you'll find restaurants and cafes replacing the kiosks, which become gradually more elegant and expensive. Where the street meets the Plaza, you'll see *Hotel Bolivar* on one side and the large *Parrilladas Restaurant* across the way. Parrilladas specializes in superb Argentine-style steak in enormous portions and at moderate prices. Recommended. Along the side streets that branch off the plaza you'll find innumerable Creole and Chinese restaurants (*Chifa*) where you can eat your fill at prices anyone can afford. Hotel Bolivar and the other luxury hotels have excellent restaurants. Exceptional among them is the *Sky Room*, on the twentieth floor of Hotel Crillon, where a folklore troupe performs every evening.

A very inexpensive restaurant which serves satisfactory and satisfying portions is *Machu-Picchu* next to Hotel Europa. Along Union Mall there are countless coffee houses and inexpensive restaurants which serve "junk food". Do not miss out on the outstanding cream cakes in the coffee shops.

A number of well-known restaurants are located downtown and are open mainly in the evening. In the Tourist Bureau building at Belen 1066 you'll find the prestigious *Tambo de Oro*, which serves Peruvian and International cuisine in a colonial atmosphere. *Las Trece Monedas*, Ancash 539, offers similar fare. Its interior design, service and quality of food justify a visit. From the Barranco quarter the superb, if high-priced, *Costa*

PERU

Verde fish and seafood restaurant overlooks the Pacific, from which most of its dishes are taken. Another fine seafood restaurant, this one in San Isidro, is *La Caleta*, at Derteano 126 (Tel. 22250).

Transportation

Urban: Buses, minibuses, *colectivos* and taxis will help you get around Lima. **Bus** fare is cheap and service is frequent, though usually slow and crowded. Route numbers are clearly marked; bus stops are usually located on corners. A student card occasionally earns one a 50% discount. **Minibuses** are really smaller buses that travel along the central routes. Because they charge slightly more than the bus, they are less crowded. They have no defined stops; drivers pull over for anyone who waves. **Colectivos** link downtown with the main suburbs, taking a number of passengers along fixed routes at fares double those of the equivalent trip by bus. This is the recommended way to get around Lima, since it's still quite cheap, and is quick and convenient. A large fleet of regular **taxis**, too, fills Lima's streets, and their drivers will take you anywhere in town. The fare is determined in advance between passenger and driver. Be sure to state your destination clearly, and bargain over the price. Try to pay drivers the exact amount, for they are likely to tell you they've got no change or put forth any number of other groundless claims designed only to empty your wallet. Tipping is not customary and it's enough to round off the price appearing on a meter – if one has been used at all!

Intercity: Aero Peru and Faucett (offices on Plaza San Martin) provide frequent and convenient air service throughout Peru. Reconfirm your flight twenty-four hours before the scheduled departure.

From Lima, **trains** set out only for the mountains, via La Oroya. They are very crowded and you must get to the station early because tickets can be purchased only one day in advance. The trains are slow, and though first class is comfortable and spacious, you still have to take every precaution against pickpockets and thieves. **Watch over your bags very carefully!** Lima's train station, **Desamparados**, is located behind the Government House; the ticket office is open 7am-noon and 1:30-4pm on weekdays, 7-11am on Saturdays. There is no Sunday train service in Peru.

Excellent **bus** service links all of Peru's cities; a large number of companies have offices and terminals in Lima, most in the vicinity of Parque Universitario on the extension of Calle Pierola (La Colmena) southeast of Plaza San Martin. Because most roads between major cities are paved, travel is relatively fast and

PERU

comfortable. For details, consult the sections on the various destinations.

Car rental: Rent-a-car firms abound in Lima. Avis, Hertz, Budget and National have airport counters; Avis and Hertz have branches offices in Lima: Avis is at the Sheraton Hotel (Tel. 327-245) and Hertz is near Hotel Bolivar, Ocona 262 (Tel. 289-477, 286-330).

Driving in Lima is difficult and we recommend that you use taxis in town.

Tourist servioes

The central Tourist Bureau for Lima and the vicinity is at Jiron de la Union (Belen) 1066, in the same building as the Tambo de Oro restaurant. Open 10am-7pm on weekdays and half-day on Saturdays, the Bureau offers explanatory material and maps along with a friendly staff who can give advice and guidelines about interesting sites, restaurants, hotels, transportation etc. The Ministry of Tourism has a branch office at the airport. On the whole, however, you won't find much material there, and it is mainly useful for making hotel reservations. Topographic maps of areas you intend to visit on foot can be bought at Instituto Geografico Militar, Avenida Aramburu 1190, San Isidro. Good road maps can be purchased at the Peru Auto Club, Vallejo 699 (Tel. 403-270, 221-451). Here special counselors will advise you about travel routes and do-it-yourself driving throughout the country.

Most airline offices and travel agencies are located along Avenida N. de Pierola and around Plaza San Martin.

Tourist sites

Downtown: The bulk of Lima's commercial activity and most of its important tourist attractions are concentrated in an area demarcated by the city's four important plazas: 2 de Mayo, de Armas, Grau and Bolognesi. Square-shaped **Plaza San Martin** lies in their epicenter and will serve as our point of departure to explore downtown. At the heart of this huge plaza stands a statue of Argentinian General Jose de San Martin, who helped Peru cast off the Spanish yoke. Surrounding the plaza are some of the city's grandest and most modern edifices, with the Gran Hotel Bolivar heading the list. Calle Pierola, lined with numerous shops, offices, restaurants and cafes, branches off to the northwest to **Plaza 2 de Mayo**, humming with hundreds of peddlers offering all kinds of food and other titbits. Around this square you can treat yourself to the strange foodstuffs sold in kiosks and get an impression of the daily lives of the Peruvians.

Calle Union, Lima's main shopping street, crosses Plaza San

PERU

Martin with its proliferation of shops offering souvenirs, clothing, jewelry, bric-a-brac and more. The quality here is superb even if relatively high-priced. Parts of the street are closed to vehicular traffic allowing pedestrians to meander freely in and out of the shops.

Turning northeast onto Calle Union (to the right of *Gran Hotel Bolivar*) and proceeding about three blocks, we come to **Iglesia La Merced**, Lima's "Church of Mercy". Its interior decor is most impressive, as is its stone facade. The church is dedicated to the merciful Virgin who, according to tradition, defends Lima from siege and attack. Her festival is celebrated each year on September 24, with the participation of the president of the Republic, army officers and public dignitaries.

Calle Union ends at the lovely **Plaza de Armas,** Lima's most important square, with a fountain more than three centuries old in its center. It was here that Pizarro founded Lima – naming it Ciudad del Reyes (City of the Kings) – and where he built his home. **The Government Palace,** which took more than twelve years to build, occupies the spot where Pizarro's home is believed to have stood. Since its completion in 1938, the Palace has served as the president's official residence, from which site state affairs are conducted. A red-uniformed honor guard patrols the front and the changing of the guard takes place daily at 12:45pm in an impressive ceremony. To the left of the Palace stands the Central Post Office.

Across Plaza de Armas we find the **Municipal Cathedral**. This impressive edifice, renovated a number of times, stands on the spot where Pizarro built Lima's first church, and in which he was buried. At the end of the last century, the remains of Lima's founder were discovered and placed in a glass coffin on public display. The cathedral houses a small museum of religious art. Beside it is the Archbishop's palace, built after World War I. Across the way is **City Hall**, constructed in 1945. It houses a small museum (open mornings Mon.-Fri.) containing works of Peruvian artists. Rio Rimac flows behind the plaza and the train station is along its bank (on Calle Ancash). A short distance from there is **Iglesia San Francisco,** with **Casa Pilatos**, an impressive mansion which serves as the Municipal Cultural Center, opposite. The church, one of Lima's loveliest, was built in 1674 in Baroque style and features a collection of art, a decorative ceiling and a painstakingly constructed tile roof. The large church library numbers tens of thousands of volumes, some of them centuries old. The vaults beneath the church were discovered and opened to the public in the early 1950s, revealing a great many mysterious tombs. Visiting hours: 9am-noon and 3-6pm.

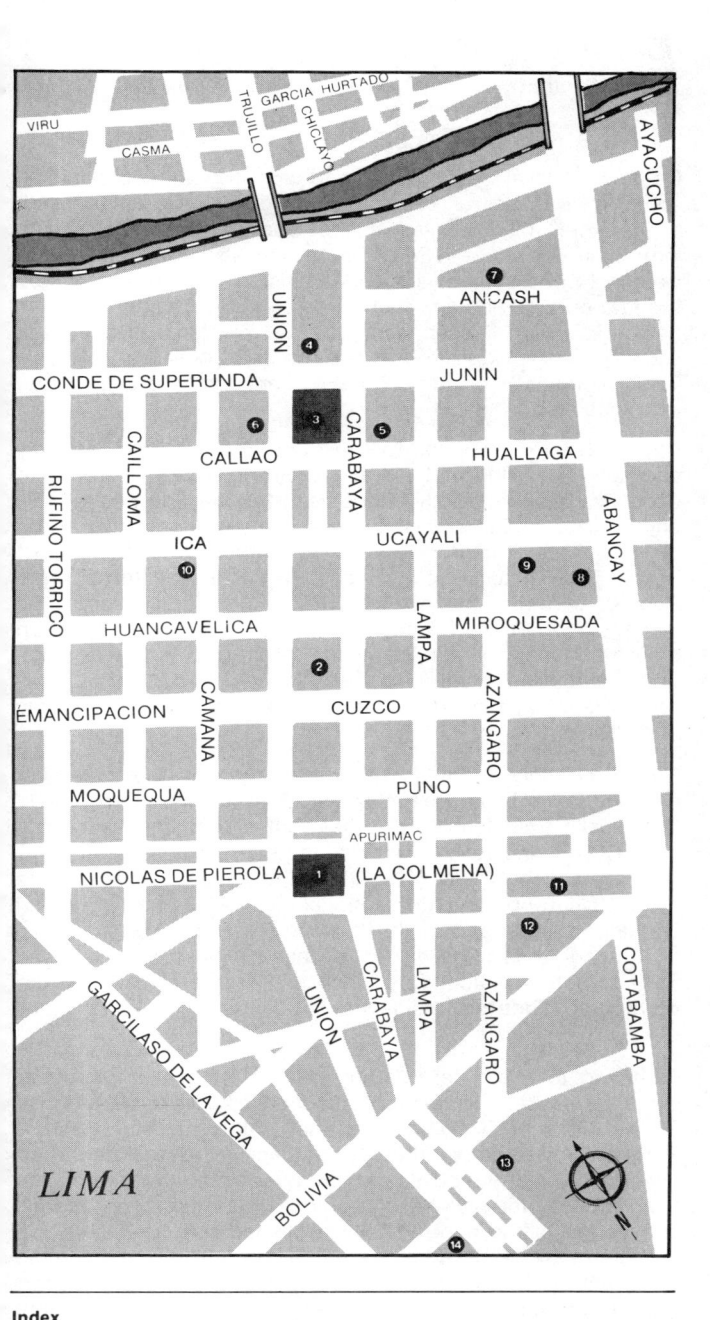

Index
1) Plaza San Martin 2) Iglesia La Merced 3) Plaza de Armas 4) Government Palace 5) Municipal Cathedral 6) City Hall 7) Iglesia San Francisco 8) National Library 9) Iglesia San Pedro 10) Iglesia San Agustin 11) Parque Universitario 12) Panteon 13) Palace of Justice 14) Museum of Italian Art

PERU

Continuing down Calle Ancash and crossing Calle Abancay we come to Plaza Bolivar, site of the **Congressional Palace** and, to its right, the building of the **Spanish Inquisition.** The Inquisition was active in Peru from the late sixteenth century and was finally abolished only in 1820. A visit to this building, where the fate of hundreds and thousands of suspected heretics was decided, is highly recommended. The courtroom itself, where you will see the Inquisitors' thrones, inspires both fear and awe. The building is open from Mon.-Fri., 9am-2pm and 3-8pm, Sat. mornings also.

Returning downtown, we walk two blocks down Calle Abancay and notice the **National Library** to our right. A right turn onto Calle Ucayali immediately brings us to **Iglesia San Pedro.** This church, also in Baroque style, was built by the Jesuits in the mid-seventeenth century and is considered one of the most beautiful in Lima. Directly across from it is the **Torre Tagle Palace**, currently the home of Peru's Foreign Ministry. The impressive building, dating from 1735, has recently been renovated and one can enjoy the beauty of its architecture, wood engravings and balconies as one strolls through its courtyard. Recommended. Open to visitors only on weekday afternoons.

Continuing along Calle Ucayali (which turns into Calle Ica after crossing Calle Union) we find **Iglesia San Agustin**. This church, two blocks from Plaza de Armas, dates from the eighteenth century, but was seriously damaged in an earthquake and only a small section of it may be visited. A famous wooden statue named *Death*, by an eighteenth-century Peruvian artist named Gavilan, is imbedded in the building's stone-chiseled facade, but cannot always be visited because it is in the damaged section of the church. One block further, we come upon the **Municipal Theater**, residence of Lima's most prestigious stage.

Returning to Plaza San Martin, we turn southeast and head down the Colmena (in the opposite direction from the Gran Hotel Bolivar). Four blocks down is a small, rather neglected park – **Parque Universitario**. Though best known as the departure point for most of the buses and minibuses that travel from Lima to its suburbs, the park boasts an additional importance, as well. In a corner of the park, teeming with peddlers and idlers, we find the national **Pantheon,** where a number of the most important figures of Peruvian history lie buried. The Pantheon was established in an eighteenth-century Jesuit church, converted to this use in the 1920s. Beside it is the **University of San Marcos**, South America's first, founded in the mid-sixteenth century. Damaged in successive earthquakes, the

PERU

University building presently serves only for conventions and conferences. Across the park is the 22-story building of the **Peruvian Ministry of Education**, which was the tallest and grandest edifice in the country at the time of its construction in 1955.

A common occurence in Latin America, which will certainly revolt most Westerners is cock fighting. Two blood-thirsty fighting cocks, with small sharp blades attached to their legs, fight each other to the death. No less interesting than the cruel fight is the enthusiasm of the spectators, especially the gamblers among them. The amount of money involved in this betting is surprisingly high, particularly considering the poverty of the fans of this "sport". These fights are held several times weekly near the Parque Universitario at 150 Calle Sandia. The fights usually begin at 4pm and continue a few hours, but one only needs a short time to get the idea.

Retracing our steps, we head south from Plaza San Martin, down Calle Union toward Paseo de la Republica (passing the Tourist Bureau). This broad promenade is lined with some of Lima's most important buildings, among them the **Civic Center** (first on the right), with the modern and luxurious Sheraton Hotel at its corner.

To the left we see **El Palacio de Justicia** – the Palace of Justice – with the **Museum of Italian Art** across the way. This museum, constructed in Renaissance style, has a collection of reproductions of Italian art in addition to changing exhibits of contemporary artists. Visiting hours: Tues.-Sat. 9am-7pm. The promenade itself, adorned with trees and greenery, is lined with benches and statues. At its end we come to the broad **Plaza Grau**, with **Avenida Colon** branching off from it. The **National Museum of Art,** one of Lima's most important, is located at the beginning of this avenue. It houses a large collection of paintings, sculptures, furniture, jewelry and more. The museum building was erected in 1868 for an international exposition held in Lima. Its spacious halls contain chronologically arranged exhibits of art dating from the first human settlement in Peru, about 4000 years ago, to our time. Highly recommended. Visiting hours: Tues.-Sun. 9am-7pm.

Other sites
Many of Lima's most important and interesting sites are rather far from downtown, but can be reached quickly and easily by bus or taxi. A general survey follows:

Pueblo Libre
About five kilometers southwest of the city center is the Pueblo Libre Quarter (bus 7, 10, or 37 from downtown, or bus 21, 24,

PERU

or 42 from Parque Universitario and many *colectivos* set out for Pueblo Libre from Plaza San Martin). Two of Lima's most important and interesting museums are located there, along with a large *artesania* (handicrafts) market. Let's explore them one by one:

El Museo de Arqueologia y Etnografia – the Archeological and Ethnographical Museum – located on Plaza Bolivar (not the one downtown), houses an impressive and highly important collection. In its many halls you will find handicrafts, textiles, ceramics, household implements, tools and sacred objects from all of Peru's pre-Columbian and pre-Incan civilizations. While the presentation is simple and uninspired, it is hard not to be impressed with the thousands of exhibits, the remnants of the Paracas, Chavin and other civilizations. The section devoted to the Incas presents a model of Machu-Picchu, while other wings contain mummies, skulls and more. A visit to this museum is a "must" for understanding Peruvian development. Visiting hours: daily from 10am-6pm (Tel. 623-282).

Nearby is the **Museum of History** and its collection of paintings, uniforms and other objects from the time of Peru's War of Independence. Open Mon.-Fri. 9am-6pm.

Fascinating **Museo Herrera**, Avenida Bolivar 1515 – a fifteen-minute walk from the Archeological Museum – contains a tremendous private collection of pottery – chiefly jugs hundreds or thousands of years old, which have been collected from all over Peru and faithfully represent the various civilizations and periods. The main building houses the ceramics exhibit, alongside a number of excellently preserved mummies, a splendid display of gold and silver jewelry (in what is, in fact, a giant vault), an exhibit of textiles and more. A separate building one story lower contains a special hall with hundreds of statuettes in various erotic positions. This hall, to which only adults are admitted, has given the entire museum a glorious reputation; a visit there is highly recommended. Even the most worldly of visitors can certainly learn something here... or at least come to realize there's nothing new under the sun.

Feria Artesanal – the artisans' market – is also located in this neighborhood, on Avenida La Marina. Here a number of large stores offer a wide variety of handicrafts and folk art, made of cloth, wood, ceramics and metal. Here is Lima's largest concentration of souvenirs of this sort with a large selection at affordable prices. We highly recommend that you stop here, compare prices – and bargain!

Museo de Oro

Ancient gold objects are undoubtedly among the most fascinating remnants of the ancient Peruvian civilizations. Since

*P*ERU

A taste of what awaits at the Museo de Oro in Lima

gold was abundant, easily mined and easy to process, much of the nobility's jewelry and other artifacts were made of the precious metal. Apart from their artistic value, it's hard to overlook their monetary value – more than worth their weight in gold! Most of the treasure was plundered by the Spanish conquistadors; the tiny remnant that has survived is displayed today in a number of museums, of which the important ones are the "gold museums" – *Museos de Oro* – in Bogota and Lima.

Lima's **Museu de Oro** allows visitors a close-up view of the artistry of the ancient craftsmen, who created stunning jewelry and ritual objects, many embedded with gems. The many halls of the well-kept museum feature a tasteful and magnificent exhibit of some of the most important displays that have survived. You shouldn't miss this museum. Part of the collection has been on loan to, and displayed in major museums throughout the world.

The "golden" section is in the basement which is actually a safe.

PERU

On the entrance level there is a large exhibit of arms from different periods and places throughout the world.

The museum is far from downtown, and getting there is a problem. A taxi will convey you swiftly and with no difficulty, but it's expensive. You can take the No. 2 bus from Plaza San Martin to the junction of Avenidas Arequipa and Angamos, and from there transfer to minibus No. 72, which goes to the museum. The entire trip takes about an hour. The museum is open daily 10am-7pm.

Miraflores

The Miraflores quarter, undoubtedly Lima's most beautiful and important suburb, is situated along the Pacific coast. Here reside the city's aristocrats and dignitaries, amid some of Lima's best hotels, movie theaters, restaurants and shopping centers. A quick trip down its streets will reveal the exclusive character of this neighbourhood. Alongside modern high-rises there are grand estates that serve as residences for diplomats, government officials, businessmen, and so on. Unless you are in Lima for a family visit, it's probably not a good idea to stay here, as it is far from downtown. A visit, however, is definitely worth your while, to get an impression of a Lima quite different from the one we've known thus far – the bustling, somewhat antiquated and faded city center. Here greenery dominates, and the broad avenues radiate a modern familiar atmosphere. Though Miraflores has no special sites, it reflects, perhaps more than anything else, the social, economic and class polarization which characterizes Peru. A visit here helps one to appreciate the severity and extent of the problem.

Colectivos leave for Miraflores from the south-western corner of Plaza San Martin every few minutes, and the trip takes less than half an hour.

Miraflores is home to the small and interesting **Museo Amano**. This private museum features an excellent collection of pre-Columbian and pre-Incan embroidery and ceramics from various regions of Peru. Visits must be arranged in advance (Tel. 412-909); small groups are given guided tours in the afternoon, Mon.-Fri. Admission is free. Take Minibus No. 13 as far as Avenida Santa Cruz, and then walk on for another block.

Entertainment and cultural events

Although Lima is an effervescent and bustling city both day and night, it is not noted for a wide range of quality entertainment. The city center has a great many cinemas (some right on Plaza San Martin), as do the new neighborhoods which screen relatively recent films, in the original languages, with Spanish subtitles. If you want to take in an evening show, buy your tickets several hours in advance.

PERU

There are performances at the Municipal Theater, private theaters and concert halls almost every evening. Tickets can usually be obtained without difficulty, and prices are not high. The Lima Symphony Orchestra, though not of a standard for discerning music lovers, performs several times a week, usually in the Miraflores concert hall.

We especially recommend that you take in a folklore performance, offered almost every evening in a *pena* (folklore club) or theater (the Municipal Theater on Mondays and the La Cabana Theater on Tuesdays). The *Sky Room*, on top of Hotel Crillon, features nightly folklore performances. The *Pena Hatachay* offers especially enjoyable folklore performances on weekends, with instrumental music and singing and dancing with audience participation. The club is located on the other side of the Rio Mapucho, behind the Central Post Office. Prices are certainly reasonable.

Nightclubs and discotheques abound in the large downtown hotels or the southern neighborhoods, especially San Isidro and Miraflores. They are open on weekends and they charge rather stiff entrance fees. This is where a great many Peruvian youths and students, etc. spend their evenings.

Banks and currency exchange

The national bank Banco de la Nacion, (open only in the mornings) has numerous branches throughout Lima where you can carry out any conventional banking transaction, including moneychanging and receiving international transfers, letters of credit, documents, etc. American and British banks also have offices in Lima, and transferring money to them is simpler. You will be paid only in local currency however, as is the case when you make cash withdrawals against international credit cards.

In the vicinity of Plaza San Martin – especially along Calle Nicolas de Pierola – there are a large number of travel agents who will change foreign currency into Peruvian intis at rates similar to the banks.

On the end of Calle Union and along the length of Calle Ocona, which turns right from Union at Plaza San Martin, there are a number of *cambio* (exchange) offices and many street moneychangers. Compare rates before changing your money. The black market rate in Lima is the highest in the country, so change enough local currency there before setting out for the provincial towns.

Postal and telephone services

It is highly recommended that you send everything by registered air mail. The Central Post Office (*Correo Central*), near Plaza de Armas, is open Mon.-Fri. 8am-8pm and on Sat. and Sun. till

PERU

noon. Parcels weighing more than one kilogram must undergo a customs inspection before you send them – a time-consuming, bothersome and exhausting bureaucratic nuisance. A centrally located post office is off Plaza San Martin, on Colmena, across from Hotel Crillon, and is open Mon.-Fri. 8am-5pm and on Sat. mornings only.

International phone calls are made from Entel, in the post office located off Plaza San Martin. You must deposit a passport or sum of money when you place your call, which is made from one of the many booths lining the hall. At times there is a long wait until the call goes through, and you'll have to listen for your name to know that your turn has come. International phone calls are very costly and collect calls are possible only to the United States and a number of Western European countries.

Books and periodicals in English

Many books are published in Peru about its culture, archeology, history and the like, and English translations are often available in many shops, primarily downtown. Bookstores abound along Calles Union and Pierola, especially in the vicinity of Plaza San Martin. They offer an adequate selection of foreign newspapers and literature – including imported books – on various topics.

Several bookstores in Miraflores and San Isidro stock mainly foreign newspapers. The local English-language weekly *Lima Times* is available at most stands in town.

Photographic supplies

If you're going to travel throughout Peru, it's best to stock up on film before leaving the capital. It is difficult, if not impossible, to find film in outlying villages and towns, and that which is available has not necessarily been kept in conditions which ensure its freshness. Developing film in Peru is not especially expensive and is done relatively quickly and well.

Shopping

Lima's major shopping street is Calle Union between Plazas San Martin and de Armas. Here you'll find anything your heart desires – from colorful buttons to elegant clothing to gold jewelry and diamonds. Dozens of shops line the street, and this is where most tourists find their souvenirs. Calle Pierola, between Plazas 2 de Mayo and San Martin, also has an abundance of stores, which specialize more in popular souvenirs, local works of art and the like. Though prices are rather high in this area, the goods are usually exclusive and of superb quality. Those interested in handicrafts will certainly find a broader selection and far lower prices in the Pueblo Libre *artesania* market (see "Tourist sites" above).

PERU

There are a number of shopping centers in the very center of town, one of which shares a building with the Tambo de Oro restaurant and the Tourist Bureau. Here and in the vicinity, along Calle Union, there are many shops that sell tourist souvenirs at reasonable prices. Another small shopping center, with slightly lower prices, is located at Calle Union 1030.

Miraflores, where the most important shopping centers are located, is the best place for clothing and footwear. Here one pays steep prices for imported goods just off the boat from exclusive manufacturers in New York or Paris.

Simple jewelry of gold or silver is extremely popular, as are woodcrafts and lovely gourd carvings produced mainly by artists from Huancayo. High-quality sweaters, ponchos, hats and wall carpets, all hand woven, are also sold throughout Lima. Most woolen products are made of lamb or llama wool. A small quantity of such goods, softer to the touch, are of the superior alpaca.

If you travel elsewhere in the country, you'll find that though prices are higher in the capital than in the periphery, there are significant differences in quality in favor of Lima-produced goods, and this must be taken into account.

Most stores in Lima close for *siesta* between 1-3:30pm.

Weather
Though Lima is relatively close to the equator, its climate is temperate. The Humboldt Current cools the air a little, but the humidity is very high, exceeding 90% in winter (May to October). Skies are usually heavily overcast. It is a little warmer between November and April, but that should present no problem for the visitor because the humidity is lower and the skies are clear. It hardly rains and the infrequent showers do not last long.

Important addresses
Peruvian Tourist Ministry: Union 1066 (Tel. 323-559).

Anglo-American Hospital: Avenida Salazar, San Isidro (Tel. 403-570).

Aero Peru: Plaza San Martin (Tel. 282-742, 274-077).

Auto Club: Lince, Avenida Cesar Vallejo 699 (Tel. 403-270).

U.S. Embassy: Corner of Avenidas Inca Garcilaso de la Vega and Espana (Tel. 286-000).

British Embassy: Edificio Washington, Plaza Washington, Avenida Arequipa (Tel. 283-830, 283-836/9).

PERU

North of Lima

In this section we will survey the sites and routes north of Lima, to the Ecuadorian border – in the mountains, along the coast and in the depths of the eastern jungles. Some sites, especially those in the vicinity of Huaraz, can be included on a tour beginning and ending in Lima, while others are best visited en route from Lima to Ecuador or vice versa. Various possibilities for each locale have been noted. Since the coastal axis between Lima and Trujillo offers no sites of special interest, the mountain route is recommended, with stops in Huaraz and the vicinity on the way.

Transportation
Many companies provide comfortable, dependable and rapid bus service to all the destinations surveyed here. Roggero (La Colmena 733, Tel. 282-044) and Tepsa (Paseo de la Republica 119, Tel. 28995) are among those we can recommend.

Huaraz
Huaraz, 408 km northeast of Lima, is a national and international center for hikers and mountain climbers who enjoy roaming through the gorgeous expanses of mountain landscape. Of Huaraz's 50,000 people, a significant number make a living by catering to the tens of thousands of tourists who throng to the city, especially from June through October, when comfortable weather and the European vacation season coincide. Though Huaraz is situated 3091 meters above sea level, it is in the middle of a valley – the Santa Valley, split from north to south by the Rio Santa and hemmed in on both east and west by tall mountain chains whose peaks soar thousands of meters farther into the sky.

The range of mountains in the west are known as *Cordillera Negra* (black range) because it is free of snow in summer and the soil is dark. The eastern Cordillera is the immense *Cordillera Blanca* (white range). Its peaks are covered in snow and glaciers and most reach heights of 6000 m above sea level. The highest in the Cordillera range is Mt. Huazcaran which is 6768 m high. Another range to the south of Cordillera Blanca is Huayhuash.

Huaraz, like many of its neighbors in this part of Peru, was severely damaged in the earthquake of May 1970, and large areas have since been rebuilt. Today it serves as a mountain climbing center and a point of departure or return for dozens of fascinating outings, some on foot, others on donkeys or horseback.

Look about from the center of town and you will see perpetually

*P*ERU

NORTHERN PERU

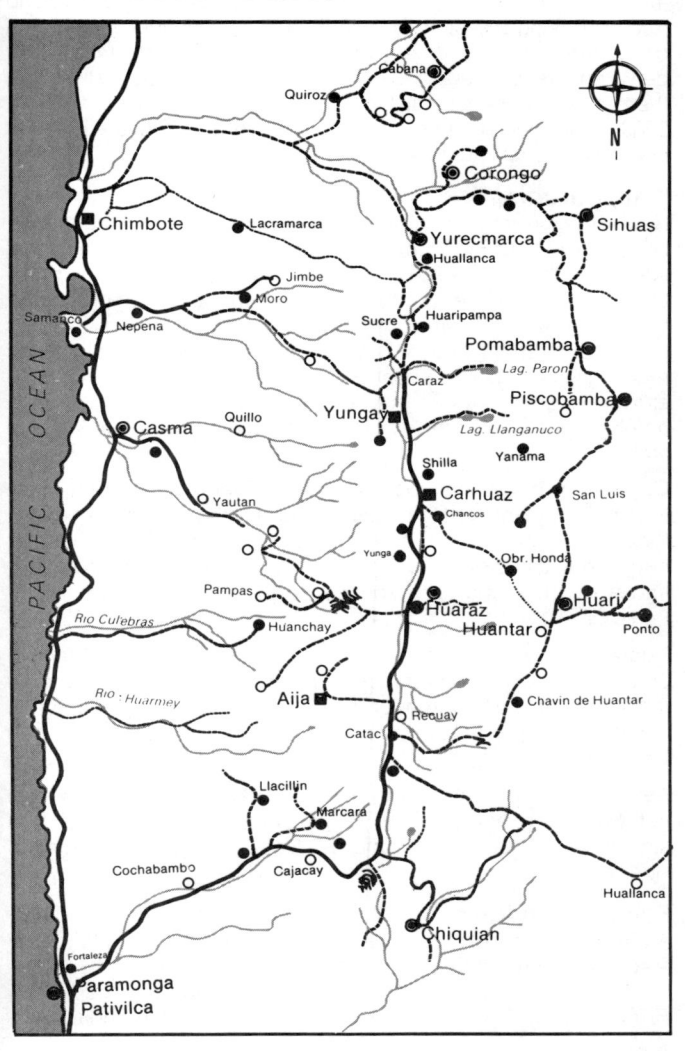

PERU

snowy peaks that surround the city. The massive glaciers which abound in this region have contributed to its stunning power and rare beauty. In my opinion, this is among the most enchanting concentrations of scenery anywhere in the world, and a hike between the glaciers and the *cochas* (lakes) trapped among them is an experience hard to equal. The snow line runs at about 5000 m, and the summits which reach about 7000 m are covered in a magnificent mantle of white.

Transportation

Bus service from Lima to Huaraz is frequent, comfortable, fast, dependable and inexpensive. Rodrigues, Expreso Ancash and Arellano Intersa are a few recommended companies of the many that provide service on this line. The trip takes about seven hours over a good, paved road. The buses set out at all hours of the day and it is best to buy tickets in advance. Travelers who reach Huaraz before sunrise may spend several hours – extremely cold ones – unable to find a hotel room, for most hotels are closed and shuttered in the small hours of the night.

Convenient public transportation links Huaraz with all the sites in the vicinity and with villages and towns that are attractions in their own right or serve as starting points for hikes. Buses set out several times daily for Trujillo and Chimbote, along the coast, and from there you can proceed northward in the direction of Ecuador.

Huaraz is very easy to reach by car, but bear in mind that relying on a private car is a problem for hikers, who must then forego the option of starting from one place and winding up in another. It is better to park your car in town and tour the area by public transportation.

Aero Peru flies from Lima to Anta several times per week. It is not worth the bother, for it takes quite a while to reach the airport and then more time is lost getting from Anta to Huaraz.

Food and lodging

As a tourist center, Huaraz naturally has many hotels and restaurants, suited to all budgets and tastes. *Hotel de Turistas* on Avenida Centenario in the city center is recommended, as is *El Pacifico*, which is on the same street and much cheaper.

Travelers will also find many cheap hotels and private *pensions*, and generally *pension* owners wait for buses to arrive in order to "enlist" tourists. A very cheap and pleasant hotel is the *Alpamayo*, opposite the soccer stadium on Avenida Confraternidad Oeste. There is a small and very congenial *pension* near Hotel Alpamayo, which is the house of Seniora

PERU

Mariela. At all of these places you can leave your unnecessary gear when you go on hikes in the area. The *Maranon Hotel*, situated conveniently in the center of the market, is pleasant and comfortable.

The local market, shops and restaurants all meet our gastronomic needs satisfactorily. Although Huaraz is not a Mecca for fussy eaters, you can certainly find plenty to eat. Here, too, like everywhere in Peru, there are lots of Chinese restaurants, along with others serving local fare. Most restaurants are downtown, near Plaza de Armas and along Av. Luzuriaga which branches off from it. One street below the avenue (boulevard), there is a popular restaurant patronized by the locals which serves large and tasty portions at low prices. Try the excellent *criolla* soup.

Fresh and canned foods which are essential supplies for your hikes in the vicinity are available in the market and shops.

Tourist services

The municipal **Tourist Bureau** is on the ground floor of the Municipality building on Plaza de Armas (Tel. 2394). It offers material concerning outings in the vicinity, shops where you can stock up on supplies, transportation and the like. Buy maps in Lima, for the ones on sale in Huaraz are nowhere near as good.

The Peruvian Auto Club has a branch at Luzuriaga 866 (Tel. 2590). Club Andino, Barron 582, will advise you about mountain trails.

Travel and tourist agencies abound as well, with most located along Avenida Luzuriaga. They offer guided tours of the area, some involving hikes of several days' duration. Though this is the quickest and most convenient way to cover the area's interesting and special sites (see below) without wasting precious time hitching rides or waiting for irregular buses, it comes at a price.

Food should be purchased in town for the entire duration of hikes, plus a reserve, for it is almost unobtainable on the road. Take nourishing and filling food that will not spoil, which does not weigh much and is easy to prepare (rice, beans, etc.).

Currency exchange

Dollars can be converted at the Banco de la Nacion. Since long lines and bureaucracy are almost inevitable, you must simply grin and bear it. Businesses and certain travel agencies change money according to black market rates, but in Lima the rate is a bit higher.

PERU

Postal and telephone services
From the post office on Plaza de Armas you can send letters and small parcels by air or sea. For international calls go to Entel, across from the post office.

Camping and photographical supplies
Many shops in Huaraz sell or rent camping equipment of various types – everything from sleeping bags to tents to gas burners. Check the condition and quality of the equipment when you rent it and do not leave an excessive deposit. Gas cylinders, rather rare in South America, can be bought here, though at high prices. Photography shops in town stock film, but only the most common types. ASA 400 is particularly hard to find. Be sure to check expiry dates.

Weather, elevation and mountain climbing guidelines
The weather around Huaraz is rather pleasant, though temperatures drop at night and the chill can be quite painful. Be very sure to bring along the best camping gear, for nights under the stars are liable to be unbearably cold without it. A two-layer tent is important for keeping out the rain, and be sure to have enough warm and comfortable clothing. When hiking in the mountains, be sure to choose protected places sheltered from the wind for your campsite at night.

Because of the high altitude – in town, and all the more so in the surrounding mountains – you must observe certain essential safety rules. The physical consequences of thin air must be taken into account when planning any outing (see "Introduction"). In Huaraz itself the average temperature is 15 degrees Centigrade (60 degrees Fahrenheit), and it tends to drop as you ascend. During the rainy season, January through April, mountain climbing is very difficult. We recommend that you try to schedule your visit between May and October, the dry season.

Most trails require three to seven days of hiking at altitudes of up to 5000 m. This demands superb physical condition and sufficient acclimatization to the area's conditions. You should therefore come to Huaraz **at least** two or three days before you begin your hike. On certain routes you can hire a guide with donkey to haul your gear, and this seems to me very worthwhile despite the expense. At high altitudes all climbers, however fit, will find it difficult to bear even their own weight, and the benefits of moving about without gear are worth their "weight" in gold.

PERU

Nature's splendor - Cordillera Wallwash

Trails and sites in the vicinity

Wallwash
One of the most difficult trails in the Huaraz area circles the Wallwash (pronounced Wai-wash) mountain range. This is a beautiful route, winding among deep blue lakes and gigantic glaciers which descend to them from the mountain tops. Many sections of the trail climb to more than 4000 m, so you must

589

PERU

make appropriate arrangements. You need ten days to complete the full "circle route", though you can scale it down by foregoing some stretches and settling for a route which is shorter, though no less impressive and enjoyable.

Pack plenty of food and excellent camping gear. Physical fitness is a prime condition before setting out, as is slow and easy adjustment to the elevation. Part of the way you may wish to avail yourself of the services of the locals, who will be glad to accompany you and load your gear on the backs of their donkeys and mules – a real help along this route.

Take the daily bus from Huaraz to Chiquian, 110 km to the south. This charming little village has a modest market where you can stock up on last-minute items. The hike begins here, first along the river and then atop the soaring mountain ridge. Llamac is the last village pass before ascending the first ridge of mountains – beyond which there is a stunning view of the glaciers. From here on, the trail leads around deep blue lakes to mighty glaciers, amidst green flora and brown hamlets, offering the hiker several days of quiet tranquility.

The lengthy trail ends in the town of Cajatambo, from which regular transportation will bring you to the coastal road and to Lima.

Santa Cruz

Though dozens of mountain trails wind around Huaraz and the vicinity, the Santa Cruz is by far the most popular. This pleasant hike lasts four to five days and reaches heights of up to 4800 m. Here, too, it is important to adjust to the elevation slowly and to pack camping gear, warm clothing and food for the trip.

The trail begins in the village of Yungay (elev. 2585 m), 56 km north of Huaraz. Here you can get organized, load up on last-minute food items, and leave behind unnecessary gear.

From Yungay set out, preferably by car, on the dirt road leading to Lake Llanganuco. From there begins the exhausting climb to the first ridge, 4700 m high, with an enchanting backdrop of glaciers and mountain peaks. Below the ridge are some sheepfolds where you can spend the night. The next day begins the descent, which continues the following day as well, until the village of Vilcabamba. Then there is a climb again from 2200 m to 4800 m. You should sleep on the way before crossing this ridge. You can rent donkeys to carry your gear – which is important and useful. The next day, the ridge summit will afford a splendid view of Punta Union, with a glacier on one side and a fertile agricultural valley on the other. Then begins the descent again – as far as the village of Caspampa, from which you can go on to beautiful Laguna Paron, 32 km away, or to Caraz and

PERU

then back to Huaraz. In the central plaza in Caraz you can rent a car and drive to Laguna Paron.

Alpamayo

Mt. Alpamayo is considered to be one of the most beautiful mountains in the world. It is shaped like a perfect pyramid with four facets, and is covered with snow. The summit is about 6300 m high and is a difficult challenge for mountain climbers. Hikers can reach the base of the summit. This trip, there and back, takes five to six days, while the truly enthusiastic may choose to continue from the mountain and cross the Cordillera – a difficult hike which demands good orientation skills. If one chooses this option the trip lasts 6-7 days.

The hike begins in the small village of Cochapampa, which can be reached with one of the *camionetas* (pick-up trucks) which leave from the market in Caraz. From the village, a long and exhausting climb lies ahead to reach the magnificent Laguna Collicocha, and the mountain saddle, which is 4900 m high. From the saddle there is a steep descent to the wide valley Quebrada Alpamayo. Several hours along the slopes of the valley brings one to the magnificent foothills of Mt. Alpamayo. One can hire a donkey to carry one's gear up to this point, but here one separates from the muleteer, and must pay for the number of days it takes him to return to his village. The remainder of the trip takes about three days, and includes the crossing of some difficult mountain passes, the highest of which is 5000 m high. The views are breathtaking from these heights. The lakes are magnificent (Lagunas Safuna), and it is worthwhile spending some time walking around them.

The route ends in the pleasant town Pomabamba, from which buses depart a few times a week to Huaraz. The return trip to Huaraz by truck is certainly an exceptional experience, even if it lasts at least 12 hours and is exhausting. Before you leave Pomabamba, you can enjoy the hot springs which are situated a few minutes walking distance from the central plaza.

Laguna Churup

This enchanting lake lies 4600 m above sea level. It is almost surrounded by straight cliffs, and the color of the water is turquoise. It is located about 35 km away from Huaraz and a good portion of the trip can be done by car. One can do a day trip to the lake, or perhaps spend a night out camping. There is an area suitable for parking not far from the lake.

The taxi will bring you to the village Pitek, and from here there is a difficult 2-3 hour climb to the lake. A glacier descends to the lake from the mighty snow-capped peak which rises above.

PERU

You can ask the taxi driver to wait for you in Pitex to return to Huaraz, or otherwise take a three hour walk back, passing friendly Indian villages on the way.

Another alternative is to combine this trip with visits to other lakes in the vicinity, using Pitex as a base, and setting up camp there. One can also ask to sleep in one of the village huts.

Las Ruinas de Yungay

In 1970 an earthquake devastated the Cordillera Blanca area. This caused a huge piece of the glacier from Mt. Huazcaran to break off and descend at high speed, destroying everything in its path. All 18,000 inhabitants of Yungay were killed, except a few who were elsewhere at the time. Not a single house was left standing.

Four date palms mark the spot of Plaza de Armas. While walking along the plain, which less than twenty years ago had been a vibrant town, you will discern a few pathetic remnants of the daily life that used to exist here; a piece of a wrecked bus, or bits of half buried furniture. From the monument built on the hill, one can clearly see Mt. Huazcaran and the glacier which caused the disaster.

A short time after the disaster, a new town of Yanguy was established not far form the former town, and today it has a similar number of inhabitants – about 20,000. It's less than an hour's ride away from Huaraz, and the buses which depart frequently for Caraz, pass through the ruins of Yungay.

Chavin de Huantar

The ruins of a temple some 3000 years old are located 110 km southeast of Huaraz. Due to damage in the 1970 earthquake, parts of it are closed to the public. The site features wonderful stone carvings, an impressive building and the remains of statues. The figures of condors and pumas, etched in precise detail on the temple walls, are especially beautiful, as are the remains of gargoyles protruding from the walls. Do not miss the temple's underground vaults, from which you can form an impression of its contruction and design.

Getting to Chavin involves about five hours of difficult travel on an annoying dirt road, and only its scenic wonders make it bearable. Daily buses from Huaraz (morning and afternoon) reach the village of Catac quickly and with no difficulty along a paved road which extends the full length of the Santa Cruz Valley. Here you turn eastward and continue another eighty kilometers to Chavin on a rough trail. Hitchhiking is very difficult once you've passed Catac, while a similar route on foot is

PERU

complicated, difficult, and not worth the effort since it offers no special attractions. Tour companies in Huaraz organize round trip excursions to Chavin, and you would do well to consider joining one. There is daily bus service between Chavin and Lima, but the route is circuitous and tiring, passing through innumerable towns and villages. We recommend that you use Huaraz's bus services instead.

Trujillo

Francisco Pizarro founded Trujillo in 1536 next to the ancient adobe city of Chan Chan and named it after the city of his birth in Spain. Though rich in modern buildings, Trujillo (pop. 750,000) seems to have retained its colonial charm. Buildings and churches dating from the sixteenth to the eighteenth centuries create a special atmosphere, dominated by Spanish architecture and imported building styles which few other cities preserve so well and so beautifully. Trujillo has many magnificent estates, which once belonged to the city's aristocratic and wealthy families. Most have been expropriated by the government. While some have been turned into office buildings and corporate headquarters, others are put to social uses and are usually not open to the public. The excellent weather (average temperatures are 25 degrees Celsius in summer and 15 degrees Celsius in winter) goes far in explaining the attraction the Spanish felt for the city and the dryness explains the wonderful preservation of archeological ruins in the vicinity.

Transportation

Frequent and convenient buses connect Trujillo with Huaraz, Lima and the Ecuadorian border. The highway from Huaraz to the coast goes via Casma (pop. 20,000). The only two things worthy of mention here are the stench of fish which permeates the city and the many thieves. Not far from Casma there are numerous temples and antiquities, the most impressive of these – Sechin – is some six kilometers up the hill from Casma in the direction of Huaraz. From Casma the road leads northward to Chimbote (pop. over 200,000), which until recently was the center of the Peruvian fishing industry. Another 135 km brings us to Trujillo. It's about ten hours from Huaraz or Lima to Trujillo and up to eleven hours from Tumbes. Roggero and Tepsa buses are recommended. The lines from Lima and back are very crowded! Make reservations. If all buses are booked for the forseeable future, you can make the trip in stages: go first to Casma or Chimbote and try to proceed from there.

Aero Peru and Faucett fly daily between Trujillo and Lima and thence to Peru's other cities. Faucett flies to Tumbes and stops over in Trujillo on the way to Iquitos.

PERU

Food and lodging
Trujillo has many hotels and restaurants. We recommend the downtown hotels, but check their cleanliness. The best restaurants are those in the large hotels. The best hotel in town is *Hotel De Turismo*, situated in a nice colonial building on Plaza des Armas. Not far from the plaza, at 538 Calle Pizzaro, is *Hotel Americano* which is very cheap, though at first glance it looks impressive and expensive. In this same street there are many restaurants and coffee shops offering excellent cakes. Trujillo's water is not suitable for drinking and you would do well to order bottled drinks. Seashore restaurants specialize in seafood; give them a try. Be sure to leave nothing unguarded while you're dipping in the ocean!

Tourist services
There are Tourist Bureaus at the airport and at Calle Independencia 509. Their staff will be happy to advise and guide you concerning accommodations, transportation and places to visit (especially important if you're interested in the colonial estates where visiting hours are irregular). For maps and road information, visit the Auto Club (T.A.C.P.), Calle Almegro 707.

Currency exchange
Banks on Plaza de Armas will convert money at the official rate and without excessive commission. If you are going on to Ecuador you can buy *sucres* (Ecuador's currency) farther north.

What to see
The giant **Plaza de Armas** lies in the heart of town, with a fountain at its center and surrounded by statues of national Independence heroes. Surrounding the square you'll find the **Municipal Cathedral**, the **City Hall**, public buildings and **Iturregui House**, one of the remaining grand estates from Colonial days, which today serves as a social club and Chamber of Commerce.

Dozens of churches and impressive buildings have survived from the pre-Independence period, when all Peru was under Spanish influence. Though some were damaged in the many earthquakes that have struck the coastal area, many have survived, and these convey the former character and style of the city. Most of the churches feature impressive stone and wood contruction and some are graced with gold and silver ornaments. **Iglesia Carmen**, next to Plaza de Armas, is an example of religious art at its best, and though it is closed in part (due to earthquake damage), you'll be impressed with its facade, balconies and spires. **Iglesias San Francisco and Santo Domingo** are also worth visiting.

*P*ERU

The interesting **archeological museum** (Bolivar 446) at the University of Trujillo contains a collection of pre-Columbian art. A private museum of pottery from all over Peru, particularly that of the Chimu civilization, is located in the **Cassinelli House**, Pierola 601.

Excursions

Chan Chan

One of Latin America's most interesting archeological sites – the remains of the "mud city" of Chan Chan and the ruins of the Chimu Kingdom – should certainly be visited. (It is five kilometers north of Trujillo.) This city, whose buildings, temples and walls are made of adobe bricks, was the capital of the Chimu kingdom, which extended from Guayaquil (Ecuador) in the north to Paramonga (north of Lima) in the south, about a thousand years ago. Chan Chan knew many kings, each of whom built and glorified the city by adding more giant walls (more than twelve meters high), mighty fortresses and magnificent temples.

The city's streets, lined with stores and workshops, once buzzed with life. The plazas served as religious and social centers. In the middle there where well-tended gardens, canals and pools, granaries and warehouses filled with jewelry and treasures. The Incas conquered Chan Chan in the fifteenth century, and ruled until the arrival of the Spanish, who destroyed and plundered it.

The dry climate has helped to preserve Chan Chan, and visitors can still get an idea of its beauty and special glory despite the ravages of time. Chan Chan can be reached by bus or taxi from Trujillo; allow yourself several hours to explore.

Besides Chan Chan there are other ruins scattered around near Trujillo, the most beautiful of which is the Arco Iris Temple. The building is well preserved, as are the many engravings on the walls. Buses which reach the temple pass the corner of avenues Espana and Mansiche near the stadium.

Huanchaco

This tranquil fishing village lies a few kilometers from Trujillo along the coast, and is a holiday spot for inhabitants in the area. Those who have been traveling for a long time will find this a good place to renew their strength. It's worthwhile going down to the beach in the morning or afternoon when the fishermen go out to sea. Their boats are similar to the famous straw boats on Lake Titicaca.

Hotel Bracamonte is very good and cheap, and the owners are

PERU

very congenial. One can sleep there in a sleeping bag for a token payment. In the house of *Seniora Violeta* one can eat decent meals for ridiculously low prices.

The typical *artesania* of the region are necklaces made with turquoise stones called *chaguira*. The local youngsters will certainly try to sell them to you. They ask for high prices, but bargaining will bring them down.

Cajamarca

It was in the mountain city of Cajamarca (elev. 2750 m), northeast of Trujillo, that Pizarro killed the last Incan king, Atahuallpa, thus gaining control of Peru. In this agreeable city of 75,000 people, 300 km from Trujillo, houses and streets seem to have preserved their character and have not allowed time to leave its mark. Buses from Trujillo (8 hours), Lima and Pacasmayo arrive frequently, most at the terminal on Calle Ayacucho. Aero Peru also flies in from Lima and Trujillo.

The most interesting place in town is the room where the Incan ruler was held captive and to which the gold for his supposed ransom was brought. This room, next to Iglesia Belen, was recently opened to visitors after centuries of being locked. Once you've seen the prison and church (closed on Tuesdays), you can visit the square where Atahualpa was taken captive, and thereafter the many churches which grace the city.

Two museums – one of archeology (at the University) and another of Colonial art – house interesting displays of the city and its surroundings, and are recommended. There are hot springs – the **Banos del Inca**, or the Incan Baths – near town. Those with wanderlust for unknown parts can hop aboard a truck for the difficult five-hour trip through wonderful scenery, to the tiny mining town of Hualgayoc, ninety kilometers north, at a height of 4000 m. It is not worth your while to go onward, and you should return by the same route.

Tumbes

Peru's northern border town (pop. app. 30,000), 1320 km north of Lima, doesn't have much worthy of mention, and serves primarily as a crossing point to and from Ecuador.

Transportation

Tumbes is linked with Lima by plane, bus and *colectivos*. Modern, comfortable buses ply the coastal route to Lima in about sixteen hours. If you wish to use Tumbes as a point of departure for your tour of Peru, you can get off at any of the coastal cities (Trujillo, for example) and proceed from there to the mountains.

PERU

Currency exchange
Change money at the branch office of Banco de la Nacion. Dealing with street moneychangers is strictly forbidden and the authorities have been known to deal harshly with offenders. The bank on the Ecuadorian side, in the town of Huaquillas, is open only until noon.

On to Ecuador
The border crossing may be reached by local bus (a thirty-minute trip) or by taxi. Border crossing procedures include a routine inspection of passport and bags, though painstaking searches of travelers' luggage have been known to occur every so often. From the Ecuadorian border town there are direct buses to Quito (12 hours) and Guayaquil several times a day. The Peruvian border station, located in Aguas Verdes, is open from 8am-6pm, but occasionally closes for siesta, when you'll have no choice but to wait. Crossing the border in either direction in a private car requires an International Driver's License and certificate from the Auto Club (which has an office in the central plaza in Tumbes).

The Amazon Basin

One of the most exceptional experiences awaiting a tourist in South America is a visit to its thick jungles, where wild and unconquered nature rules supreme. The slight progress that has penetrated the jungles – be it electricity (generators), motor vehicles (rarely more than noisy crates), or roads (twisting, narrow trails passable only during the dry season) – has not managed to hide the fact that only in recent decades has the white man been able to establish a permanent foothold in this corner of the world and begun to make substantial use of its resources. Not for nothing has the Amazon captured the imagination of tourist and scientist, adventurer and philosopher. Its mysterious green mantle conceals fascinating oddities, wild animals, a special type of people and unknown Indian tribes. The dense jungle, fed by the limitless waters of the Amazon, summons visitors to one of the most stunning experiences which man can undergo. It's an ordeal involving effort and risk, and one must prepare for it carefully. A tourist who wishes to explore this corner of the world must behave with caution and patience, freeing himself as best he can of Western prejudices, ways of thought and behavior which do not fit in here. Here one must totally submit to the laws of the area and attempt to integrate into the local way of life, where time is meaningless, cleanliness and hygiene unimportant, and safety (on the roads, for example) unworthy of attention. Here it's jungle law,

*P*ERU

do-as-you-please: cars that travel without lights; buses that either set out or don't; boats that stop for a week in mid-stream with no forewarning and any number of similar wonders liable to bring the most stable of souls to the verge of total nervous collapse. Remember that a journey into this region involves the likelihood of all sorts of difficulties, and all the preparation in the world will not serve even as a basis for the changes you will have to accept in your plans. Even your destination can be predetermined only along very, very general lines.

Where to go

A certain number of jungle routes have been opened to adventurous tourists in recent years, mainly in Brazil, Ecuador and Peru (Bolivia's jungle tours are entirely different in nature). Many tourists prefer to penetrate the depths of the jungle from Ecuador, from where it is relatively easier to reach and where the scarcity of visitors and restricted contact with modern civilization have left things much as they always were.

While most excursions in Brazil focus on the vicinity of Manaos, in this chapter we will focus on its Peruvian counterpart, Iquitos.

Peru offers the tourist two main possibilities: a jungle route northward from Lima to Iquitos and a southward route from Cuzco to the jungle town of Puerto Maldonado (see "Extended Tours in the Cuzco Area").

Equipment

It's very important to equip yourself properly before you set out for the jungles. In addition to malaria pills, pack water purification tablets, canned food and more as hygienic conditions are exceptionally poor. Mosquito repellent is essential, for these pests abound in countless numbers. You won't be able to sleep without a hammock and **mosquito netting**, whether you are under the stars or on ship. You will also need a sleeping bag, a good tent (a two-layered model to keep out the rain) and a cooking stove. Warm clothing is essential, particularly for the mountain sections of the trip, where temperatures plunge to bone-freezing lows at night. Locks and other devices for safeguarding your gear are as necessary here as they are elsewhere, and always keep a watchful eye on your jackets and packs. For the jungles we recommend light clothing – so long as it keeps you covered. Despite the heat, do not go about exposed, and be sure to keep your shoes laced at all times.

When to visit

The tropical climate guarantees high temperatures, high humidity and lots of rain most of the year. It's rainiest in the

PERU

summer, between January and May, while the driest months are August and September. During the rainy season, when many roads are flooded, moving from place to place is liable to take twice as long as it would normally.

The journey to Iquitos

There are two ways to get to Iquitos, the "rubber city" of the late nineteenth century. The faster, more convenient and more dependable method is by air: Aero Peru and Faucett fly there every day from Lima, Trujillo, Pucalpa and other cities. The second and increasingly popular way combines an overland trip with a river cruise. Though a long and exhausting trek, it passes through fascinating scenery and isolated settlements in parts that few people visit.

The land route ends in Pucalpa, 782 km from Lima, which you can reach by bus, truck, or rented car. Despite the hardships of the route – or perhaps because of them – it seems best to me to avail yourself of public transportation, which will take the **Carretera Central** (the "central throughway"), parallel to the wonderful railroad to La Oroya (see "The road to Huancayo") and then head for Cerro de Pasco (pop. 30,000), a mining town 4300 m above sea level. (Beware of breathing difficulties). The train is the most convenient way of reaching this point. It sets out from Lima for Huancayo, and you must change trains in La Oroya (where you can head eastward through lovely agricultural districts on outings to the towns of Tarma, Palca, San Ramon and La Merced). The route to Cerro de Pasco passes through a town called Junin and a plain of the same name. Here Bolivar's army defeated Spanish loyalists in August 1824, the first of many victories that led to Peruvian independence.

From Cerro de Pasco the road continues another 110 km, as far as the town of Huanuco (pop. 75,000). It's a steep climb all the way, and buses and passenger trucks crawl along. Frequent buses link Huanuco with Cerro de Pasco, with La Oroya, Lima and Huancayo to the south and with Tingo Maria to the north. Several buses per week travel the difficult route between La Union and Huaraz via Catac. That city is surrounded by Incan and pre-Incan ruins, including a temple and fortress.

Another 135 km brings us to the outskirts of the jungle town of Tinga Maria (pop. 20,000). The area is lush in natural and cultivated flora, and the combination of mountains and the beginnings of the jungle makes for exceptional scenery. From Tinga Maria there is frequent bus service to Pucalpa (5-8 hours) and Lima. In addition, Aero Peru and Faucett flights to Pucalpa and Lima touch down there almost every day.

PERU

From here the road divides: while its western branch reaches Mayobamba, about 600 km north (from which you can return to the Pacific coast), its eastern branch continues another 300 km or so to Pucalpa. At this jungle town, on the western bank of Rio Ucayali, the land route ends. The 75,000 mixed Indian-Spanish people of Pucalpa engage in river sailing, industry and commerce. In recent years the city has attracted renewed attention with hopes of finding oil in the vicinity. Thus far, however, the quantities discovered do not justify the investments of constructing a refinery and laying a pipeline.

Pucalpa has hotels and restaurants, though of no great quality and, like their counterparts in all the jungle towns, rather expensive. Faucett, Aero Peru and local airlines link the town with Lima and Iquitos. Buses set out for Lima many times each day. There's a Tourist Bureau on Calle 2 de Mayo.

In the Pucalpa area one can visit Indian villages to watch the fishermen and bustling marketplace. The Albert Schweitzer Hospital, established to care for children, is located on the shore of Lake Yarinacocha, about ten kilometers out of town. There are a number of interesting institutions and villages worth visiting in the area. You can rent a boat and go upstream or downstream for a few days, visiting Indian tribes and getting an impression of a way of life which has hardly changed in centuries.

Frequent river transportation links Pucalpa with Iquitos. Numerous sailing craft, both for freight and passengers, make the trip in three to eight days depending on the season and the type of craft (the best time is from April to October, when the water level rises and ships sail at night as well). Be sure to bring food, water-purification tablets (don't drink the river water!) and mosquito repellent. The voyage is interesting at first, but soon begins to get monotonous. With this in mind, try to select the fastest and most comfortable boat you can find. As for prices – bargain with the captain, and make sure you know his route and various stops.

Iquitos

This legendary port, Peru's outlet to the Atlantic ocean, grew out of a mid-eighteenth century missionary settlement built on the western bank of the Amazon. It was only in the 1880s, when the world demand for rubber (produced from trees that flourish in the Amazon region) increased, that the little village, 3100 km from the Atlantic, turned almost overnight into a center of world importance, with European and American commercial and diplomatic offices. Iquitos, like Manaus in Brazil (halfway to the ocean), experienced the kind of boom few cities in the world have known.

PERU

As Iquitos prospered, magnificent buildings – veritable palaces – were built, and a life of culture and luxury took root. Its people enjoyed imported food and drink, attended Parisian opera and saw the best of Europe's performing troupes. But all that ostentatious prosperity – at its peak, legends tell of people in Iquitos lighting cigarettes with $100 bills – vanished in a flash, when seeds of the rubber tree were stolen and planted in Asia. The rubber monopoly was over, and it took only a few months for Iquitos to fall into absolute economic collapse.

Today's Iquitos is no more than a grey, dilapidated port city whose population of 170,000 labors unstintingly for their sustenance, finding it hard to imagine those remote days. Even the magnificent port, the adjacent promenade, the Plaza de Armas with its grand buildings, and the rubber barons' well-kept estates are no more than neglected remnants of a glorious past.

Iquitos is totally isolated; save for visiting planes and ships no one comes and no one goes. The new neighborhoods which have gone up recently, especially since oil was found nearby, haven't broken through the barrier of isolation, and the sense of being cut off is apparent everywhere.

Transportation to Peru and neighboring countries

Aero Peru and Faucett land at Iquitos' international airport several times daily on flights from Lima and Peru's other major cities. Faucett flies several times a week to Miami. Varig, Cruzeiro del Sol and Tanc serve the area, flying to Manaus (Brazil), Leticia (Colombia) and other destinations. Since most flights in this region are fully booked, you must make reservations well in advance and confirm them the moment you arrive in town. There are no flights between Iquitos and Ecuador, an expression of an unresolved border dispute.

Propeller-driven planes fly to villages and towns in the Iquitos area, where Indians live in ancient tribal dwellings. Ships ply the Amazon and its tributaries, though most are decrepit cargo vessels that chug along slowly and are often delayed in mid-journey. Stock up on mosquito netting, a hammock, canned food, water-purification tablets and mosquito repellent before you board one of them!

Ships set out for Brazil and Colombia at irregular intervals; make inquiries at the harbor. The river route to Leticia goes via Ramon Castilla, where immigration procedures are arranged. The fastest way to Brazil is via Leticia, and on to Benjamin Constant and Manaus.

Food and lodging

There are plenty of hotels in Iquitos. Though the best and most

PERU

modern of them, the *Holiday Inn*, is a little far from downtown and rather expensive, you probably should spoil yourself after that exhausting shipboard voyage. The *Hotel Turistas*, part of the government hotel chain, is located downtown; a comfortable place, it's suitable for those on an intermediate budget. A large number of pensions (*residencials*) offer cheap rooms, without showers or air-conditioning.

Iquitos' many restaurants offer a variety of dishes, but nearly all – especially the cheaper ones – concentrate on fish. Tropical fruit is plentiful and cheap in the local market, and you should stock up before heading for outlying areas. Remember that as a rule prices in Iquitos, as in all the jungle cities, are considerably higher than those in central Peru, essentially because of the added cost of transport.

What to see

Little remains of the Iquitos of long ago. Man's neglect combined with the jungle's predatory tendency have taken their toll on the ruins of that turn-of-the-century grandeur. True, the city center – Plaza de Armas – is surrounded with public buildings from that era, but their sorry appearance doesn't compare with the glory they once knew. Even the Church of Santa Ana and the Municipality building on Plaza de Armas (with a Tourist Bureau in one corner, open only till noon) preserve but a trace of the spirit of that time.

The floating slums of Belen are perhaps more indicative than anything else of Iquitos' current condition. This suburb, in which more than ten thousand impoverished people are crowded into miserable boats, is exceptional even in terms of South American poverty. Children roam about in the mud between the boats as adults attempt to find their place in the terrible press. At high tide, when the water level rises several meters and tiny craft sail among the boats offering various goods for sale, the entire quarter looks like a huge floating market.

Near Iquitos is Lake Quistacocha, with a small and interesting zoo on its shore. Some of the water creatures common to the area can be seen at the Municipal Aquarium on Calle Huitado. A small museum in town displays local artwork, a few archeological remains and samples of local flora.

Excursions

The major reason that makes the exhausting trek to Iquitos worthwhile is the visit to the Indian villages in the area.

Many tour companies organize guided tours of one to three days' duration, which include a river voyage and hike through the thick of the jungle (the *selva*). Some of these companies

PERU

have branch offices or agents in Lima where you can make reservations and pay accordingly; others have offices in downtown Iquitos, near Plaza de Armas or on Calle Putumayo. Bear in mind that penetrating the jungle is both complicated and difficult. We therefore recommend that you utilize the services of a reliable company with a staff that is familiar with everything liable to be encountered along the way.

The Indians in the Iquitos area are in constant contact with the modern world, to the great detriment – from the tourist's viewpoint, of course – of their traditional way of life. It's become rather unusual to see colorfully painted Indians hunting with blowguns and fishing with harpoons. Wild animals too, annoyed at the disturbance, have wandered off deeper into the bush and very few tours penetrate deeply enough to encounter them.

Iquitos is therefore a rather "touristy" jungle, ready and waiting for visitors who wish a small taste of the exotic Amazon. A stroll through Iquitos itself and excursions in the area will open a window onto a strange world, where social values and concepts are so different that they seem to have been taken from another planet. It's an instructive experience, one which breaks through the barriers of the imagination and adds a new dimension to our comprehension of everything connected with man and his nature.

South of Lima

Some of the most famous places in Peru are concentrated south of Lima. We will survey them individually along two axes. One runs down the coast to the Chilean border, more or less parallel to the ancient seashore route; the other runs along the mountain ridge to Cuzco. There is also the possibility of combining the routes, going part of the way along the coast and part of it in the mountains. The order of our survey will reflect the geographical distance from Lima. Each place is mentioned for its own merit and may serve as a basis for starting, joining, or leaving the route we present – in any direction you wish.

Transportation
All the locales to be surveyed below, both along the seashore and in the mountains, enjoy frequent bus and *colectivo* connections with Lima and with each other. There are several buses every day between the capital and each of the destinations, though we do recommend that you buy tickets a day or two in advance. For intercity transportation, local service offers you great freedom and relative speed in buses that may be less comfortable and grand than those of Lima, but are no less efficient.

PERU

The roads linking the coastal route with the Andean highway are very hard to travel, and you'll find progress rather slow. The train from Arequipa to Puno is perhaps the most comfortable way of all to complete the circle, but the Nazca-Abancay highway is also a good way of linking the mountain and coastal routes, and the trip is an experience in its own right (see "Nazca").

The Coastal Axis

Pachacamac

Thirty-one kilometers south of Lima on the Pan-American Highway we come to the remains of Peru's largest coastal city in the pre-Spanish era: Pachacamac. Francisco Pizarro's brother, reaching the site in 1533 – shortly after the Spanish landed in Peru – razed the city to its foundations, slaughtering the priests and smashing statues and magnificent buildings. Pyramids, temples, grand stone figures and similar ritual objects were damaged, and only a tiny remnant is left. Entire sections of the site, however, have been restored in recent years, and today we can once again marvel at the remains of a civilization whose primary "sin" lay in its not having been sufficiently well fortified against the Spanish. A small museum on the site displays findings from local excavations – some of gold and silver, others of stone and bronze.

A number of tour companies organize outings to Pachacamac, or you can take the bus from Plaza Santa Catalina next to Parque Universitario. The trip takes nearly an hour, and the visit to the site and museum takes about two hours.

Paracas

This small town 250 km south of Lima occupies the site where one of the best-developed coastal civilizations Peru has known blossomed about three thousand years ago. To reach Paracas, go via **Pisco**, the port city after which Peru's national brandy is named. (From Pisco you can travel fifty kilometers eastward to Tambo Colorado, where a pre-Incan city has survived roofless though in excellent condition; its wall frescoes and streets are quite amazing.)

Paracas, as we said, was the center of an ancient civilization which, like many others in this area, disappeared for reasons that are still unclear.

A small archeological museum on the site displays pottery, wood and textile artifacts, which testify to an especially high level of development. Another indication of this is the advanced

PERU

mummification technique which the people of Paracas used to preserve their dead. Corpses were wrapped in fine fabrics, sealed in tightly-woven "coffins" of straw and buried on a nearby peninsula, in complex burial structures apparently meant to ensure them a pleasant wait until their resurrection.

Paracas has known strategic importance in more recent times as well. Here the Argentinian General Jose de San Martin came ashore to aid the Peruvians in their war of independence against the Spanish, setting up his headquarters not far away. Today, Paracas is known primarily for the many water fowl that congregate in the area, thereby making it an important nature reserve.

Small islands scattered offshore are home to tens of thousands of water birds and thousands of sea lions. Organized boat excursions set out from Paracas every morning and afternoon. The area has been nicknamed "the poor man's Galapagos" and rightly so, for in abundance of wildlife it can compare only to Ecuador's Galapagos Islands, and tour rates here are immeasurably lower. The entire region has been rediscovered in recent years, with attention now devoted to the needs of the wildlife. Several companies organize boat trips to the islands; during the five hours or so of the cruise, dozens of elephant seals swim around the boats, and it is not at all rare to see a flock of giant birds a few meters over your head. Such a cruise is highly recommended for nature lovers.

You can take the island cruise from Pisco or Paracas. The former offers more comfortable lodging possibilities and more convenient public transportation (four hours from Lima).

Ica

The city of Ica (pop. 150,000), 110 km south of Paracas, is important only as the center of the Peruvian wine industry (these wines are not highly recommended to the connoisseur) and as home to an archeological museum. Most of Peru's wine is made in this region, but a visit to a local winery (*bodega*), is not particularly interesting. The city itself is rather humdrum; other than the palm-spangled Plaza de Armas, there is little to see here that deserves an extended visit – apart from the archeological museum, reached by bus from the Plaza. The tastefully arranged museum displays a textile and ceramics collection, handiwork of the Paracas, Ica, Nazca and other civilizations. Mummies and skulls are also on display and will give you an impression of the manner in which the dead were treated and buried.

Of the city's several hotels, the *Turistas* (expensive) and *Ica* (inexpensive) are recommended. There is frequent public

PERU

transportation to Lima and other cities from the central bus terminal. The Tourist Bureau (Cajamarca 179) can provide a wealth of information and recommendations about where to go and how to get there.

Nazca

Nazca, inhabited by man for more than five thousand years, has known ups-and-downs in its long history. A mysterious civilization that flourished here three millenia before Christ is apparently the one responsible for the giant figures in the desert sand for which Nazca is known. Their creators vanished without a trace, replaced by a civilization no less advanced which excelled in pottery, carving and metal working, the remains of which grace most of Peru's museums today. The Nazca civilization, which peaked around 850 AD, left a legacy of painted and decorated ceramics, wood carvings, gold jewelry and wondrously patterned fabrics.

Transportation

Nazca, 450 km from Lima, can be reached easily in about six hours by Roggero or Ormeno bus, or by colectivos. Try not to arrive in the wee hours of the morning, when hotels and hostels are securely locked; you'd probably have to spend the rest of the night under the stars.

From Nazca some buses continue down the coast toward Arequipa, while others head east – climbing the mountains toward Abancay, from which one may proceed either south to Cuzco or north to Ayacucho and back to Lima. It's a tough route to travel and the trip drags on for hours. Since the buses are rarely in reasonable mechanical condition, breakdowns on the road should not come as a surprise. At the same time, the scenery on the way is lovely and worth the effort. Those choosing this route can include a visit to Nazca on their way from Lima to Cuzco and the Inca area, or on their return from Cuzco to Lima via Nazca.

Food and lodging

Some of Nazca's hotels are of high quality. Among these we can recommend the government-owned *Turistas*, whose staff can give you directions and information about excursions in the vicinity, and the *Hotel Nazca* near the bus terminal. Many local residents let rooms in their homes to tourists; though rates are rather low, it's doubtful that the cleanliness will satisfy the average squeamish visitor. Several restaurants can be found downtown; most of the menu consists of seafood. There is a nice restaurant near the small airport from where the flights over the desert figures depart.

*P*ERU

Close encounters of the art kind' - at Nazca

What to see
Only one place downtown seems worthy of a visit: the Municipal Museum on the central plaza (open 10am-1pm and 2-6pm), where artifacts of the ancient civilizations are displayed; the rest of Nazca is no different from hundreds of other towns. Our main attention will be devoted to the surroundings, which are rich in archeological ruins including temples and burial grounds. Since they are scattered all over the Nazca valley, we recommend that

PERU

you avail yourself of a local guide's services and a rented car to find them.

The main reason for visiting Nazca is, of course, the giant paintings in Pampa Colorada. Since Erich von Danniken's book and film *Chariots of the Gods*, the remains of the fascinating Nazca paintings have achieved worldwide fame. Indeed, as you fly over the area and observe a giant spider, monkey, man-as-astronaut or bird painted on the ground hundreds of meters below, you cannot escape the strange mystery of it all: giant figures, hundreds of meters long, carved into the ground thousands of years ago. Strangest of all is the astonishing fact that the figures have meaning only from a bird's-eye view; walking along the ground you wouldn't even notice them. To compound the enigma, the entire region is desertlike and quite flat, without even a single point from which those ancient people could have admired their work and designed the figures. Numerous attempts have been made to explain the meaning of these figures, but even today the unknown outweighs the known.

The venerable German researcher Maria Reiche, who has spent decades studying the phenomenon, proposes, in her book *Mystery on the Desert*, the hypothesis that the figures were intended to have an astrological significance, perhaps a calendar; she considers them to be the work of a number of local groups, working centuries apart. A more recent theory dating from the mid-1970s, attributes the paintings to a local civilization guided by people flying in balloons. Though relics discovered in the area and analysis of the figures on the ground lend some support to this theory, it sounds too fantastic, even alongside von Danniken's claim that the paintings were made by aliens from outer space. In any event, we're obviously speaking of one of those few places in the world where our understanding has not succeeded in fathoming that which our eyes behold. Here we can only gape in astonishment and grapple with the questions for many days afterwards.

A number of observation towers have been erected in recent years. It seems to me, though, that this doesn't equal the unforgettable experience of flying over them. The several competing companies charge pretty much the same rate, offering discounts only on rare occasions. Aero Condor is among the most reliable of the local airlines, with experienced pilots and properly maintained planes (not to be taken for granted here). Condor has an office in the Lima Sheraton where you can make reservations, especially recommended during tourist season. From their Nazca office they will drive you out to the little airport where the flights take off. The flights last for about 45 minutes,

PERU

alternatively climbing and falling – to get a good view of the figures. Be sure to get a window seat, for otherwise it will be hard to see and even harder to take pictures. We highly recommend an early morning flight, for later the sun will glare in your eyes and the haze will interfere with your vision. You should try to fly at the very moment when the fog lifts off the desert, exposing an astounding and incomparable scene.

Onward to Arequipa

Proceeding down the coastal highway from Nazca, about three hours' driving (172 km) brings us to the fishing village of **Chala**. In this small village, with its population of under two thousand, you can intimately view the way of life of fishermen who go about their work as their fathers and forefathers did – with simplicity, speed and grace. Restaurants serve fish just hauled out of the ocean, and you can swim and tan in the sun. We do not recommend that you spend the night there, for the water isn't fit to drink and the hotels are simple and not always clean. Continuing southward, the landscape becomes even more desertlike and arid; only after more than 200 km do we reach the town of **Camana**, another fishing center, which blossomed in the Inca period and appears not to have changed much since (apart from having been rebuilt after suffering severe earthquake damage in the late sixteenth century). Immediately past Camana, the Pan-American Highway turns east and climbs for 132 km – to the outskirts of Arequipa, one of Peru's most beautiful cities.

Arequipa

Arequipa, 1009 km south of Lima, is a lovely city built of white granite, and the Spanish influence has not yet faded from its homes, estates and churches. Arequipa served as a major crossroads in the Inca period, for it is situated on the main highways to Cuzco from both Chile and the coast. The Spanish explorer Diego de Almegro, one of Pizarro's men, was the first Spaniard to reach Arequipa, and the new Spanish city subsequently founded beside it in 1540 eventually merged with the Incan town.

Arequipa's 750,000 residents are imbued with an unusually strong brand of local patriotism. The pride they take in their city can be seen in everything and it's largely justified – for this is undoubtedly Peru's most beautiful city and one of the loveliest in all South America. Arequipa is known far and wide as **La Ciudad Blanca** (The White City), after the sillar stone of which most of its houses are built. This white stone is quarried from the many volcanoes encircling the city, of which the most famous, El Misti, soaring to a height of 5850 m, is visible from

*P*ERU

every part of town. The weather in Arequipa (elev. 2378 m) is ideal: perpetual sunshine and a year-round average temperature of 17 degrees Centigrade (63 degrees Fahrenheit).

Transportation

Bus: Many buses travel daily to and from Lima, Nazca and the other coastal cities. Tepsa runs daily buses southward to Tacna and Arica (Chile). Even though there are many buses each day to Puno, Juliaca and Cuzco, the train is preferable. For the trip to Lima, Ormeno and Roggero buses are recommended; Morales Moralitos buses are not recommended. Tickets should be bought at least one day in advance.

Train: Passenger trains head east from Arequipa to Juliaca and thence to Puno or Cuzco once or twice a day on a lovely route reaching heights up to 4000 m. Travel first-class, since the other classes are very crowded and you would be far more exposed to thieves (**Important**: see "Personal safety"!). Second-class tickets can be purchased only on the morning of your trip (get up early, or there may be no seats left) but first-class tickets are available the previous day. In second-class innumerable peddlers pass through during the trip, but they are not allowed access to first-class and the buffet car. If you're not interested in eating in the buffet, stock up in advance for the lengthy trip (10 hours to Puno, 22 to Cuzco). The trip at night is very cold, so plan accordingly.

Plane: Aero Peru (Tel. 23853) and Faucett (both have offices on the Plaza de Armas) provide daily service to Lima and Cuzco and thence to other destinations in Peru and the world over.

Tourist services

The Tourist Bureau, at La Merced 117, will offer courteous service and explanatory material. The Tourist Police Station is at the bus terminal, Jerusalem 317. Information about road conditions, service stations and the like is available from Peru's Auto Club (San Francisco 206).

Food and lodging

Arequipa's hotels and restaurants, in no short supply, are capable of meeting the needs of any tourist on any budget. Most hotels are downtown, within walking distance of the interesting sites. The many restaurants serve a wide variety of fare – Chinese, seafood and more. Typical Peruvian dishes are served at *Picanterias* – Creole restaurants famous for their cuisine.

What to see

Arequipa is known for its white granite buildings – a casual stroll through the streets will explain why. Even before we survey the

PERU

sites one by one, we cannot help but marvel at the grandeur of the Spanish architecture and the professionalism of the artists and craftsmen who carried out the work. Each of the many churches, public buildings and estates testifies to the architectural magnificence of bygone days, and explains Arequipa's special quality and character better than anything else.

In the city center we find the **Plaza de Armas**, laid out around a fountain and ringed with benches on which many locals spend their *siestas*. Amid trees and flowers one can watch the passers-by and appreciate the ambience of this pleasant city. The square ends at the **Municipal Cathedral**, rebuilt in the last century in the wake of cumulative earthquake damage since the sixteenth century. Not far from it is the **Jesuit Church of La Compania**, dating from the second half of the seventeenth century. This church, and Santo Domingo, La Merced and San Francisco churches, are Arequipa's most beautiful. The latter also houses a lovely monastery, with an impressive handicrafts market across the way.

Also downtown is the San Camilo municipal market, where various kinds of food and drink are offered alongside local artwork, household implements and the like. Not far from there is **San Agustin University**, one of two in Arequipa, with a small archeological museum displaying a collection of local pottery and mummies.

The crowning touch of our visit to Arequipa is the **Santa Catalina Convent**. Built at the end of the sixteenth century, it served as a boarding school for the daughters of the city's elite, who were sent there accompanied by servants and lived in luxurious rooms decorated in the spirit of the place and time. Only in 1970 was the convent opened to the public. The first visitors' hearts leapt at what they saw: entire streets, a sort of city-within-a-city existing in total isolation for centuries, wholly uninfluenced by the surrounding environment. The few nuns remaining there live in one wing set aside for them, while the rest of the convent is open to the public every day from morning until early afternoon. Highly recommended!

Excursions

El Misti Volcano has been in vogue in recent years, as more and more visitors climb to its summit. Ascending the towering peak requires hard physical effort and at least two days. It's important to bring food, suitable equipment and, most important, experience. If you lack the latter, you'd do well to practice somewhere else and choose more tranquil but no less interesting trails in the Arequipa area.

PERU

The attractions closest to Arequipa are the suburb of Cayma and the town of Tingo. Both preserve the way of life of bygone days and will give you a first-hand idea of an otherwise vanished way of life. The most beautiful and interesting of the sites, however, is the Colca Valley, about ten hours away, home of the Indian tribe which gave the valley its name. They maintained independence of Inca domination almost until the Spaniards arrived. The villages of Chivay and Cabanaconde afford visitors a window on a world in which time is frozen, a chance to observe how people lived in this region five hundred years ago or more.

The road to the Colca Valley is enchanting in its own right, with its scenery of volcanoes, valleys, canyons and rivers.

Tacna

About a six-hour trip from Arequipa, and 1293 km south of Lima, we reach the southern border city of Tacna (pop. app. 50,000), restored to Peruvian rule only in the late 1920s, after fifty years of Chilean occupation.

In the downtown Plaza de Armas we find a monument to Admiral Grau and Colonel Bolognesi, and beside it the municipal cathedral, designed by the famous French architect Eiffel.

Tacna enjoys daily air service to Lima, and frequent bus connections with Arequipa, Nazca, Puno, Cuzco and other destinations.

On to Chile

Tacna, 40 km from the Chilean border, is connected by buses, *colectivos*, and trains to Arica, the Chilean port city. Buses and *colectivos* are delayed at the Peruvian and Chilean border stations, where luggage is checked and passports stamped. Generally the procedure is efficient. It is worthwhile to use the service of the *colectivos*, which are new and comfortable taxis, and which do not cost much more than buses. In the city, electronic and photographic equipment similar to that sold in Arica, Chile, is sold at low prices. The border is closed at night and on Peruvian and Chilean holidays. Drivers of private cars must obtain special crossing documents, which can be purchased at kiosks. The Auto Club, on Avenida 2 de Mayo, will provide details and guidelines about documents, routes, service stations and so forth.

Street moneychangers can change currency for you, but their rates are low. If you're coming from Chile, you'll do well to buy *soles* in Arica or, if you must, to change only a small sum to cover basic needs until you reach Arequipa or Puno.

PERU

From Lima to Cuzco by the Mountain Route

Peru of yesterday was criss-crossed by highways. The ancient Peruvian civilizations, knowing the secret of the road and cognizant of its decisive importance for dominating the area and its tribes, spared no effort in pushing them through and paving them, developing and enhancing a network of roads that occasionally reach heights at which it is difficult even to breathe. The Incans, of course, carried this to its utmost and during the fourteenth and fifteenth centuries they built or upgraded hundreds of kilometers of paved roads across mountain and valley, linking the capital of Cuzco with every outlying province of their vast empire. These grand highways (see the chapter "The Incas"), of which a significant portion has been preserved to this day also served the Spanish conquerors and helped them reach their destinations with ease. Today's modern highways still follow the same routes. One of the most interesting of these roads goes east from Lima to La Oroya and from there south to Cuzco. Only part of the route runs parallel to that of the Incas, though transport along it was known far earlier. Today the railroad, a traveling experience in its own right, reaches Huancayo, after which the main highway winds southward to Ayacucho, Abancay and Cuzco.

Public transportation between Lima and Cuzco foregoes this enchanting route in favor of a shorter and easier way via Nazca and Abancay. The mountain route must therefore be traveled in stages, with visits along the way to some of Peru's most beautiful cities.

The Road to Huancayo

Although many bus lines link the two cities, the train (which does not run on Sundays) is, in my opinion, the best mode of transport. The Lima-La Oroya line is the world's highest, passing through breathtaking scenery, crossing many bridges and plunging through dozens of tunnels. The tracks wind about and climb steeply – reaching 4800 m above sea level (!!) – and in certain stretches "zigzag" in order to make the gradient negotiable.

This strange railroad line was conceived and designed by the American railroad engineer Henry Meiggs in the 1870s, though he did not live to see it built. The tremendous construction project, finished only in the 1890s by laborers brought to Peru from many countries (chiefly from China and the Orient), is one of modern Peru's most advanced engineering achievements.

PERU

The train begins its ascent almost the moment it leaves Lima, and reaches the mountain town of Chosica, a popular turn-of-the-century resort, about 40 km further. The train continues to climb past small towns, including the mining town of Casapalca (elev. 4150 m). About three hours out of Lima it reaches La Oroya, where the track splits – one line north to Cerro de Pasco (see "The Amazon Basin, the Journey to Iquitos"), the other south to Huancayo.

Like elsewhere in Peru, especially on trains and in stations, it is important to remember that thieves are in abundance, and to behave accordingly (see "Personal Security").

Huancayo

Huancayo, the buzzing commercial center of the mountain region, lies 412 km from Lima at an elevation of 3271 m. Most of its 350,000 inhabitants are of Indian descent. Their ancestors, too, lived in the city and its fertile surroundings for centuries, engaging in agriculture and handicrafts. Huancayo was important even in ancient times, long before the Spanish came. The main Incan highway passed through the city and Pizarro advanced along it on his way to conquer Cuzco. The entire mountain region is known as a politically active area, and Huancayo has been proclaimed capital of the Republic on several brief occasions. A terrorist underground who spread fear over the local population, is currently active in the area, which leads to periodic restrictions on traffic using the road to Ayacuchuo, as well as army and police searches.

Transportation

Buses and **colectivos** – ply the seven-hour route to Lima many times a day. Buses and trucks continue on to Ayacucho, the second-largest city in Andean Peru, and from there to Abancay and Cuzco. Direct buses to Cuzco set out several times weekly on a trip which takes about two days (longer during the rainy season). Bring a warm sleeping bag for truck rides in the mountains, since temperatures drop considerably at night. Buses head northward from Huancayo to La Oroya, Cerro de Pasco and Pucalpa and there are also buses and trucks which set out for Nazca on the coast

Public transportation in this area is abominable. Schedules are not schedules, tickets are not tickets ... and reserved seats? What are they? Buy your tickets early and get to the station long before the bus is supposed to leave. Do not worry, there's no danger of its leaving early. It is just that the local passengers seem to get excited about the trip, and get to the bus hours before its scheduled departure time, and proceed to get comfortably settled along with their luggage – so that there is

PERU

no room left for later arrivals. It's a local custom, and if you cannot beat them, join them – and you cannot beat them. Blend into the atmosphere, take a deep breath and fortify yourself with patience of steel.

Food and lodging
The hotels in town are of low quality and apart from the government-owned *Hotel Turistas* (Plaza de Armas) and the *Hotel Concepcion* (a little far from downtown) the selection is not promising. *Hostal Dani* on Calle Giraldez is cheap and comfortable. There are a great many small pensions around the train station. Be sure to check for cleanliness and hot water and remember not to leave valuables in your room.

The city is full of Chinese and Creole restaurants. Along the streets and in the markets, stalls offer local snacks. On Sundays fresh foodstuffs, brought in by Indians from nearby villages, are available at the market.

Tourist services
The Tourist Bureau is at Ancash 415; the Auto Club (T.A.C.P.) has a branch on the same street at No. 603.

Huancayo Tours, on Calle Real, the main street, organizes excursions in the vicinity and will be pleased to provide information on events and sites in the city and its environs.

What to see and what to buy
Calle Real, Huancayo's major artery, is the scene of most social and commercial activity. It is lined with shops, offices and agencies, while sidewalks are packed with passersby and dozens of Indians hawking their finest creations – food and handicrafts.

The bulk of activity takes place on Sundays, when a gigantic market – the *Feria* – takes place, to which the villagers bring their wares. Foodstuffs of diverse kinds – cheeses, vegetables, fruit and prepared dishes – are intermingled with artwork, silver jewelry, flutes and other musical instruments, woven fabrics, clothing of llama or alpaca wool and, above all, needle-etched gourds, produced by a technique that demands patience, precision and skill. The Huancayo market is considered Peru's finest and its prices – Peru's lowest. As in every market, here, too, you must bargain, but the final prices will probably be lower here than in Lima or Cuzco. Stroll among the thousands of vendors, men and women, size up what's available, bargain and buy. (If you are continuing southward you can buy inexpensive woolen goods in Juliaca as well, but as for the gourds – this is undoubtedly **the** place.)

PERU

Excursions

Those who reach Huancayo on a day other than Sunday or who consider the market too touristy will certainly find a visit to the nearby villages interesting. Here is where the craftsmen work and where, of course, you can buy *artesania* (handicrafts) at slightly lower prices than in town.

Two villages, Chochas Chicas and Chochas Grandes, are the centers of the gourd-engraving art. Ask local residents to show you to the artists' homes.

You can observe weaving and embroidery in Wallwash and silversmithing in San Jeronimo. The two villages, slightly north of Huancayo, are easily reached by minibus or taxi from Calle Real.

Near San Jeronimo is the town of Concepcion, from which minibuses set out for the lovely Santa Rosa de Ocopana monastery. This institution, founded more than 250 years ago to train priests for missionary activity among the jungle Indians, is built in an impressive style and is situated in an enchanting corner of nature. The monastery has a huge library, artworks and more. For a fee one can stay overnight.

The town of Chupaca, about fifteen kilometers west of Huancayo, holds a small, quiet market on Saturdays. A visit to the market, besides being an opportunity to buy souvenirs, gives you a chance to witness the local population, foods and customs and day-to-day activities, from up close.

Ayacucho

Ayacucho (pop. 30,000) was founded by the Spanish in 1539, and has served as the urban center for the area between Huancayo and Cuzco ever since. In nearby La Quinua we can visit the battlefield where Spanish loyalists were routed in December 1824, paving the way to Peruvian independence.

Ayacucho's more than thirty churches are living testimony to the town's religious devotion in bygone years. Most of the churches – Santo Domingo, San Francisco, La Merced and the Municipal Cathedral across from Parque Sucre, for example – have magnificent altars adorned with gold and silver. These are remnants from the opulence that greeted the Spaniards, relics of an era from which so little has survived.

A university was established in Ayacucho as early as 1677 but only reopened less than thirty years ago. It has since served as a center for student activity and ferment that do not always coincide with government objectives. For some reason, the "Shining Path" Maoist underground is more active in Ayacucho than elsewhere and the police react harshly and forcefully to any deviant or exceptional behavior (see "Personal Security").

PERU

The market in Ayacucho is famous for the quality of its merchandise. Local Indians display a variety of jewelry, knitted garments and the like, generally similar to those available in Huancayo and with no significant difference in price. We recommend a visit to the small Historical Museum in the Simon Bolivar Cultural Center, where archeological remains are displayed alongside items from the Independence period.

Transportation

Aero Peru and Faucett fly into Ayacucho every day from Lima and Cuzco. During tourist season the planes are full, so make reservations well in advance and confirm your return flight immediately after reaching town. There is passenger bus service to Lima (15 hours) via Pisco (12 hours, 374 km); from Pisco you can also continue southward along the coast. Buses and trucks cover the gorgeous 296 km route to Huancayo in about twelve hours.

Traveling overland to Cuzco, 593 km southeast of Ayacucho, requires great effort but has its reward. Several buses set out on this route every day, but they are generally crowded and uncomfortable. Make reservations as early as you can, and come early to grab a place to sit. The trip, though not supposed to last more than twenty-four hours, occasionally takes three or four times longer, especially on rainy days when whole sections of road become impassable. In addition mechanical troubles frequently cause extended delays. The local tour companies operate bus services of their own, but this is naturally more expensive. The route to Cuzco goes by way of Abancay, a small, boring transit town, and from there continues eastward into the lovely Apurimac valley. You can make your way to Abancay separately, and continue from there on one of the many buses that travel daily to Cuzco (200 km). The most beautiful stretch is between Abancay and Anta, and it is worth your while to traverse it during daylight. If you want to reach Machu-Picchu, get off in Anta and proceed a short distance to Izcuchaca, where the passenger train from Cuzco to Machu-Picchu makes a stop.

PERU

The Inca Empire

For hundreds of years – from the eleventh century until the arrival of the Spanish in the early 1500s – a mighty empire progressively expanded across South America, an empire with few to match her in the history of nations. The Incas extended their rule district by district, tribe after tribe, as they pushed through roads, built cities and temples and devised new and hitherto unknown social systems. The empire's hub was the city of Cuzco, which, according to tradition was built by Manco Capac, the first of the glorious dynasty of Incas (emperors). Before setting out to explore the relics, and even before exploring today's Cuzco, one should learn something of the history of that magnificent nation, which has left a deep imprint on the Andean countries, especially Peru. This will give one a better understanding of the historical and cultural phenomenon of the Incas, which even today influences the local social order.

The Incas

Pre-Columbian communities in South America were based on unique social and tribal frameworks, and reached high levels of development. Though the remains of these ancient civilizations are spread from Mexico in the north to Chile in the south, the mightiest and grandest relics are undoubtedly those of the Inca nation. Though it lasted for only a few centuries – and its zenith only a few decades – the Inca nation left its imprint on the history of the entire region, and is among the five or six best-known ancient civilizations in the world. Little remains of the Incas, due to the savage annihilation wreaked upon them by the Spanish conquest. Even so, what has survived suffices to testify to a tremendous and highly impressive empire. When we study ancient documents that have survived from the Inca period, or refer to modern research, we uncover a fascinating picture: a legendary clan which, by force of the personality of its members, founded within less than a century a mighty empire that covered about two million square kilometers – from Colombia in the north to central Chile in the south. Some twenty million people submitted to the tough yoke of their reign. The Incas ran their giant empire with astonishing efficiency, and by disseminating their faith, they created a tremendously powerful national-religious framework. Their swift collapse at the hands of the Spanish *conquistadors* – which required no more than one dramatic half-hour – completes the story of their meteoric rise, brief glory and fall. If we are to fully understand the sights we

PERU

will see in South America in general, and Peru in particular, we must know and understand the story of the Incas, a family which became a tribe which became an empire (until the name "Inca" became the name of the god-king who stood at the head of the Empire).

Historical sources

When we come to survey the annals of Incan civilization, we face a number of difficulties that are unusual in historical research. Unlike other advanced civilizations in the ancient world, including the Mayan and Aztec in Central America, the Incas' highly developed and efficient empire had no writing of any kind. Government decrees and business were handled orally, and proclamations were conveyed by special messengers who made use of the well-developed Imperial road system.

The only form of writing was *quipo* – "rope writing" – which, however, was meant mainly for noting dates and events rather than for day-to-day use. The lack of a writing system, made reliable and accurate documentation of events impossible, which apparently suited the policy of the Incan kings who habitually distorted history in accordance with their needs and understanding. They could, therefore, erase unpleasant events, defeats in battle, rebellions and the like from public memory, while leaving the imprint of military triumphs and spectacular accomplishments. Court poets were set to compose and disseminate ballads and folk songs praising the Incas' achievements, and these were sung at each of the many celebrations and thereby permeated the public consciousness.

The sources at our disposal, therefore, rely mainly on analysis of archeological findings along with letters and reports of Spanish explorers who reached the area with, or slightly after, the first conquerors. Though archeological remains are indeed abundant, we must remember that they are but a tiny remnant, for the Spaniards destroyed most of the Incas, to ensure that the Incan Empire would never again rise. Some of the surviving writings were recorded in Quechua – a local Indian language written down in Latin letters – and deciphered afterwards, while others were written directly in Spanish. Among the most important documents is a letter to the King of Spain consisting of 1200 written pages and four hundred drawings – a veritable treasure trove of information on the various tribes and their customs, ceremonies, agricultural methods, and so on. This document was lost at some point during the intervening centuries, and only in the early years of this century did it turn up again – in the Royal Library in Copenhagen.

PERU

History of the Empire

In light of all this, it is clear why it is so difficult to determine with certainty even such basic facts as the exact origin of the Incas and when they first appeared on the stage of history. Legend has it that Manco Capac, the first Inca and founder of the dynasty, was the son of the Sun, and that he founded the city of Cuzco (Quechua for "navel of the world") in his father's name, and laid the foundations for the Kingdom of the Sun. Another version has it that Manco Capac was born not far from Cuzco, and after a grueling search along with his brothers and sisters for a suitable location for a settlement, he chose Cuzco, where in the year 1200 he and his four sisters set up their household. The family expanded rapidly and became a tribe, which began in turn to establish itself and develop in a manner similar to the scores of other tribes in the region. Small wars were frequent, breaking out because of disputes over money, division of land, etc. Usually these wars ended with the imposition of taxes on the vanquished, and their scope rarely exceeded more than a few kilometers at the utmost. The Incas, too, subscribed to this local approach in their earliest days, and it was only with the ascension of the eighth Inca, Viracocha, that the tribe began to manifest new expansionist trends. The genuine turning point came when Viracocha's son, Pachacuti, assumed power as the ninth Inca in 1438, and in less than a hundred years – until their conquest by the Spaniards – Pachacuti and his son Topa were responsible for one of the most amazing imperialist developments human history has ever witnessed.

Pachacuti rose to power in an era when regional tensions were increasing and fierce armed struggle broke out among the three or four largest and strongest tribes in the area. The conflict reached its peak with an offensive launched by the Chanca tribe against the city of Cuzco, in which the Chancas almost succeeded in defeating and vanquishing the Incas. Pachacuti fought a heroic battle and by his personal valor emerged the victor, thereby safeguarding his regime against any internal subversion.

This victory accelerated the change in Incan attitudes. After a short period of military organization their campaigns of conquest and enslavement began, inspired by economic, religious and imperialist considerations. To this end Pachacuti quickly set up an elite force incorporating warriors from the conquered tribes. At the same time, the Incan policy of population exchange took shape, by which conquered tribes were deported and forced to accept the Sun religion, although they were still allowed to preserve their traditional dress and customs. At the same time Pachacuti began to design administrative and governmental

PERU

procedures, and to erect lavish palaces, temples, and public buildings.

When Pachacuti grew old and tired from his campaigns and conquests, Topa Inca, Pachacuti's declared successor from the age of fifteen, came to power. Topa, known as a mighty warrior and a superb builder, expanded the Empire's borders northward to Ecuador and southward to Bolivia. From there it was only a short jump to central Chile (near today's city of Consititucion), where the conquerors were halted by logistical difficulties caused by the distance from their supply bases and by the local Indians' spirited opposition – a resistance they maintained in later centuries against the Spanish as well.

In Topa's first years of rule Pachacuti remained titular emperor, devoting most of his time and energy to domestic affairs. The father abdicated formally in 1471, however, and Topa was crowned Inca. Lust for power seemed to be the dominant impulse during his reign and Topa devoted most of his reign to training and strengthening his army, and cruelly repressing the frequent rebellions. Throughout this period, the Incan Army, noteworthy for its iron discipline and high mobility, managed to maintain relative quiet in all parts of the mighty empire, enabling the continued development and construction of the imperial capital of Cuzco.

Topa built Sacsahuaman, a gigantic fortress looming over Cuzco and the entire region, along with many other majestic structures. His son Tital, known as Huayana Capac, was crowned Inca after Topa's death in 1493, and had nothing left to do but complete his father's and grandfather's magnificent projects. When Huayana Capac died without leaving a designated successor, the kingdom was split between his two quarelling sons. Huascar, the titular ruler, was routed by his half-brother Atahuallpa in a terrible internecine battle beside the Orobamba River. This clash, one of the bloodiest the empire had ever known, ended in the deaths of thousands of soldiers and a resounding defeat for Huascar. Atahuallpa entered Cuzco and became sole ruler – although not for long.

In May, 1532, shortly after his victory, he learned that Francisco Pizarro had landed on the Peruvian coast with 180 Spanish adventurers. Aware of the ancient tradition, which told of a white god who had departed from their land to cross the sea but promised to return, Atahuallpa assumed that the gods had in fact come back. With great enthusiasm, he set out for Cajamarca to greet them. Following a dialogue of the deaf in a babble of languages, the glorious Incan emperor was taken captive and Pizarro received an immense ransom of gold for his release. The Incan hoard of gold was sent to Spain, where it

PERU

disappeared over the years in mysterious ways. Aware of the danger involved in releasing the Inca, however, Pizarro did not keep his promise to free him, and instead put Atahuallpa on trial on a charge of threatening Spanish security. The charge sheet was then greatly expanded to include various religious and ethical offenses such as adultery, idolatry, incest and so on, some of which were no more than rites of the Incan religion. The Inca was found guilty and sentenced to death at the stake. In his last moments he accepted Christianity, and the manner of his execution was therefore changed – from burning to strangling. At the end of August 1533, the last of the Inca kings was executed and the glorious empire collapsed.

Religion and customs

The key to understanding the spread of the Inca Empire is perhaps best found in their religious outlook. This took shape during the rule of the first emperors in the two centuries preceding the tribe's expansion and constituted the point from which their later conquests and domination of the neighboring lands evolved.

At the head of the pantheon stood the sun god, *Inti*. The ruling Inca was considered his son and earthly representative, and herein lay the source of his power: his absolute, undisputed authority in every field of life, and his comprehensive ownership of all human beings and the fruits of their labor. Inti's wife, the moon goddess *Mama Kilya*, was responsible for nature's cyclical manifestations, the calendar and the setting of dates for ritual events. The rain-god, *Apu Illapu*, and the earth goddess, *Paca Mama*, also had roles to play. The Incas erected lavish temples in their honor, mainly in high, protected places. Here ritual ceremonies and prayers were conducted under the direction of specially trained priests who were "ordained" by the High Priest, the *Villac Umu*, who resided in Cuzco and whose authority was only slightly lower than that of the Inca himself. The priests were assisted by an order known as the Virgins of the Sun, trained from youth for their holy labors. These women made the clothes worn by the Inca and the priests, and were sworn to perpetual virginity – unless the Inca desired them as concubines.

The rites required a great many sacrifices, some of them human. At the beginning of each lunar month a hundred white llamas were sacrificed in Cuzco, while less "prestigious" animals, along with fruit, beverages, various treasures and the like, were offered at less important festivals. Human sacrifice was practiced on very special occasions such as severe drought, famine, military defeat, epidemics and – on the "brighter" side –

PERU

Ode to the Sun - the Inti Raimi celebration in Sacsayhuaman

upon the coronation of a new Inca, when two hundred children were sacrificed to the sun-god!

Divining was highly accepted as well, and the rite for consulting the oracle to ascertain the gods' wishes was an important preliminary to taking any decision. This ceremony involved various sacrifices (including children), mortification of the flesh, and taking of drugs. The Inca himself sometimes took part in the rite, by whose results imperial affairs would be determined.

Similar rituals accompanied the monthly holidays and festivals. The Incan nobility, cognizant of the common man's brutish soul, took pains to be generous in supplying the masses' need for entertainment and release. Festivals were set according to the religious calendar and included song, dance, eating and drinking and, of course, a religious ceremony centering around sacrifices. To this very day, a major festival which has survived from the Inca period – the sun festival, *Inti Raimi* – is celebrated every June.

The Incas believed in the cyclical nature of life, a fact which explains their great sensitivity to matters of burial. Their belief in an afterlife led to the development of a unique method of embalming and interment. The corpse was opened, the inner organs removed and the abdominal cavity was filled with special plants and treated with preservatives. Then the embalmed body was bound with the knees against the chest – the fetal position – to facilitate its rebirth. For graves the Incas built clay structures

PERU

shaped like hornets' nests, built directly against the mountain ridge, so that the departed one would encounter no difficulty in extricating himself from them when the time came.

Society and economy

Day-to-day life in the Empire followed a strict and exacting code. Imperial law defined every individual's place and saw to his or her every need, including education, marriage and occupation. A complex hierarchy of greater and lesser officials guaranteed citizens' needs and rights, even as it ensured most strictly that they fulfilled their obligations to the state. Welfare institutions safeguarded the population at times of crisis, giving rise to an economic and social tranquility that increased the subjects' willingness to bear the burden and to accept the sovereignty of the conquering Inca. The emperor, for his part, understood the importance of this calm for the peace of the Empire, and always made sure to foster his subjects' rights and respond to their needs, both material and emotional. Just as the ancient Roman emperors provided "bread and circuses," the Inca made sure to provide these to his subjects – generously.

When a new area was conquered, representatives of the Inca would take a general census and calculate the unit of land essential for existence. Afterwards, the population of the region was divided into groups, and a hierarchy of officials appointed to oversee them. The land was demarcated clearly and each family received an allocation according to its size. Groups of families were organized into a commune in the manner of a Russian *kolkhoz*. The allotment of cultivated land was three times larger than that necessary for subsistence, with one third of the crop set aside for the Sun, one third for the Inca (who built up a reserve to be redistributed to the people during drought years) and one third for the family's sustenance. The land was redivided each year according to changes in family size. The Inca's deputies drew up programs for building terraces, irrigation systems, and public buildings, and the local population was required to carry these out. Raw materials and fertilizer were a government monopoly and distributed among the populace on a fair and equal basis.

The mode of living was primitive and rather modest. Houses for the "plebeians" were low, windowless, square and simple one-room affairs made of clay and thatched with straw. The occupants slept on the ground. Interior walls were smooth and unadorned, except for niches where articles and clothing were kept.

The external appearance of the Incas was ascetic: most were rather short (about 1.5 meters), strong and dark-skinned. Their

PERU

clothing was of uniform style and fashioned of local materials – cotton in the coastal region and wool in the mountains. Both cotton and wool were government monopolies and were apportioned to citizens according to need. Workmen wore only breechcloths, while women wore cloth dresses that reached their ankles. Higher-class men wore shirts and pants, with leather pouches at their waists in which coca leaves and personal items were kept. Their feet were protected with sandals of wood or of llama skin. Men's hair was cut short, whereas women let theirs grow and gathered it together from behind.

Huge earrings (up to 5 cm in diameter) made of various materials, according to social status, were the usual articles of jewelry. The nobility habitually sported earrings of gold or silver, while simple folk had to settle for earrings of base metals or wood.

The Incas contented themselves with two meals per day – morning and evening. The menu was essentially vegetarian. Animals were hunted and meat served only on rare occasions. On a day-to-day basis the Incas enjoyed the abundant variety of local vegetables, of which some were totally unknown in Europe until the advent of the Spaniards (the most famous of these was the popular potato, first brought to Ireland from Peru in the eighteenth century and destined to become one of the most common of foodstuffs). Home utensils for cooking and eating were made of pottery or (in the case of the nobility) of gold. Cooking was done on a low flame ignited by rubbing sticks together.

The well-developed Incan road system opened the way to commerce between the Empire's various sections, enabling the people to broaden their horizons and, for the first time, to consume goods which were not of local manufacture.

The llama served to transport food and cargo. All llamas were government property. Each llama carried a fifty-kilogram load 20 kilometers per day. Thus Inca officials were able to regulate the movement of goods and supply necessary commodities to every district.

Architectural projects

Of the various remains of the Incas, their tremendous building endeavors are undoubtedly the most enduring. We can still marvel at Incan cities, temples, baths, palaces, terraces, irrigation canals, bridges and roads, all projects of stunning size, precision, and exceptional skill.

The Incas began building shortly after they appeared as a

PERU

nation, but it was the great Pachacuti who gave the construction "industry" real momentum and turned it from a periodic local occurrence into an enduring historical phenomenon. The glory and focus of Incan architecture was the city of Cuzco and its environs, which merited special attention as the center of the Empire. Cuzco was divided into twelve neighborhoods arranged around a central plaza, Huayqapata, where the most important temples stood. The Sun-Temple – Coricancha – located where the present-day Iglesia Santo Domingo stands, was one of the pinnacles of their architectural creativity and, like the Emperor's palace and the Temple of the Sun Virgins, was a source of pride for the entire nation. These structures were built of exceedingly well-fitted slabs of hewn stone which arouse amazement even in our time. Sanctuaries were built of many-faceted stones, so carefully chiseled that no mortar was required to secure them and no plants have succeeded in penetrating and taking root in the cracks between them, a phenomenon so common in other archeological sites. All the palaces and temples were adorned with gold fashioned into various forms – wall covering, statues, fountains, religious symbols and the like. (All these, of course, were plundered by the Spanish *conquistadors*.) The small remnant that has survived is prominently displayed in museums – chiefly the **Museo de Oro** in Lima and the archeolological museum in Cuzco.

The Imperial rulers paid great attention to their building projects, and superb architects, engineers and skilled craftsmen – high ranking members of the Incan nobility – were engaged for them. They had access to financial resources and unlimited manpower, which they put to use in chiseling and transporting stone by the most primitive of means. Most tools were made of stone, and a few were of bronze. A level and primitive measuring tool served to determine the exact size and location of angles, and the laborers had to be precise in their work and avoid even the slightest error. Most building material was quarried in the Cuzco area and transported many kilometers to its final destination. The Sasachuaman fortress – one of the most tremendous buildings in the entire world – is made of locally quarried limestone, and the stones of its walls – of which the largest weighs about one hundred tons (!) – were dragged to the site by primitive means. Tens of thousands of people took part in the task of constructing the fortress, using wooden rollers and ropes to haul the stones on ramps of sand to their final destination.

Inca engineering, however, was not confined to palaces and temples. Understanding the importance of controlling recently conquered areas and the essential need for a transportation network reaching all corners of the Empire, the Incas created an

PERU

impressive system of paved roads which extended for thousands of kilometers from Colombia to Argentina and Chile. Since there were no wheeled vehicles there was also no need for wide highways, so the Incas dug out narrow roadways between mountains and valleys along routes which frequently reached elevations of five thousand meters and more. These roads served for transmitting orders and transporting supplies to occupation forces at the front and for conveying government proclamations by means of the superb, specially trained courier corps. Roadside "inns" were set up to tend to the couriers' needs. The highway system was based on a coastal artery and an additional main route atop the mountain ridge, as well as hundreds of side roads between the two, by which every point of settlement, no matter how small, was linked with the capital of Cuzco. Many bridges were constructed over rivers and although these sometimes reached lengths of dozens of meters, most of them were rather weak, since they were meant to bear the weight of couriers and animals only.

To this very day, in the Cuzco area, one can see strips of mountainside carefully marked out by straight terraces. These terraces too, are the handiwork of the Incan builders, and were meant both to increase the amount of arable land and to prevent erosion. Pisac, Ollantaytambo, Machu-Picchu and many other regions were similarly developed. The impressive irrigation systems, canals and reservoirs supported a complex and extensive economic and agricultural infrastructure, which, combined with superb military capability and the strong, all-encompassing state religion, were of utmost importance in upholding and maintaining the mighty Empire.

Cuzco – Capital of the Inca Empire

Cuzco is one of those cities where as you enter, you seem to feel the enormous impact of history on the place. A major reason for this, apart from its 150,000 strong Indian population, is Cuzco's unique architecture – a combination of ancient Incan style and grand Spanish colonial construction, a style in which entire sections of the city are built.

Whether you come by bus or by train from Puno to the station at the edge of town, or by plane to the International Airport fifteen minutes from the city, you quickly sense that Cuzco is different from other cities in Peru, that it is graced with a special character, a unique temperament and an atmosphere significantly different from Peru's other cities.

*P*ERU

This is an enchanting and unique city, where nothing seems to have changed in the course of the centuries. Wherever you go, everything is saturated in the grandeur of those days, each spot with its own hidden events and stories. Though remnants of bygone worlds are preserved within and around many cities, there is something special about Cuzco. This is largely due to its citizens' traditional attire, archaic customs and unusual ways, which blend in wonderful harmony with the ruined temples and palaces that confront you on every street corner. The magnificence of Cuzco and its environs cannot leave one unmoved. Even a heart of stone, is softened by the exquisite beauty of man's creation here.

Cuzco lies 3400 m above sea level, but the thin air does not seem to affect its thieves. They wait in ambush at the train station, on the streets and in the markets, waiting for the moment your attention flags, to whip away your camera, money, watch, or jewelry. Moreover, the evil touch of Cuzco's infamous thieves has won the concurrence, at least of the tacit sort, of the local police. Remember that everything said of Peru (see "Personal Security") goes double and treble for Cuzco. Unofficial statistics relate that about 80% of Cuzco's tourists fall victim to theft or attempted theft. The thieves' organized activity has long since exceeded reasonable limits, but the authorities' unperturbed negligence provides them a comfortable and secure environment. Here you are on your own – so be warned! Protect your gear fanatically, for it will disappear within seconds should you fail! Leave your manners at home: when someone tries to block your path as if by accident (while his or her partner reaches for your purse with a sharp knife) shove with all your might and keep going. There is, unfortunately, no other way.

The danger of theft, however, cannot diminish Cuzco's special grandeur. Thieves aside, most Cuzcans treat visitors to their town with respect and affection. The treasures of the city far outweigh its hazards and no tourist visiting Peru should skip Cuzco.

Though your visit to Cuzco and the "classic" sights in its vicinity should take several days, a somewhat more thorough exploration, with visits to the remote and lesser-known sites, requires a week and one could spend a full month here with no effort at all. First of all we will stroll along the city's streets and after getting to know Cuzco's treasures, head out to the immediate vicinity – along the Urubamba Valley as far as Machu-Picchu. Later more fascinating routes will be mentioned for which you will have to organize yourself differently as most of these involve physical effort, suitable equipment, and lots of time.

*P*ERU

How to get there

Whenever you take a taxi, whether from the airport or from the train station, remember to negotiate the fare in advance. When you get out, take your gear out first, for drivers have been known to take off with passengers' luggage after they have alighted.

By air: Cuzco's modern airport is an important aviation hub, with incoming flights from all parts of Peru and from La Paz, the capital of Bolivia. Aero Peru and Faucett fly several times daily between Cuzco and Lima, Arequipa, Ayachucho, Iquitos and the jungle city of Puerto Maldonado. If you are flying to Cuzco from northern Peru, choose a seat on the left side of the plane so you can enjoy the view. Planes are very full on the Lima and Puerto Maldonado routes so be sure to book well in advance. It won't guarantee anything, but it will back up your arguments at the airport when they give you the happy tidings that the plane is full and your place has been given to someone else. Confirm your reservations a day in advance and get to the airport early. Watch out for your luggage, for Peruvians have a strange tendency to "lose" it or, at best, to send it to another destination! Take everything you can aboard the plane and refrain from sending luggage separately. Flights to and from Puerto Maldonado are frequently cancelled due to bad weather and rain which prevent landing, with the result that the next day flights are even more crowded than usual.

By bus: Buses to all parts of Peru set out very frequently from Cuzco. The three-day trip to Lima follows three major routes:

Via the mountains: first to Abancay (200 km, 8 hours), then to Ayacucho (another 12 hours) and Huancayo (another 12) and finally to Lima. On this route it is recommended to proceed from Huancayo by train (see "Huancayo").

Via the coast: first to Abancay and on from there through fantastic scenery, though on a difficult road, to Nazca on the coast and from there to Lima. It is about thirty hours to Nazca. Most bus companies go to Lima along this route, and the most recommended of these is Ormeno. Its offices in Cuzco are on Plaza de Armas.

Via Arequipa: travel by either bus or train from Cuzco to Arequipa and from there continue by bus. There are several buses per day to Juliaca, Puno, Arequipa and La Paz, traveling a difficult and dusty dirt road alongside the railroad tracks. We highly recommend covering **at least** the Cuzco-Puno stretch by train (eleven hours) and continuing from Puno to La Paz or Arequipa (see "Puno"). The train ride is lovely, following the river through enchanting and varied scenery. We strongly recommend that you travel first-class, where the thieves are less

PERU

menacing (see "Puno"). While first-class tickets can be purchased the day before, second-class tickets can be bought only on the morning of departure (from 6:30am). Moreover, second class is crowded with peddlers and passengers so burdened with luggage that it seems as if everyone in southern Peru has chosen to move on the very day you picked for your journey.

When to come

The most comfortable time to visit the Cuzco area is during the dry season, from April to July – the weather is nice with clear skies and an average temperature of 10 degrees Centigrade (50 degrees Fahrenheit) – but significantly cooler in the shade. Though temperatures are a little higher between December and March, the frequent rains make tourists' lives difficult. You'll need warm clothing the year round and raincoats during the rainy season.

On June 24 Cuzco celebrates *Inti Raimi* – the Incan Sun Festival, the largest festival of its kind in Peru and second in South America only to the famous carnival in Rio de Janeiro. Tens of thousands come to Cuzco to witness the sacrificial offering to the Sun God, which takes place exactly as it did in Incan times. The impressive ceremony is performed before crowds in the Sacsahuaman fortress overlooking the city and you must get there early to secure a comfortable place to sit (visitors to Cuzco during this period should make hotel reservations). The festivities begin with a parade through the city streets of representatives of all strata of society, as well as bands and dance troupes, with the revelry continuing in the fortress the next day. *Inti Raimi* is one of the most interesting folk festivals in South America and I strongly urge you to plan your visit to Cuzco to coincide with it.

Food and lodging

Cuzco is so popular that its dozens of hotels do not suffice and accommodation is usually hard to find without advance booking. The best hotel in town is the *Libertador*, at San Agustin 400 (Tel.3072), several minutes on foot from the Plaza de Armas and housed in a handsome sixteenth-century colonial building known as Casa de los Cuatro Bustos.

Next on the list is the *Hotel El Dorado*, El Sol 341 (Tel. 2130), and the venerable and highly recommended *Hotel Cuzco*, on Calle Heladeros, right off Plaza de Armas. *Hostal Loreto*, Loreto 115 (Tel. 2689), is undoubtedly one of the city's most unique and is recommended. It is located on an alley branching southward from Plaza de Armas in a building whose outer walls are the remains of an Incan temple! The rooms and the entrance patio

PERU

are stunningly beautiful, despite or perhaps because of their simplicity. Prices are in the intermediate range. More modest hotels also abound in the Plaza de Armas area and along nearby streets. Cheap and recommended places to sleep include the *Bambu*, on a tiny alley right alongside the train station – it is clean and safe, with a friendly owner, and it is a possibile to take one room for a number of people. The *Gran Hostal Machu-Picchu*, Quera 274, is comfortable, clean, safe and spacious. There's also *Las Casas* at Plateros 368, above Plaza de Armas, and the *Santo Domingo Church Hostel*, where you can roll out a sleeping bag at little cost. Though it is clean and safe, the gates are shut at 10pm. The *Hostal Familiar* on Calle Saphi (Tel. 2877) is clean and honest.

As in many other spheres, Cuzco's culinary offerings are a cut above the South American scene, particularly that of the Andean countries. The great number of *gringos* who visit the town has given rise to dozens of eateries of various types, flavors and price levels. A number of foods are typical of the Cuzco region. The strangest of these, at least to my taste, is stuffed guinea-pig, served whole, including head and tail. It reminds one of barbecued rat (the Spanish term is *cuy*). For reasons that remain quite incomprehensible to me, this abomination is considered to be the piece-de-resistance at Incan feasts, though for the life of me I can't understand how five centuries of western civilization have failed to shake the locals' taste for it. Recommended only for those with strong stomachs, and I'm not sure about them, either.

Crisp tidbits of pork, deep-fried in oil and well-seasoned, are called *chicharron de chancho*, and the same dish, made from chicken, is called *chicharron de gallina*. There's a local corn stew called *locro*, often served as a first course in creole restaurants (see "Food and drink").

Several cafes around Plaza de Armas serve breakfast, cake, ice cream and the like. The most highly recommended are *El Ayllu* on the northern corner of the square (left of the cathedral), *Cafe de Paris* (across the plaza), and *Piccolo*. El Ayllu is famous for its apple cake and the classical music played for customers' enjoyment. All three cafes excel in superb cakes, sandwiches and ice cream. They serve as meeting places for young people from all over the world and the atmosphere is pleasant. Another place to enjoy drinks and light food is *Vic's American Bar*, on Calle Plateros just off Plaza de Armas, where the *gringos* gather at day's end for an evening of song and drink.

Among Cuzco's dozens of restaurants, which serve Italian, Chinese, Peruvian and other varieties of food, my special favorites are those on "Gringos Street", Calle Procuradores, a

PERU

narrow pedestrian mall which branches off from the middle of Plaza de Armas' northern side (across from the Tourist Bureau). Here you'll find small, intermediate-priced restaurants one after another, each with its own special flavor – an excellent pizzeria, a steakhouse, a vegetarian restaurant and plain diners. Walk down the mall and within one hundred meters, you are bound to find at least one restaurant that attracts your interest.

More elegant restaurants are located in the better hotels and on Plaza de Armas itself. There are several restaurants behind the square, on Plaza Recogijo, among them *La Mamma Pizzeria*. Furthermore, you can eat cheaply and to satiation in Cuzco, as in any city, in and around the marketplaces.

Transportation

Most of Cuzco's interesting sites are within walking distance of one another and can be reached without difficulty. For the more remote attractions, including those in the immediate surroundings of the city, you can hire a **taxi** on an hourly basis. Remember to fix a price with the driver before you set out! There's also **public transportation** (buses, *colectivos*, and trucks) every few minutes to the villages, town, and archeological sites in the vicinity, so getting there and back presents no difficulty. Organizing a small group can lower the expense of taking a taxi to the more remote destinations, facilitating the return trip as well.

Another possibility, **car rental**, is handled either through hotels or through Avis (Avenida Sol), National, or the local Cuzco Rent-A-Car.

A **train** to Machu-Picchu leaves Cuzco each morning (see below).

Tourist services

The main Tourist Bureau on Plaza de Armas, left of the La Compania Church, will give you maps of the city and provide information about transportation to and visiting hours at the various attractions. There is also a branch office at the airport. The long lines of tourists waiting to be served here make it hard to obtain detailed, patiently given advice. To visit the museums and surrounding archeological sites you must buy a combined eleven-entry ticket for $10 ($5 for students; separate tickets for individual sites are not available). Buying it ahead of time at the Tourist Bureau will save you much time and trouble later. A Student Card will prove very useful in Cuzco, procuring significant reductions on admission fees, transportation and so on.

A special Tourist Police has been established to assist foreigners who have run into trouble (theft, accidents, etc.). Its office is

PERU

behind Plaza de Armas on the other side of the Hotel Cuzco (Calle Espinar). Its members wear olive-green uniforms with white arm-bands bearing the legend *Guardia Civil Turismo*. Despite their good intentions, however, their powers are limited. If you have a truly serious problem go the investigation police, P.I.P. (offices far from downtown).

The Auto Club office on Calle San Andres will equip you with maps. Faucett and Aero Peru have offices in town for buying tickets and confirming reservations. Faucett is on Avenida El Sol, and Aero Peru is on the corner of Quera and Matara (Tel. 3088 and 5007).

Many travel agencies organize tours and excursions in Cuzco and the surroundings. These include transportation and guides, as well as food and lodging on longer tours. Adventure outings that include river boating or hikes through the jungles to the east are organized by a number of companies, most with offices on "Gringos Street." Check the quality of the equipment, the tour route, guide and prices very carefully. Mayoc organizes such trips and does it well. Its head guide, Chando, speaks English. For solid and excellent tours, Lima Tours (Ave. Sol 567) is recommended.

Tourist sites

Any get-acquainted tour of Cuzco must begin at **Plaza de Armas**: all urban affairs and events take place in and around it, and anything you do in Cuzco will most likely either begin or end there. Most municipal institutions, important stores, offices, and the like are concentrated around the square and along the main street, Avenida Sol, which leads to the train station. The lovely plaza, packed with children and peddlers, has been Cuzco's center since time immemmorial. In the Inca period it was called Huacaypata, and some of the most important buildings and palaces were arrayed around it. Religious ceremonies took place in its center, and from it the emperors issued orders to their subjects. In the plaza's southeastern corner, occupied by the great cathedral, the palace of Viracucha once soared, and the Snake Palace, once occupied the spot where La Compania Church stands today (to the right of the Tourist Bureau). Nothing much remained, however, after the Spanish overwhelmed the Incas and divided up the loot. The Incas attempted to revolt against the conquerors, but were defeated. Nature and time also took their toll, and the ancient Inca city was razed nearly to the ground. The Spanish began rebuilding Cuzco in the latter half of the sixteenth century, and today it offers a rare blend of Spanish Colonial architecture and stonework of rare quality – the finest of the Incan heritage. Many buildings were built of stones salvaged from Inca ruins in Cuzco and its surroundings; the

*P*ERU

CUZCO

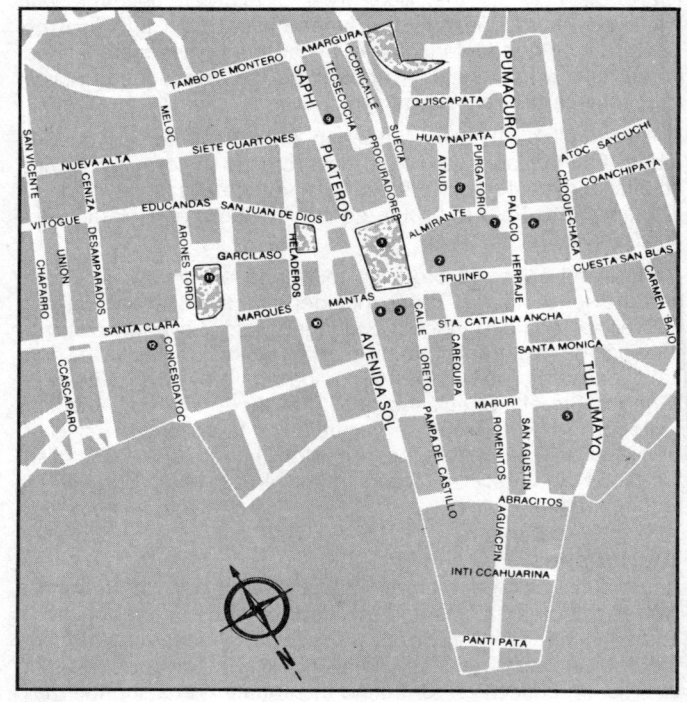

Index

1) Plaza de Armas
2) Cathedral
3) Tourist Bureau
4) Church of La Compania
5) Church of Santo Domingo
6) Art Museum
7) Plaza de las Nazarenas
8) Historical Museum
9) Archeological Museum
10) La Merced Church
11) Plaza San Francisco
12) San Pedro Church

observer can clearly discern where they join up with more "modern" stones.

The **cathedral** on Plaza de Armas, one of Cuzco's largest and most impressive edifices, is a living example of this eclectic style. Built on the ruins of the Inca's palace, the viewer can easily identify the ancient foundation, while the spires are of more modern design and construction. It took almost a hundred years, until the mid-seventeenth century, to complete the maginificent building. Today it serves as Cuzco's main church, and is home to an impressive collection of statues, paintings, and historic artifacts of the city in its early days. From atop the

PERU

left tower, the Maria Angola bell, South America's largest, sounds with a pleasant force heard many kilometers from the city. The bell, which weighs a full ton, was cast in 1659 from gold, silver and bronze.

To the cathedral's right is the **El Triunfo Church** the oldest in town. It was built on the site where the Spanish were trapped by Incan rebels in 1536 and were saved only by virtue of a miracle wrought on their be half by Virgin Mary.To the left of the cathedral there is another church, that of **Jesus Maria**.

In the plaza's southeastern corner, to the cathedral's right, the **Tourist Bureau** occupies the spot where the "House of the Chosen Women" once stood, home of those women who faithfully supplied the needs of the ruling Inca and the nobility (see "The Incas"). To its right is the prominent Jesuit **Church of La Compania**, considered Cuzco's most beautiful. About a hundred years under construction, it was completed only at the end of the seventeenth century after disputes and quarrels which echoed as far as the Vatican in Rome. The church's Jesuit builders erected it on the remains of the Snake Palace, Amarucancha, home of Inca Huina-Capac, with the aim of erecting a temple that would overshadow the neighboring cathedral in grandeur. Its two soaring towers, the rich Baroque-style interior balconies, gilded altars, and collection of paintings and other works of art, indeed constitute an impressive spectacle.

From here we can set out on a walk through the most "Incan" parts of Cuzco, to get an impression of the relics of the past and to see how they are integrated into the buildings of the present. We will start with the southern and eastern parts of town.

Along the Inca ruins

Turn down **Calle Loreto** alongside the church and walk along the longest of the surviving Inca walls. To the left is the wall of the Chosen Women's House, and to the right – that of the Snake Palace. Shortly we will pass the lovely **Church of Santa Catalina**, built in the early seventeenth century, with a small museum inside. Continuing down Loreto and Pampa del Castillo, we reach the site of the largest and grandest of the Incan temples – the Sun and Gold Temple, **Coricancha**.

Today we find the **Santo Domingo Church** on the site. The church was built directly atop the ruins of the famous temple, and only in recent decades have archeological excavations begun to expose a small portion of what is still considered to be the most precise, impressive and important of the Inca buildings. Coricancha had five sections, dedicated respectively

PERU

to the sun, moon, lightning, thunder and rainbow (the rainbow's colors were also those of the Incas). It was here that the empire's gold reserve was kept, sacrifices were offered, astronomical observations were conducted and the important religious rites carried out. Thousands of people – all noblemen especially trained for their roles, who had consecrated their lives to the holy service – performed ritual tasks in the temple. The first Spaniards to reach Cuzco spread many legends about the temple; indeed, they found quantities of gold and silver beyond imagination: statues and fountains, altars and cult objects all cast in gold, the work of unparalleled masters of the goldsmith's art.

The few remnants not plundered by the Spanish disappeared over the years and today we can only contemplate in sorrow the remains of a world that vanished almost overnight. In various corners of the church we can discern remains of walls, bath chambers, gardens – and traces of the temple itself, at the very entrance to the courtyard of the church. The entire temple complex was designed and constructed with devotion, the stones cut with an exemplary precision that arouses our amazement and admiration again and again.

Along Calle Aquacpina, which adjoins the church, we see more remains of walls, among them the external walls of the Sun Temple. Now, however, we turn left and head back to the center along Calle Rameritos. We pass the Hotel Libertador, housed in a magnificent sixteenth-century building – **Casa de los Cuatro Bustos** – and continue on **Calle San Agustin**, where the remains of Incan walls can easily be identified. A small detour to the left, to Calle Catalina, will allow us to observe the beautiful balconies of the home of Martin Concha, the last of Cuzco's Spanish governors. This house, built atop the ruins of another Inca palace, serves today as a police station.

Proceeding another block, we see on our right the **Art Museum**, which houses a collection of seventeenth-century furniture and paintings. The building has undergone many metamorphoses, first serving as the palace of Inca-Roca (the sixth emperor) then as home of the Marquis de Buena Vista, and later as the Archbishop's residence. The museum building has an impressive facade, interior decor, carefully-crafted doors and balconies, and a handsome central patio and fountain. Visiting hours: 9:30am-12:30pm and 3-6pm.

Calle Hatunrumiyoc leads north from the museum, and in its center we find one of the most famous Inca remains – the "**Dodecagon**" (a twelve-sided stone). Here's an instructive example of the Incan stonemason's rare ability to work hard stone as if it were soft clay, and to chisel precise angles that fit exactly into the surrounding stones – with no need for mortar to hold them together, and without even the narrowest chink in between!

Continuing up the street, we come to the **San Blas church**, which contains a wooden pulpit carved from the trunk of a single tree. This exquisite piece is among the largest of its type in the entire world. Many artists and a number of *artesania* dealers have set up shop around the church.

We return now to Plaza de Armas, but not before passing **Plaza de Las Nazarenas**. On the plaza's northeastern side are two impressive buildings. On the left is the **Nazarene Monastery**, built on the ruins of an Inca snake palace (one of its walls bears a relief of seven terrifying snakes), while on the right is **San Antonio Abad**, once a center of religious education, currently being renovated for its transformation into a grand hotel. In the middle is **Calle Siete Culebras** – "Alley of the Seven Snakes."

From here we return downhill to Plaza de Armas via Calle Tucuman, where we find **Casa del Admirante**, (the Admiral's House), today the **Regional Historical Museum**, where Incan artifacts and Colonial furniture and paintings are displayed (visiting hours: 9am-12 noon and 3-6pm). The building itself, damaged in an earthquake in 1950, has only recently been restored.

The Archeological Museum

To complete the picture a visit to Cuzco's **Archeological Museum**, located on Calle Tigre at the corner of Calle Saphi is highly recommended (open weekdays 8am-12:30pm and 1-6pm). This important museum houses an excellent collection of pre-Columbian relics – pottery, jewelry, tools, household implements, woven fabrics and more. A special room houses gold Incan figurines. Be sure to see them.

The **Santa Teresa Church** is across from the museum.

Calle Santa Clara and the market

Once having formed an idea of Cuzco's glorious past, especially of the Incas' impressive achievements, we need only spend a little time on the southwest side of town, an area which bustles with a different kind of activity: shops, stalls and a market. Set out from the corner adjacent to the La Compania church on Plaza de Armas to Calle Mantas, and only one block further we come upon the **Church of La Merced**, open mornings until 10 and again in the afternoon. Here we find a collection of ritual objects, a small museum and the tomb of Diego de Almegro, discoverer of Chile.

PERU

About a block farther down the street we pass the home of the Marquis de Valleumbroso, a beautiful Colonial building recently restored after having been burned in the riots of the early 1970s. To our right is **Plaza San Francisco**, with a magnificent church of the same name, which houses a giant painting of the Franciscans. As we continue, we come to the **Church of Santa Clara** (the street changes its name after Plaza San Francisco to Calle Santa Clara) and then the **Church of San Pedro**, built in 1688. Left of the church is the station from which trains set out for Machu-Picchu, with the municipal market across the way. In fact, the entire area is one great market stretching from here southward and along the railroad track, but a stroll through this area is enough to give you the idea. The market, devoted mainly to foodstuffs and footwear, is meant for the needs of the local population. A special paragraph below is devoted to purchases that interest us tourists.

A final word: remember again, especially here in the marketplace, that Cuzco takes its revenge for the depredations of the Spanish, the first foreign "tourists": no amount of defending yourself against thieves is excessive.

Entertainment

Good folk music and a rich program consisting entirely of local routines are offered every evening at *Qhatuchay*, a simple, popular folklore club on the second floor of the building with the arches along the western side of Plaza de Armas. Come early – for the Club is crowded – and have a good time until the wee hours. Recommended. Another local *pena* (folklore club), *Pena Folklorica*, at Montero 114, is more conservative. Several discotheques are active until after midnight. Among them we can recommend *Abraxas*, above "Gringos Street," and *El Muki*, on Calle Santa Catalina not far from the Church of El Triunfo. Both offer disco music and drinks (see "Food and lodging," too).

Shopping

The San Pedro market offers a rather restricted variety of local handicrafts at prices no lower than those in the stores. It is therefore best to buy your souvenirs in the shops around Plaza de Armas (the government-owned Eppa store at the corner of the square is one example) or elsewhere in town. In the San Blas Church area there are many workshops where local craftsmen create pottery, jewelry, wood carvings and other hand-wrought items. It is an interesting and pleasant quarter through which to meander and while strolling along you can visit a number of workshops and buy whatever strikes your fancy. A small, orderly market arranged around a large courtyard – Galerias Turisticas – has opened in recent years on Avenida del Sol, several

PERU

minutes' walk from Plaza de Armas. Its shops offer a wide selection of *artesania* from Cuzco and surroundings. A visit is highly recommended. Bazaars are held in the Church of La Compania from time to time, where lovely handicrafts are offered for sale. These fairs are held mainly on holiday and special occasions and there is an entrance fee – but it is worthwhile.

Wonderful markets take place on Sunday mornings in the villages of Chinchero and Pisac (see below). The two markets, particularly the latter, have earned a wide reputation which, of course, has caused prices to jump, though we must note that these very picturesque markets offer plenty of attractive buys. A visit to at least one of them is highly recommended.

It is important to note that most of the goods sold in Cuzco and the area – jewelry, woodcrafts, woven fabrics, pottery, etc. – are of local and recent manufacture. Peddlers may attempt to "prove" the antiquity of their wares, displaying moldy, torn, mud-stained or otherwise marred merchandise – just as if it has been pried right out of the hands of excited archeologists and offered straight to you at bargain prices. Don't fall for it. It has been several decades since antiquities have been found anywhere but in museums, and those could not be bought for their weight in gold. But let it be – even day-old souvenirs have their value.

Woolen goods – especially sweaters, ponchos, wall hangings and the like – are made of llama or alpaca wool, and are brought to Cuzco from Juliaca, the regional weaving center which has its own interesting market. If that is where you are headed, delay your buying because there you will find a larger selection at lower prices.

A final word: peddlers will annoy you unceasingly as you sit in Plaza de Armas or roam the city. The ones who stay put on the ground surrounding the plaza are not so bothersome, but the others, particularly the female ones, who are always on the move with their goods, will not leave you alone for a minute. Furthermore, the moment you try to give your aching legs a respite on one of the benches in the square, the cry "*Compra me!*" ("Buy from me!") will ring out time and again. Eventually it will become one long humming nuisance, and after an hour in Plaza de Armas, you will need a month to get it out of your head...

Books and periodicals in English

A number of shops sell English-language material on Peruvian and general topics. The largest of these – on Plaza de Armas, at the corner of "Gringos Street" – offers a wide though expensive selection. Try the right-hand side of Calle Plateros, at

*P*ERU

the very exit from the plaza. Here there is a small shop with books and maps at lower prices. Farther along the same street is Vic's American Bar, which has used books in foreign languages.

Postal and telephone services
The central post office, down Avenida Sol, not far from the train station, accepts letters and small parcels (open 8am-8pm). A little farther down the avenue on the left is an Entel office for international phone calls. The line is long and so is the wait. Calls are made from little booths in a corner of the hall. Bring a passport, which you have to deposit when you place your call.

Currency exchange
Though several moneychangers can be found in Plaza San Martin, it is best to convert money at Banco de la Nacion or Banco de Los Andes, both on Avenida Sol.

Camping and photographic supplies
A number of Cuzco travel and tour agencies have camping equipment to rent out to tourists preparing for hikes. Be sure to obtain a good tent, warm sleeping bag, comfortable backpack, canteen, cooking stove and comfortable walking shoes. Try the agencies on "Gringos Street" – where renting equipment is usually accepted practice.

You can buy film at the photography shops on Avenida Sol and Plaza de Armas. Special and fast films are hard to find.

Short excursions in the Cuzco Area

The Cuzco area abounds with fascinating places to visit: naturally enough, most are related to the Incas and the remains they left behind (or, to be more precise, the remains that survived the devastation and destruction wreaked by the Spanish conquistadores).

I have chosen to survey four routes here, some including a number of sites that must not be missed. These are the classic sites, which clearly and distinctly reflect the Incas and their religion, culture and construction. (Before reading the sections that follow and those pertaining to the walks through Cuzco, see the chapter on the Incas.) These four routes are meant for everyone – young, energetic backpackers, families, or retired couples on their second honeymoon. They are relatively easy routes, with convenient transportation. Most Cuzco tourist agencies provide guided tours of these sites, with most of them

PERU

well organized. It is important to remember that you buy a combined ticket to enter the sites (see "Tourist Services"). Individual tickets are not available at most of the attractions, and without the combined ticket a visitor can expect to be sorry and frustrated – which would be a pity.

The Road to Pisac

A number of the most beautiful of the Inca ruins are concentrated along the highway leading north from Cuzco to the town of Pisac, most a short walking distance from the road. To visit them, you need about a half-day walking tour, or a taxi. A third method, the best in my opinion, is to take the bus to Pisac (see below), getting off at Kilometer 9 beside the Inca baths at Tambomachay, and returning downhill to Cuzco by foot. For the sake of geographic continuity, we shall survey the sites from Cuzco outwards, and if you have opted for the bus-up/walk-down method, read the following pages in reverse order.

Sacsayhuaman

About a thirty-minute walk from Cuzco, one of the largest buildings of the ancient world looms over the town – the Sacsayhuaman ("Colored Falcon") fortress, on which twenty thousand construction workers labored for more than two generations.

The enormous stones we see today, some weighing three hundred tons or more, are only a humble remnant of what was a colossal fortress that stared down on the magnificent Inca capital. Thousands of people lived between its walls. The reasons for the construction of Sacsayhuaman have never been totally clear. Conventional wisdom holds that its planning and construction began in the mid-fifteenth century and ended only several decades before the Spanish conquest. Pizarro and his men left the fortress alone during their first years in Cuzco, and only after Manco-Inca's rebellion did they storm it, take it in a desperate bloody battle, and begin the massive task of razing it. The story of the conquest is the background for many legends, and it appears that the campaign was extensive, claiming countless victims on both sides. Once Manco-Inca was defeated and the legendary fortress had fallen into Spanish hands, it took the *conquistadores* only a few months to level it, re-using its stones for their strongholds and buildings in Cuzco, situated at the base of the mountain. Today we can only walk along the massive outer wall and contemplate the stones, chiseled with astonishing precision, which the Spaniards could not budge. Then we can gaze down at the beautiful view and

*P*ERU

INCA SITES

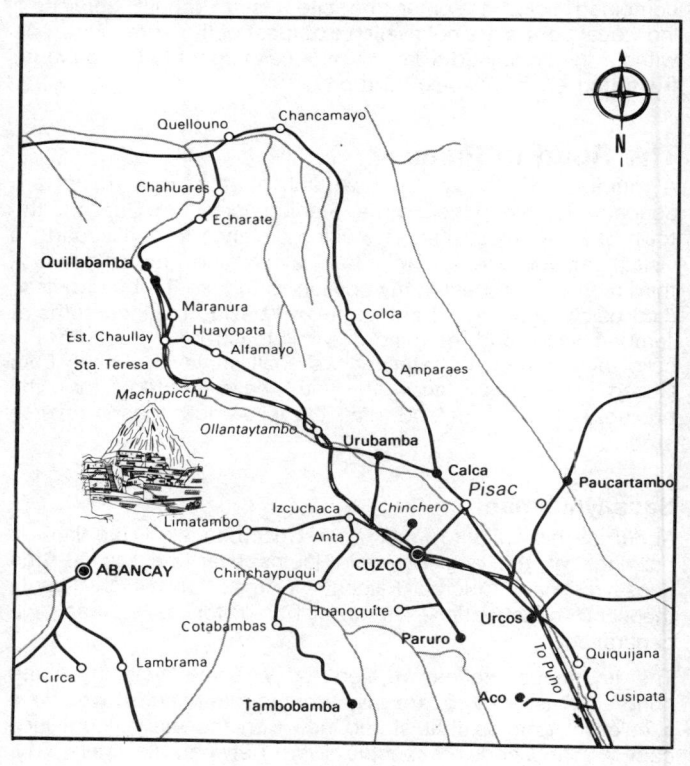

at Cuzco, spread out below in the valley, and remember the stormy glories of bygone days.

It is here, at this impressive site, that the Inca sun festival Inti-Raimi is celebrated every year on June 24 (see 'When to come"). Those who come for the festivities will certainly sense the excitement of those remote Inca days very well.

Quenco – the "Zig-Zags"

Two kilometers up the road (heading out of town) on the right is an Inca temple hewn out of local stone which, according to tradition, served as a ritual center and burial site. The entire structure is cut from the limestone, with an altar, narrow tunnels and a large amphitheater, in whose walls nineteen carved benches face a six-meter high phallic monolith in the center.

PERU

Trenches whose purpose is unknown wind in zig-zag fashion (hence its name) atop the complex. Several accounts relate that they were meant for *chicha* (local beer) to flow through, while others, more macabre, tell that they were meant as conduits for the blood of the sacrifices that were offered here.

Puca Pucara
Several kilometers farther along, the ruins of Puca Pucara ("the Red Fortress") appear to our right. Puca Pucara apparently served as a sentry post both for Cuzco and for Pisac and the Urubamba Valley. From it we can contemplate a lovely landscape of hills, terraces, paths and canals.

Tambomachay
Only a few hundred meters from Puca Pucara on our left we come upon the *Banos del Inca* (Inca baths), a complex of canals and pools known as Tambomachay. In this lovely, unusually well-preserved site, we can again note the quality of Incan craftsmanship, the precision of their work and the importance they accorded to each and every detail. Pay special attention to the circular walls whose stones fit together so perfectly that even today they are hard to match. Though known as "baths", it is hard to imagine that Tambomachay indeed served for bathing, and the site, according to the best hypothesis, was meant chiefly as a "rest stop" for the emperor and his men.

The Urubamba Valley
Along the route on which we are about to venture we find two of the most important and best-known of the Inca ruins, both highly impressive, and recommended. They are located in the Urubamba Valley, a strip of agricultural settlement that sheltered Cuzco from the north, and are very easily reached by rented car, organized tour, or ordinary public transportation.

The sites can be visited on a one-day excursion from Cuzco, or you can stop there on the way to Machu-Picchu. In the latter case, spend the night in Ollantaytambo and continue the next morning on the train from Cuzco, which stops there on the way to Machu-Picchu.

Pisac
The road that heads northward from Cuzco, passing Sacsahuaman and the sites mentioned in the previous section, now crosses the mountains and descends into the fertile Urubamba Valley at their base which still serves today as in the past, as the "breadbasket" of Cuzco. Its temperate climate and rich fertility account for the intense agriculture and settlement,

PERU

and it is certainly because of these features that the Incas invested such great efforts in constructing, fortifying and developing the valley – thereby securing the imperial capital's physical defense and food supplies.

Pisac, our first stop on the northwestern journey along the river, was and remains an important town in these respects. As we approach it, long before we cross the narrow bridge spanning the river, we discern the magnificent terraces that line the mountainside across the way and in whose shade the colorful village reposes.

The village itself is rather pleasant. Since its streets are laid out in a grid, the visitor has only to turn onto one of the narrow cobblestone alleys and walk straight to reach the square at the far end, right at the foot of the mountain. The plaza, shaded by enormous trees, is the location of the famous Indian market held every Sunday morning, with hundreds of food items, handicrafts and souvenirs changing hands. Neither in quality nor in price is this a bargain market, but the large selection and abundance of sound and color certainly justify your coming this far.

Buses traveling the 32-kilometer route from Cuzco to Pisac in less than an hour, run frequently early Sunday morning, and on weekdays there are several buses each day. Most buses set out from Calle Saphi, but you will find cars and small trucks (*camiones*) headed in that direction from other places, such as Plaza de Armas. Get to Pisac early, for everything is over by afternoon and the characteristic tranquility is restored. Pisac offers a number of places to sleep, but *Hotel Pisac* (in the plaza) is the best. Its second-floor rooms are comfortable and clean.

Above the village are found the remains of one of the largest fortresses built by the Incas. By foot it is an hour or two of exhausting ascent on a path beginning in the village (turn left at the fork, for the right-hand path is much steeper). An alternative route, paved only in recent years, is a road leading to the base of the temple in the center of the fortress. There's no regular transportation, so you have to persuade a villager to take you up, which, of course, requires the customary haggling over price.

Once up there, however, all is forgotten. Wander among the ruins of towers, pass through ancient residences, observe the high terraces (most of which are still cultivated today), and visit the Sun and Moon Temples. If you have come by vehicle, you will first see the ruins of bulidings generally considered to be the quarters for the priests and acolytes of the temple. Note the niches in the walls where ritual articles and icons were kept. Higher up, prominent in its grandeur, is the Sun Temple built of black granite slabs, with an impressive sundial at its center.

PERU

The temple, known as Intihuatana, was used for religious rites and astronomical observations. An area in its center was dedicated to Inti, the sun. Beside it, in keeping with the dualistic Inca tradition, is the Moon Temple. At the structure's southern end we can clearly discern baths fed by waters from the canal which runs alongside. The temple was protected on all sides by ramparts and towers, some of which we passed on the way from the village below. A narrow path leads north from the temple to an area uncovered only in recent years – Kallacasa, a storage facility and housing for the plebians. Opposite the temple on the rock face of the mountain to the west (past the arroyo), we see the city's burial ground, the largest of its type. The Incas buried their dead – mummified in fetal position – in conical clay structures built along the slope. Though access to the place is rather difficult, most of the graves have been visited by relic-hunters, a fact which explains the holes that make the mountainside look like a sieve.

From here we return to Pisac continuing down the Urubamba Valley, preferably via the footpath, so we can observe the scenery, the remains of defense towers and the terraces.

The Road to Ollantaytambo
From Pisac the road continues northwest, more or less parallel to the river. Buses pass through every few hours, picking up passengers at the entrance to Pisac. You can try to hitch a ride or get aboard a truck while waiting for the bus. After about nineteen kilometers of lovely scenery we reach Calca, the valley's largest town. There's no special reason to spend time there, apart from walking along its streets for a short while. Another nineteen kilometers away is the village of Yucay, and another three kilometers brings us to Urubamba. The road from Cuzco also reaches Urubamba, and the two combine northwest for another twenty-one kilometers – till our next stop.

Ollantaytambo
Ollantaytambo (elev. 2800 meters), one of the most exceptional towns in Peru, is situated 72 km from Cuzco. It is approximately two thousand inhabitants dwell in a town whose houses and streets have been preserved exactly as the Incas left them when fleeing the Spanish. Here Manco-Inca battled Pizarro's men fiercely in the futile rebellion of 1536, ultimately having to escape by a ruse to Vilcabamba, where he was finally captured by the persistent Spaniards. Today we can see the remains of the strong fortress where Manco took refuge and from which he attacked the besieging Spanish. Note the rare quality of its construction, its advanced strategic planning and the organizational, military, and economic abilities it reflects, all of which are truly difficult to comprehend.

*P*ERU

Stairway to the sky - Ollantaytambo

Ollantaytambo can be reached from the Urubamba Valley, or by bus and train from Cuzco (trains from San Pedro Station to Machu-Picchu and back stop here). Transportation to the village is rather frequent, with buses, trucks and tourist cars making the trip several times per day. When coming from Pisac, it is usual to spend the night here before continuing by train to Machu-Picchu; the same holds true for those getting off the train

PERU

here on the way back from Machu-Picchu en route to Pisac. In any event, there are a number of food and lodging possibilities – all very basic. Next to the train station there is a sort of small hostel, *Albergue*, run by some "gringos", where guests sleep in shared rooms. The *Parador Turistico* is a small, clean hotel on the central plaza, and it has a small restaurant on its ground floor. The *Alojamiento Yavar*, with clean and very basic accommodation, is also nearby. Around the square there is always someone willing to direct you to a place to spend the night but, again, do not expect too much. A floor, too, is considered a respectable place to sleep in this village. For the more energetic, of course, there is the possibility of pitching a tent at the edge of town which seems to be the nicest alternative. Remember to bring a warm sleeping bag, for nights here are very cold.

Once settled we can tour the village. A short stroll down the narrow lanes, between the simple stone walls, will suffice to give an impression of the way in which the village was built and it is crude and unsophisticated when compared with the grandeur and precision of the fortress. Most of the houses were meant for simple folk and are piled together in a sort of courtyard style along the streets, with the doors of the various houses opening onto the court. It is interesting to see the canals that carry water to the houses, and the windowless outer walls encircling the village.

At the edge of town we can clearly make out a massive terraced structure – the maginificent fortress where Manco-Inca took refuge. Its construction seems to have been begun by Pachacuti, but he did not have time to finish it before the Spaniards arrived. Entire wings, especially the upper sections (which apparently served as a temple) still seem to be in various stages of construction. Climb the hundreds of steps leading to it and walk around. The enormous stones, each weighing several tons, were brought here from a quarry located on a cliff across the river! Imagine the means and skill needed to transport them several kilometers to this site – bringing them down the slope, crossing the river, and dragging them back up the precipitous slope.

From here we can contemplate the surrounding landscape and get a fuller picture of the fortress' strategic importance. The roads to the Urubamba Valley and to Cuzco immediately come into view. A little past the temple are the ruins of houses that apparently served the local population and the defenders. Behind them a rampart wall which demarcates the western wing of the fortress is visible. By moving slightly away from the wall on the path, we reach a place which apparently served as a

PERU

prison: four cells hewn of stone, equipped with holes suitable for threading chains at the height of a man's hands and feet.

Machu-Picchu

Of all the sites in Cuzco and its surroundings the most well-known and impressive is the Lost City, the only Inca city preserved intact – Machu-Picchu. Legends were current in Latin America, Spain, and the rest of the world about the existence of such a city somewhere in the depths of the jungle but it was only in 1911, after years of searching, that it was discovered. Overnight it became one of the most famous and exciting sites of all the relics of the ancient world.

Tens of thousands stream here from all corners of the world, seeking to understand the special secret of this strange place which stood desolate for centuries, blanketed in a thick mantle of wild jungle growth that concealed it from the eye of man. To this day we do not know exactly why Machu-Picchu was abandoned, and how its existence could have eluded the Spaniards, who razed to the ground everything they came across. Some attribute this to the fact that the city was secret then as well while others explain that the Incas did not have a written history, and customarily omitted unwanted details from their oral chronicles. The latter view hypothesizes that something in the city's history displeased the Incan emperors, who ordered it erased from the national memory – thereby consigning Machu-Picchu to the depths of oblivion and saving it from destruction. The Incans did themselves a disservice, but they gave us and posterity the privilege and pleasure of beholding this special place with our own eyes and endowing the city with eternal life.

How to get there

The only way to get to Machu-Picchu, apart from hiking (see "The Inca Trail" for information concerning the foot path) is the train that sets out each morning from Cuzco. Since it takes on passengers at stations along the way, there's nothing easier than getting aboard if you've come directly from Abancay or the Urubamba Valley. Two trains run on this line and both are packed. Of these, the tourist train is more expensive (about three times the price) but also faster, more comfortable and – no less importantly – safer. The Cuzco – Machu-Picchu line is infamous for its plague of thieves, who are more easily spotted against a background of foreigners. The ride lasts nearly four hours, about an hour and a half less than on the cheaper local train. Those who wish to save by taking the local should at least go first class, for second class is very crowded and noisy, marring the atmosphere of the trip. Buy tickets at the San Pedro

P ERU

A roofless wonder - the author at Machu-Picchu, city of the Incas

station (opposite the market) a day in advance and get to the station early. Even so, you will have to fight to get a seat!

The train zigzags its way out of Cuzco, for the steep incline and sharp curves make a direct course impossible. As mentioned this stretch is a thief's paradise, so keep an eagle eye on your gear. We recommend a flashlight for the evening return trip and for when the train passes through tunnels, for when darkness strikes so do quick-handed thieves.

Upon reaching your destination, after a lovely journey, you'll find a great many buses waiting in the adjacent lot to take you up the mountain to the entrance gate. There are not enough buses so here, too, seats go to the speedy. Otherwise you'll have to wait almost an hour! Climbing by foot is exhausting and does not save any time. Another possibility, highly recommended, is to reach Aguas Calientes (Hot Waters), a village 1.5 kilometers before Machu-Picchu, the night before.

Food and lodging

You can stay at one of its small hostels in Aguas Calientes. Here you will find several agreeable restaurants and a few simple hotels, as well as hot springs which make bathing a pleasure. Get up early the next morning and make your way to Machu-Picchu on foot. That way you will get there much earlier than the train, and also enjoy the privilege of exploring the site while it's quiet and serene, before the swarms of people invade it.

PERU

The government tourist company runs a hotel next to the entrance to Machu-Picchu, but it is not large and to spend the night there you must have reservations. The self-service restaurant is relatively high-priced, and the lines are long, so it's best to bring your own food.

Visiting the site

To explore Machu-Picchu properly, a thorough tour of its various sections is needed, with careful attention paid to construction, street layout, shape of the temples, agricultural areas, etc. We'll explore the site systematically, noting as we go along its architectural wonders, the complexity of its social system, and the strength of its defenses. The well-tended lawns, neat trails and specially-constructed footpaths everywhere do not mar the authenticity of the place to any great degree.

We enter Machu-Picchu through the gate, pass a sign commemorating the city's discoverer, the American Professor Bingham, and pay the admission fee. Now, standing at the beginning of the trail, we behold the city of wonders in its full grandeur. To the right and left, above and below, are row upon row of carefully-crafted terraces where its citizens apparently grew their crops. Incidentally, one hypothesis argues that Machu-Picchu was set aside for the Sun Virgins, since the skeletons uncovered here display a ratio of three women for every man...a real paradise. Glance to the left, upward, to see a special structure accessible by steps farther along the path. The large number of bones that were found at the top of the stairs, far from the city center, has led scholars to believe that this site was a cemetery. Slightly behind it is a hewn stone on which corpses were placed to dry in the sun before mummification. If you turn around, the city in its full glory comes into view. The left section, the higher one, was set aside for ritual tasks and religious rites while the right side was residential. Look also to your left and downward – apart from the stunning view, you will also notice the steep slope that protected the city from potential attackers.

Return to the staircase and head down. Turn left onto one of the alleys and notice the buildings, all similar, and the narrow walkways between them. Soon we reach the Sun Temple, where again we see exquisite stonework, and can marvel at the giant altar stone in the temple's center. A number of mummies were found underneath the stone, in a place called the Tombs of the Kings. Continuing in the same direction we reach the nobility's quarter, with a number of gigantic carved stones in its center. From here it was possible to gaze down on the valley separating the city's two sections and see what was happening there. To

PERU

the left of the quarter we can clearly make out the remains of the quarry that supplied the city's building material.

Climbing on, we reach one of Machu-Picchu's most important sites – the Temple of the Three Windows. Though we notice the massive wall opposite us, it is impossible not to be especially attracted to the wall on our right, which runs eastward. It is made entirely of one block of stone, in which three large windows have been carved with precision.

We continue along the path. Shortly after this temple we come to Machu-Picchu's central temple, from which the path leads to the large sundial, the most beautiful and perfect of those which have been preserved. Though it is not known exactly why the sophisticated installation was built and what purpose it served, similar sundials, with faces pointing precisely to the four corners of the earth, have been found at every Incan site discovered, and they were undoubtedly of great significance in Inca life. Whether it was a clock, an astronomical facility, or a tool of some other kind, its importance cannot be overlooked and we cannot help but marvel at it.

Now we need only to continue to the other side of town and wander among its ancient houses. Notice how the construction blends into the terrain and how the builders utilised the stones in the area. At the edge of the quarter, there is a facility where prisoners were held and tortured to death. We see niches of a man's height in which detainees were held, and rocks on which they were executed.

That basically covers a tour of Machu-Picchu. The well-planned city, with its temples, fortresses and remarkable construction, testifies to an extraordinary civilization which once flourished here. A tour of the city sheds a new light on this civilization which dates back to pre-Spanish America but which still exerts an influence on the area today, five hundred years later.

Those who still have the energy, should climb to the top of the cliff above Machu-Picchu – Huayna-Picchu and enjoy the awesome view of the lost city and the incredible views around it. The steep climb takes about half an hour, and the path crosses amazing gorges.

Chinchero

The picturesque town of Chinchero, two hours from Cuzco, lies 3760 m above sea level. Inca ruins abound here, as they do in the entire area, but the major charm of Chinchero lies not in its past but, interestingly, in what's taking place here today. There's a lovely market every Sunday morning in Chinchero, the nicest and most agreeable in the area. Scores of Indians spread their

PERU

goods out on the wide lawn of the central square and engage in barter, exchanging potatoes for onions, bread for cheese and so on. Tourists will also find enough here to empty their wallets, certainly enjoying the more pleasant atmosphere if not a large selection or lower prices. It's worthwhile to spend two or three hours here on Sunday morning, coming (very early) by bus, truck, or one of the many cars from Cuzco. A neglected church in a corner of the square was once, according to the town elders, one of the region's most beautiful.

Many tourists choose to hike from Chinchero down to the Urubamba Valley (about five hours) and hitchhike back to Cuzco.

Extended Tours in the Cuzco Area

An adventurous visitor can spend weeks in Cuzco and its surroundings without being satiated. The area offers scores of mountain and river and jungle tour routes. It is impossible to mention them all, due to constraints of time and space, therefore only four have been selected – one for its popularity, another for its uniqueness, a third for its touch of mystery and the fourth, along a mountain track, is overwhelming in its beauty. Each lasts a number of days, and the visitor will require suitable camping gear, excellent physical condition, time, resourcefulness and orientation skills. The first route, the Inca Trail, is the most popular and easiest to follow of the four. The second, the jungle route, usually requires an organized tour, and the third, a journey to the last Incan city, requires preparation and special organization, and I mention it only to whet your appetite. The fourth, the Auzangate Trail, is not complicated, and can be done on horseback. You must prepare each of these outings carefully and precisely, making use of the most up-to-date and reliable maps and local information.

The Inca Trail

One of the most interesting ways of reaching Machu-Picchu – an experience in its own right – is the hike (three to five days) along one of the most famous and popular trails in South America – the Inca Trail. This route, beginning at Kilometer 88 of the railroad and ending in Machu-Picchu itself, is one of the hundreds of roads that crisscrossed the Inca empire. Most of these roads, have been widened, and have become major highways, with no surviving trace of bygone days. Others, especially those in mountainous, isolated areas, were abandoned and have disappeared, buried for centuries under sand, rock and vegetation. Only a few have survived and it's a

PERU

special experience to hike along them. The Inca Trail, the main highway from the Urubamba Valley to Machu-Picchu, is the best-known.

Remember before setting out that this is a difficult hike, more than fifty kilometers long, at elevations sometimes exceeding 4000 m above sea level. You must have suitable lightweight gear, food, maps and good spirit. Get off the train at Kilometer 88, cross the river, pay a few dollars at the entrance – and start walking.

The trail was discovered in 1915 but only several decades later was it made fit for tourists. It crosses mountains and valleys, with alternating climbs and descents. The first section is the hardest, and includes the famous climb "to the first range". Afterwards the going is easier. The trail is simply paved with Incan relics. On the way there are a number of archeological sites, among them Sayacmarca and Huinya Huayna, considered the best of the Incan antiquites in the region. Approaching Machu-Picchu from this direction is an extraordinary experience: as you round the bend of *Puerto del Sol* (the gate of the sun), the entire city suddenly appears, stretching out below.

To the eastern jungles

Several hundred kilometers east of Cuzco is a vast land of unexplored, unknown jungle. Very few people live there – only a few tens of thousands – and even fewer visit. It is a forsaken, isolated stretch of territory, a place where standards and values are utterly different, an alien, strange world. Here we find a mixture of untamed nature and human settlement, wildlife and Indian tribes together with oil drillers and prospectors. Puerto Maldonado (population app. 7000) is the largest settlement, and my personal favorite of all the jungle towns. I do not know if it is because this was the first point of settlement I reached after ten days' stormy "cruising" down Rio Tambopata, or if it is because Puerto Maldonado is actually different from its counterparts. The harsh tropical climate, the wilting heat (up to 40 degrees Centigrade or 104 degrees Fahrenheit) and the oppressive humidity fail to tarnish its extraordinary charm and should not deter one from the experience of visiting and exploring the area.

The town itself consists of several unpaved streets lined on either side with small houses. Near the river you'll find straw huts, homes of Indians who abandoned their tribal lands in the area and moved to the town. In the center of town is a broad Plaza de Armas, surrounded by a number of shops, a small hotel, a bank, a cafe and so on.

*P*ERU

Battling rapids on Rio Tambopata

How to get there
You can reach Puerto Maldonado on the daily Aero Peru or Faucett flights from Cuzco, by truck (three days in good weather and up to two weeks in rainy periods!), or by boat (only in an organized framework). The rivers leading to the town, Rio Tambopata and Rio Madre de Dios, are very rough and quite deserted. Only canoes or rubber dinghies are able to navigate the rivers, and then only with suitable equipment and a guide. Such trips are rather uncommon and very expensive (hundreds of dollars). Flights tend to be cancelled on rainy days and are otherwise usually packed to the last seat. Make reservations well in advance and be sure to confirm. Even then, nothing is assured! The two companies are most unreliable and tend to overbook heavily. Get to the airport early.

Food and lodging
The Hotels *Wilson* and *Tambo Oro* are Puerto Maldonado's best, followed by the *Central*, *Turistas* and *Moderno*. The Hotel Wilson has a good restaurant. Along the main street, too, there are a number of restaurants, cafes and stands with excellent snacks and cakes. Restaurants serve some extraordinary dishes, such as *sopa de motelo*, an excellent turtle soup, or grilled fish served with slices of grilled plantains. Castanas nuts, sold in most shops, are almost a national food here. Prices in Puerto Maldonado, as in every isolated jungle town, are very

PERU

high – as much as twice those anywhere else. Rain or storms force prices even higher, for the town depends on outside supplies, for which the demand and consequently the price, rises when bad weather delays a shipment.

Excursions

In Puerto Maldonando you can get around by foot or on a scooter, an easily-driven vehicle which you can rent on the main street. You can take it out of town, into the farm areas near town and into the forests. Be sure, however, not to stray off the main road, for the thicket is misleading and it is very easy to get lost.

Puerto Maldonado is the starting point for regional outings, meant to introduce you to the area's two highly exceptional phenomena: its nature and wildlife and its people. To behold the former in full bloom you've got to get out of town – preferably by boat – several dozen kilometers up Rio Tambopata or Rio Madre de Dios, or downstream toward Bolivia. A jungle touring center, Explorers' Inn, was erected in the late 1970s about sixty kilometers (three hours) up Rio Tambopata. Hikes set out from here into the bush and you can observe birds and wildlife (if luck is on your side) and visit Indian tribes that are totally cut off from civilization. It's a nice, if somewhat touristy place, and from there you can walk through the tangle of trees and form an impression of the wealth and density of the flora.

On the other side of Rio Madre de Dios there is an enormous nature reserve. To explore it, however, you will need a guide and lots of time. At the harbor you can rent boats for any objective and any direction, at a range of prices. By taking advantage of this you can go up and down the rivers, visit Indian villages and even reach the town of Riberalta, Bolivia (be sure to make border-crossing arrangments in town before setting out!). While cruising along the rivers, you can see animals coming out to quench their thirst, crocodiles dozing on the riverbank, turtles laying their eggs, and so on.

An encounter with the jungle people, too, is very interesting. You can meet Indians whose dress, language and way of life have not changed in centuries and no less interesting are the young prospectors, who pan innumerable kilograms of sand every day in feverish search of the precious metal. Try to stop in protected areas during extended river outings and stay out of the water! I used to bathe regularly once a day, until I met with a crocodile splashing about innocently several meters away – not a pleasant experience.

If you have time on your hands and have an adventurous spirit and the willingness for a different kind of experience, this is the place for you.

PERU

Mano Parque
Mano Parque is an area of the jungle with abundant wildlife. It is accessible from Cuzco by car, or by sailing upstream from Puerto Maldonado on the river Madre de Dios. The trip is done by canoe and takes about a week.

In Huascar street in Cuzco there are truck owners who are willing to take one, for a fee, to the village Shentuya, a day's ride from Cuzco. The road is very difficult, mostly unpaved, and starts out from the high mountains where it is cold, ending in the tropical heat of the jungles. The inhabitants of Shentuya are Indians, and those among them who have large canoes will take you on a few days' cruise down the river Madre de Dios and Rio Mano, which is one of its tributaries. On the Rio Mano there is a large concentration of wildlife – alligators, monkeys, parrots and more. It is worth spending some time at the lakes near the river, which have lovely hiking trails around them.

After the trip along the Rio Mano one returns to Madre de Dios, and from there one can return upstream to Shentuya and from there back to Cuzco, or continue down the river to Puerto-Maldondo, from which there are several regular flights a week to Cuzco. In the latter case, the owner of the canoe will sail as far as the town of Colorado, a gold hunter's town, and from there canoes depart daily for Puerto Maldondo, an additional 12 hours sailing away.

One needs a permit from the National Parks authority in order to tour Mano Parque, and this is usually obtainable in Shentuya. It is generally only issued for a few days, but can be extended at the station authority on the Madre de Dios river.

Espiritupampa
One of the most adventurous tour routes which was opened up only in recent years and which has achieved growing popularity is the journey into the thick of the jungle, where the remains of the Incas' last refuge – Espiritupampa – were discovered in the depths of Vilcabamba about twenty years ago.

Bingham discovered the site as early as 1911 while searching for the ruins of the vanished city to which Manco-Inca fled when his 1536 rebellion against the Spanish failed, and where he was captured several years later. Upon discovering Machu-Picchu, Bingham attributed the stories of the vanished capital to that city and the ruins of Espiritupampa were again swallowed up by the jungle. Only when it became clear that Machu-Picchu could not be Espiritupampa (due to its location, architecture and – mainly – the fact that the city was intact, while Manco's city had been abandoned and burned) did Espiritupampa's star rise

PERU

again. In 1964, after prolonged research and excavation, evidence was found to confirm that this, and not Machu-Picchu, was Manco Inca's last bastion. Even though the city was abandoned and desolate for centuries, the legends of Espiritupampa were passed down from father to son, ever since the Spanish conquest. Only since the mid-1960s, when an American adventurer named Savoy succeeded in returning to the site and proving that the city had existed after the Spanish conquest as well, did it become clear that Machu-Picchu was not the legendary capital of Vilcabamba, but rather, by all appearances, that it was Espiritupampa.

Reaching the site is a difficult and complicated matter requiring ten days or more. The route passes through desolate areas totally cut off from regions of human settlement. Jungle, mountains and rivers surround the hiker on all sides and a harsh climate, a multitude of mosquitoes and the terrain add physical nuisances to the spiritual experience. Come well equipped – with food, first-aid equipment, mosquito repellent and enough local currency for your needs (dollars will prove worthless). We recommend taking along a local guide and before setting out, make detailed inquiries in Cuzco concerning the safest and most convenient way to go.

Auzangate

Cuzco lies in the heart of the Andes range, and therefore a variety of possibilities for mountain hikes exist. Among these are the Salcantay and Apurimac routes, but the most enjoyable is probably that which goes around Mt. Auzangate whose summit is 6384 m high. This route is particularly enjoyable when done on horseback. The hike takes about five days and the path climbs to heights of 5000 m above sea level, which makes breathing difficult. But it is not only the great height, the beauty itself is breathtaking: majestic peaks, and glaciers which descend into many enchanting lakes, each different form the other in color.

For some reason this area is colder than other areas at similar elevation, and after sunset there is no enjoyment in walking because of the intense cold. Try to complete a day's walking early, in order to eat and snuggle up in a sleeping bag inside a good tent by nightfall. Some relief from the cold is found in the hot springs at two places along the route. Nothing is more luxurious than bathing in the hot water, when the outside temperature is hovering somewhere around freezing point.

The route begins in the Indian village of Tinki, or at Ocangate 8 km away. One can get here on one of the trucks from Cuzco which depart from Avenida Huascar and Calle Garcilaso, several times weekly. The trip, which takes about 8 hours is difficult and tiring. In either of these villages one will be able to hire horses and grooms who also serve as guides. Be sure to check the horses – a sick or tired horse is liable to ruin such a trip. Do not expect thoroughbred Arab stallions, for the horses in these high mountains look more like mules. Because the horses are, in fact, packhorses it is best to pack your gear in big sacks and not in backpacks.

Lake Titicaca

One who studies a map of southern Peru, in the immediate area of the Bolivian border, will certainly notice the broad lake – Lake Titicaca. At 3800 m, this is the world's highest navigated lake with regular transportation. Its maximum length is 150 km and is about 50 km wide, while the center it is more than 300 m deep.

A place of honor is set aside for Lake Titicaca in the history of the regional peoples, who attributed various qualities to it and its waters. According to the most important of the legends, it was here, on the Island of the Sun on the lake's Bolivian side, that Manco-Capac, the first Inca, was created and from here he went to Cuzco to found the capital of the empire-to-be. The many islands that dot the lake are populated by colorful and friendly Indians. A visit is highly recommended.

Puno

Puno (pop. 40,000), the Peruvian city on Lake Titicaca's western shore, serves as capital of the Peruvian Altiplano and is the center of most activity in, on and around the lake. This pleasant city has a number of restaurants and small hotels, all within walking distance of the central plaza. Recommended hotels here are the *Ferrocarril* (the city's best) across from the train station, the *Torino* near the bus terminal, and the *Central*, *Lima* and *Europa*, the latter being especially popular.

Puno's center is Plaza de Armas, with its Cathedral dating back to the mid-seventeenth century. From here it is not far to the port district, where boats set out to the islands (see below) and the municipal market, where there is a tremendous variety of local *artesania* of wood, pottery, metal and above all, wool including the best llama and alpaca goods brought to Puno from Juliaca, where they are made, and sold here at rather attractive prices.

Puno is known for its festivals, and dances, which are best during the first half of February when a giant carnival, rich in

PERU

dance, costumes, song, music, food and drink is held in town. In the surrounding area you'll find that some occasion is celebrated almost every month. Try to take part.

Transportation

Juliaca is linked by railroad with Arequipa and Cuzco and many taxis travel between Juliaca and Puno. The trip is short and not expensive. The daily trains to those cities are a paradise for thieves: beware!! (see "Personal security" above). **Always remember: Peruvian trains do not run on Sundays.** The trains out of Juliaca are very crowded and you must get your tickets early. The wait at the ticket counter sometimes lasts several hours! Second-class tickets are obtainable only on the day of departure, while first-class and buffet-car tickets can be bought a day earlier. We highly recommend traveling in these cars, which are far more secure against thieves. Saving a few dollars on the fare is liable to cost you many times over in misery and loss of expensive gear. The train to Cuzco covers the 400 km in eleven hours of gorgeous scenery, passing towns and villages, mountains and rivers. It makes dozens of stops along the way and at each of them crowds of locals will disturb your rest by offering bargains on various articles, food and the like. The closer you get to Cuzco, the more interesting the landscape (both natural and human) becomes, but unfortunately you've got to focus your attention on things closer at hand, keeping an eagle eye more on your gear than on the scenery. When you reach the terminal, get off last, only after the platform has emptied. When you're jostled in a crowd, thieves will have a golden opportunity to slice your baggage and empty it out. Get off in an organized group, the larger the better, have your flashlight ready and hold your gear in front of you (see "Cuzco: Transportation").

The trip to Arequipa is no different. Here, too, you'll need eyes in the back of your head. Remember again: no security measures are overdone along these routes!! The trip to Arequipa, too, takes eleven hours, passing through scenery that is interesting though not as intensive as that on the way to Cuzco. To Arequipa there are night trains, on which you can reserve a place in a sleeping car.

The roads running parallel to the railroad to Cuzco and Arequipa are not recommended. A number of companies run buses over them, but the vehicles are antiquated, uncomfortable and much slower than the train. They are worthwhile only on Sundays, when the trains do not run.

To Bolivia there are several routes by lake and land. Ferries cross Lake Titicaca to Copacabana (Bolivia) every day and from the harbor you can find transportation to La Paz with no

PERU

The floating islands on Lake Titicaca

difficulty. Local bus companies also provide direct service to La Paz once or twice daily. A beautiful and recommended way of going between the two countries is via Yunguyo (see Bolivia: "Copacabana").

The Islands

Most people who come to Puno do so on their way from somewhere to somewhere else – some from Bolivia, others from the Peruvian coastal trip and still others from Cuzco. All of them stay in town first and foremost in order to leave it for a visit to one or more of the islands in Lake Titicaca.

Two especially interesting islands, Taquile and Amantani, are a few hours' lake voyage from Puno. Both are inhabited by friendly Indians who have an affinity for tourists and their money. Both islands can be reached by boats that set out early in the morning from the port at the edge of town. (It's a good idea to get there before 7am). The two islands have a number of Indian villages organized into communes that buy and sell locally-produced *artesania*, of a quality and uniqueness that I have not encountered elsewhere. Taquile is the more popular of the two islands, while Amantani, the more remote, is quieter and far less commercial. Neither island has a hotel, but spending a night there is highly recommended. Many islanders will invite you into their homes and put you up in clean rooms for a pittance. Remember to bring a sleeping bag and a little food.

PERU

Sunrises and sunsets on Lake Titicaca are famous for their exquisite beauty. Indeed, the ones I saw on Amantani are hard to describe in words. The entire sky blazes in a fiery scarlet which bursts through the clouds as far as the horizon. Enchanting!

The boats that take you to these islands will also go – by request – by way of the Uros Indian settlements. The Indians live on **floating islands**, actually mats of reeds (which grow densely in the shallower areas of the lake) which they have compressed with their feet, with great persistence, into more-or-less rigid surfaces (be careful not to tumble into the water while walking around on them). Several hundred Indians live in rickety reed structures on dozens of islands such as these, which drift about on the lake currents. They live by fishing and raising domestic fowl and a few vegetables, making some extra money on the side by selling lovely woven fabrics to tourists. The Uros travel between their islands in tiny reed boats, probably very similar to those common on the Nile in the time of the Pharoahs. The little vessels even take them on their rather infrequent voyages into town. A visit to the Uros is very interesting and you should insist that it be included in the price you pay the boat owner for your passage to the large islands.

Juliaca

Juliaca, 45 km north of Puno, serves as an important crossroads, where the railroad branches off to Cuzco, Arequipa and Puno. Flights from Lima and Arequipa also touch down at the city's airport.

Juliaca is especially renowned as the regional center of most of the weaving done in the Peruvian highlands and products made of llama and alpaca wool are sold here at lower prices than elsewhere in southern Peru. In the city center, next to the train station, there is a rather large market offering a broad selection of merchandise. If you're hunting for genuine bargains, however, walk a few blocks to the dirty, crowded municipal market, where you'll find plenty of sweaters, ponchos, wall hangings and the like at lower prices.

URUGUAY

Uruguay is among the quietest and least known countries in South America. Its official name is the Oriental Republic of Uruguay.

From a tourist viewpoint, Uruguay is of limited interest. Tourists are generally satisfied with a visit to the capital, Montevideo, and the prestigious resort of Punta del Este.

History

The *Charrua* tribe which occupied Uruguay before the arrival of the Spanish did not relinquish their ancestral land without a struggle. The Spanish explorer Juan de Solis, who landed at Montevideo in 1516, was killed by the Charrua and for many years these Indians succeeded in preventing Spanish settlement on their land. Only in the late seventeenth century, when the Spanish (in Argentina) and the Portuguese (in Brazil) both displayed increased interest in Uruguay, was the first settlement established, at Colonia (1660). Settlement activity became truly significant only after Montevideo was founded in 1726, and fifty years later, in 1776, when a Spanish viceroy was appointed for the Rio de la Plata region, Uruguay was included in his jurisdiction. In addition, both Brazil to the north and Argentina to the south sought to annex Uruguay. The small province was bounced between the Spanish and the Portuguese. For a short period, in 1806, it was controlled by the British, who withdrew, following defeat in their attempt to conquer Buenos Aires. In 1811, the Uruguayan national hero, Jose Artigas, gathered an army which forcefully opposed the Portuguese invasion from Brazil, enjoying some Argentine support in this endeavor. Somewhat later, after Brazil took

663

URUGUAY

Montevideo in 1817, Artigas was forced to flee to Paraguay. In 1825 a group of fighters known as "33 Orientales" (the band of 33 Easterners) began to fight the Brazilians, with the aid of neighboring Argentina. Two years later, victory was theirs. In August 1828, Uruguay effectivly achieved its independence, and a constitution was adopted two years later. But Uruguay, with a population at the time of 74,000, was split between the urbanites, or *Colorados*, who tended toward liberalism and social progress, and the landowners, or *Blancos*, who favored the economic interests of the local aristocracy. The conflict between these two groups, who developed into the country's largest political parties, was accompanied by violent struggles which peaked in a twelve-year civil war that broke out in 1839. The hostilities came to an end only through the intervention of the neighboring states, and without a clear-cut victory for either side. The involvement of Brazil and Argentina in Uruguay's internal affairs, led Uruguay to take part in a war against Paraguay as the third partner in the so-called War of the Triple Alliance (1865-1870). In these and following years, the urban Colorados took firm control of the Government, while the Blanco party of the landowners failed in all its efforts to gain power.

Commercial contacts with Europe began to solidify during this period. European demand for meat and meat products, which Uruguay produces in abundance, contributed to the country's rapid development. Waves of immigration flooded Uruguay's shores and in the last quarter of the 19th century its population multiplied several times over, reaching one million by 1900.

The most significant change in Uruguay's national life began in 1903, with the election of Jose y Ordonez as president. During his first term this talented leader enacted a series of legal and social reforms which led to the political stability that would characterize Uruguay for decades to come. After a four-year hiatus between terms, Ordonez laid the foundation for Uruguay's progressive constitution, a document nourished by a democratic spirit rare in this part of the world. Its provisions included articles ensuring social welfare, a liberal system of government in which all citizens are equal in the eyes of the law, proportional representation in the legislature, and total separation of Church and State. Ordonez' successors continued in his spirit, sustaining this process: a Supreme Court was appointed, a method was devised for overseeing elections, and social welfare and pensions were established.

The First World War led to accelerated economic development. Western Europe purchased meat and related products in tremendous quantities, and Uruguay, in turn, imported many consumer goods. Post-war developments in Europe, along with

URUGUAY

changes in the investment channels of Western capital, brought about an economic depression which hit rock bottom during the 1930s. The depression forced President Gabriel Terra to declare himself dictator and to suspend the nation's elected institutions and constitution. He ruled Uruguay with an iron fist for five years, enjoying public faith and support, and was able to undertake comprehensive legal reform. General Alfredo Baldomir, an opponent of Terra's, was elected President in 1938, and Uruguay entered the World War II era under his leadership. Like its Latin American neighbors, Uruguay maintained a moderate, neutral position during the war. Although it carried out a number of actions against Germany (such as seizing German vessels and interning Germans and Nazi agents), Uruguay's unequivocal decision to align itself with the West was taken only in 1941, when the President placed the country's ports at the disposal of the United States Navy. In 1942 relations were broken with Germany, and in 1945, just before the war's end, Uruguay declared war on Germany.

While the war raged, Uruguay again enjoyed a period of prosperity. European orders for its products led to extensive renewed growth, the principles of liberal democracy were again applied in the government, and a flourishing economy contributed to parallel improvement in the educational and cultural spheres.

The 1940s and 1950s were noteworthy for political tranquility and the continuation of liberal social trends. At the end of that period, however, a severe recession caused noticeable social ferment. This was expressed in the 1958 elections with the election of the Nationalist Party, the Blancos, their first victory in ninety-three years! Even so, the hoped for improvement failed to materialize. Blanco economic policy lacked efficient means for bringing about economic recovery and halting inflation, and the Uruguayan economy progressively deteriorated. The Colorados returned to power in 1966 and undertook a constitutional reform that separated the powers of the branches of government, while greatly expanding the President's authority. Strikes, riots, and terrorism erupted in the early 1970s, leading to increased military involvement in government, with the president constantly relying on the army to prop up his regime.

But in 1984, the trek towards democracy began. In December of that year, Uruguay conducted general elections bringing her back to the exclusive club of democratic nations. The *Colorados* party received the majority of votes and their leader, Julio Sanguinetti, became president. He quickly began rehabilitating the social and economic structure of the country. During his first year in office, tranquility was restored and many Uruguayan

URUGUAY

refugees, residing in Europe, returned to their homeland. Sanguinetti was warmly received by the world's democratic leaders, who have promised to assist Uruguay both politically and economically.

Geography and Climate

Uruguay is the smallest country in South America, with an area of 177,508 sq/km. On the east it borders the Atlantic Ocean, on the north it shares a border with Brazil, while in the west the mighty Uruguay River (1850 km long, and up to 10 km wide) separates it from Argentina. The Rio de la Plata, 420 km long, serves as Uruguay's southern border. Uruguay is divided into 19 provinces, which enjoy a large measure of autonomy.

The flat pampas in the south constitute most of Uruguay's territory, while the north is largely an extension of the Brazilian highlands, with hills and low mountains. The land is generally rocky but highly fertile. Forest regions are found only near the Brazilian border and in some areas along the river. Although

URUGUAY

Uruguay is poor in natural resources and mineral deposits, little has been done to exploit what does exist.

Uruguay's subtropical climate is noted for instability, which stems from sudden and variable winds – one moment from the sea, and the next from the interior. The winters are wet, with the average annual rainfall at 890 mm. The Rio Negro is the largest river, and its tributaries drain the entire country. It joins the Uruguay River before the latter empties into the Rio de la Plata.

Population

Uruguay is home to about three million people, mostly of European extraction, whose ancestors arrived during the 19th and 20th centuries. The vigorous opposition of the native Indians to Spanish settlement led to struggles that ultimately brought about the obliteration of the Indian community. The proportion of people of Indian descent is one of the lowest in all of South America.

Eighty percent of Uruguay's population reside in urban areas. Half of all Uruguayans live in Montevideo, while the rest are concentrated in cities along the Rio de la Plata and the Uruguay River. The birth rate has remained stable for years: fewer than one-third of Uruguay's citizens are under the age of fifteen, and eight percent are sixty-five and over. This should be compared to the norm of the rest of the continent, where the proportion of children can reach 50% and life expectancy is far lower than in Uruguay.

Uruguay's official language is Spanish. Education, including higher education, is free, and the illiteracy rate is very low (10%). The great majority of Uruguayans are Catholic.

Economy

Like its larger neighbor Argentina, Uruguay has an economy essentially based on agriculture. Some 80% of its land is arable, and it is only natural that the economy has developed in this direction. Some 60% of the cultivated land is devoted to raising livestock, which accounts for 75% of Uruguay's export income. This important branch of the economy began with 100 head of cattle and the same number of horses, sent to Uruguay by the ruler of Paraguay in 1603, to breed in Uruguay's empty expanses. The pampas are divided into huge sheep and cattle ranches. Beef is Uruguay's chief export. Other agricultural activities are few; wheat and similar crops are mainly for domestic consumption and not for export.

URUGUAY

The absence of natural resources such as oil and coal, combined with the lack of a developed industrial infrastructure, result in a heavy burden on the national economy. Uruguay is forced to import most of its energy sources as well as many consumer goods – from textiles and plastics to machinery and cars. Despite encouragement of productive sectors, and customs and exchange rate policies that support export and hinder imports, Uruguay has not overcome its economic crises. Lack of efficiency and flexibility in the economy, make it impossible to rechannel production to suit the changing demands of the world market.

In the wake of the economic difficulties of the 1970s, with the rise in fuel prices and reduced meat purchases by members of the EEC, the Uruguayan government implemented a series of measures designed to stabilize the economy, but with no great success. Inflation (which amounted to 9000% between 1955 and 1970!) was slowed a little through massive support of the peso against the U.S. dollar. This, however, caused the price of Uruguay's exports to rise, which in turn led to the cancellation of orders and a significant deterioration in the country's balance of payments – the most serious problem facing the Uruguayan economy.

The government pursued a policy of monetary stability, which has had rather limited success. It also tried to implement commmprehensive reforms that would lead the country to economic independence. Export industries were established and hydroelectric plants are being built along Uruguay's rivers.

The situation since Sanguinetti became president has not improved much. The new government is valiantly struggling with the legacy left by the military regime. The currency, once the stablest in the continent, continues to fall. Its devaluation has increased internal pressure. But even so, Uruguay enjoys foreign aid and tourism. Tourists, especially from Brazil and Argentina, have returned after having stayed away during the inhospitable years of the previous regime.

General Information

How to get there
By air: The Uruguayan national airline, Pluna, flies both within the country and to neighboring countries. Madrid is its most distant destination. Lufthansa, KLM, Air France, and Iberia fly to Montevideo, either with a stopover in Rio de Janeiro or on the way to Buenos Aires. Pan American flies here from New York. Aerolineas and Pluna have frequent flights to Buenos Aires' Aeroparque Airport. Cruzeiro del Sol flies to Rio daily, and Varig

URUGUAY

makes the trip several times per week. Pluna runs a shuttle bus service from Carrasco Airport to Montevideo (a 30-minute trip), and from the company offices on 18 de Julio Avenue to the airport, at unscheduled intervals. The airport, 20 km from the capital, is small and outmoded, and lacks a tourists' bureau. It does offer a nice restaurant on the second floor.

From Argentina: The bus trip from Buenos Aires to Montevideo lasts eleven hours. The COT company (offices in Montevideo's Plaza Independencia, Tel. 984-554) has a fleet of modern, comfortable buses. The most pleasant, interesting, and inexpensive way to make this trip (10 hours) is on the passenger ship that crosses the Rio de la Plata. The ship has cabins of various classes, and restaurants. A deck ticket, the cheapest of all, includes a bed in a cabin shared by eight passengers. The city of Colonia serves as the major border crossing between Uruguay and Argentina. Colonia and Buenos Aires are linked by frequent air service (15 minutes) with the Argentinian metropolis visible across the Plata. A hydrofoil crosses the Plata several times daily – an interesting trip in a unique vehicle, though the potential traveler must bear in mind that it is noisy and apt to be accompanied by an unpleasant sensation. A ferry takes passengers and cars across the gulf more cheaply. Convenient bus transportation from Colonia to Montevideo (a 3-hour ride) is provided by ONDA.

From Brazil: The buses from Rio, Sao Paulo and Porto Alegre are luxurious, comfortable, and fast. A number of companies provide service several times daily; several of them switch buses at the border.

From Paraguay: The COIT company operates two buses weekly between Asuncion and Montevideo via Argentina (26 hours). The passenger enjoys luxurious and comfortable buses, soft drinks, light refreshments, and the passing scenery of the Chaco. The COIT offices are located on 1473 Paraguay Street (Tel. 908-906, 916-619).

Documents
North Americans and Western Europeans, with valid passports do not require a visa and may enter Uruguay for up to 90 days. This stay can be extended for an additional 90 days at the Immigration Office in Montevideo.

When to Come; National Holidays
Summer (November-April) is the main tourist season; and the hotels are full and beaches are crowded. Winter is not as nice, though not much rainier than summer.

URUGUAY

The important holidays are January 1, May 1, August 25 (Independence Day), and December 25.

Currency
Uruguay has no foreign currency restrictions, and use of credit cards is common and convenient. The same holds true for travelers' checks, with only a small difference in exchange rates when compared with cash. Many places will exchange travelers' checks for cash dollars for a small commission, an important service for a visitor planning to continue on to Brazil or Argentina, where the difference in the exchange rate for cash and travelers' checks can reach 20%!

The "new peso" has been Uruguay's official currency since 1975, when the "old peso" was abolished due to inflation. Coins are commonly used in denominations up to 50 pesos; bank notes of those values are rarely found. Common bank note denominations are 50, 100, and 1000 pesos. New bank notes bear the notation N$ beside the amount (as opposed to "old peso" bank notes which only bear $).

Business Hours
Stores are open on weekdays, with an afternoon siesta. On Saturday shops are open half day. Everything is closed on Sundays except for food stores, which are open a half day. Banks are open weekdays, from around noon, with individual hours for each bank.

Transportation
ONDA provides nationwide bus transportation with very frequent service. Trains run several routes on an antiquated, slow, and uncomfortable British rail network. Pluna provides air transportation between major cities. Automobile travel – rental or private – between the large cities is comfortable, since a network of paved roads links all the central sections of the country.

Measurements; electricity and time
The metric system is used exclusively. The electric network is 220V. The Uruguayan hour is GMT-3.

Montevideo

In addition to being Uruguay's capital and largest city, Montevideo is the country's major tourist center. This city, founded in 1726 and home to approximately one and a half million Uruguayans, is flooded each summer with tens of thousands of tourists, who come to visit its clean beaches,

URUGUAY

handsome avenues, and multitude of hotels and restaurants. Montevideo is not a "tourist city" in the accepted sense of the word. Unlike Rio de Janiero and Buenos Aires, it is not noted for a bustling tourist infrastructure. In contrast to Paris, London; or New York, it has no special sites that attract visitors intent on making the rounds from place to place. Montevideo is undoubtedly a city to which people come primarily to enjoy a general impression of it, its residents and – above all – its beaches.

Accommodations

Most of Montevideo's hotels are concentrated downtown, between Plaza Independencia and Plaza Libertad; along the Avenida 18 de Julio which is the main artery of the city; and on nearby streets from Canelones to Mercedes. Along Mercedes Street we find inexpensive hotels, while the expensive and prestigious ones are situated on Plaza Independencia. The *Victoria Plaza* (Tel. 914-209), the most expensive and luxurious of them all, occupies an impressive old 21-story building. Many good hotels – far less expensive – are arrayed around the plaza. The old quarter of Montevideo, in the vicinity of Plaza Constitucion and chiefly on Buenos Aires, Sarandi and Rincon Streets, is home to scores of inexpensive pensions, though some are dirty and run-down. Many hotels of intermediate price and quality can be found along Avenida 18 de Julio. The following are recommended: *Hotel Rex*, 870 Avenida 18 de Julio (Tel. 901-820), very close to the plaza, one flight up, with large clean rooms; *Hotel Americano*, farther down the street, near the bus terminal, with a moderate-sized lobby, clean rooms with telephones, and a rate which includes a continental breakfast.

Among the cheaper and plainer hotels, I can recommend *Hotel Ideal*, 914 Colonia Steet, and *Hotel Buenos Aires* on 204 Avenida 18 de Julio.

Many restaurants and hotels may be found in the seaside neighborhoods, particularly the Carrasco quarter, a ten-minute bus ride from downtown. Here we find the famous *Hotel Casino*, designed by the architect Baldomir. This building, opened in 1921, is beyond doubt one of the most impressive in the area. *Hotel Ermitaz* on Benito Blanco Street is far less expensive, antiquated but comfortable and clean, with a large lobby, restaurant (including grill), and suites to accommodate entire families. The two hotels are very close to the sea and appropriate for a family vacation.

Wining and Dining

Restaurants are concentrated along Avenida 18 de Julio and the vicinity, and many are relatively cheap. The pizzerias serve

URUGUAY

excellent and inexpensive fare. *Confiterias*, a sort of cross between restaurants and cafes, are also found in abundance, and offer simple dishes and sandwiches, and are good places to eat breakfast and lunch. The evening meal is generally eaten late, after 9pm. The typical Uruguayan supper is to be found, of course, in the restaurants. Most of the dishes are similar to those offered in Argentina (see "Wining and Dining" in the chapter on Argentina), and excel both in quality and quantity. The *Hotel Victoria Plaza* has a superb restaurant with an elegant atmosphere and excellent service. *Otto's Restaurant* on Rio Negro Street, corner of San Jose, serves excellent meat dishes at reasonable prices – highly recommended. Chinese restaurants are scattered along the smaller streets crossing and parallel to Avenida 18 de Julio. The few kiosks in Montevideo offer mainly soft drinks and sandwiches.

Typical foods in Montevideo are *churisco* – a sausage baked in dough or a roll – and *buseca* – a special and very spicy ox-tail soup with beans and peas. The word "steak" is unknown in Montevideo's restaurants; you have to order a specific cut: *lomo*, the finest and most expensive, or the cheaper *entricot*, which is also superb. The quality of the *asado*, which is grilled beef, and the *parrallada*, mixed grill, depends on the restaurant. Stay away from them in restaurants with poor sanitary conditions since the meat here is usually very fatty and poorly cooked. The array of side dishes is extremely limited in all restaurants, consisting usually of rice with gravy, mashed or fried potatoes, and salad.

The cafe-concert is a recommended blend of a light supper and music. This is a popular Uruguayan entertainment spot, where people spend an evening in small and pleasant cafes to the sound of a small band, generally made up of guitar, accordion, and singer.

By law, menus must be affixed to restaurant entrances. The prices displayed include service and taxes. You should also add a tip for the waiter – 5% in restaurants, and 15% in cafes.

Transportation

Public transportation downtown is very convenient. The buses are old and when you want to get off, instead of ringing a bell you say "psst" to the conductor. A mistake will usually infuriate the driver and conductor. Bus stops are marked only by small signs on streetcorners or sometimes on the wall of an adjacent building, marked with the route number. The lines at the stops are not always orderly, but people are always quiet and polite. Fares are very low, since public transportation is subsidized.

URUGUAY

Many taxis cruise the city, and are easily obtained even at rush hour. The fare tends to be reasonable, and is indicated on the meter.

Driving a private or a rented vehicle is rather easy but hardly essential, given the proximity of Mondevideo's sites.

Tourist services

The most efficient and convenient Tourist Bureau is located opposite the entrance of the ONDA bus terminal on Avenida 18 de Julio (Tel. 214). Here you can obtain all essential information concerning transportation, orientation, first aid services, special events, and anything else on your mind. The staff will provide you with color maps and a wealth of material on various topics. The Government Tourism Ministry's branch office on Plaza Libertad provides a variety of reading material and maps.

Most airline offices are located around Plaza Entrevero, near Rio Negro and Avenida 18 de Julio.

The large Exprinter travel agency has a branch at 700 Sarandi Street; one may also avail oneself of the Brenner agency in the Old Quarter.

Tourist sites

Plaza Independencia and **Avenida 18 de Julio** are the main centers of Montevideo. The enormous Plaza, the heart of the city, has an equestrian statue of Artigas in its center, above a small mausoleum. The statue, by the Italian artist Angelo Zanelli, dates from 1923.

A number of magnificent buildings surround the plaza: the monumental **Victoria Plaza Hotel** on its northern side and, opposite it, the **Government Palace** (built in 1870) which, in contrast to the rest of the nearby buildings, is relatively small and modest. The famous **Solis Theater** (opened in 1850) is on one side of the plaza, to the right of the Government Palace; beside it is an interesting **Museum of History**, open three afternoons a week. On the plaza's eastern side is the **Salvo Palace**, one of the most beautiful and impressive in the city.

The Old Quarter

The Plaza effectively marks the edge of the Old Quarter, which stretches westward to the harbor. A number of old houses remain here, and the quarter still serves as a financial and commercial center.

Rincon Street leads us toward **Plaza de la Constitucion**, the oldest of Montevideo's public squares. On its western side is the **Municipal Cathedral**. Continuing down Rincon Street we

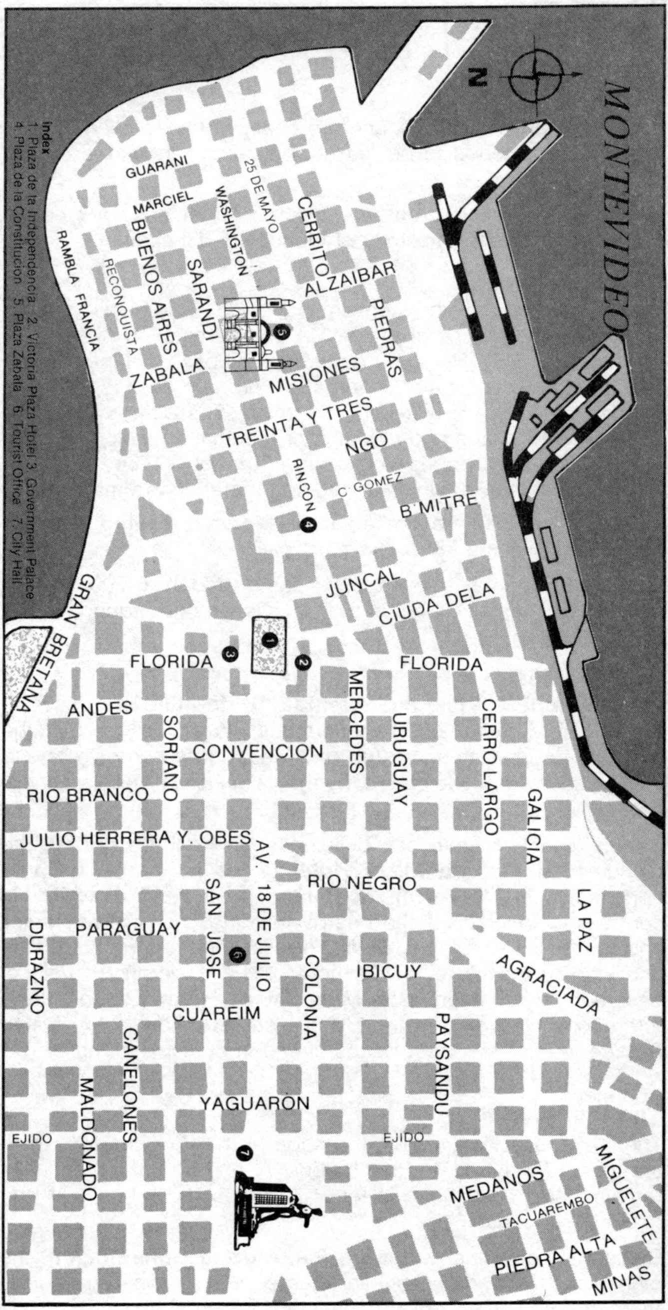
MONTEVIDEO
N
Index
1. Plaza de la Independencia 2. Victoria Plaza Hotel 3. Government Palace
4. Plaza de la Constitucion 5. Plaza Zabala 6. Tourist Office 7. City Hall
GUARANI
MARCIEL
25 DE MAYO
WASHINGTON
CERRITO
BUENOS AIRES
SARANDI
ALZAIBAR
RAMBLA FRANCIA
RECONQUISTA
PIEDRAS
ZABALA
MISIONES
TREINTA Y TRES
NGO
RINCON
C. GOMEZ
B. MITRE
JUNCAL
CIUDA DELA
GRAN BRETAÑA
FLORIDA
FLORIDA
ANDES
SORIANO
MERCEDES
URUGUAY
CERRO LARGO
CONVENCION
RIO BRANCO
GALICIA
JULIO HERRERA Y. OBES
AV. 18 DE JULIO
RIO NEGRO
SAN JOSE
LA PAZ
PARAGUAY
DURAZNO
COLONIA
IBICUY
AGRACIADA
CUAREIM
CANELONES
PAYSANDU
MALDONADO
YAGUARON
EJIDO
EJIDO
MEDANOS
MIGUELETE
TACUAREMBO
PIEDRA ALTA
MINAS

URUGUAY

reach **Plaza Zabala**. In its center is the statue of the city's founder – Zabala – astride his horse.

The monumental **Customs House** is a short walk east of here, close to the **port** which was constructed in 1901 and has been expanded several times since. This port handles 95% of the country's import and export traffic. At 234 Buenos Aires Street is the grand **Sephardi Jewish Synagogue**, with a number of halls for celebrations and events. On Jewish holidays when travel is forbidden, this building is empty, due to its distance from the residential quarters where Montevideo's Jews live.

Along Avenue 18 de Julio

On the other side of Plaza Independencia stretches Avenida 18 de Julio, a mix of business, light industry, fashion, and restaurants. The section closer to the plaza is given more to entertainment and tourism; here we find restaurants, pizzerias, cafes, cinemas, clubs, hotels, and so on. As we get farther from the plaza and head east towards Plaza Libertad, the Avenue's character changes, its buildings bursting with shops. Salesmen standing in the doorways lure passers-by to enter and are usually polite and gracious. Prices are marked clearly in the shop windows; bargaining is not only unaccepted, but arouses resentment and ridicule.

At the corner of Rio Negro Street we come upon **Plaza del Entrevero**, adorned with trees, lawns, and park benches. Two blocks further on we reach **Plaza Libertad**, with a towering statue of liberty in its center. The ONDA **bus terminal** is opposite, with the Tourist Bureau located across from its entrance. Four blocks eastward we reach **Plaza Perez**, better known as **Plaza El Gaucho** for its statue of the legendary cowboy. Here we find the new City Hall. Continuing eastward, we pass the University and the adjacent **National Library**, founded in 1816. The library is housed in an interesting and impressive building constructed in 1956; a statue of Dante graces its courtyard. At the intersection of Avenida 18 de Julio and Avenida del Artigas, is an Obelisk erected in 1956 to commemorate the heroes of Uruguayan independence.

The Avenida 18 de Julio extends to the entrance of the beautiful and well-kept **Batlle y Ordonez Park**. The park contains numerous statues and sculptures of which the most famous is *La Carreta* – six oxen pulling a cart, accompanied by a cowboy on horseback. The statue, the work of the Uruguayan artist Jose Belloni, was cast in 1934. Within the park is a 70,000-seat **soccer stadium**, built in 1930 for the World Cup. Nearby are tracks for both runners and bicycles.

URUGUAY

The **Zoological Gardens** are also not far from here, and present a variety of flora and a charming zoo. Next to the Gardens is the large **Municipal Planetarium**. The Gardens can be reached from Plaza Independencia and Avenida 18 de Julio on foot, or by buses 141, 142, and 144 – a five-minute trip.

Other Sites

The **Congress Palace**, dedicated in 1925, is certainly one of the largest and most impressive public buildings in Montevideo. The palatial marble structure is located in the center of a large plaza at the top of Lavalleja Avenue, north of Avenida 18 de Julio.

Several miles down Lavalleja Avenue is **El Prado Park**, This park – one of Montevideo's most beautiful – is home to the municipal **Art Museum** and **Historical Museum**.

The **National Museum of Fine Art**, opened in 1911, is located in **Rodo Park**. The city's largest park is located behind Ramirez Beach, and has a large artificial lake used for boating. During the summer this park is packed with local residents and visitors. In the evening, thousands flock to the amphitheater for concerts or other performances.

Montevideo (literally translated "I see the mountain",) takes its name from a hill at the western tip of the Rio de la Plata, which rises to 139 m above sea level. A small **fortress** on the top of this hill was built in 1724 to defend against the Portuguese, who had settled in Colonia. Today, the fortress serves as a **military museum**. Beside it is an old (1804) **lighthouse**. The hill affords a superb view of the city and La Plata shore.

Montevideo is surrounded by the sea on three sides; **beaches** are found everywhere. Though the beaches are sandy, wide, and fairly clean, they lack facilities such as showers. Navy personnel serve as lifeguards, and must be obeyed strictly. Ball games of any sort are absolutely forbidden, which makes life easier for the thousands of bathers, who populate the beaches chiefly during the peak months of December and January. Nevertheless, a driving rain on a sizzling summer's day, scattering bathers in all directions, is a rather common occurrence. **Ramirez Beach** and **Pocitos Beach** – the latter with a handsome promenade bordered by nine-story buildings – are the most pleasant and popular in Montevideo.

Nightlife

Unlike Buenos Aires, its neighbor across the Rio de la Plata, Montevideo is not noted for its cultural life, art, and dazzling entertainment. Yet the Solis Theater (in Plaza Independencia)

URUGUAY

La Carreta - Parque Battle y Ordonez

does present concerts, opera, and plays. Foreign artists also appear here.

Nightclubs, discotheques and folklore clubs are found downtown, along the streets adjacent to Avenida 18 de Julio, and in the neighborhoods parallel to the tourist beaches.

Cinema is popular, and American and European films with Spanish subtitles are shown at the numerous theaters throughtout Montivideo. On Avenida 18 de Julio and the nearby streets are an ample selection from which to choose. Posters for adult movies are marked with green stripes: the more stripes, the more pornography.

You can spend a typical and enjoyable Uruguayan evening in a cafe-concert, a special institution that combines a show with a light meal and something to drink. Performances begin late (10pm or later), and are packed on weekends.

Gambling (and, for that matter, prostitution) is legal here and most casinos are Government-owned. The famous hotels – especially the Casino Carrasco – feature gambling halls that operate into the early morning hours.

Banks and currency exchange

A number of **Casas de Cambio** – currency exchanges – are located downtown where dollars can be changed into pesos or other currencies. Travel agencies are generally willing to exchange currency at the going rate, unlike hotels, where the rates are lower. The dollar exchange rate varies according to the pace of inflation.

URUGUAY

Because there is no black market, and foreign currency may be purchased without restriction, travelers' checks can be cashed or purchased and bank transfers can be carried out freely. American Express and Diners Club also maintain branch offices here.

Postal and telephone services
It is best to mail letters from a post office, where they are postmarked and sent without stamps. Speed of delivery depends on the country of destination. It takes a week to ten days for a letter to reach the United States or Western Europe. Telephone service is convenient and fast. The central post office is located on the corner of Calles Buenos Aires and Missiones.

Shopping
In this sphere, too, Avenida 18 de Julio is the leader, principally along its eastern stretch (further away from Plaza Independencia). The abundant shops offer items of all kinds, with prices posted in the display windows. The streets crossing and parallel to 18 de Julio also offer a wide selection, mainly in galleries and shops. The best buys are leather goods, sports jackets, skirts, belts, purses, wallets, and woolen goods – sweaters, gloves, and the like. All are of excellent quality and reasonable price. Fashions do not always tend to be the latest so it's best to stick to classic styles. The prices of jewelry containing gems mined in Uruguay – especially topaz – are relatively low.

An exciting flea market is held every Sunday 8am-1pm on Narvaja Street, across from the University; the street is filled with goods of all kinds, from rusty nails to porcelain, crystal to antique furniture. Highly recommended.

Important addresses
American Embassy:1776 Calle Lauro Muller (Tel: 409-050).

British Embassy:1073 Marfo Bruto (Tel: 78165; 991-033).

Uruguay Auto Club: 1532 Libertador General Lavalleja.

Punta del Este
Traveling 135 km east of Montevideo we reach Punta del Este, Uruguay's most famous resort. Each summer, tens of thousands of Uruguayans and tourists – mainly from Argentina and Brazil – stream here to spend their vacations.

British forces landed in Punta del Este in 1808 on their way to conquer nearby Maldonado. Tradition claims that the little peninsula was frequented by vacationers even in Indian days. Today the city is a resort for the affluent, brimming with

URUGUAY

Yachts in Punta del Este Bay

everything needed to make a vacation prestigious and enjoyable. The city is situated between ocean and river, and at times you can distinguish between the color of water to the east – the ocean – and that to the west, the Rio de la Plata.

Punta del Este resemblances Miami Beach: a long, narrow, heavily built-up strip of land caught between the gulf and the ocean. Downtown has high-rise residential buildings; the streets are straight and clean, and the sea air is strong. Punta del Este, though, is nothing like Miami Beach. Its pace of life is far slower and the manner of vacationing much simpler. The sense of tranquility and security is relaxing and pleasurable.

The peninsula is crowded with hotels and restaurants. Despite the variety, prices are generally high. Summer visitors are best advised to make reservations, otherwise they will have little chance of finding accommodation. The area on the west side, near the yacht harbor at Mansa Beach is quieter than the other side, Playa Brava (Stormy Beach), and the wind is not as strong.

Vacationers spend most of the day at the beach, enjoying the soft white sand and the caressing sun. Most of them engage in water sports such as boating, fishing and water-skiing, as well as a wide variety of "landlubber" sports such as golf, tennis, horseback riding, and more. Evenings are spent in the excellent seafood restaurants, in nightclubs, discotheques, and... casinos. All this notwithstanding, Punta del Este remains a relatively quiet city, with no particular "touristy" aura.

URUGUAY

Slow trains, and rapid and frequent ONDA and COIT buses link Punta del Este with Montevideo. The bus trip takes about two hours, passing along the way many residential quarters constructed on all sides of Punta del Este in recent years. The bus terminal at 27 Gorlero Street houses a small information bureau that can provide details of special events and ways to spend your time.

I can recommend a visit to **Isla de Lobos**, where a giant lighthouse directs ocean traffic to the Rio de la Plata. The island, a nature preserve, is home to a large colony of sea lions. Boats set out for the island each morning from the marina and it is advisable to buy tickets in advance.

There are direct flights between Punta del Este and Buenos Aires.

VENEZUELA

Upon reaching Caracas' modern and luxurious airport, you will sense the qualities that characterize the entire country – plenitude, prosperity and modern construction – all a result of the economic boom Venezuela has enjoyed since the development of its oilfields.

For centuries Venezuela was a poor, forgotten country carved up by mountain ranges and giant rivers, on the northern periphery of South America. When the Spanish arrived in the early 16th century, their main quest was gold. When that proved an empty dream, they abandoned Venezuela to its fate, and channelled their energies elsewhere. The fact that "black gold" was discovered under Venezuelan soil four hundred years later, certainly seems like fate's last laugh.

Venezuela has bloomed since the turn of the century; cities built, roads paved, dams constructed and vast stretches of territory settled. Today Venezuela is among the wealthiest of South America's nations – some say the wealthiest – and is one of the world's leading oil exporters.

Caracas' grand streets, munificently-stocked stores and high-rise neighborhoods faithfully reflect the Venezuelans' energetic spirit – but hide the dire poverty on the outskirts of the cities. Like much of South America, in recent years, Venezuela has been afflicted by severe economic and social crisis, stemming from governmental corruption and unequal distribution of wealth.

History

Although Columbus discovered Venezuela as early as 1498 on his third voyage to America, it was only about thirty years later that the first Spanish settlement, Cumana, was founded. The Spanish, with the help of the peaceful native tribes, who had submissively welcomed them, spent several years searching for gold spurred on by the example of the discoverers and conquerors of Peru. Some tried to locate the legendary city of El Dorado on Venezuelan soil, while others prospected for ore. All suffered bitter disappointment, however, as Venezuela yielded no gold. It did give forth a respectable agricultural crop but only after great efforts had been invested in burning jungles and preparing the land.

Only those Spaniards who decided to stick to agriculture remained in Venezuela and were assimilated into the sparse

VENEZUELA

Indian population. It was not until the mid-16th century that settlement activity began in earnest. Its nature and location were dictated largely by the country's geography. These first settlers laid the foundation of urban organization that continues to dominate Venezuela to this very day.

Since its founding in 1567, Caracas, Venezuela's heart and capital, has served as the focus of national identity. Through the centuries and under all governments, Caracas has enjoyed the support and recognition of the entire population, its supremacy unchallenged.

The country's fractured geography led to the development of separate regional identities, which on several occasions refused to bow to outside control, and ignored dictates issued from the capital. It also served as the background for the anti-Spanish uprisings, which began here much earlier than elsewhere in South America. The first insurrections took place as early as the 18th century. However, it was not until 1806, and then in 1811, that a rebellion of substance erupted. The Venezuelans, led by Francisco de Miranda and Simon Bolivar, broke away from Spain and established an independent Republic. Venezuelan independence was first declared on July 5, 1811, but no fewer than twenty years of struggle and bloodshed were to pass, before it was established de facto.

Simon Bolivar was the first and greatest of Venezuela's revolutionary leaders, responsible for the liberation of Colombia, Ecuador, Peru and Bolivia. Bolivar, for whom Bolivia is named, was born in Caracas in 1783, to one of the city's wealthiest and most prestigious families. He spent long periods of his youth in Europe, where he was influenced by the current ideas of liberalism and progress. He brought these ideas back when he returned to Latin America, steadfast in his desire to liberate the local peoples from the Spanish yoke and to give them the right to an independent and secure existence. His dream was to found a "Greater Columbia" consisting of Ecuador, Columbia, Panama and Venezuela, an end to which he labored greatly. However, "Greater Columbia" did not survive long after Bolivar's death in 1830, because of the separatist ambitions of the leaders of each country.

Throughout the 19th century, as a unified national identity struggled to be born, Venezuela was plagued by severe internal strife which at times reached a state of civil war. Indian roots, Spanish heritage and Western ideas combined into a mass of contradictions that could hardly coexist. The difficulty of integrating these disparate entities ultimately led to an economic and social stagnation which has left its mark to this day.

VENEZUELA

Juan Gomez seized power in 1909 and his twenty-six years of rule which followed were characterized by terror, violence and repression. It was during this period, just when the first flames of World War I began to flicker in Europe, that oil was discovered in the Maracaibo area. By 1928, Venezuela had become the world's second largest oil producer and exporter.

"Black gold" put Venezuela on the world economic map and Caracas became a major capital. The growing purchasing power of the Venezuelans and their government attracted businessmen from all over the world, who flocked to the country with goods of every sort. Venezuela's near-total lack of industry and its limited and low-quality agricultural output, forced the country to rely on imports for just about everything – from automobiles and technological instruments to matches. During this time, the oil boom eased social tensions and helped stabilize the political structure. Thus a democratic regime, one of the most stable in Latin America to this day, was established in 1958.

Geography and climate

Venezuela, with an area of 912,000 sq/km, is bordered by Guyana to the east, Brazil to the south and Colombia to the west. The Atlantic Ocean washes 2800 km of coastline to the north.

Venezuela is divided into twenty-one administrative districts. Geographically there are only four major sections. The first is the western plains region around Lake Maracaibo. The second is the mountain range that borders the plains to the east – the Sierra Nevada de Merida – an extension of the Colombian Andes. The third, the Orinoco Basin is located in the center, and finally, to the east, Guyana Highlands, which cover more than half of Venezuela's territory.

The Orinoco River flows for 2575 km from the mountain slopes through the jungles to the Atlantic Ocean. About 80% of the country's water drains into the river before emptying through a vast delta opposite the coasts of Trinidad and Tobago.

A considerable area of Venezuela is covered with virgin forest where travel is difficult and complicated. Entire districts of the Orinoco Basin and the Guyana Highlands are nearly uninhabited. Only in recent years have trails been blazed and new settlements founded, chiefly in those areas with economic potential.

Venezuela enjoys a tropical climate: it is uniformly hot and humid the year round. The dry season, when temperatures are slightly lower, runs from December to April. Temperatures drop

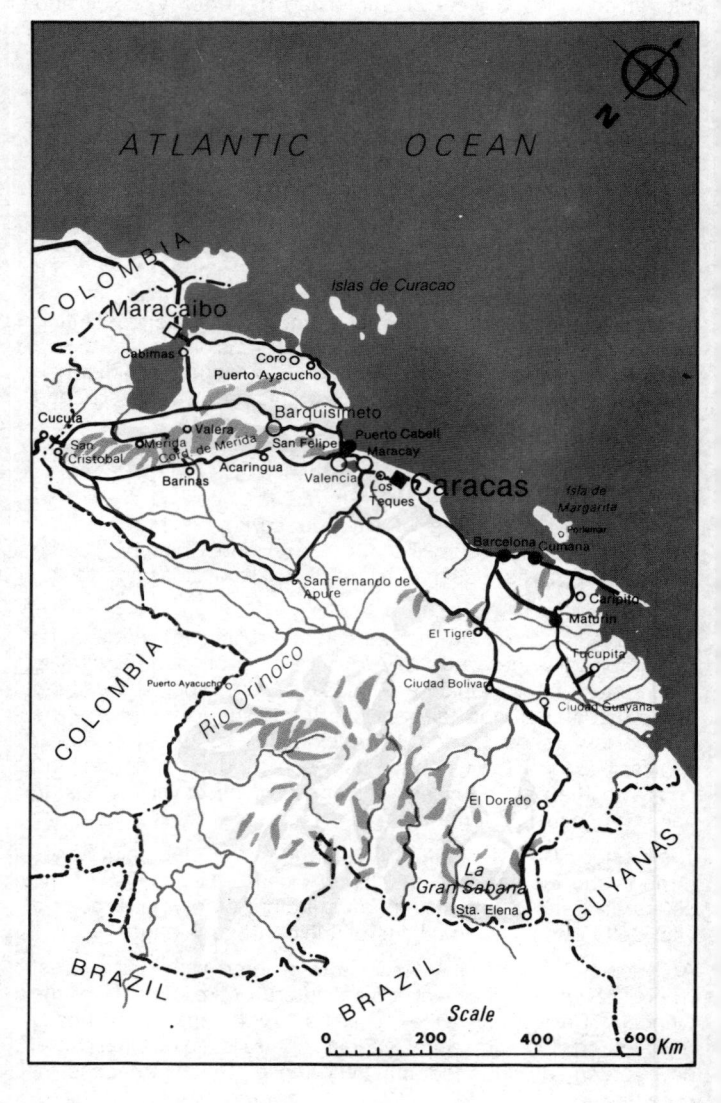

VENEZUELA

VENEZUELA

VENEZUELA

considerably at night and in the transition from sunlight to shade. The mountain regions are cooler than along the coast.

Population and government

The population of Venezuela numbers 14 million, of which more than half are children. A significant percentage of native Venezuelans are of mixed Spanish-Indian blood, with only 20% of European descent. However, since World War II, hundreds of thousands of Europeans have immigrated to enjoy the economic boom. (Today, every sixth Venezuelan was born elsewhere.)

Venezuela is a highly urbanized country due to its topography; with some 75% of its population as city-dwellers. The flight from farm to city has created severe social and economic problems. The cities cannot provide sufficient employment and housing, and tens of thousands live in slums that surround every city's downtown area. Close to half the population of Caracas – about 1,500,000 people – live in these shanty-towns called *barrios*, raising their children amid rife unemployment and crime.

Though the country's educational system is growing constantly, 19% of the population is still illiterate and less than 3% of all Venezuelans acquire a university education.

Presidential elections are held in Venezuela every five years; the minimum voting age is 18. Election campaigns are intense, and the public is very politically active. Apart from the President, 52 senators and 213 representatives are elected from constituencies.

Spanish is the dominant language in Venezuela, though other European languages are also widely spoken. The dominant faith in Venezuela is Roman Catholicism.

Economy

The economy of Venezuela is complex and problematic. Since the economic boom commenced, vast resources have been diverted to developing cities, roads, energy projects, and the expansion of public services. The national economy has come to rely on oil revenues, which account for more than 90% of exports and provide some 80% of the government budget. Meanwhile, industrial and agricultural diversification have been neglected.

Since 1982, Venezuela has been facing an economic crisis which threatens not only its economic stability but also its democratic regime. A sharp fall in petroleum sales and prices, a foreign debt of some $30 billion and the government's inability to restrain its expenses have caused an unprecendented flight of capital – estimated at $15 billion in 1982 alone! Most of that

VENEZUELA

money has found its way to banks in the United States and Europe, where Venezuela's wealthy have bank deposits and property. The country itself has had to plead with its creditor-banks for special extensions as it scrapes together funds for loan repayments.

The Venezuelan currency, the bolivar, is considered the most stable in Latin America and was once among the soundest in the world. In view of the difficulties of the mid 1980's, however, the Caracas government was compelled, for the first time in more than twenty years, to institute foreign-currency controls and to devalue the bolivar by about 100%. A system of multi-level exchange rates was introduced aimed at restraining imports, a step which caused the private sector considerable difficulties in paying off debts to non-Venezuelan creditors. As a result, external credit has also been reduced.

In Venezuela itself, the crisis is more evident in the social sphere than in the economic sphere. Unemployment runs at about 15% and the civil service – a tangled bureaucracy that employs about 25% of the workforce (1.2 million people) – has become less tolerant and more corrupt.

In an effort to restore economic equilibrium, billions of dollars have been invested to encourage agriculture, which at present employs only 16% of the workforce and provides less than half of Venezuela's food needs. Among other steps, special incentives are offered for building and developing factories in remote areas. All this, has not been enough and the import of food and essential goods still imposes a heavy burden on the economy. On January 1, 1976, all oil wells were nationalized and are now run by a special corporation established for that purpose. Exports are dwindling, due to the world oil crisis and the fact that Venezuelan oil is low in quality and high in pollutants. These circumstances have spurred the government to develop alternative industries mainly in eastern Venezuela, around Ciudad Guayana. This area has become a bustling provincial center, for iron, steel and aluminium industries.

General Information

How to get there

By air: Most airlines fly to Caracas from Europe. Air France, Alitalia, Iberia, British Caledonian, KLM, TAP and Lufthansa all fly from their respective capitals. Viasa, the Venezuelan national airline, flies to destinations in all major European countries.

From the United States, Pan American, Delta, Varig and Viasa all have daily direct flights to Caracas. At times, it may be cheaper to use certain South American carriers to reach Colombia even though they are routed through their respective

VENEZUELA

capitals. The flight takes a little more than four hours from New York and about two and a half hours from Miami.

South and Central American countries and the Caribbean Islands are serviced daily by Viasa or other national airlines. BWIA and Aeropostal fly to Trinidad. Pan American flights between the United States and Buenos Aires or Rio de Janeiro stop over in Caracas en route. You must pay a $4.50 departure tax when leaving Venezuela; passengers in transit for less than seventy-two hours are exempt.

By land: The most convenient overland route to Venezuela from Colombia is via the coastal highway from Barranquilla. To reach San Cristobal in Venezuela (for those coming from Bogota), pass through Cordillera Oriental from the Colombian city of Cucuta. From Brazil, a more difficult, complicated route passes from Manaus via Boa Vista to Santa Elena (see "Ciudad Guayana: Southward to Brazil").

Documents

Most tourists are required to obtain a visa prior to arriving in Venezuela at any Venezuelan consulate. Upon arrival at the border, a tourist card will be issued. A tourist card is good for a sixty-day stay in Venezuela and may be extended for another sixty days in the Immigration Office in Caracas. If you come by car, you'll need to present a permit from a Venezuelan consulate, registration and title papers, and a valid driver's license. Be sure to carry your passport at all times! Due to massive illegal immigration, the local police are strict and conduct searches.

When to visit: holidays and festivals

The weather is stable most of the year with the dry season running from December through April. The national holidays are January 1, May 1, July 5 (Independence Day), July 24 (Bolivar's Birthday), October 12 (Colombus Day), November 1 (All-Saints' Day), December 24-25 and December 31. There are additional bank holidays.

Accommodation

Hotels in Venezuela are clean, tidy and safe – but expensive. There are almost no cheap hotels or pensions and visitors arriving from the Andean countries are certainly in for a shock. Big city hotels are of no lower quality than their American or European counterparts, though service is not always top-grade. Camping is acceptable **only** in uninhabited areas. The coastal strip offers a long series of luxury hotels and rather expensive resorts. Most hotels accept credit cards.

Food and drink

The economic boom gave rise to hundreds of excellent restaurants with international menus. Venezuelan restaurants

VENEZUELA

are by no means inexpensive; add a 10% service charge to the bill along with a tip of equal size. Most restaurants accept credit cards and all, by law, must display a menu and price list outside their door. Inexpensive meals are available at *fuentes de soda*, kiosks found on every street corner. The most popular foods, Italian and Spanish, are available at stands and local eateries.

Breakfast and lunch are generally served at the usual hours, while dinner is late – between 9pm and 11pm. Most restaurants are closed on Sundays or Mondays. Due to the proliferation and diversity of restaurants you'll have little trouble in finding something that appeals to your taste, but we recommend that you try a number of the local specialties. These may be found at local food stands and in the Creole restaurants. Beef comes first. Venezuelans are used to the same cuts of meat as those of Argentina and to similar sized portions. Almost every restaurant serves the popular *lomito* and *parrilla*, beef filled with rice or with French fries. The *parrilla* sold at stands consists of pieces of grilled beef served shish kebab style and is excellent. Most restaurants serve instead of, or in addition to bread, *arepas* – a popular local cornflour roll, crisp on the outside and incredibly soft on the inside. At the stands, you can order *arepas tostadas* – cornflour rolls filled with meat, vegetables and more – superb! *Hervido* is a local meat-and-vegetable soup and *sancocho* is a ragout of meat and local vegetables (including *yuka*, a type of sweet potato). *Hallaca* is another popular dish – a mixture of beef or chicken with onion, vegetables and spices, wrapped in banana leaves and steamed.

To all this, add the mouth-watering *empanada* – filled with cheese or meat, vegetables, and spices. And don't forget the pizza, pasta, cake, ice cream, and wonderful and exotic fruits – pineapple, papaya, strawberries, and others.

Currency
The local currency is the bolivar, marked BS (the locals pronounce it "bess"). Common banknotes are ten, twenty, fifty, one hundred and five hundred bolivars.

Until early 1982, Venezuela was one of the most expensive tourist countries. However, since the devaluation, it has become far more attractive to visitors. Today the U.S. dollar is exchanged at the "free rate", the highest of the three exchange rates in force. Change your money at a bank, or at a **casa de cambio** where there is less red tape. Traveler's checks and credit cards are very common and are eagerly accepted.

Business hours
Banks are open from 8:30am-4:30pm, with a siesta from noon till 2pm. Government offices are open to the public at irregular

VENEZUELA

hours, but always only in the mornings. Shops and offices are open from 8am-6pm with a short midday siesta.

Domestic transportation

Aeropostal and Avensa fly between all of Venezuela's large cities. Though the flights are short and convenient, they are generally full. We recommend that you make reservations as early as possible and confirm them 24 hours before departure time. It's best to reach the airport two hours before your planned departure. The timetables are not reliable, so check by phone whether your flight has been delayed. I once flew Aeropostal from Caracas to Trinidad on a flight that was supposed to leave at 7am. I got up early, reached the airport a little after 5am, only to discover the flight had been delayed until 1:30pm. Furthermore, I was told when seeking to reserve a seat that the flight was fully booked and that I'd have to wait on standby. In the end the plane took off with only seven passengers. Such is the nature of air transport in Venezuela...

Students are entitled to a discount on internal flights through the ONTEJ student organization (see "Caracas: Tourist services").

Comfortable buses ply the modern highways which link the large cities and destinations can be reached speedily and more cheaply than by air. Some lines, especially the coastal ones, run modern buses. Others, especially in the mountain areas and the Guyana Highland industrial cities, use old and uncomfortable buses. In addition, taxis, known as *por puesto* are available – these are faster but costlier.

Avis, Hertz and local companies rent cars – all late-model Fords – at the Caracas airport, in Caracas itself or in other cities. Although the intercity speed limit is only 80 kph and most of these roads are of high quality (dirt roads are not lacking), road trouble is commonplace.

Measurements, electricity, and time

The metric system is used. Electricity is 110 volts. The local time is 4 hours behind GMT.

Caracas

Caracas (pop. 4 million) accurately reflects the results of the great boom. A modern, bustling downtown area is packed with skyscrapers, plazas, parks and public buildings. A superb road system, the most advanced in South America, serves the city and its suburbs, and thousands of cars, mostly large North American models, crowd them day and night. Shopping centers,

VENEZUELA

Plaza Venezuela - view towards Sabana Grande

giant stores and sport and entertainment centers all adorn the city.

Elsewhere in Caracas poverty, want, unemployment and crime abound – the seamier side of life in the gleaming metropolis. There is a constant stream of people from the rural countryside to the urban centers – all moving toward the city in search of a better future. This has given birth to slums where hundreds of thousands live in unbearable conditions in the shadow of all the opulence which is beyond their reach.

Generally, Caracas is not a pleasant city. The atmosphere is cold and estranged. Local residents, the *Caraquenos*, will usually treat you as nicely as they have to, but no better. The rising crime rate has led most *Caraquenos* to sequester themselves in their homes by early evening, and in the residential quarters it's rare to see anyone strolling about after dark. By contrast, downtown, in **Sabana Grande** and the entertainment centers, the city remains alive and bubbling well into the small hours of the night.

Climate

Almost 1000 m above sea level, Caracas enjoys a temperate climate. Its elevation and distance from the coast (20-45 km) contribute to its coolness and moderate the influence of the harsh tropical climate. Average temperatures range from 30 degrees Centigrade or 86 degrees Fahrenheit in summer (July August) to 9 degrees Centigrade or 48 degrees Fahrenheit in

VENEZUELA

winter (January-February). Warm rain falls mainly in the summer, and wet clothes can become sticky and unpleasant. Due to the heat, clothing begins to "give off steam" but dries within minutes after the rain has stoped. Synthetic fabrics will prove unpleasant; light cotton clothing is best. Shorts are not acceptable attire and weaing them on the street is liable to cost you dearly – it's against the law and the police issue fines.

How to get there

By air: Caracas' modern **Simon Bolivar Airport** is 30 km out of town. Immigration, customs and currency exchange procedures are quick and easy. The airport Tourist Information Office will provide you with information, maps, and even assist in making hotel reservations. The international car-rental firms have airport offices. The facility does not offer a baggage-checking service – a considerable inconvenience, particularly for transit passengers. Next to the Simon Bolivar Airport is Caracas' old airfield, **Maiquetia**, used for domestic flights. A special bus leaves every half hour from the airports to Parque Central, the bus terminal at the foot of the downtown Caracas Hilton. Parque Central is rather isolated and can be unpleasant after dark, and from there we recommend taking a taxi straight to your hotel. A taxi from the airport into Caracas costs more than $20 and the trip on the Autopista (freeway) la Guaira, takes close to an hour depending on traffic. Buses marked **Catia la Mar** head for the airport from Parque Central every half hour. Arrive early.

By land: Buses to and from Colombia, Guyana, and various Venezuelan cities generally use the Nuevo Circo Central Bus Terminal, where a Tourist Information office is located. It's advisable to make reservations several days before departure, particularly if you intend to travel on a holiday or weekend. When booking an intercity trip, you must present a passport. Taxi service also runs between cities.

Where to stay

Most Caracas hotels are rather expensive in comparison to those in the United States or Europe, and much more so than those elsewhere in Latin America. Caracas, unlike other South American cities has almost no cheap pensions or hostels, and it is hard to find rooms in the cheaper hotels. For intermediate class hotels we highly recommend reservations. Make them at the airport, if not from your country of departure. Wandering through Caracas with your luggage is liable to be exhausting and unpleasant, especially after nightfall. A concentration of relatively inexpensive hotels along Avenida Las Acacias in Sabana Grande allows you to go from one to another in search

VENEZUELA

of a room. This is the best area to stay in, both in terms of price and location. Caracas' best hotel is the *Intercontinental Tamanaco* (Tel. 914–555) in the Las Mercedes quarter away from downtown. This very elegant hotel has restaurants, art galleries, a swimming pool, offices and more. Reservations must be made at least two months in advance. The two Hiltons - the *Hilton Caraca* (Tel. 571–2322) and the *HIlton Anauco* (Tel. 573–4111), one beside the other, are similar in price (the latter is slightly less expensive). They are more conveniently located than the Tamanaco, and are especially suitable for businessmen.

Less expensive hotels are the *Crillon* on Avenida Las Acacias (Tel. 714-411) and the *Tampa* on Avenida Solano Lope (Tel. 723-711), both in Sabana Grande. The Hotel Tampa is slightly less expensive and its rooms are spacious and the service good. Recommended for businessmen. For the more budget-minded (as much as one can be in Caracas), we can recommend the *Hotel Myriam*, also on Las Acacias in Sabana Grande. For those with a tight budget, this seems to be the most suitable hotel – clean, very centrally located, comfortable, and (relatively) inexpensive.

A final tip – a new association of inexpensive hotels and hostelries has lately come into being. They'll give you information about inexpensive places to stay in Caracas and elsewhere in the country (Tel. 752-3135).

What to eat, when and where

As in Buenos Aires, here too I abandon any pretentions of compiling a list of the best restaurants. Unlike other South American cities, where the best eateries could be chosen with no great difficulty, the Venezuelan and Argentinian capitals have such high standards and offer such a large variety, that to try to list them all would be futile. Changes are so frequent that an "in" place would be "out" and a superbly grilled steak would become steak tartare before my ink had dried.

Here are a number of hints to help you choose, what, where, and how expensively to eat. First, all hotels (intermediate and upwards) have at least one restaurant, while the genuinely elegant offer two or three. Though I'm not a great fan of eating in hotels – whose function, in my opinion, is to keep rain off people's heads and not to provide gastronomical delights – a number of Caracas hotel restaurants are certainly commendable, though not as bargain selections. For more economical eating it's best to stroll through Sabana Grande, especially the main boulevard shopping centers where you'll find cafeterias, hamburger stands, kiosks and cafes. Prices at the latter are liable to be very high since they are considered more prestigious. Elsewhere you can eat in a much less elegant,

VENEZUELA

though no less satisfying, atmosphere. The Sabana Grande area is full of diverse places to eat, and it's a nice place to explore at any hour.

You'll find Chinese restaurants around Avenida Naiguata, most of which are relatively inexpensive. Most good restaurants charge lower prices in the afternoons, when a standard three-course fixed-price meal called *menu* or *cubierto* is served. As to what exactly to order – see the Introduction on "Food and drink".

Transportation

The modern subway – Line 1, leading to Chacaito, which began operating early in 1983 – is the fastest, quietest, most convenient and pleasant alternative to surface transit. The latter consists chiefly of noisy, crowded, buses, moving slowly, with poorly marked stops and irregular "schedules". Most buses depart from the Nuevo Circo Terminal. Try to avoid them. The taxis, which will stop at a wave of a hand, are faster and less problematic for finding your way around the city.

Taxi fares are metered; add 20% after 10pm and on Sundays and holidays. Taxis are hard to find in the downtown area and it's best to get one at the stands. Driving in Caracas is not recommended. The city's tangled traffic, congestion and complicated street system – the bright signs don't elucidate it sufficiently for a foreigner – all combine to make driving a harrowing experience. Nonetheless, experience has taught me that one learns the rules of the road here within a day or two, after several wasted kilometers, getting off at the wrong interchanges, etc. Rental cars, not for those on a limited budget, are available at Avis (Tel. 719-451), Budget (Tel. 283-0023), National (Tel. 782-5202) and Hertz (Tel. 715-332 or 727-255). All have airport branches (the above phone numbers are for their city offices).

Due to problems of congestion, all cars are forbidden to enter Caracas one day a week, according to the final license plate digit. When renting a car, remember to verify the day on which its movement is restricted.

Tourist services

The central Tourist Office, **Corpoturismo,** is located in Centro Capriles on Plaza Venezuela (Tel. 782-5911). It has a great deal of explanatory material and information, and a hotel reservation service for other Venezuelan cities. Corpoturismo has branches at the airport and the bus terminal.

Good maps may be purchased at gasoline stations. *Adonde Vamos*, a magazine available free of charge at the hotels, has information on shopping, entertainment, restaurants as well as

VENEZUELA

maps. The English-language *Caracas Daily Journal* is a good reference source for up-to-date information on entertainment and restaurants.

A new reservation service for inexpensive hotels and pensions is now available (see "Where to stay"). For other tourist services, contact Caracas' various travel agencies, some of which are located around Plaza Venezuela. The **Viasa** offices are not far from Plaza Venezuela, near the Tourist Office.

ONTEJ, an ISSTA-like students' organization which offers tourist services to holders of valid student cards, is located at Parque Central in the Catuche Building (Tel. 573-3722 or 572-7621). They'll help you with thrifty tourism options, and offer significant discounts (up to 50%) on flights within Venezuela and occasionally to the surrounding countries. ONTEJ offers holiday and tourist packages to the Carribbean and elsewhere.

Venezuela's auto club – *Touring y Automovil Club de Venezuela* – is located in the Auto Commercial Building on Plaza Altamira Sur (Tel. 324-108/9). Maps and information concerning recommended travel routes and service stations, are available here.

Tourist sites

Little remains of the Caracas built by Diego de Losada and his fellow founding fathers in 1567, or of the city built by the Spaniards who followed. The city center, in the Plaza Bolivar area, has been redone into a packed agglomeration of office and commercial towers. Traces of the past in Caracas are hard to find; the compulsive drive for "progress" seems to dominate. Visitors will find a humming cosmopolitan city which displays the whole gamut of urban ailments – slums, filth, air pollution and traffic jams. It is however, at the same time, a fascinating city. New buildings were designed by creative architects who enjoyed free artistic rein and innovative construction methods that would have certainly been rejected by many a city council were encouraged and supported here. The results speak for themselves: dozens of imposing ultra-modern buildings made of concrete, steel and glass.

Index
1) Chacaito Commercial Center
2) Plaza Venezuela
3) University City
4) Los Caobos Park
5) Botanical Gardens
6) Museo de Bellas Artes
7) Parque Central
8) Central Bus Terminal
9) Plaza Bolivar
10) Municipal Cathedral
11) El Capitolio (Congress Bldg.)
12) El Panteon Nacional
13) Museum of Colonial Art

CARACAS

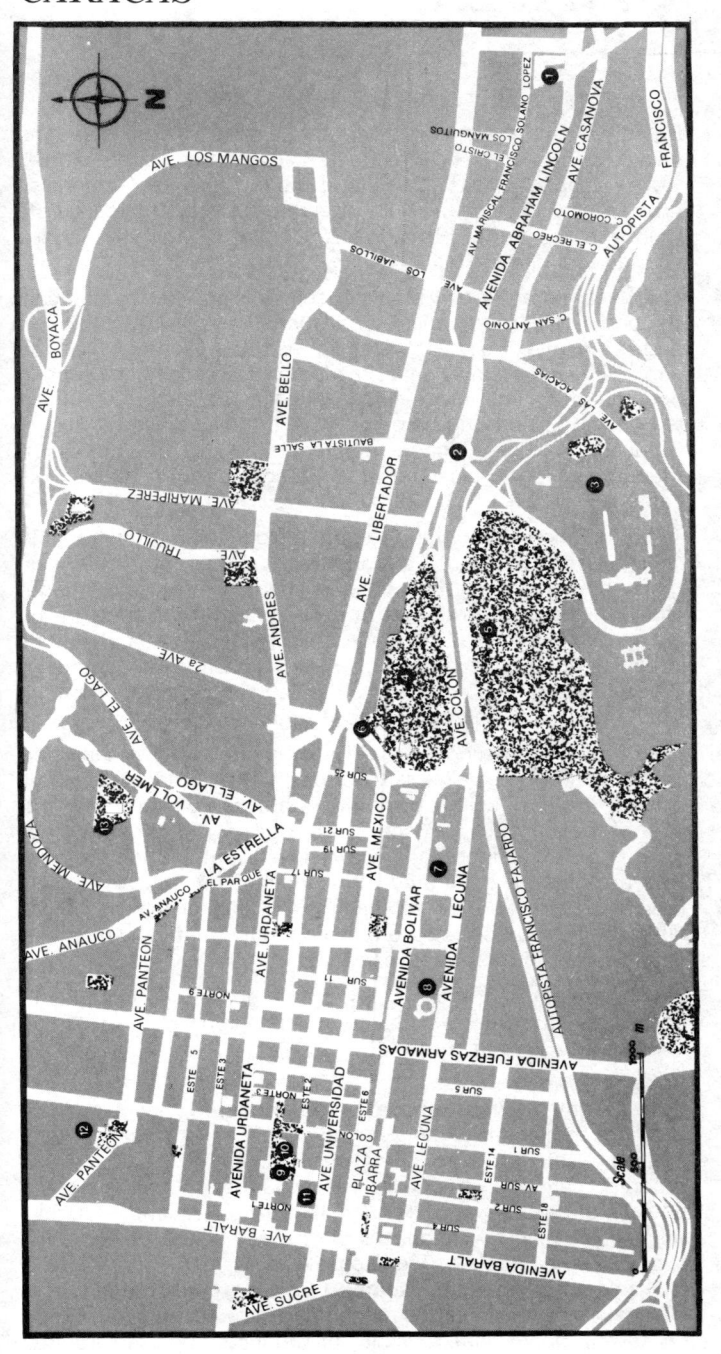

VENEZUELA

Enormous sums were invested in Caracas' magnificent and showy buildings, new streets, multi-lane expressways, well-developed plazas, parks and more. The latest grandiose urban renewal plan is the building of the subway. The results are visible in the lovely Plaza Venezuela, the revitalized Sabana Grande and elsewhere.

The best vantage point for an encompassing view of Caracas, trapped in the Muarnac Valley between Monte Avila to the north and the gentler slopes to the south, is atop **Monte Avila**. The cablecar (*teleferico*) from the Mariperez station has not been in operation for some years, so the only way to reach the summit is to climb it. From up here you have a totally different view of Caracas: a homogeneous concrete block of impressive proportions, with clusters of buildings protruding from its center.

To the left, notice the grand El Este residential quarter, home to only the very wealthy. It abounds with multi-story residences, green boulevards and prestigious shopping centers. Straight ahead is the downtown area, between Sabana Grande to the east and Plaza Bolivar to the west. To the right, Catia, the city's industrial zone can vaguely be seen. Rich tropical vegetation covers Monte Avila and on the summit a restaurant, a roller-skating rink and sports facilities are found.

Most of the interesting sites in Caracas itself are concentrated in the center of the valley, laid out one after another like a spinal column. We shall survey downtown Caracas from east to west, one attraction after another, straying only briefly in other directions. Remember that distances are great and that one site may at times be separated from another not only by several kilometers but also by several main traffic arteries that are difficult, if not impossible, to cross on foot. Most museums and national shrines are closed on Mondays.

We shall begin from the eastern end of the Sabana Grande, an entertainment center which, due to the subway project, has been given a new image.

Sabana Grande

Until the late 1970s, Sabana Grande suffered the plagues of bustling commercial centers; traffic congestion, air pollution, peeling plaster and so on. The subway and urban renewal program changed the area entirely. Sabana Grande's main boulevard became a pedestrian mall (repaved and tastefully illuminated), lined with dozens of coffee houses, restaurants, shops, movie theaters, ice cream parlors, and more. At the mall's eastern end is the **Chacaito Commercial Center**, one of Caracas' largest. Hundreds of magnificent, well designed shops on several floors offer a wealth of products imported from all

VENEZUELA

over the world. This is also the end of subway Line 1 and thousands of people flock out of its tunnel onto the promenade and disappear into surrounding offices and businesses.

A stroll through Sabana Grande is one of the best-loved *Caraqueno* pastimes, and the boulevard is packed day and night. The coffee houses are crowded at almost any hour with people engrossed in conversation over coffee, beer, or milk shakes. Stroll down the mall to the western end to **Plaza Venezuela**. The impressive plaza (one of the city's loveliest), with its central fountain illuminated at night by colored spotlights, is surrounded by a number of high-rise office buildings, the first skyscrapers built in Caracas. The Tourist Office and the Aeropostal offices are located here.

Before proceeding westward to Parque Los Caobos, turn left for a moment to the modern Ciudad Universitario – University City. Note that all the crowded freeways are hard to cross; so access to the university is easier through the park.

Ciudad Universitaria

"University city" is a prime example of modern architectural development, with acre upon acre of unusual concrete buildings interspersed with works of modern art that serve both ornamental and practical needs. Tens of thousands of students, lecturers, workers and staff members – throng the enormous campus every day. Nearby, a bit to the west, are the huge **Botanical Gardens**, boasting a large collection of plant species from all over the world.

Parque Los Caobos

One of Caracas' jewels, a green enclave amidst the mountains of concrete, is the Los Caobos (mahogany tree) Park. It lies sandwiched between Plaza Venezuela and the giant Parque Central building complex. The concrete walkways, stone buildings and paved plazas in its midst, fail to mar the vitality of the exquisite park, which is also graced by works of art throughout its grounds.

At the park's western end is **Museo de Bellas Artes** (Fine Arts Museum), one of the loveliest of its kind in Latin America (second to the one in Buenos Aires). The museum, housed in an impressive building, has a rich collection of European and Oriental art, alongside a wide range of Venezuelan art works from various periods. The spacious exhibition halls and the ramps between the floors add to the quiet and serene atmosphere which envelops its visitors. Highly recommended. Open Tues.-Fri. 9am-noon and 3-5:30pm, Sat.-Sun. 10am-5pm. Closed Mondays. Tel. 571-1813.

Stop by next door at the **Museo de Ciencias Naturales** (Museum of Natural History) for a look at it's collection of stuffed

VENEZUELA

Parque Los Caobos

animals and archeological finds. Visiting hours are the same as for the Fine Arts Museum.

Across from the museums, but still within the park, is the **Teresa Carreno Cultural Complex,** housing theaters, concert halls and the like. From here we cross a special pedestrian bridge to our next destination.

Parque Central

Perhaps the most impressive structure in Caracas is Parque Central, at the end of Avenida Bolivar and across the street from Parque Los Caobos. Construction of this complex, whose towers soar 56 stories skyward, began in the mid-1960s at the peak of the "boom". Plans call for its ultimate development into one of the world's largest residential complexes (designed for some 10,000 people). The current economic doldrums have, however, prevented its completion. Even as it stands today Parque Central is undoubtedly a considerable edifice. It not only houses hundreds of offices and shops, but also a luxurious convention center, museums, the Anauco Hilton Apartment Hotel and much more. While strolling along the various floors of the giant building and wandering about its hundreds of corridors, staircases, elevators, gardens and so on, you'll feel its city-within-a-city atmosphere. Everything seems to be at arm's reach – there's no need to abandon the air-conditioning for the noisy, sweaty city.

Parque Central has four museums – **Museo de los Ninos** (children), **Museo de Instrumentos del Teclado** (music), which

VENEZUELA

are in the same building, **Museo Audiovisual** and **Museo de Arte Contemporaneo** (modern art). The latter displays an exhaustive collection of primarily 20th-century Venezuelan and foreign artists. Recommended. Open Tues.-Fri. noon-7pm; Sat. and Sun. 11am-7pm. Closed Mondays.

Centro Simon Bolivar

Continuing from Parque Central westward, along the broad Avenida Bolivar or on one of the parallel streets, we pass the Nuevo Circo Bus Terminal and arrive at the twin towers of Centro Simon Bolivar.

Centro Bolivar was erected in the 1950s and reflects the prosperity which then reigned in Caracas. Avenida Bolivar lined with parking lots, restaurants, stores and offices on either side passes under the thirty-story towers. The center is surrounded by important public buildings: to the left (looking from Parque Central) is the **Basilica de San Pedro,** followed by the **National Theater** and one block further, the **Municipal Theater** and **Plaza Miranda.** To the right (the north) is the **Church of San Francisco,** one of the few buildings surviving from the 16th century, worth noting for its design and impressive wood carvings. Beside it is the **National Library,** housed in what was once the University. The National Library, which faces the Capitol, contains hundreds of thousands of volumes, some of them centuries old.

We now turn right onto Calle San Francisco and two blocks up, we reach the historical center of Caracas – Plaza Bolivar.

Plaza Bolivar

Handsome trees shade the equestrian statue of the liberator in the heart of the attractive square bearing his name. Although the nerve center of Caracas has shifted elsewhere, Plaza Bolivar is still the heart of town in the eyes of many, and Venezuelans look upon it with great affection. In its eastern corner is the **Municipal Cathedral**, built in 1595 but restored about a hundred years ago after having been destroyed in an earthquake. The cathedral has a wooden altar, impressive carvings and several paintings by Rubens. Across the way is a reconstruction of Bolivar's birthplace – **Casa Natal de Simon Bolivar** – displaying many belongings from his youth, military service and personal life. The Colonial-style house reflects the appearance of Caracas about two hundred years ago, and gives an idea of the interior layout, furniture and other items typical of the local aristocracy of the time. The **Museo Bolivar** next door has an exhibit of artifacts and documents from the period of struggle for independence. Both the house and museum are open daily, except Monday.

Still on the Plaza, we come to the city hall – **Concejo Municipal**

VENEZUELA

which houses a museum of Caracas' history on its ground floor. The city's past is depicted here through miniature houses and streets. Various artifacts dating from the earliest period, maps, flags and more are also on display. Across the square is **Casa Amarilla**, site of the Foreign Ministry and of a Venezuelan art exhibition.

At Plaza Bolivar's southwest corner is the Congress Building, **El Capitolio**, which was built in 1873 – in only 114 days! Its golden dome shelters a beautiful tropical garden along with the offices. Dozens of portraits of national heroes are on display in **Salon Eliptico**. Look at the ceiling which has scenes from the War of Independence depicting battles against the Spanish painted by Venezuelan artist Martin Tovar y Tovar.

Additional sites

In addition to the sites surveyed thus far (in geographical order), a number of other important and recommended places to visit, dispersed throughout Caracas, must not be overlooked.

Heading north up Avenida Norte from Plaza Bolivar to the old La Pastora quarter, we reach the National Pantheon – **El Panteon Nacional** (The Pantheon). It was founded in 1874 in memory of Venezuela's heroes and fallen soldiers, and Simon Bolivar is buried here.

The Museum of Colonial Art is located on Avenida Panteon in San Bernardino, a placid residential quarter in Caracas's north between Avenida Urdaneta and the slopes of Monte Avila. The gorgeous colonial-era building, dating from 1720, houses a fascinating collection of paintings, furniture, books and other displays from the Colonial period. All are attractively arranged and reflect the spirit of the period. Like the other museums, it's closed on Mondays. Tel. 518-517. Highly recommended.

Cuadra Bolivar is a reconstruction of the house in which Simon Bolivar spent his youth. It is located six blocks south of Centro Bolivar. Closed Monday.

Miraflores is the President's Palace where the affairs of state are conducted. The lovely 19th-century building, four blocks west of Plaza Bolivar and parallel to Avenida Urdaneta, is open to visitors on Sundays only by previous arrangement.

Parque del Este, an expansive park at Caracas' eastern extremity offers playgrounds, artificial lakes, lawns, sports fields and more. Closed Monday.

Parque Los Proceres is located on Avenida Los Proceres in Santa Monica. Dedicated to Caracas' and Venezuela's founding fathers, it boasts well-tended gardens, benches, statues, fountains and more. Impressive and interesting.

VENEZUELA

Entertainment
Caracas blossoms at night throughout the week but even more so on weekends. Cinemas are open around the clock. The Municipal Theater, south of Centro Bolivar, has performances (in Spanish) almost every evening as well as ballet, opera and concerts by local and foreign artists. Sunday morning concerts are often held at the Municipal Theater and in Plaza Bolivar.

The liveliest after-dark activities take place in nightclubs, bars and discotheques. Just walk around the Sabana Grande pedestrian mall for a taste of drinking, eating and talking in the coffee houses. A bit farther on, toward Plaza Venezuela, you'll find the popular discotheque *Reflections*. Continuing to the Chacaito commercial center, you'll reach the *La Eva* discotheque (in the basement) and the *Hipocampo* nightclub. Avenida Venezuela in El Rosal has a "strip" of clubs, bars and discotheques such as the *Juan Sebastian Bar* and *Memories* discotheque. There's another "strip" around Plaza Altamira Sur which is recommended.

Sports
Caracas offers a selection of sports events which are exceptional in South America. There are numerous sports facilities for almost every imaginable sport – soccer, tennis, golf, boxing, and more. Soccer matches are held in the university stadium. **La Rinconada**, Caracas' elegant racetrack, has exciting photo-finish races. *Caraquenos* are sports-minded and many are members in a variety of private sport and recreation clubs. The seashore abounds in water-sports clubs – fishing, sailing, diving and more. Equipment may be rented at the Macuto Sheraton. Many beaches are privately owned and used by the city's wealthy for weekend recreation.

Banking and currency exchange
Caracas' many banks (branches can be found around town) have morning and afternoon hours and exchange money at a fluctuating rate (see Introduction "General Information"). The exchange process is somewhat exhausting and can be handled far more simply at private moneychangers, along the Sabana Grande pedestrian mall.

Postal and telephone service
The Venezuelan mail and telephone services, like most government services, are slow and complicated. A letter sent to Venezuela from Europe or the United States (and vice versa), takes a few weeks (sometimes more than a month) to reach its destination. Mail your letters from a post office, and not from a mailbox in town; you can grow old waiting for some of those mail boxes to be emptied.

VENEZUELA

Parcels up to 10 kilos can be mailed from post offices. There is usually no problem sending parcels from Venezuela by surface mail.

The international telephone service is operated by the CANTAV government corporation whose offices are in the El Silencio building on the west side of Caracas (branches in Centro Simon Bolivar and in the Miranda Building on the east side). It's very expensive to call from Venezuela, but the quality of the connection is satisfactory. Waiting for a call can also take rather a long time. Discount rates to certain countries, the United States among them, are in effect evenings and Sundays.

From a private phone one can call abroad directly. Dial 109 for "directory assistance".

Shopping

Caracas is generally the best place in Venezuela for shopping.

If you're on the way to other South American countries, save time and money and shop there. If you're returning from those countries, you've certainly bought everything you can possibly carry. If you are visiting only Venezuela and find it hard to go home empty-handed, you'll have to shell out for some rather kitsch souvenirs. Except for gold jewelry, Venezuela as a country offers a tourist little that is worthwhile or unique.

Nevertheless, take the time to walk through Caracas' modern shopping centers, among the most modern in the world. There are hundreds of shops offering an abundance of goods of every type, imported from all over the world.

Important addresses

First aid: Tel.283-9733

Ambulance: 454545

Police: 169

U.S. Embassy: Av. Francisco de Miranda and Av. Principal de la Floresta. Tel. 248-7111.

British Embassy: Edificio Torre Las Mercedes, Av. La Estancia, Centro Ciudad Comercial, Tamanaco, Chuao Caracas. Tel. 911-255 or 911-077.

Tourist Office (Corpoturismo):Plaza Venezuela, Centro Capriles. Tel.782-5911.

Touring y Automovil Club de Venezuela: Auto Commercial building, Plaza Altamira Sur. Tel. 324-108.

VENEZUELA

Excursions

The Beaches

Given Caracas' summer weather, ocean bathing is the most popular weekend activity. On those days it seems that the entire city empties into the blue waters. **El Litoral**, past Monte Avila, offers a handsome strip of shore although its most beautiful sections are closed to the public. Located here are the exclusive private clubs, among them the famous **Playa Azul, Playa Grande** and **Camuri Chico**. The area may be reached by bus or taxi (*por puestos*). Both depart every few minutes from every part of town.

The beach at **Macuto** is one of the most popular, but neglect and dirt have turned this town, once the favorite stamping ground of Caracas' wealthy, into a seedy, graceless place. Rental equipment for sailing, fishing and diving are available at the Macuto Sheraton. Continuing eastward, we come to **Naiguata**, where the beach is also rather dirty.

A few hours on the road heading west from Caracas will bring you to far more tranquil cities which have clean and enchanting beaches. North of Maracay are two beautiful and popular beaches, **Ocumara de la Costa** and **Cata**. From Maracay you may set out for nearby **Lake Valencia**. About 100 km west of Caracas is the industrial port town of Puerto Cabello. Several of Venezuela's most beautiful and well-tended beaches lie to its west.

Isla Margarita

Isla Margarita, east of Caracas, is a popular resort. Its 90,000 inhabitants make a living chiefly from the sea and from tourism. Most devote their weekends and holidays to serving the thousands of tourists who flood **Porlamar**, the largest town (pop. 25,000) on the island.

Isla Margarita has kilometer after kilometer of pristine beach, wonderful weather, good restaurants, comfortable hotels and good bargains. As a duty-free zone, luxury goods are available at low prices. The most popular beach is palm-shaded **El Agua**, north of Porlamar and easy to reach by bus or hitchhiking. On the island's west side is **Golfo de Juan Griego**, famous for its gorgeous sunsets. Tourism on Isla Margarita has developed rapidly in recent years. New hotels have been built, beaches developed and roads paved – all to create a tourist resort similar to the nearby Caribbean Islands.

A one-hour flight and $100 separate Margarita from Caracas and Aeropostal will be glad to help you overcome the former in

VENEZUELA

View on Margarita Island

exchange for the latter. If you intend to fly on weekends or during holiday periods, reservations should be made several weeks in advance. A less expensive way of reaching the islands is via the ferries which ply the sea lanes from the coastal cities of Puerto la Cruz and Cumana every day. They may be reached by bus or *por puesto* (7-8 hours). It's a wonderful place, with a taste of the Caribbean. Be sure to bring a sun-screen lotion to prevent sunburn.

Colonia Tovar

In 1843, a group of Bavarian emigrants founded a small town on the mountain slopes, 60 km from Caracas. Colonia Tovar has remained isolated from the rest of Venezuela and its descendants have preserved their Bavarian origins – language, dress, customs, food and architecture. Tovar, at 2000 m above sea level, enjoys wonderful weather. Its people, who speak the Black Forest German of their ancestors, are warm and friendly.

This picturesque town, which has a number of souvenir shops, good Bavarian restaurants, and quiet hotels, is recommended for a short visit. But stay away on weekends when it can be very crowded and the trip may take hours. Regular public transportation to Colonia Tovar is not available from Caracas, though *por puestos* do set out from time to time. The most convenient way to go is either to rent a car or to organize a small group and hire a taxi. Tovar is easier to reach from the town of El Junquito either by public transit or hitchhiking.

VENEZUELA

San Juan de los Morros

Only 150 km southwest of Caracas, on the edge of a broad plain covering hundreds of thousands of square kilometers between the Andes and the Orinoco are the **Llanos** ("plains"). This is the birthplace of Venezuelan folklore, folk music, song and dance. The cattle-raising **llaneros** ride their horses barefoot, leading their large herds over vast pasturelands. This flood-prone stretch of territory is totally submerged for months every year, driving cattle and cowboys to higher, drier ground.

The *llaneros* live exactly as their forebears did, decades or centuries ago. Cattle raising is a full-time job and the only recreation is quiet singing and joyous dancing. Most of the songs tell of village life and the nomadic cowboy's life on horseback. Lyre and *cuatro* (similar to a small guitar) provide the accompaniment.

San Juan de los Morros is the *llaneros'* town. Here they gather to rest and recuperate. They bathe up in the nearby hot springs, revel in the stormy *joropo* dance, and compete in rodeos. The atmosphere is almost like the set of an old movie, where the scent of bygone days delicately lingers on.

Buses set out for San Juan every day, via Maracay. The town has small hotels, restaurants and pleasant taverns.

Western Venezuela

Venezuela's western section is dominated to a great extent by Lake Maracaibo and the surrounding plains – the country's oil center. The other attraction is the picturesque mountain town of Merida which has integrated old and new to preserve a disappearing old-time charm. It also boasts a large university.

Maracaibo

It was only about sixty years ago that Maracaibo was a small provincial town of little importance. 20,000 people scraped out a living in the hot, humid climate from the export of coffee and other crops. Today Maracaibo is the second-largest city in Venezuela, (pop. 1 million) and is the heart of the country's oil industry.

Maracaibo rests on the northeastern shore of Lake Maracaibo, the largest lake in South America. It is 150 km in length, and stretches more than 100 km at its widest point, with a total surface area of 14,347 sq/km. A canal links it to the Gulf of Venezuela which empties into the Atlantic Ocean. Using this route, tens of thousands of barrels of petroleum set forth

VENEZUELA

worldwide every day, accounting for about 75% of Venezuela's total exports.

Lake Maracaibo, surrounded by broad plains, is pinned between mountain spurs to the east and west – both extensions of the eastern Andes (Cordillera Oriental) of Colombia. Its shores are pocked with thousands of oil derricks.

Maracaibo, approached by the enormous Ordante Bridge, is a busy oil city. Apart from the port area and the adjacent streets, where one may still find old houses, it is no different from any other industrial city.

As an important economic center, Maracaibo enjoys convenient transportation to and from Caracas both by air (1 hour) and via the Pan American Highway (10 hours). Good connections are available to most of Venezuela's other large cities as well as to the Caribbean Islands, Miami and New York.

Food and Lodging

Hotels in Maracaibo are rather expensive and reservations are recommended. The best and most expensive hotel in town is the *Hotel del Lago International*, which is situated on the lakeshore. It has a swimming pool, restaurant, bar and nightclub. *Kristof Hotel*, not quite as expensive, is situated on Avenida 8 in Santa Rita. *Roma Hotel* at Calle 86 is popular and reasonable in price. The hotel restaurant serves good Italian food. The *Yocambu Hotel* is on a similar level, clean and centrally located on Av. Liberdade.

The city offers good (expensive) restaurants and less inexpensive ones which serve light meals and snacks. *Chez Nicholas Restaurant* serves very good continental dishes. You will find good meat dishes at *Rincon Buricua Restaurant*, at Av. 23 between Calles 66 and 67. The most inexpensive restaurant is *Central Lunch* on 96th street.

Excursions in the area

The Lake Maracaibo area offers much more than drilling towns and oil rigs. North and west of the city itself live two Indian tribes, one southwest of Maracaibo and the second north of the city, mostly in Colombia.

The Motilones Tribe

A little more than three hours south of Maracaibo, on the expressway to San Cristobal, is the town of Machiques. This is the departure point for a visit to the Motilone Indian-settlements.

From the arrival of the Spanish, until the end of the 1950s, there was little cooperation between these Indians and the new

VENEZUELA

settlers. All offers of friendship were aggressively rejected. Had it not been for Venezuelans' urgent need to enter Indian territories in search of new drilling sites, these Indians might have been left alone to this day. However, after several years of bloody conflict, an agreement was reached and the Motilones are now a tranquil and friendly tribe.

The Motilones' villages are situated amidst the swamps, a good distance from Machinques. It can be reached on foot from one of the local monasteries.

Guajira Peninsula

North of Maracaibo, on the other side of the Gulf of Venezuela, lies the Guajira Peninsula. This is one of the few places where authentic Indian life can still be seen. Though most of the peninsula lies in Colombia, the close tribal relations on either side of the border make for simple and speedy crossing procedures.

There are buses from Maracaibo to various places on the peninsula and to Maicao, the Colombian border town. From Maicao you can continue to the peninsula villages (see "Personal Security" in our Introduction to Colombia!).

Here, in the Guajira villages, you'll encounter a vanishing world. The women, who dress in colorful canvas dresses called *manta*, keep house and support the family. The locals live in structures almost straight from Indian tales set at the onset of the Spanish conquest. Both men and women paint their faces and wear their traditional dress. A fascinating place to visit. From here you may proceed to Colombia.

From Maracaibo to Merida

The Maracaibo-Merida expressway – the Pan American Highway – runs first along Lake Maracaibo at the base of the mountains and then climbs steeply towards the city. There's an alternate route between the cities passing through the towns and villages located in the mountains themselves. On this route, be sure to visit Valera and Bocono (where the garden-enveloped houses are built on the steep mountainside), as well as the village of Timotes and the resort towns of La Mesa and La Puerta. About 50 km past Timotes, the road passes through the Aguilar Gap. This is the very place where Simon Bolivar and his army crossed the mountains during their famous campaign to liberate Colombia in 1819. An eagle-capped monument commemorates the historic trek. Continuing, you descend toward Apartaderos, a valley of Indian houses and stone terraces, which are still plowed by oxen. The road then forks; one branch continues to Santo Domingo (and from there to the Llanos Plains and

VENEZUELA

eastward to the Venezuelan heartland), the other heads south to the town of Mucuchies and Merida.

The stretch between Apartaderos and Mucuchies abounds in small lakes and shady groves, all accessible by foot (preferably early in the morning). It's a lovely route through the lesser known and more enchanting parts of the country, winding through scenery and flora of rare beauty. The green-gold hues of the *frailejon* plant intermingle with the Indians' blue-red clothing to create a matchless mosaic.

Merida

At the foot of Monte Bolivar in the middle of the Sierra Nevada de Merida, 1640 m above sea level, lies Venezuela's highest city and one of the most enchanting in the country – Merida. Almost 20% of its 120,000 residents are students at the local university, one of South America's oldest. The city itself was founded in 1558 and has always been noteworthy for its enchanting scenery – snow capped peaks in the distance and gorgeous vegetation all around as well as its tranquil way of life.

Merida has been damaged more than once by earthquakes and only a few pre-Independence buildings have survived. The central plaza is graced with a cathedral, rebuilt in colonial style, while modern buildings have sprung up elsewhere in town.

Transportation

Aeropostal and Avensa airlines fly to Merida from Caracas. Buses link the city with Caracas (15 hours), Maracaibo and San Cristobal, from which you can cross into Colombia. Merida has a wealth of hotels and restaurants. A Tourist Information Office is located next to the Hotel Mucubaji.

Food and Lodging

Merida, being a tourist city, has a variety of hotels, but they are crowded in the tourist season, and it is advisable to book in advance. *Holiday Inn Merida* is the best hotel in town, centrally situated on Calle 37, with a swimming pool, restaurant and discotheque. *Prado Rio Hotel* on the foothills of the Sierra Nevada has a swimming pool, bar and restaurant. It is built in a distinctive design; a few of the rooms are in a central building, and the rest are cabins. Expensive. The *Mucubaji Hotel* on Av. Universidad is pleasant and less expensive. The *Italia Hotel* is cheap, clean and comfortable.

As for restaurants, *Pabellon Criolla* on the corner of Av. 8 and Calle 18 serves a selection of local dishes at low prices, *Monte Carlo Pizzeria* makes good pizzas, and *Comedor Popular* at 6 Calle 23, is a good and reasonably priced restaurant.

VENEZUELA

The temperate climate and suitable geographic conditions have created a garden city. It boasts more than twenty public parks and gardens, where natives and visitors spend afternoons and weekends. **Parque Los Chorros de Milla**, rather far from downtown, is the best developed and has a zoo, flowing streams and more (closed Mondays). On Third Avenue, next to Plaza Bolivar, are the **Museums of Colonial** and **Modern Art.**

Merida's main attraction, however, is actually overhead: the world's highest cablecar, reaching a height of 4765 m on **Monte Pico Espejo**. This point offers a spectacular view of mountains and glaciers. The cablecar does not run every day and mechanical breakdowns are frequent. When the service does operate, lines are long and its advisable to arrive early, preferably before 7am. On certain days, (usually Fridays), a 50% discount is given. The trip itself takes more than an hour.

At the top, there are various hiking trails, some of several days' duration. These include a trek to the ice cave in the **Timoncitos Glacier** and a hike to **Los Nevados** – Venezuela's highest village. Details and guidance are available at Club Andino de Merida. Don't forget that it's very cold up there and, except at the cablecar terminal, food is not available. Accurate maps and reliable equipment are a must. Hiking permits must be obtained from the Parks Authority and Police.

On to Colombia

From Merida, the Pan American Highway continues on to San Cristobal, about 80 km from the Colombian border. From here you can go on to San Antonio, the Venezuelan frontier town and cross the bridge into Colombia after completing border-crossing procedures. Final immigration procedures are handled in Cucuta (pop. 350,000). Bogota may be reached from here by land or air.

Currency exchange here is not simple and only cash dollars are accepted. All exchanges should be made on the Venezuelan side.

It's important to mention that there's no border station on the bridge. Immigration procedures must be made in the cities **before** you cross the border.

Southeast Venezuela

One of the more interesting and lesser known of Venezuela's regions runs along the length of the Orinoco Basin, across the 2575 km between its sources somewhere in the heart of the jungle, to the Atlantic Ocean, into which it empties through a tremendous delta.

VENEZUELA

The Orinoco Basin covers more than half of Venezuela's total area. It is sparsely settled, chiefly by indigenous Indians and by prospectors in search of buried treasures – gold, diamonds, oil, aluminium and copper.

Venezuelan governments have worked for decades to develop and promote the Orinoco Basin. Aware of its economic potential, they are fighting to overcome the tremendous financial burden involved in opening up the region. Roads have been paved, cities built, dams constructed and several industrial projects established. This is only the beginning.

Few roads lead to the Guayana Plateau, to Sabana and to the Amazon Basin, and even fewer are suitable for passenger cars without front-wheel drive. Few airplanes serve the remote towns whose inhabitants seldom leave in favor of the crowded, noisy Venezuelan heartland. Two cities, Ciudad Bolivar and Ciudad Guayana, are the largest in this part of Venezuela. From these cities one can penetrate deep into the tangles of a lost world of arid plateaus, bald mountains and dense jungles.

Ciudad Bolivar

Four hundred km up the Orinoco, on the river's southern bank, is Ciudad Bolivar, the city of Simon Bolivar. He declared it his capital in 1817, and from here, organized his army and set out on the famous campaign across the Andes en route to the battle of Boyaca (Colombia). There, by defeating the Spanish loyalists, he reached a turning point in Venezuela's War of Independence.

A little of the spirit of those days is still preserved in Ciudad Bolivar. Colonial buildings line its streets and the atmosphere is pleasant and easygoing. Along the riverbank are Indian peddlers who engage in lively commerce.

The city was originally called *Angostura* because of its location on the Orinoco's narrowest stretch, but today only the large suspension bridge over the river still bears the old name. Ciudad Bolivar, once a trading center for gold and diamonds, preserves a quiet, restrained character. It's worthwhile to buy gold and gold jewelry here, and is one of the few places in Venezuela where locally produced *objets d'art* have artistic merit. Its climate is hot, though it eases a bit in the afternoons and evenings.

Transportation
Ciudad Bolivar is easy to reach from Caracas. Follow the coast east, 350 km, as far as Puerto La Cruz and then another 300 km via Barcelona and El Tigre on the Pan American Highway. If coming from San Juan de los Morros, the Llanos road is

VENEZUELA

preferable, via El Tigre (467 km) and another 130 km to Ciudad Bolivar. A number of buses set out daily to Caracas (10 hours) and many more to Ciudad Guayana, close to El Dorado. Aeropostal and Onesa link Ciudad Bolivar with important cities in Venezuela and Santa Elena, on the Brazilian border (see "Guyana: Southward to Brazil").

Food and Lodging

The little city of Ciudad Bolivar (pop. 12,000) has several hotels and restaurants. *Gran Hotel Bolivar*, which is expensive, is pleasantly situated on the banks of the Orinoco in the Paseo Orinoco area. It has a good restaurant. On Av. Tachira you will find a number of reasonable hotels. *Italia Hotel*, also on the banks of the river, is not expensive and its restaurant is recommended.

On the eastern end of Paseo Orinoco there are a few inexpensive hotels, and also a market where you can buy cheap local foodstuff.

Excursions in the area

The road south from Ciudad Bolivar leads to La Paragua, a primitive mining town where most of its inhabitants prospect for diamonds and gold (not without considerable success). It's a 200 km trip on a difficult route which passes near Cerro Bolivar – the massive "iron mountain" whose ore fuels one of Venezuela's most important industries – iron production. From La Paragua you can set out for nearby villages where the main employment is diamond-hunting.

Energetic tourists who wish to visit Angel Falls economy-style can leave from La Paragua on a combined river cruise and hike toward Canaima, – the tourists' camp near the falls. It's a difficult, complicated route which requires not only superb physical condition but also navigation and jungle skills, suitable equipment, food and lots of time and perseverance. There are also flights to Angel Falls (see "**Angel Falls**").

Ciudad Guayana

Like Manaus and Iquitos, which blossomed almost overnight into centers of international economic importance with the discovery of rubber, so did the graceless industrial city of Ciudad Guayana. It has been developing at an astonishing pace – thanks to the growth of the iron and steel industries in the vicinity. Mining and processing metals rank second only to oil in the Venezuelan economy. In recent decades, the government has made great effort to develop these industries and increase their share in the national product. Ciudad Guayana was established as the center of the mining and metal processing industries. A large

VENEZUELA

harbor, an airport and a rail link to the important mines were constructed to accommodate the growing industries. Some of Venezuela's largest factories producing steel, aluminium and iron were built in and around the city.

The Venezuelan government plans to settle a million people in the heart of the Guayana Plateau, despite the hot, harsh climate and unfavorable geographic conditions. The population of Ciudad Guayana and its surroundings has reached about 300,000 and is rapidly increasing. Ciudad Guayana is situated on the Orinoco, about 100 km from the beginning of the delta and an equal distance from Ciudad Bolivar, at the confluence of the Orinoco and Caroni Rivers.

Ciudad Guayana's Puerto Ordaz Airport has daily flights to and from Caracas and stopovers en route to Angel Falls (see below). Buses head south to El Dorado and northwest to Caracas. The city has hotels and restaurants and serves as point of departure for interesting excursions: east to the Orinoco Delta and south to Sabana and the Brazilian border.

Food and Lodging
Intercontinental Guayana Hotel offers a swimming pool, two restaurants and a discotheque. Its standards are high and so are the prices. *El Rasil Hotel* in Centro Civico is somewhat less expensive and offers good services. Reasonably priced hotels are found in the historical town San Felix.

Excursions in the area
The first three routes surveyed are loops, with Ciudad Guayana at their beginning and end. The last two – east to the delta and south to Sabana – may be taken either separately or en route to the coast (in the first case) or Brazil (in the second).

Guri Dam
Several dozen kilometers up the Caroni River we come to Guri which is destined, upon completion, to be the world's fourth-largest dam and the third-largest hydroelectric facility.

The trip takes upwards of an hour and half by taxi and you must get there before 9am, when the guided tour begins. Upon completion, the dam will soar to 272 m at its highest point, create a lake 70,762 sq/km and will help generate eight million kilowatts of electricity! One of the world's great construction projects, Guri is an exceptionally interesting place to visit.

Cerro Bolivar
Venezuela's largest iron mine (annual output: two million tons of ore) is 134 km south of Ciudad Guayana near the town of Ciudad Piar. A new railroad leads from Ciudad Guayana to the area and

VENEZUELA

brings the ore back into town – where it's loaded onto freighters for export to many countries.

The government corporation that runs the mine, Ferro Minera Orinoco, organizes guided tours almost every day from its Ciudad Guyana offices. You can visit the site yourself by going directly to Ciudad Piar, near the mountain, though it's harder to enter that way and guides are not always available.

Angel Falls

When Jimmy Angel flew over the falls in 1935, he didn't know he'd discovered the world's highest waterfall (980 m). Returning two years later, Angel tried to land atop the mountain (from which the mighty waters descend) in hope of finding gold there. Though the mountaintop looks rather flat from the air, Angel and his party barely survived the rough landing. The falls have borne his name ever since, and their great height – seventeen times that of Niagara – has attracted many tourists and visitors.

Angel Falls are about 250 km south of Ciudad Guayana and there's no road or proper land access to them. The conventional method of getting there is with Avensa, which flies every day to the Canaima camp from which one sets off to the falls.

Canaima has two visitors' centers, one belonging to Avensa and the other to Rudy ("Jungle") Truffino, Canaima's founder and veteran director. The flights from Caracas are rather expensive and include lodging, food and a tour of the falls. You can economize by reserving only a flight and foregoing the accommodation, but then you'll need food and camping gear unless you decide to stay at the hotel (if there's room) and pay separately. The Avensa flights stop over at Puerto Ordaz Airport in Ciudad Guyana, so you can board there at far less expense. Planes fly to Canaima from Ciudad Bolivar from time to time as well, but they are usually private or chartered and are not always willing to take on passengers. A difficult route – a combined river voyage and hike – leads from Ciudad Bolivar to Canaima and Angel Falls (see "Ciudad Bolivar: Excursions in the area").

The Orinoco Delta

One of the most interesting ways of returning to the coastal plain from Ciudad Guayana is to trek down the Orinoco and visit the villages on the shores of the gigantic Orinoco Delta. Take the paved highway from Ciudad Guayana to Tucupita, a town of some 30,000 Indians who lost their lands upstream in the wake of the Guri Dam project and were resettled here. Automobile and *por puesto* travel between the two cities is frequent, as is river freight and passenger traffic (inquire about boats and

VENEZUELA

directions along the river in Ciudad Guayana). Aeropostal flies here several times weekly from Ciudad Bolivar with a stopover in Maturin (by way of which one may continue afterward to the coastal area and Caracas).

Tucupita is a good point of departure for a small boat cruise among the riverside villages, where you can form an impression of the local Indians and view their way of life, work, and dress. Another interesting possibility is to head about 60 km upstream to the village of Barrancas. From Tucupita you can also set out by boat to Curiapo Island, right in the middle of the river, where there's a large and impressive Indian village. It is here, a little before the river splits into thousands of branches in the delta region, that the Orinoco reaches its greatest width – more than 18 km.

South to Brazil

From Ciudad Guayana a mostly unpaved road leads south to Santa Elena – the Venezuelan town on the Brazilian border. From here you can go on to Manaus. This difficult route requires either a front-wheel-drive vehicle or the patience and persistence necessary for slow progress by bus, truck and hitchhiking. Bring food (although there are enough restaurants on the way, it's hard to know where you'll get stuck), camping gear and enough local currency. Public transportation, fuel, lodging and food are very expensive here.

You'll pass through gorgeous scenery, thick vegetation and flat-topped mountains called *tapuies* (table mountains). These mountains, among South America's strangest and oldest geological structures, jut out with surprising steepness. At times the gradient is 90 degrees – and is nearly impossible to climb. The road passes between the mountains, crosses the Gran Sabana and descends to Santa Elena.

The paved road leads south from San Felix in Ciudad Guayana for 285 km, skirting the town of Upata and the pleasant little jungle village of El Callao. It continues to Tumeremo and finally reaches El Dorado.

El Dorado came into existence when hordes of prospectors began to pan for gold in the vicinity. Since the great hunt ground to a halt due to lack of success, the town appears to have kept running by sheer inertia. It is quiet, passive, and uninspiring. Buses come from Caracas, Ciudad Guayana and Ciudad Bolivar. There are several hotels and places to eat and you can organize river outings here to various villages and even to Canaima and Angel Falls.

VENEZUELA

From El Dorado, the "highway" continues to **Kilometer 88,** a half-settlement half-crossroads, the starting point for the climb to Gran Sabana. It's a lovely trip amid lush vegetation, streams, lakes, waterfalls and table mountains. Kilometer 88 is the last stop for taking on supplies and it's a good idea to top off fuel tanks, take on extra water and stock up on food.

The road used to end here and was pushed through to **Santa Elena** only in the mid-1970s. The road is full of ruts and pot holes and the climb over La Escalera is exhausting and lengthy. The road continues on through Gran Sabana, crossing rivulets and streams until it reaches Santa Elena. This border town came into being in the early 20th century as a by-product of the diamond hunt and has since become a center for diamond miners and traders. Its several hundred inhabitants live in simple houses and are almost totally out of touch with the modern world.

Santa Elena is also accessible by Aeropostal flights, but reservations must be made well in advance. Jeeps run the routes between Santa Elena and Ciudad Bolivar every few days, according to need.

From Santa Elena you can head for the countryside – to Monte Roraima, the Indian village of Peraitepuy, or the mining camps in the vicinity.

The border station is open until evening on weekdays and sometimes on weekends as well. If you're going on to Brazil, complete the crossing procedures in Santa Elena and cross the border at the nearby checkpoint. From here it's 220 km to Boa Vista, Brazil. Trucks travel the route almost every day, as do small cars. From Boa Vista there are plane and bus connections to Manaus (760 km, 20 hours) and from there, to the rest of Brazil.

INDEX

A
Abancay (Peru) 617
Aguas Calientes (Peru) 649
Alcantara (Bra) 311
Alpamayo (Peru) 591
Amantani (Peru) 660
Ambato (Ec) 514
Ancud (Chi) 385
Angel Falls (Ven) 713
Angra dos Reis (Bra) 246
Anta (Peru) 617
Antofagasta (Chi) 365
Apurimac Valley (Peru) 617
Aracati (Bra) 310
Arani (Bol) 172
Arequipa (Peru) 609
Arica (Chile) 362
Armacao dos Buzios (Bra) 242
Arraial de Ajuda (Bra) 284
Asuncion (Par) **542**
Atacames (Ec) 532
Auzangate (Peru) 657
Ayacucho (Peru) 616

B
Banos (Ec) 515
Barranquilla (Col) 430
Belem (Bra) 313
Belo Horizonte (Bra) 273
Benjamin Constant (Bra) 323
Benjamin Constante (Col) 466
Boa Vista (Bra) 322
Bogota (Col) 410
Brasilia (Bra) **331**
Bucaramanga (Col) 422
Buenaventura (Col) 448
Buenos Aires (Arg) **81**

C
Cabanaconde (Peru) 612
Cabo Frio (Bra) 242
Cajamarca (Peru) 596
Cajatambo (Peru) 590
Calafate (Arg) 124
Calama (Chi) 368
Calaya (Bol) 164
Cali (Col) 445
Camana (Peru) 609

INDEX

Campo Grande (Bra) 329
Canoa Quebrada (Bra) 156
Caracas (Ven) **689**
Carahue (Chi) 373
Caraz (Peru) 590
Carmen de Viboral (Col) 444
Cartagena (Col) 425
Caruaru (Bra) 304
Casma (Peru) 593
Caspampa (Peru) 590
Castro (Chi) 385
Catac (Peru) 592
Caxias do Sul (Bra) 265
Cerro Bolivar (Ven) 712
Cerro de Pasco (Peru) 599
Chacaltaya (Bol) 162
Chala (Peru) 609
Chan Chan (Peru) 595
Charazani (Villa Gnl. Perez) (Bol) 163
Chavin de Huantar (Peru) 592
Chiloe Island (Chi) 384
Chimborazo (Ec) 515
Chimbote (Peru) 593
Chinchero (Peru) 651
Chiquian (Peru) 590
Chiquicamata (Chi) 367
Chivay (Peru) 612
Chochas Chicas (Peru) 616
Chochas Grandes (Peru) 616
Chojilla (Bol) 165
Chosica (Peru) 614
Chulumani (Bol) 167
Chuy (Bra) 267
Ciudad Bolivar (Ven) 710
Ciudad Guayana (Ven) 711
Coca (Ec) 527
Cochabamba (Bol) 169
Cochapampa (Peru) 590
Colca Valley (Peru) 612
Colonia Tovar (Ven) 704
Comodoro Rivadavia (Arg) 123
Concepcion (Peru) 616
Congonhas (Bra) 277
Copacabana (Bol) 160
Cordoba (Arg) 110
Coroico (Bol) 167
Corumba (Bra) 330
Cota (Bol) 164
Cotacota (Bol) 161
Cotopaxi (Ec) 493
Cucuta (Col) 423
Cuenca (Ec) 512
Cuiaba (Bra) 327

INDEX

Curitiba (Bra) 260
Cuzco (Peru) **627**

D
Darien Gap (Col) 439
Diente del Diablo (Bol) 161

E
El Beni (Bol) 168
El=Bolson (Arg) 120
El Dorado (Ven) 714
El Penol (Col) 444
Encarnacion (Par) 543
Escoma (Bol) 163
Esmereldas (Ec) 531
Espiritupampa (Peru) 656
Esquel (Arg) 120

F
Farellones (Chi) 362
Feira de Santana (Bra) 295
Fitz Roy Mountain (Arg) 125
Florianopolis (Bra) 262
Fortaleza (Bra) 306
Foz do Iguacu (Bra) 269

G
Galapagos Is. (Ec) 505
Goiana (Bra) 337
Guaibu (Bra) 304
Guajira (Col) 435
Guajira (Ven) 707
Guarapari (Bra) 283
Guaruja (Bra) 249
Guayaquil (Ven) 499
Guri (Ven) 712

H
Hualgayoc (Peru) 596
Huancayo (Peru) 614
Huanchaco (Peru) 595
Huanuco (Peru) 599
Huaraz (Peru) 584
Humahuaca (Arg) 109

I
Ibarra (Ec) 535
Ica (Peru) 605
Iguacu Falls (Arg) 98
Iguacu Falls (Bra) 267
Ilhabela (Bra) 249
Ilha do Marajo (Bra) 316
Ilha do Mel (Bra) 262

INDEX

Ilha Grande (Bra) 247
Ilha Paqueta (Bra) 240
Inca Trail (Bol) 165
Inca Trail (Peru) 652
Ingapirca (Ec) 513
Ipiales (Col) 460
Iquitos (Peru) 600
Isla Magdalena (Chi) 390
Isla Margarita (Ven) 703
Itaipu (Bra) 272
Itaparica (Bra) 294
Itatiaia (Bra) 243
Itaugua (Par) 551
Izuchaca (Peru) 617

J
Joao Pessoa (Bra) 304
Jujuy (Arg) 108
Juliaca (Peru) 661
Junin (Peru) 599

L
La Ceja (Col) 444
Lago Agrio (Ec) 521
Laguna Churup (Peru) 591
Laguna San Rafael (Chi) 383
La Mitad del Mundo (Ec) 492
La Oroya (Peru) 599
La Paz (Bol) **145**
La Quiaca (Arg) 109
La Quinua (Peru) 616
Las Palmas (Ec) 532
Letitia (Col) 464
Lima (Peru) **568**
Limon Cocha (Ec) 522
Limones (Ec) 533
Llamac (Peru) 590

M
Maceio (Bra) 297
Machu Picchu (Peru) 648
Manaus (Bra) 317
Manizales (Col) 444
Mano Parque (Peru) 656
Maracaibo (Ven) 705
Mar del Plata (Arg) 114
Marinilla (Col) 444
Mayobamba (Peru) 600
Medellin (Col) 440
Mendoza (Arg) 111
Merida (Ven) 708
Misahualli (Ec) 527
Mitu (Col) 463

INDEX

Montevideo (Uru) 670
Morro de Sao Paulo (Bra) 285
Mosqueiro (Bra) 316

N
Natal (Bra) 305
Nazca (Peru) 606
Nino Corin (Bol) 164
Niteroi (Bra) 240
Nova Jerusalem (Bra) 304
Nova Friburgo (Bra) 246
Nuevo Rocafuerte (Ec) 523

O
Ocangate (Peru) 657
Olinda (Bra) 302
Ollantaytambo (Peru) 645
Osorno (Chi) 377
Oruro (Bol) 169
Otavalo (Ec) 533
Ouro Preto (Bra) 277

P
Pachacamac (Peru) 604
Pana Cocha (Ec) 523
Pantanal (Bra) 325
Paracas (Peru) 604
Paracuru (Bra) 310
Paranagua (Bra) 262
Parati (Bra) 247
Parque Nacional Lauca (Chi) 365
Parque Nacional Torres del Paine (Chi) 392
Pasto (Col) 459
Patagonia (Arg) 121
Patagonia (Chi) 387
Peninsula Valdes (Arg) 122
Petropolis (Bra) 243
Pichincha (Ec) 493
Pisac (Peru) 643
Pisco (Peru) 604
Pitek (Peru) 591
Pomabamba (Peru) 591
Pompeya (Ec) 522
Pontal da Barra (Bra) 298
Popayan (Col) 448
Portillo (Chi) 361
Porto Alegre (Bra) 266
Porto Seguro (Bra) 283
Porto Velho (Bra) 324
Posadas (Arg) 98
Potosi (Bol) 178
Providencia Is. (Col) 438
Pucalpa (Peru) 599

INDEX

Puca Pucara (Peru) 643
Pucon (Chi) 374
Puerto Asis (Col) 461
Puerto Iguacu (Arg) 101
Puerto Iguacu (Bra) 269
Puerto Madryn (Arg) 123
Puerto Maldonado (Peru) 653
Puerto Montt (Chi) 381
Puerto Natales (Chi) 391
Puerto Porvenir (Arg) 128
Puerto Porvenir (Chi) 391
Puerto Varas (Chi) 380
Puerto Suarez (Bol) 173
Puerto Villaroel (Bol) 168
Punata (Bol) 172
Puno (Peru) 658
Punta Arenas (Chi) 388
Punta del Este (Uru) 220
Punta Tumbo (Arg) 123
Purace, parque (Col) 451
Putumayo (Col) 461

Q
Quenco (Peru) 642
Quito (Ec) **480**

R
Recife (Bra) 298
Rio Abajo (Bol) 161
Riobamba (Ec) 514
Rio de Janeiro (Bra) 213
Rio Gallegos (Arg) 124
Rio Grande (Arg) 128
Rio Grande do Sul (Bra) 265
Riohacha (Col) 435
Rio Napo (Ec) 522
Rionegro (Col) 443
Rio Sao Francisco (Bra) 281
Rio Turbio (Arg) 126
Rio Yasuni (Ec) 524
Rosario Is. (Col) 430

S
Sabara (Bra) 277
Sacsahuaman (Peru) 641
Salta (Arg) 106
Salvador (Bra) 287
San Agustin (Col) 456
San Andres Is. (Col) 436
San Andres de Pisimbala (Col) 451
San Antonio de Ibarra (Ec) 535
San Bernadino (Par) 551
San Carlos de Bariloche (Arg) 116
San Jeronimo (Peru) 616

INDEX

San Juan de los Morros (Ven) 705
San Lorenzo (Ec) 533
San Martin (Col) 467
San Martin de los Andes (Arg) 115
Santa Catarina Island (Bra) 265
Santa Pedro de Atacama (Chi) 367
San Sebastian (Arg) 128
Santa Cruz (Bol) 172
Santa Cruz (Peru) 590
Santa Elena (Ven) 715
Santa Marta (Col) 432
Santarem (Bra) 317
Santiago de Chile (Chi) **349**
Santo Antonio de Leverger (Bra) 329
Santo Domingo de los Colorados (Ec) 530
Santos (Bra) 250
Sao Luis (Bra) 310
Sao Paulo (Bra) 253
Sao Sebastiao (Bra) 249
Sierra Nevada de Santa Marta (Col) 434
Silvia (Col) 450
Sua (Ec) 532
Sucre (Bol) **173**

T

Tacna (Chi) 364
Tacna (Peru) 612
Tairona, parque (Col) 434
Tambo Colorado (Peru) 604
Tambomachay (Peru) 643
Taquile (Peru) 660
Tarabuco (Bol) 176
Tarija (Bol) 181
Temuco (Chi) 369
Tena (Ec) 527
Teresopolis (Bra) 245
Tierra del Fuego (Arg) 127
Tierra del Fuego (Chi) 387
Tierradentro (Col) 451
Tinga Maria (Peru) 599
Tinki (Peru) 657
Titicaca, Lake (Bol) 163
Titicaca, Lake (Peru) 658
Tiwanaku (Bol) 157
Trancoso (Bra) 285
Trelew (Arg) 123
Trinidad (Bol) 168
Trujillo (Peru) 593
Tucuman (Arg) 104
Tulcan (Ec) 535
Tumaco (Col) 462
Tumbes (Peru) 596
Tunja (Col) 420
Turbo (Col) 439

INDEX

U
Ubatuba (Bra) 248
Ulla Ulla (Bol) 165
Urubamba Valley (Peru) 643
Ushuaia (Arg) 128

V
Valenca (Bra) 285
Valle de la Luna (Bol) 161
Ventilla (Bol) 165
Vila Velha (Bra) 261
Vilcabamba (Peru) 590
Villa de Leyva (Col) 421
Villarica (Chi) 373
Villa Rivero (Bol) 172
Villavicencio (Col) 466
Villazon (Bol) 182
Vina del Mar (Chi) 359
Vitoria (Bra) 283

W
Wallwash (Peru) 589

Y
Yungas (Bol) 167
Yungay (Peru) 590

Z
Zipaquira (Col) 418

NOTES

Notes

Notes

Notes

NOTES

Notes

Notes

QUESTIONNAIRE

In our efforts to keep up with the pace and pulse of South America, we kindly ask your cooperation in sharing with us any information which you may have as well as your comments. We would greatly appreciate your completing and returning the following questionnaire. Feel free to add additional pages. A complimentary copy of the next edition will be sent to you should any of your suggestions be included.
Our many thanks!

To: Inbal Information (1983) Ltd.
2 Chen Blvd.
Tel Aviv 64071
Israel

Name: _____

Address: _____
_____

Occupation: _____

Date of visit: _____

Purpose of trip (vacation, business, etc.): _____
_____

Comments/Information: _____
_____
_____
_____
_____
_____
_____
_____
_____
_____
_____
_____
_____
_____
_____
_____
_____
_____
_____

SA/8/1

INBAL Travel Information Ltd.
P.O.B. 39090 Tel-Aviv
ISRAEL 61390